JAMES LARKIN
LION OF THE FOLD

Editor
DONAL NEVIN

Gill & Macmillan
in association with RTE and SIPTU

Gill & Macmillan Ltd
Hume Avenue, Park West, Dublin 12
with associated companies throughout the world
www.gillmacmillan.ie
© Kenneth Brown, Breda Cardiff, Fergus D'Arcy, Joe Deasy,
John de Courcy Ireland, Francis Devine, Theo Dorgan, John Gray,
James Kavanagh, Dermot Keogh, Emmet Larkin, Patrick Lynch,
F. X. Martin, Theresa Moriarty, Donal Nevin, Ulick O'Connor,
Cormac Ó Gráda, Manus O'Riordan, James Plunkett, John P. Swift
and Eric Taplin 1998, 2006
ISBN-13: 978 07171 4154 8
ISBN-10: 0 7171 4154 3
First published in 1998
Published in this format 2006
Design and print origination by Carole Lynch
Printed by ColourBooks Ltd, Dublin

*The paper used in this book comes from the wood pulp of
managed forests. For every tree felled, at least one tree is planted,
thereby renewing natural resources.*

A catalogue record for this book is available
from the British Library.

1 3 5 4 2

Contents

Part 2: Jim Larkin: His Life and Turbulent Times

Preface

James Larkin died on 30 January 1947. In 1996 the National Executive Council of the Services, Industrial, Professional and Technical Union (SIPTU) decided to mark the fiftieth anniversary of his death with a number of commemorative events in 1997.

James Larkin founded the Irish Transport and General Workers' Union (ITGWU) in 1909 and was its general secretary until 1924. He then became the general secretary of the Workers' Union of Ireland (WUI) and continued in this position until his death. He was thus general secretary of these two unions for a period of thirty-eight years.

In 1990 the ITGWU and the Federated Workers' Union of Ireland (which the WUI had become) merged to form SIPTU. It was appropriate therefore that this union should organise the commemorative events marking the fiftieth anniversary of Larkin's death. These events included a lecture in Liberty Hall, Dublin, by Prof. Emmet Larkin of the University of Chicago, the biographer of Larkin, whose book *James Larkin: Irish Labour Leader*, published in 1965, remains the authoritative work on Larkin; a celebration in poetry, prose, music, and song, 'Salute to Big Jim', in Liberty Hall and in Transport House, Belfast; a 'SIPTU Tribute to James Larkin' exhibition in the National Library of Ireland; and a special production in Liberty Hall of Seán O'Casey's play *Red Roses for Me*. Finally, SIPTU arranged for this compendium on Larkin and his times to be prepared.

Radio Teleffs Éireann also commemorated the fiftieth anniversary of Larkin's death with a Thomas Davis Lecture Series, 'James Larkin: Lion of the Fold', which was broadcast between January and May 1997. The fifteen lectures were given by historians from the University of Chicago, University College Dublin, Queen's University, Belfast, the University of Liverpool, and University College Cork, by other historians and writers, and by trade union officials.

The general editor of the RTE Thomas Davis Lecture Series is Michael Littleton, and the consultant editor of the Larkin series of lectures was Donal Nevin. The Thomas Davis Lectures, in most cases extended and revised, are given in part 1 of this book. Part 2, 'Jim Larkin: His Life and Turbulent Times', and part 3, 'Big Jim', were compiled by Donal Nevin. Unattributed chapters in parts 2 and 3 were written by Donal Nevin.

The editor acknowledges the help of a great many people in preparing this compendium but especially Prof. Emmet Larkin for his help and co-operation, Prof. Patrick Lynch for his wise counsel, and Theresa Moriarty for her considerable research assistance and archival expertise. His special thanks are due to Shirley Cosgrave (a colleague from far-off Irish TUC days, when the total staff of the Congress in Dublin and Belfast was six!) and Tom Dunne (SIPTU), both of whom bore with patience and serenity the editor's persistent importunities and impositions over a prolonged period.

The editor wishes also to express his appreciation to the seven contributors to part 3: Breda Cardiff, Prof. Fergus D'Arcy, Joe Deasy, Dr John de Courcy Ireland, Bishop James Kavanagh, Rev. Prof. F. X. Martin, Theresa Moriarty, and Ulick O'Connor.

The editor acknowledges also the assistance given by Hilda Larkin Breslin, Patrick Cardiff, Francis Devine, Enda Dunleavy, Tom Geraghty, Celia Larkin, Michael Littleton, Proinsias Mac Aonghusa, Stella Larkin McConnon, Evelyn MacMahon (New York), Seán Mac Réamoinn, Mary Maher, Sylvia Meehan, John Murphy (SIPTU), Anne Nevin, Maura Nevin, Manus O'Riordan, Deirdre Price, the US Ambassador, Jean Kennedy Smith, Fergal Tobin (Gill & Macmillan), and Freida Wiles (Brown University, Rhode Island); also the staff of the National Library (especially Theresa Biggins, Kevin Browne, Eugene Hogan, and Dónall Ó Luanaigh); Gerald Whelan (RDS Library); Jennifer Hunter (Irish Labour History Museum Library), Dr Jack McGinley (TCD Library), John Gibson (*Irish Times* Library), and the staff of the National Archives and the City of Dublin Public Libraries (Gilbert Library). The editor's special appreciation and thanks are due to Séamas Sheils (SIPTU) for his extensive work on the pictures and the design.

Finally, the editor would like to express his thanks to the general officers of SIPTU: Jimmy Somers, general president; Des Geraghty, vice-president; and the now retired general secretary, W. A. Attley. Billy Attley, a hard taskmaster but wholly supportive, gave unstinted encouragement to the editor's work in putting together this compendium marking the fiftieth anniversary of Ireland's greatest trade union leader and an important figure in the history of this century.

The publication of as large a volume as this is involved substantial subsidy. In very large part this was provided by SIPTU, but other organisations that contributed to the cost were the Department of Arts, Heritage, Gaeltacht and the Islands and the Irish-American Labor Coalition, New York.

Contributors

Kenneth Brown is Professor of Economic and Social History at Queen's University, Belfast, since 1988 and is the author of several books on British labour history, including *John Burns* (1976) and *The First Labour Party* (1984).

Breda Cardiff was on the staff of the Workers' Union of Ireland in the last years of James Larkin's life.

Fergus A. D'Arcy is Associate Professor in the Department of History and Dean of the Faculty of Arts, University College Dublin. He is joint editor of *Workers in Union: Documents and Commentaries on the History of Irish Labour* (1988) and author of *Horses, Lords and Racing Men: The Turf Club, 1790–1991* and has contributed chapters to many books, including Art Cosgrave and D. McCartney (editors), *Essays in Irish History in Honour of R. D. Edwards* (1979), D. McCartney (editor), *The World of Daniel O'Connell* (1980), Kevin B. Nowlan (editor), *The Materialist Messiah* (1984), Art Cosgrave (editor), *Dublin through the Ages* (1988), and Donal Nevin (editor), *Trade Union Century* (1994). He is the author of *Daniel O'Connell: A Biography* (forthcoming).

Joe Deasy is president of the Irish Labour History Society and author of *Fiery Cross: The Story of Jim Larkin* (1963).

John de Courcy Ireland is the author of *The Sea and the Easter Rising* (1966), *Ireland's Sea Fisheries: A History* (1981), and *Wreck and Rescue on the East Coast of Ireland* (1983), as well as numerous papers and articles on maritime affairs and socialist politics.

Francis Devine is a tutor in the Education and Training Department of SIPTU. He was joint editor, 1979–1997, of *Saothar: Journal of the Irish Labour History Society* and is the author of *Red Star, Blue Moon: A Collection of Poems* (1997).

Theo Dorgan is the Director of Poetry Ireland, the author of two collections of poems, *The Ordinary House of Love* (1991) and *Rosa Mundi* (1995), editor of *Revising the Rising* (1991) and *Irish Poetry after Kavanagh* (1996), and joint editor of *The Great Book of Ireland* (1991).

John Gray is Librarian of the Linen Hall Library, Belfast, and author of *City in Revolt: James Larkin and the Belfast Dock Strike of 1907* (1985).

Bishop James Kavanagh was appointed in 1966 to the newly established Professorship of Social Science in University College Dublin. In 1973 he was appointed an Auxiliary Bishop of the Archdiocese of Dublin.

Dermot Keogh is Professor of Modern History at University College Cork. He is the author of *The Rise of the Irish Working Class: The Dublin Trade Union Movement and Labour Leadership* (1982), *The Vatican, the Bishops and*

Irish Politics (1986), *Ireland and Europe, 1919–1989* (1989), *Twentieth-Century Ireland: Nation and State* (1994), *Ireland and the Vatican: The Politics and Diplomacy of Church and State, 1922–1960* (1995), and *Jews in Twentieth-Century Ireland* (1998). He also edited *Ireland and the Challenge of European Integration* (1989) and *Church and Politics in Latin America* (1990).

Emmet Larkin is Professor of British and Irish History at the University of Chicago. He is the author of *James Larkin: Irish Labour Leader* (1965), *A History of the Roman Catholic Church in Ireland in the Nineteenth Century, 1780–1918* (of the twelve volumes projected, seven have been published, covering the period 1850–1891), and *The Historical Dimensions of Irish Catholicism* (1976).

Patrick Lynch is Professor Emeritus of Political Economy at University College Dublin, and joint author of *Guinness's Brewery in the Irish Economy, 1759–1876* (1960), and joint editor of *Essays in Memory of Alexis Fitzgerald* (1987).

Rev. Prof. F. X. Martin OSA was Professor of Mediaeval History at University College Dublin, from 1962 to 1988. He is the author of many books and is joint editor of *A New History of Ireland*, which is being published under the auspices of the Royal Irish Academy. He was joint editor of *The Scholar Revolutionary: Eoin MacNeill, 1867–1945, and the Making of the New Ireland* (1973) and of *The Course of Irish History* (1967, second edition 1984).

Theresa Moriarty is Vice-President of the Irish Labour History Society. She is the author of *Work in Progress: Episodes from the History of Irish Women's Trade Unionism* (1994) and joint author of *Women's Voices: an Oral History of Women's Health in Northern Ireland, 1900–1990* (1992) and a forthcoming study on the 1913 lock-out.

Donal Nevin is a former general secretary of the Irish Congress of Trade Unions. He is the editor of *1913: Jim Larkin and the Dublin Lock-Out* (1964), *Trade Unions and Change in Irish Society* (1980), *Trade Union Priorities in Social Policy* (1981), and *Trade Union Century* (1996), and has contributed essays to the RTE Thomas Davis Lecture Series published in Francis MacManus (editor), *The Years of the Great Test, 1926–39* (1967), Kevin B. Nowlan and T. Desmond Williams (editors), *Ireland in the War Years and After, 1939–52* (1969) and Kevin B. Nowlan (editor), *Karl Marx: The Materialist Messiah* (1984) and the essay 'The Irish Citizen Army' in Owen Dudley Edwards and Fergus Pyle (editors), *1916: The Easter Rising* (1968).

Ulick O'Connor is the author of many books, including *Oliver St John Gogarty* (1963), *Brendan Behan* (1970), *Lifestyles: Poems* (1973), *A Terrible Beauty is Born* (1975), *Irish Tales and Sagas* (1981), *The Celtic Dawn* (1984), *All the Olympians* (1984), *The Yeats Companion* (1990), and *Biographers and the Art of Biography* (1991). His plays include *Dark Loves* (1974), *Three Noh Plays* (1981), and *Executions* (1993).

Cormac Ó Gráda is Associate Professor in the Department of Economics, University College Dublin, and the author of *Ireland Before and After the Famine: Explorations in Economic History* (second edition, 1993), *Ireland: A New Economic History, 1780–1939* (1994), *An Drochshaol: Béaloideas agus Amhráin* (1994), *A Rocky Road: The Irish Economy since the 1920s* (1997), and *Black '47 and Beyond: The Great Irish Famine in History, Economy, and Memory* (forthcoming).

Manus O'Riordan is Head of Research with SIPTU and the author of *James Connolly in America* (1971), *The American Trial of Big Jim Larkin* (1976), and *The Voice of a Thinking Intelligent Movement: Jim Larkin Junior* (1995).

James Plunkett is the author of *Big Jim* (radio play, 1954), *The Risen People* (play, 1958), *The Trusted and the Maimed* (1955), *Strumpet City* (1969), *The Gems She Wore: A Book of Irish Places* (1972), *Farewell Companions* (1977), *Collected Stories* (1977), and *The Circus Animals* (1990).

John P. Swift is an official of SIPTU and the author of *John Swift: An Irish Dissident* (1991).

Eric Taplin is an Honorary Fellow in the Department of Economic and Social History, University of Liverpool, and the author of *Liverpool Dockers and Seamen, 1870–1890* (1974), *The Dockers' Union: A Study of the National Union of Dock Labourers, 1889–1922* (1986), and *Near to Revolution: The Liverpool General Transport Strike, 1911* (1994).

Abbreviations

AOH	Ancient Order of Hibernians
ASRS	Amalgamated Society of Railway Servants
CIU	Congress of Irish Unions
DMP	Dublin Metropolitan Police
DUTC	Dublin United Tramway Company
FWUI	Federated Workers' Union of Ireland
GFTU	General Federation of Trade Unions
ICTU	Irish Congress of Trade Unions
ILP	Independent Labour Party
ITGWU	Irish Transport and General Workers' Union
ITUC	Irish Trades Union Congress
IWW	Industrial Workers of the World
IWWU	Irish Women Workers' Union
NUDL	National Union of Dock Labourers
RIC	Royal Irish Constabulary
SDF	Social Democratic Federation
SIPTU	Services, Industrial, Professional and Technical Union
TUC	Trades Union Congress
WUI	Workers' Union of Ireland

PART 1
THOMAS DAVIS LECTURES, 1997

General Editor
MICHAEL LITTLETON

Consultant Editor
DONAL NEVIN

Thomas Davis Lectures

Every year since 1953, Radio Telefís Éireann has been broadcasting half-hour radio lectures named in honour of Thomas Davis, one of whose sayings was 'Educate that you may be free.' The fifteen lectures that follow were broadcast between January and May 1997 in commemoration of the fiftieth anniversary of the death of James Larkin.

Chapter 1

James Larkin: Labour Leader

Prof. Emmet Larkin

James Larkin was a remarkable man. On the day he died, Seán O'Casey, his lifelong admirer, wrote: 'It is hard to believe that this great man is dead, for all thoughts and all activities surged in the soul of this Labour leader. He was far and away above the orthodox Labour leader, for he combined within himself the imagination of the artist, with the fire and determination of a leader of a down-trodden class.'

It is most appropriate, therefore, that we should honour James Larkin's memory in this distinguished series of Thomas Davis Lectures on the fiftieth anniversary of his death. Before any meaning can be drawn, however, from the life and work of this remarkable man, something must be said about that life and work. He was born in the slums of Liverpool in 1874, raised in poverty, received only a few years' formal schooling, watched his father die slowly of tuberculosis, was thrown on a brutal labour market, struggled to keep his family from sinking into a more abject poverty, stowed away to escape unemployment and find adventure, and then returned to Liverpool at the age of twenty to take his place among that vast army of casuals who prowled the docks in search of a day's work.

He finally found regular work as a docker and was soon promoted to dock foreman. When his men went out on strike in the summer of 1905 he went with them and became their leader. The strike was lost, but he was asked to become a full-time organiser for the union, the National Union of Dock Labourers. He quickly organised the Scottish ports, and was then assigned the more difficult task of reorganising the Irish ports.

Soon after his arrival in Ireland in January 1907, Larkin was involved in a series of strikes in Belfast, Cork, and Dublin, which the executive of the National Union was reluctant to support. He then broke with the union and founded the Irish Transport and General Workers' Union at the end of 1908. The Transport Union, after a shaky start, rapidly gained in numbers and strength over the next several years, and by 1913 it was the largest and most militant union in Ireland. In the great Dublin strike and lock-out of 1913, Larkin challenged the employing class in the persons of William Martin Murphy and his Employers' Federation. The epic struggle, which lasted some six months and involved twenty thousand workers and their eighty thousand dependants, resulted in a crushing defeat for the workers, in spite of massive support from the British labour movement. The Transport Union was decimated and financially wrecked. In early 1914, therefore, Larkin decided to make a speaking tour in America to raise the necessary funds for the rebuilding of his union.

By the time he was able to sail for America, in late October 1914, however, the First World War had already broken out, and it would be nearly nine years before Larkin was to return to Ireland. While in America, Larkin was by turns a lecturer, a union organiser, a German secret agent, an Irish propagandist, a socialist agitator, a founder of the American Communist Party, and finally a 'martyred' political prisoner who served nearly three years in prison. Two over-riding themes, however, give his American career some coherence and consistency in the face of what might otherwise appear to have been mere rootless activity. The first was his implacable opposition to the First World War, and the second was his enthusiastic acceptance of the Russian Revolution in November 1917. For the four years that the war continued, Larkin agitated and worked against it, going even so far as to become a German agent. With the news of the Russian Revolution, Larkin declared himself to be a Bolshevik of the reddest hue. Both these stands, needless to say, especially after the United States entered the war in April 1917, were very unpopular, and when the celebrated Red Scare of 1919 followed hard on the heels of the end of the war, Larkin was arrested, tried, convicted, and sentenced to a very stiff term in prison.

Governor Alfred E. Smith eventually pardoned Larkin in early 1923 in the interests of free speech, and he was shortly after deported to Ireland. On his return home he found that the successful war against the British had degenerated into a fratricidal civil war among the Irish, and he immediately called for peace. Within a month of his arrival, however, a fierce struggle for power broke out in the Transport Union, which was soon extended to the Irish labour movement, and Larkin was at the centre of it. The eventual result was that Larkin was suspended as general secretary of the Transport Union and finally expelled. He then approved the founding of the Workers' Union of Ireland but was only able to carry a remnant of the Transport Union, mainly based in Dublin, with him. With the advent of the Great Depression in 1929, Larkin's power and influence on both the trade union and political sides of the labour movement were further impaired, and the man who had long been seen as the Irish labour movement incarnate now was only a part of it.

These are, however, only the bare bones of James Larkin's life and work, and a good deal more needs to be understood if the meaning of his achievement and its significance is to be appreciated. What made Larkin unique as a labour leader, as O'Casey pointed out, was both his imagination and his fire and determination. 'Seán could see', O'Casey later wrote with regard to Larkin's imagination, 'that here was a man who would put a flower in a vase on a table as well as a loaf on a plate. Here, Seán thought, is the beginning of the broad and busy day. The leisurely evening, the calmer night ... never [more] to be conscious of a doubt about tomorrow's bread, certain that while the earth remaineth, summer and winter should not cease, seedtime and harvest never fail.'

Besides this tribute to Larkin's imagination, O'Casey has also left a poignant account of his fire and determination, couched in the prophetic language of scripture.

> Through the streets he strode, shouting into every dark and evil-smelling hall-way.
> The great day of change has come; Circe's swine had a better time than you have; come from your vomit; out into the sun. Larkin is calling you all! And many were afraid, and hid themselves in corners. Some ventured as far as the rear and dusky doorway to peer out, and to say, Mr. Larkin, please excuse us, for we have many things to do and to suffer; we must care for the cancerous and tubercular sick, and we must stay to bury our dead. But he caught them by the sleeve, by the coat collar, and shouted, Come forth, and fight with the son of Amos who has come to walk among the men and women of Ireland. Let the sick look after the sick, and let the dead bury the dead. Come ye out to fight those who make the ephah small and shekel great; come out that we may smite the winter house with the summer house; till the houses of ivory shall perish and the great houses shall have an end. And Seán had joined the Union.

But how—and, even more important perhaps, why—did this 'son of the prophet Amos' become the idol of the Dublin workers? It all began in fact in a poverty-stricken English Catholic school, where he was taught the rudiments of Christian morality. 'I was taught', he explained many years later, 'the truth of eternal justice and that the brotherhood of man was a true and living thing, and the fear of God was a thing that ought to cover all my days and also control my actions. And then I had occasion to go out in the world and found there was no fatherhood of God, and there was no brotherhood of man, but every man in society was compelled to be like a wolf or hyena …

'And so at an early age,' he further explained, 'I took my mind to this question of the ages—why are the many poor? It was true to me. I don't know whether the light of God or the light of humanity, or the light of my own intelligence brought it to me, but it came to me like a flash. The thing was wrong because the basis of society was wrong; that the oppression was from the top by forces that I myself for a moment did not visualise.' As Larkin listened to that small band of socialist street-corner orators in Liverpool in the eighteen-nineties, his understanding of what was wrong with the world became clearer. They said that the system, which produced such degradation among the working class, could not be defended and would eventually perish in its own corruption, and he listened. They promised that they could close the awful gap between what was and what should be, and he was heartened. They told him that he could have a real part in the making of their brave new world, and he was converted to socialism.

For some ten years Larkin preached the new socialist gospel in the evenings and on Sundays in and around Liverpool. Some years later he reflected on these years of preaching in the wilderness. He asked his readers if they understood what it was like to get up on a box or a chair, physically and mentally tired ... amongst strangers ... and then suffering from want of training, want of education, but filled with the spirit of a new gospel ... You try to impart to that unthinking mass the feeling which possesses yourself. The life all around you seems to stagnate; everything seems miserable and depressing. Yet you want them to realise there is great hope for the future—that there is something worth working for, if the workers will only rouse themselves. You plead with them to cast their eyes upward to the stars, instead of grovelling in the slime of their own degradation; point out to them life's promised fullness and joy if they would only seek it.

What little time Larkin had after his work on the docks, his burgeoning family and his socialist preaching he gave to the Social Guild of Liverpool, visiting the sick and the poor. His description of one of his visits is at once an example of his rhetoric and his deep compassion as well as his moral indignation in the face of social injustice.

I and two of these people one night went down into Christian Street. We went down to one of those subterranean dwellings they have in Liverpool, down below the earth, where the people who were born in the image of God and His likeness were drawn down by this economic vortex and driven into this damnable hell down below, driven out of the light of day into these dens that have no background at all, but only have an entrance to get in.

It was dark, bitterly dark. We passed into the first orifice and then the next, and then we heard a moan, and we looked through and saw nothing, it was so dark, and I went out and got a candle and came back and lit the candle, and then we found it. In the corner lay the body of a woman, and on its dead breast, on its dead breast was the figure of a child, about two months old, sucking, trying to get the life blood out of the breast of the dead woman. And then there were two little girls, one seven years old, and one of nine, and that was in the year 1902, and the City of Liverpool, in a Christian City, in a street called Christian—Christian Street, and Christian people; and they foully murdered that mother and they left those three children to march with the world, and none in that City of a million people cared about that mother or about her children; and even God sent no one down to the gloom, except in as much as He had sent us.

Each new horror experienced in Liverpool only served to confirm James Larkin in his new-found socialist faith.

When Larkin first arrived in Dublin in 1907, however, he was shocked, even after what he had experienced in Liverpool, at the degradation of human life in the capital city of Ireland. Some 26,000 families, or nearly a third of the people of Dublin, lived in 5,000 decayed tenements, in which 20,000 families lived in one room. Of these 5,000 tenements, 1,500 had actually been condemned, not only as unfit for human habitation but as incapable of ever being rendered fit for human habitation. Death, disease, immorality, insanity, crime, drunkenness, unemployment, low wages and high rents were the pestiferous concomitants of this Dublin slum life. By founding the Irish Transport and General Workers' Union, of course, Larkin was able to do something about raising the workers' wages, shortening their hours, and ameliorating their working conditions, thereby improving the narrow margin on which they and their families existed.

In these years, however, Larkin attempted to make his Transport Union something more than an instrument for the material advancement of the workers: he made it a vehicle for their social and cultural improvement as well. When the Transport Union acquired Liberty Hall as its headquarters in early 1912, the old hotel was also transformed into a centre for the social and cultural activities of the union. The 'Hall' soon housed the Irish Workers' Choir, and the Juvenile and Adult Dancers' class, while an Irish-language class was formed, followed by the founding of the Irish Workers' Dramatic Company. Sunday evening socials with a lecture and concert became a standard feature, at a nominal charge for union members and their families. Larkin also early organised both a fife and drum and a pipe band and later two football teams and a boxing team for the sports enthusiasts in the union. Every Christmas, moreover, there was a party for the workers' children, with presents and ice-cream for everyone.

The crowning achievement, however, of Larkin's imaginative social and cultural efforts was his renting of a house and three acres in Fairview as a recreation centre for the union members and their families. On Sunday 3 August 1913 Croydon Park was officially opened with a 'Grand Temperance Fete and Children's Carnival'. There was dancing and singing and games for the children as the band played all day. That Christmas, in the midst of the lock-out, one observer noted 'the surprises that Santa Claus is preparing for the kiddies … Three large marquees are to be pitched close to the house in Croydon Park, and in these 5,000 children are to be fed and entertained. A Christmas tree is rearing its bravery of light and colour in the conservatory of the fine old house …'

A short time later Larkin wrote to a Liverpool seed merchant that 'I want to interest our people in the culture of vegetables and flowers and window-box displays … The gardens have been neglected. We have vines and hot houses … I want to get good results, so as to encourage our people.' He also bought a cow and calf to familiarise the Dublin slum-dweller with another side of Irish life.

These were the reasons Larkin was the idol of the Dublin working class. He gave them more of his time, his energy and himself than anyone had ever given them before. He gave them a social life besides the public house and the tenement porch or window, and he brought a measure of hope and happiness into their narrow lives by providing them with new outlets for their neglected humanity. The achievement was modest, because the resources were slender, but a great deal was done with very little where nothing had ever been done before.

In the last analysis, however, Larkin's ascendancy over the Dublin workers was rooted in his remarkable ability to identify with them. He was at one and the same time only one of themselves and yet something more than each. He said as much when he told them:

> Don't bother about cheering Larkin—he is but one of yourselves. It is you that want the cheers, and it is you that deserve them. It is you and the class from which I come—the down-trodden class—that should get the cheers, and all the good things that follow the cheers. I don't recognise myself—a mean soul like myself in a mean body—as being the movement. You are the movement and for the time being I have been elected as your spokesman.

It was Constance Markievicz, however, on listening to Larkin for the first time at a mass meeting in Dublin in October 1910, who later summed up his impact best:

> Sitting there listening to Larkin, I realised that I was in the presence of something that I have never come across before, some great primaeval force rather than a man. A tornado, a storm-driven wave, the rush into life of spring, and the blasting breath of autumn, all seemed to emanate from the power that spoke. It seemed as if his personality caught up, assimilated, and threw back to the vast crowd that surrounded him every emotion that swayed them, every pain and joy that they had ever felt made articulate and sanctified. Only the great elemental force that is in all crowds had passed into his nature for ever.

In May 1911, Larkin increased both his presence and his influence in Dublin with the launching of the *Irish Worker and People's Advocate*. This novel production was, and remains, unique in the history of working-class journalism. Week after week, Larkin attacked with a monumental perseverance and determination the sweating, exploiting employers and the corrupt, cynical politicians who were, in his view, responsible for the reprehensible social condition of Dublin. He gave no quarter and expected none as he vilified any and all, high and low, who had the misfortune to come under the notice of his pen. Within a year no less than seven cases for libel were begun against the *Worker*, none of which proved successful.

'Another Sweating Den' was a typical example of Larkin's editorial technique in dealing with the unwholesome exploiters of the poor.

> We have discovered another philanthropist. He has a drapery establishment in Earl street, and his name is Hickey. Now, Hickey is a tricky boy, and instead of paying his porters a reasonable wage, he gives them the magnificent sum of 9s. a week, and allows them to eat the scraps left over after the shop assistants have dined. Most of the men who work as drapers' porters are married and have families. Hickey's are no exception, and some of his men have as many as five children. We would like to know does Mr. Hickey think it possible to support a family, buy clothes for them, and pay rent in Dublin out of this amount? If he will let us know how to do it we will be very thankful. Hickey knows it can't be done, but Hickey doesn't care.

Larkin justified these exposures and denunciations by pointing out:

Thousands of working men and women have had the burden of late lightened owing to the *Irish Worker*. Light has been shed on dark places, the truth has been told for the first time about some of the impostors who are trading under the cloak of religion, and hiding behind the mantle of Nationality, and untold benefits have accrued to the slaves who work for them.

Still, even while exposing all these sordid tales of mischief, misery, jobbery, and injustice, Larkin never failed to call for something more for the workers. 'We are going to rouse the working classes out of their slough of despond,' he insisted—'out of the mire of poverty and misery—and lift them to a plane higher. If it is good for the employers to have clean clothing and good food and books and music, and pictures, so it is good that the people should have these things also—and that is the claim we are making to-day.'

It was in that claim for social equality, in fact, that the true greatness of James Larkin is really rooted. Indeed it was this demand for social justice for the working class that not only gave real meaning to his life as an agitator and his work as a trade union leader but was also his inestimable gift to the class from which he sprang. As an agitator he raised the social and political consciousness of the Irish working class by preaching the gospel of divine discontent and prophesying for them a brave new world. As a trade union leader he mobilised the power inherent in their aggregate numbers by organising them for the winning of that brave new world. Without his socialist faith, however, Larkin could never have convinced the Irish working class of their real worth as human beings, and without that raised consciousness they could never have been persuaded to make their world a less terrible place for their posterity; and it was this better world that was James Larkin's legacy to the class to which he devoted his life and his work.

Chapter 2

Ireland, 1907–1947
The Socio-Economic Context

Prof. Cormac Ó Gráda

When the 33-year old James Larkin arrived in Belfast from Liverpool in 1907 to organise that city's dockers, Belfast was the biggest city in Ireland. Even tagging the population of the middle-class townships of Pembroke and Rathmines-Rathgar onto Dublin's still left Belfast with a slight numerical edge over Dublin by 1901, an edge that it would maintain for a generation. Belfast's status as one of the great industrial cities of the United Kingdom, having quadrupled its population since 1850, must have made it seem like the right place for Larkin to begin his career in the Irish labour movement. Belfast was Linenopolis; but it was much more. It contained the biggest shipyard in the world and thriving engineering plants, distilleries, ropeworks, and much else. Its big, brand-new city hall, built in 1906, aptly reflected civic pride and achievement.

By contrast, Dublin, which would become Larkin's main focus after some dramatic months in Belfast and where he died in 1947, had been losing out in a relative sense for decades. From being one of the great cities of Europe at the beginning of the nineteenth century it had dropped back to the second division by its end. Still, though bloated somewhat by Famine immigration in mid-century, its population of a quarter of a million in 1850 would rise to nearly 400,000 on the eve of the First World War. Of course, Dublin's share of a declining population continued to grow (to 4 per cent in 1850, 8 per cent in 1911), and therefore so did its relative economic importance in Ireland.

The occupational profiles of Ireland's two biggest cities almost a century ago make for interesting comparisons. In 1911 slightly more than half of Dublin's labour force worked in what the census deemed 'industrial' occupations, but the 55,000 men in such occupations included 9,000 builders and decorators and 19,000 unskilled mechanics and labourers, many of whom belonged to the 'stagnant pool' of casual workers. Using different occupational categories, Prof. Mary Daly estimates that 20.4 per cent of Dublin's male workers and 31.7 per cent of its females were employed in manufacturing.

Belfast's profile was very different. There, 36.2 per cent of the men and 70 per cent of the women in the labour force had manufacturing jobs.[1] Linen employed about 11,000 men in Belfast and the shipyards another 7,000, engineering works 6,000, and iron and steel a further 5,000. Half the 48,000 women employed in the industrial sector worked in linen mills, while another quarter worked in clothes factories.

As the numbers suggest, Dublin's industrial base was rather weak. It is symptomatic that the leader of Dublin's employers, William Martin Murphy, a tycoon with a background in construction, was a newspaper, tramway and department store proprietor—hardly your classic industrial capitalist. The industrial troubles of 1913 were associated with transport workers and dockers rather than factory operatives or miners.

The contrast between Ireland's two biggest cities was just as striking in housing. In the nineteen-hundreds Dublin's poor housing and ill-health were notorious. In 1911 the city contained over five thousand one-room tenements in which five or more people lived; of these, 643 housed eight or more people. Overcrowding was greatest in the Mountjoy, Merchants' Quay and Inns Quay wards in the inner city. Belfast's housing stock was newer, and therefore better. Tenement accommodation there was a rarity, and the city contained only thirty-four of those one-room tenements occupied by five people or more. Partly because sectarian tensions confined most of Belfast's Catholics to the oldest parts of the city, they were at a disadvantage in housing terms, but even they were much better off than Dublin's poor.

Larkin moved to Dublin before the end of 1907. There his early efforts fed on Dublin's notoriously bad housing. In the wake of the events in O'Connell Street on 31 August 1913, the *Irish Times* claimed that Larkin's followers lived 'for the most part in slums like Church Street,' adding that 'if every unskilled labourer in Dublin were the tenant of a decent cottage of three or even two rooms, the city would not be divided into two hostile camps.'[2]

That contrast between rich and poor in Dublin before the Great War is emphasised by the extremely detailed tables of death produced at the time. The death rate per thousand was 16.5 for the professional class and 17.5 for the middle class, in contrast to 40.2 for the general service and workhouse category. The far higher mortality rates of the poor were largely the product of higher infant and child mortality, but overcrowding also meant that the poor were much more vulnerable to killer diseases such as tuberculosis and pneumonia.

In 1911 women constituted a majority in both cities, but men far outnumbered women in the prisons, hospitals, mental institutions, and workhouses. In Dublin such institutions contained over twice as many inmates as Belfast (15,533 against 7,735), more a reflection of Dublin's status as capital city than anything else.

Neither city had much in the way of a labour—never mind socialist—movement, though both nationalist and unionist movements contained a labourist tendency. Though Jim Larkin's stay of half a year or so 'shook Belfast to its roots' in 1907, according to his biographer Emmet Larkin (no relation), 'in the long run he achieved little of a tangible nature' there, and the événements of the spring of 1907, which began by uniting workers, ended up by increasing sectarian tensions.[3] Labour would never win control of either Dublin or Belfast, though the Labour Party, founded by

Larkin and James Connolly in 1912, would get close in Dublin in 1942, when it became the biggest party in the city council.

By the nineteen-forties Dublin had regained its numerical superiority over Belfast. The population of most towns in the South grew after independence. In history, increasing urbanisation usually means industrialisation, and the policy of import-substituting industrialisation introduced in 1932 was partly responsible for the rising population of Ireland's cities and towns. The increasing urbanisation of the population should have provided a fertile field for trade unions, but the rise in union membership was by no means as smooth as the rise in town populations. Huge increases in membership in the nineteen-tens were followed by drastic declines in the twenties. After 1932, rival trade unions competed for the affiliation of workers in Seán Lemass's new factories, driving up membership again.

The course of wages over Larkin's years in Ireland is well documented. A wide-ranging survey conducted by the Free State Fiscal Inquiry Committee in 1923 showed that before the Great War skilled workers in Ireland were paid almost as much as their British peers. The gap in unskilled wages in the towns was still about one-quarter, however.[4] But what of changes over time? In summary, the story is one of rapid rise between the early nineteen-hundreds and the early twenties, followed by little sustained rise thereafter till the nineteen-forties. Comparing wages for a broad range of skilled trades in 1914 and 1947, the year of Larkin's death, suggests a nominal rise of about 250 per cent over the period; the rise in unskilled wages would not have been very different.[5] Real wages rose in the wake of the Great War, but, after adjustment for rising living costs, the rise in real wages between the mid-twenties and the mid-forties was minimal.

The nineteen-twenties were years of retrenchment and what would later be called 'fiscal rectitude'. Though the contrast between Cumann na nGaedheal and the young Fianna Fáil can be overdone—because by 1930–31 world conditions and political pressures were forcing Cumann na nGaedheal into measures undreamt of earlier—the changeover was nevertheless probably the most radical to occur in independent Ireland. Under Fianna Fáil, the nineteen-thirties were worse for farmers but better for urban dwellers than they would have been under Cumann na nGaedheal. The industrial work force rose considerably. Comparing wage data in Irish and British cities at the end of the thirties presents a mixed picture: bricklayers and local authority labourers were paid as much in Ireland as in Britain, for example, but the same could not be said for transport workers.

However, Irish wage levels lagged behind after 1939. Comparing industry-wide levels in 1938 and 1946 suggests that the gap between Irish and British men's wages rose from a sixth to a third; for women the rise was from 8 to 31 per cent.[6] Was this because of the weakness of a famously divided labour movement? Larkin, after all, hated not only bosses; nor was he guiltless in his feuds with Tom Johnson, the mild-mannered leader of the Labour Party, or the more difficult William O'Brien of the ITGWU. Some of the significant drop in the share of wages and salaries in net manufacturing output (from an average of 48.9 per cent in 1936–40 to 46.0 per cent in 1941–43) and in labour's share of domestically generated national income (from 51 per cent in 1938 to 44.3 per cent in 1944) might be explained in this way; but over the longer period it is the poor performance of the economy, not labour's declining share of the proceeds, that mattered most. War's end produced a rash of strikes, beginning in 1946 with a strike by teachers in Dublin. The Labour Court was set up to improve industrial relations in August 1946, but the strikes continued. On the night before the end of a two-month bus and tram strike in November 1947, passers-by in the streets cheered trams making trial trips.

Let us focus for a few moments on social conditions towards the end of Larkin's life. Before the introduction of BCG, tuberculosis was a deadly disease that hit large numbers of young people in the prime of life. It was most likely to attack in conditions of overcrowding and big families. In the nineteen-hundreds tuberculosis claimed more than 11,500 lives a year in Ireland; it was then the most common cause of death among Irish people. The disease must have had a macabre resonance for Larkin: it had claimed the life of his own father, an immigrant from Armagh, in Liverpool in 1887. In the nineteen-thirties it still caused about 3,500 deaths annually in the South, or about one death in twelve.

The death rate from TB was a sensitive barometer of deprivation; tellingly, it rose during the years of the Second World War. James Deeny, chief medical adviser to the Minister for Health in the nineteen-forties, wrote in his memoirs that 'to visit some of these places and see long lines of people, mainly young men and women, in bed in old-fashioned wards, under miserable conditions, without even a hot-water bottle in winter, hopeless and helpless, most of them slowly dying, was heart-breaking.'[7] The need to provide isolation facilities for TB patients had proved an intractable problem for decades. By the time this was finally agreed, in 1945–46, the technology that would make prolonged stays in sanatoriums unnecessary had already been discovered. In the thirties and forties mortality rates from TB were twice as high in Ireland as in Britain. As the latest chest surgical treatments became available to the poor, the death rate fell from 1.25 per thousand in 1945 to 0.54 in 1952.

The victory, or near-victory, over TB and other infectious diseases curable by antibiotics came late to Ireland, and the result was a dramatic fall in mortality from TB in a short space of time. In the nineteen-forties increased concern with public health found its less controversial representations in postage-stamp cancellations of the time, such as *Are you sure your food is clean?* and *Cosain do leanbh ar an diftéir.*

Infant mortality, often invoked by both historians and development experts as a guide to living standards, claimed about one young life in fifteen in the early nineteen-twenties. The rate was twice as high in the cities as in rural districts. Infant mortality also rose significantly during the Second World War; the rise, mainly due to gastro-enteritis, was particularly marked in Dublin.[8]

The Southern economy remained open in one important sense during 1939–45: the emigrant outflow during the war years was very high, a reflection of both depressed conditions at home and the buoyant demand for labour in Britain. Between 1940 and 1945 136,000 travel permits or passports were issued to men and 62,000 to women. Those seeking them were people, mainly young and unskilled or semi-skilled, about to seek work in Britain. Since each trip required a permit, these numbers exaggerate the true emigration rate,[9] but the net figure was perhaps two-thirds of the total. The widening real wage gap helps explain the rise in emigration, but employment opportunities were also much better in Britain. The low proportion of females among emigrants and the small number of permits issued in 1944 reflected the severe controls imposed at the time; the female proportion rose again after 1945. The Emigration Commission later interpreted the youthfulness of the emigrants— particularly the women—as evidence that emigration to Britain was 'not looked upon as involving a permanent or complete break which results from emigration overseas.' Throughout, the rate of emigration was highest in the west and in the border counties.

In what would become the Republic in 1949, economic conditions improved somewhat during Larkin's last years.[10] Personal expenditure rose and investment recovered, doubling in real terms between 1944 and 1946. Following a decade or so of virtual stagnation, industrial output rose by about two-thirds between 1946 and 1951, and the increase was destined mainly for the domestic market. The census of 1951 offered another sign of hope: it was the first since 1841 to register an increase in the Twenty-Six Counties. Unemployment as a proportion of the total insured labour force fell from 10.6 per cent in 1946 to 7.5 per cent in 1950.

But the main boom in the late forties was in consumption, as people tried to make up for time lost during the war years. The number of cars registered for the first time rose from 2,848 in 1946 to 17,524 in 1950. Imports of nylon stockings rocketed from a few thousand a year during the war to an average of over 230,000 pairs in 1946–51. Still, tea and sugar continued to be rationed; in late 1947 the Government subsidised necessities at the cost of increasing duties on the 'old reliables', doubling the duty on fur and cosmetics and enacting huge increases in cinema prices. Royal Baking Powder offered a way 'to make light puddings in spite of dark flour.' On the eve of one of the worst cold spells on record, Fuel Importers (Éire) Ltd improvised by offering Dubliners a hundred tons of firewood clippings, which were 'not regarded as rationed fuel.' Eggs continued to do their vanishing act in late autumn in the towns, and consumers pretended not to understand 'why eggs should disappear as soon as prices are pegged.' The early months of 1947 saw the longest cold spell in memory, producing more hardship than any time during the war years.

Still, the report of the Social Service Department of the Rotunda Hospital, Dublin, for 1947 recorded 'a marked improvement in the general economic conditions of the patients. Increased wages and supply of goods made it possible for the average skilled workman in regular employment in the city to maintain himself and his family, at least as well as he did before the war.' For the unemployed and casually employed, things were also better, but they were still unable to support themselves without assistance from voluntary charities.

The Rotunda's social workers interviewed nearly seven thousand new patients; the slight decline from previous years was put down to the transport strike and the severe weather early in the year. The development of new public housing estates in Donnycarney and Cabra West meant that half the Rotunda mothers lived three miles or more from the hospital. One-third of those interviewed were found to need assistance. Their main requirements were extra nourishment and clothing; a few needed a maternity ambulance, help with housing accommodation, follow-up, and supervision.

The following account from the Rotunda's report for 1946 offers a revealing glimpse of conditions faced by the poorest inner-city Dubliners at the time:

Mrs. N. developed Phlebitis following her discharge from the wards on her 7th confinement and was advised to rest in bed at home. We were asked to arrange for a district nurse to call daily to dress her leg and also to ensure that she could obtain adequate rest and nourishment. We discovered that her home consisted of one small, attic room. There were holes in the floor, the outside walls were dripping with wet whilst the plaster was falling off the inside walls and ceiling and all water had to be carried up from the ground floor. Mrs. N. was in bed; the head of the bed was against the damp wall and beside an open window: as a result the baby had developed a cold. Mrs. N. and her husband and five children—the eldest was six and a half years—lived in this room and slept on the only bed. In spite of the difficulties, the home was reasonably clean. Mr. N., an unemployed cattle drover, was dependent on 18s. 4d. unemployment assistance, 12s. 6d. food vouchers and 5s. children's allowance per week and his rent was 10s. Occasionally he obtained a day's work and earned about £1. In addition the Society of St. Vincent de Paul was giving him a food voucher, value 4s. per week and the Catholic Social Service Food Centre was giving Mrs. N. dinner and milk every day. We applied at once to the Corporation Housing Department for accommodation for this family and seven months later they moved to a four-roomed Corporation house.

Such conditions provided an ideal breeding-ground for TB. But in general, housing had made considerable strides in Dublin and in the country as a whole since the nineteen-hundreds. The average number of people per room in Dublin had dropped from 1.55 in 1926 to 1.29 in 1936 and 1.14 in 1946. The proportion of families having more than two people per room fell from 45.3 per cent in 1926 to 27.3 per cent in 1946.

Social change has been much more rapid in the four decades after Larkin's death than in the four decades that straddled his time in Ireland. To take one example, on the face of it, sexual attitudes were as rigid in the nineteen-forties as they had been in the nineteen-hundreds; the 'illegitimacy' rate was about the same in 1950 as it had been in the early twenties. Even in Dublin, births outside marriage were very much the exception. As a young Dublin woman put it to the American sociologist Alexander Humphries about 1950, 'if a girl got into trouble the boy who was responsible would always marry her. And if he didn't, nobody would have anything to do with him. Even his own parents would make it hard for him. So the boy usually does marry the girl.'[11]

All the same, census data suggest some change in sexual mores during this period. Direct evidence on premarital conceptions is lacking, but the census reports for 1911 (for the whole country) and 1946 (for the Twenty-Six Counties only), which contain special studies of marital fertility, offer some tantalising clues. They show a marked increase between 1911 and 1946 in the proportion of couples married less than one year at the time of the census who had at least one child. Among teenage brides the proportion rose from 12.7 per cent in 1911 to 30.6 per cent in 1946. The proportion in 1911 is consistent with minimal premarital sex, but the 1946 proportion indicates that one-fifth or more of those marrying in 1945–46 may have done so after conceiving. Among all brides of less than a year the proportions were less but the rise just as striking: 6.8 per cent to 15.9 per cent. The 1911 levels are consistent with little in the way of premarital sex. In 1946 the incidence of teenage premarital pregnancy or 'shotgun weddings' was very much less in Connacht and the three counties of Ulster than in the rest of the country. This is an important, previously unremarked on, change.

Attitudes to family limitation were also changing, though the big changes would come later. Even at the beginning of the century the middle classes were practising family limitation in Dublin. Humphries cites a man with a clerical job about 1950: 'People have to curtail their families. If I were to have another baby this year I'd be down on my uppers. The cost is terrible and this business about free maternity is bunk. It is inefficient and no one is going to avail himself of it unless he is a pauper.'[12] But the control was through 'rhythm' and continence, not through contraception.

Larkin's early years in Ireland coincided with the beginnings of what we know as the welfare state; in his final years, the welfare state was entering its glorious phase. One of the measures introduced by Asquith's reformist Liberal administration of 1906–11, the Old Age Pension Act (1908), was a particular boon to Ireland. The pension was means-tested, so Ireland's relative poverty entitled a higher proportion of people to its provisions. But the fact that one in twenty-five of the entire population of Ireland had been granted the pension by early 1909, against one in eighty-eight in England, was only partly a reflection of Ireland's greater poverty: there was also a good deal of what would today be called 'welfare fraud'.

The trouble was that hard evidence on people's ages was not easily come by: throughout the country the elderly and not-so-elderly testified to 'eating a potato out of [their] hand on the night of the Big Wind' in 1839. As Augustine Birrell, Chief Secretary at the time, reminisced much later, 'the "Big Wind" eventually played such havoc with the Treasury chest that it had to be discarded as untrustworthy evidence of age.' Birrell's department was put to the pin of its collar by 'the complexity of the budgets sent in by applicants, some of whom farmed over three hundred acres, and possessed horses, cows, and implements of husbandry.' A complete revision of the list was made, but thousands below the required age of seventy still benefited.

Still, the measure did much for the quality of life of old people, and it produced a massive income transfer to many of those who needed it most. Many elderly couples must really have believed, with their five shillings each, 'nach mbeadh siad aon lá bocht lena mbeo arís.' The old age pension also produced an amazing increase in filial piety and for some old folk a shift from the workhouse to family care. It was said that 'if an old age pensioner begins to cough, so much anxiety is displayed by his family that the doctor is dragged out of his home ... to prolong the life of this eligible member of the family.'[13] Ernest Blythe, the first Minister for Finance of the new state, is perhaps best remembered nowadays for having cut the old age pension in 1924—an understandable ploy, perhaps, in that this item alone absorbed one-tenth of the Free State's public expenditure and that falling prices had been increasing the real value of the pension since 1921, but mean-minded and regressive all the same.

As noted, the nineteen-twenties were not propitious years for advances in social welfare. In this era of de Valera-bashing it is no harm remembering that in this sphere the Fianna Fáil administrations of the nineteen-thirties were far more radical than their predecessors. They alleviated the miserable lot of the unemployed, they gave thousands of small farmers a modest 'dole', and in the towns they considerably expanded the stock of public housing. In the thirties the alternative to them was not a compassionate and 'enlightened' administration of the modern kind but more of Cumann na nGaedheal nineteen-twenties-style.

A measure enacted towards the end of Larkin's days, the payment of children's allowances to families with three children or more from 1943, created its own controversies. The Department of Finance fought a rearguard action against it. Though neither as generous nor as fair as the old age pension, it proved a boon to many hard-pressed families. More generally, the slow growth of the economy firmly constrained the scope of welfare reform.

Economically and socially, Larkin's years in Ireland were ones of modest progress and missed opportunities. Part of the problem was that Ireland, a newly independent economy, made its share (and perhaps more than its share) of policy mistakes. By the late forties it should have been clear that the road to economic self-sufficiency was a cul-de-sac. Some, in their enlightened moments, realised as much; but it would take longer for politicians, trade unionists and the people to realise that the aphorism 'no man is an island' applied to small economies, even island economies, as well.

Chapter 3

Liverpool: The Apprenticeship of a Revolutionary

Eric Taplin

Irish people—and I speak as an Englishman—have a profound sense of their historical heritage. Within that heritage are a number of influential figures, and, as far as the Irish labour movement is concerned, none is more important than Jim Larkin. He is remembered as the stormy petrel of Irish trade unionism and the prophet of revolutionary socialism. In the years immediately before the First World War he enjoyed an international reputation as the champion of the Irish unskilled workers. On the other hand, employers, the governing classes and to some extent the British trade union establishment looked upon him as a notorious trouble-maker. But whatever one's view of him, Larkin was a working-class leader who left a major imprint upon his and subsequent generations.

He is best remembered as the leader of the Belfast strike of 1907, the founder of the Irish Transport and General Workers' Union in 1909, and the leader of the memorable Dublin strike and lock-out of 1913. What is less well known is that the roots of his socialist and trade union activities were in Liverpool, where he lived for most of the first thirty years or so of his life. It was there that he served his apprenticeship; and the thrust of this chapter is to give a brief account of his working life in those early and eventful years.

Jim was born in Liverpool at 41 Combermere Street, Toxteth, on 4 February 1874. At eleven years of age, following his father's death, he started work as an engineer's apprentice, but he left to take on better-paid though less secure jobs, including work at the docks. He became a socialist by the time he was seventeen years of age and was a member of the Liverpool Branch of the Independent Labour Party. Rising unemployment in 1893 drove him to stow away on a ship to Montevideo. He returned to Liverpool a year later, and although he picked up jobs as a dock labourer, he experienced periods of great poverty. Nevertheless he was powerfully built and a hard and conscientious worker who neither smoked nor drank.

He was noticed by T. and J. Harrison, a large firm whose ships docked at the south end of the Liverpool waterfront, and became a regular employee for them. In 1903 he was promoted to foreman dock porter. This was a major step up for Larkin: it was a permanent job with a regular wage of £3 10s a week, and none but the most trustworthy and reliable men were recruited. On the strength of this security Larkin married in September 1903 and at twenty-seven years of age enjoyed some of the smaller luxuries of life. Although he remained fiercely teetotal, he began smoking a pipe, and bought a good suit and a broad-brimmed hat.

To Harrisons he was a model employee. Temperance was a rare quality among dock workers, and Larkin was honest and diligent. He had power over men, in that he chose his gangs from the many who clamoured for work each day, but was hardly popular among them. He drove the men hard to complete the job in hand and was nicknamed 'Rusher Larkin'. But he was respected for his honesty and fairness. He took no part in the petty corruption of bribery and so forth that was the common practice of most foremen.

All this appears to be a far cry from a revolutionary socialist. But in his spare time he spoke at street-corner meetings, sold copies of the *Clarion* and *Labour Leader*, and involved himself deeply in the expanding labour movement. It was here that he learnt the skills of public speaking and preached the socialist revolution that would end working-class degradation. Although he had reservations about the value of trade unions, he joined the National Union of Dock Labourers in 1901, though he did not play an active role in branch affairs. In brief, Larkin, the model foreman, kept his politics separate from his work.

The NUDL, which Larkin had joined with some reluctance, had been formed in Glasgow in 1889.[1] Its progress was rapid at first, with branches being established in many of the ports of northern England, Scotland, and Ireland. Indeed, within a year of its foundation there were thirty-four branches, with a membership of 25,000; but its main strength was on Merseyside, where it proved to be immensely popular—so much so that its head office was moved from Glasgow to Liverpool in 1891. However, in the early eighteen-nineties, rising unemployment and an employers' counter-attack led to the collapse of many branches, and by 1905 there were about 12,000 members, about half being in the Merseyside branches.

A factor weakening the union had been a three-week strike on Merseyside in 1890 with mixed results. The union was virtually stamped out at the north end of the dock system, where the large steamship companies, such as Cunard and the White Star Line, had permanent berths. Posters on the walls of the dock sheds declared: *Men wearing union buttons will be immediately discharged*.[2] However, the strike had achieved one notable victory, which probably saved the union from extinction: employers at the south end of the docks recognised the union, accepted the union's port working rules, and gave preference of employment to union members. Harrisons probably chafed under this restriction on their management freedom, but the issue was apparently not serious enough for them to take on the union.

It is now time to bring another actor onto the stage. James Sexton was general secretary of the NUDL, having been elected to the post in 1893.[3] His early life was, if anything, more poverty-stricken than Larkin's. He was born in 1856 of Irish parents who were living in St Helens, Lancashire, and he was at work at the age of nine. In his teens he became a seaman but returned home on the death of his father, becoming a dock labourer in the late eighteen-seventies, when he was in his twenties. In 1882 he suffered a severe injury at work that disfigured him for life. His cheekbone was smashed, one eye temporarily dislodged, and his skull slightly fractured. He was in hospital for two months; on returning to the docks he was offered light work at boy's pay.

Even before his accident, Sexton was an outspoken critic of the working conditions of labour. As he later wrote, 'no day passed without my registering at its close ... a vow that the rest of my life would be devoted to awakening the consciences and the courage of those slaves of industry, and striving to arouse within them some knowledge of their dignity and responsibilities as men.'[4] He joined the NUDL in 1889, though he played little part in the 1890 strike. He achieved local prominence during the eighteen-nineties, when he emerged as a leader of the unemployed movement in Liverpool, where, incidentally, he first met Larkin.

Sexton was an Irish nationalist and a socialist. He favoured Home Rule by constitutional means, under the influence of T. P. O'Connor, the Nationalist MP for the Scotland division of Liverpool. But his interest in Ireland waned as he became absorbed into the British labour movement. Similarly, his socialism became increasingly reformist rather than revolutionary. By 1905, at the age of forty-nine, he was a figure of local, indeed national, importance as the leader of the largest union on Merseyside and a member of the Parliamentary Committee of the British Trades Union Congress.

The event that transformed Larkin into a notorious trade union agitator was the Liverpool dock strike of 1905. It was confined to the firm for which Larkin worked, T. and J. Harrison, but it was prolonged and increasingly bitter.

Foremen were required to be union members, but by mid-June 1905 seven of the thirty-five foremen had allowed their union membership to lapse, and on 27 June eight hundred union dockers struck, demanding that the foremen rejoin. Within a fortnight all but two or three had rejoined, but the damage had been done. The strike provided Harrisons with the opportunity they had long waited for. They condemned the men, imported blacklegs, and repudiated their recognition of the union. This was serious. If Harrisons were successful, other firms at the south end might follow suit. Both the firm and the union therefore dug in their heels. After thirteen weeks of acrimony, the men capitulated and returned to work on the firm's terms. The strike had been a tragic failure.[5]

The dispute, however, proved to be the making of Larkin. It is not clear whether Larkin provoked the strike, though he did claim that the men had grievances that had not been dealt with about the foremen in question other than union membership. In any case, he flung himself into their cause. His compelling oratory, his infectious enthusiasm, his determination, his fearlessness and his devotion to the men on strike transformed him from the model foreman to the militant leader of men, known throughout the Liverpool waterfront. The man who had previously regarded trade unionism as little more than a reformist tool within capitalism was now converted to the vision of organising all workers into unions to crusade against capitalist exploitation and, through militant industrial solidarity, to forge the socialist revolution. It was a vision that remained with him throughout his subsequent career.

Sexton, however, viewed the dispute with foreboding. As soon as the strike began he sought to get the men back to work and to resolve the problem by negotiation with the firm. Indeed he was prepared to waive the question of the foremen's membership of the union if the firm continued to recognise the NUDL. However, when this failed he fought with tenacity to restore the status quo. Blacklegs housed in the dock sheds, he claimed, were contravening the Public Health Act concerning smoking, which constituted a fire hazard, and sanitary regulations were being ignored. To secure publicity, he went as far as entering one of the docks, and was arrested for smoking in a forbidden area. In court he claimed that blacklegs were permitted to smoke at work; but he lost the case and was fined 5s, with 4s 6d costs. The Health Committee of the city council ultimately met to debate the use of dock sheds for housing workers; it was a rowdy meeting, but it decided by a narrow majority not to prosecute. 'It's a fraud!' Sexton shouted from the public gallery. 'You are a lot of whited sepulchres!'[6] The legal strategy had failed. All Sexton could secure was the support of the Liverpool Trades Council and financial assistance from the General Federation of Trades Unions.

The loss of the strike was a damaging blow, although Sexton's worst fears, that other firms at the south end would repudiate the union, proved to be groundless. It also posed a personal problem for Sexton. Larkin's meteoric rise in popularity was a potential threat to his leadership. Larkin's dazzling oratory and selfless devotion made him the hero of the waterfront; he offered a clear alternative in style, attitude, and philosophy, possessing a charisma that Sexton lacked. Yet at the same time Sexton could not help but admit a grudging admiration for the energy and dedication of his rival.

I have dealt at some length with this dispute for two reasons: firstly because it was a turning-point in Larkin's career, and secondly because it sowed the seeds of the rivalry between Larkin and Sexton that was to have important consequences.

Nevertheless, relations between the two men remained cordial for a time. Both sought reform and were agitators in the cause of the working class, and both held a vision of a new and better society. Both had the immediate aim from 1905 of organising waterfront workers to reduce the abuses so prevalent at the docks. On two occasions Larkin assisted Sexton's political ambitions. In the autumn of 1905 Sexton successfully secured election to Liverpool City Council, with the help of Larkin. In 1906 Sexton was the Labour candidate for the West Toxteth constituency in the general election; Larkin was his election agent. Although he was unsuccessful, Sexton recalled in his autobiography that Larkin 'plunged recklessly into the fray ... displayed an energy that was almost superhuman ... nothing could frighten Jim ... I am convinced that it was largely owing to Larkin's overwhelming labour that we reduced a Tory majority from four thousand to five hundred, but I would rather not give an opinion on some of the methods he adopted.[7]

But in spite of this mutual support, deeper differences inevitably surfaced. Sexton was pragmatic, cautious, and conciliatory, seeking to achieve a strong dock workers' union, recognised by employers, so that working conditions could be improved and the dignity of labour recognised. Progress should be made through persuasion, moral force, and legal reform; militancy was a weapon of last resort. On the political front he sought to reform society through constitutional means—hence his lengthy efforts to become a Labour member of Parliament, not achieved until 1918. This was in sharp contrast with Larkin's impatient revolutionary fervour to harness all workers within militant trade unions to overthrow the capitalist system.

It was clear that when the 1905 strike was over Larkin could not return to Harrisons or, indeed, secure work anywhere on the docks. The NUDL executive appointed him national organiser, at a salary of £2 10s a week. Although Sexton later claimed he had reservations about the appointment, it did at least get Larkin out of Liverpool. Larkin threw himself into his new job with characteristic enthusiasm, establishing new union branches and reviving old ones in Scotland and Ireland. But apprehension grew in Sexton's mind as a result of the Belfast dispute of 1907, which lasted five months. It cost the union £7,000, and although the establishment of Irish branches was welcomed, Sexton was not prepared to watch the union bled white by expensive disputes to secure them.

To Larkin, however, working-class solidarity demanded sacrifices by the union in the interests of the weak and defenceless. A clash between the two men was therefore inevitable. In 1908 Larkin was instructed to inform the union executive of all ports he visited, in spite of his success in establishing branches in Dublin and Cork. In November 1908 he was instructed to go to Aberdeen to resolve a local problem. Larkin refused and instead went to Derry and Dublin, where trouble was brewing. Sexton then secured the right to suspend Larkin if he thought fit.

The response of Larkin was immediate. He defied the union, claiming that an opportunity now existed to organise *all* unskilled Irish labour, not only dock workers. This proved to be the last straw. Sexton had no interest in embracing within the union Irish workers from a multiplicity of occupations—a perilous enterprise that might undermine and destroy his patient work of the previous fifteen years. On 7 December 1908 Sexton suspended him.

The reaction of Larkin was characteristically belligerent and dramatic. He immediately formed the Irish Transport and General Workers' Union, and the battle commenced in Derry, Belfast, Dublin and Cork between the NUDL and the Irish union for membership among waterfront workers, a battle that was largely successful for the new Irish union.

Larkin's Liverpool apprenticeship was now at an end. He was, as it were, coming home. It is doubtful that he had seen the country of his forebears before being sent to Ireland in 1907. The impact on him was immense. Although never narrowly nationalistic, he was with his own people, witnessing depths of degradation at least as bad as if not worse than those in Liverpool. It fired his anger to see so many of his fellow-countrymen and their families so abused and exploited, and gave an added edge to his furious determination to transform the situation.

That was not quite the end of the stormy relationship between Larkin and Sexton. Two legal actions kept the wounds festering. In 1909 Larkin was arrested and charged with conspiracy to defraud the NUDL. Sexton was a witness for the prosecution, and Larkin was sentenced to twelve months' hard labour, later reduced to three months. In 1911 Sexton sued for libel over a publication that alleged that he had instigated the prosecution against Larkin. Larkin gave evidence for the defence, but Sexton won the case. This proved to be their final confrontation. Larkin concentrated on his crusade in Ireland, while Sexton retained his hold on what was essentially a dock workers' union within the British trade union movement.

Neither Larkin nor Sexton emerges creditably from their increasingly stormy relationship. Sexton used dubious tactics to discredit Larkin and used the union executive and the British trade union movement to block Larkin's progress. Larkin in turn exaggerated Sexton's failings and was contemptuous of the union that employed him. He expected blind admiration and support for his endeavours.

Larkin's experience in Liverpool was crucial. It gave him the opportunity to discover his powers of leadership and oratory, to harness his restless energy to a practical cause, and to use the trade union movement as a vehicle for the realisation of his vision of a new society of brotherhood and unity. His ambitions could not be contained within the traditional structure of British trade unionism, with its limited objectives and cautious tactics. To Larkin, trade unionism embraced the totality of people's lives—not only industrial change but also political and social revolution, to create a dignified life for all. To Sexton this was 'Larkinitis'.

Like all men and women of action and high ideals, those who devote their lives to a cause, Larkin is relatively easy to criticise. He had his faults. He was reckless, thoughtless on occasion, ignoring the less savoury aspects of his crusade. He rarely thought through a plan of action. He acted intuitively, spontaneously, instinctively, with a verve and audacity that take the breath away. He made enemies quickly and bickered with those with whom he disagreed. He dismissed adverse criticism too lightly.

But he gave himself totally, without fear of the future. Those who do so, who remain unswervingly dedicated and optimistic, irrespective of setbacks, for a vision that would enrich the quality of human life are rare indeed. It is for this reason that this remarkable man should be commemorated fifty years after his death.

Chapter 4

City in Revolt
Belfast, 1907

John Gray

It is by courtesy of a police report that we know that James Larkin arrived in Belfast on 20 January 1907 as an obscure delegate to the British Labour Party conference, which had honoured the fastest-growing city in the British Isles with its presence. Larkin represented the National Union of Dock Labourers, a British union, and also hoped to organise dockers in the city.

He came as no Irish evangel, rather, as contemporary descriptions have it, like a 'big burly docker from Liverpool or London,' who spoke in the 'approved manner of an English slum.' No-one foresaw the explosive consequences of his arrival: the prevailing view of the British and Irish trade union leaderships was that the strike was an outmoded weapon, that a new age of arbitration and conciliation was dawning, helped by the election of a Liberal government in 1906.

Belfast seemed the last centre where a major challenge to this new orthodoxy could arise. The grandiose new City Hall was a symbol of the city's overweening pride in its industrial success. Edwardian Belfast could claim the world's largest shipyard, linen mill, ropeworks, and tobacco factory. When in 1898 the Lord Mayor told delegates to the Irish Trades Union Congress that the city was 'an elysium for the working classes,' no-one contradicted him. Certainly skilled workers, also the backbone of the existing labour movement, shared in the prosperity, enjoying rates of pay governed by the British market and unequalled outside London.

The tinder that Larkin set alight lay rather in the abyss that separated this 'labour aristocracy' from the far larger mass of the unskilled. It is no accident that Belfast's most successful industries were labour-intensive and dependent on that very Irish factor, the never-ending tide of cheap labour flowing in from the countryside. Typical were the 3,100 dockers, mainly casual workers, often earning no more than 10s a week. Lindsay Crawford, an Independent Orangeman but also a radical journalist, estimated the minimum cost of keeping a family at 22s 5d; so women and children too were pressed into service in the low-wage economy of the mills.

Tommy Carnduff, a young unskilled worker at the time and later the 'shipyard poet', remembered how the 'labouring classes ... were bordering on starvation' and yet did not make mobilisation easier. Efforts by skilled workers to encourage unskilled organisation had signally failed, and the strategies they suggested—essentially the humble petitioning of employers—led to nothing but humiliating reverses.

Then there was the special difficulty of sectarianism—remember that although Catholics were relatively disadvantaged, Protestants remained a majority at every level of degradation. Poverty was shared, but every minimal advantage could be contested on sectarian grounds, and that contest was at its fiercest among the unskilled. Early efforts in the eighteen-nineties to organise the dockers had run foul of such divisions, and in 1907 the demarcation between Protestant cross-channel dockers and Catholic deep-sea dockers was a clear one.

No reports of Larkin's early street-corner speeches survive. All we have is anecdotal memory of mesmerising effect, a new sense of empowerment. William Long heard 'as fine a speech as ever I heard' at the corner of Corporation Street. The response was extraordinary: by the beginning of April, Larkin had recruited over two thousand men, and both the police and the press were beginning to take notice. So too were the employers.

On 26 April a coal-importer, Samuel Kelly, dismissed union members among his coal-heavers because 'a union … should not embrace such a class of employment.' Almost his entire work force walked out. Simultaneously the Belfast shipping companies were contacting the Europe-wide Shipping Federation, warning that they might need blackleg labour.

Rank-and-file union enthusiasm made restraint difficult. On 6 May, Belfast Steamship Company men walked out rather than work with a non-union man. Larkin conceded that this 'was a mistake' and instructed the men to return to work; they were locked out and replaced with blacklegs imported from Liverpool. The great Belfast dock strike was under way.

Thomas Gallaher, owner of Belfast Steamship Company, was one of Belfast's self-made businessmen, with a fortune founded on his great tobacco factory. He was to prove an inflexible and single-minded opponent. He may have banked on an early climb-down by his men, but humble petitioning was suddenly out of style; the following day union men stormed both Kelly's coal quay and the Steamship Company's sheds and chased the blacklegs.

Kelly promptly capitulated, granting union recognition and a pay rise. A victory march, led by a Union Jack with the men singing 'Britons never shall be slaves,' passed through the town. Gallaher, by contrast, spurned an intervention from the Lord Mayor, who relayed Larkin's willingness to go to arbitration. Only when this overture was rejected did Larkin fight back, denouncing Gallaher as 'an obscene scoundrel' and on 16 May urging the mainly women workers at Gallaher's tobacco factory to join a union and declaring in millennial terms: 'There was a strike of quay labourers at New York and Montreal, and before long it was not improbable that there would be a general strike all over the United Kingdom.' A thousand tobacco girls walked out; and yet they had to return the following day: the NUDL had no means of supporting them.

Foiled in one direction, Larkin moved elsewhere and in early June presented all the coal-importers with demands for union recognition and pay increases; and by 17 June all had conceded. Sailors in the coastal trade were threatening to come out, and an unrelated strike by five hundred iron-moulders led to the laying off of thousands of men in the shipbuilding and engineering industries. With time on their hands, they proved ready recruits for increasingly rowdy strike activity on the streets.

On 20 June, Larkin played for the highest stakes yet with a general demand to all the shipping companies. Success would isolate the obdurate Thomas Gallaher, but he was also taking on the great British railway companies, which also owned cross-channel steamers, companies that had refused recognition elsewhere to the members of the Amalgamated Society of Railway Servants. Larkin's Belfast ultimatum was undoubtedly timed to encourage ASRS members, who were simultaneously meeting in Birmingham to take industrial action. They failed to do so, and the Belfast men were left to go it alone on 26 June. Seven smaller firms gave in; but the larger companies held out.

More blacklegs arrived, and soldiers guarded an extended perimeter on the quays. Larkin tested the new Trade Disputes Act and its rights of peaceful picketing but failed to persuade any blacklegs to defect. He dismissed the new legislation as the 'Trades Act folly'. Strikers stormed the monthly meeting of the city corporation; a cry from the gallery, 'The Lord Mayor is no use. I'd shoot the Lord Mayor,' confirmed the angry mood but did nothing to resolve the new impasse in the dispute. But Larkin had another powerful card to play.

Almost overnight the union had recruited most of the city's carters, and now an ultimatum was issued on their behalf. For some it was a step too far: Robert Gageby, a veteran moderate labour leader, urged the carters 'to carry on their work.' At the same time the Presbyterian *Ulster Echo* made the first sectarian attack on the union leadership—they were 'extreme and rabid nationalists and Roman Catholics.'

Disagreements about strategy precipitated a crisis marked by Larkin's dramatic resignation as strike leader at a mass meeting on 2 July and his nomination of Alex Boyd, an Independent Orangeman and leader of the Municipal Employees, as his replacement. Larkin emphasised that Boyd was a Protestant and sought to vindicate himself in the face of two charges: that 'he was the great dictator' and that he was 'a hindrance to negotiations.' His willingness to step down provided an immediate answer to his critics behind the scenes.

The following day moderate strategy collapsed in ruins when the Lord Mayor sought to intercede with the employers and met a flat rebuff. At Dublin Castle, Sir Anthony MacDonnell sent the Chief Secretary, Augustine Birrell, a memo observing that 'you will notice deadlock is due to refusal of employers to consult Trades Union leaders.' The effect on the trade union movement was electrifying. Alex Boyd declared that it was now 'war to the knife' and denied that Larkin had ever resigned the leadership. There was, however, a new, wider organisational framework, with a strike committee involving other unions and inevitably curtailing Larkin's powers of independent action.

Now, on 3 July, Larkin's instruction that 'no carter's wheel of any union man would turn on the streets of Belfast' was enthusiastically obeyed. It no longer mattered if blacklegs were free to work at the quays behind military guard if no carts could get through to them. The *Northern Whig* reflected gloomily: 'We are on the eve of an experience something akin to that which has paralysed Russian cities during the last couple of years.'

And this was on the eve of the Twelfth of July, so often a season of working-class division in Belfast. At the Independent Orange Order demonstration £80 was collected for strike funds. Even within the more conservative 'old' Orange Order there were many supporters, typically Walter Savage, now a dockers' delegate to Belfast Trades Council, who wrote to the newspapers claiming that he could get '1,000 Old Orange Order Orangemen who belong to the union to sign this letter. Our fervent prayer is that James Larkin may long be spared—to work for the emancipation of the unskilled workers in his native land.'

Mass meetings were now organised in all the working-class areas of the city. Larkin was well received on the Shankill Road; Alex Boyd and others from Sandy Row were enthusiastically received on the Falls Road. All culminated in a massive march on 26 July through all the working-class areas of the city. The *Irish News* noted the new contrasts in the movement, as

> the older established societies preceded by banners, many of which were designed with much taste … marched two and two with almost military precision, whilst members of the more recently organised unions were collected in an irregularly formed but solid body, sometimes twenty abreast, rendering a computation of the total number taking part … out of the question.

Four platforms were needed at the City Hall to address the multitude. What was once a purely industrial dispute, and indeed one that was never to involve more than four thousand strikers, was becoming a popular mobilisation.

Yet by late July problems were crowding in apace. Threats to further extend the strike movement came to nothing. As the Police Commissioner, Hill, noted, there was much talk of 'socialism and generalities,' but this could not disguise tactical inertia. Instead the coal quay employers took the initiative and locked their men out. Meanwhile the carters' strike led to the laying off of thousands in industry. In this war of attrition, the strikers faced starvation.

Larkin now sought outside help to refill the war chest, but others no doubt hoped that the august authority of the British trade union movement could extract them from all enveloping crisis. James Sexton, general secretary of the NUDL, arrived on 16 July to announce executive backing but brought only £200. Delegates from the General Federation of Trades Unions arrived too; they were to provide a mere £1,692 throughout the strike, and their priority was always damage limitation, made easier by the exclusion of the Belfast leaders from all negotiations.

The employers, offered the prospect of piecemeal settlements, listened, and in short order both the iron-moulders' and coal quay disputes were settled. At the great rally on 26 July, Larkin announced that the coal quay men 'had won a great victory,' including increases of 11s per week; only on 5 August was it admitted that 'nothing had been committed to writing.' Larkin bitterly conceded that they had 'withdrawn one of the wings of their army and allowed the employers to surround the rest.'

Meanwhile that other peril so feared by all, the raising of political and national as opposed to purely industrial issues, surfaced, and as a direct consequence of the non-sectarian mass mobilisation of the strike movement. Pressures on the RIC in the city brought about by long hours of strike duty in the face of universally hostile working-class communities led to the emergence of a 'more pay' movement within the force, and insensitive leadership provoked virtual mutiny. On 27 July between 500 and 800 out of the RIC force of 1,000 seized control of Musgrave Street Barracks and admitted civilian strikers to an almost night-long meeting. Larkin was not in the city, but other labour leaders advised the policemen to petition for redress and return to barracks, the course eventually adopted. If in this way civilian strike leaders hoped to win kudos for their role in maintaining law and order, they were to be cruelly disappointed.

As were the mutinous police! The Liberal government had been happy to allow Belfast employers to stew in their own juice; it was another matter when law and order in Ireland as a whole was threatened. The leaders of the police mutiny were dismissed and their supporters transferred post haste out of the city. Simultaneously, six thousand troops were hurried into place, the greatest military concentration in Belfast up to 1914.

Unionists denounced the mutiny as a nationalist conspiracy, and nationalists, including Joe Devlin MP and the Dungannon Clubs, precursors of Sinn Féin, who had ignored the dock strike, now denounced the introduction of the army reinforcements. British trade union delegates from the GFTU now saw the continuance of the civilian strikes as a security risk and sought to force a settlement on the carters. As one of them, a Mr Appleton, put it, 'I felt that it would be of the greatest use to remove one of the elements of danger'—a bizarre reflection on the men he was supposed to defend. At the last moment the carters repudiated his proposal on a technicality: they were not yet prepared to 'blackleg' on the dockers. Once again it was a 'fight to a finish,' but this time with a real army.

The decisive Assistant Inspector-General Gambell, now commanding the RIC, drew up a scheme for 'showing the turbulent classes how easily we can cover the city with military pickets.' This was put into effect with overwhelming force on 7 August. At a stroke the strike pickets lost their month-long dominance of the streets, and blackleg carting got under way. The angry rhetoric of the strike leaders was in inverse proportion to their ability to do anything about the new situation. Larkin told the men that 'he was not a believer in bombs, but if a bomb would settle the matter he would not hesitate'; more prophetically, Joseph Harris asked, 'Were they [the strikers] to be blamed if riots resulted?'

They did indeed, and yet stemmed from moderate tactics—a mass meeting to which all the city's four MPs were invited. Only Joe Devlin came, and he used the opportunity to denounce the military presence. The following day minor disturbances in the Lower Falls were exacerbated by the heavy-handed introduction of the military. Full-scale rioting broke out, essentially a battle between nationalists and the army and one that would-be peace-makers, whether priests or trade unionists, were powerless to halt. Troops shot three bystanders dead, and calm was only restored when they withdrew. Although the English left mourned the Belfast victims as martyrs, mainstream labour's inclination to distance itself from the Belfast strikes intensified; Philip Snowden condemned 'that portion of the Belfast population which is almost as much accustomed to rioting as a savage tribe is to constant warfare.'

Heightened sectarian and political tensions compounded the strikers' difficulties. Larkin complained about press efforts 'to make it a political or religious dispute' and in desperation sought government arbitration. The government, now anxious to close the whole episode, agreed, provided the employers consented. In the case of the carters they saw their chance, and by 17 August the men had grudgingly accepted terms available weeks earlier. Now, as the employers had hoped, the dockers were isolated. For them it was a return to the old days of humble petitioning. As one veteran put it, 'I felt a pity about the fate of the men I knew—they were never again employed by the shipping company.'

By the middle of September it appeared that the strike was over. There was a final bitter flourish, provoked by the efforts of the coal quay employers to form a bogus union and eliminate the NUDL. In November the men came out on a final desperate strike; but any little chance they had was scuppered by the NUDL leader, James Sexton, who paid a one-day visit from Liverpool, denounced the action, spoke to the employers on his own, assured the men that 'all would be plain sailing,' and departed. The following day union men found they had been permanently replaced by blacklegs.

For all its pioneering heroism, the Belfast dock strike was, then, for most of its participants, a defeat, despite its enormous potential. The creation of the real possibility of change owed everything to Larkin, not as the espouser of revolutionary theory but as a millennial visionary speaking from the heart and bringing new tools to Ireland in the form of the sympathetic strike. The concept of a solidarity that made the individually weak strong suddenly had meaning. Certainly a new syndicalist intention can be read into Larkin's challenge to the great British railway companies; but, as even James Sexton pointed out, these were also the tactics that had marked the original formative struggle of the NUDL in Liverpool in 1889. Certainly the existing labour leadership in Belfast had misgivings at first about Larkin, but they were soon swept together with him by the force of events. The critical distinction between Larkin and others at this time was that he did not flinch from the discovery that the tactics of English militancy had revolutionary implications in Ireland.

It was the misfortune of all that in Belfast they were faced by a particularly malevolent conjunction of forces. A confident and obdurate employing class never shrank from the toughest strategies, including, increasingly, the playing of the sectarian card. They may have been in some measure pariahs in the British body politic, and especially to a Liberal government, but when issues of Irish law and order came to the fore, Liberals had viceregal priorities, even if that meant using overwhelming force. Meanwhile the British labour movement, the most obvious source of support, was unprepared for explosive developments of the kind seen in Belfast. From an early stage their interventions were all about resolving the disputes, and regardless of the interests of the strikers, while for some the violence in Belfast provided the excuse for a retreat into narrow English chauvinism.

Thus the would-be progressives of British society abandoned their exemplars in Belfast; but in Belfast the consequence was not merely a temporary reverse. The defeat of the dock strike, which weighed particularly heavily on the mainly Protestant cross-channel dockers and coal-heavers, played into the hands of resurgent unionism, and by 1912 all strands of the movement that had contributed to the 1907 strike, whether in the new unskilled unions, in moderate or left-wing Labour, or in the Independent Orange Order, had been virtually eliminated.

Certainly Larkin left no coherent rearguard, armed either with theory or with rhetoric, with which to resist Belfast's counter-revolution. He was not that sort of man: rather he moved restlessly onwards to wherever the flame burned brightest. Even as Belfast's coal-heavers faced their final defeat, a sympathy strike in Newry was taking on a momentum of its own. Belfast had shown what was possible elsewhere in Ireland; indeed events in Belfast foreshadowed the later dramatic breakaway of the Irish Transport and General Workers' Union and the road to the great Dublin lock-out. The tragedy was that Belfast was left behind.

Chapter 5

Larkin and the ITGWU, 1909–1912

Francis Devine

Lost in the shadow of the drama of the Belfast dockers' and carters' strike, James Larkin's organisational energies were quickly directed to the formation of a Dublin branch of the National Union of Dock Labourers on 11 August 1907 in the Trades Hall. A year later the branch claimed two thousand members.

While the NUDL's arrival in the city did not, as Charles McCarthy contended, bring 'the new unionism a generation late'—for there had been activity on the Dublin quays in the eighteen-eighties to parallel events in England—it is undoubtedly true that Larkin's personality and leadership recast 'new unionism' in fresh ways, which allowed him to 'introduce general unionism into Ireland and to invent Larkinism,' in a way that not only transformed Irish working-class politics but, as has been claimed, 'surely prefigures the rising of all transport workers in 1911' in Britain.[1] As Dublin employers made ready for the great battle of 1913–1914, Larkin had laid the foundation-stone of the modern labour movement, industrially and politically, with the creation of the Irish Transport and General Workers' Union and the Irish Labour Party and, most spectacularly, the transformation of the supine Dublin working class into a fighting force inspired by a socialist vision.

Larkin's activities in the first half of 1908 were so frenetic as to suggest that he was capable of bilocation. In addition to the demands of his position as national organiser of the NUDL, from January to March he regularly attended meetings in London of the official committee to investigate dock wages. Continued political involvement saw him attend the Independent Labour Party conference in Huddersfield in June, representing the Dublin Branch, and, later the same month, the Irish Trades Union Congress in Belfast as a delegate from the NUDL, where he gained election to the Parliamentary Committee. A new force to be reckoned with had come onto the industrial relations stage and drew immediate antagonistic attention, both from the older, craft trade unionists, whose sectional, conservative outlook was suddenly under threat, and the employers, who, as they increasingly saw it, feared for their very existence.

In July 1908 the Dublin Coal Masters' Association tried to break the NUDL by lock-out. Larkin was conciliatory but could not compromise on the issue of recognition. Despite support from Dublin Trades Council, where Larkin was already a prominent figure, and loyal backing from the members, the NUDL general secretary, James Sexton, intervened and brokered a settlement in London on 30 July. The deal included an arbitration clause but excluded Larkin from further participation in negotiations.

The NUDL was becoming impatient with Larkin's increasing commitment to Ireland and his regular refusal to follow instructions. The executive gave Sexton powers to discipline Larkin, whose intention of conforming was hardly indicated by his decision to move his family from Liverpool to Dublin. Sexton perhaps saw Larkin as a challenger to his position. Others were increasing their agitation for a separate organisation for the Irish unskilled. The violence that accompanied NUDL activity in Cork—where Larkin had despatched the Newry man James Fearon, who cheerily exchanged strong-arm tactics with the employers—further increased tensions between Larkin and his executive.[2]

Larkin obtained an arbitrated settlement in Cork in December. In November he had pushed for increases for Dublin carters, returning to the city from Derry as the strike broke rather than, as instructed, proceeding to Aberdeen. By 18 November, Dublin was a city 'under siege'. Sexton replied to Larkin's telegram plea for support with the terse 'Stew in your own juice.' He had already refused to accept any consequences for the Cork action. As Dublin reached fever pitch, Sexton suspended Larkin on 7 December, pointing out that any further 'action taken by you will be on your own responsibility.' Dublin dockers had found a leader but were losing their union.

Having finally established peace on 21 December, Larkin had time to reflect on his suspension and possibly 'took the disciplinary action to mean that British unions would never represent the true interests of Irish workers and drew some logical conclusions.'[3] Many historians believe that until his expulsion from the NUDL, Larkin had little interest in forming an Irish union. This may well be true, but the day after his expulsion it was reported that, having had his boat 'cut adrift from the other side,' he was prepared to 'fight out an existence in Ireland ... to start a new organisation of his own.'[4] On Tuesday 29 December 1908 delegates from Dublin, Cork, Belfast, Dundalk and Waterford met in the Trades Hall, Capel Street, Dublin, as the non-existent NUDL Irish Executive, to create a new union. On 4 January 1909 William O'Brien wrote in his diary: 'The Irish Transport and General Workers' Union founded officially from this date.' It was the date on which the new union was registered with the Registrar of Friendly Societies.

It has been suggested that the new union was called the Irish Transport Workers' Union, with the words 'and General' being added later. This is not so, although the initials ITWU were used regularly in the early years and appeared on the first badges, issued in January 1909, giving some credence to William O'Brien's claim that at the last moment he convinced Larkin to broaden the appeal of the union.[5]

The ITGWU heralded a new form of organisation. In the preface to its rules, registered in May 1909, it asked, 'Are we going to continue the policy of grafting ourselves on the English Trades Union movement, losing our own identity as a nation in the great world of organised labour?

31

We say emphatically, No!' Some criticise the vagueness of this ITGWU creed, but it must be remembered that it was constructed hurriedly and served a limited purpose.

The actions of the ITGWU demonstrated from the beginning that four new propositions guided and inspired them and would lead to the transformation of the entire labour movement: belief in the tactics of militant 'new' unionism; support for a socialist philosophy; Irish unions for Irish workers; and strong labour political action. Larkin's success in the last six months of 1908, not to be judged in terms of wage increases but of trade union recognition, has gone largely unnoticed. Emmet Larkin rightly hails the achievements won in the face of economic depression, serious unemployment and a hostile NUDL executive as 'remarkable.'[6] A new, militant class consciousness had been stirred in Dublin, and the ITGWU was its organisational and psychological expression. Larkin, shocked by the squalor and abject nature of Dublin's tenement poor, had undoubtedly developed a sense of mission; and his commitment to Ireland, with or without his NUDL expulsion, seems, with hindsight, almost pre-ordained.

The ITGWU met predictable resistance from Sexton, who held on to the NUDL branches in Derry, Drogheda, and partly, by playing the sectarian card, Belfast. With an ally, Joseph Harris of the Workers' Union, Sexton successfully secured Larkin's removal from the ITUC Parliamentary Committee. In 1908 Harris had sought Larkin's assistance—willingly given—in trying to establish Workers' Union branches, and in March 1909 Harris offered to transfer those branches to the ITGWU. Larkin declined. At the congress of the ITUC in Limerick in May, Sexton, supported by other Larkin enemies, such as E. W. Stewart, blocked the ITGWU's affiliation. D. R. Campbell, a Larkin ally from Belfast Trades Council, succeeded in getting the NUDL-ITGWU dispute referred to a committee that would report back to the next congress.

Worse problems for the ITGWU were to follow in Cork, where in April and May strikes took place among tram workers and builders' labourers and the city saw its first Labour Day rally in years. Alarm among businessmen resulted in the formation of the Cork Employers' Federation. When Harris was invited to recruit for the Workers' Union on the docks, trouble quickly broke out as coal-porters, dockers and railwayman struck in rapid succession in early June.

On 17 June the Cork Employers' Federation adopted a policy that was to prove the precursor of employers' strategy in Dublin in 1913:

That we, the employers of Cork, hereby bind ourselves and the firms we represent as follows:
(1) to immediately dismiss any employee who shall wilfully disobey any lawful order out of sympathy with any other strike or trade dispute;
(2) that the vacancy so caused shall be filled forthwith by local labour if procurable, failing this that the vacancy be filled from any available source;
(3) that any such employee discharged shall not be employed by any member of the Federation.[7]

Their statement was a jumbled mixture of the prevailing belief among employers in the 'philosophy' of 'free labour' and their horrified reaction to the new legitimacy of peaceful picketing contained in the Trade Disputes Act (1906). Ill-prepared ITGWU involvement in an internecine dispute was a blunder. The strike was lost; Cork Trades Council split, with the skilled unions forming a separate body; the Workers' Union in Ireland did not survive the defeat; and the Cork Branch of the ITGWU collapsed, to lie dormant for nearly four years.

Larkin, Fearon and two branch members were arrested in August and charged with 'conspiring to defraud.' Fearon got six months' hard labour in December, suffered a breakdown, and finished in a mental asylum. It was July 1910 before Larkin appeared before a packed County Dublin common jury that 'excluded Catholics and Nationalists' on twenty-four charges, including criminal conspiracy, false pretences, and 'having received and misappropriated certain sums of money.' The essence of the case was that money collected for the NUDL was handed over instead to the ITGWU. Sexton, in a final act of revenge, appeared as a prosecution witness. Larkin, having successfully appealed for the release of his co-accused, the docker Coveney, was given a year's hard labour. Dublin Trades Council launched an immediate campaign for his release.

Larkin was released on 1 October 1910 and was welcomed by a gigantic torchlight procession. Despite the setback in Cork, the ITGWU was boosted by his release. By the spring of 1911 Larkin's influence was paramount in both Dublin Trades Council and the ITUC. At the Galway congress, thanks to William O'Brien's 'masterpiece of manipulation and electioneering,' Larkinites secured control of the Parliamentary Committee.

The year 1911 was one of upheaval internationally. Workers sought to take advantage of boom conditions, but in Ireland employers increasingly thought that they were victims not of the trade cycle but, as Desmond Greaves has observed, of

> the malignant personality of Larkin. He was now in the high spring of his career, bustling, businesslike and confident. He had a vision of a great bloodless revolution in which the half-starved, ill-clothed denizens of the slums could win a new life that would include leisure and culture. He thought that all that was necessary was the will and he made himself the embodiment of that will.[8]

ITGWU membership increased significantly. The Registrar's figure for membership at the beginning of 1912 was 18,089, with 13,009 having joined in 1911. New branches were established in Dundalk, Bray, and Sligo, while the Irish Women Workers' Union was launched on 5 September, with Larkin as president and his sister Delia as secretary. The IWWU remained under the aegis of the ITGWU until 1917. ITGWU support for British dock and rail strikes in June and August was not fully reciprocated later in the year, although there were so many strikes—all characterised by spontaneous and sympathetic action—that the *Freeman's Journal* opened an 'Irish Labour Troubles' column in August, which ran until February 1913.

Things were hotting up, and, after a 'wildcat lock-out' by Pierce's Foundry in Wexford against the ITGWU, the *Irish Times* (on 24 August 1911) reflected the increasing determination of employers to meet fire with fire.

> We are getting into a position in which the fight between capital and labour will have to be fought out to the bitter end. If this is the case, most people would rather have the contest now and get it over. Anything is better than these constant strikes and threats of strikes, which dislocate business in all directions and do an infinity of harm ... The strikers must be taught that they are not omnipotent.

Dublin employers followed their southern brethren's lead and formed a federation, at first to seek repeal of the 1906 Act. In Wexford class conflict reached a crescendo with a general lock-out, imported scabs, extra police, much violence, and Arthur Griffith of Sinn Féin thundering against the ITGWU and inviting the workers to join another union. Larkin had transferred P. T. Daly to Wexford from Cork. Daly was badly beaten before eventually being 'deported' from the town as an unashamedly partisan judiciary sought to force victory. Deadlock ensued. Support for the workers was impressive and solid. Shopkeepers supplemented strike pay with extensive credit; many unions gave donations, particularly the local branches of the Trades and Labour League; and, as evidence of the depth of public support, on a motion of Seán Etchingham the Leinster Council of the GAA donated the entire proceeds of the hurling final between Dublin and Kilkenny to the strike fund.[9]

James Connolly, who had returned from America in 1910 and was now an ITGWU organiser, took over from Daly and succeeded in achieving a settlement in February 1912, when the exhausted employers, while still adamant in their refusal to deal with the ITGWU, acknowledged the men's membership of the Irish Foundry Workers' Union—the Transport Union by any other name. Connolly created another ITGWU subsidiary in Belfast in October 1911 with the setting up of the Irish Textile Workers' Union.

In June 1911 Larkin launched the *Irish Worker and People's Advocate*. There had been previous, short-lived attempts to produce a labour paper.[10] The *Irish Worker* said that its aim was 'to raise the working class,' and it was read avidly by a hungry readership. Its circulation at first was 26,000, rising to 64,500 in July, 74,750 in August, and an astonishing 94,994 in September, before settling at 20,000. Given that *Sinn Féin* never reached 5,000 and averaged about 2,000 copies, these figures are extraordinary, and it is not an exaggeration to say that the *Irish Worker* was read by the entire Dublin working class. A masthead slogan encouraged readers, having read it, to 'pass it on.'

Larkin, who had 'appointed himself as keeper of the public conscience,' ingeniously translated his street-corner style to paper; the *Irish Worker* was

'Larkin's oratory congealed in print.'[11] Dermot Keogh feels that the *Irish Worker* 'contained no original labour philosophy' but that it was 'vitriolic, scurrilous,' with many issues a 'libel a line.' Nevertheless this 'confused and palpitating sense of grievance and unrequited appeals for redress became known pejoratively as Larkinism.'[12] Such analysis misjudges the paper and its purpose. John Newsinger rightly concludes that the 'scabrous attacks on slum landlords, sweat-shop employers, lying journalists, various scabs, corrupt politicians, bullying policemen served a definite and calculated purpose. He was out to diminish them by ridicule, to cut them down to size and show them up as moral pygmies.'[13] It galvanised the Dublin workers. Larkinism gave them 'an ethical vision', forging 'an alternative morality by the patient construction of a workers' counter-culture,' as Emmet O'Connor has observed. The paper was a significant personal achievement for Larkin, who over forty months not only edited it but wrote over four hundred articles, at a time when he was general secretary of the ITGWU, general president of the Irish Women Workers' Union, a frequent election candidate, and a regular public orator.

The *Irish Worker* was staunchly republican, rebutted church attacks on Larkin and the union without being anti-religious, and exposed every form of exploitation of the masses. Its unremitting solution was the 'one great union' as part of a continuous campaign to make the union 'central to the lives of its readership and endowing its trade union concerns with spiritual significance.' There were pathetic attempts to produce right-wing alternatives, but the *Irish Worker* remained unchallenged as the informed and rousing voice of working-class grievance, expectation, and hope. To read it even today is to experience excitement and a joyous self-confidence and to access the most significant expression yet of Irish working-class culture on a sustained basis. The paper was doing much to strengthen the spine of a class whose backs would have to endure so much in 1913.

The ITGWU continued to grow in 1912 and by April had four branches in Dublin, with premises at Liberty Hall, James's Street, and High Street, and eleven other branches, in Belfast, Bray, Dundalk, Dún Laoghaire, Enniscorthy, Kill of the Grange (County Dublin), New Ross, Newry, Sligo, Waterford, and Wexford. Some expansion may have been due to the union's new role as an 'approved society' under the National Insurance Act. Membership was now 24,000. Industrial disputes continued, with Sligo dockers winning the right to elect their own stevedores in June, a right maintained by the union to the present time. A mild recession occasioned unemployed demonstrations in Dublin.

The main event in 1912, however, was on the political front. At the ITUC meeting in Clonmel, Connolly moved and Larkin seconded the ITGWU motion that led to the formation of the Labour Party. The motion was vaguely worded, perhaps to avoid the sort of opposition similar motions had engendered in the past, and simply sought 'the independent representation of Labour upon all public boards.'

Larkin had joined the Independent Labour Party as a seventeen-year-old in Liverpool. He believed that trade unionism was a 'played-out economic fallacy' and put his faith in the creation of a socialist party pursing working-class interests. He served as Sexton's election agent in 1905 when they fought an unsuccessful campaign for Labour. In Ireland Larkin never joined the Socialist Party of Ireland, which had invited Connolly to return from America in 1910. It was the influence of the SPI that permeated labour politics. In January 1911 Dublin Trades Council formed a Labour Representation Committee to fight local elections. Larkin held sway on the committee. By January 1912 the Dublin Labour Party, as it was now called, fought the corporation election. Five of the eight candidates were successful, including Larkin, who had a huge victory despite attacks in the *Irish Independent* and elsewhere suggesting that he was an atheist, a believer in 'free love' and, by innuendo, an advocate of abortion. It was a short-lived triumph, as he was ousted from his seat as a 'convicted felon', an unfortunate residue from his conviction after the Cork dispute in 1909.

A largely unmentioned side of Larkin's character is summarised by his statement to a government inquiry into industrial disputes in 1913 that he did 'not approve of strikes at all.' Set against the usual image of the recklessly militant Larkin, this seems an odd statement, a possibly mischievous one, given its timing. While accepting that workers had no defence other than their trade union, and that its main weapon was the strike, as early as 1909 Larkin had been advocating compulsory arbitration courts and enshrined the policy in the first ITGWU rules. Larkin later enlarged the concept, calling them compulsory wages and arbitration boards. It is clear that he did not want, as many employers did, some mechanism that would 'simply prevent strikes.' In an open letter to the *Irish Worker* on 26 April 1913 (before the start of the lock-out) Larkin outlined an elaborate plan on 'how to stop strikes.' Equal numbers of employers' and workers' representatives were to be elected to a sectoral trade wages board. Failure to reach a settlement there would see the matter referred to a city wages board of ten members equally representative of employer and worker. Failure to comply with eventual decisions from such bodies precluded assistance and were to be penalised by 'money or prison.'

The amended rules of the ITGWU, issued in October 1912, nevertheless had deleted all reference to compulsory arbitration. The precise reasons for this change are not known, but it may illustrate a pragmatic side to Larkin's nature. As the union grew in strength, the need for any form of arbitration—and with it a subtle way of gaining employer recognition—diminished. By 1912, ITGWU might was such that it could enforce recognition from employers, with no need to rely on state or any other arbitration intervention. Emmet Larkin argues that 'the new syndicalist ideas were in theory opposed to all contracts and working agreements' and that Larkin's advocacy of arbitration was in conflict with 'the temper of the times.' It is nevertheless clear, however, that this period saw the ITGWU, and by extension the emerging modern Irish labour movement, embrace the possibilities of conciliation and arbitration, from a position of growing strength, as a civilised and occasionally necessary means of resolving industrial disputes peaceably. The state's and even the employers' reluctant acceptance of the permanence of the labour movement—although about to be severely tested in one last great battle—was an indication that labour had arrived to stay and would need to be integrated into the daily affairs of the nation.

Such sentiments might have seemed absurd in 1911, but already the foundation-stone had been laid by Larkin. The formation of the ITGWU was the cornerstone of the new advance for labour. As Emmet O'Connor has argued, Larkinism 'encompassed a strategy, a method, a morality and a politics,' and by 'ennobling solidarity to a moral duty, Larkin revolutionised the ethics of industrial conflict. With this transformation went the politics of self-reliance and socialism.'[14] Larkinism promoted an alternative morality in this period and contributed to the possibilities of syndicalism that lay ahead.

The years 1909–1912 saw Larkin irrevocably committed to the cause of labour in Ireland. He created the ITGWU—part of what some have seen as the 'decolonisation' of the movement—which transformed trade unionism from the narrow and sectional to the visionary and all-encompassing. Opponents within the older craft trade unions, as well as among employers unused to such unrelenting challenge to their economic power and authority, were overcome on a tide of support inspired by Larkin's passionate oratory, the daring advocacy of the *Irish Worker*, and the growing confidence of people inspired by a belief in socialist politics. The creation of the Labour Party opened the way for working-class political representation, while the success of industrial action was to lead to careful consideration of schemes for avoiding or at least mediating the worst of the battles between the warring factions.

Labour had risen to take its place. That place was about to be challenged in one of the bitterest and most protracted disputes in Irish history, but, at least on the workers' side, Larkin had created structures of permanence and had inspired the workers by association with his heroic style.

Chapter 6

Larkin and the Dublin Lock-Out

Prof. Fergus A. D'Arcy

The strikes here do not seem to be coming to a head though the magistrates say the trouble will not commence before next week when the strike pay goes out and they begin to feel the pinch and loot shops.

Yesterday they were weak enough to let Larkin, the agitator, out on bail. Only a fortnight ago he broke his bail. I and the remainder of the Regiment here have to stand to every night in case we are wanted for riots.

Their [the DMP's] methods have been criticised freely as over severe etc. but on the other hand they prevented looting and the military being called out.

In this place the danger is not from the strikers but from the thousands of looting roughs who eke out an existence here doing nothing and wait an opportunity of looting shops. In comparison with its population there is no other city on earth I believe where there is less industry. Guinness's brewery and the tramway are the only employment in the town ...[1]

So wrote a Capt. Vane de V. M. Vallance to his mother on 13 September 1913.

The celebrated great strike and lock-out in Dublin in 1913 began in mid-morning on Tuesday 26 August, in the midst of Horse Show week, when two hundred tram drivers and conductors left their vehicles and passengers stranded in the city centre. As members of the ITGWU they took this action in protest against the dismissal of two union members from the parcels department of the Tramway Company. They returned to work at the end of January 1914, bringing the strike and lock-out to a virtual end, although the last workers affected, women workers in Jacob's biscuit factory, did not go back till mid-March 1914.[2]

It is the most important labour dispute in Irish labour history. It involved everyone: workers, skilled and unskilled, employers, large and small, chambers of commerce, Dublin Castle, City Hall, the British government, the Catholic Church, and the British TUC. It lost 1,700,000 working days and involved over 20,000 trade unionists, and £150,000 was raised in support of those workers affected. The two giants of the conflict were Larkin and William Martin Murphy, whose attitudes and actions precipitated the conflict. Both men were, and remain, enigmatic.

Murphy was a well-known figure long before the strike and lock-out of 1913.[3] He was born in Bantry in 1845, educated at Belvedere College, Dublin, went into his father's contracting business in 1864, and made a fortune in Ireland and overseas through railway construction. By 1900 he owned the *Irish Independent* and the Imperial Hotel and was the principal owner of the Dublin United Tramway Company. He had already represented Dublin as an Irish Party MP from 1886 to 1892. He was a well-respected man of moderation and discipline, a classic individualist unashamed of making money, whose boast in January 1913 was that he had never had to face a strike of his employees, because he treated them well. He had no time for employers who created labour unrest by abusing their workers, and he enjoyed a reputation as a progressive and moderate employer—a reputation at one time acknowledged by Dublin Trades Council.

Remembered for private acts of kindness to individual workers or their dependants, Murphy was also harsh and ruthless when it came to trade unionism, and it is not too cynical a view that suggests that he never faced a strike because he never used unionised labour where unorganised labour could be had instead. He was not prepared to tolerate the unionisation of the unskilled, as represented by the ITGWU with Larkin at its head. Murphy had a strike-free record to 1913 because his absolute authority was not challenged until Larkin challenged it at that time.

Larkin was a younger man by twenty-nine years, having been born in Liverpool in 1874, the son of a fitter who died of TB in 1887, who in turn was the son of an Armagh tenant farmer.[4] Larkin was a restless character, who gave up an engineering apprenticeship to earn more in a succession of odd jobs, ending on Liverpool docks. He had become a socialist at the age of seventeen, embarking on a career that made him one of the greatest enigmas of modern Irish history—Catholic, nationalist, revolutionary, syndicalist, communist.

The most striking feature of Larkin's early years was his complete lack of interest in trade unionism. From 1892 to 1905 he was first and foremost a socialist, a member of the Independent Labour Party. His reputation for sobriety, honesty and hard work brought him the coveted position of foreman docker by 1903. Around this time then he was in the paradoxical position of being a respected and trusted employee, earning good money, and at the same time a preacher of revolutionary socialism. As a doctrinaire socialist he was originally hostile to trade unionism, but under ILP influence he came to accept the view that the unions could become the instruments of socialism. He joined the National Union of Dock Labourers, set up in Glasgow in 1889 by two Ulstermen and which was run from 1893 by the second-generation Irishman James Sexton. Larkin joined the NUDL in 1901 but was not an active member till 1905.[5]

The Liverpool dock strike of 1905 brought Larkin into active trade unionism, cost him his job, and in 1906 secured him the position of organiser for the union. Larkin now burst into prominence, from nowhere, it seemed, and became the most exciting organiser in the British labour movement, and to staider trade unionists the most reckless. The workers lost the 1905 Liverpool strike, and their position after it was worse than before it, as far as Sexton was concerned. Larkin as a revolutionary socialist could afford to take a different view: his tactics raised political awareness, even if they cost a lot of trade union money. This was the effect of his brilliant agitation in Scotland and the north of Ireland during the period 1906–08.

The Belfast strike of 1907 had united Protestant and Catholic unskilled labour, but it also cost the NUDL £7,000 of English members' money—more than Sexton was prepared to tolerate. Sexton wanted gradual, painstaking advance through negotiation, not dramatic victories through confrontation that ended in defeat. Sexton wanted a better deal for labour within society; Larkin wanted society to become labour through the collapse of capitalism. The differences resulted in Larkin's suspension in December 1908 and his defiance of this by setting up the ITGWU in 1909. It also resulted in his first prison term in 1910 for three months.

The years from 1908 to early 1911 were ones of great difficulty for Larkin and his new union, but by 1911 he had become the leading figure in the Irish labour movement. He had been released from jail in October 1910 after serving three months of a twelve-month sentence. His new union had won affiliation to the Irish Trades Union Congress in May 1910—a significant moral victory. He, William O'Brien and other socialist trade unionists had come to dominate Dublin Trades Council, and in June 1911 they came to dominate the Parliamentary Committee of the ITUC.[6] At the same time Larkin achieved the remarkable feat of launching the *Irish Worker* and making it the most widely circulated journal in the country and the most famous Irish working-class newspaper.

Although the intense mutual hostility between the patriarchal Murphy and the messianic Larkin made a big contribution to the bitterness and horror of the 1913 conflict, it cannot be said either to have caused it or to have decisively determined its course and outcome. Too many other complex factors were at work, both immediately and over the long term. Some were objectively economic and material, others were cultural, and others yet again ideological.

For example, if economically conditions were bad in the late nineteenth-century and early twentieth-century cities and towns, then in Dublin they were very bad. One of the ironies of the age was that it was not the great manufacturing towns of the classical Industrial Revolution, such as Manchester, Leeds, and even Belfast (although Salford was no heaven *circa* 1913), that presented the worst examples of poverty and human degradation: curiously, it was the non-industrial administrative and ecclesiastical centres, like York and Dublin, that served up the ugliest examples of poverty, exploitation, and unemployment. It is now a commonplace that housing conditions in Dublin surpassed in horror anything to be found elsewhere in a city of its size in Europe. At the same time, in general, wages since 1900 had seriously failed to keep pace with prices. The increase in unemployment between 1906 and 1910 made any trade union growth difficult.

Cultural factors that may well have shaped the particular ferocity of the 1913 conflict in Dublin could well be ascribed to the special conditions of the Irish historical experience. Compromise and conciliation were not characteristics of the Irish social and political climate, as the Land War and the struggle of Orange and Green made plain. Furthermore, the landlords of capital were by no means disposed to treat the tenants of labour generously, or to encourage in them notions of partnership. The churches, Catholic and Protestant alike, were in Ireland—unlike those in Britain, the Continent, and even the United States—singularly innocent of and ignorant of the social gospel. A few exceptions in Dublin in 1913 only served to prove the rule. Deeply divided by sectarian self-righteousness and mutual mistrust, they were united only in a fear of socialism.

With regard to the shaping effect of changing ideology, the most notable influence on the labour movement was the rise of syndicalism, alike in Britain, the Continent, and America, over the period 1890–1910. Essentially it embodied a disenchantment with politics and parliaments as a means of securing working-class redemption. Equally it involved a critical attitude towards labour establishments, whether in the craft-dominated trade union congresses of Britain, Ireland and the Continent or in the various parliamentary labour and socialist parties. Above all it involved a messianic belief in the transforming power of the One Big Union, the general strike, and the sympathetic strike. Finally, it offered a special appeal to and exerted a special influence on the poorest and most marginalised of workers. By the end of the first decade of this century syndicalism was already exercising a powerful influence on some leaders even of the Irish labour movement, most notably on James Connolly and Jim Larkin.

From 1910 trade picked up, unemployment fell, trade unionism expanded, and a new militancy and confidence developed in the labour movement. By that time Larkin was very well placed to make the most of both the objective conditions and the changing mood, and he did so successfully in the summer of 1911 among the Dublin carters, significantly by use of the sympathetic strike. Membership of his union rose from 3,000 in 1911 to 8,000 in 1912 and to 10,000 in 1913, the majority of them in Dublin.

The famous 1913 conflict was precipitated when Larkin tried to extend this growth into the empire of William Martin Murphy in the *Irish Independent* and the Tramway Company and when Murphy determined to resist. In the Tramway Company unionisation certainly was needed, in that working conditions were exceedingly harsh. Murphy resolved to defeat Larkin's attempts to unionise in this area by offering his men an increase and by claiming he had no objection to their joining a 'legitimate union'. When he discovered that some employees had thrown in their lot with Larkin, he dismissed half the workers in the despatch section of the *Irish Independent* and about two hundred of those in the parcels section of the Tramway Company. This was on 21 August 1913, and it was followed a few days later by the issuing of the notorious document to drivers and conductors calling on them to renounce Transport Union membership.

Instead they went on strike on Tuesday 26 August and inaugurated the struggle.

That six-month struggle had a number of turning-points, marked not only by heroic endurance and visionary politics but also by decisive misjudgments, disastrous errors and irreconcilable divisions within the labour movement.

Precipitated by Murphy's dismissal of tramway and newspaper workers on 21 August and by the tram workers abandoning their vehicles on 26 August, the conflict quickly intensified in bitterness even as it spread in extent.

On the evening of that famous Horse Show Day, when Dublin passengers were abandoned in Sackville Street (O'Connell Street), three of the labour leaders, Larkin, Lawlor, and Partridge, spoke trenchantly at a meeting in Beresford Place and next day were arrested for sedition and conspiracy.[7] Bail was given on condition of no further illegal meetings or inflammatory speeches, but two days later, now joined by James Connolly, the union's Belfast organiser, Larkin again spoke defiantly and planned for a major public meeting in O'Connell Street for the following Sunday. On Saturday 30 August Connolly and Partridge were arrested, Connolly being held in custody and a warrant issued for the arrest of Larkin. He made his way safely to the house of Constance Markievicz until the fateful Sunday. Meanwhile the Dublin Employers' Federation decided to convene a general meeting to consider their own plan of action.

The day of Connolly's arrest saw the climate in the city turn very nasty indeed, with ugly clashes between the tough and overwrought Dublin Metropolitan Police and the strikers. Clashes and baton charges in Burgh Quay and Eden Quay led to the death of a Transport Union member, James Nolan, and the death of John Byrne from head wounds some days later.

Then came Sunday 31 August and the demonstration. It was ironic indeed that, having been prohibited from meeting in O'Connell Street and its vicinity, the union leadership and strike committee, led by William O'Brien and without Larkin, negotiated with the police and agreed to stage a march from Liberty Hall to the peaceable suburban surroundings of Croydon Park, Fairview, where the union had a recreational centre. Some fifteen thousand set out peaceably enough for this venue, and only a small body of some three hundred strikers gathered round the GPO, in the expectation of Larkin's appearance.[8] Unluckily for them, many hundreds of Sunday strollers and church-goers added substantially to this number. Larkin's remarkable appearance at a balcony of William Martin Murphy's Imperial Hotel (now Clery's department store), a typically dramatic and defiant gesture, was the signal for an attempted arrest by the enraged DMP. It resulted famously and notoriously in Ireland's first Bloody Sunday.

Bloody Sunday, August 1913, was a disastrous blunder by the authorities, and at the stroke of a baton Larkin's hitherto uncertain hold over the movement was re-established and enhanced. What began as a strike became in effect a lock-out when the next day Jacob's locked out their workers, followed by the Dublin Coal Merchants' Association the day after. By Thursday 4 September the majority of Dublin employers had fallen in behind Murphy and the Coal Merchants; by Friday the notorious document compelling workers to abjure the Transport Union was in general use. By the last week of September over 20,000 were dismissed and some 100,000 were in a state of destitution and dependence.

With Larkin and Connolly still in custody, peace talks sponsored by the Lord Mayor foundered on the intransigence of both sides and on the determination of Murphy and the Employers' Federation to smash the Transport Union. With Larkin and Connolly's release on 12 and 13 September, the union leadership moved rapidly to secure support.

On 23 September Dublin Trades Council agreed a substantial levy on all its trade union members in support of the strikers, and by late October the Transport Union itself was paying 10s a week to ten thousand dismissed workers. Larkin's efforts to raise money in Britain were successful too. The carpenters voted £1,500 a week and the Miners' Federation £1,000 a week. In addition, and dramatically, the British food ship *Hare* arrived in the last week of September, followed by the *Fraternity* in the first week of October. As the cavalry officer Vallance confided ruefully to his mother in a letter of 19 October, 'strikes still on here but no excitement except a few evictions—the strikers seem to be living quite comfortably on the ship load of supplies from England while Dublin loses £60,000 a week in trade.'[9]

At that stage the British government intervened to attempt a settlement. George Askwith of the Board of Trade arrived in Dublin to chair a public inquiry to which both sides made their case, the employers represented by T. M. Healy, the workers by Larkin, described by Vallance in a letter home to England as 'quite imperturbable I am told—he never gets rattled in the hottest discussion but sticks to the point and keeps cool.' But not all his coolness was sufficient for the day.[10]

Sympathy for the workers and the union cause, which had been growing since Bloody Sunday, was further strengthened by the employers' public refusal to compromise. Something of that shift in opinion can be seen in a letter sent privately by Archbishop Walsh to the Lord Lieutenant, Aberdeen, on 10 October, in which he remarked that

> the labour leader has an exceeding strong case ... I must say that on the merits of the case generally, my sympathies are altogether with them [the workers] and I trust that the outcome of the present case will be a radical change for the better in the position of the employed in Dublin.[11]

By the beginning of October, then, while there was no end in sight, support for Larkin and the workers was strengthening. This, however, was to change rapidly, for two reasons. The first was the highly personalised attacks Larkin made in England on the Labour Party, the labour movement, and some of its leading personnel, notably Philip Snowden.

Larkin wanted from them not just sympathy, food, and cash: he wanted a general sympathetic strike and economic blockade of Dublin by British workers. The second was the well-intentioned but ill-advised scheme of two London sympathisers, Dora Montefiore and Lucille Rand, to offer support by providing a scheme of holidays in England for the children of the strikers. The offer was welcomed by the strike leadership but immediately fell foul of Archbishop Walsh, the Catholic Church, the nationalist press, and the nationalist movement. As the first of the children left Ireland on 22 October, unseemly scuffles at the points of departure brought the whole endeavour into disrepute. Worse still, it deflected attention from the real issue of the struggle and allowed the employers to recover ground in the battle for public opinion.

As the conflict entered its third month, Vallance informed his mother in England:

> Still standing to in case we are called on to suppress strikers. The men are getting rather fed up with it, none more so than the officers. The officers here have a tour of twenty-four hours' duty every four days, escorting coal carts and guarding the tramway depots. Two strikers the other night tried to climb over the railings of one of the depots; the sentry promptly rushed at them with his bayonet, just missed them but they left in their haste some of their underwear on the rails.[12]

Even as Larkin and his colleagues faced this setback, he himself was tried and sentenced to seven months' hard labour for his part in the events leading to Bloody Sunday. The sentence caused uproar, even in Britain, where pressure upon and then pressure from the government led to his release after a week. The unsympathetic Vallance wrote home in November:

> Afraid you were rather premature in your congratulations of Dublin being at peace again with Larkin jailed. Larkin is out again and making some apt statements such as 'The government made a mistake in sending me to jail but a worse one in setting me free.'[13]

As the conflict continued into November, one of its most interesting developments was the establishment of the Irish Citizen Army as a protective force for the strikers, following a call from Connolly that the workers should arm. But, for all the good intentions of its original organisers, it was during the lock-out never more than a gesture, and its real historical significance was not to emerge until three years later in profoundly altered circumstances.

As for the conflict itself, the next step towards ending it came from the British Labour Party, when a delegation led by Arthur Henderson arrived in early December to meet the employers. That deputation yielded crucial ground by promising to abandon sympathetic strikes, to hold ballots before strikes, and to give notice of intention to strike; yet the employers declined to offer full reinstatement in return. On this rock the hopes of a resolution foundered.

Thereafter, for Larkin, the Transport Union and the Irish labour movement it was downhill all the way. A most critical setback was the convening of a special meeting of the British Trades Union Congress in London on 9 December 1913. The Irish delegation was made up of Larkin, Connolly, O'Brien, and McPartlin. It ended in wretched acrimony and division when Larkin's colourful and impassioned attacks and his insistence on support for a general strike were rejected. Although the Congress voted to continue financial aid to Dublin, Larkin had fatally alienated the British labour leadership. They continued to urge a fresh meeting with the employers, although the workers' position had already been fatally compromised. When, therefore, on 18 December 1913 the Dublin employers met representatives of the workers, they agreed to withdraw the notorious document. The workers were asked to renounce the sympathetic strike, and secured no guarantees of reinstatement.

By the early weeks of January 1914, with continued funds from Britain in jeopardy, the workers began to drift back to work on whatever terms they could get. By late January the Transport Union was having to sanction significant sectoral returns to work; by the end of January it was all over in the port of Dublin, and the Transport Union, in the short term, was on its knees. Women workers in Jacob's, the first to be locked out on a large scale, were the last to return, in March 1914. For most who managed to return to work it was on conditions no better and often far worse than those on which they had left. For the uncountable many who never recovered their jobs, the end was enlistment or emigration.

Small consolation it was therefore to Larkin to be elected president of the Irish Trades Union Congress in June 1914. Already serious tensions had developed within the labour movement and within the Transport Union, where relations between Larkin on the one hand and Connolly and O'Brien on the other had become strained. When he left Ireland for the United States in October 1914 for a few weeks that turned into a few years, Larkin left the Transport Union with certain tensions unresolved.

The strike was led by a man who regarded himself as a revolutionary socialist, aided by others who were in some cases also revolutionary socialists, such as Connolly, or evolutionary socialists, such as William O'Brien. The sympathetic strike and the sympathetic lock-out quickly made it into a direct class struggle. It was indeed a major occasion of class conflict. The situation had revolutionary potential but one that was never realised. The rhetoric of conflict was dramatic and alarming, incidents of the conflict were violent, bloody, and in some cases fatal; but the object of the conflict, even from the revolutionary socialist Larkin's point of view, was not revolution but union recognition, and the object from the point of view of Larkin's lieutenants and rank and file was clearly identical: the defence and recognition of trade unionism, not the initiation of workers' revolution. Despite conflict with the police, missing from the long and embittered struggle was any conception of a blow being directed at the state. Although employers chose to believe that the essence of the conflict was a combination of socialism and syndicalism, it was far from this. If Larkin was prepared to risk confrontation, the strike committee, led by O'Brien and P. T. Daly, was not.

In the short term the defeat was a major one for the labour movement; in the long term it proved to be a victory, because never again did employers as a class attempt to destroy trade unionism. The right of the unskilled to unionisation was in reality accepted. And this general picture was true more particularly of the Transport Union. At first devastated, it recovered over the next five years to grow to unprecedented dimensions: membership rose to 14,000 by 1918, to 68,000 by 1919, and to 100,000 by 1923. Most important of all perhaps was the fact that in the long term the real moral victory went to labour.

However, coupled with the sense of 1913 as ultimately a great victory is a sense also of it as great tragedy—not least because in some ways its greatest hero was also its greatest casualty.

Chapter 7

Clash of Titans: James Larkin and William Martin Murphy

Prof. Dermot Keogh

James Larkin died in Dublin on 30 January 1947. The Archbishop of Dublin, John Charles McQuaid, celebrated the Requiem Mass before a large congregation, which included the President of Ireland, Seán T. O'Kelly, the Taoiseach, Éamon de Valera, and most members of the Government. Liam Mac Gabhann described the scene as the cortege passed through the frozen, muffled streets of the capital on its way to Glasnevin Cemetery:

> There were crowds at Jim Larkin's funeral—just as there were crowds in Jim Larkin's life. A half century of history marched through Dublin yesterday morning ... And the men in the dungarees, and women grown old who have borne children since they struck instinctively at the 400 bosses at Larkin's will, seemed to be there because they just had to be there.

Overshadowed in Irish labour history perhaps only by James Connolly, Larkin was laid to rest in the presence of the leaders of both church and state. Both de Valera and Archbishop McQuaid acknowledged, by their presence, the country's appreciation of the man who had done most to win recognition for the inalienable rights of the worker. It was difficult to argue with success. As the poet Austin Clarke wrote,

> What Larkin bawled to hungry crowds
> Is murmured now in dining-hall
> And study ...
> His name endures on our holiest page,
> Scrawled in a rage by Dublin's poor.

Dublin's poor, most particularly, had come out in strength on that bitter morning in February 1947 to pay their last respects. Seán O'Casey wrote at the time: 'There was a man sent from God whose name was Larkin. Jim Larkin is not dead, but is with us all, and will be with us all.' While there is obvious irony in O'Casey's use of biblical language, he nevertheless invests Larkin with messianic and transcendent powers. Larkin was, for O'Casey and his other followers, a man apart, a leader and a charismatic personality whose great act of promethean defiance is captured today in the fine bronze statue in O'Connell Street, the scene of the infamous baton charge in 1913.

History has not been quite so kind to Larkin's great rival, William Martin Murphy. He died in Dublin on 25 June 1919, during the War of Independence; and, according to a report in the *Irish Independent*, which he owned, the funeral was private, 'in keeping with the deceased's unassuming character throughout his great career.' There was nevertheless a very large congregation in the Church of the Three Patrons, Rathgar, for the Requiem Mass. As the funeral made its way to Glasnevin, his *Irish Independent* again reported that 'there were many manifestations of sympathy all along the route with the deceased and the members of his family.'[1] The remains were received at the cemetery by a large number of clergy, including a number of Jesuits from Belvedere College, where Murphy had been a pupil. He was buried in the O'Connell Circle—in fitting company, as the *Irish Independent* said—with 'many other famous Irishmen whose names add lustre and honour to the history of the country.'

Murphy's passing brought tributes from many quarters: he was 'simple, kind and generous' and 'a very lovable personality,' according to one anonymous writer. Calm under pressure, he was incapable of bitterness, had 'qualities of greatness' and a 'passionate hatred of injustice,' and 'his great soul knew no fear.' He had a mind like a searchlight. That was Murphy, according to the main appreciation in the *Irish Independent*.[2] Industrialist, constitutional nationalist, parliamentarian, home ruler, imperialist—Murphy represented that contradictory world of the Irish Party that was passing away. Politically, he was one of yesterday's men.

Unlike Larkin, there is no statue anywhere in the country to acknowledge Murphy's not inconsiderable contribution to the making of modern Ireland. Poets and novelists have not been sympathetic to him. There is an indirect disparaging reference to him in Yeats's 'September 1913': 'for men were born to pray and save … [but] fumble in a greasy till.'

Murphy's name stirred strong emotions. Much hated after the 1913 lock-out by trade unionists, Murphy, according to the employers' apologist Arnold Wright, enjoyed 'the entire confidence of the citizens of the more substantial class.'[3] His fellow-employers, many of whom did not particularly like the crude building contractor from the Beara Peninsula in County Cork, gratefully acknowledged his contribution to the defeat of Larkin in 1914 with a commissioned portrait by William Orpen. The painting shows a slight, white-bearded, ascetic figure. He looks particularly spry and fit for his age. His suit is somewhat crumpled, revealing perhaps his lack of interest in matters sartorial. He wears a watch and chain in his waistcoat. The depiction of his hands is particularly striking. They are not those of a dandy or of a man unused to manual work. But what is really known about the man who exercised great economic power in Irish society for over thirty years?

The early historiography of the labour movement in this period has been most unhelpful in trying to provide an answer to that question. Not surprisingly, it lent itself very easily to the presentation of a clash between two dominant personalities—James Larkin and William Martin Murphy—

a clash of Titans, as this lecture title (which I was given) suggests. The Titans were the race of gods begotten of the union between sky and earth, and the Greeks thought of them as gigantic beings who had ruled the world in a primitive age. Using this title, it is seductively easy to slip into an analysis that deals with the evil Murphy on one side and the enlightened Larkin on the other.

In the absence of a business history tradition in Ireland, William Martin Murphy is almost exclusively perceived in the scholarly and popular literature through labour eyes. His first biography, by the Jesuit Father Tom Morrissey, was published in 1997. Let me try to sketch Murphy's early formation and his later career as an industrialist and a politician.

He was born in Derrymihan, Castletown Bearhaven, on 6 January 1845. His father, Denis William Murphy, moved to Bantry to open a timber yard and became a successful building contractor. He built a house at New Street. His mother was Mary Ann Martin of Castletown Bearhaven, the daughter of a coastal sea captain;[4] she may have been descended from Huguenot stock. She died on 1 March 1849, aged twenty-eight, when Murphy was three.

Under the influence of the editor of the *Nation*, A. M. Sullivan, a friend of his father, Murphy was sent to the Jesuit-run Belvedere College, Dublin, in 1858. He lodged in South Circular Road with Donal Sullivan MP and his younger brother Richard Sullivan, who was the ablest scholar at Belvedere in Murphy's time. He also spent time working in the offices of the *Nation*, where he gained his first experience of journalism. He also worked on the *Irish Builder*, which was run by John J. Lyons. While still at secondary school Murphy received an early but intense political education in the household of the Sullivans—that distinguished family of Bantry intellectuals and politicians, where he would also have met their political friends in the Irish Party.

In Belvedere the Jesuits introduced Murphy to Latin and Greek. A member of a leading Cork family, Father Frank Murphy, whose brother became an MP, took personal care of the thirteen-year-old. Only in the school a few days, Murphy found himself being bullied in class by a boy sitting behind him. Forgetting where he was for a split second, he reached out and 'gave my tormentor a back-hander across the face.' Murphy thought he was going to be expelled, but then Father Murphy said: 'That's right. He deserved that—I was watching him.'[5] In later life, Murphy employed equally robust tactics to defeat his trade union opponents.

At school Murphy had a particular flair for mathematics, winning the first prize in Belvedere in that subject the year after he entered the school. He remained top of his class, on his own admission, through very hard work. As president of the Belvedere College Union in 1909, Murphy recalled his days in the school with 'nothing but pleasure.' He wrote how he 'always counted amongst the famous order some of my dearest and staunchest friends.' Murphy wrote in 1909 of how he gained a knowledge of the world and 'a reliance on myself at an early age,' which he felt could not have been acquired at boarding school. He found those acquisitions of 'inestimable value when I lost my father, whose only son I was, and had to take up the responsibilities of the business in which he was engaged.'

Murphy was just nineteen when his father died in 1863. That put an end to his formal education and dashed his hopes of ever becoming an architect. It may also account for his arrested aesthetic sense, for which he was noted in later life.

Although a minor when he returned to Bantry to take over the family business, he quickly made it prosper through very hard work. Murphy's great physical energy and entrepreneurial ability made him a successful building contractor in the Munster region. He was a fine horseman, and he rode great distances over mountain roads to supervise contracts such as the building of bridges and churches. Little is known about industrial practices in west Cork at that time; but he had the reputation of being a hard, tough but fair-minded employer, who ought to be judged by the unenlightened standards of the time.

A combination of luck and skill made his business prosper, and soon his interests were centred beyond Bantry, then beyond Cork, and finally beyond Dublin. As Murphy's business expanded he moved first to Cork and then to Dublin in 1875. He married Mary Fitzgerald Lombard in 1870; they had a large family. In the capital Murphy combined his work as an international businessman with the life of MP between 1885 and 1892. His many talents did not include that of the parliamentarian. He took the anti-Parnell side, and lost his seat in 1892. Two subsequent attempts failed to get him re-elected to the British House of Commons.

Murphy's interests were primarily in the business world. His success was partly due to good timing. He was a beneficiary of the railway boom of the late nineteenth century; he was also to the fore in building tramway systems in Dublin, Belfast, and Cork. He helped build, and he retained an interest in, tramway companies in a 'good many towns in the United Kingdom, ranging from Paisley to Ramsgate and Margate.'[6] He was associated with the building of a railway line in west Africa, which, according to Arnold Wright, 'will help forward the wonderful development that is proceeding in that part of the Empire.'

Murphy made Dublin the base of his personal financial empire. He had a controlling interest in the Dublin United Tramway Company; he also owned a drapery business and a large hotel in the city. Newspapers, however, were a major personal business and political interest. By 1907, the year James Larkin first came to Ireland to work as a trade union official, Murphy was no longer a mere building contractor from Bantry. He had made good.

By 1907 Murphy was a man of means and an international financier with a burgeoning press empire. He was the owner of the *Irish Independent*, a halfpenny daily that he bought in 1900; by 1909 that loss-maker was turning a profit.[7] He also acquired ownership of the *Irish Catholic* and the *Evening Mail*. Murphy was an outstanding business success story, but he was also perceived as rather unorthodox. After all, he was a Catholic and a nationalist, with not a little contempt for many of his employer colleagues.

Murphy was a nationalist and a conservative Home Ruler. His political ideas, however, were very much out of sympathy with the cause of radical nationalism as represented by Michael Davitt, and he believed that Ireland's natural place of advantage was in the British Empire. According to Arnold Wright, he saw no incompatibility between 'a strongly held conviction of Ireland's right to mould her own destiny and a complete loyalty to the King.' That attachment to the service of the empire was much the ethos of Belvedere College, which he had attended. The school prepared many of the best and the brightest to go to university and then to serve throughout the British empire as doctors, engineers, military officers, or civil servants. Murphy was a nationalist, as indeed were many of the Irish who held positions in the empire. The two positions were not incompatible.

However, Murphy was not an uncritical admirer of British rule in Ireland. He had watched too many Chief Secretaries come and go, each with a tourist map and a geography of the country in their pockets, to remain in awe of the superiority of British administrative wisdom. Although he believed in empire, he did so for very pragmatic reasons. He was never part of the Dublin Castle set. The symbols and trappings of monarchy did not attract him. He caused consternation when he refused a knighthood when King Edward visited Dublin in 1907 to attend the International Irish Exhibition, which Murphy had helped to organise. It would appear that rumours were circulating in the city claiming that Murphy had played a prominent part in the venture in order to get a knighthood; that is believed to have been part of the reason for his refusal to accept the honour.

The Dublin business community acknowledged his achievements by electing him president of the Chamber of Commerce in 1912 and 1913. A rough diamond, Murphy, the Catholic nationalist from the Beara Peninsula, did not fit in that readily with the Horse Show-going Dublin employer class. Many of the more cultured—the old money—would not have been pleased at Murphy's determined stance in 1912 in preventing Dublin Corporation taking a decision to build a gallery on the Liffey to house the priceless art bequest of Sir Hugh Lane. Murphy won, and the country almost lost that extraordinary collection of paintings. Here was an example of Murphy's uncouth side.

If Murphy had a soft side to his character it was a nostalgia for Beara. In later life, when he had moved to Dartry, Dublin, he continued to take his annual holidays in Bantry. A keen yachtsman, he liked to sail his boat— the *Myth*—off the Beara Peninsula. The local historian Gerard Harrington records his 'passionate love for his native place' and his willingness to give the locals 'a leg-up.' That 'leg-up' placed a number of local people on the staff on the *Daily Independent*, which he bought in 1900. It may also have been that he employed men from Beara in his other concerns, the Dublin United Tramway Company, the drapery shop, and the hotel; that may account for the personal loyalty of many to him and for the terrible bitterness caused by the strike in 1913.

The justice of Larkin's case that employers should recognise the Irish Transport and General Workers' Union was never in doubt; he was defending the fundamental right of the worker to join the union of his or her choice. The son of impoverished Irish parents, 'Big Jim' had been born in Liverpool in 1874. That made him twenty-nine years younger than Murphy. Since his arrival in Belfast in 1907 as an organiser for the National Union of Dock Labourers, Larkin had transformed the indifferent fortunes of organised labour in the country. He had helped found the Irish Transport and General Workers' Union in 1909 and later the Irish Women Workers' Union. His success as an organiser, in such a short time, was remarkable.

Unlike Murphy, Larkin was a gifted public speaker and mass orator. Indeed Murphy regretted that during his time at school he had not 'availed myself more of the training which the old Belvedere Elocution Master was fully capable of giving me.' He felt that he was 'always too self-conscious and diffident when I had to stand alone before an audience … This is a feeling I never got over.'[8] Larkin, who never enjoyed the benefits of secondary education or of an elocution teacher, learned his craft as a public speaker in the trade union movement in Liverpool and later on the streets of Belfast, Cork, Wexford, and Dublin. That great gift as a public speaker enhanced his standing among his followers. Larkin was tall and very strong. He knew the drudgery of heavy, physical work. He was a natural leader. Some may have believed him to be a Titan. Murphy was not counted among them. Larkin's actions and what was now being termed 'Larkinism' had called into question future respect for industrial agreements.

Murphy always made the claim that he was a good employer. He had said in 1887:

> I am not going to say that the workingmen of Ireland are any more perfect than any other class in the community … My own experience, extending over 20 years, is that by meeting workingmen fairly and by treating them as possessing equal rights, I have never failed to make reasonable and amicable arrangements.[9]

Nearly twenty-five years later, in 1911, Murphy attempted to stop his more panicky employer colleagues calling on the government for extreme measures to deal with a series of strikes.

> The government had given some protection, but the government might have done more; but to suggest that the government should have brought out an army to mow down peaceful pickets was neither possible or thinkable. What was known in the early days as the massacre of Peterloo was not going to be repeated in their time.[10]

That was in 1911. Within two years, Larkin's tactic of the sympathetic strike had united the fragmented and factionalised Dublin employers. There was employer solidarity for the defeat of 'Larkinism'. Murphy, too, felt that decisive action needed to be taken to halt Larkin. He was made leader of the 400-strong Employers' Federation, set up in 1913. Even if Murphy was not 'one of us', many unionist employers found that his single-mindedness had its uses.

Larkin had made a particular effort to unionise the Dublin United Tramway Company. Murphy, in response, called a meeting of his workers at midnight in the Antient Concert Rooms, Great Brunswick Street (Pearse Street), Dublin, on 19 July 1913. He addressed the tramway workers as 'My friends—and I may truly call you my friends, because every employee of any undertaking that I am connected with I look upon as a friend.' As a director of the Dublin United Tramway Company since 1880 he had all that time 'had the most pleasant relations with the employees of this Company.' He wanted the meeting to understand clearly 'that the directors of this company have not the slightest objection to the men forming a legitimate union.' Murphy promised a shilling a week pay rise. He exhorted the men at the end of the meeting to say in unison, 'God save Ireland'—an old nationalist toast that Murphy would have heard many times in the Sullivan household while boarding there as a schoolboy.

A month later, on 21 August 1913, Murphy had distributed to some of his 'friends' a notice that dismissed all ITGWU members from his employment in the Dublin United Tramway Company. Larkin called a strike at 9:40 a.m. on 26 August. At a meeting of the Employers' Federation a resolution was passed stating that the ITGWU was 'a menace to all trade organisation, and has become intolerable.' They pledged, therefore, not to employ any person who continued to be a member of that union. Employees faced instant dismissal, no matter to what union they belonged, if they failed to carry out 'lawful and reasonable instructions.'

In Larkin's eyes, Murphy was neither a Prometheus nor a Titan. As editor of the weekly *Irish Worker*, Larkin conducted a highly personalised campaign against the leader of the Dublin employers. Murphy was lampooned as an 'industrial octopus', a 'tramway tyrant', a 'blood-sucking vampire', the 'sweater', and 'this whited sepulchre'.[11]

Let us take at random the editorial in the *Irish Worker* for 7 September 1912, which focused on Murphy's ownership of the *Evening Mail*.

> This vicious, immoral sheet is owned and controlled by a creature named William Martin Murphy, a creature who never hesitated to use the most foul and unscrupulous methods against any man, woman, or child, who, in the opinion of William Martin Murphy, stood in William Martin Murphy's way, a soulless, money grabbing tyrant.[12]

Larkin, in the heat of the struggle, had denied Murphy 'the creature' and 'blood-sucking vampire' a share in a common humanity.

Murphy responded in kind. In the *Irish Independent, Irish Catholic* and *Evening Mail* (all owned by Murphy), Larkin was portrayed as an internationalist, a social revolutionary who was both anti-Catholic and anti-Irish. The exchanges were robust and demagogic. Murphy's *Irish Catholic* was not very Catholic when it wrote in 1913 of the poor of Dublin:

Into these thoroughfares there have poured nightly all the foul reserves of the slums, human beings whom life in the most darksome depths of a great city has deprived of most of the characteristics of civilisation. In the majority of instances they are beings whose career is generally a prolonged debauch ...[13]

The *Irish Catholic* warned on another occasion that 'Socialism is essentially Satanic in its nature, origin, and purpose.'[14] Compromise, therefore, was not possible. Murphy felt obliged to secure a victor's peace.

I have made reference to the demogoguery of the *Irish Independent* and the *Irish Catholic*. Having dealt with prejudice on Murphy's side, it is important also to draw attention to prejudices on the labour side. Murphy was not the only target of Larkin's demagogic style of journalism: John Redmond and the Irish Party, Dublin Corporation and City Hall officials and, of course, the Dublin Metropolitan Police were all unrelentingly criticised. One issue of the *Irish Worker* in 1911 contained an anti-Semitic poem. Larkin, who was not anti-Semitic, showed very bad editorial judgment in allowing such a poem to appear in a paper that professed to defend international working-class solidarity. His judgment was even more suspect on other occasions.

The quotations from the *Irish Catholic* given earlier and the publication in the *Irish Worker* of the poem just referred to provide examples of the personal limitations of the 'Titans', Murphy and Larkin. Both men became too fixated on one another; the outcome was tragedy.

Larkin failed to unify the trade union movement, and his behaviour during the lock-out alienated a large section of the leadership of British labour. He had, however, helped unify the divided employers of Dublin. Murphy regularly referred in his speeches to the lack of backbone shown by a number of employers. He told the Chamber of Commerce on 1 September 1914: 'I consider that some employers in Dublin have bred "Larkinism" by the neglect of their men, and then these same employers continued to support him by not having the courage to stand up against him.' On the same occasion Murphy—who was behaving like a commander-in-chief recently returned from a victorious campaign—was reprimanding his subordinates. He told his triumphant audience that the question he had fought in the tramway company was not one of wages or the treatment of those he employed there: the issue was

the supremacy of Mr. Larkin and whether he was going to rule the trade of Dublin, and whether men could carry on their business and in fact be able to call their bodies and souls their own, unless they went cap in hand to him. The position was becoming intolerable.

But Murphy did not consider the fight against Larkin 'difficult'. Once the strike started

> the employer had to get his back to the wall, and the workman had fired his last cartridge. The employer all the time managed to get his three meals a day, but the unfortunate workman and his family had no resources whatever except submission, and that was what occurred in 99 cases out of 100. The difficulty of teaching that lesson to the workmen was extraordinary.

Here was a Carthaginian peace. A strange way to treat friends, as Murphy had described his workers.

Perhaps history might have been kinder to Murphy if he had not been so ruthless and won so decisively against Larkin. He remains today in popular perception—a perception reinforced by literary fiction—an uncouth contractor from County Cork who made good. The contemporary Catholic writer G. K. Chesterton reinforced that view of the heartless entrepreneur and radical individualist. Setting Murphy apart from his English capitalist contemporaries, he wrote that 'he was more like some morbid prince of the fifteenth century, full of cold anger, not without perverted piety.' Another contemporary comment reinforced the image of the 'grand inquisitor' in saying that Murphy had gone through life with the Companies Act in one hand and the *Imitation of Christ* in the other.[15]

Murphy has remained a one-dimensional figure, all the time viewed in the context of the drama of 1913. He is the anti-hero in a social drama where Larkin towers over him as his moral superior: vested interest versus the salvation of the working class. For all his faults, Murphy remains the most important Catholic businessman of late nineteenth and early twentieth-century Ireland. A full investigation of his life might yield interesting insights into the world behind the public world of the Irish Party. Murphy, a power-broker in the worlds of business and politics, opened his home in Dartry to a range of important visitors. While he may not have held office, he was recognised by successive British governments as an important figure in the world of Irish politics, a world he remained active in right up to his death in 1919. In 1917 he served on the Irish Convention. His economic philosophy continued to have a strong influence on the policy positions taken by John Redmond and the Irish Party.

Murphy may not have been particularly charismatic. He was no Titan. But all too often he has been presented through the eyes of his main adversary, Larkin. While the latter has—for his early biographers—remained on a plinth, Murphy has been consigned to a historical Hades. The narrowness of that historical approach has closed off as a subject for investigation the world of the Catholic nationalist businessmen of Murphy's generation, who were a significant force in the establishment of the new state.

Chapter 8

The Strikes of 1911–1913: Their International Significance

Prof. Kenneth Brown

The clash between Jim Larkin and William Martin Murphy, which culminated in the Dublin lock-out of 1913, was so significant, proclaimed a writer in the *Irish Worker*, that future chroniclers of Ireland's history would have to devote an entire chapter to it. This injunction has been well heeded ever since. Although recent work on the history of the labour movement has brought into the light the contribution of other, less celebrated figures, most remain in the shadow still cast by Larkin. George Bernard Shaw pronounced him the greatest Irishman since Parnell; and certainly few other figures have inspired so much literary and artistic endeavour. The pivotal years of Larkin's influence, between 1907 and 1913, continue to exert a magnetic attraction on labour historians, possessing the same emotive, even climactic connotations that the years 1921–26 have for historians of the British labour movement.

The events that began in Belfast in 1907 and culminated in Dublin six years later have invariably been considered in the context of Ireland and its national history. Such an approach is perfectly proper and entirely natural, given both the magnitude of Larkin's achievements and his own outstanding personal attributes. Yet national histories themselves have a wider, international context, and ignoring this broader perspective can obscure important insights. Irish labour historians have generally been reluctant to place the pre-war strikes in a British context, still less in a European or global one. The reason may be that, superficially at least, contemporary British industrial unrest had different causes from that in Ireland.

In a buoyant labour market, strike activity was encouraged by the failure of real wages to sustain the rises of the previous decades. While some of the Irish unrest was concerned with issues of wages and conditions for workers, among the worst-treated in Europe, the main issue at stake in 1913 was the very right to organise—a battle won in Britain some twenty years before. Therefore, with some token nod at events on the other side of the Irish Sea, Irish writers have generally tended to ignore the wider importance of events in Dublin. Yet neither Britain nor Ireland was alone in experiencing industrial and working-class turmoil in the years before the First World War; and it is in this particular setting that I propose to consider the strikes of 1911–13.

It appears that virtually every country in the industrialising world before 1914 was racked with civil unrest, manifest in popular disturbances and strikes. There were massive strikes in German and Russian textile factories in 1903. Employers in Germany's heavy industrial sector organised company unions and used 'free labour' to defeat strikers. The Swedish government passed laws allowing pickets to be imprisoned, a measure that the Kaiser wished to replicate in Germany. In Britain the Taff Vale judgment rendered union funds liable to legal actions for damages, as did the Loichot case in France. General strikes occurred in Belgium, the Netherlands, Luxembourg, Sweden and Italy between 1902 and 1904. The year 1905 saw particular problems in eastern Europe, with revolution in Russia, mass popular demonstrations forcing the introduction of universal suffrage in Austria, and a virtual state of civil war in Hungary. Further west, Sweden and Norway split, the formal separation of church and state in France was followed by widespread rioting, and Germany experienced some of its worst strikes ever. In 1907 a peasant revolt in Romania resulted in 20,000 deaths. Barcelona was rocked in 1909 by an orgy of violence involving the widespread sacking of convents and churches, while the Portuguese monarchy was overthrown in the following year.

With the exception of rioting by the unemployed in 1905, Britain at first escaped relatively mildly, though a heavy electoral defeat by the Liberals prompted the Conservative leader, Arthur Balfour, to observe in 1906 that Britain was 'face to face (no doubt in a milder form) with the socialistic difficulties which loom so large on the continent.'[1] From 1910, however, Britain was caught up in the wave of industrial unrest that swept over Europe and the United States. On the other side of the Atlantic, attempts to organise migratory workers invariably degenerated into violent battles. Trade unionists dynamited the buildings of the *Los Angeles Times* in 1910, and a year or two later the state militia burned down a tent colony of striking Colorado miners, killing two women and eleven children. The British government was sufficiently concerned by the increasing incidence of violent strikes to establish a Commission on Industrial Relations. General strikes occurred in Barcelona and Ancona; industrial unrest in Spain, a country with a very small industrial base, reached a peak in 1913 with more than three hundred strikes. In the same year Italy was hit by 810 stoppages, and striking Italian railway workers, like their counterparts in France a year or so before, were forced back to work only when served with conscription notices by the government, which rendered them liable to military law. Hundreds of casualties in the Lena goldfields in 1912 led to demonstrations in Russia's big cities. The rash of strikes reached some 2,400 separate stoppages in 1913, culminating in a virtually total cessation of work in St Petersburg in July 1914.

As for Britain, major stoppages on the railways and in the docks in 1911 were followed a year later by a miners' strike. In 1913 the number of separate strikes was 1,459, many of which were unofficial, that is, organised by rank-and-file militants against the advice of union officers. The number of days lost through industrial action reached 10 million in 1911, 40 million in 1912, and 11.6 million in 1913. These figures include not only the two Dublin stoppages but the upsurge of unrest that occurred throughout Ireland—so much so that the *Freeman's Journal* had to launch a special column in August 1911 headed 'Irish Labour Troubles'.

This strike activity was accompanied by an upsurge in violence. This of course was by no means a new characteristic of industrial unrest, but contemporaries detected in it a new readiness, almost perhaps an eagerness, to abandon discussion in favour of force. Sir George Askwith, the British Board of Trade's industrial relations expert, wrote that 'nobody could understand the rapid and alarming spread of many of the strikes.'[2] One town councillor told him that although he had been in Paris at the time of the Commune in the early eighteen-seventies he had not then witnessed such scenes as he saw in Hull during the 1911 seamen's strike. 'He had not known there were such people,' he said: 'women with their hair streaming and half nude, reeling through the streets, smashing and destroying.'[3] The Foreign Secretary, Edward Grey, opined that the 1912 coal strike presaged the onset of revolution, convinced that 'unless we meet the men, there would be civil war.'[4] Winston Churchill was so exasperated by what he regarded as trade union intransigence that, according to one colleague, he was in a 'shoot 'em down attitude,' a state of mind that was to have fatal consequences at Tonypandy when, as Home Secretary, he authorised the deployment of troops.[5] Not surprisingly, recent general surveys have confirmed that levels of British strike violence rose dramatically in those years.

Irish labour was equally convulsed. Belfast was shaken to its roots by the carters' strike of 1907, which produced both rioting that led to civilian deaths and a mutiny in the ranks of the RIC. Attempts by employers in Sligo to replace striking dock workers with blackleg labour from Liverpool also resulted in serious casualties. If the 1911 Dublin strike was relatively peaceful, the same was not true of 1913. In the first eight months of the year thirty separate disputes broke out, and the eventual lock-out was accompanied by protests and riots. Prof. Charles McCarthy has appropriately described the situation as representing 'a growing sense of impatience and a hunger for catharsis.' Social restlessness, he adds, 'was building up to a dangerous level.'[6] Larkin's most eminent biographer has referred to the 'insidious crescendo of violence in these years,' quoting a contemporary reviewer of John Galsworthy's play *Strife*, which opened in Dublin in August 1913: 'Labour and Capital have got to fight it out to the end some time and though Compromise may delay the final issue it will never prevent it.'[7]

What, if any, are the common threads running through these manifestations of popular discontent? As far as industrial action is concerned, it used to be fashionable to treat the British unrest as part and parcel of the syndicalist agitation occurring in parts of the Continent and the United States. Syndicalism was an ideology that had developed out of internal disputes among Marxists about how best the proletariat could achieve its historic destiny of seizing control of the state. Put simply, pure

Marxists favoured the acquisition of power through indirect or parliamentary means, while syndicalists advocated strike action by trade unions, culminating in a general stoppage of all workers.

There is no doubt that syndicalist influences were at work in both Europe and the United States. They were apparent, for example, in the establishment in 1905 of the Industrial Workers of the World at Chicago. This organisation's tactics and propaganda were based on a constitution that proclaimed baldly that 'the working class and the employing class have nothing in common,' and it openly advocated the use of industrial sabotage. Italy had its own independent syndicalist union federation, and its members organised the short-lived general strike in 1904. By 1912 syndicalists dominated the Italian socialist party. German trade unions flirted with Rosa Luxemburg's resolution in favour of a politically motivated general strike in 1905 and again in 1910. Many French trade unions adhered to a revolutionary syndicalist ideology, and these militants had some influence on the 1910 railway strike there. It found organisational expression in the alliance of the Confédération Générale du Travail and the Fédération des Bourses du Travail. In Spain the events of Tragic Week in July 1909, when 175 striking workers were shot down in the streets of Barcelona, led ultimately to the establishment in 1910 of the Confederación Nacional del Trabajo (CNT). As an openly syndicalist organisation it was subjected to severe state repression after an anarchist assassinated the Prime Minister in 1912.

Research has suggested, however, that such syndicalist influences were relatively unimportant in both Britain and Ireland. The 'Triple Alliance' between the railway workers', miners' and transport workers' unions was sometimes portrayed as a British version of the one big union advocated by syndicalists, but it owed little to syndicalist theory and much more to the practical consideration that it made sense for major unions to co-ordinate strike action. Studies of individual unions and strikes have suggested that political philosophies of any sort had little real appeal, except to a few isolated and unrepresentative groups in a work force more noted for its pragmatism than its ideological fervour.

At best, therefore, it could be argued that economic circumstances led British workers to respond enthusiastically to charismatic figures such as Ben Tillett and Tom Mann, whose own commitment to syndicalism provided that sense of conviction and purpose that effective leadership always required. In exactly the same way they had responded positively to James Keir Hardie and John Burns in the eighteen-eighties without necessarily espousing or sharing their socialist principles. As for Ireland, the thrust of Dermot Keogh's book is that Belfast in 1907 and Dublin in 1913 were roused essentially by Larkin the man rather than Larkin the revolutionary ideologue. It is perhaps significant in this respect that when in 1912 Charles Watney and James Little published their important study, *Industrial Warfare*, they did not even mention Larkin in their list of leading syndicalist personalities. Larkin's reputation as a revolutionary syndicalist owed more to the attributions of others than to his own beliefs: indeed, he is on record in 1911 as claiming that he neither believed in nor favoured the use of the strike weapon.

Syndicalism, then, is probably best discounted as the common thread linking Dublin with Liverpool, Berlin, Barcelona, Paris, and even Colorado. In any case, the resort to violence was by no means confined to industrial relations. As we have already seen, in Europe generally in these years demands for constitutional or political change frequently became the occasion for violence. This was equally the case in Britain. Beatrice Webb suggested that the whole of the British public was caught up over the issue of whether men were to be governed by reason in harmony with the will of the majority or by emotion and the fervent aspiration of militant minorities. Virginia Woolf put it more dramatically perhaps in claiming that in or about December 1910 human character changed. Both women were reflecting a general concern that in several different spheres of British public life, violence and passion appeared to be displacing rational discourse. The constitutional crisis arising from the rejection of the budget by the House of Lords created tensions that, in the opinion of the American ambassador in Britain, Walter Page, were reminiscent of the days before the outbreak of the Civil War. Similarly, the militancy of the suffragists, if mild by standards of late twentieth-century terrorism, was a profound shock to the orderly Edwardians, and the Marquis of Crewe said later that it would not have been a surprise to him or to Scotland Yard if members of the government had been assassinated. In Ireland itself, of course, nationalists and unionists alike were preparing to settle their differences by force, and David Lloyd George warned that the coincidence of fighting in Ireland with labour unrest would create a very dangerous situation, 'the gravest with which any government has had to deal for centuries.'[8]

The general situation in Britain, therefore, paralleled that in other parts of the advanced world; and the Dublin strikes of 1913 can be seen as part of this much wider tendency to eschew accepted methods of conflict resolution. In presenting such an interpretation of pre-war Britain I am going back to a thesis first advanced in 1934 by the American historian George Dangerfield under the title of *The Strange Death of Liberal England*. In his book he wove together the various strands of civil unrest in Britain—suffragists, Home Rulers, and trade unionists—suggesting that between them they undermined and then destroyed the liberal values on which British society had rested since the early part of the nineteenth century. 'Fires long smouldering in the English spirit', he wrote, 'suddenly flared up so that by the end of 1913 Liberal England was reduced to ashes.'[9] The ensuing turmoil somehow culminated in a final and cataclysmic rejection of rationality in August 1914.

As a thesis this has not found much support among British historians. They have generally dismissed the idea that there was any significant link between these various movements of unrest, concluding that they were coincidental or connected only in the sense that they were the products of legislative bottle-necks. Such scepticism may well reflect the fact that they find it difficult to come to terms with the notion of serious upheaval in Britain, because ever since the civil war of the seventeenth century the country had remained largely free of serious civil strife, apart from the Jacobite rebellions and intermittent troubles in Ireland. Britain proved impervious to military dictatorship, civil war, and the sort of destabilising swings characteristic of continental Europe, though it was perhaps more affected by revolutionary fervour in 1848 than is sometimes suggested.

Interestingly, non-British scholars coming from different traditions, whether European or American, have been far more receptive to Dangerfield's hypothesis. The great French historian Halévy actually anticipated Dangerfield by a couple of years, giving the dramatic title 'On the Brink of Catastrophe' to the third part of the epilogue to his *History of the English People in the Nineteenth Century*. It contains a chapter on syndicalism, feminism, and labour unrest, under the subtitle of 'Domestic Anarchy', a phrase that the American scholar Alfred Havighurst refuses to dismiss as mere rhetorical flourish. Barbara Tuchman's account of the pre-war world contains echoes of Dangerfield, and another Frenchman, François Bedarida, also devoted some pages to discussing his interpretations, unlike some more recent British histories of the period. The only significant British scholar who has taken Dangerfield seriously is Norman Stone. Indeed he has suggested that what Dangerfield said about Britain could be applied with equal force to most European countries in the pre-war period. Pretty well everywhere, he suggests, a new irrationality was gaining currency.[10] Generally, it can perhaps be suggested that the old consensus values that had held European societies together were being challenged.

This was certainly happening in Britain. Nineteenth-century British society had been built on a corpus of values summed up in the notion of respectability. This entailed notions of sobriety, morality, self-help, and a general commitment to capitalism, *laisser-faire*, individualism, and the maintenance of the existing social order, with its assigned (some believed divinely ordained) roles for capital, labour, and women. General subscription to this set of values provided the common faith that, in the view of Émile Durkheim, is all that is necessary to hold a society together. In Dangerfield's view, these values were being increasingly challenged in the years before 1914.

As far as industrial relations are concerned, whatever they may have thought in private, British trade union leaders had generally paid lip-service to the principles of classical economics, especially the notion of industrial harmony. The image of trade unionism as it was carefully presented to the 1867 royal commission was that of institutions that, while primarily concerned to protect their members against the worst excesses of industrial life, clearly envisaged doing so within the prevailing economic and social system. But the growing scale of industry had created a new group of business plutocrats increasingly remote from their work force, and this process of alienation was furthered by technical innovation in many industries, leaving workers feeling that they were being subjected to more oppressive working conditions and a faster pace and rhythm of work. These changes, coupled with the spread of socialist doctrine of class war and the increasing evidence of widespread poverty, all served to place considerable stress on the convention of industrial harmony.

Socialist economic theory undermined the notion that wages should be determined by profit and left to find their own level in the market. From the turn of the century British trade unionists increasingly rejected the sliding-scale agreements that embodied this idea, and they proved increasingly reluctant to participate in the conciliation schemes that had grown up in the nineteenth century. The tenets of free-market economics were also increasingly difficult to defend in the light of the findings of various contemporary social surveys that in 1900 a third of Britain's urban population was living on or beneath the poverty line. Small wonder that Ben Tillett could proclaim openly in his union's annual report that the class struggle was the most brutal of wars and the most pitiless towards the weak.

Yet if Dangerfield's hypothesis is credible, it merely raises a further question: what was it about the early years of the present century that aroused the consciousness of hitherto quiescent groups and encouraged political, social and industrial establishments everywhere to react so strongly? Why did employers and governments dig their heels in so resolutely against the increasing articulation of popular demands for industrial and political rights? This was essentially what happened in Dublin. Into a city with some of the most poorly housed citizens in Europe and certainly some of the lowest-paid casual workers, Larkin appeared as a saviour. To the establishment that had presided over such a state of affairs, he was demonised as a major threat.

In any healthy liberal society, values and norms are constantly being reassessed, and many of the movements that, as it were, went critical in the Edwardian period had their origins much earlier in the nineteenth century. In the same way, while the challenge to existing values involves a threat to those who espouse them, this is always the case, whatever period we consider. What marks the Edwardian period out as unique is that these processes of re-evaluation were characterised, as I have suggested, by an unprecedented degree of violence. It was this phenomenon that so struck Dangerfield and that provides a common theme in contemporary protest movements and strikes throughout Europe and the United States. How can it be explained?

Two influences were important. In a situation of rapidly expanding international trade, the long economic depression of the later nineteenth century put pressure on industrialists to improve efficiency and competitiveness. Their ensuing attempts to constrain wages and increase work rhythms did not go down well with labour forces that had benefited from rising real wages and in general were now better educated, better informed and better organised than before. Rising living standards were not universal, however, and part of the troubles in the pre-war industrial unrest came from those, as in Dublin, who reacted against the growing evidence of their economic inferiority.

The second influence might be described as national uncertainty. Not only did international tensions grow considerably after the turn of the century but nationalism also began to exert itself. In eastern Europe particularly, nationalist aspirations threatened the integrity of the Ottoman, Austro-Hungarian and Russian empires. In the west the growing power of Germany appeared as a threat to both France and Britain. British imperial sensitivities had been roused by the Boer War, in which one of the world's strongest military and economic powers had struggled to defeat an undeveloped colony of farmers. At a time of growing international uncertainty, therefore, it was only natural that establishments everywhere should seek to sustain national identity and unity by reasserting the values on which nineteenth-century certainties had been built. Thus, just as the demand for change became more insistent, so the resistance to change was hardening.

This clash between old and new value systems took different forms in different European countries. Sometimes it occurred as a conflict between the church and socialism, sometimes between labour and capital, sometimes between imperialists and nationalists. In Britain, as Dangerfield argued, it was perceived as a challenge from socialism to liberalism. 'Socialist agitator' became a convenient tag to apply to those who appeared to be set on destroying the cosy status quo. Socialists were certainly prominent critics of empire; they generally favoured Home Rule, supported the attack on the House of Lords, and advocated votes for women. Industrial unrest was widely—though, as we have seen, wrongly—attributed to the malign influence of socialist syndicalists. Larkin's opponents in Dublin constantly overlooked his espousal of the old—Catholicism—and emphasised his proclamation of the new—socialism.

Whatever form it took, however, the conflict between old and new social values became increasingly violent as a result of the economic and international tensions that formed its backcloth and that culminated in the final violence of world war. Predictably, the events of Easter 1916 and the winning of independence subsequently endowed the interpretation of this period of Irish history with a nationalist, somewhat parochial colour. It should not be forgotten, however, that the Dublin strike of 1913 arose out of more than purely Irish considerations. As Ireland's version of the clash between new and old social values, it was part of a much wider social current.

Chapter 9

Larkin in America: The Road to Sing Sing

Manus O'Riordan

On 12 May 1947, three months after burying his father, James Larkin Junior told an audience of New York trade unionists:

> There is hardly a state in the Union in which Jim Larkin did not lie in jail because of participation in and leadership of some union fight, either of Irishmen or Germans or Italians or of Poles, or any other race on God's sod, and in every quarter of these United States they fought.

It was in late October 1914 that Big Jim Larkin, general secretary of the Irish Transport and General Workers' Union, had set sail for the United States on the *St Louis*. In the aftermath of his leading of Dublin's workers in the epic struggle of 1913 he had reached the edge of nervous and physical exhaustion. James Connolly had seen more clearly than most how much Larkin required a change of environment. But the America that Larkin entered was no less an arena of bitter class conflict. So here too he gave it his all.

Within a few days of his arrival in New York, on 8 November 1914, Larkin was addressing a rally of fifteen thousand people in Madison Square Garden. This was to celebrate the election to Congress of the Socialist Party candidate Meyer London, who had been counsel for the Jewish and Italian clothing workers of the Triangle Shirtwaist Company both before and after 146 of them were to perish in the infamous fire of March 1911. And, echoing an uncompromising poem of Connolly's, Larkin told his audience:

> We Socialists want more than a dollar increase for the workers. We want the earth.

What was central to Larkin's speech on that occasion, as on many others yet to come, was his opposition to the mass slaughter that had been unleashed by the imperialist war in Europe. A few weeks later he declared to an audience of 'Wobblies'—members of the Industrial Workers of the World—

> No working-class organisation or propagandists advocate bomb throwing as a remedy for the evils of capitalism; but in the European holocaust the bomb thrower who, from his aviation machine, destroys human life or

property is considered a hero and decorated with Victoria or Iron Crosses by the capitalist governments engaged in the War.

Larkin's active opposition to the war during his first year in the United States did not, however, remain exclusively that of an international socialist. He had brought with him a letter of introduction from Thomas Clarke of the IRB to John Devoy, Fenian veteran, Clan na Gael leader, and editor of the *Gaelic American*. While America was not formally to enter the war until April 1917, it was economically supportive of the war effort of the British Empire. Larkin saw it as his duty to support American labour disputes that would disrupt it. John Devoy and the Irish-American judge Daniel F. Cohalan brought Larkin into contact with Germany's military attachés as early as November 1914. They offered to put him on the payroll at $200 a week, but he refused outright, although willing to accept financial assistance towards labour disputes, which would be channelled to him via Devoy. At the same time he was adamant in refusing to have any association with German sabotage operations.

While Devoy was to remain a steadfast 'friend in need' to the very end of Larkin's sojourn in the United States, it was otherwise with the Clan na Gael organisation as a whole. The Irish-Americans whom Larkin was drawn to were not the lace-curtain variety but those like Elizabeth Gurley Flynn, for whom Joe Hill would compose his song 'The Rebel Girl' while lying on Death Row in 1915. Larkin's visit to Flynn's home in the Bronx prompted her to unfurl once again the banner of the Irish Socialist Federation, which she had helped Connolly establish in 1907 and which now could feature Big Jim as its key speaking attraction on the New York waterfront. Recalling that period, Flynn provides a vivid portrait of how Larkin 'was very poor and lived in one room in a small alley in Greenwich Village called Milligan Place.'

By the summer of 1915 Larkin had begun a lecture tour on the west coast. This was to constitute much of his activity over the next couple of years. As he was to tell the court in his 1920 trial,

> throughout this period I worked with the Socialist Party of America, speaking for them and interpreting the philosophy of the Socialist movement under their auspices, in the States of New York, Connecticut, Rhode Island, Massachusetts, Maine, Illinois, Montana, Idaho, Washington, Oregon, California, Arizona, Nevada, Pennsylvania, New Jersey, Delaware, Texas and for a short time Alaska.

Larkin became increasingly drawn in to the wider struggles of American workers. Following the framing of the IWW troubadour Joe Hill on a murder charge and his subsequent execution in Salt Lake City, Larkin was chosen to give the English-language oration at the Chicago funeral service, attended by five thousand mourners in November 1915. As he went on to write,

> Joseph Hillstrom, one of the Ishmaelites of the industrial world, was to hand and they 'shot him to death' because he was a rebel, one of the

disinherited, because he was the voice of the inarticulate downtrodden. They crucified him on their cross of gold, spilled his blood on the altar of their God—Profit.

In 1916 Larkin joined with his fellow Liverpool-Irish socialist Jack Carney in bringing out a Chicago edition of the *Irish Worker*, in which he singled out for attack the tenor John McCormack for his support of America's economic war effort on behalf of Britain. Later that year both Larkin and Carney also campaigned for Eugene Debs, the Socialist candidate for Congress, whose election platform was one of uncompromising opposition to the war.

America's formal entry into that war in April 1917 was to inaugurate an era of outright repression of dissident opinion. The Espionage Act of June 1917 was intended to function as a grab-all act against all forms of anti-war activity. Larkin was one of the first to be arrested that month, merely for saying that there were not enough soldiers in New York State to make him go to war. As the rule of law had not yet been thoroughly compromised, those particular charges against him were dismissed. Right-wing terror went on to have recourse to murder in August, when an IWW leader, the Cherokee Frank Little, was lynched for leading an anti-war strike of copper miners in Larkin's old organising ground of Butte, Montana.

By September 1917 the rule of law had been sufficiently bent to facilitate the arrest of over two thousand IWW members during the following few months. Mass show trials were staged, such as the one in Chicago with 165 defendants and in Sacramento with 146. The sentences handed down ranged from five to twenty years. In June 1918 the Socialist Party leader Eugene Debs was himself arrested for an anti-war speech and was sentenced to ten years' imprisonment.

Although Larkin had already spent three years lecturing for the Socialist Party, it was not until the end of 1917 that he became a party member, in order to more effectively confront the forces of reaction. The pressures of the war, coupled with the impact of the Russian Revolution, were already leading to sharp right and left-wing divisions in the party. One of his associates in the emerging split, Bertram Wolfe, later recalled Larkin's pivotal role.

The Connolly Club which he founded at 43 West 29th Street in New York City—by the simple expedient of leading a band of his followers in capturing for the left wing of the Socialist Party the old Party headquarters by breaking the lock, and then moving in bodily, with his cookstove for frying eggs and Irish bacon, his Irish Worker, his mimeograph machine [duplicator], and his hangers on—had room for workingmen of all nationalities, Jewish cloakmakers, Scotsmen and Englishmen, Germans, Bulgarians, Yugo-Slavs, Russians, Greenwich Villagers. Wide-eyed they listened to the poetry of Larkin's speech, his intemperate polemics, his crotchets, his mixture of creeds. To his home in Patchin Place, where he likewise held forth, there came men of all nations. His lieutenants included a Canadian Irishman named Curley, Tom O'Flaherty, Patrick Quinlan of the IWW, Sheamus O'Shiel, Eadhmonn MacAlpine. It was through his rebel network of seamen and longshoremen in New York Harbour that he fixed up the trip that took John Reed to Soviet Russia with seaman's papers, wearing a fisherman's shirt and passing as a sailor on some Scandinavian ship.

Larkin's contribution to the birth of an American Communist Party can be said to have begun in May 1918. The James Connolly Socialist Club, which he had established just two months previously, was addressed by John Reed within a few weeks of the latter's arrival back from Russia. Reed was of course to achieve international fame primarily as the author of *Ten Days that Shook the World*, and his eye-witness report fired Larkin, Carney and the Belfast-born MacAlpine with such enthusiasm for the Russian Revolution that they plunged headlong into the activities of the left wing of the Socialist Party of America in attempting to transform it into a Communist Party. Larkin's campaigning drew the following response from the *New York Times* on 3 February 1919:

When a man speaking in an American city excites the applause of numerous auditors by telling them that 'Russia is the only place where men and women can be free,' the fact raises a good many rather serious questions. Mr. Larkin has been credited with ability of a kind and moving eloquence. That is what makes him dangerous, but one observes that he prefers America to Russia as a place in which to preach.

Before the year was out, however, Larkin would experience with full force the reality of the fact that America was very far from being the home of free speech. In the meantime, February 1919 also saw Larkin helping to organise a distinct left-wing section of the Socialist Party in New York. The left had been particularly incensed by the fact that the New York Socialist aldermen from the party's right wing had joined in voting for the erection of a Victory Arch across one of the city's main thoroughfares, to celebrate not alone America's success in the imperialist war but also its military intervention aimed at crushing the new Soviet Republic in Russia.

That spring, fresh elections for the Socialist Party executive indicated that the left wing would win twelve of the fifteen seats. The old right-wing executive responded in May by expelling about two-thirds of the party's membership, which accordingly slumped from a peak of 110,000 in January 1919 to a mere 40,000 six months later.

On 21 June 1919 a National Left-Wing Conference was held at the Manhattan Lyceum, New York, at which the majority view was that the left should attempt to win majority control of the Socialist Party conference on 30 August and if that failed should then split and form a Communist Party. The minority view, led by Nicholas Hourwich of the party's Russian-language Federation, was dogmatically in favour of forming a Communist Party straight away, and they accordingly marched out of the conference in protest against having any more dealings with the Socialist Party. The majority of the conference proceeded to elect a National Council of nine, with Larkin topping the poll; the other Council members were Louis Fraina, Charles Ruthenberg, Isaac Ferguson, John Ballam, Eamonn MacAlpine, Benjamin Gitlow, Maximilian Cohen, and Bertram Wolfe. Ferguson was named national secretary, and Fraina and MacAlpine became editor and assistant editor, respectively, of the *Revolutionary Age*. A few weeks later a Left-Wing Manifesto was drafted and published by Fraina, and it was this document that was to form the basis of the prosecution of Larkin at the end of that year. Larkin, however, took exception to some of the Continental jargon used in the Manifesto— coming, as he would say himself, from the 'British School of Socialism'.

At the end of July the majority of the Left-Wing Council, including Ruthenberg, Fraina, and Ferguson, decided to reverse their previous position and join the Russian Federation in proceeding straight away to form a Communist Party. The minority, consisting of Gitlow, Larkin, and MacAlpine, decided to stick to the previously agreed strategy and were later joined by Reed. This strategy came to naught, however, when the Socialist Party leaders called in the police on 30 August to eject Reed and the other left-wingers from their national convention at the Machinists' Hall, Chicago. Accordingly, September 1919 saw the birth of two new parties: the Communist Party of America, with Ruthenberg as national secretary and Fraina as international secretary, and the Communist Labor Party, with Alfred Wagenknecht as national secretary and John Reed as international secretary.

The combined membership of the two parties came to between fifty and sixty thousand, of which the CLP had only ten thousand. The CLP had the larger English-speaking membership, but even so the combined English-speaking membership of both parties only came to 10 per cent of the total. In the CPA, English-speaking members formed only 4 per cent, with the semi-autonomous east European federations as a whole making up 75 per cent, of which one-third was the Russian Federation. As Ruthenberg argued in May 1920, the basic problem with the CPA was that it had not got five speakers 'who could present its cause in English, and the same was true in regard to writers and editors.' The CLP partisan Larkin was even less impressed with the CPA's English, and in November 1919 he had denounced that party 'because of the love of its leaders for long words and abstract reasoning which went over the brows of the masses. Their talk is full of stuff against "Parliamentary Government". The people can't understand them.'

After much factional bickering, the two parties would finally unite in May 1921. In the meantime their combined membership had fallen to ten thousand in 1920 as a result of the wave of arrests and deportations unleashed by the US Attorney-General, A. Mitchell Palmer, assisted by the future FBI Director J. Edgar Hoover. Between November 1919 and January 1920 an estimated ten thousand people were arrested. New York State called into operation a Criminal Anarchy Statute that had been passed upon the assassination of President McKinley in 1902 but never before used until 1919. New York accordingly became the centre of a series of political trials, where each of the defendants was sentenced to five to ten years by Judge Bartow Weeks. Gitlow of the CLP was tried in January 1920, Winitsky of the CPA in March, Larkin of the CLP in April, and Ruthenberg and Ferguson of the CPA in October 1920.

Larkin had been arrested in New York on 7 November 1919, the second anniversary of the Russian Revolution. Three days later he was charged with 'criminal anarchy' before the Chief City Magistrate, McAdoo, who was to express arithmetical as well as political hysteria by declaring 'that every member of the Communist Party in this state, numbering 75,000 or more, was guilty of criminal anarchy in becoming a member of the party.'

Thanks as much to John Devoy as the American left, Larkin was released on bail on 20 November 1919 and went immediately back into the fray. As the *New York Times* reported on 29 November, a rally was held at which more than five hundred men and women rose to their feet and took the Communist oath administered by Larkin.

Larkin finally came to trial on 7 April 1920, and the proceedings continued until the twenty-seventh. The transcript of the trial was to take up 924 printed pages. Since Larkin conducted his own defence, he had to state his case by posing questions to himself, as well as answering the interjections of Judge Weeks and the cross-examination of the Assistant District Attorney, Alexander Rorke. Larkin's final contribution was to be a $3\frac{1}{2}$-hour summation to the jury.

Back in January 1915 Larkin had declared:

> The English working class is as dear to me as that of my own country or any other, but the Government of England is the vilest thing on the face of the earth.

But now it was the American government that was putting him on trial, and Larkin unleashed his fury against the role played by the Irish-American establishment in that repression. He pointed out that officers of the court were members of Clan na Gael, most notably the Chief City Magistrate, McAdoo, who had first arraigned him. Defiant in the face of the prosecutor, Rorke, who was boasting of his own Irish parentage, Larkin charged:

> After some few weeks they discovered that I was not talking as they wanted me to talk; they discovered that instead of my charging crimes against the English people, I was charging the crimes against the English government. Well, you know that it is foolishness for any Irishman to come to America to prove a case against the Government, for mark you, gentlemen, once the English and Irish people get to understand the problem, they will settle the problem between themselves, and your American-Irish politicians, they would have no reason to exist.

Larkin was also audacious enough to prick the bubble of America's own xenophobic chauvinism.

America will be the greatest nation on earth when it absorbs the present element within her borders. But it is not a nation now. You have no cultural expression. You are confined to a few great men like Twain and Emerson and Whitman. But America shows a parochial mind. The defendant thinks that some of the best that Americans possess by way of men and women, and the mental expression in applied knowledge, has come from the alien within her borders.

But, as Larkin pointed out, Aryan New York was still discriminating against what it regarded as alien New York.

I am a comrade of Gitlow. He is a Jew and I am a Gentile. Did you notice, gentlemen, that every Jew who got in that box was dismissed by peremptory challenge, but not by the defendant? And yet the Jews have given something in the way of service to America, and why they were debarred from sitting in judgment upon this man who is tried for trying to overcome the Constitution, I fail to understand. And yet they tell you that this is a country, homogenous in itself, where everybody has a right to free expression and all the responsibilities both of citizenship and of service.

Larkin also came into conflict with colour prejudice. With reference to a meeting he had addressed in the Manhattan Lyceum, he was asked by Rorke:

Q. Did you in the course of the remarks say that the white men believed that they have a white God?
A. Yes, I did.
Q. Did you say that in Mexico you will find that the God down there, in painting and sculpture, is the coloured God?
A. I said in paintings they symbolised the idea of God, and that they were dark in colour.
Q. Did you say that the Negro has a special God all his own?
A. No, I did not.
Q. Did you say that the Negro got salvation?
A. In a portion of the story I said that.
Q. Did you say to those people there 'You have been praying for a new world'?
A. Yes.
Q. Did you say to them 'The international basis of our movement is the same everywhere'?
A. Something the same.

Larkin undoubtedly gave maximum offence to the American establishment, to the point where in his summation for the prosecution Rorke would fume:

The trails of the serpents that are swarming to this country are already here, the work that was carried on in Liverpool and in other countries is brought here, and behold, throughout the United States, this archangel of anarchy.

Larkin nonetheless insisted that it was he in fact who was adhering to the best of America's own radical traditions.

How did I get the love of comrades, only by reading Whitman? How did I get this love of humanity except by understanding men like Thoreau and Emerson and the greatest man of all next to Emerson—Mark Twain? Those are the men I have lived with, the real Americans—not the Americans of the mart and the exchange who would sell their souls for money and sell their country too.

Larkin went on to invoke Abraham Lincoln's words:

Listen to what one of the great citizens of the world that was honoured by you says: 'If by mere force of numbers a majority should deprive a minority of any clearly written constitutional right, it might in a moral point of view justify revolution'—an address delivered by President Lincoln, a man that has been a world force, who speaks out as the First Citizen and a man who is admitted to have saved this Union. 'This country,' says he, 'with its institutions, belongs to the people who inhabit it. Whenever they shall grow weary of the existing Government they can exercise their constitutional right of amending it, or their revolutionary right to dismember and overthrow it.' That is Lincoln ... The defendant says that he was trying to infuse a new spirit and understanding of real socialism, revolutionary socialism. Of course you are all fearful of that term, and yet here is a man, Lincoln, who is not fearful of it.

Larkin maintained that what was at stake in his trial was in fact freedom of thought itself.

Einstein and men like him would not be allowed to function, would not be allowed to think.

Reduced to its essentials, Larkin summed up the case against himself as follows:

The Defendant claims here now that he is not getting tried for any overt act, he is not getting tried for any intent to commit an overt act, he is getting tried for within his mind focusing the idea of the centuries, and trying to bring knowledge into a co-ordinate form that he might assist and develop and beautify life. That is the charge against the defendant—that he preached a doctrine of humanity against inhumanity; that he preached the doctrine of order; that he preached the doctrine of brotherhood as against that mischievous, hellish thing of national and brute, herd hatred.

Larkin was found guilty. On 3 May 1920 Judge Weeks sentenced him to a term of five to ten years' imprisonment, whereupon he was promptly despatched to Sing Sing Prison. In vain did Felix Frankfurter of the

Harvard Law School join with others that same month in issuing the Twelve Lawyers' Report, in which they denounced the Attorney-General for a grossly illegal campaign of terror whereby 'working men and working women suspected of radical views have been shamefully abused and maltreated.'

How did Larkin respond to the prospect of prolonged incarceration? There is a vivid image of his old self and his fighting spirit on St Patrick's Day, 1921. With a naïve sense of judgment, the prison warders—many of whom were themselves Irish—momentarily softened towards the famed Irish orator in their charge and invited him to relate the story of St Patrick to the assembled prison population. Larkin's version was conventional enough until he reached the legend of how St Patrick had driven all the snakes out of Ireland. 'And where did they go?' he enquired rhetorically before providing his own conclusion. 'They came to America, to become politicians, policemen, and prison guards.'

The uproarious applause that Larkin thus provoked among his fellow-prisoners was the exception that proved the rule. Oscar Wilde's biographer, Frank Harris, discovered on a visit to Sing Sing that the prisoners generally regarded Larkin as a damned fool in going to jail for standing up for others. There is indeed an image of a different Larkin, diffident and defensive, if not yet despondent. It was provided by none other than Charlie Chaplin, as great a humanitarian as he was a comedian. Having accompanied Harris on that same visit, Chaplin later recalled:

> Prisons have a strange atmosphere, as if the human spirit were suspended. At Sing Sing the old cell blocks were grimly mediaeval: small, narrow stone chambers crowded with four to six inmates sleeping in each cell. What fiendish brain could conceive of building such horrors! Larkin was in the shoe factory, and here he greeted us, a tall handsome man, about six foot four, with piercing blue eyes but a gentle smile. Although happy to see Frank, he was nervous and disturbed and was anxious to get back to his bench. Even the warder's assurance would not allay his uneasiness. 'It's bad morally for the other prisoners if I'm privileged to see visitors during working hours,' said Larkin ... He said he was treated reasonably well, but he was worried about his wife and family in Ireland whom he had not heard from since his confinement. Frank promised to help him. After we left, Frank said it depressed him to see a courageous, flamboyant character like Larkin reduced to prison discipline.

The right-wing hysteria that had sent Larkin to Sing Sing did not abate until November 1922, when Al Smith was elected Governor of New York and inaugurated in the New Year. On 17 January 1923 Larkin received a free pardon from Smith, who added:

> I pardon Larkin not because of agreement with his views, but despite my disagreement with them ... Political progress results from the clash of conflicting opinions ... Full and free discussion of political issues is a fundamental of democracy. Stripped of its legalistic aspects, this, to my

mind, is a political case where a man has been punished for the statement of his beliefs.

The *New York Times* of 20 April 1923, in reporting on Larkin's deportation from the United States, quoted him as saying before he boarded the *Majestic* that henceforth 'you'll find me at Liberty Hall in Dublin.' Perhaps he felt that the best part of a decade that he had spent in America had come to naught. Not least among his disappointments would have been the fact that his complaint in January 1915 about the failure of American socialists to organise New York subway workers, 40 per cent of whom were Irish, had remained as valid as ever.

But Larkin need not have despaired. In 1926 two other Irishmen emigrated to New York and became subway workers. Mike Quill and Gerald O'Reilly would progress from New York's Clan na Gael clubs to join Jim Gralton's Irish Workers' Clubs and thereafter the Communist Party of the USA. In April 1934, with the help of the party that Larkin had been so instrumental in forming fifteen years previously, Quill and O'Reilly founded a new union with just a hundred members from among the largely Irish work force of the New York transit system. In honour of, and inspired by, the Irish union that Larkin had founded twenty-five years previously, they named theirs the Transport Workers' Union of America. By the time of Larkin's death this union had grown to encompass 35,000 transit workers in New York alone and a total membership of 68,000.

It was the Transport Workers' Union of America that sponsored the crowded rally in the Manhattan Centre, New York, at which James Larkin Junior recalled his father's legacy in May 1947. The greatest tribute they had paid on the passing of Big Jim was to have steadfastly implemented the injunction that he himself had handed down in his Chicago funeral oration of November 1915, Joe Hill's last words: 'Don't mourn for me—organise!'

Chapter 10

Titan at Bay

Donal Nevin

Opening the final chapter of his biography of James Larkin, the American historian Emmet Larkin remarks that 'to chronicle nearly twenty years of decline is depressing. That so rich, so active, and so fruitful a life should come to such an end is nothing less than anti-climactic.' But, he added, 'sustained by his sublime faith in the working class, he was still convinced that he would lead them out of their land of bondage. He struggled in his declining years to keep the flickering hope alive that the working classes, if they had only the courage to will it, would finally come into their own.'[1]

If there were the best of times and the worst of times in Larkin's life, then assuredly the twenties, with which this chapter is concerned, were by far the worst.

Released by order of the Governor of New York, Al Smith, from Sing Sing Jail in January 1923, where he had served nearly three years of a five to ten-year sentence on a charge of criminal anarchy—that is, seeking to overthrow the US government by violence—Larkin was deported as an undesirable alien. He arrived back in Dublin on 30 April to a tumultuous welcome from Dublin's workers, whom he had led in the epic struggle during the great lock-out ten years before.

He had returned after almost nine years' absence. During those years dramatic political changes had taken place in the aftermath of the Easter Rising: the War of Independence, the setting up of Stormont, and a bloody and vicious Civil War, which had claimed more casualties than the 1919–21 struggle. Internationally, the Russian Revolution in 1917 and the end of the Great War had seemed to presage widespread revolutionary struggle in Europe and confrontation with capitalism. 'The whole of Europe is filled with the spirit of Revolution,' wrote Lloyd George to Clemenceau in 1918. 'The whole of the existing order in its political, social and economic aspects is questioned by the masses of the population from one end of Europe to the other.' At the western end, Ireland had not been immune from this questioning.

Larkin was now just under fifty years of age and had spent less than eight years in Ireland, from January 1907 to October 1914. Several efforts to return home had been thwarted by the British and American authorities. He had not been in any close contact with the ITGWU—of which he remained the general secretary—and did not seem to realise the implications, or the extent, of the changes in the union's membership, organisation and leadership that had taken place since 1914.

Larkin's position on his return was not helped by the acrimony that had developed from 1917 between the old guard of the union, whose loyalty was wholly to Larkin, such as his sister, Delia Larkin, P. T. Daly, Barney Conway, Michael Mullen, Seán O'Casey, and others, and the new leadership, notably William O'Brien, a master tailor who, though prominent in the trade union movement from the early years of the century, had only joined the ITGWU in January 1917, becoming general treasurer the following year.

From being largely Dublin-based, the union now had the bulk of its membership outside the capital city, in about 350 branches, in virtually all the cities and larger towns and in rural areas. From being confined mainly to workers in transport and the distributive trades, it now embraced workers in manufacturing industries, general operatives, and, not least, agricultural workers. Its membership had grown from perhaps 10,000 in 1913 to 120,000 in 1921; but by the time of Larkin's return, membership was declining rapidly.

In addition, Larkin may not have appreciated the people's weariness and their demoralisation, which was so marked after the Civil War. Trade unions were facing a massive drop in membership, declining economic activity, the imposition of wage cuts, an alarming increase in unemployment, and a signally unsympathetic government. The ascendancy of William O'Brien, backed by Thomas Foran, the first president of the union, marked a break with Larkin's style of leadership. Only one of the eight ordinary members of the Executive Committee had been active before 1914, and the power of the committee had been firmly underwritten by rule changes made in 1918. In the past, Larkin had ruled supreme, some would say imperiously, even if necessarily so at that stage of the union's development.

In the power struggle with O'Brien, Larkin may well be accounted largely responsible for his own defeat, in that he probably overestimated O'Brien's conspiratorial influence, and he made a serious blunder in antagonising Foran and the new members of the Executive Committee. His massive support in Dublin was further eroded by his fierce denunciations of, and unfair attacks on, virtually the entire leadership of the labour movement and in particular the greatly respected Thomas Johnson. Less impetuousness, greater patience, more tolerance towards those who disagreed with him might have avoided the situation where O'Brien came so to dominate the union that its industrial unionism motto, OBU (one big union), came in time to be interpreted in popular parlance as 'Old Bill's Union'. O'Brien's victory in the bitter struggle between the two men not only meant that Larkin was ousted from the Transport Union but led to disastrous splits both in the trade union movement and the political labour movement that were to persist for over three decades.

Larkin's behaviour at the time was highly erratic, to say the least. This may in part be explained by the effects of his years in the United States, where he had engaged in continuous intensive trade union and political labour activity, agitating and organising in most states of the Union. He had been arrested a number of times and had more than once been in danger of lynching in the western mining states by hired anti-union company gunmen, as had happened to his friend Frank Little in Butte, Montana. (Larkin was with Frank Little in Butte in the days before the lynching.) He had been involved in numerous strikes throughout the United States. Above all, perhaps, his health had been affected by his years in jail, which seem to have had a serious psychological effect, as has been attested to by those who visited him in Sing Sing, including Charlie Chaplin, Frank Harris, and Robert Monteith.

The rift that erupted between Larkin and the leadership of the ITGWU directly on his return from America had all the elements of Greek drama. Larkin assumed he would take up the reins of control of the union in his uniquely individual style, as had been the case before 1914; it was clear that O'Brien was determined that this would not be. Larkin was readily convinced that there was a conspiracy against him, engineered by O'Brien, and this seemed to be confirmed by the fact that major changes in the rules of the union had been rushed through just as Larkin was arriving in Dublin.

Essentially, the struggle between the two men was less a conflict about ideology or union structures than one between antagonists with contrasting personalities and differing views on the role of trade unions in the circumstances of the time. O'Brien was cautious, conservative, aloof, dull, calculating, but with considerable administrative ability—the type of official who would later attract the Russian term *apparatchik*. To quote Seán O'Casey in his autobiographical *Sunset and Evening Star*, O'Brien was 'a self-centred man, the clever, sharp mind at white heat behind the cold, pale mask, forever boring a silent way through all opposition.'

In sharp contrast, Larkin was impetuous to the point of recklessness, impatient, unpredictable, given to flamboyant gestures, intemperate in language, and careless of financial and administrative details. An English commentator in 1913 was to describe Larkin as a born revolutionary who believed that the Kingdom of Heaven must be taken by violence today and tomorrow and the day after. Both shared an arrogance, an inability to compromise, and an unwillingness to forgive enemies, real or imagined.

The conflict between them was to only a limited degree occasioned by differences in strategy and tactics, or indeed ideology. For Larkin, action was everything, not ideology. As Bertram Wolfe, who with Larkin was one of the founders of the American Communist Party, put it, Larkin had no taste for theory at all.[2] He wanted to move things forward, not to get to any place in particular. Though given to extravagance of language, once he mounted a public platform his considered statements could be surprisingly moderate. His socialism was in large part a great humanitarian love of his fellows, an acknowledgment of the brotherhood of man, a hatred of injustice, an instinctive, intuitive understanding of the clash of class interests in a harsh capitalist society. His whole turbulent life was spent resisting the attacks of the capitalist class against the working class.

On the national question there were basic differences between O'Brien and Larkin. Writing from America, Larkin had been extremely critical of the labour leadership, which after 1917 allowed Sinn Féin to dominate the political scene, with labour taking a back seat. Peadar O'Donnell put the situation pithily when he said of William O'Brien that he confused the prompter's stool for a place on the stage. As well, Larkin had been opposed to the Treaty.

In his first address after his return to the crowds outside Liberty Hall, the 'old spot by the river,' Larkin set out the course he was to follow. 'Comrades,' he told the crowd,

> this is a meeting of the old guard and the new guard. They all knew the old rule of the Union 'Each for all and all for each.' Unity is strength but there has been a lack of faith and a limitation of vision. Those who had founded the Union had dreamed great dreams and were going to realise them. There are many ways to win freedom and liberty. The three important things were unity, solidarity and charity.

Two days after Larkin's return he met O'Brien in the union's new office premises in Parnell Square. It was not a cordial meeting on either side. Larkin, according to O'Brien's account, was sitting down and did not stand up or offer to shake hands but simply said, 'Hello, Bill. You've got grey.' 'Yes, Jim,' O'Brien replied, 'and you've got white.'

At his first meeting with the Executive Committee, held on 4 May, after much disagreement with the committee members Larkin was persuaded to make a tour of the union branches. At an adjourned delegate conference ten days later Larkin, in Emmet Larkin's view, was more than reasonable, he was statesmanlike. However, following his provincial tour Larkin accused O'Brien of being behind a conspiracy against him and being out to break him.

On 3 June, at a meeting of the Dublin No. 1 Branch, the heart of the union, held in the La Scala Theatre, Larkin declared war on O'Brien, charging that he had instigated rule changes so as to limit Larkin's authority and that he had fixed the delegates to the special conference. 'Tammany Hall', he thundered, 'never had a machine like this, and all to down one man.' Claiming that the new rules were illegal, Larkin appealed to a mass meeting of the members of the Dublin branches and secured an overwhelming vote for the suspension of Foran, O'Brien, and others.

The following week, supporters of Larkin seized the head office of the union in Parnell Square and occupied Liberty Hall, whereupon the Executive Committee suspended Larkin as general secretary and applied to the courts for an injunction, while the military removed those—led by Barney Conway—who were occupying the union premises.

There followed a series of legal actions, which culminated in a hearing of a consolidated action before the Master of the Rolls, Judge Charles O'Connor, which opened in Dublin Castle on 12 February 1924. Given the two main antagonists and Larkin's tempestuous personality, there were moments of high drama during the six days of the hearing, with bitter exchanges between Larkin and O'Brien, whom Larkin referred to as Field-Marshal and the Pooh-Bah of the union, and impatient admonitions from the Master of the Rolls. It was not Larkin's finest hour.

Larkin had dispensed with his counsel and conducted his own case, which, as a result, was totally disorganised. His questioning of witnesses was marked by insinuation and abuse and frequently was grossly unfair. According to one observer, Larkin 'ignored procedure, made irrelevant statements, side-tracked major issues and on the whole prejudiced the Court against himself.' The judge felt obliged at one point to point out that Larkin was wasting his time calling evidence to prove absolutely irrelevant facts and accused him of having a mind so constituted that he could not distinguish what was relevant and what was irrelevant. Larkin insisted that he would not be bullied and that if he was not allowed to speak he would sit down. 'I cannot say that I would be sorry,' remarked the judge. More often than not, however, Larkin had the last word and showed flashes of wit as, refused permission to admit as evidence the official organ of the ITGWU, he retorted: 'I think everybody else ought to refuse it too.'

In the course of Larkin's cross-examination, O'Brien persistently taunted and baited Larkin, who too often rose to the bait. Asked by Larkin whether everything he had sworn was true, O'Brien replied that everything he had ever sworn was true. To Larkin's comment 'We will test that later on,' O'Brien taunted: 'Test it now. Now is the time. Come on, James, I will face you as I always did.' 'Now, Field-Marshal,' retorted Larkin, 'don't get so warlike.'

Larkin's case rested largely on his claim that the 1918 rules (drafted by O'Brien with the assistance of J. J. Hughes, who later became the first general secretary of Cumann na nGaedheal) had not been properly passed. The court found that the rules were valid. Larkin had relied mainly on the fact that while about 6,900 members had voted in favour of the rules, the two largest branches, Dublin No. 1, with ten thousand members, and Dublin No. 3, with three to four thousand members, had not even met to consider them. While this was true, it was not of course relevant in the legal sense. Understandably, Larkin insisted that only a small minority of the members had approved the rules.

The outcome of the widely publicised court case had the most damaging effect on Larkin's standing within the union and among the public. Not only had he lost the case on legal grounds but to the public he was seen to have been bested by O'Brien and Foran in every argument that arose—and worse, Larkin's serious allegations against them were shown to be unfounded. Furthermore, the bitter and vindictive attitude of Larkin, and a petty streak evident in his questioning of officials and certain members, must have alienated many of his potential supporters in the union.

A second court action the following year completely alienated those who continued to support Larkin in the political labour movement. Larkin had been making persistent attacks on the Labour Party, vitriolic even by his standards. The *Irish Worker*, which he had founded in 1911 and edited up to October 1914, had been relaunched in 1923, with Larkin again as editor. It was now but a pale reflection of the paper it was before the war, when, in the words of Emmet Larkin, it was unique in the history of working-class journalism and what another American scholar, Robert Lowery, was to describe as 'an extraordinary newspaper, a milestone in the history of working-class journalism.'[3]

The *Irish Worker* in its issue of 24 May 1924 carried a particularly scurrilous attack on Thomas Johnson, the leader of the Labour Party in Dáil Éireann and secretary of what was then the Irish Labour Party and Trades Union Congress. The language used was outrageous even when allowance is made for the extremely slanderous language that at the time was the stock in trade of post-Civil War political rhetoric. It seems probable that Johnson was pressed by his parliamentary colleagues, who included William O'Brien, to take an action for libel, more for the purpose of demonising Larkin than vindicating Johnson against the absurd charges that were made in the article. To compound matters, Larkin accepted responsibility for the article, while admitting that it had been written by his eldest son, James Junior, adding gratuitously that if he himself had written it it would have been written with more bitterness and invective.

The court awarded the then huge sum of £500 in damages against Larkin, who refused to pay and, not for the first time, was declared bankrupt. As a result he was debarred from taking his seat in Dáil Éireann when elected in the general election of 1927.

I am happy to add a footnote to this unsavoury episode. Many years later Johnson and Young Jim Larkin became the closest of friends and colleagues, and Johnson spoke in support of Big Jim at Labour Party meetings in the 1943 general election. Indeed Larkin made handsome amends at the annual conference of the Irish TUC in 1946, after the split and when Johnson had been acting general secretary of the Congress. At the conclusion of the conference, James Larkin said:

It would be unfair to leave this room without giving thanks to the man who has been guiding Congress since the crisis came upon us. I refer to one of my old colleagues, Comrade Johnson. Whether mistakes were made or not they were not due to him personally. I feel there is new life, new spirit and a new atmosphere in this Congress and I hope he will live long to assist you. We will always be glad to co-operate with him and to ask him to be still one of the apostles of Labour in this country. There has been no time in all the years that I have ever thought of doubting his honesty of purpose and his great gift of conciliation. He was able at all times to deal with hotheads like myself, who were young and enthusiastic and who were running, possibly, out of line. I say this and I hope he will appreciate it in the spirit in which it is offered.

On 14 March 1924 Larkin was expelled from the union he had founded. Again his supporters, led by Barney Conway, took over Liberty Hall for several days, eventually being ejected by the military and jailed. By now Larkin had gone to Moscow to attend the congress of the Communist International (Comintern), and in his absence his brother Peter was in charge.

In the middle of June 1924, at a meeting in Beresford Place, Peter Larkin launched the Workers' Union of Ireland. The first of its rules was that the union 'existed to organise the workers of Ireland for the attainment of full economic freedom.'

There developed over the next few months a virtual civil war in the trade union movement in Dublin. There were inter-union disputes in the docks, the coal trade, the building industry, and the cinemas. The WUI struck against the employment of ITGWU members; the Transport Union sought to oust WUI members from their jobs. It seems that about two-thirds of the Dublin members of the Transport Union transferred to the WUI, but some went back later. Very few provincial members transferred.

The WUI slowly consolidated itself, though funds were virtually non-existent and the union was usually in debt, but it boasted that it never failed to pay strike benefit, which was then 15s a week. The weekly contribution was six pence. By the end of the decade the union was claiming about 15,000 members.

Larkin's return to Dublin in April 1923 had coincided with the suspension of all offensive operations by the Republican forces in the Civil War. His first address to the people was a passionate plea for peace. He attacked the new Free State government, coupling these attacks with onslaughts on the Labour leadership expressed in extremely intemperate language.

In practical terms, Larkin's involvement in political activities on his return to Ireland revolved around the Irish Worker League,[4] which he had set up in September 1923, not as a political party but rather as a support group for the re-launched *Irish Worker*. Indeed Larkin pointed out that it was a social and not a political or economic organisation; it seems to have been intended to be akin to the Daily Herald League or the Clarion Fellowship, which Larkin would have been familiar with in pre-war Britain. Young Jim Larkin was later to describe it as 'somewhat in the nature of a kind of personal political organisation established by my father.'

The league's constitution, which was not adopted until April 1924, when Larkin became its honorary president, declared its purpose to be the organisation of 'a militant working-class movement to achieve in our time economic, political and intellectual freedom.' It never, however, showed any sign of winning significant public support, nor indeed did it constitute an organisation in any real sense. Even so, such was Larkin's prestige that the league was accepted as the Irish Section of the Communist International, displacing the Communist Party of Ireland, which had been set up by Roddy Connolly, the son of James Connolly, in 1921.

After the foundation of the Workers' Union of Ireland, the *Irish Worker* became in effect its organ. The league's activities included occasional lectures, the organisation of lotteries for prisoners' dependants, dances in support of striking workers, the sale of low-price foodstuffs, and the like. It organised large demonstrations to commemorate the Russian Revolution and the first anniversary of the death of Lenin.

Even though it had neither finance nor organisation, the Irish Worker League ran three candidates in Dublin in the September 1927 general election, securing a creditable 12,500 votes. Larkin was elected on the first count in the North Dublin eight-seat constituency; however, as an undischarged bankrupt he was disqualified from taking his seat. In the subsequent by-election Larkin came third after the candidates of Cumann na nGaedheal (Vincent Rice KC) and Fianna Fáil (Kathleen Clarke); he had hoped that Fianna Fáil would not contest the by-election and was bitter when it did.

In the Dublin Corporation elections in September 1930 the league fielded twelve candidates (including candidates associated with it) who polled more than the Labour Party's nineteen candidates. Both Larkin and his son, Young Jim, were elected. By 1932, however, the Irish Worker League had ceased to exist.

In June 1924, Larkin, though denied a passport by the authorities, had travelled to Moscow to attend the Fifth Congress of the Communist International. There he was acclaimed as a revolutionary hero. He had been described by Lenin as 'a talented leader possessing remarkable oratorical talent, a man of seething Irish energy, who had performed miracles among the unskilled workers.' In 1917 Larkin had acclaimed the October Revolution and at the height of the anti-red hysteria in America had proclaimed himself a Bolshevik. On Larkin's release from jail in New York, Zinoviev, then the president of the Comintern's Executive Council, had cabled 'warmest greetings to Larkin, the undaunted fighter.'

In Moscow for three months, Larkin did little to commend himself to the communist leaders. He spoke twice at the congress sessions. The first time was to support the policy of the Communist Party in Britain that it should form a united front with the Labour Party. In his second intervention, on the situation in Ireland, made at the request of Zinoviev, he confined himself to little more than reminding the assembled communists that the Irish proletariat had risen in 1916, not in 1917, and pointing out that the Irish proletariat was not confined to Ireland but that there were millions more Irish in other countries.

According to C. Desmond Greaves, Connolly's biographer and author of the official history of the ITGWU (1909–1923), Larkin in Moscow explained the setbacks that the working-class movement in Ireland had suffered in terms of the treachery of individuals. Greaves was informed by Bob Stewart, the British communist leader who had spent some time in Ireland seeking to assist in the setting up of a Marxist party and who was a delegate to the congress, that at a meeting at which Zinoviev asked

Larkin his opinion of various labour leaders, he had dismissed each of them with colourful epithets. Zinoviev then asked him whether there might not be some general political reason for this apparent mass betrayal. Greaves commented that Larkin could only argue *ad hominem*—a reasonable enough conclusion.[5]

At the congress of the Profintern, the Red International of Labour Unions, to which the Workers' Union of Ireland was to affiliate, Larkin stressed the importance of the co-operative movement to the trade unions in their revolutionary struggle, echoing his frequent references over the years to a co-operative commonwealth. He dismissed any idea that England was on the verge of revolution and derided the notion that strikes could be directed from an information bureau, meaning of course the Profintern itself.

On his second visit to Moscow, in February 1928 for the Sixth Congress of the Comintern, Larkin was invited by Bukharin, now the president of the Comintern, to speak on the Trotsky-Stalin controversy, but he refused, explaining that it would be an impertinence on his part to take sides in an internal Soviet matter. According to Jack Carney, who accompanied him to Moscow, Larkin on one occasion debated into the night with Bukharin about the existence of God. To Bukharin's surprise, Larkin insisted that he had faith that there was a God and that he would hold to this belief until he had been proved wrong.

Larkin quarrelled with Losovsky, the chairman of the Profintern, so violently that, according to Young Jim Larkin, who was with his father in Moscow, the two very nearly came to blows. (Young Jim Larkin remained in Moscow, where he spent nearly two years at the International Lenin School.) Recently opened archives in Moscow quote Losovsky as saying, sarcastically no doubt, that according to Larkin, Ireland had the very best revolutionaries and the very worst reactionaries in Europe.[6]

Larkin had no further involvement with the communist movement after 1930.

As the twenties come to a close, James Larkin, agitator without equal, one of the greatest orators in the English-speaking world of his time, a revolutionary of world fame, was by now tired and exhausted from his herculean efforts in Ireland and in America to arouse the working class to struggle against what he saw as the wage-slavery of capitalism. He had by now become politically isolated, ostracised by almost all the leaders of the labour movement. He had no national platform, or publication, from which to fire his thunderbolts against injustice and oppression or to launch another revolutionary movement. He had become the Ishmael of his era.

As Prof. Larkin put it in his biography of Larkin, there was at that time 'little room in Ireland for men or movements intent on perpetuating the Revolution rather than consolidating it.' By now 'circumstances had deprived him of his role, and time would not allow for the creation of another. To a man whose way of life was action, such a sentence was death.'

By 1931, now aged fifty-seven, it was unlikely that Larkin would achieve his dreams. In an editorial in the *Irish Worker* for 11 October 1930, headed 'The world in chaos', Larkin had quoted lines from Tennyson's 'Locksley Hall':

For I dipt into the Future,
    as far as human eye could see
Saw the Vision of the World,
    and all the wonder that would be
Till the war-drum throbbed no longer,
    and the battle-flags were furled
In the Parliament of Man,
    the Federation of the World.

To these lines of the poet Larkin added: 'What a beautiful dream! Can it be realised of a surety if and when the peoples of the world determine it? To realise this glorious dream requires an acceptance of the dream and determination to realise it. It cannot be achieved under a Capitalist form of society; that surely must be patent to all men and women who possess intelligence.'

But Big Jim remained undaunted. A fortnight later he was to quote William Morris:

Come then! For what are you waiting?
The day and the dawn is coming
And forth the banners go!

Sadly, in the last fifteen years of his life James Larkin was to see the dream shattered by fascism and war.

Chapter 11

The Last Years

John P. Swift

The final decade of James Larkin's life embraced the entire period of the Second World War. Although what is now the Republic was not a participant in that momentous event, the labour movement was greatly affected by the war. During those years social conditions deteriorated significantly, the country's small industrial sector suffering severely from inadequate and poor-quality fuel, the lack of essential imported raw materials, and shortages of new equipment and spare parts for machinery. By 1944 industrial output had fallen by approximately 25 per cent of the pre-war level. With the notable exception of the building industry, industrial employment fell less dramatically.

Frequent periods of unemployment or short time working were experienced by many thousands of industrial workers. In the ten years ending in 1946 average annual unemployment was 47 per cent higher than over the previous decade. Yet in the same comparative period trade union membership soared by 55 per cent, from 146,000 to 227,000. Social welfare payments as well as wages failed to keep pace with inflation, and wage increases were rigidly controlled. In the years from 1939 to 1947 the cost of living index rose at twice the rate of increase in average industrial earnings.

The consequences of factors such as these were widespread poverty of a kind unknown in Ireland since then, evidenced, for example, by the common sight of undernourished, barefoot children. Housing remained a major problem, particularly in Dublin, with thousands existing in appalling conditions in tenements.

Throughout that decade, from roughly the mid-thirties to the mid-forties, this was a very conservative and illiberal society, where the politicians of all the main political parties, including the Labour Party, danced to the tune of a reactionary Catholic hierarchy. Extraordinary power was wielded by the church, and the influence of Catholic social teaching was evident in virtually every facet of Irish life. In that oppressive and claustrophobic atmosphere there was an intolerance of dissent, and for many, even on the left, the cost of challenging this situation was apparently prohibitive.

Catholic social teaching had been boosted in 1931 by the publication of Pope Pius XI's encyclical *Quadragesimo Anno*, commemorating the fortieth anniversary of Pope Leo XIII's encyclical *Rerum Novarum*. Condemning socialism, both documents recommended as a solution to class war the establishment of corporations resembling the mediaeval guilds. Echoing those doctrines were the corporate policies of several European fascist states, where workers were compelled to become members of joint workers' and employers' corporations, controlled by employers and fascist party functionaries. In all these fascist regimes trade unions were suppressed and union activists were imprisoned and in many instances executed.

Influenced, apparently, by events on the Continent, the Irish hierarchy responded to these developments by advocating corporatism and denouncing communism. While a crusade of that kind might seem farcical in hindsight, its reverberations in the Irish labour movement were considerable.

It was in this environment that James Larkin, then in his sixties, found himself during this final era of his life. He had long ceased to be a figure of international significance and was never to re-establish himself as the outstanding revolutionary labour leader he had been in the earlier part of the century.

It was as a Dublin city councillor and as a leading figure in Dublin Trades Council that Larkin made his greatest mark during those final years. While his achievements in these fields, particularly as a city councillor, remain undervalued, it is difficult to escape the conclusion that Larkin's political decline, which had begun more than a decade earlier, continued up to the time of his death. Possibly the most obvious manifestation of that decline was his uncharacteristic silence, or mild statements, on many of the key issues of the time. In relation to such fundamental issues as de Valera's Constitution of 1937, with its sectarianism and anti-feminism and its emphasis on the rights of private property, this was particularly regrettable.

Another de Valera initiative in the late thirties was the establishment of the Commission on Vocational Organisation, a response to the clamour by influential elements for the adoption of a vocational or corporate state modelled on some of the fascist regimes in Europe. Larkin was one of four labour representatives on the 25-member commission, which was chaired by the Bishop of Galway, Dr Michael Browne. Among the other members were several prominent academics and Catholic clerics, all enthusiastic corporatists. In its report, published in 1943, the commission recommended measures for implementing what was termed vocational organisation.

Signing the report, two of the commission's labour members, Louie Bennett, general secretary of the Irish Women Workers' Union, and Senator Seán Campbell, treasurer of the Dublin Typographical Provident Society, dissociated themselves from any suspicion of fascist tendencies that might be read into the recommendations. Another labour member, Luke Duffy, the Labour Party's general secretary, published an alternative document criticising the commission's recommendations. Larkin declined to sign the report, apparently holding the commission and its work in silent contempt. As one observer later commented, 'What a pity the contempt was silent!' That Larkin had been aware of the threat posed by the commission is beyond doubt, for he had earlier anticipated the main thrust of its findings, warning the trade union movement of the dangers of such a development.

Larkin's political decline was more starkly revealed during the Spanish Civil War. As with the great majority of Irish labour leaders, he failed to distinguish himself on that issue. Much more disquieting, however, was his acquiescence in the WUI's prohibition on its officials speaking on public platforms other than on union affairs, designed to prevent its officials from supporting publicly the Spanish republican cause. The chief victim of this undemocratic directive was Larkin's friend and colleague Jack Carney. When Carney's representations to Larkin on the matter fell on deaf ears, he resigned his position in the union and emigrated to England.

Other examples of Larkin's political deterioration became evident in the years following his departure from the communist movement around 1930, none more telling than his frequent and unjustified attacks on British unions operating in Ireland. The Communist Party of Ireland was not alone in interpreting such behaviour as a mask for his abandonment of militant policies.

There were also in this period some disturbing developments in the labour movement itself that demanded the most vigorous resistance. It was not forthcoming from Larkin. Where, for example, was the famous Larkin rage in the late nineteen-thirties when the Labour Party was abandoning core sections of its constitution to appease the Catholic hierarchy? Nor was there evidence of that rage in the forties when a number of his socialist colleagues were being expelled from the Labour Party.

In his final decade Larkin was twice elected to the Dáil, as an independent labour candidate in 1937 and as a nominee of the Labour Party six years later. On both occasions he was to lose his seat in the following year's general election. As an independent deputy in his first term of office he normally supported the policies of de Valera. His record generally in the Dáil was unimpressive, and he had surprisingly little to say. But for someone like Larkin, who was in his element addressing the throngs on the streets of Dublin, Dáil Éireann must have been a rather formal and restrictive forum, and to some extent this may explain his disappointing contribution as a parliamentarian.

Much more impressive was his performance as a member of Dublin City Council. Elected in 1936 as an independent candidate, he was re-elected as a Labour Party nominee in 1942. As the long-serving chairperson of the Council's Housing Committee he worked diligently and effectively on behalf of the working people of Dublin, playing a leading role in rehousing in new suburban dwellings thousands of Dublin workers and their families, many of whom had existed in one room in tenements.

It was also on Larkin's initiative that the impressive St Anne's estate in Clontarf was purchased by the city council for the citizens of Dublin. His vision that in its redevelopment the estate be divided equally for housing, playing-fields and a public park and gardens was realised some years following his death.

Another Larkin initiative as a councillor was the conferring on George Bernard Shaw of the Freedom of the City of Dublin. Joe Deasy, a fellow

Labour councillor, described as 'most articulate' Larkin's nomination of Shaw, showing an intellectual aspect of Jim that is not widely understood. Incidentally, GBS once declared that James Larkin was the greatest Irishman since Parnell.

In contrast to his relative inertia on some key political and social issues, Larkin worked effectively during this period in the trade union movement. For twelve years, beginning in 1924 with the split in the ITGWU and the formation of the WUI, he had been virtually isolated in the movement by his arch-opponent, William O'Brien. O'Brien had obstructed the WUI's affiliation to both Dublin Trades Council and the Irish Trades Union Congress. However, in 1936 the Workers' Union had finally secured affiliation to the trades council, and Larkin, as a delegate from the council, attended the annual conferences of Congress from 1937 to 1942. In 1937 he was elected to the trades council's executive committee, a position he retained until his death ten years later, being president from 1943 to 1945.

It was in this state of disunity that the trade union movement was confronted in 1941 by the Fianna Fáil Government's Emergency Powers Order No. 83, popularly known as the Wages Standstill Order, and the Trade Union Bill. Implemented on 7 May 1941, the Order, in effect a wage freeze, withdrew from unions striking for pay increases the legal protection of the Trade Disputes Act (1906). No such restrictions were imposed on prices or profits. Only from April 1942 were workers permitted to secure wage increases, and these were to be related to future increases in the cost of living.

The most controversial feature of the Trade Union Bill was a provision to establish a Trade Union Tribunal, with powers to award exclusive negotiating rights for particular categories of workers to a single union where that union organised a majority of the workers. This was seen as a means of consolidating and extending the areas of organisation of the ITGWU. That section of the Act was later found to be repugnant to the Constitution.

The proposals in the Trade Union Bill were perceived by the British unions, and others, as an O'Brien-inspired strategy aimed at realising the Transport Union's long-held objective of 'one big union'. That largely explains the rather muted opposition to the Bill, and indeed the Wages Standstill Order, by the Transport Union and Congress, both then dominated by O'Brien.

There was nothing muted about Dublin Trades Council's opposition to the Order and the Bill; nor was Larkin found wanting in the council's campaign. It was Larkin who proposed, in May 1941, that a Council of action be established by the trades council to oppose the Government's legislation. Composed of representatives of affiliated unions and the Labour Party, with James Larkin Junior, or Young Jim Larkin, as he was known, as secretary, the Council of Action lobbied TDs, held many public meetings throughout the city, issued handbills and other material, and published the militant journal *Workers' Action*. Contributions to this periodical, which was co-edited by John Swift of the Bakers' Union, Dr Owen Sheehy-Skeffington of Trinity College, Dublin, and the radical *Irish Press* journalist Paddy Staunton, included Roddy Connolly, son of James Connolly, and the playwrights Seán O'Casey and Paul Vincent Carroll.

Under the leadership of Larkin Junior and in conjunction with the Labour Party, the campaign was extended to other social issues, such as unemployment, housing and prices, and food and fuel supplies. Larkin was an enthusiastic and active participant in the campaign, being particularly effective as an orator at the many public meetings that were held.

An echo of the Larkin of 1913 was evident in College Green, Dublin, on 22 June 1941, the day Hitler invaded the Soviet Union, when the council's campaign culminated in a mass demonstration by the affiliated unions against the Bill and the Order. In the course of a typical rousing and defiant speech, Larkin expressed his utter contempt for the Bill by producing a copy and setting it alight with a match. Speaking of this occasion later, Larkin declared: 'I never felt so lifted up as I was that day in Dublin.'

Although essentially unsuccessful in its immediate aims, the Council of Action's campaign contributed much towards increased public support for the Labour Party, particularly in Dublin. In 1942, for example, by winning 13 of the 35 seats, Labour recorded its greatest success, becoming the largest party in Dublin City Council. Larkin was among those elected, having been by now admitted to the Labour Party. In the general election of 1943 the number of Labour deputies rose from nine to seventeen, the Larkins, father and son, being among those returned in the party's best result since the early twenties.

In those final years of his life Larkin was principally preoccupied as general secretary of the Workers' Union of Ireland, devoting much of his time to union affairs and dealing not alone with normal union activities but with wider concerns of members, and indeed non-members, on such issues as housing and social welfare, to which he was particularly committed.

It was to the union's premises that most of those working-class people came to visit Larkin. Originally based in Unity Hall in Marlborough Street, the union later transferred to the Thomas Ashe Hall in College Street (named after the first hunger-striker to die during the national struggle; Ashe had been both an admirer and a friend of Larkin during the 1913 lock-out). But for Larkin the union's new offices had more vivid and dramatic memories, for in 1913, on the day of the legendary proclaimed meeting in O'Connell Street, Larkin had been imprisoned in a small cell in the premises, then a headquarters of the Dublin Metropolitan Police.

Coinciding with Larkin's final decade was a period of greatly increased dissension in the labour movement, culminating in disastrous splits in the Labour Party and the Irish TUC. That dissension had its origin mainly in the bitter personal enmity between Larkin and O'Brien.

The admission to the Labour Party of the Larkins, senior and junior, in December 1941, and Big Jim's adoption as a candidate in the general election of 1943, were strongly opposed by O'Brien. By a margin of eight votes to seven the party's Administrative Council failed to ratify Larkin's nomination, the eight Transport Union members of the council opposing ratification. However, with one exception, Labour's Dáil candidates for Dublin city and county, in conjunction with the party's Dublin Executive, later decided to nominate Larkin as an official candidate, and that decision was accepted by the party leader, William Norton. At a subsequent meeting of the Administrative Council on 3 December 1943 the Transport Union members sought unsuccessfully the expulsion from the party of the chairperson and secretary of the Dublin Executive, James Larkin Junior TD and John de Courcy Ireland, respectively, on the grounds that in promoting the candidature of Larkin Senior they had breached the party's constitution.

The Transport Union responded in January 1944 by disaffiliating from the Labour Party, with five of their eight deputies seceding to form a rival body, the National Labour Party. That same month, in a circular to Transport Union branches, O'Brien charged the party's Administrative Council with having allowed and encouraged admission into the party of people who had been active members and well-known propagandists of the Communist Party. Moreover, a pamphlet issued by O'Brien on behalf of the ITGWU charged that communists had taken possession of the Labour Party in Dublin and that the party had allowed communism to permeate it to such an extent that there was no hope of it recovering its independence. In pursuance of his campaign, O'Brien, who in 1918 had welcomed enthusiastically the Bolshevik Revolution, had recourse to the then influential weekly journal, the *Catholic Standard*.

These extravagant claims of communist influence in the Labour Party were based on several factors, including Larkin's former open involvement, at home and abroad, in the communist movement. Moreover, having attended the Lenin School in Moscow in the late nineteen-twenties, Young Jim Larkin had been a prominent and active communist in the early thirties, presiding in June 1933 at the re-formation conference of the Communist Party of Ireland and contesting on several occasions, as a communist candidate, Dáil Éireann and Dublin municipal elections. Furthermore, in July 1941 the Dublin Branch of the Communist Party of Ireland had disbanded, its members subsequently enrolling in the Labour Party.

The anti-communist campaign by O'Brien and others had drastic consequences for the Labour Party, its vote declining by 74,000, or one-third, in the 1944 general election. Four of the twelve Labour Party seats, including Larkin's, were lost, as was one of the five seats formerly held by the breakaway National Labour Party, though Young Jim Larkin was returned. Reunification of the Labour Party occurred after the 1948 general election, when the leaders of both parties joined the first inter-party Government.

Considerably more complex and of much greater duration was the split in the Irish Trades Union Congress, which occurred in April 1945. At the root of that rift also was the Larkin-O'Brien conflict. As mentioned earlier, Larkin had been a Dublin Trades Council delegate to the Congress's annual conferences from 1937 to 1942. However, in a vindictive move directed against him, the 1942 conference decided that only trades council delegates from affiliated unions would be eligible to attend future conferences. The Workers' Union of Ireland was not affiliated to Congress.

Another important factor in the Congress schism was the long-standing tension between the British and Irish affiliates, complicated by the all-Ireland character of Congress. Moreover, aside from the normal conflicts of personalities and ambition, there were divergent views on the rationalisation of the movement.

An invitation to the Irish TUC from its British counterpart in November 1943 to participate in a World Trade Union Conference to be held the following year in London was, ostensibly, the immediate cause of the split. Deeply divided on the issue, the National Executive of Congress decided to decline the invitation. But at the following year's conference, Senator Sam Kyle, leader of the largest British union, the Amalgamated Transport and General Workers' Union, moved a motion regretting the executive's decision. In the ensuing debate O'Brien warned ominously that if the motion was carried it would be 'the first step in the break-up of Congress.' O'Brien and others opposed to the motion contended that the Congress's participation in the London conference would infringe Irish neutrality in the war.

It was further alleged, falsely, by the opponents of the motion that for several years the Congress had been dominated by the votes of British unions. In fact the British unions had never sent enough delegates to annual conferences of Congress to form a majority.

With less than one-fifth of the membership in the Twenty-Six Counties, the British unions were portrayed as the principal obstacle to restructuring the movement. In fact much greater scope for restructuring lay with the Irish unions, seventeen of which had a membership of less than two thousand. Furthermore, three of the four general workers' unions, and three of the four painters' unions, were Irish, and there were no fewer than six Irish unions catering for engineering workers.

By a margin of 96 votes to 73, the 1944 conference carried the motion regretting the National Executive's decision to decline the London invitation, and in February 1945 two Executive members attended the international conference. This was followed two months later by the formation of a rival body, the Congress of Irish Unions, when ten Irish unions disaffiliated from the Irish TUC. Dominated by O'Brien and the ITGWU, the CIU represented 77,500 members, or about one-third of the total affiliation of the two Congresses, its membership being confined almost exclusively to the Twenty-Six Counties. While the ITUC retained several significant Irish unions, such as the Irish National Teachers' Organisation, the Irish Women Workers' Union, the Post Office Workers' Union, the Irish Bakers,' Confectioners' and Allied Workers' Union, and the newly affiliated Workers' Union of Ireland, a substantial proportion of its membership was in British unions in Northern Ireland. The ITUC's immediate post-split membership was 146,000, almost two-thirds of the combined figure for the two Congresses.

As Donal Nevin, former general secretary of the ICTU, stated later: 'The existence of two Congresses created great difficulties for trade unions, weakening their efforts, dissipating their resources and making impossible a common front against the employer organisations ...' Indeed this development occurred at precisely the time when the Federated Union of Employers, a precursor of the present Irish Business and Employers' Confederation, was growing in strength and unity. It also occurred the year before the enactment of the Industrial Relations Act (1946), introducing the Labour Court, arguably the most fundamental development in industrial relations in Ireland.

Efforts to reunite the movement began almost immediately following the split, facilitated by the retirement of O'Brien as general secretary of the ITGWU in early 1946, followed a year later by the death of Larkin. With no major ideological or organisational differences separating the two Congresses, nor personal animosity between their leaders, the climate for reunification gradually improved, culminating in February 1959, some fourteen years later, in the inauguration of the present Irish Congress of Trade Unions. The chief architects of unity were Young Jim Larkin, general secretary of the Workers' Union of Ireland, and John Conroy, general president of the Irish Transport and General Workers' Union.

In his book *Jim Larkin: The Rise of the Underman*, R. M. Fox offers this description of Larkin in his later years:

> Almost any day he could be seen striding about the city, with his big cloth cap pulled down on his massive head, his shoulders hunched as he walked, with a touch of a swagger, like a seaman's roll. He had a big pipe, too, which demanded constant attention and many matches. The only sign of stressful years was his silvery hair which made him look older than he was and the deepening lines of his strong-marked features.

It was possibly the stressful years that prompted Larkin to declare, at his final ITUC conference in 1946, that he was going down rapidly to the grave. Whatever the reason, the immediate cause of his death was an accident that occurred towards the end of 1946 when, during an inspection of repairs to the union's premises, he fell through the floor, sustaining internal injuries. Characteristically, he stubbornly refused medical attention and continued to work normally. However, he was eventually admitted to the Meath Hospital, where he died on 30 January 1947. He was seventy-three years of age.

From the Meath Hospital he was taken to the Thomas Ashe Hall in College Street, where he lay in state for two days. There came from the working-class districts of Dublin and elsewhere a constant stream of citizens to pay tribute to someone who had not alone improved their living standards but given them dignity and self-respect, as well as hope. On 2 February 1947, in what is still recalled as the severest winter in living memory, with a blanket of snow and ice on the ground for several weeks, Larkin's funeral took place. Following Requiem Mass in his parish church, St Mary's, Haddington Road, and in appalling blizzard conditions, the funeral procession of many thousands made its way to the city centre, halting at Thomas Ashe Hall and Liberty Hall, and thence to Glasnevin Cemetery, where Larkin was buried.

At the subsequent annual conference of the Irish Trades Union Congress in July 1947 its president, John Swift, who succeeded Larkin as president of Dublin Trades Council, paid this tribute to James Larkin's outstanding contribution to the Irish and international working-class movement:

> Then came Larkin and his co-workers. Soon thousands of the despised rabble became ennobled with the dignity of trade union organisation. Larkin taught them the duty of struggle, the imperative of rebelliousness. He breathed fire into the dead eyes and the cringing breasts of slaves. They heard him, and their supplications to their masters became defiance, their despair became a challenge. He taught them self-reliance. They followed Larkin because he had convinced them in his person and in his teaching that there was no more noble duty or destiny for men and women than that of raising themselves from bondage.
>
> Some of us are old enough to remember how Dublin throbbed to Larkin's fiery slogans. A Titan of a man, he needed no banners on which to scroll his burning poetry. He made banners of the air: his voice wrought magic patterns compelling attention and exultation. In the city's gutter, in the fetid slum, in the stinking holds of ships, on the quayside, where men fawned and flunkeyed for wretched bread, in the poorhouse, even, and the prison, there was exultation when Larkin spoke. Men and women, made dumb and abject by injustice and destitution, listened.
>
> What new hurricane from the heavens was this that said, 'The great appear great because we are on our knees. Let us rise!'
>
> Larkin was a great artist, working towards the ideal that consumed him. His music was livid thunder, hurtled at injustice and hypocrisy. At times his harmonies were strange, as of forces eruptive and elemental. But who could doubt the main chords of the symphony he sought to fashion, with its tones and overtones that told of chains breaking and dungeons tottering, and the wild elation of serfs made free!

A fitting epitaph for a great working-class leader.

Chapter 12

Larkin and the Women's Movement

Theresa Moriarty

When James Larkin founded the Irish Transport and General Workers' Union in 1909 there were no unions for women industrial workers in Dublin. Ireland's trade union movement was overwhelmingly male. In Belfast a women's union, the Textile Operatives' Society of Ireland, had organised linen workers since 1893, with limited success. This union was the only female presence at the annual meeting of the Irish Trades Union Congress for almost twenty years.

Apart from the linen unions in the north, whose combined women members totalled around four thousand, only another thousand or so women were union members, out of a total of seventy thousand Irish trade unionists.[1] Mixed unions, admitting women and men as members, were the exception and counted their women members in hundreds.

Women were regarded as unskilled workers. They were concentrated in a small number of industries, where their low pay, long hours and poor conditions were characterised as 'sweated labour.' They worked outside those trades and crafts where the trade union movement had taken root.

Many have seen Larkin as an unlikely organiser of women workers. He arrived in Ireland as an organiser of the National Union of Dock Labourers. His trade unionism was formed in the exclusively male world of the quayside workers, the dockers and carters, first in Liverpool and from 1907 in Belfast and Dublin. In the turbulent years before the First World War, 'Larkinism' was the Irish expression of an international industrial and political revolt, manifest in the unionisation of unskilled workers, large-scale strikes and lock-outs, and a revival of socialist ideas within the trade union movement. This rebellion was paralleled by an international movement of women, whose protest at their exclusion from public life and political rights had been gathered beneath the suffragist banner of '*Votes for women!*'

From 1909 Larkin's programme for the ITGWU included adult suffrage and equal voting rights in parliamentary and local elections for all women and men at the age of twenty-one. In 1912, when Dublin's first woman councillor, Sarah Harrison, was elected to the city council, he was among the guests who attended the suffragists' celebrations. He was acknowledged as an ally by the suffrage paper, the *Irish Citizen*. In September 1913, at the height of the Dublin lock-out, the paper paid him this tribute:

> Mr. Larkin was the initiator of the vigorous resolution passed by the Irish Trades Congress, last Whitsuntide, in condemnation of the Government's

attack upon freedom of speech and freedom of the press, and calling for the resignation of 'that incapable irresponsible McKenna' [the Home Secretary]. He also assisted to carry suffragist resolutions at the Dublin Trades Council, and his paper, the Irish Worker, has repeatedly attacked the Government for its coercive policy towards the suffragists.

The men of Mr. Larkin's Union also frequently interfered, at the rowdy meetings in Dublin last year, to protect Suffragettes from the hooliganism of the Ancient Order of Hibernians—the body that is now organising the strike-breakers.[2]

Socialists like Larkin often distrusted those whose political loyalties, in whatever cause, stopped short of full support for working-class demands. A brief but telling exchange took place at the Dublin gathering of the Irish Trades Union Congress in the summer of 1914. Larkin, as president, refused to allow a guest speaker from the Irish Women's Reform League to address the delegates on women's suffrage, on the grounds that Miss Moser, the league's nominee and a Poor Law guardian in the Dublin township of Pembroke, had failed to sign an agreement to employ only trade union labour. He instructed his union delegates to oppose her and warned that 'the suffrage could be used for or against their class.'[3] He was a suffragist, he later assured Francis Sheehy-Skeffington, 'in spite of the suffragists.'[4]

The man whose declared mission was to be an apostle of divine discontent welcomed the rising of women in its most militant form. In his dismissal of the woman suffrage speaker at the ITUC conference, Larkin had declared that delegates would not object to a militant suffrage speaker. His gospel of divine discontent spoke to the new militancy of women. While socialists and feminists laid different stress on issues of class and sex roles, they often sought each other's support in various campaigns. The two movements contested the same political terrain and occupied the same public territory of meetings, protest, and agitation. Both experienced arrest, jail, and hunger-strike. In the small political world of Dublin there were overlapping friendships and common personnel between feminists and socialists who belonged to the same circles and organisations. When Francis Sheehy-Skeffington launched the Irish Citizen he was president of the Socialist Party of Ireland.

The contending priorities of organised labour and suffrage feminism found a common cause in the movement to unionise women industrial workers. Trade union men and suffrage women came together on 5 September 1911 in the Antient Concert Rooms, Dublin, to launch the Irish Women Workers' Union. The two most popular speakers in the packed hall were James Larkin, who was 'wildly cheered,' and Constance Markievicz, 'who was greeted with great applause.' In their speeches both she and Hanna Sheehy-Skeffington linked membership of the new union with winning the vote.

Plans to unionise women in Dublin had been considered months ahead of this meeting. Bean na hÉireann, the monthly nationalist women's journal, reported in March 1910 that 'leading members' of Dublin Trades Council had been approached to organise women workers in the city and urged 'prominent public ladies' to take up the question in the face of any male reluctance.

Many trade unionists believed women workers could not be organised. Even Delia Larkin, James Larkin's sister, who was appointed as the new women's union secretary, reported her surprise at the enthusiasm of the first meeting, 'because an idea has always been uppermost in the people's minds that it was utterly impossible to get a number of women to come together for any demonstration. In fact I myself have always felt that women were apathetic in their attitude towards their own betterment, but Tuesday's meeting has once and for all, dispelled that feeling.'[5]

On 12 August 1911 Delia Larkin began contributing a 'Women Workers' Column' in the *Irish Worker*, the weekly paper of the ITGWU, edited by James Larkin. An appeal for recruits to the Irish Women Workers' Union followed a week later. Within days of this advertisement a strike by three hundred workers in Jacob's biscuit factory heralded the public launch of the union in September.

There are no surviving records to illuminate the decision to set up the IWWU. William O'Brien, Larkin's lifelong adversary, records that Larkin had insisted that the definition of the ITGWU member was a 'male person'. O'Brien wrote: 'Many people (including myself) did not see any necessity for such a union believing it was not desirable to organise workers on a sex basis, Mr. Larkin had his own reasons (or prejudices) and had his way.'[6]

This claim has become the orthodox historical explanation for a separate women's union. But it was not simply prejudice that inspired the strategy of separate women's organisation. The segregated workshops where women and men worked, and women's poorer pay and conditions, militated against their membership and participation in the trade union movement. Labour organisations, like the Women's Trade Union Leagues in the United States and Britain, helped the organisation of women's unions, with notable success. Even mixed unions of men and women increasingly resorted to separate women's branches or 'ladies' committees'; for a decade before 1920 the Irish National Teachers' Organisation even reserved seats on the national executive to accommodate the specific interests of women and their work.[7] William O'Brien himself followed this direction when his own union, the Amalgamated Society of Tailors, admitted women as members. In July 1917 O'Brien presided at a meeting of women to set up a branch in the Dublin district.

The Irish Women Workers' Union offered membership to all women workers, regardless of their industry or the type of work they did, which mirrored the organisation of the ITGWU. Delia Larkin described her union as being 'affiliated' to the ITGWU. In some respects the IWWU of this era was closer to a women's section than an independent union. Its president was James Larkin; its trustees were officials of the ITGWU, and the women workers' officers were paid by it.[8] When the ITGWU moved into Liberty

Hall in March 1912 the women workers took a room in the building. The IWWU never registered as a separate organisation legally, as trade unions were obliged to do; yet it affiliated independently to the ITUC, paying a fee of one guinea for a thousand members in the spring of 1912.

Its organisation was informal. It had no functioning executive committee. It had its own rules; and its enrolment fee of sixpence, with twopence a week subscription, was less than men paid in the ITGWU, acknowledging women's lower wages. Its record of activity indicates that it had autonomy in practice. James Larkin's presidency of the women's union served to strengthen the bond between the two unions. When James Connolly formed an Irish Textile Workers' Union among some Belfast women spinners, he was instructed by Larkin to transform it into a branch of the IWWU.

The women who had welcomed the union so enthusiastically in 1911 had a record of militancy, which they brought into their own union. They struck in small workshops and large factories, they aired their grievances, and they called their employers to account in their own column in the *Irish Worker*. Union activity was intense. The IWWU rooms in Great Brunswick Street (Pearse Street) and then Liberty Hall were open nightly. The members were in the main very young, often in their early teens. The record they have left in both actions and words conveys a lively, militant membership that, though small in numbers, was strong in spirit.

In their organising secretary, Delia Larkin, they had a champion equal to their cause. R. M. Fox recalled: 'She was tall and commanding in appearance, like her brother, and had a similar temperament, implacable to opponents, but with a friendly warmth to the people she trusted.'[9] In her weekly column in the *Irish Worker*, Delia Larkin wrote the vivid pieces that highlighted the working conditions of Dublin's laundry workers, food producers, domestics, clerical workers, and nurses. She opened a space to women members and campaigners alike. She quoted Shakespeare and Burns in her argument. She would advocate the sweeping away of dust-gathering domestic furnishings and bric-a-brac as vigorously as she denounced a recalcitrant boss in the cause of women's freedom.

Delia Larkin shared with her brother a broader view of trade unionism, which reached beyond the work-place. She felt that 'there was not enough time and attention given to the social side of Trade Unionism.' Weekly socials, New Year dances and a summer excursion were features of the union calendar. Delia Larkin started a drama society within the union, from elocution classes that she ran in Liberty Hall, training the actors herself. She formed the union choir. Both drew on the talents of the IWWU and the ITGWU.

Most Dublin work-places where the women's union had members were small. In Keogh's sack factory in May 1912 thirty-nine women went on strike. In the Pembroke laundry a month later fourteen women struck. It was only in Jacob's biscuit factory, employing three thousand women, that the IWWU had a substantial membership. In September 1913 six hundred women were locked out there. In the spring of that year the IWWU sent two delegates to the annual ITUC conference, Ellen Gordon from Belfast and Delia Larkin.

But by the summer of 1913 the union's recruitment drive had faltered. Activity had slumped; membership was down to six hundred. Finances were poor, and Delia Larkin and her drama group, the Liberty Players, left Dublin to tour Britain to raise funds.

As the crisis of the August challenge to members of the ITGWU lengthened into weeks, and then the autumn months of 1913, the IWWU was soon added to the employers' lock-out of union members. A British suffragist, Mary Neal, reported in her newspaper, *Votes for Women*:

> The significant thing is that so long as the girls only wore the general badge of the men's Union the masters took very little notice. But they had always depended on the women to break the men's strike by working at a lower wage, so that as soon as the women began to organise themselves, form their own Unions, and wear their own badges, notices were put up saying that if they wore the Union badge they would be dismissed. The girls wore the badge and were locked out.[10]

James Connolly explained to the Scottish readers of the socialist weekly *Forward* that the employers barred help to the ITGWU, which spread the dispute even further among members of the IWWU. His observant eye contrasted the poverty of the women's circumstances with the strength of their solidarity:

> and in every shop, factory and sweating hell-hole in Dublin as the agreement is presented, they march out with pinched faces, threadbare clothes, and miserable footgear, but with high hopes, undaunted spirit, and glorious resolve shining out of their eyes.[11]

The lock-out spread swiftly through the city as a result of sympathetic strikes, when workers refused to handle either strike-bound goods or the bosses' agreement and were then in turn locked out themselves. Funds were raised by donation and levy throughout the city, the country, and abroad. Food was shipped to Dublin by trade unionists in Britain.

Delia Larkin was out of Dublin, six weeks into the fund-raising theatrical tour, when the lock-out began. She returned early in September to take charge of administration in Liberty Hall. That same month James Larkin appealed for help from British workers, speaking to packed halls in England and Scotland. At one London meeting Larkin's account of seven weeks of slow starvation moved Dora Montefiore, a fellow-speaker, to suggest that families in Britain could offer homes and care to Dublin's children who were suffering so severely in the dispute.

> When Larkin had finished speaking I wrote out a slip of paper and passed it across to him, asking him if a plan like this which had already been

carried out by Belgian comrades, and in the Lawrence strike, in the United States, could be arranged through the Daily Herald League, would it have his blessing. He wrote a few words in the affirmative, and I then passed along a line to Lady Warwick, who was also on the platform, asking her if she would act as Treasurer to the Fund, which she agreed to do.[12]

James Larkin's passionate appeals combined with a socialist and feminist experience of previous disputes. Both Dora Montefiore and the Countess of Warwick, Frances Greville, were members of the left-wing Social Democratic Federation and knew from first hand the importance of such solidarity. A year earlier Frances Greville had planned a similar strategy for children during a London dock strike.

On 10 October, Dora Montefiore launched her appeal to the women of the Daily Herald League, a support organisation of the British socialist newspaper. The request for the names of families willing to take children and for funds to pay their travelling expenses met an immediate response. Within days, 350 homes were offered to Dublin children and their relatives.

Dora Montefiore came to Dublin with Grace Neal, former organiser of the Domestic Workers' Union, and Lucille Rand, a young American woman whose father had been governor of California. Here they joined the daily task force at work in Liberty Hall.

> Orders for food coming by the foodship are distributed there in the upper rooms, while in the basement meals are always being cooked and distributed to the mothers and children who come with tin cans and jugs for stew or cocoa and carry away under ragged shawls big loaves baked at the Co-op bakery. Every passage and landing is crowded with patient people, none of whom go empty away, for the organisation as far as one can see is perfect.

A Ladies' Committee headed by Delia Larkin mobilised women, employing their domestic skills in the struggle. Liberty Hall's kitchen became the hub of the solidarity effort. 'The cooking, cleaning and attendance is performed by a number of locked-out women and girls as well as by the daughters of locked-out workers.'

Mothers flocked to Liberty Hall meetings to hear the arrangements to bring the children to supporters' homes during the lock-out.

> Last night the mothers' meeting in one of the largest rooms in Liberty Hall was a sight none of us will ever forget. Miss Larkin told me it was the 'surprise of my life.' The meeting of mothers and babies overflowed, blocking the stairs, and struggling out into the street.

The first group of children travelled to the home of Emmeline Pethick Lawrence, co-editor of *Votes for Women*, under the guardianship of Mary Neal, secretary of the English suffragists. Five children and their mother journeyed without incident. She reported:

Every working man and woman on the way gave us a greeting and wished us luck, from the stevedore on the quay who gave them 3d for sweets to the stewardess of the first class saloon who could not resist going in to see them and share with the third class stewardess in what was evidently considered the privilege of looking after them.

The following morning all the Dublin newspapers published the letter of the Catholic Archbishop of Dublin, William Walsh. He wrote of his 'consternation' at the scheme, and went on to say:

> The Dublin women now subjected to this cruel temptation to part with their helpless offspring are, in the majority of cases, Catholics. Have they abandoned their Faith? Well, if they have not, they should need no words of mine to remind them of the plain duty of every Catholic mother in such a case. I can only put it to them that they can be no longer held worthy of the name Catholic mothers if they so far forget that duty as to send away their little children to be cared for in a strange land without security of any kind that those to whom the poor children are to be handed over are Catholics, or indeed persons of any faith at all.

The *Daily Herald* described Walsh's warning to the mothers of Dublin as hitting the scheme 'like a bombshell.' The public good will for the first group of children was eclipsed by the angry crowds mobilised to prevent any further groups leaving Dublin. Anyone travelling with children was challenged. On the Kingstown (Dún Laoghaire) train and at the mail boat a group of fifty children and their mothers was intimidated and assaulted. Every night that week, as children prepared to travel to Liverpool, Belfast, even Hazelhatch, Dublin ships and railway stations were picketed by crowds organised by the Ancient Order of Hibernians and fired up by their speakers.

In an effort to reassure families in Dublin, Delia Larkin went to Liverpool, where eighteen children and two relatives were being looked after in the district, to report on the children's accommodation, religious attendance, instruction and schooling during their stay. Delia Larkin now had overall responsibility in Liberty Hall. She had to stand in for her brother, as James Larkin was imprisoned awaiting trial. Dora Montefiore reported:

> I want to tell you how the outward fort of Liberty Hall, and the inner fort of high resolve and loyalty to the least and greatest of Jim's wishes, are being held by his sister and comrade, Delia Larkin. Although racked with anxiety as to the result of the trial I find her on Monday afternoon at Liberty Hall, moving outwardly serene among the girls and men whom it is her daily work to organise.
> I came to talk to her about the temporary frustration of our scheme for placing the kiddies among our English comrades. She led me into our room, now deserted by the swarming mothers and kiddies of last week, but used at present as a storeroom for the beautiful and loving gifts of fathers, mothers and sisters in England and Scotland.

There she stood, a tall alert presence with the fringed blue eyes and black hair of an Irishwoman, and with quietly undulated voice she told me how things were to be organised in Jim's absence.

At the great London rally in the Albert Hall on 1 November, Delia Larkin replaced him on the platform of speakers.

Delia Larkin was the living embodiment of the heart of the new Labour movement. Few people in the hall perhaps realised what an ordeal it was for this quiet woman, who has spent her life in working and not talking, to face such a vast audience. In a few simple dignified words she went to the root of the matter.

In Dublin the plans of the Daily Herald League for the children were halted, but its solidarity work continued. For another four months, from November until March 1914, Delia Larkin and Grace Neal oversaw a staff of twenty-two people preparing the three thousand breakfasts at Liberty Hall every morning and providing clothing for more than three thousand children and babies. They served free dinners to nursing mothers from mid-December until the end of February. A Christmas party, with three marquees and a decorated tree for the children, was held at Croydon Park, Fairview, the ITGWU's recreation centre.

Throughout the crisis James Larkin maintained his support for the women's effort. He mobilised his members as bodyguards to protect the children and families. Dora Montefiore recalled a procession of children leaving Liberty Hall, each carried high on the shoulders of a stalwart docker. Forced for their safety to suspend the children's trip, James Larkin defiantly declared it had been 'the finest tactical error ever made in the workers' fight.'

By the summer of 1914 relations at Liberty Hall had soured. A dispute had begun over the use of facilities in Liberty Hall by the women's union. In the autumn James Larkin left for the United States. Financial difficulties in the union centred on the administration of the insurance section, from which Delia Larkin drew her wages, and in July 1915 she left Liberty Hall and Dublin. James Connolly approached Helena Molony to take over the running of the IWWU. When she was jailed after the Easter rising, Louie Bennett and Helen Chenevix stepped in. All three women became long-serving officials when the IWWU was reorganised in 1918.

Dublin's women workers paid a high price in the lock-out. Between four and five hundred women never got their jobs back. They had been arrested and imprisoned, like fourteen-year-old Lily Kempson, who died in January 1996. Fifteen-year-old Alice Brady was shot by a scab and died in the new year of 1914.

In three short years before the First World War, the IWWU, with its inchoate organisation, had created a new space for women industrial workers at the heart of Dublin's trade union movement. They had inspired suffrage and nationalist women in their cause and exposed the system of exploitation that underpinned their poorly rewarded labour.

The Irish Women Workers' Union went on to become a permanent presence in Irish trade unionism. Those who took that route paid tribute to James Larkin. Shortly after he died, Louie Bennett wrote to his eldest son, James Larkin Junior: 'We on our side give to your father the credit of having initiated and encouraged the career of the IWWU.'[13]

The *Daily Herald* reported James Larkin's own tribute, made in January 1914, at the graveside of Alice Brady: 'In their seventeen weeks' fight, no section had shown more pluck and endurance and solidarity than the women workers.'

Chapter 13

Larkin through the Eyes of Writers

Theo Dorgan

To the poets and writers whose gifts answered to the raw character of James Larkin he appeared larger than life, a man of biblical stature, a giant or a prophet whose rage of the heart called forth in them an urge to portray a hero out of the ancient world.

Look back to 'Gilgamesh', to 'Táin Bó Chuaille', to the 'Odyssey', the 'Iliad'—our earliest beginnings in the craft have to do not just with gods and goddesses but with the lives and being and doing of heroes. Now in our time we know too much of human frailty, the irony has entered into our souls. After Auschwitz, says Paul Celan, no more poetry. Meaning, in part, no more heroic poetry. And yet that unillusioned man Frank O'Connor could make a simple hero of Jim Larkin, that sceptical countryman Patrick Kavanagh could, as could the worldly Brendan Behan and the fastidious Austin Clarke.

The impulse to honour heroes has two origins. Those who live in the time of the hero will struggle to fix in memory some sense of their own times. The hero in some way is an emblem of the times, and by extension or mimesis the poet participates in the life and stature of the hero. To have known a hero, to have lived in the same streets and halls and times as the hero is in some way to participate in the heroic. And for those who come after, for those who have not known the hero directly, the hero becomes an icon, an incarnation of virtues the author wishes to possess, or of human qualities he would wish us to share.

The trouble of course is that the icon is a simplified portrait. Thus in the New Testament, Matthew, Mark, Luke and John write of Jesus as a hero figure in whose literal steps they have walked, while for the later Church Fathers Jesus becomes icon, they write of him in a continuous present though they live centuries after him. His icon becomes the emblem of his living presence, and when we stand inside the nimbus of the icon we stand inside the charmed radius of the very life itself. Absence supplies a living presence.

I introduce the religious frame of reference because so many of those who attempt Larkin's incarnation give him to us as a Christ-like figure. Perhaps the most vivid example of this is Frank O'Connor's bleak poem 'Homage to Jim Larkin'.

> Roll away the stone, Lord, roll away the stone
> As you did when last I died in the attic room;
> Then there was no fire as well, and I died of cold
> While Jim Larkin walked the streets before he grew old.

Larkin was a young man then, all skin and bone;
Larkin had a madman's eyes, I saw them through the stone;
Larkin had a madman's voice, I don't know what he said,
I just heard screeches ringing in my head.

Something screeched within my head as in an empty room;
I felt the lightning of the pain run through every bone;
I couldn't even scream, Lord, I just sobbed with pain;
I didn't want to live, Lord, and turned to sleep again.

But with the screeches in my head I couldn't settle right,
At last I scrambled to my knees and turned to the light;
Then I heard the words he spoke, and down crashed the stone
There was I with blind man's eyes, gaping at the sun.

Things are much the same again, damn the thing to eat;
Not a bloody fag since noon and such a price for meat;
Not a bit of fire at home all the livelong day—
Roll the stone away, Lord, roll the stone away.

O'Connor published this poem in the *Irish Times* on 9 December 1944. The picture he offers us draws for its power on oblique references to the teachings of Christ, the Christos docens, the teaching Christ whose words sometimes fell on deaf ears, sometimes on ears suddenly attuned to their inner meaning. It is the fate of prophets that their words sound to some like the ranting of madmen; to others they ring with the clear true note of direct revelation. To the very poor, the destitute, what Marx and Engels termed the lumpenproletariat, the appearance of a Messiah figure is always problematic. The very exigencies of their situation can make it impossible to assign a true value to the words of salvation offered them, the charismatic leadership embodied in the hero. Thus they have ears to hear, and hear not; eyes to see, and they see not. O'Connor makes plain that Larkin was indeed, in a limited sense, a Messiah, one who came with the word that heals and saves; equally, he makes it plain that neither Larkin's words, nor deeds nor person are sufficient to bring about transformation; the rock of hopelessness still stands in the way.

In this sense it might be truer to say that O'Connor sees Larkin more as an Old Testament prophet, since it was not required of a prophet that he actually change anything, merely that he be right about the necessity of change. Eerily enough, in this regard if in no other, O'Connor follows in the footsteps of the Dublin employer whom Lord Askwith quotes as having said, 'I don't know how you can talk to that fellow Larkin, you can't argue with the prophet Isaiah.'

James Plunkett in his epic *Strumpet City* also explicitly finds the Christ in Larkin, and even has Rashers Tierney say of him words to the effect that 'there goes Jesus Christ' when Larkin sweeps by him on a street at evening.

The Christian text implicit in O'Connor's poem is of course the famous and troubling proposition that 'the meek shall inherit the earth.' The

Dublin poor were, however, far too demoralised to believe this, to find any shred of comfort in it. Plunkett again, in *Leaders and Workers*, hints at both the practical and impractical Christ in Larkin when he says: 'It remained to Jim Larkin to see the slum dweller as a human being—degraded, yet capable of nobility; perceptive, capable of living with dignity, capable even of music and literature. That was the message he began to address to the city at large—a message of love, delivered one must concede, by a man swinging wildly about him with a sword.' Plunkett's words bring irresistibly to mind Yeats's 'Cuchulainn fought the ungovernable sea.' Here, with his usual perceptiveness, Plunkett locates the fatal, one might even say dramatic or tragic fault in Larkin's character. It was the Christian heart that filled with rage at injustice, the pagan heroic heart that laid blindly about him in the *taom feirge* or *taom buile* of our Bronze Age epics.

Larkin of course was a great orator, a man whose words could ignite the dampest tinder, coaxing a spark that he would fan and foster into a roaring, devouring flame. He was a master of that long-lost art, the rhetoric of civic rage. The Greeks of the ancient world recognised and valued rhetoric, the true art of moving men's minds in a mass. What we now call rhetoric they would have called sophistry, for true rhetoric sought to move men to the pursuit of justice by the power of the spoken word. This heroic art found a great master in Larkin, and I think it was this dramatic quality in the man that quickened the interest of writers.

Seán O'Casey in *The Star Turns Red* gives us a Larkin figure in Red Jim, the labour leader who answers the question of the Brown Priest, why he should stay with the workers in revolt, with this vivid passage: 'To be with us when the star turns red; to help us carry the fiery cross. Join with us. March with us in the midst of the holy fire.' Yeats again here, of course—'O sages standing in God's holy fire'—and Moses also, the Biblical deliverer of his people, to whom God appeared in the midst of a burning bush.

In *Red Roses for Me*, two years later in 1942, O'Casey's Larkin figure is given the words 'Friend, we would that you should live a greater life; we will that all of us shall live a greater life. Our strike is yours. A step ahead for us today; another one for you tomorrow. We who have known, and know, the emptiness of life shall know its fullness.' At the end of this act he has him say further:

> We swear to release thee from hunger and hardship,
> From things that are ugly and common and mean;
> Thy people together shall build a great city,
> The finest and fairest that ever was seen.

These last lines are, admittedly, sentimental, scarcely rising above the level of greeting-card verse, but the image reached for is that of the Biblical prophets, or of William Blake, the image of Jerusalem, the golden city shining on a hill.

O'Casey, scourged by the church he delighted in baiting, nonetheless reaches for the Biblical treasury of word and image when he portrays this giant, dramatic figure. Patrick Kavanagh, in many ways a far more conservative man, takes a different, a more modern and a more radical note in his poem entitled simply 'Jim Larkin'.

Not with public words now can his greatness
Be told to the children, for he was more
Than a labour-agitating orator—
The flashing flaming sword merely bore witness
to the coming of the dawn: 'Awake and look!
The flowers are growing for you, and wonderful trees
And beyond are not the serf's grey Docks, but seas—
Excitement out of the Creator's poetry book.
When the Full Moon's in the River and the ghost of bread
Must not haunt all your weary wanderings home,
The ships that were dark galleys can become
Pine forests under winter's starry plough
And the brown gantries will be the lifted head
Of man the dreamer whom the gods endow.'

And thus I heard Jim Larkin above
The crowd who wanted to turn aside
From Reality coming to free them. Terrified
They hid in the clouds of dope and would not move.
They eat the opium of the murderer's story
In the Sunday newspapers; they stood to stare
Not at the blackbird but at a millionaire
Whose horses ran for serfdom's greater glory.
And tyranny trampled them in Dublin's gutter
Until Jim Larkin came along and cried
The call of Freedom and the call of Pride
And Slavery crept to its hands and knees
And Nineteen Thirteen cheered from out the utter
Degradation of their miseries.

First published in the *Bell* in 1947, Kavanagh's poem is unusual in a number of respects. We tend to forget how urban a poet he was, how lively and unillusioned his eye was, not just for 'every blooming thing' in the pastoral sense but for the nuanced, inflected speech of the poor. To be sure, his Larkin too is the great exhorter, the leader come to call the huddled masses from their knees, casting off chains real, metaphorical and metaphysical. But he is cleverly situated here in his true setting, the somewhat old-fashioned Biblical orator striving to waken from a drugged befuddlement these demoralised readers of tabloids and gawkers at the passing spindrift of wealth and position. Kavanagh's Larkin moves and acts in a milieu where his real but in some ways backward-looking powers must operate in a world of the alienated, the sceptical, the disbelieving.

In the same month that great-hearted son of the Dublin poor Brendan Behan published in *Comhar* his poem 'Jim Larkin'.

Ba mise é! Ba gach mac máthar againn é!
Sinn féin. Láidir. Mar ab áil linn a bheith,
Mar ab eol dúinn a bheith.
Eisean ag bagairt troda is ag bronnadh fuascailte—
Is sinne ag leanúint a chónra trí chlab na cathrach
I mbéiceacha móra feirge.

Ag leanúint a chónra trí chlab na cathrach aréir
An sinne a bhí sa chónra?
Níorbh ea: bhíomar sa tsráid ag máirseáil
Beo, buíoch don mharbh.

In my own English version:

He was myself, and every mother's son of us,
Ourselves indeed strong as we would love to be,
As we know how to be,
Following his hearse through the clamouring din of the city,
Offering unrelenting fight, or liberty
In great roars of rage.

Last night as we followed his hearse through the great din of the city
Is it we who were there, cold in that coffin?
No, we were there on the street, marching,
Heads up, hearts full of gratitude to the dead man.

Of all the tributes in prose and verse to Larkin, I find Behan's especially touching. First of all because it was written in Irish—not very good Irish, perhaps, but written, as were all his poems in that language, from a genuine urge to possess himself as an Irishman. Secondly, because it is written on the move, by a man who in his own way and for his own reasons was by every instinct a true working-class rebel. And thirdly, because he manages a deft piece of footwork: this is a lament for a great man dead, but the focus is displaced onto the pride of the living. It is a very Dublin tribute, somehow, recalling the words alleged to have been uttered by an old shawlie on seeing Behan's own coffin go by: 'He was pure straight, God love him, not like us.'

Behan's poem is also, ironically, the saddest of all the literary tributes. The blunt fact of course is that neither the Dublin nor the larger Irish working class possess Larkin's rage for justice alive in their hearts. I say this with no disrespect to working men or women, nor indeed to the unions that have fought so valiantly for them and with them, but the game has changed out of all recognition now. We live in a state entirely dominated by financial institutions and multinational companies undreamed of in the old syndicalist days. Larkin at least had this advantage: he could stand in a Belfast or a Dublin street and point to the owners of our small patch of the world. He could point to William Martin Murphy and say to the starving worker, there is your slave-master, there is the man who owns you, body and soul. Who, in our time, can point at the owners? We are owned by machines now, and not by men; behind what coffin should we march to find strength in ourselves and in our numbers?

The truth is that the hero's day is done. If a new Isaiah were to rise up in the desert, a new Moses appear to lead us out of the modern deserts of alienation to the promised land of true human community, what language would she employ, what vision would she offer us? Her visions would be smoothly derailed and explained away as the ravings of a disturbed mind, her followers dismissed urbanely on the television news as the latest in a series of inconsequential cults. And of course, so polished now are the practitioners of our black arts, should she become dangerous to the interests of our owners, she would be surgically, and deniably, removed. We are back where Kavanagh locates us:

> They hid in the clouds of dope and would not move.
> They eat the opium of the murderer's story
> In the Sunday newspapers; they stood to stare
> Not at the blackbird but at a millionaire.

This brings me to a further reflection on the hero: that he or she begins always from the margins, working steadily into the centre of a nation's life as destiny and the play of social forces permit. More exactly, being pulled to the centre in a complex play of personal energy and will with impersonal dialectic. All the commentators on Larkin, especially those on the left, emphasise his instability. At heart he was a syndicalist, closer to the ragged battalions of anarchism than to the sober ranks of organised Marxists. For those of us whose hearts are on the left, this is a perennial anguish: rage or discipline? No-one as yet has found a third way that advances the interests of the underclass while allowing free play to originality and spontaneous, cheerful self-contradiction. Larkin's instinctive genius for the theatre of the streets made him a natural ally of the American IWW, the Wobblies, who had all of Woody Guthrie's heart. But the American left, unlike the European, always knew itself outgunned, understood that the life of a working man or woman was an endless and bloody rearguard action. The pride was always and only in the refusal to serve, to bow the knee. In this particular political sense, Larkin was and is a doomed figure, perhaps best caught by the poet Lola Ridge.

Born in Dublin in 1871, she went to America in 1907 and lived there until her death in 1941. Her poetry deals unswervingly, single-mindedly, with the lives of the martyred poor and dispossessed. Here is her poem 'To Larkin':

> Is it you I see go by the window, Jim Larkin—you not looking at me or anyone
> And your shadow swaying from East to West?
> Strange that you should be walking free—you shut down without light,
> And your legs tied up with a knot of iron.

One hundred million men and women go inevitably about their affairs,
In the somnolent way
Of men before a great drunkenness ...
They do not see you go by their windows, Jim Larkin,
With your eyes bloody as the sunset
And your shadow gaunt upon the sky ...
You and the like of you, that life
Is crushing for their frantic wines.

The figure evoked here is heroic, marginal, and doomed, a hero but a Gothic one, not a shining-browed warrior out of the archaic Irish or Greek but an outcast, a Steppenwolf of the Revolution. Ridge's gaunt, bloody-eyed figure is uncannily close to the pen-picture Seán Ó Faoláin offers in his *Countess Markievicz*:

> Larkin had come out of the dark netherworld with the eyes and face of a poet. He burned with a fiery simplicity of belief in his fellow-man and his speech to them was like a lava. He had ... the hollowed cheeks and high cheekbone of an ascetic.

The difference here, naturally, can be understood as political. Ó Faoláin, the disillusioned national revolutionary, is interested in Larkin as a vivid character study. Ridge sees him as a doomed actor on the stage of the actual world. Ó Faoláin quickens to the human type. Ridge sorrows for the lost leader of the downstruck.

The great Scots poet Hugh MacDiarmid was once asked what he thought of the left-wing poets of the thirties. His reply was as devastating as it was unfair: 'Unlike Auden and Spender and MacNeice, I am *of* the working class, not *for* it.' Larkin was of his class, not for it; he loved the poor, as perhaps nobody in Irish public life before or since has loved them, with a Christ-like and heroic, often wrong-headed generosity. But just as the hero is spurned by his people, just as Christ is everywhere mocked in the words and deeds of so many of his alleged followers, Larkin has fallen from our words and from a world where his heart and deeds are now unintelligible.

He was of course a complicated and complex man. A bull in a china shop. Indisciplined. Given to destructive rages and to admiring Rabelais and Ibsen. Modest and simple yet devastating in argument, a man of contradictions. Now, reviewing certain writings about the man, and thinking of others I have not had time to mention, I am struck by what can only be called a reductive simplicity in the imaginative portrayals of the man. The clear-headed prose portraits—of Æ, say, or James Plunkett, or Connolly, seem in some sense to give us more of the man's essence. Perhaps Larkin's true poet or dramatist has yet to appear.

I'll end this lecture with a contemporary poem, a short lyric by the Galway poet Jack Mitchell.

A family likeness—
Venus and Big Jim?
Don't laugh.
Look again at that old photograph:
Jim blossoming from that crowd—
Larkin rising
Perfect from the slaves,
Like a sudden dancer in a ring,
Or a bird
Bursting from its nest.
Yes, this is the people caught
In the act of taking wing
That crowd wears Larkin like a crest!

Now contemplate
His stony image in O'Connell Street,
Based on that picture they say.
Vanished all the fine sway and tilt
Of body and arms and head—
The lilt that was Larkin banished,
Instead—
This ponderous colossus
Lead-footed on its squat column,
This dead Golem
Erected after rigor mortis had set in,
Arms raised, rigid as girders,
Trumpet mouth turned to an idiot O,
Haranguing the void.

That said,
I'll take a drink
To the grand old sculptors of Greece.
Just think
What would have happened
To love and sex and all the fun and fuss
Had they carved Aphrodite thus!

The lilt that was Larkin is good, I think, and perhaps points us to what
may yet come, a full-blooded portrait of a full-blooded man, alive,
glorious and surprisingly heroic in his unbowed, unillusioned humanity.

Chapter 14

Big Jim: A Loaf on the Table, a Flower in the Vase

James Plunkett

Jim Larkin was born in Liverpool in 1874. He worked from an early age, first at delivering papers and then as a messenger-boy for a butcher. In his teens he began to work in the Liverpool docks and became a very active member of the National Union of Dock Labourers, so much so that he was sent as an organiser for the union to Ireland, arriving in Belfast in 1907. Here his militant methods and aggressive techniques stirred up so many strikes that he shocked not only the Belfast employers but the executive of the union back in Liverpool as well. Its general secretary, James Sexton, who eventually had him dismissed, said about him later: 'James Larkin crashed upon the public with the devastating roar of a volcano without even a preliminary wisp of smoke.'

Larkin then formed his own union, the Irish Transport and General Workers' Union, and operated in many other centres. Dublin, however, became his base, and it was there that he conducted the epic lock-out of 1913. After that, in 1914, he travelled to the United States to raise funds. While there he was tried in New York by the Supreme Court on a charge of criminal anarchy and sentenced to Sing Sing Jail for a period of between five and ten years.

His return to Ireland in 1923 resulted in a split in his union and caused considerable alarm and antagonism among the leaders, both lay and religious, of the still very young Free State, who dreaded his return as a dangerous source of menace to the social order they were intent on establishing. In no time he was leading a new union and was troubling the even tenor of a new middle class, which Seán Ó Faoláin described as representing 'laissez faire in social reform, a hypocritical pietism in religion … a class which breed censorship, lay priests and arid traditionalism.'

When I was growing up in the thirties, Larkin was sometimes one of the orators to be seen on Sunday mornings at Foster Place or outside the City Hall, a compelling speaker and demagogue who always brought me to a standstill to listen and admire from a distance. Then circumstances ordained that I should meet him in person.

It was in 1938 and I had begun working in the Dublin Gas Company, where moves were afoot among the clerical workers to become unionised. Eventually the decision was taken to approach Jim Larkin to ask him to accept us in his Workers' Union of Ireland. The task of making the approach was placed on the shoulders of myself and a close friend, Paddy Phelan.

The LARKIN FAMILY

James Larkin c. 1903.

James Junior, Denis, Bernard and Fintan Larkin with their mother, Elizabeth Larkin, c. 1916.

Elizabeth Larkin c. 1903.

Strike meeting at Queen's Square, Belfast, 1907. On the platform from left: Michael McKeown (National Union of Dock Labourers), Alexander Boyd (Municipal Employees), James Larkin, W. J. Murray and James O'Connor Keesock.

BELFAST 1907

Above and left: Larkin addressing strike meeting, Belfast 1907.

Strike meeting at
Queen's Square,
Belfast 1907.

Above and right:
The Royal Irish
Constabulary escort a
convoy of delivery
vans, Belfast 1907.

Funeral of Charles McMullen and Maggie Lennon killed by police fusillade
during rioting in Belfast, August 1907.

RIC Constable William Barrett, being chaired by colleagues during the
police mutiny, Belfast 1907.

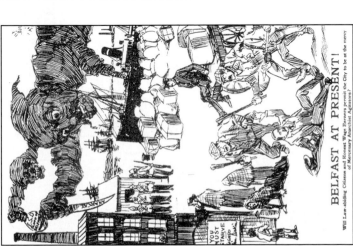

Cartoons from *Nomad's Weekly*,
left: 20 July 1907, *centre*: 10 August 1907,
right: 14 September 1907

IRISH TRANSPORT AND GENERAL WORKERS' UNION

Right: James Larkin, General Secretary ITGWU, 1900–1924.

Below: ITGWU Badge, 1913.

The chief who raised the Red Hand up
Until it paled the sun,
And shed such glory o'er our cause
As never Chief had done.

Inscription on banner in 1913

Left: William O'Brien, General Treasurer ITGWU 1918–1924 and General Secretary 1924–1946.

Below left: Thomas Foran, General President ITGWU 1909–1939.

Below right: James Connolly, Acting General Secretary ITGWU October 1914–May 1916.

Liberty Hall, Beresford Place, Dublin – ITGWU Head Office from March 1912.

Left: Strike notice signed by James Larkin, 26 August 1913.

DUBLIN
1913

Above, right and below: Dublin slums.
(Royal Society of Antiquities of Ireland)

Manchester: cartloads of potatoes for loading on the *s.s. Hare* for the relief of the families of locked-out workers in Dublin.

Larkin prepares to board the first relief ship at North Quays, Dublin.

The first truckload of food is rolled on to the quay.

Left and below: Food is distributed from a warehouse on the quay to hungry families.

Drawing of the food kitchen in Liberty Hall in 1913 by Sir William Orpen, RA.

ENGLISH FOOD FOR DUBLIN STRIKERS.

Left: 'English Food for Dublin strikers': a page of pictures from *The Irish Independent* (Dublin), 18 September 1913.

Below: Front page of the *Evening Herald* (Dublin), 15 September 1913.

EVENING HERALD

VOL. 22. NO. 222.   DUBLIN, MONDAY, SEPTEMBER 15, 1913.   PRICE

DRIVING LARKINISM OUT OF DUBLIN

Three Thousand Builders Labourers Locked Out

ANOTHER SEVERE BLOW FOR SYNDICALISM

Two Thousand Farm Hands Leave Work To-Day

JACOB'S VICTORY OVER STRIKE TRUST

LARKIN TELLS A CROWD OF ENGLISHMEN

That the Great Question in Ireland is Not Home Rule

FARM HANDS STRIKE

In Anticipation of the Lock Out

2,000 MEN DISEMPLOYED

The scene in O'Connell Street, Dublin, on Bloody Sunday, 31 August 1913. *(Photograph: J. Cashman)*

Jim Larkin (disguised) following his arrest on Bloody Sunday at the Imperial Hotel, O'Connell Street (now Clery's Department Store).

Below: Funeral of James Byrne, who died from injuries received in a police baton charge, passes along Eden Quay, Dublin.

Larkin and P. T. Daly outside the police court.

Captain Jack White (left) and Francis Sheehy Skeffington.

The Daily Mirror

THE MORNING JOURNAL WITH THE SECOND LARGEST NET SALE.

THURSDAY, SEPTEMBER 4, 1913.

WOUNDED IN THE DUBLIN RIOTS; MAN WHO SAYS THE POLICE RAIDED HIS HOUSE AND BROKE UP HIS FURNITURE.

Front page of *The Daily Mirror* (London), 4 September 1913: Keir Hardie is seen on sidecar in bottom centre picture in the funeral procession of James Nolan who died from injuries received in police batoning on Eden Quay on 30 August 1913.

The Daily Mirror

THE MORNING JOURNAL WITH THE SECOND LARGEST NET SALE.

PEACE OR A SWORD? LARKIN SET FREE THREATENS TO RAISE THE FIERY CROSS

DUBLIN

KINGSTOWN

BRAY

Front page of *The Daily Mirror* (London), 14 September 1913.

So, on a sunlit summer evening when work was finished, the two of us stepped out from the door of the Gas Company office into D'Olier Street and set off in a mood of nervous anticipation for Unity Hall, which stood (or rather staggered: it was in the extremities of decay) almost directly opposite the Pro-Cathedral. Inside the door of the hall we found a bare hallway leading to a bare staircase and a room with bare floorboards and a rough wooden table at which, under a bare electric light-bulb suspended from its cobwebbed flex, the man himself was seated.

He was tall, heavily built, obviously at one time of much physical strength, with a lock of white hair that fell down over his forehead and a large bent pipe that seemed to require vast quantities of matches to keep it up to the mark. He asked us a number of exploratory questions in an easy and friendly tone, which relaxed and reassured us. It ended with his agreement to admit us as members. That settled, he drifted into a welter of notions, topics and opinions that touched on a hundred and one things, which poured out in a ceaseless flow from the powerhouse that was Jim Larkin's mind.

His accent was a strange mixture of Liverpool and Dublin, with now and then an echo of his years in America. He was then around sixty-four, in good shape physically for his age but with a face much lined by hardship, long and bitter battles, and the constant wear and tear of his passionately held ideals.

In 1946, eight years after that first meeting in Unity Hall, I became a branch secretary and a full-time salaried employee of his union. I was twenty-six years of age and the youngest branch secretary on his staff, and he treated me with an old man's indulgence. Over the succeeding eight years I had learnt something of his make-up—his sometimes sudden and almost ungovernable outbursts of fury when he encountered what he regarded as injustice, his flights of soaring oratory as he warmed to a theme, his unpredictability. But there was also a contrasting side: his tenderness towards the weak and unfortunate, and his almost feminine sensitivity to human suffering. If he asked your opinion on something and you showed any unease or uncertainty, he had the habit of quoting at you Mr Hardcastle's line from Goldsmith's play *She Stoops to Conquer*: 'This is Liberty Hall, young fella, you may say as you please.'

By that time the union had moved from Unity Hall to Thomas Ashe Hall in College Street. As a branch secretary it was part of my duties to attend on Sunday mornings to meet the shop stewards, to collect the members' weekly dues from them and to listen to their reports. On my first Sunday I was surprised to find a queue, made up mostly of working-class mothers, lining the stairway leading to the upstairs offices. Frank Cluskey, also a branch secretary, who later became a very popular Labour TD, happened to be standing at the hall door, and I asked him what was going on. 'This happens nearly every Sunday,' he told me. 'The Big Man is above in his office hearing confessions.' It was the custom for the members or the wives of members to come on Sundays to look for his help and advice with the things that caused problems in their everyday family lives. This was a form of trade unionism with a broader field of concern than the early guilds or the contemporary craft unions: it was concerned with the deprived and forgotten, the unskilled and jobless, mostly uneducated tenement dwellers whose plight had gone either scorned or unnoticed by both church and state. Emmet Larkin (no relation) in his biography of Jim Larkin commented on this feature of Larkin's style of trade unionism: 'Larkin made his Union something more than an instrument of industrial advance. He made it an instrument for social and cultural advancement as well.'

Seán O'Casey in his autobiography described the impact on him of Jim Larkin's appearance in Dublin as far back as 1908. He heard Larkin arguing that the work of the unskilled labourer should be honoured as a gift and not as something demeaning. O'Casey decided that here was a leader 'who would put a flower in a vase on a table as well as a loaf on a plate.'

Larkin himself in his presidential address to the annual Irish Trades Union Congress on 1 June 1914 confirmed the breadth of his aspirations. 'I submit that the working class have as much right as any section or class in the community to enjoy all the advantages of science, art, and literature. No field of knowledge, no outlook on life, no book should be closed against the workers. They should demand their share in the effulgence of life and all that was created for the enjoyment of mankind.'

Liberty Hall, which was first acquired by his union in 1912, became an outlet for practising what he preached. W. P. Ryan in *The Irish Labour Movement* records that 'Liberty Hall soon became a joyous institution, a place of social rallies and studies as well as affairs.' This was followed soon afterwards by the acquisition of Croydon Park, a house and three acres in Fairview, as a leisure and educational centre for union members. It was opened with a 'Grand Temperance Fete and Children's Carnival', with dancing and singing and games for the children and a band that played all day.

Emmet Larkin has described Croydon Park as the crowning achievement of Larkin's social programmes. It and Liberty Hall became centres for choral singing and practice, for dancing classes and Sunday evening socials, which continued even during the height of the epic struggle of 1913. There was also an Irish Workers' Dramatic Company, and Larkin himself was persuaded on one occasion to take the part of the Ballad Singer in Lady Gregory's *The Rising of the Moon*. His son, Young Jim Larkin, told me about the hilarious outcome. His father decided that there was no necessity to learn the lines, because he believed that in so fine a play they would come naturally and spontaneously to him in the course of the performance. The outcome was that while he could keep going through improvisation, the rest were scuppered. His sister, Delia Larkin, was the prompter, and the performance deteriorated into an argument in full view of the audience between prompter and performer about whether the script or Jim Larkin had the correct lines. The audience hailed it as the most entertaining presentation of the season.

Young Jim also asserted that his father continued throughout 1913 and after to keep in touch with his interest in Irish, in the Citizen Army, in books and paintings, in housing, temperance, sports, the Abbey Theatre, and even in growing crops and fruit in Croydon Park. There is a letter dated 2 April 1914 (published in *The Attempt to Smash the Irish Transport and General Workers' Union*) that Larkin wrote to a seed merchant in Liverpool regarding Croydon Park. It reads:

> Dear Bulley,
> We are running a co-operative Hostel here in Dublin. We have some three acres of gardens. I want to interest our people in the culture of vegetables and flowers and window-box display. The gardens have been neglected for some years. We have vines and hothouses. I myself have not had the experience I would like in these matters. We have two gardeners employed. I want to get good results so as to encourage our people. Would it be too much trouble to ask you to interest yourself in the matter by sending me the best seeds, plants, etc., up to the value of £20-0-0d delivered in Dublin and also any information you could send me.
> Yours fraternally, etc.

In the same book there are extracts from minute-books showing the extreme financial difficulties afflicting the union during Larkin's absence in the United States. One is concerned with the financial drag of Croydon Park on union funds. It reads:

> The sale of the cow and calf was next considered, when the chairman explained the offers he had been made. John Farrell moved and Thomas Duff seconded that the sale be closed with the highest bidder.
> Agreed.

During my own years as a branch secretary, from 1946 to 1955, I reported for the most part to Jim Larkin Junior, known to us as Young Jim, and became very close to him. He was born in 1904, and he spoke to me about the early years and their effect on the young family. He told me that in the first place they could get little of their father's company. He appeared always to be at meetings or going to—or into, or coming out of—jails. During the 1909–1914 period he had advocated a rent strike and had stopped paying his rent for their small house in Auburn Street. A long-drawn-out skirmish developed, which proved extremely unpleasant for his wife and young family: summonses; court hearings; visits from bailiffs; last-minute postponements of evictions; furniture being taken out into the street and then being brought back into the house. Eventually they tried to hold possession by living only in the top part, but finally they were evicted.

When no landlord could be found to rent his father accommodation for his family, they were installed in an empty house in the North Strand by the forcible actions of some men on strike. However, the house was in very bad condition and so infested with rats that they had to get out. Finally they found shelter in two or three rooms over the stables at the rear of Croydon Park, in what had previously been the servants' quarters.

It was at that period that his father began to have his wages (£2 10s per week) sent home directly to his wife. Young Jim explained why: 'As far back as 1912 or 1913 it was his practice to get his wages sent home directly rather than receive them himself, otherwise invariably by the time he would arrive home some or all of his wages would have been given away.' On the occasion of Big Jim Larkin's death the veteran campaigner and labour leader Thomas Johnson referred to this. He wrote: 'Jim … always listened to any tale of hardship and generally helped immediately out of his own pocket or by instruction to his Branch Officials. Very frequently, indeed, he was imposed on by hardship stories after his generous nature became known.'

During his trial on a charge of criminal anarchy before the Supreme Court in New York he attempted to explain his outlook to the court. He said: 'How did I get the love of comrades, only by reading Whitman. How did I get this love of humanity except by understanding Thoreau and Emerson and the greatest man of all next to Emerson—Mark Twain.' He also told them in the course of his defence: 'At an early age I took my mind to this question of the ages—why are the many poor? … I don't know whether the light of God or the light of humanity, or the light of my own intelligence brought it to me, but it came to me like a flash. The thing was wrong because the basis of society was wrong; that the oppression was from the top by forces that I myself for a moment did not visualise.'

During the same trial he was asked if he was a graduate of a college. His answer was typical. 'I am a graduate', he replied, 'of the school of adversity.'

Big Jim Larkin had been elected to Dublin Corporation as early as 1912 but was disqualified from taking his seat because he had been imprisoned on a criminal charge. However, in 1930 he was elected to a newly constituted Dublin Corporation and immediately devoted much of his attention to the problem of working-class rehousing, becoming chairman of the Housing Committee in 1942. The slums angered him passionately, because he held them responsible, among other things, for ill-health and excessive drinking, and he regarded their influence on the quality of life as being worse even than poor wages. He fought especially for newly-weds and deplored the circumstances that could force them to begin their married life under the evils of slumdom; so he persuaded Dublin Corporation to set aside a proportion of newly built houses for newly-weds. These were allotted through a draw for some of the new houses, which were kept aside specifically for newly-weds. His goal was not blocks of flats but separate houses, with civilised amenities for each family. He was very closely involved in acquiring such estate sites as Croydon Park, Ellenfield (Unity Park), and St Anne's.

While involved in all this, he found time to persuade Dublin Corporation to honour the city's debt to one of its famous sons, George Bernard Shaw, which it did in 1946, despite opposition from three councillors, on mainly religious grounds. One of them was Alderman Bernard Butler. On the way home with Big Jim and Barney Conway, Joe Deasy asked him what he thought of Butler's objection. 'Alderman Butler is a very decent man,' was Larkin's comment, 'but he would burn you at the stake for the good of your own soul.'

I have already referred to how Jim Larkin explained to the American court how the truth came to him, as he put it, like a flash. In a long life of dedication to the oppressed everywhere, ideas and insights had the habit of coming to him like a flash, invariably to the grave discomfiture of his enemies and often, let it be said, to the consternation of his friends. He relied by nature on the intuitive rather than the rational. As a result, some regarded him as an unbiddable menace, while others hailed him almost as a prophet. W. P. Partridge, for example, said that he believed Jim Larkin was sent by God to save the Dublin worker from slavery. W. P. Ryan asserts that in Ireland he became mythological and legendary within a year of his arrival.

If his methods did everything to encourage such a belief, and if he took the whip time and time again to the money-changers, it must at least be conceded that the Dublin working-class scene, and indeed the condition of unskilled workers everywhere in those evil days, justified him. His weapon almost always was direct action, and he was prepared to suffer without flinching whatever consequences his methods might entail. His life was a series of forays. He pursued his own visions and objectives with seldom a backward glance to count the strength of his followers. His lifelong crusade won the approval of the country's most respected spirits. These included W. B. Yeats, George Russell, Maud Gonne, Constance Markievicz, Lady Gregory, Seán O'Casey, James Stephens, Daniel Corkery, Sir William Orpen, and Francis Sheehy-Skeffington, to name a mere sample.

When death put an end to his lifelong crusading he lay in state in Thomas Ashe Hall, where four candles burned about the open coffin and veterans of the Citizen Army took turns to stand guard. The queue that filled the stairway leading up to the union's assembly room had picked their way through a blizzard and snowbound streets to pay their final homage and consisted to a large part of the humblest citizens and the poor of the tenements. They were determined to show that he would live on in their hearts. He himself had kept faith. In worldly goods he left behind him a few personal articles and £4 10s in money, the balance of his weekly wages.

Chapter 15

Larkin in History

Prof. Patrick Lynch

In 1885 James Larkin was eleven years old and a casual labourer on the docks at Liverpool. Little did he know then that within three years the word 'unemployment' would for the first time enter an English dictionary. People had been out of work before 1888, but the new word described the collective plight of groups, not of individuals.

Victorian prosperity probably reached its high noon in the summer of 1897, the year of the queen's diamond jubilee. The celebrations seemed excessive compared with those of a decade earlier; but their grandiosity was an intimation of the end of an era. The queen's passing, it was felt, must surely be approaching, and that historic event, a matter of mourning for some, would also be the culmination of an age and of the millennium. These jubilee festivities of 1897 had been an anticipation.

Strange forces, not always understood, were at work; to some these were ominous, to others exciting. Fears and hopes abounded around the crumbling pillars that supported the empire of which the aged queen had been the unique symbol. Indeed Rudyard Kipling, laureate of that empire, sounded a warning in the first verse of his prophetic 'Recessional':

> God of our fathers, known of old,
> Lord of our far-flung battle-line
> Beneath whose awful hand we hold
> Dominion over palm and pine—
> Lord God of Hosts, be with us yet,
> Lest we forget—lest we forget!

Middle-class claims and values had been challenged nearly half a century earlier in the Communist Manifesto of 1848, and the challenge was intensified as unskilled workers formed industrial unions. Radical leaders hoped that the new unions would be used as weapons to undermine the social and economic order.

In these declining years of Victorian prosperity, Larkin found in socialism a new faith, which was to be the inspiration of his life, something broad and deep, nourished by a passion for justice. As he said, 'at an early age I took my mind to the question of the ages—why are the many poor?' His first concern was to raise the dispossessed from material poverty. Victorian prosperity had been for the few, poverty for the many.

From the beginning of his mission, Larkin insisted that the deprivation he deplored was more than material destitution. As C. Desmond Greaves observed, 'he had a vision of a great bloodless revolution from which half-starved, ill-clothed denizens of slums could win a new life that would include leisure and culture.' In his lecture in this Thomas Davis series, James Plunkett quoted from Larkin's presidential address to the annual Irish Trades Union Congress in June 1914 when he declared 'that the working class have as much right as any section or class in the community to enjoy all the advantages of science, art and literature.' Plunkett adds that Liberty Hall, acquired by Larkin's union in 1912, soon became, in the words of W. P. Ryan, 'a joyous institution, a place of social rallies and studies as well as affairs.'

Larkin's vision, therefore, had always been a broad and clear one. In excoriating vice and scorning the spoils of avarice, he never succumbed to despair or despondency. Undeviatingly, he aimed to end the segregation of an underclass and integrate it into civilised society.

The Liverpool in which Larkin grew up had been a world of poverty, disease, and squalor. He was not yet sixteen when an accident left him out of work for nineteen weeks. He spent his days in the local public library; reading was to become the habit of a lifetime. At open-air evening meetings he was persuaded that socialism could transform society; he became a socialist before he was seventeen and joined the Independent Labour Party, confident that his new creed could raise slaves of toil to decency and dignity.

By 1893 'unemployment' was no longer a strange word in Liverpool. The number of people out of work had trebled in a few years. After a brief and disappointing spell in South America, Larkin returned to Liverpool and became a foreman dock porter with a good regular wage. His employers regarded him as a model worker—honest, diligent, and fiercely sober when teetotalism was rare on the docks. He married in 1903, at the age of twenty-nine, and began to enjoy life. Sampling a few of its minor luxuries, he smoked a pipe and bought a good suit and the broad-brimmed hat that was later to seem an extension of his personality.

This comfortable and complacent routine did not last long. The pipe and the hat, or their successors, did survive, but his behaviour was changing, and in some respects radically. At street corners he was beginning to advocate socialism, to sell its newspapers and to revise his earlier misgivings about the value of the unions. Soon he would be convinced that industrial unions of unskilled and general workers could achieve results that conventional unions of skilled workers had never sought. The new unions might help to change the structure of society; the older ones accepted society as it was if they were able to preserve and advance the status of members.

He reached a crossroads in his career in 1905, and then took a decisive step. During a strike, the model foreman joined in action against his own employers. He was becoming an inspiring agitator whose dedicated leadership, captivating oratory and organising ability left him unchallenged as the most prominent personality on the Liverpool waterfront. Trade unions, which previously seemed to him to be smugly satisfied with the existing economic order, could now, he believed, be turned into weapons for changing the world. Militant industrial action might give reality to his vision of the socialist revolution.

He had lost patience with traditional trade unionists, who moved slowly and cautiously, by persuasion and legal reform, to create strong unions reluctantly recognised by employers. Restlessly desirous of change, and disregarding caution and even prudence, the impulsive Larkin was now ready to patch together anywhere the makings of a militant work force to destroy the capitalist system.

Arthur Balfour once said that Gladstone was 'a Tory in everything but essentials.' Larkin had now become a syndicalist in everything but essentials, even if he knew little about syndicalism. He had no use for patient research, careful preparation, or even consistency. Often reckless and seemingly thoughtless, he had an abiding conviction that his creed could transform human existence. One big union and militant industrial action must change society.

Larkin's friend and associate Jack Carney left an account in 1948 of the impression made on him forty-two years earlier when he first heard the voice of the recent convert to socialism. He had heard other socialist orators, but Larkin was different.

> What impressed me most about Larkin was his ability to translate the feelings of his audience in sympathetic speech. One felt that through some mysterious means, he had investigated your personal position and was taking the opportunity of saying for you what you could not say for yourself. His language was not the language of tears but the language of hope ... More than any other man, Jim Larkin taught me that Socialism does not spread by itself because of its own inner beauty or logic or consistency. It spreads when there is something in it that makes it a response to the needs of the hour ... He had an uncanny insight into the worker's mind. He was without equal in the English-speaking world as an organiser of the masses ...[1]

When the strike in Liverpool in 1905 left Larkin without work on the docks, he became an organiser for the National Union of Dock Labourers and enthusiastically began to establish new branches in Ireland and Scotland. Conflict was inevitable with James Sexton, general secretary of the union; Sexton represented the reforming type of union that the militant Larkin rejected. Larkin was now recruiting not only dock workers but unskilled labourers. The clash between the two men came to a head, and in December 1908 Larkin formed the Irish Transport and General Workers' Union.

He had arrived in Ireland in 1907 and found social conditions in Dublin even worse than in Liverpool. Nearly one-third of the population of Dublin lived in poverty. Many were in hovels officially condemned as unfit for human habitation. Water was usually available only in yards alongside the toilets. These dilapidated tenements, architectural reminders of the Georgian homes of prosperous residents, now sheltered the Dublin poor, rife with squalor, disease, immorality, and early death. Larkin's biographer, Emmet Larkin, quotes an observer in 1910 who stated: 'O'Connell Street is crowded with English soldiers to whom Irish girls have flocked from the Coombe and other parts of the city where they have no fit homes ...' and it was the custom for women to board the ships in port and sleep with the crew. Larkin refused to allow his dockers to work on these ships and eventually restricted the practice but lacked the support that he had had in Belfast from a strong, vigorous socialist and labour movement.[2]

It was to be nearly a decade and a half before Frank Duff organised the Legion of Mary, a lay Catholic social movement, to curb prostitution. Larkin and Duff had respect for each other. In 1927, when the parish priest denied the Legion the use of his Francis Street parochial house, Larkin offered them accommodation in his union's premises nearby, an offer that Frank Duff accepted. Larkin fully satisfied the Legion's requirements and later gave them a meeting place in Unity Hall.[3]

It has been said that even if Charles Stewart Parnell was not known for his interest in poetry, the day would come when poets would be interested in him. James Larkin had indeed an interest in poetry, which he often quoted, and, like Parnell, was to inspire poets as well as historians and social and political writers. When George Bernard Shaw linked James Larkin as an outstanding Irish historical figure with Parnell, he was thinking no doubt of Larkin as a leader and organiser. One of Parnell's achievements was to demonstrate the effect of a tightly disciplined party on the House of Commons. Larkin in 1913 had an international rather than a local significance. Wages and conditions of work were certainly an issue, but more important was the right of workers to defy their employers and join the union of their choice. As a pragmatist, Larkin did not declare it as a principle, but it was so recognised by his great opponent, William Martin Murphy.

Larkin had discovered in 1907 in Belfast the gulf between the trade unionism of the skilled workers and the plight of the unskilled masses of cheap labour when efforts to organise them failed. He was not successful in Belfast, but he had learnt many lessons, among them the necessity for organising unskilled general workers.

Larkin in 1913 may have been a syndicalist without knowing it. The syndicalist movement had been active in the United States since 1905, when the Industrial Workers of the World was set up in Chicago. Labour activity in Ireland may have suggested a movement resembling syndicalism, but such activities owed nothing to syndicalist theory. As the historian Dermot Keogh has demonstrated, Larkin the man rather than any theorist explained what happened in Belfast in 1907 and Dublin in 1913. In 1913 Larkin may have failed to win immediate rewards, but he demonstrated to the world that he could organise the unskilled working class into a defiant force. This was the international dimension of 1913;

inevitably its significance seemed diminished by the political consequences of the Easter Rising of 1916, which, leading to Irish independence, placed more emphasis on national achievement than on working-class aspirations.

In 1911 Larkin launched the *Irish Worker and People's Advocate*. In a short time this paper had reached a circulation more than four times that of Arthur Griffith's *Sinn Féin*. Edited and mainly written by Larkin, the *Irish Worker* pursued the cause of 'one big union,' much as the syndicalists had.

By 1913 the Irish Transport and General Workers' Union, which Larkin had formed in 1908 after he had broken with the National Union of Dock Labourers, was the largest and most militant Irish union, but its membership was greatly reduced and its finances weakened by the defeat in the strike and lock-out of 1913. In October 1914 Larkin began a speaking tour of the United States. He was physically and emotionally drained after his epic efforts in Dublin; but soon after his arrival in New York he was again active and embarking on implacable opposition to the First World War. This was to be one of the two causes he supported consistently during his stay of nearly nine years in the United States.

The second cause was his unqualified support for the Russian Revolution. He was now an international socialist, supporting labour disputes to interrupt American economic aid for the British war effort. He played many parts during these nine years in the United States: union organiser, Irish propagandist, lecturer, member of the Socialist Party of the United States, a founder of the American Communist Party, and political prisoner in Sing Sing.

He became a close observer of American life. In speeches, journalism and particularly in the astonishing conduct of his own defence at his trial for criminal anarchy in April 1920, he reveals a convincing familiarity with the character and traditions of America. This was the America so vividly evoked in the novels of Theodore Dreiser, a rapidly expanding country with its meretriciously commercial society, its skyscrapers, railroads, stocks, bonds, vast riches and squalid poverty. But, like Dreiser's America, Larkin's was a vision of a country of great potential and immense bounty, the country he admired, the America of Abraham Lincoln, Walt Whitman, Ralph Waldo Emerson, of those for whom the evolution of the United States offered an expectation not of the pursuit of money and mammon but a land of promise and reward for all.

There was much to eradicate from the squalor of contemporary America, but there was also the unrealised beauty of the modern city and flourishing countryside to be shared by those at present doomed to drudgery. Larkin's vision had no place for a futile and romantic return to pre-industrial fantasy. Like characters in Dreiser's novels, he knew that history may oppress men and women but it can also be an expression of them, that men and women create and change history.

Marx found a pattern in history where variations in the modes of production lead to new social groups, whose cultural values are shaped by these material changes. The English economic system in the nineteenth century, inherited from the industrial revolution, was for Marx approaching the end of economic change and leading to the dictatorship of the proletariat. It is doubtful whether James Larkin ever accepted such a doctrine or, indeed, any rigid variation of it. Class conflict, yes; but he wanted a sharing of the fruits of production, not the social domination of any one class. As he never pretended to be a theoretician, and as there was no rigorous consistency in his beliefs, there were often contradictions in them and in his unrehearsed declarations. But his ultimate objective was never in doubt: social justice.

One learns little of his character and spirit by enquiring whether or not he was an economic determinist. His biographer records that Larkin had a strong dislike of the abstract, of the self-appointed interpreters of the Marxist holy writ, and that 'he denounced the Communist Party because of the love of its leaders for long words and abstract reasoning that went over the brows of the masses.'

What Larkin was determined to change was a society of the few who had, and the masses who were condemned to live and die in poverty unless they were aroused and inspired to obtain their rightful inheritance. Larkin was not alone in his generation, or indeed in a later one, in seeing prospects for human advance in the great Russian Revolution of 7 November 1917. He was heartened ten days later when, as he saw it, Lenin and his small band of followers had achieved a successful socialist revolution in the most backward country in Europe. More than a century earlier the poet William Wordsworth had hailed another revolution with his declaration that 'bliss was it in that dawn to be alive; but to be young was very heaven.'

Larkin's radical temperament impelled him to intemperate outbursts against those who failed unreservedly to welcome the new Jerusalem of Soviet Bolshevism. Events in Russia had captured his imagination; his idealism was not to be restrained by lack of knowledge.

By the end of the world war, in November 1918, he was a leading member of the American communist movement. The new left-wing Boston paper *Revolutionary Age* reported social disruption spreading across Europe. On 2 February 1919 Larkin was the main speaker in Boston at a meeting marking the memory of the German communists Karl Liebknecht and Rosa Luxemburg, who had been killed by government forces in Berlin. He aroused the indignation of the *New York Times* by stating that Russia was the only place where men and women could be free, and incited that paper to comment that it was the ability of a kind and the moving eloquence with which he is credited that made Mr Larkin so dangerous.

Throughout 1919 the United States had the most serious strikes in its history. The strikes had no political significance; as an expression of nationwide dissatisfaction with the prevailing economic order, however, they were feared by conservative groups as part of a communist plan for the overthrow of society. In characteristic rhetoric, and words of a familiar vocabulary, Larkin denounced the investigators of the social disruption as 'microbes of society', 'men with the minds of an amoeba' and 'a body with the vile odour of the skunk.' By the end of 1919 he and others were being charged with criminal anarchy.

In the trial, defending himself, Larkin, according to his biographer, 'gave one of the finest of those remarkable virtuoso performances of which he was so capable.' But it was all to no avail. Found guilty, he was sent to Sing Sing for nearly three years. Early in 1923 the new Governor of New York, Alfred E. Smith, granted him a free pardon, and in April he was deported for Ireland from Ellis Island on the *Majestic*. His friend Jack Carney had signed on the same ship as a French chef, but when the absence of his credentials as a chef was exposed, he ended up stoking the boilers.

In character, but unexpectedly, Larkin dramatically arrived in Dublin five hours after the cease-fire in the Civil War, on 30 April 1923. He urged his audiences, not always successfully, to end the Civil War and concentrate on a constitutional struggle. Meanwhile a clash with William O'Brien led eventually to a final split and a destructive fissure in the labour movement. The conflict between O'Brien and Larkin had roots deeper than personal antagonisms or differences about union organisation. For Larkin, a trade union was now a militant revolutionary weapon; for O'Brien, the traditionalist, it was a conventional means of achieving reform.

In May 1924 James Larkin left Dublin for Moscow to represent Ireland on the Communist International at its Fifth Congress. He was already well known to the Soviet leaders; Lenin had praised him in 1913, and Zinoviev, first in the communist hierarchy after Lenin, had congratulated him in 1922 when he was temporarily released from jail in the United States. In July 1924 he was elected to the Executive Committee of the International and on returning to Dublin was welcomed in the Mansion House as one of the twenty-five commissars ruling the world. His private sense of humour must have been aroused by the additional announcement that he had been appointed an officer of the Red Army. As far as Dublin was concerned, this was illusory; the reality was that on his return from Russia, Larkin found his position undermined through inter-union rivalry. The result was a gradual decline in the trade union movement, aggravated by a worsening in the general economic climate.

In February 1928 he was in Moscow for the last time to attend a meeting of the Sixth Congress of the Comintern. Much had changed in the four years since his last visit. Zinoviev and Trotsky had been banished, and Stalin's ascendancy was beginning, but Larkin does not seem to have appreciated its significance. He returned to Ireland, where trade unions were divided and dispirited on the eve of a convulsion of capitalism in the great depression of the nineteen-thirties. Conditions were more catastrophic than his most reckless rhetoric could have described.

Trade unions were diminishing in numbers and funds; the Labour Party was reduced in size and bereft of leadership. Larkin was no longer the outstanding personality, a source of admiration and inspiration; yet memories of his greatness were indestructible and endured. He had preached his doctrine of divine discontent to workers formerly helpless and disorganised; he had aroused a new faith in workers as human beings. He refreshed lives that had withered, and gave promise that their posterity would enjoy self-esteem and confidence.

Larkin had a special love for Ireland. But his message was for all lands where wealth and privilege deprived the poor of social justice, where industrial society could enrich lives denied the fruits of harnessing new ideas, inventions, and technology. Despite the vigour of his speech and the vehemence of his metaphors, he, as he repeatedly asserted, was a man of peace. His eloquence and conviction had identified the condition and fate of the general worker everywhere. Even today, at the end of the twentieth century, a large part of the increasing volume of employment, particularly in the service industries, is made up of lowly paid contract workers with little hope or confidence in their future. Larkin's message is a reminder that workers are likely to be hired and fired according to new gospels of deregulation and the excesses of privatisation. Strong unions are still needed to protect the victims of unplanned casual work as part of the flexibility of the free-market economy.

Many have lamented the wilderness of Larkin's declining years. Decline indeed it was; but all was not waste. In 1928, when he was only fifty-four years old, some detected the beginning of the end. Momentous achievement and international acclaim were now followed by a falling off. Larkin might have argued—but he didn't even try to argue—that the world in which he had fought was being replaced by a nightmarish miasma he had never foreseen.

The great depression of the thirties did not surprise him: he had always predicted the malaise of capitalism. But what followed in a large part of Europe was not the social revolution of his hopes and beliefs but fascism and Nazism; elsewhere it was the supine acceptance of mass unemployment—a new tyranny more oppressive than the old, and the dehumanising reality behind the word 'unemployment' that had entered the dictionary nearly half a century earlier.

By the early thirties Larkin was unobtrusively discarding links with communism as former Soviet friends and colleagues succumbed to the vengeance of Stalin. He never repudiated his past; yet he was now being visited, it must have seemed, by a god that failed. In 1941 he was again active in Dublin, opposing a restrictive Trade Union Bill. He had only six years to live but was becoming accepted as a prophet of the economic depression that was leaving jobless many who for the first time now understood the meaning of Larkin's mission in the years of his greatness.

I first met him in the early forties in the Gaiety Theatre, Dublin, as he smoked his pipe during an interval of Emlyn Williams's play, appropriately entitled Night Must Fall, with Micheál Mac Liammóir in the lead. We discussed the play, and then he talked about drama and novels, mainly American. I later heard him speak at a meeting of the Literary and

Historical Society in UCD, when he could still reach heights of eloquence that brought cynical students to their feet in admiration of his denunciation of Nazism. In the same society twenty-five years earlier Larkin, then a world figure, had courteously corrected a careless student speaker who attributed to Longfellow a quotation that rightly belonged to Swinburne.[4]

In the nineteen-forties, I recalled not the commissar who had once been charged by the Comintern to share in ruling the world; no, I remembered instead Prof. George O'Brien telling me of a meeting of a small dining club in the Moira Hotel in the nineteen-twenties whose members included W. B. Yeats, Lennox Robinson, Thomas McGreevy, Brinsley MacNamara, and P. S. O'Hegarty. The guest was James Larkin, back from the Soviet Union; he held his audience in thrall, discussing with Yeats the contributors to the Yellow Book in the 1890s; and the same evening he told George O'Brien that he admired William Martin Murphy, 'because he was a hard but clean fighter for his own side.'[5]

PART 2

JIM LARKIN
HIS LIFE AND TURBULENT TIMES

Who is it speaks of defeat?
I tell you a cause like ours
Is greater than defeat can know—
It is the power of powers.

As surely as the earth rolls round
As surely as the glorious sun
Brings the great moon wave
Must our Cause be won!

From the masthead of the *Irish Worker* (1911–14)

James Larkin

Born: Liverpool, 28 January 1874
Died: Dublin, 30 January 1947
General organiser National Union of Dock Labourers 1905–1908
General secretary Irish Transport and General Workers' Union 1909–1924
Cork Prison 1910
Parliamentary Committee Irish Trades Union Congress 1908, 1911–1914
Mountjoy Jail Dublin 1913
President Irish Trades Union Congress 1914
Vice-chairman Irish Citizen Army Council 1914
Editor *Irish Worker* 1911–1914, 1916 (Chicago), 1923–1925, 1930–1932
President Irish Women Workers' Union 1911–1917
Convict no. 50945 Sing Sing Prison, New York, May 1920–January 1923
Elected to Moscow City Soviet 1922
General secretary Workers' Union of Ireland 1924–1947
Elected to Executive Committee Communist International 1924
Elected to Dáil Éireann 1927, 1937, 1943
Elected to Dublin City Council 1912, 1930, 1936, 1939, 1942, 1945
Chairman, Housing Committee Dublin City Council 1939–1947
President Dublin Trades Union Council 1944–1945

Chapter 16

Prologue

Prof. Emmet Larkin

In those exciting years before the First World War, Socialism was the most revolutionary element in the European complex. Socialism had posed a threat to the traditional concepts of property and the State since the Communist Manifesto and the Revolutions of 1848. But it was not until the turn of the century that the threat actually became a menace. The increasing economic strength of the working classes, and their growing political awareness were, of course, the obvious reasons for the ferment. More important, in the particular sense, at least, was the addition at this time of a still more revolutionary dimension to Socialist thought—Syndicalism. The blow that would destroy Capitalism, the Syndicalists argued, was not to be struck either at the ballot box, or even at the barricades, but rather where the worker was invincible—at the point of production. When the proletariat, therefore, was properly organized along industrial lines, and led by men who could not be corrupted by bourgeois concepts of compromise, it would withdraw its labour, and with folded arms, serenely contemplate the capitalist collapse. This wonderfully simple technique for the achievement of a very complex end—the Social Revolution—gained a very wide following among left-wing Socialists, and particularly among trade union leaders with a revolutionary bent.

Syndicalist theory developed out of the pressing need to make Socialist thought harmonize with proletarian practice. The roots of syndicalist theory were actually first struck in the pioneer efforts to organize the unskilled worker into industrial unions. This attempt not only produced a dynamic new rationale in Socialist thought, but it resulted in the emergence of a remarkably vital new leadership. The old Socialist leadership had been made up almost entirely of converts from the intellectual middle classes. The new men, however, were almost all strictly proletarian in their origins, and could hardly be called intellectuals. They were self-educated, pragmatic, class-conscious, articulate, and individualistic to the point of being anarchic. Since they had come up through the ranks, they were as confident, as dogmatic, and often as arrogant as only self-made men can be. They were full of the truth of their mission and determined to awaken the working classes by preaching their 'divine gospel of discontent.' Their faith was Socialism, their work was industrial unionism, and their vocation was Syndicalism.

The English-speaking world proved very receptive to these prophets of the new order. In America Eugene Debs and 'Big Bill' Haywood, in Britain Tom Mann and Ben Tillett, and in Ireland James Connolly were the outstanding personalities in this broad movement to organize the workers of the world. The most remarkable man, however, among this remarkable generation of proletarian leaders was the Liverpool Irishman—James Larkin. His accomplishment was unique and representative—unique partly because it was representative. His rich and complex personality allowed him to harmonize the three most dissonant themes of his day. For he claimed to be at one and the same time a Socialist, a Nationalist and a Roman Catholic. It was representative because his career mirrored to a larger extent than did that of his equally colourful comrades those attributes that were the hallmark of this generation of working-class labour leaders. 'It is hard to believe this great man is dead,' wrote Seán O'Casey on the day Larkin died, 'for all thoughts and all activities surged in the soul of this Labour leader. He was far and away above the orthodox Labour leader, for he combined within himself the imagination of the artist, with the fire and determination of a leader of a down-trodden class.'

Born in the slums of a great English city in 1874, like so many Irishmen of his generation, Larkin saw and suffered all that was the lot of his ghettoed class. He received hardly any education, watched his father die of tuberculosis, began to earn his living at the age of eleven, was duly exploited in a precarious labour market, struggled to keep his family from sinking into abject poverty, stowed away to escape unemployment and find adventure, and finally returned to Liverpool to take his place among that vast army of casuals who prowled the docks in search of a day's work. Still, Larkin emerged from this grim reality more fortunate than most, for in these bitter years he found the faith that was to sustain him for a lifetime. His Socialism was rooted deep in his comprehending humanity and in his passionate longing for social justice. As he tried to explain many years later when he was on trial for allegedly attempting to overthrow the United States Government—'And so at an early age, I took my mind to this question of the ages—why are the many poor? It was true to me. I don't know whether the light of God or the light of humanity, or the light of my own intelligence brought it to me, but it came to me like a flash. The thing was wrong because the basis of society was wrong.'

Before he was seventeen Larkin had translated his inspiration into action by joining the Liverpool branch of the Independent Labour Party. For the next fifteen years he was always to be found in the front rank of militant British Socialists, preaching and prophesying the coming of the Social Revolution. Though Larkin thus early discovered his Socialist faith, he was not to find his work until much later. In earning his bread he graduated from docker to foreman, the youngest on the Liverpool docks. He had not joined the local labour union, the National Union of Dock Labourers, until 1901, although he had been a convinced and militant Socialist for almost ten years. When, however, a strike broke out in his firm in the summer of 1905, he walked out with the men and soon emerged as their leader. The strike was bitterly fought, and when the men lost Larkin was appointed organizer for the National Union. His first assignment, which he successfully completed within a year, was the re-organization of the Scottish ports. Then, early in 1907, he undertook the more difficult task of effecting a re-organization of the Irish ports. He had now found his work, and like all converts to the new cause, Larkin became a veritable St. Paul, in that he would now go and compel them to come in.

In beginning his Irish career at the age of thirty-three, Larkin terminated his long apprenticeship, for he discovered in Ireland the vocation in which his faith and work could find expression—he became an agitator. In the next seven years, until the outbreak of the First World War in 1914, he laboured to build and perfect the most revolutionary labour union of its day—the Irish Transport and General Workers' Union. Larkin thought it was a union's responsibility to do more than merely wring better wages, hours and conditions from reluctant employers. He viewed his Union as a revolutionary instrument with which he hoped to effect both economic change and social advancement. In his mind equality could never be real unless it was complemented by a genuine fraternity. This fraternity was not to be achieved merely by uniting the workers in a common and militant effort to shake their employers and the State, but also by introducing them to those cultural and educational advantages that give the grandeur and the beauty to life as well as the power and the glory. In those years Seán O'Casey could say, 'here was a man who would put a flower in a vase on a table as well as a loaf on a plate. Here, Seán thought, is the beginning of a broad and busy day, the leisurely evening, the calmer night.'

The building of the Transport Union, and with it the foundations of the Irish Labour movement, was undoubtedly the most creative achievement of Larkin's long life. These seven years, however, both in and out of Ireland, were not only heroic and creative but tragic and violent as well. The terrible paradox was that there could not have been the one without the other. In Ireland those tragic features in the narrative—the human weaknesses, the humiliating defeats, the heart-breaking defections, and cruel reversals of fortune were all redeemed by Larkin's sublime confidence and dogged perseverance. Even at the end of seven painstaking years, when his Union was wrecked by an overwhelming combination of Dublin employers, he could only be brought to grief, not to heel. But the insidious crescendo of violence in these years, that was both to be consumed and born again in the First World War, and which seemed to permeate every class, would neither be stemmed nor redeemed by any act of heroism or sacrifice. For those who were most capable of making such an act were themselves becoming increasingly committed to the use of force in order to effect those changes they felt to be necessary for society. James Larkin, alas, was an outstanding case study in a period which itself was merely the prologue to an era where the continued depreciation of reason has resulted in the apotheosis of force.

The epic struggle of the Dublin workers against their employers in 1913 made Larkin an international figure in the world of labour. For nearly six months 20,000 men and women, on whom some 80,000 others depended for their support, were locked out because they refused to sign a pledge that they would never join Larkin's Union or resign from it if they were already members. In defence of the basic right of the worker to combine, the British Labour Movement contributed over £150,000 and shipped large quantities of food and clothing to their beleaguered brethren in Dublin. By his revolutionary public appeals and his militant demands for extreme measures against the Dublin employers, Larkin and 'Larkinism,' at the end of 1913, were household words in Britain. In America too the left-wing took him up in their journals and periodicals as a prime example of what a Socialist of the meat-eating variety was like. Even Lenin was impressed by Larkin's revolutionary posture in 1913. When the war finally came in August 1914, Larkin cemented his international reputation as a revolutionary Socialist by immediately and unequivocally denouncing it as a Capitalist plot. With his effectiveness being seriously limited by the wreck of his Union, as well as the obviously inhibiting effects of the war on civil liberties, Larkin decided to tour America to raise some badly needed funds. When he left Ireland in late 1914 he planned to stay in the United States for only a short time, but he remained nearly eight and a half years.

In the United States Larkin was by turns a lecturer, a union organizer, a German secret agent, an Irish propagandist, a Socialist agitator, a founder of the American Communist Party, and a 'martyred' political prisoner. Two themes, however, dominated his American career and gave a kind of coherence to what might otherwise appear to be a mere rootless activity—the war and the Russian Revolution. During the four years in which the war was waged, Larkin agitated and worked against it. By lecturing, propagandizing, and even becoming a German agent, he did all he could to frustrate the war effort. With regard to the Russian Revolution, Larkin enthusiastically agreed with Eugene V. Debs, who had described himself as a Bolshevik from the top of his head to the tips of his toes. During the 'Red Scare' of 1919–20, Larkin was arrested, tried and convicted of advocating the overthrow of the Government, and sentenced to a term of from five to ten years in Sing Sing, of which he served nearly three years before he was pardoned by Governor Alfred E. Smith in the interests of free speech.

To follow Larkin's American career is indeed to chronicle the decline of Socialism as a political force in the United States. The first world war had seriously shaken the façade of Socialist Unity in the United States, as it had destroyed it almost everywhere else in the world. What temporarily saved it in America was that this country did not immediately become involved, and the Socialist Party did not insist on a 'hard' line in opposition to the war. The Russian Revolution, paradoxically enough, was the beginning of the end for American Socialism. The great event at first seemed to provide a common ground for agreement among all shades of Socialist opinion, but the Bolshevik seizure of power in November 1917 soon resulted in a civil war in the Socialist Party of America. While the 'Reds' were numerically superior, the 'Yellows' controlled the Party organization and funds. By the summer of 1919 the Socialist Party was in ruins, and the emergence of two mutually hostile Communist Parties made a shambles of the movement. Larkin, needless to say, always took up his position on the extreme left, and was counted a 'Red' of the deepest hue. He was, indeed, a man who insisted on his version of the truth; and the price he paid was imprisonment, poverty, isolation and loneliness, but he paid it without a whimper. When he was being deported at Ellis Island in New York in 1923, for example, and an attendant asked about his baggage, Larkin could still reply with a chuckle—'Everything I own is on my back. I'm like the man in Whitman's poem, "Free and light-hearted I take to the open road."'

When he arrived in Ireland, however, he soon discovered it was no longer a land for light-hearted men. A successful revolution against the British had degenerated into a tragic civil war among the Irish. The Irish Labour Movement, pressed by an intolerant Nationalism and an aggressive Catholicism, gave up the ghost of Socialism. The employers, badly frightened by the economic convulsion that had followed on the heels of the First World War, were in a truculent and wage-cutting mood. Larkin had few doubts about what was to be done. The still smouldering civil war must be brought to an end, the Labour Movement must be purged by a strong dose of left-wing laxative, and as for the employers, they must simply be fought—as always. Larkin did as much as one man could do to persuade Éamon de Valera and his Republicans to take up an active political opposition in the Irish Parliament. His efforts, however, to turn Irish Labour in a revolutionary direction only produced in its turn a raging civil war in the Labour Movement. The employers, furthermore, pleading a deteriorating world economic situation beyond their control, and backed by a sympathetic Government, forced their demands for wage cuts on a divided Labour Movement. By 1929 Larkin's power in Dublin was the merest shadow of what it had been, and his influence in the world of Labour was negligible. The Great Depression all but buried him in an unmerciful oblivion.

When Larkin died nearly twenty years later in 1947, most people outside Ireland were surprised, for they had assumed he had been dead for a long time. His last years are a sad testimonial to a man whose way of life was action. Why the fire should have gone out in so vital a man is a question that is as historically important as it is artistically awkward. The answer to that question is also complex. In the early thirties the world in which Larkin believed was disintegrating. The collapse of the old order in the Great Depression did not surprise him because he had been predicting it all his life. The result, however, was not his prophesied Social Revolution, but the rise of a new order, more menacing and more inhumane than the old—Fascism. The European convulsion and its attendant evils were magnified in Ireland by problems implicit in the attempt to consolidate the Revolution recently made against the British. The consequence was that there was little room in Ireland for men or movements intent on perpetuating the Revolution rather than consolidating it. By 1936 Larkin also realized that at sixty-two he was too old to begin again. Circumstance had deprived him of his role, and time would not allow for the creation of another. To a man whose way of life was action, such a sentence was death.

[Reprinted, with permission, from Emmet Larkin, *James Larkin: Irish Labour Leader* (1965), xii–xviii.]

Chapter 17

Early Years in Liverpool

The first printed reference to James Larkin's place of birth will be found in a series of articles published in the Glasgow socialist paper *Forward* by George Dallas, the secretary of the Scottish ILP Federation. In the opening article of the series Dallas wrote that 'Jim Larkin was born in a place with an unmentionable—at least unspellable—name in County Down.' The source of this information was most likely Larkin himself, or a close friend of Larkin, both of whom are quoted extensively in the series.

When W. P. Ryan, an experienced journalist and editor, came to write what was the first history of the Irish labour movement, published in 1919,[1] he drew heavily on Dallas's articles in *Forward* about Larkin and stated that he had been born in the neighbourhood of Newry.

In the 1911 census, the household return for 27 Auburn Street, Dublin, where the Larkin family was then living, gave Larkin's place of birth as *Co. an Dúin* (County Down). (The return was completed in Irish.)[2] It seems unlikely that Larkin, after spending less than three years in Dublin (and absent from the city quite a lot over that period), could have acquired the ability even to transcribe the details on the form in Irish script, in tiny, rather florid writing. It is probable that the form was completed by Michael Mullen, who was a strong supporter of Larkin and a close colleague. He had been born and brought up in the Aran Islands; in later years he was to be known as 'Micheál Ó Maoláin as Árainn'.

Larkin always insisted that he had been born in County Down. It may well be that he believed it, if he had been so informed by his parents, who were intensely nationalistic and who may have wanted to strengthen their son's national feeling by assuring him that he had been born in Ireland. However, no documentary evidence about his birthplace was ever forthcoming.

This had grotesque consequences. In 1913 a viciously anti-Larkin paper called the *Toiler*, edited by J. P. McIntyre, an arch-enemy of Larkin's (who was to meet his death in Portobello Barracks during the Easter Rising at the hands of the same British army officer who had shot Francis Sheehy-Skeffington), ran a campaign seeking to prove that Larkin was the son of James Carey, the notorious informer on the Invincibles, and that he was masquerading as 'James Larkin from Killeavy, Co. Armagh.' In the issue for 17 January 1914 there is a letter from 'An Old Kildare Farmer' citing how alike the two men were. 'Six of us [old men from Kilcock] who knew James Carey well, and who knew all his relatives in the locality went to see Larkin, and whether he is Carey's son or not, without a doubt he has the Carey eye ... Everyone who has seen Larkin in this locality and who is old enough to remember Jim Carey are fully convinced that Larkin is his son.'

Those who were hostile to Larkin referred to him as the 'English agitator'. Obviously Larkinites countered this by insisting on his Irish birth.

Twice in the course of his evidence to the New York Supreme Court in 1920 Larkin referred to his birth in Tanniharry, County Down (this is how the court reporter recorded the place-name). There is a townland called Tamnaharry in south County Down, near Newry. There is no question but that Larkin's father came from Lower Killeavy in south County Armagh and his mother from the Burren in south County Down.

In *The Attempt to Smash the Irish Transport and General Workers' Union*, issued by the ITGWU in 1924, it is stated categorically in the introduction (assumed to have been written by William O'Brien) that 'his [Larkin's] birth certificate shows that he was born on May 2, 1879, at No. 2 Court, Back Berry Street, Liverpool.' This birth certificate clearly was of another James Larkin, and this should have been obvious to the writer if he possessed the certificate. At the hearing of his legal action against the ITGWU in 1924, Larkin denied that he had been born in Liverpool but accepted that he had been 'registered and christened' there; this we now know to have been correct. Larkin's statement is consistent with his repeated *belief* that he had been born in County Down, presumably because he had been so told by his parents.

Larkin's family accepted that their father had been born in County Down, but, tellingly, his eldest son, also James, was to write to Joe Deasy, then preparing his pamphlet *Fiery Cross: The Story of Big Jim Larkin*, that 'as far as he was aware' his father had been born outside Newry.[3] More importantly, Young Jim was explicit that his father had been brought back to Liverpool 'within some weeks and spent all his younger life in that City.' This contradicts George Dallas's statement that Larkin had been taken to England when a few days old, returning to Ireland again at six years of age, attending Byrne School, County Down, for some six months.

In his address to the jury at his trial in New York, Larkin makes no reference to getting any schooling in Ireland. On the contrary, he stated explicitly that he went to school for three-and-a-quarter years altogether, in an English Catholic school named earlier in the trial transcript as 'the church school, Lady Mount Carmel, High School, Liverpool.' (There was a Church of Our Lady of Mount Carmel in Liverpool, to which was attached a school in adjacent Chipping Street.)

Neither of Larkin's biographers, R. M. Fox (1957) and Emmet Larkin (1965), questioned that Larkin was born in Liverpool; both writers acknowledged assistance from Young Jim Larkin in writing their books. It was not until 1980 that documentary proof was forthcoming that Larkin had been born in Liverpool. In the *Irish Democrat*, September 1980, the Marxist historian C. Desmond Greaves revealed that he had found the entry of Larkin's birth in the register of births for the Toxteth district of Liverpool.[4]

Why, it might be asked, had this obvious source not been researched earlier? The answer is a simple one. Everyone had been mistaken about

Larkin's year of birth. Larkin himself, his family, colleagues and historians had taken for granted that he had been born in 1876, simply because that was the year that had been given by various sources. The year was never questioned till the entry of Larkin's birth traced by Greaves showed that he was born in 1874.

Yet conflicting dates had been given by Larkin himself, suggesting that he was not sure of his year of birth. George Dallas wrote in 1909 that Larkin was then some thirty-two years old, indicating that he was born in 1877. Larkin was married in September 1903, and the entry in the register gives his age as twenty-seven, implying that he was born about 1876. The 1911 census return gave his age as thirty-one, suggesting that he was born about 1880. (This figure is in a different handwriting from the other entries—probably Larkin's own.) In court in New York in 1920 Larkin gave evidence that he was born 'about 1878' and later that he was forty-two years of age, inferring that he had been born in 1878.

Fox in his biography and Emmet Larkin in his authoritative work did not call into question Larkin's year of birth as 1876. This also was the year inscribed on Larkin's gravestone in Glasnevin Cemetery and on the Larkin statue in O'Connell Street, Dublin, which was unveiled by the President of Ireland, Dr Patrick Hillery, in 1979. (This has since been corrected.)

A copy of Larkin's birth certificate was on display at the SIPTU 'Tribute to James Larkin' exhibition in the National Library, Dublin, in 1997. The details given are:

Born	February 4, 1874, 41 Combermere Street, Liverpool
Name of father	James Larkin
Name of mother	Mary Ann Larkin formerly McNulty
Occupation of father	Forge laborer
Informant	X mark. Bernard Larkin, occupier 41 Cumbermere Street, Toxteth Park
When registered	Eleventh March 1874

Also on display at the exhibition was a photocopy of the entry on page 632 of the baptismal records for 1874 of St Patrick's Church, Park Road, Toxteth, Liverpool. An English translation of the Latin entry reads:

In the year 1874 on the 28th day of January was born and in the year 1874 on the 4th day of February was baptised James Larkin.
Son of James and Mary Larkin (nee McAnulty), married.
By me Edward Garthale Pro reat Misc
No godfather Godmother Anna McAteer

Both the birth certificate and the baptismal record give a single Christian name, James.[5] However, James Larkin's marriage certificate gives the names James Joseph, and when arraigned in New York he was charged under the name James Joseph Larkin.

It will be noted that there is a discrepancy between the date of birth given in the baptismal record (28 January) and that in the birth certificate

(4 February). This is probably explained by the fact that James Larkin's grandfather, Bernard, who was illiterate, gave the date of the baptism when registering the birth on 11 March. It seems certain that the date of Larkin's birth was 28 January, as given in the baptismal record.

There is an account of Larkin's schooldays in Liverpool in the autobiography of his socialist colleague and friend Fred Bower, *Rolling Stonemason* (1936). The Protestant school Bower attended was near a Catholic school. On St Patrick's Day and on 12 July, while their fathers, Orangemen and Catholics, fought real gory battles in deeply sectarian Liverpool in the last decades of the nineteenth century, their sons had their battles too. Bower relates that after school the boys from the two schools would charge each other with sticks and stones. The leader of the Catholic boys was 'a tall raw-boned Liverpool-born son of an Irishman.' 'Let that tall leader catch me by myself,' wrote Bowers, 'and I went through it. Two marks I will carry to the grave where he cut my head open, or rather the skin that covers it.'

The 'Liverpool-born son of an Irishman' was James Larkin. Later in life the two men joined the local Socialist Party and became the best of comrades. When the Liverpool Anglican Cathedral was being built, Fred Bower thought up the idea of burying a message for posterity at the point where the foundation-stone was to be laid by King Edward VII on 19 July 1904. The two men got a piece of tin and compressed a copy of the *Clarion* and the *Labour Leader* of 24 June 1904, with a note written by Fred Bower, '*To the finders, hail!*' The note read:

We the wage slaves employed on the erection of this cathedral, to be dedicated to the worship of the unemployed Jewish carpenter, hail ye! Within a stone's throw from here, human beings are housed in slums not fit for swine. This message, written on trust-produced paper with trust-produced ink, is to tell ye how we of to-day are at the mercy of trusts. Building fabrics, clothing, food, fuel, transport, are all in the hands of money-mad, soul-destroying trusts. We can only sell our labour power, as wage slaves, on their terms. The money trusts to-day own us. In your own day, you will thanks to the efforts of past and present agitators for economic freedom, own the trusts. Yours will indeed, compared to ours of to-day, be a happier existence. See to it, therefore, that ye, too, work for the betterment of all, and so justify your existence by leaving the world the better for your having lived in it. Thus and thus only shall come the Kingdom of 'God' or 'Good' on Earth. Hail, Comrades, and—Farewell.

This was the ideal by which both men lived throughout their long lives.

When Larkin went over to Liverpool to bury his mother, Bower joined him at the cemetery. 'Never had a mother such a worshipping son,' commented Bower. 'As we came from the cemetery we sat together. Not a word was spoken, but I sensed his hurt.' Fred Bower contributed eight articles and three poems to the *Irish Worker* between 1911 and 1914. In

October 1914, when Larkin was sailing to America from Liverpool, Bower was again visited by Larkin, who stayed his last night in Britain with him.

Larkin had a good deal to say about his early years in Liverpool when he conducted his own defence during his trial in New York in 1920. He recounted details of his working life, going to work as a half-timer at the age of seven, a full-timer at eleven, spending altogether in school three-and-a-quarter years, working at many occupations, travelling a great deal in England and Wales. At thirteen (in fact probably fifteen) he had shipped out from Liverpool in the American full-rigged ship *A. G. Ropes* and plied the seas both in sailing-ships and steamers. He joined the American cruiser *Boston*, going around Rio de Janeiro in 1901 or 1902, worked on the *Tallahassie* from Buenos Aires backwards and forwards to ports in the United States, Newport News, Norfolk, and Galveston, returned to England, and again went to work along the docks in Liverpool.

From the age of nine, he told the court (in fact probably eleven), he had carried a card in the Social Democratic Federation; with Jack Jones he joined the Independent Labour Party at Bradford in 1893,[6] and up to 1905 he was actively engaged in propagating socialism and agitating against the Boer War.

Later, in his submission to the jury, he spoke eloquently and movingly of the poverty he had seen when a young man in Liverpool. The following are extracts from the transcript of the trial:

In an English Catholic school, a poverty-stricken school, I was taught the truth of eternal justice and that the brotherhood of man was a true and living thing, and the fear of God was a thing that ought to cover all my days and also control my actions.

And then I had occasion to go out in the world and found there was no fatherhood of God, and there was no brotherhood of man, but every man in society was compelled to be like a wolf or a hyena, trying to tear down the other man that he might gain an advantage either by the other man's suffering or the other man's sorrow, or, which was more important, the sorrow of his wife, the sorrow of his daughter, the sorrow of his children.

Let me talk to you for a moment about what I saw as a boy, and I have been engaged in community service for many years. I joined the Socialist Party when I was nine years old. I have been a member of a labour union since I was thirteen years old. I have always taken my place as far as I could in the battle front of the world of labour as against the aggressor, and I had occasion to join what was called the Civic Community in Liverpool. Dr. Root, an American, is one of the men who controlled it.

[Its members' function] was to go down in the slums of Liverpool. I and two of these people one night went down into Christian Street [off London Road] into one of those subterranean dwellings they have in Liverpool, down below the earth, where people who were born in the image of God and His likeness were drawn down by this economic vortex and driven into this damnable hell down below, driven out of the light of day into these dens that have no back ground at all, but only have an entrance to get in.

137

It was dark, bitterly dark. We passed into the first orifice and then the next, and then we heard a moan, and we looked through and saw nothing it was so dark, and I went out and got a candle and came back, and lit the candle, and then we found it. In the corner lay the body of a woman, and on its dead breast is the figure of a child about two months old, sucking, trying to get the life blood out of the breast of the dead woman. And then there were two little girls, one seven years old, and one of nine, and that was in the year 1902, in the City of Liverpool, in a Christian City, in a street called Christian—Christian Street, and Christian people; and they foully murdered that mother and they left these three children to march with the world, and none in that city of a million people cared about that mother or about her children; and even God sent no one down to the gloom, except inasmuch as he sent us, and we were there to see them.

I saw the streets in Liverpool where the women of our class, daughters of the working class, were out on the street selling their body to lustful brutes, earning the price that they might eat bread; and I saw these women manipulated and controlled and exploited by the forces that ruled the City of Liverpool, some of the most respectable citizens were controlling that industry, and took the product in the brothels around the district.

And so at an early age, I took my mind to this question of the ages—why are the many poor? It was true to me. I don't know whether the light of God or the light of humanity, or the light of my own intelligence brought it to me, but it came to me like a flash. The thing was wrong because the basis of society was wrong; that the oppression was from the top by forces that I myself for a moment did not visualize.[7]

The only other source of information about Larkin's boyhood and youth is to be found in George Dallas's articles in *Forward* in 1909, which were drawn upon by Ryan, Fox and Emmet Larkin in their books. The first three of the four articles, dealing with Larkin's early years, are reprinted at the end of this chapter.

W. P. Ryan, a Gaelic scholar, remarks that the Irish literature of the Middle Ages was rich in stories of weird and wondrous voyages, but that in all that wealth of tale there is nothing like the realism of the eventful voyage of Larkin as he recounted it to George Dallas.

Eric Taplin deals in chapter 3 with Larkin's activities in the trade union movement in Liverpool in the early years of the century. He relates how Larkin's compelling oratory, his infectious enthusiasm, his determination, his fearlessness and his devotion to the men on strike transformed him from the model foreman into the militant leader of men, known throughout the Liverpool waterfront. He further points out how the man who 'had previously regarded trade unionism as little more than a reformist tool within capitalism was now converted to the vision of organising all workers into unions to crusade against capitalist exploitation and, through militant industrial solidarity, to forge the socialist revolution. It was a vision that remained with him throughout his subsequent career.'

In the course of this transformation, Larkin—as James Sexton, the general secretary of the National Union of Dock Labourers, wrote in his autobiography—was 'to crash upon the British public with the devastating force and roar of a volcano exploding without even a preliminary wisp of smoke. He swept down upon us, indeed, with the startling suddenness of the eruption of Mont Pele, and, proportionately, his activities were hardly less serious in their results.' (The volcanic eruption of Mont Pele in 1902 destroyed Saint-Pierre, the capital of Martinique, killing all but one of its thirty thousand inhabitants.)

Larkin's life history

George Dallas

Jim Larkin was born in a place with an unmentionable—at least unspellable—name in County Down some 32 years ago. He was taken across to England when a few days old, and sent to school before his third birthday. Returned to Ireland again at six years of age, attended Byrne School, County Down, for some six months—returned to Liverpool at the expiration of the six months referred to, and immediately started to work. He carried milk morning and evening; and all day on Saturday worked in a butcher's shop. The proprietor, who was a strict Wesleyan, would not allow any work to be done by any of his family on a Sunday (he termed it the Sabbath). For the better carrying out of this principle he had a glass window inserted in a wall which separated the shop from the living apartments, so that he and his sons might retire at 12 on Saturday nights, and be able to watch through this window the three wage slaves working in the shop until two and three o'clock on Sunday morning.

For working some 40 hours per week (part of the time engaged in chopping up fat at 2d. per lb. to mix among the suet sold at 8d. per lb.) young Larkin received 2/6 per week, and 1d. currant bun and glass of milk on Saturday night. These early experiences are responsible for what some of the respectable Trade Union leaders call Larkin's want of tact.

He suffered some 18 months' torture with this Christian, and during this time passed the necessary standards at school. He was then just 9 years old, but being a big boy for his age, he started as a full-timer with a jobbing painter and paper-hanger, who, although one of the best men in Liverpool at this business, was a confirmed drunkard, and his weakness was Larkin's opportunity. The lad had arranged to accept three shillings as wages as an apprentice. During the first few months his wages were risen twice, and had reached 9/– per week. Owing to his master's periodic drinking, Larkin had perforce to do, not only gurresic work, colouring ceilings, hanging paper, etc., but became a fairly good brush hand. On three or four occasions he had to make up the wages, and saw that his 'boss' had been charging the full standard rate of $8\frac{1}{2}$d. per hour for him. He demanded half the wages charged, also 6d. per hour overtime. This was his first successful strike as a worker.

He then joined the S.D.F. (at that time Jack Jones, now of West Ham, and Tom Jennings were the leading lights), and came to the conclusion that he was doing a man out of a job. Then he went to serve his time as a French polisher with another religious hypocrite, who (of the same faith as Larkin) would go to mass every morning himself, but would not allow his apprentices to go even on a Holy Day of Obligation. This refusal on his part led to a disagreement. After a wordy warfare which culminated in a fistic encounter, Larkin sacked the boss and took the road for London. During the next seven weeks (like Gorki) he passed through the depths, slept in fields, barns, dykesides—anywhere and everywhere between Liverpool, London, and Cardiff. Was in a lodging house or dossing den in Warrington the night the landlady killed one of the inmates because he would not leave the hot-plate! And all this before his eleventh birthday!

He then went to serve his time as an engineer in Liverpool, and started with 3/– a week with the same firm as his father had worked for for many years. Although he was thus early left to fend for himself, Larkin has nothing but tender memories of his parents. In a recent letter to a friend, he said:

My father was one of the best men I have ever known, one of nature's gentlemen, and who from a boy had been in every movement for Irish independence, both physical and constitutional. I will never forget Michael Davitt coming to Liverpool during the dock strike, along with Cunninghame Graham. My father, who had had no conversation with Davitt since that escapade at Chester Castle, had an appointment with him in Lord Nelson Street, and took me with him. Davitt had been addressing a meeting of dockers the same day, I think at the waste ground in the South end of Liverpool. When they met my father reminded Davitt of some little incident that had taken place some years previous. You know what glorious eyes Davitt had, at least I, who though but a boy then, can still see the fire flashing from them. My father in the course of the conversation mentioned he had not only joined the Irish National League, but he had also enrolled me some years previous, but that I refused to remain any longer a member and had joined a lot of fanatics called Socialists. Davitt turned, and patting me on the head, said—'Let the boy think for himself, Jemmy!' The next time I saw Davitt he was speaking in favour of Hyndman, I think at Burnley. I believed then, as I believe now, that Davitt was a Socialist, but knew the time was not ripe in Ireland to speak out. The only two Irishmen I have ever had a regard for were Finton Lawler and Michael Davitt. I hope the sod lies light on both!

For two years he worked with the engineers, but on a 'Grand National' day, refusing to be implicated in some racing sweepstake or other, he incurred displeasure and with other four apprentices who had followed him, was 'sacked.' He was unemployed for some time, and attended the unemployed meetings addressed by Manson, 'The Lone Scout' of the *Clarion*, John Edwards, I.L.P., and Fabian Taylor, O'Brien, and a lot of others. It had been decided to hold a town's meeting to start a fund to relieve the sufferers from a foreign earthquake. Manson knew the moment had arrived; suggested the unemployed should storm the meeting, and demand that the starving unemployed of Liverpool should be looked after first. The suggestion was acted on, and Larkin had the honour of carrying a bannerette with some strange devices. The outcome of the meeting was instead of a fund for the earthquake, some thousands of pounds were subscribed for the unemployed.

Then Larkin got a job on relief works at 4/8 per day, worked odd days at the docks, worked his passage to Cardiff in search of work, and took his share in open air agitation in the ranks of the S.D.F. One day an accident befell him, an apprentice engineer accidentally striking him with a huge key, and Larkin went to hospital. The young apprentice's father being a wealthy man, paid Larkin's expenses and gave him £1 a week for 19 weeks. This was Larkin's crowded hour of glorious life. Picton Library by day, open-air-meetings by night. Before he reached his 14th birthday his father died, and, as he said, he 'lost his truest and best friend.'

'My mother and self,' says Larkin, 'fought along for some time to keep the house together. We became vegetarian from necessity, and had a fast day every day. Finally I decided to throw up the trade and go down to the docks so that my eldest brother might finish his time. I joined the National Union of Dock Labourers in 1901, and worked at anything and everything; stevedoring, portering, carting, coal-heaving, carrying bags, bushelling— in fact at every job aboard ship and ashore. Things getting slack, I along with a chum decided to stowaway to the River Plate. So I drew my wages, sent them home to the mother, and went aboard. Going down the river that night, we were run into off the Victoria Pier, I was on the 'breakers, and when the water came pouring in, and no way out, hatches battened down (my chum was down the fore-peak); and as the water rose around my knees, I thought my career had closed. But they latterly got the ship back to dock. When they opened the hatches, I kept quiet, and they, knowing I worked aboard the ships of the firm, never suspected me when I came ashore. I assisted in discharging the coals, that they might put in four plates, and after two days' delay, I again took my berth—in the same bunker. This time I had arranged with one of the firemen I knew, to open a hatch during the 12 to 4 watch, so that I might get out. During the following two days not less than 11 other stowaways were found. The voyage out to the Plate was relieved by a little dispute with reference to the grub. By the way, stowaways were not objected to at that time on these boats at all events. They had been used to carrying coals in fore-hatch, and the stowaways came in handy in getting coals out of fore-hatch and brought down to amidships bunkers. The mate, who knew me on account of working at the boats loading them, gave me charge of the crowd.

After we had broke bulk, I called them together, pointed out we had only one change of clothing, and it would be destroyed working coal; they were giving us burgo and molasses for breakfast instead of hash, and those of us who smoked had no tobacco. I suggested writing out our demands, and a deputation sent to the skipper about it. Some said we would be shot for mutiny, but they agreed that an old shell-back named White and I

141

should go. Our demands were—I have the copy before me as I write—'No watches, work from 6 to 6, regular meal hours, same food as crew, each man to be supplied with one set of dongarees and one shirt, plug of tobacco a week, and no work on Sundays.' The captain, Evans by name, was a little chap, and refused point blank. We told him we would work no more, and he replied we would get no food. Knowing some of the firemen, I had them posted, and the first thing next morning, as soon as the sailors turned out and as the fore-castle crowd were coming forward with the grub, we waylaid them and relieved them of the grub, returned to the fore-castle, and had breakfast. Then the row commenced; the firemen refused to work without breakfast, and the upshot of the affair was we gained our point. White and I were sent for by the 'old man.' He tried bluffing us, putting us in irons, get us gaoled on arrival in Monte Video, and then not only conceded all we asked, but granted us also an allowance of 1 bottle of square-faced gin each day. It is unnecessary for me to state that I had no gin, and further I got the crowd to give the gin to the firemen who had stood by us. Before arrival in Buenos Ayres, I was agreeably surprised by the mate giving me 25 dollars, Argentine, worth at that time 1/2.

I remember a stowaway being discovered the morning after we left Monte Video. He was a bricklayer belonging to Liverpool; they took him ashore in a boat, and landed him about 50 miles from anywhere. What became of him Providence only knows. On the way up to Mobile, I again got at loggerheads with the chief engineer, who was always wanting me to assist the greaser. One night about 2 bells after I had turned in, he sent the donkey man forward to tell me I had to take one of the firemen's places. I refused; pointed out that I had been working hard all day at coals, and refused to do any more. The chief sent for me; as I entered the alleyway, I was seized by the chief donkey man, second engineer, and third mate, who with other assistance, carried me into No. 3 hold, and ironed me to a stanchion, leaving me only a tin of water. What a night I passed! The rats came around me in hundreds. *They ate all my finger-nails and toe-nails.* It makes me shiver even now!'

Last week I described how Larkin was chained down below on board ship for mutiny, till the rats ate off his toe nails. He was released the next morning, and his first act was to 'pay back' the chief engineer. For this he was again put in irons. Released at St. Lucea, and lived by beach-combing for a few months, getting 2/– a day from the British Consul for grub. He worked a spell in a smithy kept by a black, who had married a white woman. His bed was in the mortuary attached to cantonments. He shipped from there as a fireman on a steamer. Was in Rio the year of the fever, where his ship's Company lost 11 men, including 3 officers. Upon arrival in Galveston, not being signed on, the captain, an Aberdeen man, had him placed in city gaol. He appealed to the Consul, and during his incarceration was visited by a Mrs. Russell, vice-president of the Temperance League of America, who offered to adopt him if he would change his name. Fell in with Jack Johnson, the champion boxer. While in city gaol four horse thieves, Mexicans or greasers, lay there awaiting an escort to take them to Austin to the penitentiary, the captain, a youth of 17, was the happiest cuss Larkin ever met, singing all day, although he had been sentenced to 44 years' imprisonment.

Later Larkin joined the American cruiser, *Boston*, as a marine, which was in commission, and ordered to Valpariso to demand satisfaction for the death of some American sailors who had been assaulted on a tram-car.

Then he joined a schooner trading between the Windward Islands. Then got a job as coal passer on an American Revenue cruiser, on patrol between Galveston in Texas, and Key Western Florida, watching for gun-runners between mainland and Cuba. This was a good job, good pay but the fly in the ointment was a big slouch of a lieutenant, who was half Chinese. His amusement consisted of watching you dumping ashes. If you spilled any he would maul you on the bare skin with his side arms. He met his Waterloo one day, and Larkin was amissing. Larkin then worked his way down the coast.—Pernau, Rio, Santos, and then into Buenos Ayres again, where he picked up a job here and there, got engaged by an American Irishman at $5 a day, along with some others, to take a gun in the revolution to overturn the Government. He helped to overturn a few tram-cars to make a barricade, fired a few shots in the atmosphere, though supposed to be at the vigilantes; in fact, enjoyed himself until, as he says, 'it got too warm for our crowd, so a few of us walked into the Cathedral, and forgot our deadly weapons. Mine was a Snider rifle, more dangerous to me than anybody else, and then I skinned out for Eusanada up to Rosario, and back to Compagru, and joined a four-masted schooner, and worked back to the gulf, landed at Port Levine, and then into Galveston, when I got a job on a lighter, shipping cotton from Houston, witnessed the lynching of a notorious gambler while in Galveston. A real bad man, as they call them, chummed up with a bum named Toommay of Phil., who I found was writing letters to Congressmen asking for assistance, etc.; he made something like a thousand dollars while I was with him. I then jumped freights from Houston, until I arrived in Boston. There joined No. 2 Branch of the longshoremen's Union, and worked the blind badger for a few moons. Things being bad, I bent my way to Newport, Maryland, and shipped for home.'

Before this he attended a meeting of the Socialist Party of America. Ben Harriman was the big gun. Father Hagarty was just coming to the front. He also heard Dan De Leon, who was still playing the Trade Union ticket, but was arrested shortly afterwards.[8]

Chapter 18

Belfast in Revolt

On 20 January 1907 a delegate to the first annual conference of the Labour Party, successor to the Labour Representation Committee, arrived on the Belfast Steamship Company steamer from Liverpool and came down the gangplank at the cross-channel quays near the Queen's Bridge in Belfast. He was described as distinctive in appearance, like a 'big burly docker from Liverpool or London,' dressed in 'a fading greatcoat' and 'big rimmed hat.' When he spoke it was in the 'approved manner of an English slum.'

As a rank-and-file delegate to the conference, which was being attended by James Keir Hardie, Ramsay MacDonald, Arthur Henderson, and other leaders of the newly formed party, there was no immediate reason to single him out from many others.

This, in summary, is how John Gray in his book *City in Revolt: James Larkin and the Belfast Dock Strike of 1907* (1985) describes the arrival in Ireland of James Larkin, for that is who the obscure delegate was. The national organiser of the Liverpool-based National Union of Dock Labourers, he had also come to organise the dockers in what was then the fastest-growing city in Ireland or Britain.

Thus it was that James Larkin first set foot on the soil of the land of his forebears. He was thirty-three years old. This visit to organise the dockers of Belfast was to mark the beginning of Larkin's mission to the sweated, exploited, largely unorganised unskilled workers of Ireland's cities and towns, the start of a fiery crusade against poverty and injustice in a land where the voice of social justice was scarce a whisper and where the poor were an ignored sub-class, living under the harshest of conditions in fetid slums and hovels.

The events in Belfast in 1907 have been set out by John Gray in chapter 4. That year Belfast was to experience strikes and industrial disorder on an unprecedented scale, clashes between strikers and the police, rioting, something of a mutiny by the police, the introduction of the army onto the streets, mass meetings and demonstrations, culminating in a huge demonstration of 100,000 workers, who marched under the banner of Belfast Trades Council on 26 July in support of the strikers. Throughout the year, over the labour scene, over the city, loomed the giant figure of Larkin, who was to remain in the city for about a year. What was achieved in this turbulent year?

George Askwith, a new member of the Board of Trade, arrived in Belfast on 13 August to attempt a resolution of the industrial disputes that had crippled the city for two months. He went to see Larkin.

He was very surprised to see us, but after intimating that the British Government and all connected with it might go to hell, launched into long exhortations on the woes of the carters and dockers and denunciation of the bloodthirsty employers, collectively and individually. I said all this might be true, though not having been an official for more than ten days, I could scarcely be responsible for the acts of the British Government and in fact wanted some help. Could he tell me what the carters wanted, and put it on paper?

Askwith, in his *Industrial Problems and Disputes* (1920), went on to suggest that since Larkin himself did not seem to know what exactly the carters wanted, they might jointly try to find out. With that, some carters were sent for, chairs got from somewhere, and then all sat down to work it out.

So great was Mr. Larkin's zest on this new tack, and so angry did he get at the carters' differences of opinion and changing proposals, that he did most of the talking, with an occasional phrase from me, and gave them lectures which no employers would dare to utter.

Thirteen years later George Askwith, now Lord Askwith, remembered Larkin as 'a tall man, with long dark hair and blue-grey mobile eyes, at that time wearing a very heavy black and drooping moustache, a large black sombrero hat, and a kind of black toga.' Askwith found him an interesting man. 'I don't know how you can talk to that fellow Larkin,' a Dublin employer remarked to Askwith. 'You can't argue with the prophet Isaiah.' To Askwith it was not an inapt description of a man who came to believe he had a mission upon earth, adding that 'Isaiah must have been rather a difficult person and liable to go off at a tangent.' Whatever his shortcomings with regard to the employers, Askwith discovered that Larkin was adored in Belfast, as he later came to be in Dublin.

The American historian J. Dunsmore Clarkson, purely on the basis of the accounts of the Belfast disputes as recorded in the city's chief Orange newspaper, the *Northern Whig*, concluded that the essential fact was that 'Larkinism meant a revolution in the ranks of Irish Labour.'[1] Clarkson's Irish contemporary, the historian W. P. Ryan, quotes approvingly Thomas Johnson's view that 'the start and stir of life in the Irish labour world' dated from Larkin's visit to Belfast.[2] C. Desmond Greaves, in *The Irish Transport and General Workers' Union: The Formative Years, 1909–1923* (1982), points out that Larkin, 'a vigorous, rumbustious organiser,' had begun his work in Belfast circumspectly enough, even though his activities were accompanied by a propaganda war in which he was 'vilified in every possible way. On the one hand, he was the English agitator. On the other, he was a "papist".'

Clarkson, with some exaggeration, concluded that when the strike was over, its lessons remained. 'Never had Ireland witnessed such a practical demonstration of the "solidarity of labour". The fact that it had been staged in Belfast and in July at that—made the demonstration magnificently impressive.'[3] He was correct in adding that from Belfast the new evangel was carried to Cork and back again to Dublin.

Two myths about Larkin in Belfast in 1907 must be dispelled. It has been said that he led a parade of Catholic and Orange bands, and nationalists and unionists, through the Falls and up the Shankill on the Twelfth. In fact Larkin was not in Belfast on the day, which was quiet and uneventful, though support for the strikers was forthcoming in varying degree at the demonstrations of the official Orange Order and the Independent Orange Order. On 26 July, however, a massive demonstration organised by Belfast Trades Council, some two to three miles long and in which more than 100,000 took part, did pass through the main working-class areas, Ballymacarrett, Falls Road, Shankill Road, and York Street, to the City Hall, where four separate platforms were used to address the masses.

The second myth concerns Larkin and the RIC mutiny in the city in 1907. A detailed and authoritative account of the events concerning the mutiny and its crushing will be found in John Gray's *City in Revolt* (p. 111–36). Sir James Sexton—no friend of Larkin—claims in his autobiography (1936) that Larkin had 'actually succeeded in calling out the members of the Royal Irish Constabulary and holding a strike meeting in the yard of their own barracks.' There is no corroboration of this in the newspapers of the day, even though Sexton claims to have been present at the meeting.[4] It is true that on 17 July, Larkin was reported in the *Irish News* as saying that the police were working eighteen hours a day and were not getting a penny extra, adding that 'if they dared, many of them would also go on strike.' Two days later Constable William Barrett refused to sit by a scab driver on a motor wagon and was suspended from duty. At a meeting of some hundreds of police in Musgrave Street Barracks he had urged his colleagues to 'stand together, comrades, and all will be well.' The headlines in the *News Letter* (29 July) told the story:

BELFAST CONSTABULARY IN REVOLT

MEN DEFY THEIR OFFICERS

MEETINGS AT MUSGRAVE STREET BARRACKS

EXTRAORDINARY SCENES

DEMAND FOR INCREASED PAY

Regrettably, an article on Constable Barrett in the *Garda Review* (November 1974)—stating that 'one of the extraordinary results of the police outburst was the spectacle of Big Jim Larkin marching shoulder to shoulder with the police representatives through the streets of Belfast'— would appear to be without foundation.

Sir Anthony MacDonnell, the Under-Secretary for Ireland, gave evidence to the Select Committee on Employment of Military in Cases of Disturbances (1908) that 'out of a police force of 1,000, 600 struck.' Constable Barrett was suspended, but not before he had been borne by his uniformed and helmeted colleagues in procession to the Custom House steps, where he addressed his colleagues. Large reinforcements of military were drafted into Belfast, until there were some seven thousand troops quartered in Belfast.

The mutiny was crushed. Barrett was dismissed, and six others suspended. Hundreds were transferred to other districts.

According to John Gray, Barrett remained active in politics—he was a bodyguard for Winston Churchill on his stormy visit to Belfast in 1912—and his photograph hung in the Hall of Martyrs in Moscow in the early nineteen-eighties. He died in 1940, aged sixty-five.[5]

Fred Bower, an old comrade of Larkin in Liverpool, was in Belfast during the strike and spoke at strike meetings. In his book *Rolling Stonemason* (1936) he recalls seeing 'a band composed of Orangemen and Catholics marching together, units all in one workers' army.' In the boarding-house where he stayed, the white-haired, motherly landlady said to him: 'Are you a Protestant?' 'Yes,' he said, 'I was brought up so.' 'Well, do you know,' she went on, 'a month ago, I would have cut your throat before I would have let you enter my house. But Mr. Larkin has changed all that.'

On 14 August the *Northern Whig* reported that handbills were posted up throughout the Falls area: '*Not as Catholics or Protestants, as Nationalists or Unionists, but as Belfast men and workers stand together and don't be misled by the employers' game of dividing Catholic and Protestant.*'

Seventy years after the events of 1907 a veteran of the carters' strike, 84-year-old Billy Hunter, recalled to Eileen O'Brien in the *Irish Times* (9 May 1977) something of the dramatic atmosphere of those hectic days. He recalled Larkin as 'a big man, a strong personality,' addressing the meeting on the Custom House steps on 11 July 1907. He told the workers not to fall out over the Twelfth holiday. 'Those who wanted to go to the Field could go, and those who wanted to go to the sports in Celtic Park could go, but not to fall out, under no circumstances to fall out. That was the employers' aim. If there would be a fall out the strike would collapse.' He spoke colourfully about the blacklegs imported from Glasgow to break the strike, of how the strikers and their wives drove them off the streets, and of how lorries were set on fire or shoved into the Lagan. There was a woman scab who lived in the Markets and who decided to take a horse out with a load. 'They put her into the horse-trough at Great George's Street. They gave her a bath. She did not try it again.' He remembered the strikers stopping a traction engine drawing stuff to the ropeworks, by throwing a big heavy plank across the road, blocking it on the Connswater Bridge.

'You could talk to Larkin,' Billy Hunter said. 'You could approach him and he would give you advice. He was a splendid organiser.'

What, it might be asked, was achieved in that turbulent year in Belfast? John Gray concludes:

The Belfast strike movement of 1907 failed to achieve most of its immediate objectives, and the hopes of those involved who had wider aspirations were soon dashed, at least in a Belfast context. That in no way detracts from the importance of the events in the summer of 1907 as a turning point in the fortunes of the northern working class and of the Irish labour movement as a whole.

Considered purely as an industrial dispute, the Belfast dock strike, while of pioneering importance, never directly involved more than 3,500 workers. Its impact stemmed rather from the largely spontaneous and non-sectarian mobilisation associated with it, whether measured numerically, in terms of the daily attendances of 5,000–10,000 at strike meetings and the 100,000 or more who marched on the Trades Council demonstration on 26 July, or measured in terms of action on the quays and elsewhere with its cumulatively dramatic consequences.

In so far as there is a heroic and revolutionary mythology associated with the events of 1907, it quite legitimately revolves around James Larkin. His revolutionary instinct, made all the more potent because it was combined with exceptional talents as a populist orator and enthuser of men, had an immediate and profound impact and ignited tinder where others had failed for years past.[6]

The American historian Emmet Larkin in his biography of Larkin concluded the chapter on Belfast:

The myth that has grown up around James Larkin claims Belfast as one of his great achievements. What happened in Belfast can, of course, be conceived in the most grandiose terms. It could include the destruction of political and religious bigotry, organising the workers for the revolutionary act, and contributing to the dignity and integrity of the working classes. The rub is that Larkin did achieve all these things, but only to a limited extent. He did blend, for example, Orange and Green on a Labour canvas, but the pigment proved soluble in the religious wash. He did explain that he was a Socialist, but his winning better wages and conditions cannot be offered as a laying of the foundations for a change in the social order. He did appeal to what was best in the Belfast workers, but how much their store of dignity and integrity was increased by him is certainly impossible to say. Still, is the attempt to count for nothing? No!— only beware of confusing it with the achievement. In the long run Larkin achieved little of a tangible nature in Belfast, not because he was something less than what he should have been, but because his enemies were too powerful and circumstances too adverse. In the short run he shook Belfast to its roots.[7]

Chapter 19

Founding the ITGWU

William O'Brien, who was to replace James Larkin as general secretary of the ITGWU in 1924, first heard Larkin speak in July 1907 in Beresford Place in Dublin. In his old age he told Edward MacLysaght that he had been favourably impressed. 'It struck me that Larkin was the kind of man to rouse up the workers in a way that had not been done before ... I attached myself to Larkin.'[1]

Within six months O'Brien was to write in his diary for 4 January 1904: 'Irish Transport and General Workers' Union founded officially from this date.' In December the *Irish Times* reported that at the weekly meeting of Dublin Trades Council, Larkin had told the members that 'the genesis of a great movement had been started in Ireland' and that he intended to stay in the city 'to see what he could do to organise men of his own class—the bottomdogs—as they were sometimes called.'[2]

Earlier in the month Larkin, according to O'Brien's diary, had said that while he had always believed in the solidarity of labour the world over,

> it might be that the best way to bring Irish workers into line with the workers of the world was to organise them on Irish lines first. He couldn't say yet whether he would put his hand to the plough—but if he did he would not turn back. In any case he meant to organise the port and docks board men, the tramway men and the shop porters in the immediate future.[3]

It was at a meeting in the Trades Hall, Capel Street, on 28 December 1908, attended by representatives from Belfast, Cork, Dublin, Dundalk, and Waterford—members of the National Union of Dock Labourers—that it was decided that a new union would be set up. Its rules were registered on 6 May 1909 by the Registrar of Friendly Societies, D. O'Connell Miley. The rules were signed by

>Joseph Whelan
>John Purcell
>Thomas Foran, president
>John Bohan
>Thomas Fearon, vice-president
>John Murray
>James Larkin, General Secretary

The American historian J. Dunsmore Clarkson recorded that at its foundation the ITGWU's material resources consisted of a table, a couple of chairs, two empty bottles, and a candle.[4]

Seán O'Casey was to describe the foundation of the union in *Drums under the Windows*:

> In a room of a tenement in Townsend Street, with a candle in a bottle for a torch and a billycan of tea, with a few buns for a banquet, the Church militant here on earth of the Irish workers, called the Irish Transport and General Workers' Union, was founded, a tiny speck of flame now, but soon to become a pillar of fire into which a brand was flung by Yeats, the great poet, Orpen, the painter, AE, who saw gods in every bush and bramble, Corkery the story-teller, James Stephens, the poet and graceful satirical jester, Dudley Fletcher, the Rector of Coolbanagher, and even Patrick Pearse, wandering softly under the Hermitage elms ... even he was to lift a pensive head to the strange new shouting soon to be heard in Dublin's streets ... to say No private right to property is good as against the public right of the people.[5]

That 'tiny speck of flame' bursting into 'a pillar of fire' in 1913 was to make the Dublin workers' heroic struggle resound throughout the world, making the city's name glorious among the cities of the earth.

What was the miracle performed by Larkin's creation of the ITGWU? How did it achieve the impossible and transform supine oppressed slaves into upstanding citizens demanding their right to live as human beings enjoying the fruits of their labours and savouring the good things of civilisation, humankind's heritage of art and culture?

When Larkin came to Dublin town
When Larkin came to Dublin town
When Larkin came to Dublin town
He said the poor have mighty weapons
To fight, to bring the tyrants down.

We are the poor of Dublin town
We are the poor of Dublin town
And where will the poor find mighty weapons
To fight, to bring these tyrants down?

Come follow me, said Larkin then
Come follow me, said Larkin then
And I will show you these mighty weapons
To make you all free working men.

No ship must sail, no wheel must turn
No crane must swing, no furnace burn
And these are far greater weapons
Than guns and bombs or uniforms.

So the sun comes down each dreary day
The sun comes down each dreary day
On tenement but inspired people
Who want, who starve but won't give way.

So come all you good working men
Come join with me for liberty
And we will forge a mighty Union
To break the bonds of slavery.[6]

* * *

ITGWU Red Hand badge

At the beginning of the century, union badges were a significant part of the organisation of dock workers. Dockers being employed casually, and commonly illiterate, membership cards were an inconvenient method of receipting and recording membership, and so dockers' unions issued members with 'quarterly control' buttons. These buttons remained the property of the union and were exchanged each quarter—January, April, July, and October—for the new badge, provided the member paid up arrears and remained in benefit.

The ITGWU, founded by Larkin in 1909, maintained this practice, although some sections, like the carters, retained separate badges as an indication of their entry into the ITGWU from previous organisations. By 1913 the ITGWU replaced the quarterly badge with an annual or bi-annual issue. As emblems the union chose the arms of the four provinces. In 1913, the year of the great lock-out, it happened to be the red hand of Ulster.

The ITGWU issued further Four Provinces badges from 1915 to 1918 but in 1919 reverted to the red hand permanently, in commemoration of 1913. In 1920 the hand was reversed—probably by accident—from a right hand to a left hand, and the slogan *One big union* was added, a style that remained standard throughout the union's existence.

The Workers' Union of Ireland adopted the red hand as a motif when it was founded in 1924, and it remained a permanent feature until the merger of the FWUI and ITGWU in 1990 to form SIPTU. The WUI commemorated the fiftieth anniversary of 1913, and both unions issued seventy-fifth anniversary badges in 1988.

[This note was prepared by Francis Devine.]

Chapter 20

The *Irish Worker*, 1911–1914

In the first issue of the *Irish Worker*, in 1911, its editor, Jim Larkin, declared: 'Too long, aye! far too long, have we, the Irish working people been humble and inarticulate ... The Irish working class are beginning to awaken. They are coming to realise the truth of the old saying "he who would be free must strike the blow."'

Addressing the workers, he told them:

> At present you spend your lives in sordid labour and have your abode in filthy slums; your children hunger, and your masters say your bondage must endure for ever. If you would come out of bondage yourself must forge the weapons and fight the grim battle.
>
> The written word is the most potent force in our modern world. The *Irish Worker* will be a lamp to guide your feet in the dark hours of the impending struggle; a well of truth reflecting the purity of your motives, and a weekly banquet from which you will rise strengthened in purpose to emulate the deeds of your forefathers, who died in dungeon and on scaffold in the hopes of a glorious resurrection for our beloved country.[1]

Larkin reminded his readers that principles are better than persons. 'Stand by your principles,' he admonished them. 'Let them be fixed as the sun.'

> Bide your time, the morn is breaking
>   Bright with Freedom's blessed ray,
> Millions from their trance awaking
>   Soon shall stand in firm array.
> Man shall fetter man no longer,
>   Liberty shall march sublime,
> Every moment makes us stronger,
>   Calm and thoughtful, bide your time.

Subsequent issues of the paper exposed the sweat-shop conditions in many employments. Naming names, it pointed out that men racking vaults in 'one of the richest breweries in the country' got 16 shillings a week for sixty-three hours; sandwich men employed by Allen's Billposters were paid 1 shilling a day; porters at Hickey's drapery in North Earl Street earned 9 shillings a week, working 8 a.m. to 8 p.m. and on Saturdays from 8 a.m. to 1 a.m. the following morning; girls in Jacob's were receiving 3s 6d a week and men a maximum of 16 shillings.

Language crude and direct was used to castigate those employers, however powerful, who sought to oppose the union. As early as June 1911 Larkin had turned his attention to none other than 'W. M. Murphy, the industrial octopus, the importer of swell Cockney shopmen, and Cockney ideas, the gigantic captain of industry, the owner of the advertising sheet y-clept the 'Independent' whose function is to herald forth the necessity for allowing W. M. Murphy to run this little island, not forgetting Uganda, in the interests of W. M. Murphy.'[2]

In the paper Larkin quoted the early Fathers of the Church, including St Jerome ('Opulence is always the result of theft, if not committed by the actual possessor, then by his predecessors'), St Ambrose ('The soil was given to rich and poor in common. Wherefor, oh ye rich, do you unjustly claim it for yourselves alone?'), St Clement ('Private property is the fruit of iniquity'), and St John Chrysostom ('To rich men: Do you not exhaust others with labour, while you enjoy in indolence the fruits of their misery?'). Larkin described himself as 'a man who has more enemies than any other man in this country—a man who totally disagrees with the present system, and lives for the day when there will be no employee nor employer, when we will all be workers, working together like brothers believing in the brotherhood of man, and fulfilling the fatherhood of God.'[3] He claimed in 1913:

> The *Irish Worker* is doing its share in educating the working class to their own want of knowledge, want of class loyalty, want of solidarity, want of earnestness, want of spirit, and their rights which they have forgotten to demand. A new nation is in birth, a newer type of man and woman is being formed amongst the working class; a new era opens out to us, and the *Irish Worker* is one of the instruments to that end—the end being a mutual Commonwealth built on service, a broadening out of the perspective of life, a fuller and more complete life, the obliterating of class rule and distinction of caste—a day when work, useful and beautiful, will be the test ...[4]

Here was Larkin's philosophy expressed. He had absolute faith in the working class achieving these aims, if they would only bestir themselves. At times he may have seemed to lose hope and appear to give way to pessimism and despair but quickly had his belief restored that the workers would take their future into their own hands.

In one of the early issues of the paper Larkin gave vivid expression to these alternating feelings of despair and hope.

> We are living in stirring times. Those of us who during the last years have been preaching the need of organisation in the industrial field have much to be thankful for. Many times we have had to pause and consider—will anything come of our labours?
>
> The apathy of the workers seemed to stultify all our efforts; it seemed that with the advance of education a spirit of selfishness had been imparted and self-sacrifice had died out. Men replied to your appeal for fellowship and brotherly love in the words of Cain—'Am I my brother's keeper?' You whose lives flow on like a placid stream cannot appreciate the temperament of those who, like myself, go down amongst the exploited in the field,

factory, workshop and aboard the great argosies that convey the products of fellow-workers from one area to another. We who are born with the microbe of discontent in our blood must of necessity live the strenuous life; one day down in the depths of despondency, the next day lifted up on the peak of Mount Optimism. The appeal of the fettered and harassed worker, the cry of the poor sweated exploited sister, and beyond their pain, the heartrending bitter wail of the helpless, unfed, ill-clothed, uncared for child, drives us down to the seventh Hell depicted by Dante; and then comes a moment in our lives, such a moment as we are passing through now, when we feel the very atmosphere moving in harmony, crying out in one triumphant refrain: 'Brotherhood one in spirit, oneness in action, oneness amongst the workers the world over.'

It is good to be alive in these momentous days. Reader, have you ever got up on a box or chair, physically and mentally tired, perhaps suffering from want of food; amongst strangers, say a mass of tired workers, released from their Bastilles of workshop or factory; and then suffering from lack of training, want of education, but filled with the spirit of a new gospel. You try to impart to that unthinking mass the feeling which possesses yourself. The life all round seems to stagnate, everything seems miserable and depressing. Yet you want them to realise that there is great hope for the future—that there is something worth working for, if the workers will only rouse themselves. You plead with them to cast their eyes upward to the stars, instead of grovelling in the slime of their own degradation; point out to them life's promised fullness and joy if they would only seek it. You appeal to their manhood, their love of their little ones, their race instinct, but all these appeals seem to fall on deaf ears: they turn away apparently utterly apathetic, and one tramps on to the next town or meeting, feeling it was hopeless to try and move them. You then creep into a hedgerow, pull out a cheap copy of Morris's 'News from Nowhere', 'The Dream of John Ball, Franciscan Friar', Dante's 'Inferno', John Mitchel's 'Jail Journal', or last but not least, 'Fugitive Essays' by Fintan Lalor, then forgetting the world 'and by the world forgot,' one lives.

And then suddenly when things seem blackest and dark night enshrouds abroad, lo! the Sun, and lo! thereunder rises wrath and hope and wonder, and the worker comes marching on. Friends, there is great hope for the future. The worker is beginning to feel his limbs are free.[5]

Larkin's contribution to the production of the 189 issues of the *Irish Worker* that he edited over forty-one months was remarkable. The American scholar Robert Lowery estimated that, in addition to writing one or more editorials each week, he contributed over four hundred articles.[6]

Larkin was assisted in the editing of the paper by Jack Carney, and early contributors included Seán O'Casey, whose first writings appeared in the *Irish Worker*, James Connolly, R. J. P. Mortished (later to be the first chairman of the Labour Court when it was set up in 1946), Desmond Ryan, and Andrew P. Wilson (Abbey Theatre playwright and actor). Larkin's sister Delia was a regular contributor. During the 1913 lock-out eminent writers, including W. B. Yeats, George Russell, Pádraic Colum, Séamus O'Sullivan, Stephen Gwynn, Susan Mitchell, and James Stephens, submitted contributions to the paper. Taking the 189 issues of the paper, one can compile a long list of well-known women and men, or people who were to become well known in various spheres, who either wrote for the paper or agreed to have their work reproduced in it. Such a list would include Fred Bower, Maeve Cavanagh, G. K. Chesterton, Tom Clarke, Jim Connell, James Cousins, St John Irvine, Rev. Dudley Fletcher, Maud Gonne, Canon James Owen Hannay (George A. Birmingham), Sarah C. Harrison, Big Bill Haywood, Thomas Johnson, George Lansbury, Mary Lawless, Peadar Macken, Rev. Vincent McNabb, Michael Mallin, Constance Markievicz, Dora Montefiore, Robert Monteith, Grace Neal, Standish O'Grady, Liam P. Ó Riain, and Francis and Hanna Sheehy-Skeffington.

Essays by Mark Twain, Jean Jaurès, George Bernard Shaw and Fintan Lalor were reprinted, and Larkin frequently included poems by Elizabeth Barrett Browning, Tennyson, Walt Whitman, and Ella Wheeler Wilcox. Connolly's *Labour in Irish History* was serialised in the paper.

At first, nominally at any rate, the paper was run by a co-operative printing company, with Michael Mullen (Micheál Ó Maoláin) as secretary.[7] In March 1912 the Irish Co-operative Labour Press Ltd was founded by a committee consisting of Delia Larkin, Michael Mullen, William O'Brien, and others, but apparently nothing came of this effort to put the paper on some kind of business footing.

Robert Lowery, who compiled a 67-page index to the *Irish Worker*,[8] described the paper as 'an extraordinary newspaper, a milestone in the history of working class journalism, and it is unlikely that Dublin or Ireland will ever see its like again.' Larkin's flamboyant personality, he added, set the tone for the articles, songs and poetry that found their way into its pages, with 'nearly every issue containing something bordering on libel.' As Lowery pointed out, Larkin found himself in court seven times on libel charges in the first year of publication, though, significantly, he never lost a case.[9]

The primitive printing facilities available limited the average circulation to about 20,000 a week. Its readership would have been vastly greater. Larkin wrote that the paper was printed on Irish-made paper, set by hand labour, that the editor got no wages, and the writers were all voluntary workers. Understandably, he boasted that the newsboys who sold the paper received 75 per cent more commission than from any other paper.[10] Almost all the sales were in Dublin.

Lowery described Larkin's editorials as 'fresh and lively and, as often as not, explosive.' He rarely wrote of his own achievements, and his articles revealed a fairly modest person. Lowery concluded that as an editor Larkin must be judged a success. He recruited correspondents from important areas, including Belfast, Cork, Dundalk, Limerick, Sligo, and Waterford, correspondents who served as his eyes and ears.

Lowery commented that 'Larkin the editor was a fair man.'[11] He concluded his article:

Almost all the articles in the *Irish Worker* have more historical importance than literary merit ... Those looking for literary masterpieces will be disappointed. That was not what was most exciting about the *Worker*. Instead one will find the living documents of Ireland's exploited working class whose rage, sorrow, wit, humour and pathos were the material from which movements were fashioned and from which leaders like Larkin and Connolly and writers like O'Casey emerged.[12]

The English historian John Newsinger, in *European History Quarterly*, contributed a thoughtful study of the *Irish Worker* as a help in mapping out 'the ideological contours of Dublin's labour revolt' and in establishing the nature of Larkinism.[13] In it he analysed the paper's contribution to Larkin's mission of discontent, its role 'in the time of dream,' and its attitude to such issues as the great lock-out, the Catholic Church, working-class nationalism, republicanism, war, and the road to Easter Week. From Newsinger's analysis it is clear that the *Irish Worker* was indeed 'a lamp to guide the feet' of Dublin's working class 'in the dark hours of the impending struggle,' as Larkin intended it to be and as he wrote in the first issue of the paper in May 1911.

As on so many aspects of Larkinism and events in the years before 1914, Prof. Emmet Larkin has best expressed the real significance of the *Irish Worker*:

This novel production was and remains unique in the history of working-class journalism. It was less a newspaper than the spirit of four glorious years. To read the *Irish Worker* of these years is to feel the quickening pulse of Dublin. Week after week the sordid tales of mischief, misery, jobbery, and injustice poured forth in a plaintive and never-ending painful dirge. Week after week, while working and waiting for the millennium, Larkin attacked with a monumental perseverance the sweating, exploiting employers and the cynical, corrupt politicians, who in his eyes were responsible for the reprehensible social condition of Dublin. He gave no quarter and expected none as he vilified any and all, high or low, who had the misfortune to come under the notice of his pen.[14]

Workers of Ireland

Jim Connell

Workers of Ireland, why crouch ye like cravens?
Why clutch an existence of insult and want?
Why stand to be plucked by an army of ravens
Or hoodwinked for ever by twaddle and cant?
    Think on the wrongs ye bear,
    Think on the rags ye wear,
Think on the insults endured from your birth;
    Toiling in snow and rain,
    Rearing up heaps of gain.
All for the tyrants who grind you to earth.

Your brains are as keen as the brains of your masters,
In swiftness and strength ye surpass them by far,
Ye've brave hearts that teach you to laugh at disasters,
Ye vastly outnumber your tyrants in war.
    Why, then, like cowards stand,
    Using not brain or hand,
Thankful, like dogs, when they throw you a bone!
    What right have they to take
    Things that ye toil to make?
Know ye not, comrades, that all is your own.

Rise in your might, brothers, bear it no longer,
Assemble in masses throughout the whole land;
Show these incapables who are the stronger
When workers and idlers confronted shall stand.
    Through Castle, Court, and Hall,
    Over their acres all,
Onward we'll press like the waves of the sea,
    Claiming the wealth we've made,
    Ending the spoiler's trade;
Labour shall triumph and Ireland be free.[15]

The Uprising

Fred Bower

Don't you hear the rumbling, comrade,
    Like the surf on fog-bound coast
Hear the rising, rising rumble
    Of the toil-worn Labour's host?
Who are they that preach contentment
    Whilst our babes in hunger die?
Who would pacify resentment?
    Shut their ears to victim's cry?
Yes; we hear the rumbling storm-shock
    Rising ever nearer home,
Rising as each freighted vessel
    Bears our loved ones o'er the foam;
Rising as each broken brother
    Bends and falls to rise no more,
Rising at each groan of anguish.
    Wrung from hearts and bodies sore.
Just a little longer, comrade,
    Labour yet shall own its own;
Soon shall pass that time for ever
    When they reap who ne'er have sown.[16]

Battle Hymn of the Workers

Marcus Kavanagh

Gaze around, comrades, and hearken to the Cause
It is breaking down the barriers of capital's cruel laws,
It is wresting back our freedom from the sweaters' greedy claws—
    The brave Cause that's marching on.

See the workers, grim, determined, as they hasten to the fight—
To batter down the strongholds reared by hated Mammon's might—
To journey back from darkness to the glory and the light
    Of the Cause that's marching on.

They are coming from the factories, sweated sore with heavy toil,
They are climbing from the death-pits hollowed deep into the soil,
They are hastening to the battle, for every man is loyal
    To the Cause that's marching on

From the horrid fetid squalor of the sordid city slum,
Pallid-faced, yet still determined, see the hungry women come;
They too, shall help to battle 'gainst the filthy, sweating scum
    For the Cause that's marching on.

For a weary age they've ruled us with a hard and heavy hand,
For a weary age they've spread themselves like fever o'er the land;
Now at last the battle's joined, and face to face with them we stand
    For the Cause that's marching on.

Why should we let them rule us, this idle bestial brood?
Why should our lives depend upon their every savage mood?
Those dogs who've robbed us of our all—our liberty—our food
    When no Cause was marching on.

We shall smite them without mercy in the conflict that's to be
We shall clean the nation of them from the centre to the sea;
From their greedy claws we'll rescue what belongs to you and me
    And the Cause that's marching on.

Only when the workers stand together in a compact strong
In the holy faith of freedom, in the wish to right all wrong;
Only when the fruits of Labour unto Labour shall belong
    Will the Cause cease marching on.[17]

Chapter 21

Tenement City

'It is something terrifying to see how the people lived in the streets and slums of Dublin,' James Larkin was reported as saying in the *Ulster Guardian* (Belfast) in September 1907.[1]

For the poor, Dublin before the First World War was a social inferno, the slum areas in the inner city a swamp of disease, squalor and death—and degradation. Tens of thousands of families lived in overcrowded, foul-smelling tenements and in filthy, unsanitary lanes and alleys. Low pay and casual labour and long bouts of unemployment meant that workers' families eked out a precarious, impecunious existence. The unemployed had to make do with Poor Law hand-outs and with begging or seek refuge in one of the two Dublin workhouses, which sheltered 6,500 paupers.

The statistics of poverty in Dublin at the time are stark and startling. A mass of factual and survey material on low pay, public health, housing conditions and mortality rates by class is available in reports of commissions and other official inquiries and reports and in papers read to the Statistical and Social Inquiry Society of Ireland.

A brief selection of the facts of poverty was set out in the Larkin Exhibition in the National Library of Ireland in 1997, commemorating the fiftieth anniversary of Larkin's death:

- Population of city: 305,000
- Out of 9,000 deaths in a year, 1,600 occurred in workhouses
- 26,000 families lived in 5,000 tenements, over 21,000 in one room
- 1,500 tenements had been condemned as unfit for human habitation
- One-third of the population lived in the 'slum jungle'
- The death rate was 35 per 1,000 population, compared with 20 in Belfast
- Infant mortality among the poor was the highest in Ireland or Britain: 142 in Dublin, compared with 103 in London
- Because of tuberculosis, the vast majority of deaths occurred among the poorer classes
- There were 3,800 paupers in the South Dublin Union (James's Street) and 2,700 in the North Dublin Union (North Brunswick Street)
- Over $4\frac{1}{2}$ million pledges were taken in pawnbrokers in a year
- The average wage of 18,000 labourers was 18 shillings a week
- In a survey it was found that earnings per family averaged 22s 2d a week, of which 78 per cent was spent on food and rent.

This handful of facts can only hint at the terrible misery of the reality that lay behind the figures. Emmet Larkin has summarised the position: 'From these festering tenements oozed all the fearful concomitants of Dublin slum life. Death, disease, immorality, insanity, crime, drunkenness, unemployment, low wages, and high rents rolled on in a seemingly interminable vicious cycle.'[2] Death, for the working class of Dublin, Prof. Larkin noted, was at least the end of a frightful existence.[3] 'It was common knowledge that O'Connell Street and Grafton Street were crowded with prostitutes,' with one side of O'Connell Street being reserved for 'respectable people.'[4]

The most compelling and comprehensive account of social conditions, poverty, crime and housing in Dublin in the early years of the century is given in *'Dear, Dirty Dublin': A City in Distress, 1890–1916* by Prof. Joseph O'Brien of the City University of New York.[5] Here will be found the details of the life of the city's slum denizens, the hunger, squalor, prostitution, and disease.

In a paper read to the Catholic Truth Society in October 1910 Rev. John Gwynn referred to the streets 'crowded night and day with bands of children, the waifs and strays who had no permanent home or parents and begged and hawked a living from the passers-by.'[6]

Terrible though the reality was, and abundant the evidence, the real disgrace was that the situation was largely ignored by the authorities, notably the corrupt city council, and also in large part by the churches and other leading influences in society. Regularly, the *Irish Worker* revealed the names of slum landlords, and these included members of the Irish Party and Dublin City Council, leading national figures, businessmen, prominent citizens. A veil was discreetly drawn by the press over the city's disgrace. For some citizens the poverty was an irremediable problem.

That is, until 'Jim Larkin came to Dublin town' or, as Prof. O'Brien put it, descended 'like a thunderbolt among the cowed and dispirited masses of unskilled labourers in the city of Dublin.'[7]

On the evening before the funeral of James Nolan, batoned to death by the police in Eden Quay, beside Liberty Hall, two tenement houses collapsed in Church Street. At about 9 p.m. on 2 September no. 66 Church Street, a four-storey tenement, suddenly collapsed, and brought no. 67 down with it. Seven bodies, including three adults and four youths and small children, were taken from the rubble. Fortunately, most of the forty-six members of the eleven families living in the two tenements were not at home at that early hour on an autumn evening: otherwise the death toll would have been far greater. Among those who died were seventeen-year-old Eugene Salmon and his eight-year-old sister, whom he died trying to save. A few hours earlier he had been dismissed from his employment in Jacob's factory because he refused to forswear Larkin's union. A few months before this Larkin himself had been burned in saving people from a fire in Capel Street.

These two incidents were written about in the *Irish Worker* by one of the strike leaders, a member of Dublin City Council, William Partridge.[8] This was one of some seventy-five articles Partridge wrote in the paper between 1911 and 1914; he also contributed five poems.

Heroes led by a hero

W. P. Partridge

The mantle of night had fallen over the busy city. The once thronged street became deserted and silent; the huge business houses whose electric lights had illuminated the surrounding thoroughfares now loomed like giant shadows in the calm light of the placid moon—Dublin was asleep. But out of the dark shadows there crept a crimson glare—sharp crackling noises like the report of small arms, awoke the sleeping echoes, and these noises increased as the darkness faded before the crimson rays.

A man hurrying home stopped before the door of a shop whose windows crackled in the wreathing flames and from the apertures over the door issued one volume of black smoke. Instantly the cry of fire pierces the midnight air, bringing terror to all who hear. Feebly the lone man strives to arouse the sleeping inmates of the burning house; in vain he beats upon the closed door with his hands and feet, striving in vain to burst it open, and as he staggers back exhausted, out of the surrounding darkness into the circle of lights dashes a giant form. The huge form is hurled against the stubborn door, the walls crash, the door is borne inward by that superhuman effort and the tall form disappears in the fumes and smoke within, to return in an instant guiding two girls who have been rescued from an awful fate.

But there is still one life more in danger. Again the tall form disappears in the flames, anxious eyes without see it spring lightly up the burning staircase, and as the top is reached the structure crumbles beneath the hero's feet and he falls amidst the burning debris and lies still. A shout—a rush—and the still form is dragged through the flames out into the cool reviving breath of Heaven. The giant springs to his feet and would again enter the building on his mission of mercy, but is held back by the saving hands of brave friends.

The fire king has won one victim—Ireland has won one hero more. The hero who would have died to save is Jim Larkin, the faithful founder and fearless leader of the Irish Transport Workers' Union, that 'Bloody' Murphy and his crowd of blood-sucking, soul-killing gang of moneybags would destroy.

From the debris of the fallen houses in Church Street they bore the hero's lifeless body—this time it was that of a boy of 17 years who worked in the factory of the sweater, Jacob, and who, through the miserable wages paid by this exploiter of the working classes, was compelled to risk his life in the tenements of the city. A few hours previous he had been dismissed because men refused to betray the hero leader, Larkin, and desert the faithful ranks of his gallant little Union fighting the fight of the oppressed and defenceless of the city.

Young Eugene Salmon returned to the death-trap he called home, and as the mountain of blinding debris piled around him the young hero saved his baby sister and five others of the family. Still one remained, and in a gallant effort to save the child he gave his young life, and the lifeless bodies of both were found where they had fallen.

161

Young Salmon, the hero, was a member of the Union led by the hero, Larkin. He was dismissed by the employer who paid such miserable wages as compelled the poor lad to reside in the pile that was not a home but a tomb. Before God, Jacob has killed this lad. Such are the men who stand in the ranks of the Irish Transport Workers' Union—young Salmon is a sample. Such is the man who leads and directs them—Jim Larkin.

From the martyr's silent grave; from the grief-stricken group of sobbing men, women and children; from the fearless form standing proudly erect in the dock, I turn away. Another vision comes before my mind—it is the vision of my crucified, outraged Saviour hanging bleeding and torn upon the Cross. He preached Justice. He, too, loved the poor. He was spat upon and despised; He was persecuted and crucified. He was crushed by the very powers that now prevail against a frail, weak mortal who, like our Saviour, has fought for Justice, who loved the poor, and has done his best to do his duty.

And I pray to God that it may be my privilege to follow the lead of such a man as Jim Larkin, so long as it pleases the Almighty to spare him to lead; and when the end comes—as it will come for us all—'Bloody' Murphy and the robbing gang behind him not excepted—then I ask no greater favour than I be permitted to die the martyred death of brave young Salmon whose name will live in the prayers and in the hearts of the Irish people, when those who now wage war on the union to which he belonged will be remembered only to be despised.

* * *

Prof. Emmet Larkin has described William Partridge as Larkin's most loyal and faithful lieutenant, who had stated that he believed Jim Larkin was sent by God to save the working classes of Dublin.

Partridge was born in Sligo and reared in Claremorris. He settled in Dublin at the turn of the century and worked as an engineer for the Great Southern and Western Railway at Inchicore, becoming a member of the Amalgamated Society of Engineers. He was dismissed from his job in August 1912 for making a collection for the victims of the Belfast riots of the preceding month.

He was one of the leaders of the Dublin lock-out in 1913 and was twice arrested in August. From 1914 he was a 'travelling organiser' of the ITGWU and later an official of the union at Emmet Hall, Inchicore.

Partridge contributed about 120 articles, poems and other items to the *Irish Worker* between 1911 and 1914. He was active in Dublin labour politics. In January 1913 he was elected to Dublin City Council. As a member of the Irish Citizen Army he stood guard in Liberty Hall in April 1916 when the Proclamation of the Irish Republic was being printed. He was a member of the St Stephen's Green garrison under Michael Mallin; arrested after the surrender, he was imprisoned in England. He was released on 20 April 1917 and died on 29 July. Constance Markievicz delivered the funeral oration.

Chapter 22

The Battle Opens

At midnight on Saturday 29 July 1913 the chairman of the Dublin United Tramway Company, William Martin Murphy JP, addressed seven hundred men of the company's traffic department in the Antient Concert Rooms, Great Brunswick Street (Pearse Street), Dublin. He promised them a pay rise of one shilling a week and a half-day's pay for every man who had attended the meeting. But that was not his reason for calling the meeting.

> My friends—and I may truly call you my friends, because every employee of any undertaking that I am connected with I look upon as a friend—the position I hold to-night, and the occasion on which we have met, are rather unusual. In fact, I think they are without precedent. We cannot disguise from ourselves the fact that an attempt is being made by an organiser, outside the Company, to seduce the men for the purpose of inducing them to go on strike. Well, I can tell you, when I ask you to come here to meet me to-night I have not the least apprehension that there is even a remote possibility of such an event occurring. But I know there are hot-heads—young men, who have very little experience of the world—among you, who might be endeavouring to seduce other people to go against what I may call their bread and butter.
>
> I want you to clearly understand that the directors of this Company have not the slightest objection to the men forming a legitimate Union. And I would think there is talent enough amongst the men in the service to form a Union of their own, without allying themselves to a disreputable organisation, and placing themselves under the feet of an unscrupulous man who claims the right to give you the word of command and issue his orders to you and to use you as tools to make him the labour dictator of Dublin ... I am here to tell you that this word of command will never be given, and if it is, that it will be the Waterloo of Mr. Larkin.
>
> A strike in the tramway would, no doubt, produce turmoil and disorder created by the roughs and looters, but what chance would the men without funds have in a contest with the Company who could and would, spend £100,000 or more. You must recollect when dealing with a company of this kind that every one of the shareholders, to the number of five, six or seven thousands, will have three meals a day whether the men succeed or not. I don't know if the men who go out can count on this.
>
> I have been a director of the Dublin United Tramway Co. since 1880 and all that time I have had the most pleasant relations with the employees of this Company. I respect them as a fine body of men and flatter myself that they have a regard and respect for me ...

About a month later, on 21 August, the following notice was handed to some of the DUTC's employees:

As the directors understand that you are a member of the Irish Transport Union, whose methods are disorganising the trade and business of the city, they do not further require your services. The parcels traffic will be temporarily suspended. If you are not a member of the union when traffic is resumed your application for re-employment will be favourably considered.

On Monday 25 August the Dublin correspondent of the *Times* (London) wrote: 'These are great days in Dublin. The weather continues perfect, great crowds throng the city, and tomorrow what all Irishmen not unjustifiably believe to be the greatest horse show in the world will open with a record entry of stock.'

The following day the *Times* reported: 'It was a shock to most people this morning when they prepared to go out to Balls Bridge, to find the tramway system tied up. Tramcars on all lines were brought in as far as College Green and there deserted. The game began at 10 o'clock and by 10.30 long lines of idle trams occupied the rails for half a mile in all directions from the Green.'

The Irish Transport and General Workers' Union had called their members in the DUTC out on strike. That morning Councillor William Partridge brought the demands of the men to the company and then 'had the honour to stop the first car,' as he put it when he spoke at Beresford Place that evening. At 9:40 a.m. on Tuesday 26 August the trams had stopped; the ITGWU members stuck their union's red-hand badge on their coat lapels and struck.

That evening Jim Larkin addressed a huge crowd outside Liberty Hall, the head office of the ITGWU.

This is not a strike, it is a lock-out of the men who have been tyranically treated by a most unscrupulous scoundrel. Murphy has boasted that he will beat Larkin. What a wonderful boast that was for the mighty man of Gath walking in the fear of the Lord. He said he would spend £100,000 to break Larkin, a man who is going to lead you out of bondage into the land of promise.

They had to get up the RIC and the Buffs [a British army regiment] to Dublin, and the great Scotchman [Lord Aberdeen, the Lord Lieutenant] and the Liberal Government have again to bow at the knee of a labourer's son. They talk about victory and breaking Larkin. Given the intelligence and discipline you ought to have and taking the advice and leadership that I give you, I would wipe them off the street in one hour, and they know that. In Belfast, in 1907, all the forces had to keep their noses clean, and keep behind the four walls. I promise that, living or dead, they will never break me and dead, I will be a greater force against them than alive.

Police brutality has been shown to-night. I advise the friends and supporters of this cause to take Sir Edward's advice to the men of Ulster. If Sir Edward Carson can call on the people of Ulster to arm, I will call upon you to arm. Sir Edward Carson told the people of Ulster that they had a right to arm. If they have a right to arm, the working men have an equal right to arm themselves, so as to protect themselves. If at every street corner there is a hired assassin ready to kill you, then you should arm. I don't offer advice which I am not prepared to adopt myself. You know me, and you know when I say a thing I will do it.

My advice to you is to be round the doors and corners, and, if one of our class should fall, then two of the others must fall for that one. We will demonstrate in O'Connell Street. It is our street as well as William Martin Murphy's. We are fighting for bread and butter. We will hold our meetings in the streets, and if any one of our men fall, there must be justice. By the living God if they want war they can have it.[1]

A mass meeting was called for Sunday afternoon, 31 August. It was promptly proclaimed by the Chief Divisional Magistrate of the Dublin Metropolitan Police District, E. G. Swifte. On Friday night, 29 August, Larkin again spoke at Beresford Place.

To-morrow we are going to issue our proclamation not signed by the King or signed by Swifte. Before I go any further, with your permission, I am going to burn the Proclamation of the King. I care as much for the King as I do for Swifte the Magistrate. People make kings and people can unmake them and what the King of England has to do with stopping the meeting in Dublin I fail to see.

If they are going to stop the meeting at the dictation of William Martin Murphy then I say that for every one of our men that fall two must fall on the other side. If they assault and murder men let them take the responsibility. I hope to hold a meeting in O'Connell Street and we will meet in O'Connell Street. If the police and soldiers stop the meeting let them take the responsibility. We want no men but men that will stand. They have no right under law to proclaim the meeting. You have every right to hold the meeting, but you have been too supine and too cowardly in the past to hold the meeting. If they want revolution there that day, there will be revolution.

The police have said they will take my life and I am going to give them a chance, but in taking my life they will raise a new spirit and a new hope and it won't be a question of paying no rent, but a question of His Majesty, God Save Him, losing another part of the Empire, and the sooner the better for Ireland. I am a rebel and the son of a rebel. I recognise no law but the people's law.

To-morrow night we hold five meetings, Ringsend, Inchicore, Terenure, Cabra and here. We are going to raise a new standard of discontent and a new battlecry in Ireland.

Remember if they are going to use the weapon of starvation there is food in the shops and clothes in the shops; there is coal on the banks. Cheerful homes want fires in grates and a man who is faced with hunger wants bread.[2]

Soon Seán O'Casey was penning an article for the *Irish Worker*.

The whole forces of the Transport Union are wheeling into the battlefield, dressing their ranks, cheering with enthusiasm, deploying to their several places, looking up at the banner that shall never weaken in the grasp of those who carry it, the symbol of their hope—the banner of the Red Hand. Look over in the distance at the army of opposing Generals in their gaudy uniforms, which greed and plunder with deft hands, have decorated. Look

165

at Marshal Murphy with his drum-head courtmartial at his back, with his manifesto on the drum-head draped with the Union Jack—swear away the Transport Workers' Union! If not, then starve!

Have a care, Marshal Murphy. Starvation is not a pleasant anticipation, it is always a difficult thing to starve thousands unwilling to suffer where food is plentiful. Hunger makes men weak; it often makes men desperate, and the ferocity of hungry men and hungry women is a dreadful thing. Other countries have experienced it. Let Murphy take care that Ireland does not furnish another dreadful example of men mad whom the capitalists would destroy.

'That ancient swelling and desire for liberty' is again stirring in our souls. The workers have lifted up their eyes unto the hills. They have no friends but themselves; but in their own strength they can conquer. Their only hope is their Union. 'Sacrifice the Union,' say the employers, 'and all is gained.' Sacrifice the Union—all is lost.

What life would remain in a human body if the heart were plucked out and cast away? We know that the Transport Union is the heart of all our strength and all our hope. We are not deceived. The workers can do as much without their Union as Caesar's body when Caesar's head is off!

'Men, be men!' Who shall stop the onward march of the people?[3]

Meantime, the editor of the *Irish Independent* (2 September 1913) was throwing down the challenge.

It is necessarily incident to the 'sympathetic strike' ordered by the Transport Union despot that skilled workmen may be peremptorily bidden to leave their work. Was ever greater tyranny attempted to be set up in the name of freedom of association? Yet this is what Larkinism means and stands for … If the employers of Dublin join forces to overturn and destroy this attempted tyranny, it can be done in a comparatively short time. It is infinitely better for Dublin that whatever suffering and loss may be involved should be endured for a few weeks at most than that the city should be left helpless in the toils of Larkinism for an indefinite term of years.

The employers of Dublin must lead the way in emancipating the city from the thraldom of the international Socialist disguised as a Labour leader. In fighting their cause the employers will be battling for the real liberty of labour. This will never be until the pernicious influence of Larkinism has not merely been scotched, but killed.

In the *Irish Worker*, James Connolly set out the real issues in the dispute.

Perhaps before this issue of the *Irish Worker* is in the hands of its readers the issues now at stake in Dublin will be brought to a final determination. All the capitalist newspapers of Friday last join in urging, or giving favourable publicity to the views of others urging the employers of Dublin to join in a general lock-out of the members of the Irish Transport and General Workers' Union. It is as well. Possibly some act is necessary in order to make that portion of the working class which still halts undecided to understand clearly what it is that lies behind the tyrannical and brow-beating attitude of the proprietors of the Dublin tramway system.

The fault of the Irish Transport and General Workers' Union! What is it! Let us tell it in plain language. Its fault is this, that it found the labourers of Ireland on their knees, and has striven to raise them to the erect position of manhood; it found them with all the vices of slavery in their souls, and it strove to eradicate these vices and replace them with some of the virtues of free men; it found them with no other weapons of defence than the arts of the liar, the lickspittle, and the toady, and it combined them and taught them to abhor those arts and rely proudly on the defensive power of combination; it, in short, found a class in whom seven centuries of social outlawry had added fresh degradations upon the burden it bore as the members of a nation suffering from the cumulative effects of seven centuries of national bondage, and out of this class, the degraded slaves of slaves more degraded still—for what degradation is more abysmal than that of those who prostitute their manhood on the altar of profit-mongering?—out of this class of slaves, the labourers of Dublin, the Irish Transport and General Workers' Union has created an army of intelligent self-reliant men, abhorring the old arts of the toady, the lickspittle, and the crawler and trusting alone to the disciplined use of their power to labour or to withdraw their labour, to assert and maintain their right as men.

To put it in other words, but words as pregnant with truth and meaning: the Irish Transport and General Workers' Union found that before its advent the working class of Dublin had been taught by all the educational agencies of the country, by all the social influences of their masters, that this world was created for the special benefit of the various sections of the master class, that kings and lords and capitalists were of value; that even flunkeys, toadies, lickspittles and poodle dogs had an honoured place in the scheme of the universe, but that there was neither honour, credit, nor consideration to the man or woman who toils to maintain them all.

Against all this the Irish Transport and General Workers' Union has taught that they who toil are the only ones that do matter, that all others are but beggars upon the bounty of those who work with hand and brain, and that this superiority of social value can at any time be realised, be translated into actual fact, by the combination of the labouring class. Preaching, organising, and fighting upon this basis, the Irish Transport and General Workers' Union had done what? If the value of a city is to be found in the development of self-respect and high conception of social responsibilities among a people, then the Irish Transport and General Workers' Union found Dublin the poorest city in these countries by reason of its lack of these qualities. And by imbuing the workers with them it had made Dublin the richest city in Europe to-day, rich by all that counts for greatness in the history of nations.

It is then upon this working class so enslaved, this working class so led and so enriched with moral purposes and high aims that the employers propose to make general war. Shall we shirk from it; cower before their onset? A thousand times no!! Shall we crawl back into our slums, abase our hearts, bow our knees, and crawl once more to lick the hand that would smite us? Shall we, who have been carving out for our children a brighter future, a cleaner city, a freer life, consent to betray them instead into the grasp of the blood-suckers from whom we have dreamt of escaping?

No, no, and yet again no! Let them declare their lock-out; it will only hasten the day when the working class will lock out the capitalist class for good and all. If for taking the side of the tram men we are threatened with suffering, why we have suffered before. But let them understand well that once they start that ball rolling, no capitalist power on earth can prevent it continuing to roll, that every day will add to the impetus it will give to the working class purpose, to the thousands it will bring to the working class ranks and every added suffering inflicted upon the workers will be a fresh obstacle in the way of moderation when the day of final settlement arrives.

Yes, indeed, if it is going to be a wedding, let it be a wedding; and if it is going to be a wake, let it be a wake; we are ready for either.[4]

About a week later the Chief Secretary for Ireland, Augustine Birrell, was to write to the British Prime Minister, Herbert Asquith:

The issues in the dispute are only about Larkin and his methods which everybody in all ranks, outside the anarchical party, agree are impossible. Larkin's position is a very peculiar one. All the powers that are supposed to be of importance are against him: the [Irish] party, the whole Catholic Church, and the great body of Dublin citizens, to say nothing of the government, and yet somehow or another he has support and is a great character and figure. The fact is that the dispute has lifted the curtain upon depths below Nationalism and the Home Rule movement ... I should not be surprised if Carson holds out some sort of a hand to Larkin as a fellow rebel against nationalist tyranny![5]

An Irish-born newspaper magnate, Lord Northcliffe, boldly declared: 'Larkinism is more than a strike, it is a revolution. Either you crush it now or be prepared to be crushed.'

Chapter 23

The Struggle of 1913: An Overview

W. P. Ryan

The principal Dublin employers combined in 1913 to destroy the Irish Transport and General Workers' Union and to crush Larkin, Connolly, and their militant colleagues. They came to a common conclusion as to the formidable menace to the industrial order, as they understood it and desired it to remain, which the new Union and the new leaders constituted. They were quite correct from their point of view: Larkin and Connolly were a danger to the socially selfish and spiritually stagnant society in which the Irish employing parties lived and moved and had their being. They wanted as a beginning to curtail profits, and eventually to abolish them; or, as capitalist moralists would express it, to 'plunder' the 'princes of business.'

The theory of toilers being on the same human plane as employers, the conception of industrial unionism, the vision of a co-operative commonwealth, were much farther from the imagination of the masters and their friends than was the picture of independent peasant proprietors from the minds of Irish landlords when an 'unknown strolling man' began operations in Mayo over thirty years earlier.[1] The masters, like the landlords, professed to be aghast at the methods employed, and probably were: the methods were sometimes unlovely, like the system. In each case, however, the greater objection was to the ends in view.

The struggle that ensued in 1913, in consequence of the employers' league and decision, was stormy, heroic, and, through no fault of the Irish workers, indecisive—at any rate on the questions avowedly at issue. For the workers it had precious permanent results. It brought into play unexpected power, splendid traits and capacities in the humblest toilers; it brought skilled artisans and craftsmen, long aloof, to their side; it brought the best in intellectual Ireland to realise the shame of their conditions and the worth of their humanity. Labour at its close, to those who thought amongst the more favoured classes, was no longer an obscure, unregarded slave element; it was a part of the 'household', and there was searching of heart, there was fraternal resolve as to its treatment and its future. Nothing in all the previous hundred years was so definite in the psychological effect for Labour as this desperate and, in some measure, this drawn battle.

Various employers had been planning the overthrow of Larkin since 1911, when the Transport Union had already given earnest of its power to obstruct profiteering. A salient part of the scheme was the introduction, on a bold scale, of strike-breakers, so-called 'free' labourers, from Britain. Lord Aberdeen, the Lord Lieutenant, deeming the tactics of the masters rather crude, as well as dangerous, intervened at the time, called Larkin to confer with him, and heard straight talk about the pitiful community of the quays, the grossly under-paid women, and the toilers generally. He initiated a conference of employers and employed, at which there was a proposal for a Conciliation Board. All conciliation boards take the capitalist system and profiteering for granted, and some of the employers were willing to try the experiment, but the scheme got no further, while the Union went ahead ...

In January, 1913, quay porters at the North Wall came out in protest against non-union foremen as well as for better pay and less hours of working. Several other shipping firms came into the battle on the side of the Dublin Steam Packet Company, but Larkin and his men stood strenuously by their demands, though to the poor porters and their families it all meant strain and suffering week in week out. It was evident, however, that there was a new spirit in this long-despised proletariat, and eventually the masters were compelled to come to terms. The men secured a substantial share of their claim, and the moral effect of their victory was felt by many other workers. The 'least' of the toilers began to hold their heads high, and all to grow unreasonable from the master's point of view. After the quay porters, building workers and engineers gave them trouble: hurting their pride of power and profit.

Larkin's fighting methods and Connolly's doctrine of industrial control began to look more serious to the possessing classes. They were as gravely concerned as the landlords had been when the farmers' leaders left the modest demand of the 'Three F's'[2] for the programme of 'The Land for the People.' But how to act was the problem. Some were much in advance of the majority. The most militant was William Martin Murphy. He decided that in his royal sphere he would be master of the common people. He would abolish the Irish Transport and General Workers' Union; he would utter the word and thereafter it would be a memory in his wide domain.

He called the *Irish Independent* despatch corps before him and declared his imperial will. If they elected to belong to the union run by the man-from-God-knows-where called Jim Larkin they would know the service of William Martin Murphy no more. There it was, a sheer issue between a new William and a new James. And the upshot of it was that they declared for James. The spirited folk showed William Martin Murphy that the prospect of unemployment and hunger was not enough to deter them from belonging to the Irish trade union of their choice. William thereafter summoned the tramway-men to his presence, but this time he was not altogether so imperial in his commands. However, he warned propagandists out of his tramway world. Those who introduced the doctrines and ways of the dreaded union would be dismissed straight away. There were dismissals at a later stage, with consequent unrest and action amongst the men. Meanwhile the *Independent* trouble had led to hostilities in other quarters, notably in the case of the multiple newsagents, Easons, whose parcels, containing the militant employer's journal, workers averse from 'tainted goods' objected to handle.

Tram men, sore over dismissals of comrades, struck work in Horse Show week in August, to the indignation of snobs and pleasure-hunters, who thought it positively scandalous on the part of the 'lower classes' to interfere with the distractions of the rich. It was a feverish time amongst the wealthy and socially insensitive, and the ill-feeling spread to their servants the police. Larkin condemned the rough and bullying tactics of the latter (speaking at a great meeting in Beresford Place) and declared that the workers did not mean to take brutality patiently. They would arm themselves for their own protection. He made some pointed allusions to Carsonian expedients in the north-east of Ulster. The Dublin Castle authorities, who had given the Carsonites their way, interfered promptly in the deepening struggle between the masters and the under-men, taking, as ever, the side of the former—Connolly said later that the employers 'obtained beforehand [before they precipitated the struggle] the promise of swift and relentless use of government forces.'

Larkin was arrested, with four of his chief associates: William O'Brien, William Partridge, P. T. Daly and Thomas Lawlor. They were returned for trial, but admitted to bail, all the time the excitement growing apace. A meeting announced for the next Sunday in O'Connell Street was 'proclaimed' by the government but the workers had grown grimly determined that their voice and case should be heard. Their spirit received strident expression at the monster meeting which welcomed Larkin and his associates after their release from the police-court. Intense as it was, the spirit of the meeting was orderly, but this did not prevent violent baton-charges by the police at the close.

On the Saturday afternoon there was a further clash at Ringsend, where workers resented the presence of 'scabs' in a football team, thereby bringing themselves under the ban of the offended police. In the charges that followed the police met fierce resistance. Later in the evening in Brunswick Street,[3] where 'loyal' tram-men provoked popular feeling, there was another encounter, in which the batoning police were again hard pressed. After nightfall, in the neighbourhood of Liberty Hall, a great popular rallying centre, their temper and tactics were still more boldly resented and resisted. Again and again the people threw themselves against the baton-men, and bore them back, for which defensive temerity they were described as 'howling rabble' and other graceful things, by writers in the capitalist press. James Nolan, a bright and promising Dublin worker, was a victim of the police onslaught, dying early on Sunday morning. His fate caused a thrill of pity and passion in all his class.

The general public was in doubt that the proclaimed meeting would be attempted in O'Connell Street on the Sunday. Great forces of police, including Royal Irish Constabulary from the country, were at hand and in readiness, with military in the background. Larkin had not been to the fore on Saturday. Sight-seers and strollers came into the popular parading place, as usual on the early afternoon of the Sabbath. Suddenly, sensation broke the mingled expectancy and enjoyment. At the moment announced for the meeting, Larkin, who had disguised himself, began to address the people from a window of the first floor of the Imperial Hotel,[4] one of the establishments in which William Martin Murphy was interested. He was quickly arrested, and scarcely had those in the vicinity recovered from the first feeling of surprise when the long lines of police down the great thoroughfare fell upon the workers and sight-seers, men, women and children and in a series of savage charges and batoning indulged their fury relentlessly.

The police had not matters their own way in other quarters, then or afterwards, Larkin's escort being a centre of storm, and the Bridewell, to which he was taken, being menaced by an angry crowd; while on the Inchicore tram line 'loyal' drivers had to receive not only police but military protection. However, it was the wild scene in O'Connell Street, the indiscriminate savagery towards men, women and children, that burned into the mind of those who saw, or heard the details of, the atrocity. And the details went far and wide.

Exciting as were those events they were only the prelude to the real struggle. Already the employers had taken steps towards the formation of an alliance which they believed would smash the Irish Transport and General Workers' Union and divide the members into ineffective groups or units again—the linking up and harmonising of so many different orders and grades, all ready to help one another, had been a prime cause of offence. After the batoning in O'Connell Street the coal merchants decided to lock out all employees who belonged to the offending body.

A day or two later 404 employers, the business potentates of the metropolis, 'bound themselves by solemn vows, and by still more binding financial pledges' (in Connolly's words), that they would not employ thenceforward any worker who did not sign an undertaking that he or she would neither belong to nor help the Irish Transport and General Workers' Union. Not only did they attack the Union itself, they challenged all unions and all workers. The clearing out was to begin after three days. It was well understood of course that the outrageous edict would be sturdily resisted, and that the attempt to enforce it would mean the starvation and agony of a host of women and children. The employers on their own admission were entirely alive to the bearing of the hunger-factor in the contest.

Meanwhile it happened that the British Trade Union Congress had assembled at the beginning of September in Manchester for its annual meeting, and Dublin leaders, after the battle in O'Connell Street, decided to send over a delegation to let English and Scottish workers know that the Dublin Castle authorities, for whom as British voters they were to some extent responsible, were using their power to the full to assist the employers in their evil work. Thomas MacPartlin, the President of the Dublin Trades Council that year, William Partridge, and Thomas Lawlor, were the delegates. The Congress, having heard the facts at first hand, condemned the action of the Castle, urged all the affiliated unions to support the Dublin toilers in their struggle, and took upon itself the responsibility of providing food for those affected, no matter how long the fight might last. In its turn it sent a delegation across the Irish Sea. At home in Dublin the funeral of James Nolan was an extraordinarily impressive and affecting sight; and while still the people brooded over it the collapse, one evening, of slum tenements in Church Street, with grievous loss of life, showed another tragic side of the toilers' lot in the capital of Ireland.

The delegation from the British Trade Union Congress included some amiable and optimistic men—the veteran Keir Hardie was a visitor at the same time—and the body got into communication with the Dublin masters. In two sittings at the Shelbourne Hotel, at the second of which representatives from the Dublin Trades Council were present, the Britons tried to show the employers to the fore that the proposal to stamp out trade unionism in the twentieth century was unworkable. The masters professed that they were not averse from trade unionism of the old and respectable kind, but they had decided that the brand invented by Larkin must go. It was felt that a settlement was possible on general issues, and on the one contested question of dictation to the workers over the union to which they should or should not belong reflection might do something, so the conference adjourned.

The masters proceeded left and right to carry out the attack upon the Transport Unionists, and incidentally on other unionists who would not declare against it. Workers were locked out on all sides, and then the masters informed the British trade unionists that no good purpose would be served by their coming to the adjourned conference. The delegates wrote to express their astonishment at the 'serious, wilful, and indefensible breach of a common understanding.' But the masters did not mind. They took no account of the sensibilities of workers and they were not anxious about meals and the morrow. They had locked out the wage-slaves who would not forswear the Transport Union, and they awaited developments.

Some were unexpected and disconcerting. Transporters were firm, and workers of other unions proceeded to make common cause with them. The builders' labourers, who the masters understood were unfriendly to 'Larkinism', stood out promptly against the ban, while skilled artisans in their turn showed plainly that they had come to take the doctrine of solidarity seriously and would put it into practice. The women and girls were splendid from the start. For the sake of principle they lost the poor posts that had stood between them and starvation, and went out with defiance and resolution in their hearts. The general labourers spurned the masters' ultimatum, and went forth to tramp the streets and swell the crowds of the dismissed and unemployed.

The industrial dislocation that followed the pressing of the masters' mandate was unprecedented. Thousands of humble homes, and many that had been comfortable, were faced with ruin, but a rare coherence and fine courage marked the hosts who were thrown on the defensive—thirty-seven unions altogether were brought into the fight. The employers had the police and the 'judicial' class at their service. 'They were able to

173

override the law,' as Connolly wrote, 'and to fill the prisons with old and young, men and women, boys and girls, who attempted to exercise the picketing rights guaranteed to them by English law.'

There was a reign of terror as well as the shadow of starvation. (A whitewashing police inquiry by a couple of lawyers later on was treated with derision by the workers).

Withal it was plain and palpable that Labour in Dublin had suffered a spiritual revolution. Larkin was under lock and key, but there were leaders to the fore who were worthy of the heroic men and women they led; and incidentally they set the pace to the official Britons at a rate the latter found embarrassing. Connolly, who had been arrested and released after a hunger-strike, was a tower of strength in public and in private: in his addresses abroad, in his campaign directions, in his tactics in council. The spirit of the men, women, and children in the dismal deeps of Dublin seemed to kindle his heart and give fire and inspiration to his utterances. The incoming of men and women, more socially favoured, to help in any and every fashion, from street-corner speaking to cooking and serving in Liberty Hall and elsewhere, was a new feature in labour struggles in the capital. Francis Sheehy-Skeffington, his wife, and the Countess Markievicz were three out of many who threw themselves heart and soul into the work of feeding the spirits and the bodies of the locked-out wage-slaves and their families.

Larkin was released on bail, and went over to England to spread in his unsparing way the facts of the Dublin issue, and incidentally to hurt the pride of some official-minded trade union leaders of Britain, with whose methods he and other human-hearted people had little patience. Thousands of the rank and file in Britain were intense in their sympathy with the Dublin workers: the *Daily Herald* of those days is an eloquent index of the fact, and Connolly said afterwards that the spirit of the working folk on both sides of the Irish Sea in those early stages showed the highest point of moral grandeur yet reached by the Labour movement.

Sympathetic strikes took place amongst the rail-men in Liverpool, Manchester and Birmingham; they were stopped by officialdom, but there were other indications of fraternal revolt to follow. The Trade Union Congress delegates to Ireland issued their report, declaring that the Dublin employers were 'determined to crush out trade unionism.' This stirred the rank and file anew, and it began to seem that direct action on a wider scale than that of the rail-men would be the outcome. British capitalists met and came to the assistance of their kind in Dublin. Emboldened, the latter refused the request of the Lord Mayor to meet Labour leaders in conference; they proved no more amenable to Professor Kettle and the Dublin Industrial Peace Committee. The British Government, whose forces in the Irish capital were doing the work of the capitalists all the time, sent over a commission with Sir George Askwith at its head.

More and more workers came out or were locked out week by week, and the problem of feeding the hungry, even though food-ships—a dramatic feature of the situation—began to come in from Britain, became more and more serious. Amongst the most faithful of subscribers from the ranks of Irish toil were Orangemen. The commission gave T. M. Healy,[5] as leading counsel for the employers, an opportunity of denouncing in 'Larkinism' what in his younger days he had applauded in farmers who struggled to bring landlords to reason. One intense feature of the inquiry was an address of Larkin's in which he dealt in scathing and impassioned terms with the social degradation and shame of Dublin.[6] The commissioners in their report, which appeared with unexpected promptitude, showed an effort to be placid and judicial. They declared, however, with decision, that the document in which workers were asked to forswear the Transport and General Workers' Union 'imposes on the signatories conditions which are contrary to individual liberty, and which no workman or body of workmen could reasonably be expected to accept.' They suggested a conciliation court. But the masters, trusting in their united might and the power of the hunger factor soon or late, remained as obdurate as ever, treating censure and suggestion with equal indifference.

At this stage 'Æ' addressed to them the memorable letter which is sure to be the most enduring document of the struggle, the one thing through which those masters of Dublin, so proud and cruel in their little day, will live in history: '... You determined deliberately, in cold anger, to starve out one-third of the population of this city, to break the manhood of the men by the sight of the suffering of their wives and the hunger of their children ... It remained for the twentieth century and the capital city of Ireland to see an oligarchy of four hundred masters deciding openly upon starving one hundred thousand people, and refusing to consider any solution except that fixed by their pride. You, masters, asked men to do that which masters of labour in any other city in these islands had not dared to do. You insolently demanded of those men who were members of a trade union that they should resign from that union; and from those who were not members you insisted on a vow that they would never join it.'[7]

A little later, a sympathetic lady, Mrs. Dora B. Montefiore, who was blissfully unconscious of Irish clerical susceptibilities, set in train a scheme to take many of the workers' children out of the hunger zone, and to leave some for a time in friendly homes in Britain, homes of Catholics as far as possible (more were to be sent to ultramontane Catholic homes in Belfast). The 'danger to faith and morals' roused ecclesiastics, and the passionate but innocent hearts they could influence, to a stormy crusade to retain the little ones in the pious environment of Dublin slumdom. Archbishop Walsh, with a grim candour, put the matter in a different light when he said that taking away the children to comfortable quarters for a while would make them discontented afterwards with their poor homes in Dublin! The onsets to 'save the children' brought a frenzied interlude, yet a wildly unreal one, in those days of battle between tyranny and principle. Here again 'Æ's' review will be classic. It is part of his address at the Albert Hall, London, on 1 November, 1913, when Connolly also spoke from the heart to a vast gathering of working Britons (and not a few Irish) presided over by George Lansbury.[8]

Larkin's trial, begun on the 27 October, had ended, after class-lawyers had expressed their sense of his iniquity, in a sentence of seven months' imprisonment. But working British voters had grown not merely restive but wrathful, and a couple of electoral knocks for the Government led to the hasty opening of the prison doors on the 13 November. Larkin went to Britain with his 'Fiery Cross' and the Dublin masters, failing to bring the under-men to their knees by starvation, began to import British 'scab' labour. Whereupon the dock labourers in the port of Dublin came out. The police, who all the time had been violently partial, sometimes ferocious, were becoming unbearable.

Archbishop Walsh made a plea for a conference. The masters could not well ignore the Archbishop. The conference met and failed, the masters being determined to retain the 'free' slave labour they had secured. All those terrible days the golden fact was the grit and endurance of the often hungry toilers and their ill-clad folk in the bleak homes in winter-swept Dublin.

The pressure of the rank and file in many quarters of Britain grew embarrassing to the official leaders. A general strike in sympathy, a 'blockade' of Dublin to bring the masters to reason, were urged by the more militant spirits. Those who knew the official trade union leaders were certain that in the last resort they would 'trim' and fail, on one pretext or another. As it happened, at the special Trade Union Congress which they were obliged to call in London, one that was largely made up of the obedient official element of their own stamp, they secured a huge majority—on the misleading 'card' vote system—against the drastic action of a 'blockade' of Dublin, though they still gave lip-support to the fighters. Larkin ruffled their feelings, as he often did before, and they roundly abused him. Connolly, in one of his finest speeches, brought them back to realities and principles. But they did nothing beyond preparing for another conference with the Dublin autocrats, who feared direct action but did not object to talking while those locked-out and on strike went hungry. Their delegates met those of the trade unionists, but refused to unbend, especially over the retention of their 'free' slaves.

It would be a grave injustice to overlook or minimise the spirit of the best of the British rank and file in the whole battle, or to fail to emphasise the whole-hearted efforts of independent leaders and pioneers, of whom George Lansbury is the most popular example. They responded to the ideas that dominated the under-men of Dublin and their champions. The officials at the best never thought in anything higher than breadstuff.

The struggle lasted eight long months, in some quarters more, and ended indecisively. A couple of unions went back on their brethren in the end—the variety of unions and plans did not make the battle easier. Larkin dwelt forcibly on this aspect of things, and the need of the One Big Union, in his slashing address as President of the Irish Trades Union Congress in Dublin in the summer of 1914. The masters had not prevailed against them, although, he said, they had to retreat to their base. On the central and original issue the employers were unsuccessful on the whole, though, some workers for tactical reasons signed the obnoxious document, and awaited events. The masters, while refusing to recognise the Union, were obliged to tolerate the individual unionist who remained loyal to it both in the spirit and the letter; they could not get on conveniently without them. Even those autocrats of Dublin had discovered that a frontal attack on trade unionism was vanity; it conduced to the solidarity they dreaded. They held out, however, for the power to employ 'free' labour also, and could not be compelled for the nonce to give preference to organised workers. It rested with the unions to go on more zealously with the organising of the 'free' who were not free. In the ensuing couple of years those who stood loyally by the Transport Union were able to secure appreciable increases of wages. Connolly thus summed up the result (*Irish Worker*, 28 November, 1914):

'The battle was a drawn battle. The employers, despite their Napoleonic plan of campaign, and their more than Napoleonic ruthlessness and unscrupulous use of foul means, were unable to carry on their business without men and women who remained loyal to their unions. The workers were unable to force the employers to a formal recognition of the Union, and to give preference to organised Labour.

'From the effects of this drawn battle both sides are still bearing heavy scars. How deep those scars are none will ever reveal.'[9]

In many cases the feeling was not the positive, poisonous one of scorn. It was often one of frigid indifference; often also, there was the shallow sense that the under-workers were merely animals in crude human form, born for coarse and muddy toil, for things as low as their own (supposed) personalities. That they had any fineness of nature, that their employments were essential social services which could be and ought to be beautified: such things were unthinkable when the struggle of 1913 began. That struggle against the powers of cash and arrogance, class-law based on sophistry and brutality, ecclesiastical pessimism worlds removed from the Christian vision of human divinity and brotherhood, a lying press, and a parasitical 'society', was a grand moral and spiritual exhibition on the part of Poverty in revolt, Poverty finding its soul; and its challenge and its message went wide and deep.

In 'Æ' is one striking example of the fire it struck in responsive spirits; in Pearse, brought up with a shock from his ideal mental home among the lowly Gaels of Connacht to the terrible yet beautiful realism at his door in Dublin, we have another; and there were many, many more: like W. B. Yeats, who wrote with passion of the quasi-religious fanaticism that in the 'Save-the-Children' (!) frenzy was a factor in support of the oppressors of the poor; like James Stephens with his scathing reminder to clerics and other powers of how backward in culture, art, and true living was the Ireland they dominated; like those sensitive artists and rare individualities, Thomas MacDonagh and Joseph Plunkett (who incidentally gave

177

prominence in the *Irish Review* to Connolly's defence of the cause of his brethren in the battle). In sooth the struggle brought more than will ever be told towards the chastening and intensifying of Irish hearts and minds in the crucial, unique years that were at hand.

[Extracts from W. P. Ryan, *The Irish Labour Movement from the 'Twenties to Our Own Day* (1919), chapter 16.]

* * *

William Patrick Ryan was born near Templemore, County Tipperary, on 28 October 1867. He emigrated to England and worked as a journalist on the *Catholic Times,* the *Sunday Sun,* and the *Morning Leader.* Returning to Ireland at the end of 1906, he edited successively the *Irish Peasant,* the *Peasant,* and the *Irish Nation,* and for several years he was a member of the Coiste Gnó (Executive Committee) of Conradh na Gaeilge. He went to London in 1911 and shortly after became assistant editor of the *Daily Herald,* with which he remained up to his death on 31 December 1942.

He was the author of many books in Irish and English, including *The Pope's Green Island* and *Caoimhghín Ó Cearnaigh,* as well as *The Irish Labour Movement.*

Chapter 24

Dublin's Bloody Sunday

Prologue

The strike of the ITGWU members in the Tramway Company began on Tuesday 26 August. Over the following days there were a number of 'incidents', clashes with the police and disturbances. However, police action was muted on these occasions. On the night of Friday 29 August, after Larkin had declared before a crowd of ten thousand people that the meeting proclaimed by the Chief Magistrate, Swifte, would be held on Sunday afternoon, the police took action as the crowd was dispersing after the meeting in Beresford Place, and there was a succession of baton charges.

On the following day, Saturday 30 August, there were serious disturbances in the Ringsend area, and mounted police were called in to clear a bridge blocked by strikers and their supporters. Trams were attacked, and there were several baton charges. By six o'clock substantial reinforcements of police had arrived on the scene. Police escorting arrested men to College Street police station were attacked, and a further series of baton charges followed in Great Brunswick Street (Pearse Street).

A meeting was due to be held that evening in Beresford Place, and a large crowd had gathered by eight o'clock. Soon there were battles between sections of the crowd and the police on duty there. Stones and bottles were thrown. Inspector Campbell ordered the police to charge. Following repeated charges, the main crowd was dispersed. Ambulances removed the many injured to hospital.

Shortly afterwards there were further disturbances near the Abbey Theatre. The section of the crowd involved were driven off by police charges, but skirmishes continued into Abbey Street. There the head of the police, Sir John Ross, who had arrived on the scene, ordered the street to be cleared. The police, now reinforced, charged in great force down the street against the angry crowd.

There was also trouble around Store Street police station, in Talbot Street, and later in Tyrone Street, the centre of the slum area. An unsympathetic journalist gave a graphic though one-sided description of the scene there:

> So furious was the rain of bottles—broken and whole—and bricks that the place seemed more like the haunt of howling demons than a Dublin street within a few hundred yards from the cathedral. The shameful, filthy expressions shouted at the top of women's voices, formed a very painful exhibition. To the accompaniment of hoarse, ribald execrations and shrieks from the rioters, the combined police force charged up towards Tyrone Street, but had to withdraw owing to the hail of bottles and stones. Each time the police drew back, the howling rabble followed them and made

havoc in their ranks with the hail of missiles that poured on them from all directions. The little barefoot urchins—girls and boys—more daring than their elders, rushed out every now and then and gathered up fresh stores of 'ammunition' for the mob. Darting out into the street, they had little trouble finding plenty of broken bottles and bricks which had been used on the police a moment before. Women, with dishevelled hair and looking like maniacs, were even more persistent than the men and youths in belabouring the police.[1]

During the disturbances that Saturday, hundreds of people, including thirty policemen, were injured and required medical attention in the hospitals. Two civilians died from their injuries: James Nolan, who died in the early hours of Sunday morning from the effects of a fractured skull, and James Byrne, who died subsequently from injuries received in one of the baton charges.

Eye-witness accounts of the batoning of James Nolan were subsequently given to the Dublin Disturbances Commission, which reported in 1914. One of the witnesses, Patrick Carton, a member of the ITGWU, had gone to Liberty Hall to pay his weekly contribution.

As far as I can remember on the night of the occurrence, when the first baton charge took place, I was at Liberty Hall, and I noticed about twenty police on duty outside Tuck's entrance. There were about 300 people round Liberty Hall. I noticed a number of children singing national songs. The police advanced and drew their batons and commenced batoning the people owing to the children singing national songs. I was on the steps and I heard a voice stating, 'Clear the steps of Liberty Hall!' I then made my way out to Eden Quay, but got a blow on the way which my cap saved me from. I saw a man lying on the ground after being batoned, whose name subsequently turned out to be James Nolan. I saw a policeman going in front of Nolan and looking at him after, as I thought, striking him. I took the constable's number, which was 224C. After the constables had retreated I rendered all the assistance possible to the man, and, as a matter of fact, went with him to the hospital. I called the attention of Inspector Campbell to the state of the man on the ground, and he ordered the constable to disperse the men about. Inspector Campbell sent 52C in a cab to the hospital with the man. I insisted on going also, and after a lot of argument I managed to step into the cab and accompanied the constable to the hospital. The man never spoke after he went into the hospital, and on looking at him his eyes and head were all swollen and battered.

The second witness, Stephen Gilligan, was on his way to the post office with a telegram.

I saw the charge of the police. The people were talking in threes and fours, and got no chance of moving. The first thing they knew was the batons coming down on them. I heard a voice saying, 'Now give it to them, boys!' I pretended I was a reporter and got safe. I saw the police charge the doorway and smash the sidelights. They charged round Eden Quay. The majority went on the footpath charging the people there. The people for the most part kept to the quayside. I stood in the shadow of the Corporation weigh-house and saw poor Nolan trying to get away. I saw a police constable, 224C, Constable Bell, strike him with a baton. I saw him fall on his knees. The constable ran on, and then 149C struck him across the neck. I went back towards the Butt Bridge.

A third eye-witness to the baton charge at Eden Quay was Henry Nicholls, a graduate of Trinity College. A member of the IRB, he was a friend of Thomas Clarke, the first signatory of the Proclamation of the Republic in 1916.

On the evening of 29 August I went to Beresford Place, about 8.30, to listen to the speeches. The crowd was very peaceable, and remained quiet under the provocation given by the police forcing a way through them to let a motor car pass. When the speaking was over I was making my way home along Eden Quay when suddenly, without any provocation, about twenty police charged the crowd, of which I was one. The majority fled. I walked on and was knocked staggering by a blow between the eyes by a constable. When turning to notice his number, I was struck by another constable in the mouth, my pipe being smashed. I got the numbers of both constables (33B and 188B) and immediately went to College Street to lay a charge against the constables ...

Nicholls subsequently insisted on getting a written apology from the police, which an Inspector McCaig gave.

Another eye-witness wrote about what he saw on that fateful Saturday night. He was Robert Monteith, who accompanied Roger Casement to Banna Strand, County Kerry, in April 1916. The following is an excerpt from his book *Casement's Last Adventure*:

I witnessed the murder of Nolan. He was walking quietly down Eden Quay when he was met by a mixed patrol of Dublin Metropolitan Police and the Royal Irish Constabulary. The strength of the patrol was about thirty-five, all more or less drunk. One of the constabulary walked from the centre of the road on to the sidewalk and without the slightest provocation felled the poor man with a blow from his staff. The horrible crunching sound of the blow was clearly audible fifty yards away. This drunken scoundrel was ably seconded by two of the Metropolitan police, who, as the unfortunate man attempted to rise, beat him about the head until his skull was smashed in, in several places. They then rejoined their patrol, leaving him in his blood. For saying: 'You damn cowards' I was instantly struck by two policemen and fell to the ground, where I had sense enough to lie until the patrol had passed on.

The following day, Sunday 31 August, was to see the bloodiest manifestation of the police violence against the locked-out workers and citizens in general that was so evident throughout the dispute. In the House of Commons the leading Labour MP Josiah Wedgewood (later Lord Stansgate) was to comment that they had not seen in Britain for over a hundred years any such action on the part of the police as was witnessed in Dublin during 1913.

Bloody Sunday

On Saturday, the eve of the prohibited meeting in Sackville Street (O'Connell Street) at which Larkin had pledged himself to speak, William O'Brien was informed by Francis Sheehy-Skeffington that a warrant had been issued for Larkin's arrest.[2] Larkin, in Liberty Hall when he received this information, decided to go 'missing'. Eventually he ended up in the home of Constance Markievicz and her husband, Surrey House, in Leinster Road, Rathmines, even though the house was under police surveillance. That night the Markieviczes gave a party, and as the guests arrived the police, assuming that Larkin must be elsewhere, called off their surveillance.

On Sunday, Larkin donned a frock coat and top hat belonging to Markievicz and was made up as an old man with a beard by Helena Molony, an actress with the Abbey Theatre company. Then, accompanied by a 'niece' (Sydney Gifford), he left Surrey House for O'Connell Street.[3] He was to pose as someone who was deaf, and the 'niece' would answer any questions put to them. At about 1:30 p.m. their carriage pulled up in front of the Imperial Hotel in O'Connell Street, the property of William Martin Murphy.

Assisted by the 'niece', the old bent figure entered the hotel, lit a cigar, and went to the dining-room on the first floor, walked unsteadily to the french window, stepped onto the balcony, straightened his back, and began to speak. Immediately a crowd surged towards the hotel and the cry went up, 'It's Larkin!' Within seconds Larkin was seized and arrested and led out of the hotel by four policemen.

What followed can be reconstructed from the report of the Dublin Disturbances Commission, the Dublin newspapers of the following day, notably the *Freeman's Journal*, eye-witness accounts, and Arnold Wright's *Disturbed Dublin*.

During the Sunday morning there had been few police on duty in O'Connell Street, which was thronged with the usual Sunday crowd of people going to or returning from church services in the many churches of all denominations in the vicinity. About midday, however, strong detachments of police were deployed at strategic positions along the thoroughfare and in the streets leading off it. Apart from the DMP, a large force of RIC men had been drafted in from provincial areas.

At about one o'clock several hundred men wearing the red hand badge of the ITGWU gathered in front of the GPO. At about 1:30 a man attired in a silk hat and a frock coat appeared on the balcony of the Imperial Hotel and began to address the crowd. The shout went up, 'It's Larkin!' Wild cheering marked the surge of the crowd across the street towards the hotel. According to Arnold Wright, the words spoken by Larkin were: 'I am here today in accordance with my promise to address you in O'Connell Street, and I won't leave until I am arrested.'

Superintendent Murphy, with about twenty policemen, rushed into the hotel to arrest Larkin, who simply said, 'It's all right; I'm satisfied.' Still wearing the false beard, and surrounded by police, he was led out of the hotel. There was tremendous cheering from the throng that by now had gathered outside the hotel. A cab drew up in which was Constance Markievicz and a companion. She described the events that followed:

We had driven down with a few friends to see if the proclaimed meeting would be held. There were no unusual crowds; our car trotted down O'Connell Street and pulled up at Prince's Street, opposite the Imperial Hotel. We noticed a great number of police everywhere. Larkin was just finishing his speech, and went into the hotel a few seconds after our arrival. A few people gathered. They were all laughing and very much amused at Larkin's appearance. A friend recognised me, and called on me for a speech. I did not want to create a disturbance, so I jumped down off the car and walked across the street.

As I reached the other side Larkin came out of the hotel, between two policemen, and surrounded by an escort of about thirty police. I ran across in front of him and shook his hand, saying, 'Good-bye, good luck.' As I turned to pass down O'Connell Street the inspector on Larkin's right hit me on the nose and mouth with his clenched fist. I reeled against another policeman, who pulled me about, tearing all the buttons off my blouse, and tearing it out all round my waist. He then threw me back into the middle of the street, where all the police had begun to run, several of them kicking and hitting at me as they passed.

I saw a woman trying to get out of the way. She was struck from behind on the head by a policeman with his baton. As she fell her hat slipped over her face, and I saw her hair was grey. She had a little book, which fell out of her left hand as she fell. I saw a barefooted boy with papers hunted and hit about the shoulders as he ran away. I shall never forget the look on his face as he turned when he was struck.

I could not get out of the crowd of police, and at last one hit me a back-hand blow across the left side of my face with his baton. I fell back against the corner of a shop, when another policeman started to seize me by the throat, but I was pulled out of the crowd by some men, who took me down Sackville Place and into a house to stop the blood flowing from my nose and mouth, and to try and tidy my blouse.

I noticed that the policeman who struck me smelt very strongly of stout, and that they all seemed very excited. They appeared to be arranged in a hollow square, and to be gradually driving the people into the street, and then closing in on them and batoning them. I tried to go up, down, and across O'Connell Street, but each time I was put back by them into the crowd of charging police. The people were all good-tempered, and there would have been no row. They were also out-numbered by the police round about where I was.

By this time the police had formed into a long line extending from the GPO to the O'Connell Monument. Truncheons drawn, they awaited the order to charge. Arnold Wright described what followed:

The constables fell upon the crowd with an energy which created momentary surprise but which ultimately produced a panic. Individuals fled in all directions in their attempt to escape the blows which were dealt with fierce intensity by the infuriated members of the police force. Innocent sightseers along with rowdy demonstrators shared in the terrible punishment that was meted out by the guardians of the law. A number were knocked down and trampled upon in their vain efforts to escape. Again and again the police charged up and down the street. One section of the flying crowd made off down Prince's Street (beside the GPO), only to be met here by a body of police who were held in reserve and who, joining in the fray, dealt out blows indiscriminately to the wretched fugitives. The piteous cries of the injured and the shrieks of the frightened women filled the air. 'Terror and panic were let loose,' observes a spectator, 'and a state of frenzy seemed to possess police and people alike.' The scene of the disturbances was strewn like a battle field with the bodies of injured people, many of them with their faces covered with blood and with their bodies writhing in agony. The whole episode only lasted a few minutes, but in that brief space of time hundreds were injured, some seriously.[4]

The clearing of O'Connell Street had been effected. But disturbances continued elsewhere. The police escorting Larkin to College Street police station were attacked.[5] The Bridewell, to which he was later removed, was attacked repeatedly, with the crowd being dispersed by many baton charges.

The worst rioting was experienced on the tramway route from Christ Church Cathedral to Inchicore. There the trams were attacked. The police being unable to control the angry crowd of Larkin supporters, a battalion of the West Kent Regiment was called out from Richmond Barracks (now McKee Barracks). As Wright put it, 'it was not until the night was far advanced that the last stone was thrown and the last charge made by the police.'

The headlines in the *Freeman's Journal* the following day (1 September 1913) summed up the events of Bloody Sunday:

BLOODSHED IN DUBLIN

APPALLING SCENES IN THE CITY

FIERCE BATON CHARGES

HUNDREDS INJURED

TWO MEN DEAD

HOSPITALS OVERCROWDED

MR. LARKIN ARRESTED AT IMPERIAL HOTEL

Up to four hundred civilians had been injured, about half of them requiring hospital treatment. Some thirty DMP and RIC were injured.

A dramatic picture of the police onslaught in O'Connell Street taken by the photographer J. Cashman from the nearby 'Picture House' was reproduced in newspapers throughout the world and had an enormous impact on foreign opinion and corresponding embarrassment to the

British government, who were responsible for the actions of the Dublin Castle authorities. As C. Desmond Greaves pointed out, 'the historic baton charge had gripped the imagination of Europe.'[6] Arnold Wright admitted that 'a tremendous sensation was caused throughout the United Kingdom' by the events of Bloody Sunday.[7]

Another witness to Bloody Sunday was Ernie O'Malley, the IRA leader in the War of Independence, who almost a quarter of a century later was to write in his book *On Another Man's Wound* (1936):

> Police swept down from many quarters, hemmed in the crowd and used their heavy batons on anyone who came in their way. I saw women knocked down and kicked. I scurried up a side street; at the other end the police struck people as they lay injured on the ground, struck them again and again. I could hear the crunch as the heavy sticks struck unprotected skulls.

An impartial witness, a guest in the Imperial Hotel on Bloody Sunday, was the English Liberal MP Handel Booth. This is how he described what happened:

> Just before my wife and I sat down to lunch we looked out from the balcony and noted to each other that there was nothing going to happen, that everything was perfectly quiet. There was no riot, no meeting, no anything. My wife had seen the demonstrators go away, and I had seen them start off for Croydon Park. Looking up and down the street, we said there could have been nothing more peaceful when we sat down to lunch.
>
> Larkin appeared. I did not know him. He wore a false beard. He appeared immediately in front of our table, and addressed a few words to the street below. What he said I do not know because of the hum of the passing traffic. We were within a yard of him. We understood him to say that he was going to speak until the police arrested him. Immediately he said that he turned on his heel, passed our table, and went, I understand, to the kitchen of our hotel, where he was arrested by Superintendent Murphy.
>
> We stepped back into the balcony to see what was happening in the street. While on the balcony somebody shouted that it was Larkin, or that it might be Larkin. What else was shouted did not reach our ears; but we were interested in seeing Larkin brought out of the hotel. He was brought out peaceably enough.
>
> We were just thinking of turning to go back to lunch when the mad scene broke out. We looked down and saw the shouting and excitement in the street. The police had drawn their batons. Some of the police had gone one way, some another, and were being met by others and by the people, many of whom, girls and others, wore straw and sailor hats. It was an ordinary Sunday crowd. They were certainly bewildered, and did not know which way to turn.
>
> I was back on the balcony when Mr. Larkin was removed by the police, who had been rushing excitedly into the hotel. The puzzled crowd could not tell what was happening. Policemen came in view from all sides, girls hastened away with their companions, and excited women shouted for

cheers for Larkin. A few responded as the prisoner was marched away; then silence ensued save for pattering feet and sickening thuds. The noble street was in the hands of the most brutal constabulary ever let loose on a peaceful assembly. Up and down the road, backwards and forwards, the police rushed like men possessed. Some drove the crowd into side streets, to meet other batches of the Government's minions wildly striking with truncheons at every one within reach. In escaping many ran the gauntlet until the third or fourth blow knocked them senseless. The few roughs got away first; most respectable persons left their hats, and crawled away with bleeding heads. Kicking the victims when prostrate was a settled part of the police programme. Three such cases occurred in a direct line with our window.

Shocked by the 'inhuman savagery' of the police during the 1913 lock-out, Tom Clarke wrote a letter of protest to the *Irish Worker* (27 September 1913) and to *Irish Freedom*, the organ of the IRB. Clarke had spent sixteen years in jail, much of the time in solitary confinement.

Sir—Will you kindly allow me the courtesy of your columns to touch upon one phase of the recent happenings in this City. I have witnessed a number of fierce riots in Ulster in bye-gone times; was present when buckshot in volleys was fired into an unarmed crowd in Dungannon which so infuriated them in their frenzy they closed in on a strong possé of police who were sweeping through them with fixed bayonets and the crowd with naked hands came to grips with the police and put them to flight. I saw brutal things done that day on both sides, as might be expected there was much bloodshed—one man killed outright and a long list of wounded was the toll. Later on I witnessed the Bowery hooligans and New York police have a 'set-to'. The fight was fierce and some savage acts were witnessed. It has fallen to my lot to get considerable first-hand knowledge of the ruffianism of the criminal classes of London's underworld.

Yet nothing I know of during my whole career can match the downright inhuman savagery that was witnessed recently in the streets and some of the homes of our city when the police were let loose to run amok and indiscriminately bludgeon every man, woman and child they came across, in many cases kicking them on the ground after felling them with the baton. They have wrecked the homes of dozens of our citizens, smashing windows, fanlights, doors, furniture, china, pictures—everything breakable—murderously assaulting the inmates, irrespective of age or sex. The new-born babe at the mother's breast wasn't safe any more than the sick mother herself—in one instance she was dragged out of bed and clubbed and the poor wee babe got it, too, and showed the result in a black eye. An avalanche of evidence is just now available to sustain everything I am stating.

Dublin with its people, the most easy-going and peaceful of any city I know, is staggered by what has happened. Totting up the 'casualties' we find two dead and about a thousand maimed and battered citizens have received treatment in the public hospitals and private surgeries of the city! A bloody holocaust surely! but a fitting one to be dedicated to Dublin Castle and its idea of 'Law and Order'.

Aftermath

On the day after Bloody Sunday, Larkin was again charged by the police. Bail was refused. As a result he was not able to attend the funeral of James Nolan, the victim of the police baton charge near Liberty Hall on the Saturday, which was held on 3 September.

A great crowd assembled at Liberty Hall to march up Eden Quay, where Nolan had been repeatedly batoned by several policemen, through O'Connell Street and on to Glasnevin Cemetery. Seán O'Casey was to write of a similar funeral of another victim of police violence in 1913, taking the same route:

> Here it came, the Dead March in *Saul*, flooding the street, and flowing into the windows of the street's rich building, followed by the bannered Labour unions, colours sobered by cordons of crepe, a host of hodden grey following a murdered comrade.[8]

Walking at the head of the funeral procession was James Keir Hardie. That evening he addressed a memorial meeting at Liberty Hall. Hardie, a Scotsman, was the first independent Labour member to be elected to the House of Commons.

> James Nolan is no longer with us in the body, but those of you who know a little of astronomy are aware that the light that comes from the stars takes a long time to reach earth. The American poet, Longfellow, took advantage of that fact to pen a beautiful moral. It was this—
>
> When any good man dies,
> For years beyond our ken,
> The light he leaves behind him lies
> Across the paths of men.
>
> James Nolan has gone from our midst, but his influence remains and his martyrdom will inspire thousands of young men to follow in the path along which he trod.
>
> Why is Larkin so much feared by the employing classes in Dublin? I shall tell you. It is because he has got down to the foundation and the whole superstructure rises with the foundation. Yes and the employers know it and William Martin Murphy knows it. It is all very well for him and for Jacobs to express their sympathy with the working classes and to say, 'Oh yes, some employers don't treat their workingmen fairly and don't give them sufficient pay.' That is all very well but the one man and the one movement which has shown how to get better pay for the down-trodden is Jim Larkin and his policy. My friends, they say they don't like Larkin's methods, very likely not. When you go down to a dentist with a bad tooth, his methods are not very agreeable but you get the tooth out and then comes relief.
>
> Jim Larkin's methods are not those of the rose leaf or the kid glove. He is a man with more heart than head as any good man the world has ever seen, has been. He doesn't sit down and calculate and weigh up chances. He sees a wrong to be righted and by God, Jim Larkin is going to do it.

Talk about the brutality of coercing people to join the union. Why, my friends, there was more brutality shown on the streets of Dublin by the armed forces of law and order in one short hour on Saturday last, than has been shown by the Irish Transport Union workers in the years of their existence.

An attempt has been made by the Jacobs and the Martin Murphys to get a general lock-out proclaimed of all who are connected with the Transport Workers' Union, but I don't think such a thing is possible. There must be employers of labour in Dublin, who are ashamed of the conditions of the working classes in the city. If my voice either through the press or otherwise, could reach the more enlightened section of the employers of labour in your great city, I would respectfully appeal to them not to allow themselves to be dragged at the heels of Martin Murphyism with all the poverty and moral and physical degradation which the continuation of the present system entails. Better a thousand times to take sides with Jim Larkin in fighting for a cleaner city and a healthier and a happier race of people than try to break down the most potent agency for elevating the working classes which Ireland has yet produced.

The power of landlordism has been broken. Absentee landlordism has been wiped out, and now a new power for evil has grown up in our midst—the power of Capitalism. Here you have one man in Dublin owning your tramways, with shares in all kinds of public works, and that man is to you what the landlords of old were to your fathers. He has power over you. He said cynically the other day, at the Chamber of Commerce, that he would starve you into submission. My friends, most of us have served too long an apprenticeship to privation to be very much afraid of it. There is going to be no starvation in Dublin; but the Trade Union Movement in Ireland will stand by you, and I believe, though I have no power to speak with authority, the Trade Union Movement of Great Britain will stand by you. I know this, that the section of the movement with which I am most prominently identified in past years—the Socialist movement—will stand by you firmly.

Within two years Hardie was dead, his heart broken by the insanity of war, the betrayal by his socialist comrades in so many countries of their pledge to oppose war, and the intense hostility of his fellow-countrymen to his stand against the war.

In his speech at the funeral of James Nolan, Hardie had looked to 'the great international working-class movement to be a new power to battle against war and militarism, fighting equally for the coming of the time when the races of the world would remember that first of all they were human beings, and instead of combating and fighting one with the other, they would co-operate together for the promotion of the common good.' That was the principled stand too of his fellow-socialists in Ireland, Jim Larkin and James Connolly, on the outbreak of war.

Notwithstanding Hardie's disbelief that the Dublin employers would proclaim a general lock-out, on the very day of James Nolan's funeral a meeting of 404 employers was held at 35 Dawson Street, presided over by

William Martin Murphy. The meeting unanimously adopted two resolutions:

Resolution I
That this meeting of employers, while asserting its friendly feelings to Trades Unionism, hereby declares that the position created by the Irish Transport and General Workers' Union (a Union in name only) is a menace to all trade organisation, and has become intolerable.

Resolution II
That, in order to deal effectively with the present situation, all employers should bind themselves to adopt a common line of action by signing the agreement presented herewith.

Agreement
We hereby pledge ourselves in future not to employ any persons who continue to be members of the Irish Transport and General Workers' Union, and any person refusing to carry out our lawful and reasonable instructions, or the instructions of those placed over them, will be instantly dismissed, no matter to what Union they belong.

Within days, the following document was handed to tens of thousands of Dublin workers:

I hereby undertake to carry out all instructions given me by or on behalf of my employers, and further I agree to immediately resign my membership of the Irish Transport and General Workers' Union (if a member) and I further undertake that I will not join or in any way support this Union.

Chapter 25

The Askwith Inquiry

During the period 1910–1913 there were major strikes and lock-outs in the main industries in Britain. Following strikes among miners, railway workers and textile operatives and in other industries in 1910, the climax was reached with the setting up of the famous Triple Alliance of miners, railwaymen, and transport workers. There were conflicts between strikers and police and in some cases, as in Tonypandy in Wales, the involvement of the military. Tom Mann's syndicalist propaganda had resulted in the Transport Workers' Federation—led by Robert Williams and catering for dockers, seamen, and carters—becoming a highly militant body. A general strike of seamen affecting every port compelled the Shipping Federation to withdraw its ban on the employment of members of the National Union of Seamen and Firemen. The port of London was brought to a complete stop by a strike of dockers led by Ben Tillett.

Tom Mann led a transport stoppage in Liverpool. The city was in a state of siege, and there were pitched battles in the streets. The settlement conceded practically all the strikers had demanded. In August 1911 the four railway unions called a strike, to which 200,000 workers responded. Winston Churchill, the Home Secretary, mobilised 50,000 troops. Soldiers opened fire at Liverpool and Llanelli.

In 1912 a coalmine stoppage, beginning on 1 March, affected a million workers. The strike was ended by the Miners' Federation on 6 April. Things came to a head in London in May when the port employers refused to meet the Transport Workers' Federation. Some eighty thousand London dock workers answered the federation's call for a strike; after two months the strike was broken, and there was widespread blacklisting of port workers by the employers.

In January 1914 all London building workers were locked out, on the issue of union recognition. Borrowing a leaf from William Martin Murphy's book of the previous year, the building contractors presented all their workers with a document requiring them to agree to work with non-union workers, under pain of a £1 fine. Not only did the union members refuse to sign but large numbers of non-union workers did too. Dublin's example was catching.

Altogether, the number of workers involved in strikes and lock-outs in Britain and Ireland increased from 170,000 in 1909 to 1,230,000 in 1912, while the number of days lost rose from 2,800,000 to 40,900,000.

The authorities feared that behind these industrial upheavals were forces of violent social revolution—syndicalism—of which Tom Mann was the leading exponent. Mann saw industrial action primarily as an instrument of social and political revolution—as did James Connolly and, to a lesser degree, James Larkin.

These years too were years of rapid expansion in union membership, which increased from 2,369,000 in 1909 to 3,987,000 at the end of 1913.

Events in Dublin from early in 1913 were perceived to be a re-run of the British experience during the previous three years. A distinct whiff of social revolution was in the air. After the events of Bloody Sunday and the riots leading to the deaths of two civilians at the hands of the police, the Chief Secretary for Ireland, Augustine Birrell, wrote to the Prime Minister, Herbert Asquith: 'The whole atmosphere is still charged with gunpowder.' Noting that Larkin's position was a peculiar one, he added: 'All the powers that are supposed to be of importance are against him; the [Irish] party, the whole Catholic Church, and the great body of Dublin citizens, to say nothing of the Government, and yet somehow or another he has support and is a great character and figure. The fact is that the dispute has lifted the curtain upon depths below Nationalism and the Home Rule movement ...'[1]

The reverberations in Britain of the repression by the police called for action, and the Chief Secretary, under great political pressure from England, decided to get the president of the Board of Trade, S. C. Buxton, to set up an inquiry under the Conciliation Act (1896) to inquire into the facts and circumstances of the dispute and to take steps to effect a settlement. He was not hopeful that, apart from clearing the issues, 'any modus for the future could be worked out,' he informed the Prime Minister.

Sir George Askwith, the Board of Trade's chief conciliation officer, chaired the court of inquiry. The other members were Thomas R. Ratcliffe-Ellis, secretary of the Mining Association of Great Britain, and J. R. Clynes MP, chairman of the Gas Workers' and General Labourers' Union. The inquiry opened in Dublin Castle on 29 September 1913. A formidable legal team was assembled by the employers, including T. M. Healy KC MP, Mr Hanna KC, and Sergeant Sullivan. Harry Gosling represented the Trades Union Congress, together with Havelock Wilson and Robert Williams (all of whom had been involved in the major disputes in Britain in the years preceding), while Thomas Johnson and David Campbell attended on behalf of the Irish Trades Union Congress.

The written submission of the workers' case was prepared by James Connolly. It was as follows:

> With all due respect to this Court, it is neither first nor last in our thoughts to-day, nor at any other stage of the inquiry. The ultimate tribunal to which we appeal is not this Court, much as we desire to assist its operations, but rather the verdict of the class to which we belong. We do not claim to be philanthropists labouring to preserve social amenities for the sake of some nebulous, changing thing known as 'the public'. We do not pretend to be animated by a fierce zeal for public order, though we hope we shall never wantonly disturb it, nor do we profess to be inspired by a single-minded desire to aid capitalists to conduct their business at all costs. No, we are banded together for the purpose of elevating our class, of organising that

class for the conquest of its rights. If the public, the forces of law and order and the capitalist class are willing to co-operate with us towards that end, well and good. If, on the other hand, the social and political forces represented by these three terms unite to defeat and subdue us and to thwart our just aspirations as we believe they have done in this case, we shall still press onward believing that eventually victory, and the verdict of history will be on our side. This mental attitude of ours explains our position in this dispute. The learned counsel for the employers says that for the past five years there have been more strikes than there have been since Dublin was a capital. Practically every responsible man in Dublin to-day admits that the social conditions of Dublin are a disgrace to civilisation.

Have these two sets of facts no relation? We believe that they stand to one another in the relations of cause and effect. The long period of stagnation in the labour ranks of Dublin was responsible for the growth in your midst of labour and housing conditions scarcely to be equalled outside Bombay or Constantinople. Now that the Irish Transport and General Workers' Union and its officials have set out to arouse the people; now that fierce, and it may be sometimes reckless, fighting has inspired the suffering masses with a belief in their own ability to achieve some kind of emancipation; now, in short, that the luxury, comfort, and even the security of the propertied classes are menaced, we see the quickening of a faint sense of social conscience in Dublin. But until aroused by the shock of industrial war, the propertied classes of Dublin have well deserved their unenviable notoriety for, like the typical Irish landlords of the past, 'enforcing their rights with a rod of iron and renouncing their duties with a front of brass.'

They tell us that they recognise trade unions. For answer we say that when they did so, it was wherever the necessity of a long apprenticeship made it difficult to replace a worker if he went on strike, but whenever no such apprenticeship existed to protect the worker the Dublin employers made fierce and relentless war upon trade unions amongst the unskilled labourers. Messrs. Tedcastle and M'Cormack is an instance among shipping firms. The Tramway Company has seen at least two attempts to organise its men. It fought and crushed the attempts, and the workhouse, the insane asylum, and the emigrant ship received the ruined lives of those who made the efforts. They complain that the Irish Transport and General Workers' Union cannot be trusted to keep its agreements. The majority of shipping firms in Dublin to-day are at present working, refusing to join in this mad enterprise engineered by Mr. Murphy, and with perfect confidence in the faith of the Irish Transport and General Workers' Union. They complain of the sympathetic strike, but the members of the United Builders' Labourers' Trade Union, a union recruited from the same class of labourers as the Irish Transport and General Workers' Union, have been subjected to a sympathetic lock-out because of their refusal to pledge themselves not to help the latter body if they so desired it at any time in the future. A more unreasonable pledge was never asked for. It is as if, instead of waiting until the contingency arose, the Irish Transport and General Workers' Union were to call a strike in a shop because the employer would not sign an agreement not to lend his own money to another employer if he needed it. To such an extent has the madness of the employers led them. We on our side say that we are proud of the spirit of solidarity exhibited in Dublin; we are proud of the manner in which organised labour in these islands has rallied to help us in defeating the attempt of the employers to dictate to the workers to what Union they should or should not belong.

T. M. Healy's address to the inquiry extended over two days. According to Arnold Wright (whose book *Disturbed Dublin*, published in 1914, had been commissioned by the employers), the address would 'live amongst [Healy's] happiest efforts of forensic oratory.' The address sought to demonstrate that the Larkinite movement was a purely anarchical one, in which the most subversive principles were backed by an insidious system of moral and physical intimidation.

Healy—to George Russell 'the bitterest tongue that ever wagged in this island'—described the workers as puppets in the hands of three of four of their leaders and alleged that trade unionism in the mouths of these people was a mockery existing only in name. 'Mr. Larkin acts the part of a Napoleon; he orders this or that, and the men obey him, and that had brought about the strikes. Why,' Healy plaintively cried, 'the present system is the most finished system of tyranny that was ever started in any country. These haughty masters have worn out their marrow bones in kneeling at the shrine of Larkin!'

Healy expatiated on the scandalous character of the *Irish Worker*. Larkin's abuse of Murphy he quoted with relish: his description of Murphy 'as the greatest ogre, as a monster in human shape, a sweater,' was among the milder epithets used. Healy had conceded that from 1911 until 1913 'Mr. Larkin's organisation, with great skill and ability, had extended its operations. He believed it had done some good. He was far from saying that Mr. Larkin had not done some good. He believed he had.'[2]

When he came to be cross-examined by Larkin, Murphy stood up, as did Larkin. This was the first occasion on which the two men had met. The writer John Eglinton (William Magee) wrote in *A Memoir of Æ*:

> I looked in there one day and have a vivid recollection of the dark inchoate face of Larkin and of his tall ungainly figure, craning forward as he bellowed forth his arraignment; and opposite him the calm handsome face of Murphy, with his trim white beard, speaking just above his breath and glaring occasionally at his angry foe; near him rose from time to time the robust form of his counsel, Thersites Healy, releasing effortlessly his biting speech.[3]

Another observer, later a distinguished writer, Liam O'Flaherty, was to write:

> The dock workers idolized Larkin. Someone has said of him that he 'seized the Dublin workers by the scruff of the neck' and made them erect ... In October 1913, a Board of Trade Inquiry was set up to examine the causes of the Labour troubles in the city. In this inquiry Tim Healy represented the employers; Larkin represented the workers ... In the struggle of wits, Healy was easily defeated. Larkin's cross-examination of William Martin Murphy

was masterly, and were it not for Healy's help the great employer would have cut a very sorry figure indeed ... We are exceedingly sorry to relate that Healy played this part in the most scandalous episode in recent Irish history.[4]

Murphy, memorably, had been described by G. K. Chesterton as 'more like some morbid prince of the fifteenth century, full of cold anger, but not without perverted piety.'[5] Less elegantly, a friend of Tim Healy was to comment that Murphy went through life with the Companies Act in one hand and the *Imitation of Christ* in the other.[6] Murphy, apparently, had been 'very reluctantly' driven by the other employers to appear at the inquiry.[7]

Frank Callanan in his biography of Healy expresses the intriguing view that Healy's antipathy towards Larkin remained finely counterbalanced by his hatred of the Irish Party.[8] Healy, he wrote, was 'loath to diminish the challenge Larkin posed from the left to the hegemony of the Irish party in Dublin.'[9] In a letter to his brother, Maurice Healy, on 10 October 1913 Healy had written: 'I told Murphy he was fighting Redmond's battle, and he was well aware of it. Personally I should prefer Larkin to Devlin, and I told Murphy so. It is deplorable that his overthrow will mean the victory of the Mollies, and that we should be fighting their corner!'[10] (The Ancient Order of Hibernians was pejoratively designated the 'Molly Maguires'. It was intensely hostile to Larkin, denouncing him at every opportunity.) On 11 October, Healy wrote to his brother pointing out that Larkin had been useful in destroying the Mollies, and 'that is why I was keen to come to an understanding with him.' He added, however, that Larkin was 'utterly impossible, and I think a little astray in the head.'[11]

Even as late as January 1914 Healy did not believe that Larkin had been vanquished. Murphy, he wrote on 12 January, 'thinks he is up against a strike, while I think he is up against a theory.' Because of what Healy considered to be 'the pusillanimousness of the Catholic church in the face of Larkin's challenge,' Dublin had ceased to be the capital for Redmondites.[12]

Strangely, a somewhat similar view had been expressed by the Chief Secretary for Ireland, Augustine Birrell, in a letter to the British Prime Minister, Herbert Asquith. 'Were there to be an election in Dublin tomorrow two of the four Nationalist MPs would lose their seats.' Birrell added that he 'would not be surprised if Carson holds out some sort of a hand to Larkin as a brother rebel against nationalist tyranny!'[13] Healy had been primarily responsible for the overthrow of Parnell as leader of the Irish Party. In this he had the active co-operation of the Catholic Church, and the wholehearted support of William Martin Murphy.

One of the papers owned by Murphy was the *Irish Catholic*.[14] It had been particularly vicious in its references to Larkin almost from his arrival in Dublin and offensive to Dublin's slum-dwellers. At an early stage of the dispute the paper wrote:

Into these thoroughfares there have poured nightly all the foul reserves of the slums, human beings whom life in the most darksome depths of a great city has deprived of most of the characteristics of civilisation. In the majority of instances they are beings whose career is generally a prolonged debauch, seldom broken by the call of labour ... wrecks which litter the floor of life as many a foul and pest-haunted hulk lies amidst the rocks and weeds at the bottom of the ocean ...[15]

Healy did not hold out any hope of the Askwith Inquiry resolving the dispute. He had written to his brother, after the Chief Secretary had announced the setting up of the inquiry, expressing the view that 'the strike will continue until the men are exhausted.'[16] Later he wrote: 'I fear the strike can only be settled as the Port of London strike was, by the surrender of the men.'[17]

There was a political issue involved in the efforts to resolve the Dublin dispute. The Redmondite leadership of the Irish Party was as hostile to Murphy, the anti-Parnellite, as it was to Larkin. F. S. L. Lyons in his biography of John Dillon quotes a letter from Dillon to T. P. O'Connor: 'Dublin is hell. And I don't see the way out. Murphy is a desperate character, Larkin as bad. It would be a blessing if they exterminated each other.'[18]

Without doubt the highlight of the hearings at the Askwith Inquiry was Larkin's impassioned onslaught on the forces that had made Dublin a hell for up to one-third of its citizens, whose right to the barest living was actively contested by the authorities and the employers and scarcely defended by the churches. In his address Larkin was less concerned with the rights and wrongs of the industrial relations situation in Dublin or with the terms of settlement that might emerge: rather he was concerned to put on the record the appalling social conditions of Dublin's poor and to ensure that the authorities and the public realised that what was at stake was not a mere strike or indeed lock-out but a basic issue of human liberty, the right of workers to organise themselves to advance their interests and to choose their own leaders, and, more particularly, his insistence that at issue was a social revolution, the revolt of the underman and woman striving to create the conditions for a better life for all.

In this context it is extraordinary that Archbishop Walsh—not at all unsympathetic to the workers, though hostile to their leaders' methods in pursuit of their claims—should have seen fit to complain to the Lord Lieutenant, Lord Aberdeen, criticising Askwith's conduct of the inquiry. Walsh wondered how any competent commissioner, let alone one known to be an able lawyer, 'could have conducted an inquiry in such an extraordinary fashion.'[19]

The following are extracts from Larkin's address to the Askwith Inquiry:

The first point I wish to make is that the employers in this City, and throughout Ireland generally, think they have a right to deal with their own as they please, and to use and exploit the workers as they please. They assume all the rights and deny any to the men who make their wealth. They deny the right of the men and women who work for them to combine and try and assist one another to improve their conditions of life.

195

The masters assert their right to combine. I claim that the right should be given to the workers. The employers claim that there should be rights only on one side. The employers are the dominant power in the country and they are going to dominate our lives. As Shakespeare says, 'The man who holds the means whereby I live holds and controls my life.'

For fifty years the employers have controlled the lives of the workers. Now, when the workers are trying to get some of their rights, the employers deny the right of their men to combine. Man cannot live without intercourse with his fellow beings. Man is, as has been said by an eminent authority, a social animal. But these men—these 'captains of industry'—draw a circle round themselves and say, 'No one must touch me.' But they have no right to a monopoly. The workers desire that the picture should be drawn fairly. But these able gentlemen who have drawn the picture for the employers have found that they could not do it! They have the technique, the craftsmanship but they have not got the soul. No man can paint a picture without seeing the subject for himself. I will try to assist our friends who have failed. As I say, they have the pigments and the craftsmanship, but they have not been able to paint a picture of life in the industrial world of Ireland.

Let us take the statement by Sir Charles Cameron. There are, he says, 21,000 families, averaging $4\frac{1}{2}$ to each family, living in single rooms in this City. Will these gentlemen opposite accept responsibility? They say they have the right to control the means by which the workers live. They must therefore accept responsibility for the conditions under which the workers live. Twenty-one thousand families living in the dirty slums of Dublin, five persons in each room, with, I suppose, less than one thousand cubic feet. Yet it was laid down that each sleeping room should at least have 300 cubic feet for each person. In Mountjoy Gaol, where I had the honour to reside on more than one occasion—criminals (but I am inclined to believe that most of the criminals are outside and innocent men inside) were allowed 400 cubic feet each. Yet men who slave and work, and their women—those beautiful women we have among the working classes—are compelled to live, many of them, five in a room, with less than 300 cubic feet each. They are taken from their mothers' breasts at an early age and are used up as material is used up in a fire. These are some of the conditions that obtain in this Catholic City of Dublin, the most church-going city, I believe, in the world.

The workers are determined that this state of affairs must cease. Christ will not be crucified any longer in Dublin by these men. I, and those who think with me, want to show the employers that the workers will have to get the same opportunity of enjoying a civilised life as they themselves have.

Mr. Healy has drawn a picture from the employers' viewpoint. I want to show the other side, the true side. I will use other pigments and more vivid colours. Go to some of the factories in Dublin. See some of the maimed men, maimed girls, with hands cut off, eyes punctured, bodies and souls seared, and think of the time when they are no longer useful to come up to the £1 a week or some other standard. Then they are thrown on the human scrap-heap.

See at every street corner the mass of degradation, controlled by the employers, and due to the existing system. Their only thought was the public house, and, driven to death, they made their way thither to poison their bodies and get a false stimulant to enable them for a time, to give something more back to the employers for the few paltry shillings thrown at them. These are the men whom the employers call loafers.

The employers bring up from the country poor serfs who know nothing of Dublin or city life so that they would bring down the wages of men already here. The employers do this because their souls are steeped in grime and actuated only by the hope of profit-making, and because they have no social conscience. But this lock-out will arouse a social conscience in Dublin and Ireland generally. I am out to help to arouse that social conscience and to lift up and better the lot of those who are sweated and exploited. But I am also out to save the employers from themselves, to save them from degradation and damnation.

Mr. Murphy said he had had no strikes of any moment during his connection with industrial concerns, but I have proved that his life has been one continuous struggle against the working classes. I give him credit that in a great many cases he came out on top. Why? Because he has never been faced by men who were able to deal with him, because he has never been faced by a social conscience such as has now been aroused, and, according to which the working classes would combine to alter the present conditions of Labour. He had said he would drive 'Larkinism' headlong into the sea— I evidently have the honour of coining a new word. But there is such a thing as human thought—and nobody has killed it yet, or driven it into the sea, or kept it from making progress.

We have seen the multifarious operations of Mr. Murphy all over the world. He is an able man with the power and capacity to buy up the ablest men of the working classes, and he has used his power relentlessly. He may use that power for a while but the time always comes when such power would be smashed and deservedly smashed. There must be a break

The Irish workmen are out to work for a living, and to get access to the means of life. They are not going to be slaves; they are not going to allow their women to be the slaves of a brutal capitalistic system which has neither a soul to be saved nor a soft place to be kicked.

I am engaged in a holy work. Of course, I cannot now get employers to see things from my point of view, but they should try to realise my work. I have worked hard from an early age. I have not had the opportunities of the men opposite, but I have made the best of my opportunities. I have been called anti-Christ. I have been called an Atheist. Well, if I were an Atheist I would not deny it. I am a Socialist. I believe in a co-operative commonwealth, but that is far ahead in Ireland.

Has there been a reason why there were not strikes long ago? Is the reason not to be found in the fact that the men have been so brutally treated that they had not the strength to raise their heads? Why, when I came to Dublin I found that the men on the quays had been paid their wages in public houses, and if they did not waste most of their money there they would not get work the next time. Every stevedore was getting ten per cent of the money taken by the publican from the worker, and the man who would not spend his money across the counter was not wanted. Men are not allowed to go to their duties on Sunday morning. After a long day's work they get home tired and half drunk. No man would work under the old conditions except he was half drunk.

I have tried to lift men up out of the state of degradation. No monetary benefit has accrued to me. I have taken up the task through intense love of my class. I have given the men a stimulus, heart and hope which they never had before. I have made men out of drunken gaol-birds. The employers may now drive them over the precipice, they may compel them, after a long and weary struggle, to recognise the document submitted to them not to belong to the Irish Transport Workers' Union, but it will only be for a time. The day will come when they will break their bonds, and give back blow for blow.

Is it any wonder a Larkin arose? Was there not a need for a Larkin? If the employers want peace they can have peace, but if they want war they will get war.

The members of the court of inquiry unanimously agreed a report, which was finished quickly, being read at the session held on 6 October. It condemned 'the sympathetic strike' and 'the sympathetic lock-out'. It roundly condemned the document that the employers had insisted on their workers signing as a condition of employment, and found that 'this document imposes on the signatories conditions which are contrary to individual liberty, and which no workman or body of workmen could reasonably be expected to accept.'

The report also put forward methods of settling differences that existed or might arise thereafter that 'might well be accepted as a basis for discussion.' These included the appointment of conciliation committees, to which the workers would elect by ballot representatives from among themselves. It also outlined procedures that might be used in the event of disputes arising. The members of the court of inquiry declared that they were not in favour of 'compulsory arbitration'.

The workers' representatives indicated that they were prepared to enter into discussions where the report left off. In its formal response to the report, on 14 October, the Employers' Executive Committee repeated their refusal to recognise the 'Irish Transport Union' until the union 'be re-organised on proper lines' and 'with new officials who have met with the approval of the British Joint Labour Board.' Until then the employers would 'continue to insist on the undertaking referred to being signed.'

The battle of attrition between the locked-out workers and the 404 Dublin employers continued.

Chapter 26

Fiery Cross

Following his trial on three charges, the jury, after a half-hour deliberation, found Larkin guilty on the first count of the indictment, of using seditious language, and he was sentenced by Mr Justice Madden to seven months' imprisonment. 'With an imposing escort,' he was removed to Mountjoy Prison.

British public opinion was outraged at the sentence, and there were immediate political repercussions. The government lost seats in by-elections, and this resulted in their deciding unanimously that the sentence was 'grossly excessive' and should be reduced. Lloyd George had already stated that the 'most prominent explanation' for the Liberals' setback was probably Larkin.

Larkin was released after serving sixteen days of his sentence. At 7:30 a.m. on Thursday 13 November he walked out the gates of the prison, went home for 'a brush-up and a cup of tea,' and then walked down to Liberty Hall. That night at Beresford Place, Larkin denounced the British government, which, he told the crowd, 'had made a mistake in sending me to prison and have made a greater mistake in letting me out.' He announced that he was going 'to raise a fiery cross in England, Scotland and Wales.' Shortly afterwards, in a speech in Bristol, the Chief Secretary's constituency, Larkin attacked the government for exercising something he insisted he had not asked for—the royal prerogative.[1]

Within a few days Larkin held the first meeting of his Fiery Cross campaign in the huge Free Trade Hall in Manchester, which was packed, with twenty thousand waiting outside. This meeting prompted a remarkable editorial in the *Manchester Guardian*:

> The enthusiastic welcome given to Mr. James Larkin when he visited Manchester yesterday is something which cannot be lightly passed by even by those who distrust his methods, fear his influence, and are in doubt about the justice of the cause he pleads. When a man's imprisonment raises such a storm of protest that Cabinet Ministers and Members of Parliament cannot speak even in the remotest parts of the country without having his name shouted at them, when the chance of hearing him speak fills the Free Trade Hall, and leaves thousands blocking the street outside for a sight of him, even the most convinced and implacable opponent, if he is honest, must admit that he is a man to be reckoned with—must admit, too, that a personal influence so extraordinary must be backed by a cause or a principle that deeply moves his fellow-countrymen.[2]

That same day the *Manchester Guardian* published a letter from William Martin Murphy, in which he wrote that 'the sole reason for this audacious attempt [the Dublin tram strike] ... was the colossal vanity and vaulting ambition of Mr. Larkin' and that 'the real question at stake is the personal supremacy of Mr. Larkin.' The editorial writer gave the reply:

> To this the impartial observer must simply retort, with respect, that of Mr. Larkin's personal supremacy there is no question at all. He may be—his speech, which we report verbatim, shows it—a man labouring under the stress of overmastering emotion, and therefore incoherent, violent; one who states rather than reasons, and a man of masterful and domineering temper, and therefore difficult to deal with. But if that were the whole truth about him he could not wield the immense influence he does over, not only the men he works amongst, but those he has never seen.

The editorial went on to quote a special correspondent of the *Times* (London), who wrote on 20 September that he found outside the ranks of the workers people who, while objecting to the 'sympathetic strike', were impressed by the personality of Mr Larkin and recognised his sincerity. After remarking that he was 'virulent and ill-mannered' on the platform, the correspondent said that 'those who approach him for an exchange of views find neither bitterness nor malice in his conversation.' 'Mr. Larkin's methods may be those of the Syndicalist,' the *Times* correspondent added, 'but he has no aim but to discover and increase the discontent of the under dog.'

The *Manchester Guardian* concluded:

> It is idle to dismiss Mr. Larkin with a sneer at the demagogue or abuse of the opponent of capitalism. The conditions of labour and housing in Dublin are now, thanks to the exposure by him and those who work with him, fairly well-known by the British public. It is sufficient to say that nothing so appalling, so shocking even to the slackest and most easily satisfied social conscience has been discovered in our time.

The enthusiasm of Larkin's reception at other centres in Britain was without precedent for a labour speaker. In city after city—Birmingham, Cardiff, Edinburgh (Connolly's birthplace), Glasgow, Hull, Leicester, Liverpool (Larkin's own birthplace), Newcastle, Preston, Stockport, Swansea—workers flocked to his meetings and rallies.

J. T. Murphy, a leader of the Communist Party of Great Britain and the Comintern in the twenties, recalled in his autobiography, *New Horizons* (1941), how the struggle of the poorest of Dublin's workers stirred all sections of the working class movement as never before since the days of Chartism. He remembered a great demonstration in Sheffield at which Larkin and George Lansbury were the speakers: 'Six-foot Jim Larkin and his powerful torrentially passionate eloquence swept the audience off its feet. He finished his speech with a rendering of William Morris's "The Day is Coming".' Murphy had never seen an audience so roused to demonstrative enthusiasm. After Larkin's death the Scottish Communist MP William Gallacher 'remembered well when Larkin came over to

Britain how he electrified not only Irish workers but all workers who had the opportunity of hearing him.'[3]

The greatest of the meetings at which Larkin spoke was at the Royal Albert Hall in London. This 'Great Rally for Dublin', as it was billed, was organised by the *Daily Herald*. On the eve of the rally the *Daily Sketch* reported that among the thirty thousand applications for tickets were peers, knights, twenty-six MPs of all parties, bishops, university professors, authors, and clergymen. The Prime Minister's daughter was among the early applicants for four tickets. The paper's reporter wrote of a belated applicant, a young Catholic priest 'trembling with eagerness' to join in the rally. The *Daily Sketch* was in no doubt that 'Jim Larkin was the star of the programme, the man whom peers and politicians, parsons and poets alike are suddenly anxious to hear.'

The Albert Hall can seldom have witnessed a scene such as on that night of 20 November 1913. One of the speakers was Big Bill Haywood—billed as the undesirable citizen from the States—soon to become general secretary of the Industrial Workers of the World. In his autobiography, *Bill Haywood's Book* (1929), he wrote that it proved to be 'a wonderful meeting'.

> Twenty-five or thirty thousand people, more than could get in the hall, had gathered. Some students attempted to disrupt the meeting but the stewards were well organised and ejected the noisy bunch in quick order. A son of George Lansbury came over the railing of the first balcony and dropped into a struggling group which was fighting to get into the hall ... I have never spoken in any meeting with more satisfaction than in this auditorium.

Haywood described Larkin as 'a big bony man with a shock of iron-grey hair and marked features such as are appreciated by the sculptor or cartoonist.' It so happened that among the speakers at the meeting was a cartoonist, the Australian-born Will Dyson, who was to become one of the great cartoonists of his day. He did a full-page cartoon of Larkin for the *Daily Herald*, which was reproduced in the WUI publication *1913: Jim Larkin and the Dublin Lock-Out* (1964).

The students referred to were from the Royal College of Mines. Among them was David Garnett, later to become one of the most distinguished writers of his generation—he was not among the interrupters but was in fact sympathetic to Larkin and had warned the organisers of the threatened disruption. Hence the presence of a group of burly workers led by Con O'Lyhane from Cork, as big a man as Larkin, who had been associated with Connolly in 1898 and later went to England, where he was a socialist propagandist. Garnett, in the first of his three volumes of autobiography, *Golden Echo* (1970), wrote about the attempt to disrupt Larkin's speech:

> The interruptions had aroused Jim Larkin to fury. He walked up and down the platform like a caged tiger and his tremendous voice roared out angrily. Once the sound of fighting outside the hall penetrated, but Larkin roared a

little louder, telling us of the infamies of the Dublin employers and the corruption of the city fathers.

When Will Dyson was speaking, students dropped from the boxes to the tiers of seats beneath. The speaker hesitated, and Larkin sprang forward on the platform and boomed: 'Don't mind these little fellows. We have some hefty boys from the London docks who will soon attend to them.'

Other speakers at the Albert Hall meeting included the suffragist leader Sylvia Pankhurst and Robert Williams, secretary of the Transport Workers' Federation.

Chapter 27

Larkin at Liberty Hall

Sir William Orpen

Jim Larkin suddenly appeared in Dublin. No matter how much people may think that Jim has jumped off the deep end since, in those days, in all truth I must admit, to me he seemed a most godly, honest, straightforward man. I used to go down to the dirt and filth of Liberty Hall and sit in Jim Larkin's office in the afternoons just for the interest of watching the man. He was always sincere, always modest, always thinking of others, during those terrible strike times when he was out against 'graft', drink, and starvation in the city. The poverty in Dublin during that time of riots and strikes was terrible, and the basements of Liberty Hall were used as soup kitchens. I remember a few little things that may show some reason for my admiration for this man.

On a certain Saturday afternoon I was with him. A letter had come in saying that the Roman Catholic Archbishop was going to speak against him from the pulpit on Sunday morning. About 4.30 up came a man and said a priest from some village near Dundalk insisted on seeing him. 'Show him up,' said Jim. In came a very excited priest. 'Well,' said Jim, 'what is it all about?' 'About!' he shouted. 'I hear they are going to speak against you from the pulpit to-morrow, and that your people are going to have a procession through the city. I want you to let me lead them. You are the Saviour of Dublin.' Jim rang his bell. A man came in. He muttered something to him and the man departed. Jim lit a cigar slowly and said, 'I thank you from my heart for your goodwill, and what you wish to do for me, but I cannot allow you to do it. Now, will you really trust me and do what I tell you?' 'Surely,' said the priest. 'Then,' said Jim, 'you are to go back to your village at once and carry on your duties there, and forget that you ever came to Liberty Hall.' Then turning to one of the clerks he said, 'Show his Reverence downstairs. There is a cab waiting at the door. Take him to Amiens Street Station and see him off in the train to Dundalk.' Then turning to the priest he said, 'Good-bye, Father. This is the best thing you can do for me and for yourself. Pray for me.' And out went the poor priest in tears, with his head bowed.

One of the next visitors that afternoon was a high prelate of the Church. He thundered at Jim. Did he not realise that on the morrow he was going to be spoken against from the pulpit; that 'the Church' had ordered him not to hold his meeting on that Sunday afternoon in the Phoenix Park; that if he did he was defying the Church? So he railed on at him for a long time, his arms flying about, and occasionally thrusting his forefinger close to Jim's face. All this time Larkin was sitting back in his chair puffing his cigar, with his clear eyes fixed on the prelate. Not a move did he make. When the prelate's outburst ceased from want of breath, Jim got slowly out of his chair and said very gently, 'Pray God, Holy Father, that when you rise to-morrow morning you will be able to say your prayers to your God with the same peace of mind that I will say mine.' And turning to one of his men he said, 'Show the Holy Father the way out.' And he departed amid great silence. And Jim continued his work and his cigar.

As I stated, there was great poverty in Dublin during these strikes, much starvation and many deaths, especially amongst the children. One of Jim's plans was to get these starving children out of the city to whoever would take and keep them. He, indeed, got a lot sent to England; and here his enemies pulled all their strings against him. The anti-Larkin newspapers were full of it. 'Larkin sends Dublin children to England. The Sassenach influence will destroy them. It is an anti-Irish act.' And so on. It is strange, but something like this always used to crop up in Ireland, at such times against all who were really trying to do things for the good of the people. Sometimes we can explain the cause, sometimes not. Parnell fell in love. Who can blame him for that? Hugh Lane tried to get rid of pictures he could not sell. An abominable lie. John Synge wrote a criminal play against the morals of his own countrymen and countrywomen. What stupidity! In Horace Plunkett his countrymen refused to believe. No one knows why in this case, unless perhaps he was born too well-off, and worked for nothing. Even that great man, Douglas Hyde, who perhaps did more for Ireland than any living man, seems nearly forgotten. And as to the poor English politicians who were broken by being given office in Ireland, their names are too numerous to mention. And so they got at Jim Larkin and his idea of saving the children from starvation!

One afternoon Professor Sheehy Skeffington was to take two children to the Kingsbridge Station and hand them over to Lady X., who was going to keep them at her place in Meath. The professor did not turn up in time, and Larkin said, 'Orpen, would you be good enough to take them?' 'Certainly,' said I, and went off downstairs with the two poor little things. About half-way down I met the professor hurrying up. 'What are you doing with these children?' said he. I explained that as he was not there, Larkin had asked me to see them to Kingsbridge. 'This is my business,' said the professor, and held out his hand to the children, and went on downstairs. So I returned to Jim, told him what had happened, and took my place to watch and wonder at the strange things to be seen in that dirty room, which was on the second storey. But even there the air was pungent with the smell of the cauldrons of soup from the basement, and of the Dubliners who came with their bottles, tin cans, or any kind of utensil that would hold this hot, life-giving stuff. All day long lines of starving people waiting for their turn, very quiet and silent, no rough words or jostling; they were too weak for such things. It was a sad sight. Suddenly we heard great noises and loud words. The door burst open, and in came a lot of people with Sheehy Skeffington. He had nothing on except a blanket wrapped round him. When he was delivering the children to Lady X. at Kingsbridge, the anti-Larkinites attacked him and tore all his clothes off. I nearly got that!

Later, there was a lull of work in Jim's room, and he said to me, 'I suppose you think I smoke too many cigars?' 'You do smoke a lot,' said I. 'Well,' said he, 'it's like this. I am up before the Court on Monday. They are sure to give me at least six months, and not a smoke will I get in prison all that time, so you must forgive me if I'm overdoing it a bit now. I'm making up for lost time—ahead.' That night Sinclair and I asked him to come out and have something to eat, and go to the Tivoli Music Hall. 'Ah, no,' said Jim. 'Sure, you're asking for trouble to go out with me. There would be sure to be hell, for or against me, if I showed my face at the Tivoli. Go and enjoy yourselves, and I'll go back home and have a good long sleep in my own comfortable bed, for I'm told the beds in Kilmainham Jail are not too comfortable at all.' And that was the last I ever saw of Jim Larkin, but I have never forgotten him.

[From Sir William Orpen, *Stories of Old Ireland and Myself* (1924), chapter 10.]

William Orpen was a visiting professor at the Dublin School of Art. In a letter to Sir William Rothenstein, the distinguished painter and principal of the Royal School of Art, London, Orpen wrote: 'Larkin is the greatest man I ever met' (quoted by Konody and Dark in *Sir William Orpen: Artist and Man*).

Chapter 28

Larkin Goes to Jail

On 28 October 1913 Larkin was tried and sentenced to seven months' imprisonment for using seditious language. The articles that follow Jim Larkin's message—by Constance Markievicz, Ben Tillet, George Lansbury, and Maud Gonne—were published in the *Irish Worker* on 1 November 1913.

From the prison gates

Jim Larkin

At the entrance to Mountjoy Gaol I desire to address a few words of encouragement and hope to you. We have now been associated together for the past seven years. Throughout that period of time we were in a chronic state of sturm-und-drang, always and ever advancing from position to position. Attacks on us have been made in front and flank, and we have always proved unconquerable. The fort is as impregnable to-day as in the past days when we hoisted the flag.

This great fight of ours is not simply a question of shorter hours or better wages. It is a great fight for human liberty, liberty of action, liberty to live as human beings should live, exercising their God-given faculties and powers over nature; always aiming to reach out for a higher betterment and development, trying to achieve in our own time the dreams of great thinkers and poets of this nation—not as some men do, working for their own individual betterment and aggrandisement.

It has always been in our mind the building up of this nation not that we ourselves might enjoy the fulfilment of our own work, but that those who come after us may enter into the promised land. This work requires the right not only to combine, but to use that combination for our own economic and industrial emancipation.

Now, I will be away from you in body, but I will be with you in spirit. I have faith that those men who are honoured by being left to bear the standard will get your heartiest, honest and sustained support, that there will be no compromise. Trust no one but yourselves; have faith in the men you have elected and will elect; they must be the men who will decide what settlement shall be arrived at in our present conflict.

Without wishing to cast any reflection upon our friends across the Channel, this fight must be settled by the men here at home in our own Union. Without in any way disparaging any order or section of the organised working-class, we of the Irish Transport and General Workers' Union cannot only claim but can make good our claim of being the pioneers in this grand class war.

History speaks in no uncertain way; it tells us that the pioneers must suffer, but suffering brings satisfaction, and to us who have been pioneers, we must during the period of this class struggle which we have entered into depend upon the loyalty, the faithfulness, and the determination of what is known industrially as the unskilled workers. Sometimes compelled to retreat, we have come back again into the battle with renewed strength and courage.

Men such as Daly, Partridge, McKeown and Connolly—any of these may be at liberty. These and these only must we allow and authorise to act for you. There will be an attempt to seduce you from your allegiance, but no one can mislead truth. Everyone hopes such a deep and just cause as that in which you and I are engaged must win out. Don't forget the RED HAND that struck terror in the hearts of the sweaters and slum property owners, the publicans and all who may be out to destroy life.

We live to give life, hope and joy. And now for the sake of your children, and children's children, be true to yourselves; and, moreover, may you by the stress of the attack of this struggle learn anew; stand by the Union and live out the motto of your Union—'Each for All, and All for Each.' I enjoin, even to the humblest, and I so convey to all good luck till the prison gates are open.

In jail

Constance Markievicz

Jim Larkin is in jail. In jail for fighting the workers' cause. In jail for championing the poor against the rich, the oppressed against the oppressor. For daring to speak straight and fight straight he is sentenced to seven months for 'using seditious language.'

He dared attack 'Capitalism'. Under the flag of 'Capitalism' you find the British Crown with all its minions, its judges, magistrates, inspectors, spies, police, the Antient Order of Hibernians—even some of the clergy—all the worshippers of Mammon, all these were ranged against Jim Larkin.

The case was tried by his enemies, his accusers; the 'just' judge, a capitalist; the 'twelve honest men', men of the capitalist class—some Hibernians, some interested in the various businesses now combined against 'Larkinism'; all the craft and cunning of trained police witnesses, and of Castle note-takers; the whole power of Capitalism and English rule were ranged against the man, Jim Larkin.

In the little Court House in Green Street, Jim stood—a noble figure, fearless, with no thought for himself, strong in his faith, certain of ultimate success. He had faced jail before without flinching, and he will face it again. Many a fight in the cause of Freedom has been fought in Green Street Dock; it was one of the last stations on Robert Emmet's road to Calvary. It bears a great tradition of noble souls who gave their all in the cause of freedom.

Jim Larkin has given his youth, his strength, his brains, his courage, his greatness to the cause of freeing the enslaved; his liberty is his last gift. To the wage slaves—his brothers—whom he loves, his life is theirs should they require it. All honest men and women must love, respect, and honour him; all true hearts must be prepared to follow him; to carry on the fight as he would have it carried on; to give their all in the cause of freedom— the workers' cause. Let his last message be written in flowing letters in our hearts. Remember you are Irishmen. Stand fast! Let there be no weakening.

Jim is in jail for us; what sacrifice can we make for Jim? What offering of work and self-sacrifice can we lay at his feet?

Let none of us think that we are of no importance and that we don't count; every little one of us is something to Jim. Let not the least of us forfeit the right to look him in the face and take his hand when he comes out of jail.

To the Dublin strikers

Ben Tillet

Dear comrades, men, women and children of the labour movement!

Ireland was never, as now, face to face with the real enemies of Ireland and the Irish people. Judge and jury were alike, the puppets of the master-despots; even the Crown Lawyer is forced by the compulsion of the real masters of the people, to crucify a good man in the person of Jim Larkin, and his fellow fighters for justice.

There was never a more cruel and brutal persecution in the history of Irish torture than the present conspiracy of capitalists, using the English forces to coerce a great people. I am sure, though, that if the workers of Dublin and Ireland responded to the great heroic call to save their children from the sweater, the thief and the political charlatan, that Ireland will be freer for having brave good men to fight for them. I should be proud to stand in the position of Jim Larkin, equally as I am proud of the workers who are with him, to fight for the God-given right of life and freedom.

The workers of England are also having their eyes opened to the brutality of the conspiracy against the workers, and the heart of every English worker loving freedom and truth is with you. Not only food, but money will be sent you. We shall try on this side to make the movement even still more significant. The Irish workers here join with their English mates, and we shall be making a movement that will be handed down to history as an epoch. The brutes and the Bench of wrong-doers may crucify the man, but the cause will be stronger and mightier for the atrocities practised on the leaders.

I glory in the magnificent fight you are making. There is some Connemara away in the veins of me, and I want to see you win. Tell the men to keep together and we shall be able to win, for England is awakening to the dreadful atrocities and the murdering of the innocent children and the men and women who are denied a bare subsistence and the elementary rights of living.

A new Jerusalem

George Lansbury

We ask you to remember that the darkest night is that which precedes very often the most glorious dawn. Your country has suffered much, sometimes at the hands of the possessing classes of this country, but the common people over here have suffered at the hands of these people just as you have suffered, but we have learnt, and we are not going to fight against one another merely because we live on two sides of the Irish Channel. Looking across the water at you, we know very well that you are men and women just like ourselves, sweated and robbed, many of you pauperised and destitute because of the evil that men do to one another.

But all of us have now awakened and the fight that lies before us is the fight, not for sectarian domination, not even for national domination, but it is a fight for the workers of the world to come together and join their hands with one another and march forward, not to conquer other people, but to conquer their own conditions and out of the misery and the destitution and the other evils amid which we now live to build a new Jerusalem.

Therefore it is that we men and women who belong to the 'Daily Herald League' bid you hope, be true to one another, don't let anything divide you. The most sacred thing in life is the unity of men and women, and so come together, let the spirit of love for one another animate and dominate you all the time.

Think of the other men's children, the other men's wives, the other men's mothers, as you would of your own and inscribe on your banner the words, 'Do unto others as you would they should do unto you.'

You will hear a great deal of religion. The Founder of our religion said that there were two great Commandments, the first of which was 'To love the Lord thy God with all thy heart, with all they soul, and with all thy strength'; and the second was like unto it, 'To love thy neighbour as thyself.' It is still true and the words of the Master ring down through the centuries—'This do and ye shall live.'

It is because society has forgotten this, because many of the so-called religious people have forgotten this, that Dublin and other industrial centres of this and every other land witness the scenes that are witnessed every day, and it is because I believe that the Irish people will once more be in the van of that progress which means the uplifting of the whole of the human race that I join with all my fellow-members in sending you this message, and conclude by asking you in your heart of hearts to cheer and keep alive the idea of the solidarity—the oneness of the great human family of men and women the world over.

The real criminals

Maud Gonne

The employers of Dublin have asked their workers to sign a document which no self-respecting man could sign. They would oblige them to sign away their free will. For the honour of our race, the men have refused; there would have been small hope for the Irish nation if they had consented. It would have meant that foreign domination had destroyed all manhood.

Because the workers have shown, that poor and down-trodden as they are, their souls are not enslaved and that they are worthy of Ireland, the employers have declared they will starve them into submission, and that their women and children shall die of hunger in the streets.

In a free country employers of labour would never have dared to propose such a thing, for they would have been treated as the criminals they are. In Ireland they are protected by a police force over which Ireland has no control, and encouraged by a magistracy whose object seems to be to make justice a derision.

What wonder that the labour leader, James Larkin, was condemned by a packed jury, some of whose members said themselves they should not act because they were parties in the trouble.

Until Ireland is free such things are inevitable. We can only stand by the workers, remembering that they are fighting for Ireland's honour.

Chapter 29

Æ and the Dublin Lock-out

We hold the Ireland in the heart
   More than the land our eyes have seen
And love the goal for which we start
   More than the tale of what has been ...

No blazoned banner we unfold—
   One charge alone we give to youth,
Against the sceptred myth to hold
   The golden heresy of truth.

This extract from George Russell's poem 'On Behalf of Some Irishmen Not Followers of Tradition' was included in his *Collected Poems*, published in 1913.[1] That year George Russell, widely known by his pseudonym 'Æ'— poet, playwright, painter, and mystic—was to give practical evidence of his commitment to a new Ireland that he could hail.

Russell was born in Lurgan, County Armagh, in 1867. He liked to think that he was related to Thomas Russell, the 'Man from God Knows Where', friend of Wolfe Tone and Robert Emmet and one of the leaders of the United Irishmen, who had been hanged in Downpatrick in 1803.[2] From 1897 he had worked with Sir Horace Plunkett in the Irish Agricultural Organisation Society, setting up co-ops in the congested districts of the west of Ireland, and by 1913 had become one of the leading figures in the co-operative movement. From 1905 he had edited the influential weekly *Irish Homestead*, the journal of the IAOS, and in its columns he had campaigned against social injustice.[3]

It was not surprising, therefore, that Russell should have passionately espoused the cause of Dublin's workers in their struggle in 1913. The paper he edited sought to promote a Peace Committee to negotiate a settlement, but, given the intransigence of Murphy and the employers, this had come to nothing. Prophetically, Russell had written in an editorial in the *Irish Homestead* in 1912: 'We anticipate labour troubles during the next two years which will make the labour troubles of the past seem a mere murmuring of gnats.'[4]

Russell's letter to the editor of the *Irish Times*, published on 7 October 1913, came as a bombshell to the complacent citizens of the country. It was to be described by W. P. Ryan, the first historian of the Irish labour movement, as the 'memorable letter which is sure to be the most enduring document of the 1913 struggle, the one thing through which those masters of Dublin, so proud and cruel in their little day, will live in history.'[5] This famous letter is in a real sense the Irish equivalent of Émile Zola's great indictment 'J'accuse' in his letter to *L'Aurore* on 13 January 1898 concerning the Dreyfus case.

Russell addressed his letter to 'the Masters of Dublin':

Sirs—I address this warning to you, the aristocracy of industry in this city, because, like all aristocracies, you tend to go blind in long authority, and to be unaware that you and your class and its every action are being considered and judged day by day by those who have power to shake or overturn the whole Social Order, and whose relentlessness in poverty today is making our industrial civilisation stir like a quaking bog. You do not seem to realise that your assumption that you are answerable to yourselves alone for your actions in the industries you control is one that becomes less and less tolerable in a world so crowded with necessitous life.

Some of you have helped Irish farmers to upset a landed aristocracy in this island, an aristocracy richer and more powerful in its sphere than you are in yours, with its roots deep in history. They, too, as a class, though not all of them, were scornful or neglectful of the workers in the industry by which they profited; and to many who knew them in their pride of place and thought them all-powerful, they are already becoming a memory, the good disappearing together with the bad. If they had done their duty by those from whose labour came their wealth they might have continued unquestioned in power and prestige for centuries to come.

The relation of landlord and tenant is not an ideal one, but any relations in a social order will endure if there is infused into them some of that spirit of human sympathy which qualifies life for immortality. Despotisms endure while they are benevolent and aristocracies while *noblesse oblige* is not a phrase to be referred to with a cynical smile. Even an oligarchy might be permanent if the spirit of human kindness, which harmonises all things otherwise incomparable, is present.

You do not seem to read history so as to learn its lessons. That you are an uncultivated class was obvious from recent utterances of some of you upon art. That you are incompetent men in the sphere in which you arrogate imperial powers is certain, because for many years, long before the present uprising of labour, your enterprises have been dwindling in the regard of investors, and this while you carried them on in the cheapest labour market in these islands, with a labour reserve always hungry and ready to accept any pittance. You are bad citizens, for we rarely, if ever, hear of the wealthy among you endowing your city with the munificent gifts which it is the pride of merchant princes in other cities to offer, and Irishmen not of your city who offer to supply the wants left by your lack of generosity are met with derision and abuse. Those who have economic powers have civil powers also, yet you have not used the power that was yours to right what was wrong in the evil administration of this city.

You have allowed the poor to be herded together so that one thinks of certain places in Dublin as of a pestilence. There are twenty thousand rooms, in each of which live entire families, and sometimes more, where no functions of the body can be concealed and delicacy and modesty are creatures that are stifled ere they are born. The obvious duty of you in regard to these things you might have left undone, and it be imputed to ignorance or forgetfulness; but your collective and conscious action as a class in the present labour dispute has revealed you to the world in so malign an aspect that the mirror must be held up to you, so that you may see yourself as every humane person sees you.

212

The conception of yourselves as altogether virtuous and wronged is, I assure you, not at all the one which onlookers hold of you. No doubt, some of you suffered without just cause. But nothing which has been done to you cries aloud to Heaven for condemnation as your own actions. Let me show you how it seems to those who have followed critically the dispute, trying to weigh in a balance the rights and wrongs. You were within the rights society allows when you locked out your men and insisted on the fixing of some principle to adjust your future relations with labour, when the policy of labour made it impossible for some of you to carry on your enterprises. Labour desired the fixing of some such principle as much as you did. But, having once decided on such a step, knowing how many thousands of men, women and children, nearly one-third of the population of this city, would be affected, you should not have let one day to have passed without unremitting endeavours to find a solution of the problem.

What did you do? The representatives of labour unions in Great Britain met you, and you made of them a preposterous, an impossible demand, and because they would not accede to it you closed the conference; you refused to meet them further; you assumed that no other guarantees than those you asked were possible, and you determined deliberately in cold anger, to starve out one-third of the population of this city, to break the manhood of the men by the sight of the suffering of their wives and the hunger of their children. We read in the Dark Ages of the rack and thumb screw. But these iniquities were hidden and concealed from the knowledge of man in dungeons and torture chambers. Even in the Dark Ages humanity could not endure the sight of such suffering, and it learnt of such misuses of power by slow degrees, through rumour, and when it was certain it razed its Bastilles to their foundations.

It remained for the twentieth century and the capital city of Ireland to see an oligarchy of four hundred masters deciding openly upon starving one hundred thousand people, and refusing to consider any solution except that fixed by their pride. You, masters, asked men to do that which masters of labour in any other city in these islands had not dared to do. You insolently demanded of those men who were members of a trade union that they should resign from that union; and from those who were not members you insisted on a vow that they would never join it.

Your insolence and ignorance of the rights conceded to workers universally in the modern world were incredible, and as great as your inhumanity. If you had between you collectively a portion of human soul as large as a threepenny bit, you would have sat night and day with the representatives of labour, trying this or that solution of the trouble, mindful of the women and children, who at least were innocent of wrong against you. But no! You reminded labour you could always have your three square meals a day while it went hungry. You went into conference again with representatives of the State, because dull as you are, you know public opinion would not stand your holding out. You chose as your spokesman the bitterest tongue that ever wagged in this island, and then, when an award was made by men who have an experience in industrial matters a thousand times transcending yours, who have settled disputes in industries so great that the sum of your petty enterprises would not equal them, you withdraw again, and will not agree to accept their solution, and fall back

213

again upon your devilish policy of starvation. Cry aloud to Heaven for new souls! The souls you have got cast upon the screen of publicity appear like the horrid and writhing creatures enlarged from the insect world, and revealed to us by the cinematograph.

You may succeed in your policy and ensure your own damnation by your victory. The men whose manhood you have broken will loathe you, and will always be brooding and scheming to strike a fresh blow. The children will be taught to curse you. The infant being moulded in the womb will have breathed into its starved body the vitality of hate. It is not they— it is you who are blind Samsons pulling down the pillars of the social order. You are sounding the death knell of autocracy in industry. There was autocracy in political life, and it was superseded by democracy. So surely will democratic power wrest from you the control of industry. The fate of you, the aristocracy of industry, will be as the fate of the aristocracy of land if you do not show that you have some humanity still among you. Humanity abhors, above all things, a vacuum in itself, and your class will be cut off from humanity as the surgeon cuts the cancer and alien growth from the body. Be warned, ere it is too late.

—Yours, etc.,

Æ.

Russell knew that in writing his 'Open Letter to the Masters of Dublin' he was jeopardising his future in the co-operative movement. Already the Ancient Order of Hibernians, an organisation that spewed forth the more vicious of the calumnies against James Larkin, had taken secret though unsuccessful steps to have the *Irish Homestead* suppressed.

Sir Horace Plunkett, in a letter to F. S. Oliver, an English writer and friend of Russell's, referred to the letter as a 'glorious indiscretion', adding that 'to attack the Dublin employers, Dublin Castle, the police, the nationalist M.P.s, the A.O.H., the R.C. Church, over the condition of the Dublin slums was a magnificent exhibition of moral courage—so magnificent that I can forgive all his recklessness of consequences to my own little schemes.'[6]

Just weeks before the lock-out of the workers, Russell had commented in the *Irish Homestead* on the controversy then raging about the building of an art gallery for the Sir Hugh Lane collection of French impressionist and other paintings that he wished to donate to the city of Dublin.[7] The proposal was opposed by the Dublin Chamber of Commerce, whose president was William Martin Murphy. Russell wrote that the businessmen responsible for the refusal of Dublin City Council to build the gallery, which was to be designed by Sir Edwin Lutyens, had revealed themselves 'as the meanest, the most uncultured, the most materialistic and canting crowd which ever made a citizen ashamed of his fellow-countrymen.'

James Larkin, who on 28 July 1913 had moved a motion at Dublin Trades Council supporting the building of the gallery, was even more direct in his comment: Murphy, he declared, should be condemned to keep an art gallery in Hell. This thought was echoed by Stephen Gwynn in a letter to W. B. Yeats declaring that he 'hoped to God that Murphy and the Ardilauns may be damned to an eternity of Dublin Corporation.'[8]

214

Lady Gregory described Murphy as 'a vulgar man' in a letter to John Quinn,[9] and this description is well exemplified by what Murphy, a millionaire newspaper proprietor, transport magnate, draper, and hotelier, wrote in his own paper, the *Irish Independent*, replying to what he termed 'an insolent letter' from Sir Hugh Lane:

> There has been much eloquence wasted on this subject over the last few days and all the old platitudes have been trotted out about the 'priceless collection', the 'envy of Europe', the 'resort of pilgrims', the educational effect on the taste of the citizens, the answer to which may be summed up in the word—Fudge.[10]

Yeats too had something relevant to say on the matter in his poem 'September 1913', the first verse of which was:

> What need you, being come to sense,
> But fumble in a greasy till
> And add the half pence to the pence
> And prayer to shivering prayer, until
> You have dried the marrow from the bone;
> For men were born to pray and save:
> Romantic Ireland's dead and gone
> It's with O'Leary in the grave.

It was first published in the *Irish Times* on 8 September 1913, with the title 'Romance in Ireland (On reading much of the correspondence against the Art Gallery)'.

In a poem composed on 16 September 1913,[11] 'To a Friend whose Work has come to Nothing,', Yeats, addressing Lady Gregory, asks:

> But how can you compete,
> Born honour bred, with one
> Who, were it proved he lies,
> Were neither shamed in his own
> Nor in his neighbour's eyes?

The reference is to William Martin Murphy. In another poem, composed on 29 September 1913, 'To a Shade' (Parnell), Yeats refers to Murphy, who took a leading part in the anti-Parnellite movement:

> Your enemy, an old foul mouth had set
> The pack upon him.

The reference here is to Sir Hugh Lane, who was Lady Gregory's nephew.

During the controversy about sending children from the slums to English families to be fed and looked after while the lock-out continued, and the subsequent turmoil and riots at the railway stations, at the North

Wall and at Dún Laoghaire pier directed at preventing children leaving Dublin, organised by the AOH and other Catholic organisations, Yeats wrote a vehement protest, headed 'Dublin Fanaticism', to Larkin's paper, the *Irish Worker*.[12] (The article will be found on pages 224–5.)

Russell had not corresponded with Yeats for nine years, but following his protest in the *Irish Worker* he wrote on 5 November:

> My Dear Yeats,
>   Please let me congratulate you on your speech at the Peace Meeting[13] and above all on your article in the Irish Worker. I have differed from you in many things but I felt all my old friendship and affection surging up as I read what you said. It falls on us to make a fight for social and intellectual freedom. I have a long battle before me and the Church is raging against me over Ireland and is trying to make my continuance in the co-operative movement an impossibility, and I am glad to see you, [Stephen] Gwynn, Séamus O'Sullivan, [James] Stephens are all on the same side of life. Please accept my assurance of my deep regard.
>   Yours sincerely,
>   Æ.[14]

Dr Monk Gibbon has suggested that this letter was 'almost certainly the olive branch which marked the end of this coolness.'[15]

During Larkin's 'Fiery Cross' campaign, mass meetings were held in the main cities in England and Scotland in support of the Dublin workers' fight. At a meeting in the Royal Albert Hall, London, on 1 November 1913 in support of the locked-out workers and demanding the release of Larkin, then imprisoned in Mountjoy Jail, Russell made a memorable speech:

> I stand for the first time on a public platform in this country. The great generosity of English to Irish workers has obliterated the memory of many an ancient tale of wrong. I come from Dublin, where most extraordinary things have been happening. Humanity long dumb has found a voice, it has its prophet and its martyrs. We no longer know people by the old signs and the old shams. People are to us either human or sub-human. They are either on the side of those who are fighting for human conditions in labour or they are with those who are trying to degrade it and thrust it into the abyss.
>   Ah! but I forgot; there has sprung up a third party, who are super-human beings, they have so little concern for the body at all, that they assert it is better for children to be starved than to be moved from the Christian atmosphere of the Dublin slums. Dublin is the most Christian city in these islands. Its tottering tenements are holy. The spiritual atmosphere which pervades them is ample compensation for the diseases which are there and the food which is not there. If any poor parents think otherwise, and would send their children for a little from that earthly paradise, they will find the docks and railway stations barred by these superhuman beings and by the police, and they are pitched headlong out of the station, set upon and beaten, and their children snatched from them. A Dublin labourer has no rights in his own children. You see, if these children were even for a little out of the slums, they would get discontented with their poor homes, so a

very holy man has said. Once getting full meals, they might be so inconsiderate as to ask for them all their lives. They might destroy the interesting experiments carried on in Dublin for generations to find out how closely human beings can be packed together, on how little a human being can live, and what is the minimum wage his employer need pay him. James Larkin interrupted these interesting experiments towards the evolution of the underman and he is in gaol.

You have no idea what the slums in Dublin are like. There are more than 20,000 families each living in one room. Many of these dens are so horrible, so unsanitary, so overrun with vermin that doctors tell me that the only condition on which a man can purchase sleep is that he is drugged with drink. The Psalmist says the Lord gives sleep to his beloved, but in these Dublin dens men and women must pay the devil his price for a little of that peace of God. It maddens one to think that man the immortal, man the divine, should exist in such degradation, that his heirship of the ages should be the life of a brute.

I beseech you not to forsake these men who are out on strike. They may have been to blame for many an action. The masters may perhaps justifiably complain of things done and undone. But if the masters have rights by the light of reason and for the moment, the men are right by the light of spirit and for eternity. This labour uprising in Ireland is the despairing effort of humanity to raise itself out of a dismal swamp of disease and poverty. James Larkin may have been an indiscreet leader. He may have committed blunders, but I believe in the sight of Heaven the crimes are all on the other side. If our Courts of Justice were courts of humanity, the masters of Dublin would be in the dock charged with criminal conspiracy, their crime that they tried to starve out one-third of the people in Dublin, to break their hearts and degrade their manhood, for the greatest crime against humanity is its own degradation.

The men have always been willing to submit their case to arbitration, but the masters refuse to meet them. They refused to consult with your trade union leaders. They would not abide by the Askwith report. They refused to hear of prominent Irishmen acting as arbitrators. They said scornfully of the Peace Committee that it was only interfering. They say they are not fighting trades unionism, but they refuse point blank to meet the Trades Council in Dublin. They want their own way absolutely. These Shylocks of industry want their pound of flesh starved from off the bones of the workers. They think their employees have no rights as human beings, no spirit whose dignity can be abased.

You have no idea what labour in Ireland, which fights for the bare means of human support, is up against. The autocrats of industry can let loose upon them the wild beasts that kill in the name of the State. They can let loose upon them a horde of wild fanatics who will rend them in the name of God. The men have been deserted by those who were their natural leaders. For ten weeks the miserable creatures who misrepresent them in Parliament kept silent. When they were up for the first time in their lives against anything real, they scurried back like rats to their hole. These cacklers about self-government had no word to say on the politics of their own city, but after ten weeks of silence they came out with six lines of a letter signed by all the six poltroons. They disclaimed all responsibility for what is happening in the city and country they represent. It was no concern of theirs; but they would agree to anything the Archbishop might say. Are they not heroic prodigies! Dublin is looking on these men with alien eyes. It was thought they were democrats, we have found out they are only democratic blathers.

We are entering from today on a long battle in Ireland. The masters have flung down a challenge to the workers. The Irish aristocracy were equally scornful of the workers on the land, and the landlords of land are going or have gone. The landlords of industry will have disappeared from Ireland when the battle begun this year is ended. Democratic control of industry will replace the autocracy which exists today. We are working for the co-operative commonwealth to make it the Irish policy of the future, and I ask you to stand by the men who are beginning the struggle. There is good human material there.

I have often despaired over Dublin, which John Mitchel called a city of genteel dastards and bellowing slaves, but a man has arisen who has lifted the curtain which veiled from us the real manhood in the City of Dublin. Nearly all the manhood is found among the obscure myriads who are paid from five to twenty-five shillings per week. The men who will sacrifice anything for a principle get rarer and rarer above that limit of wealth. I am a literary man, a lover of ideas, but I have found few people in my life who would sacrifice anything for a principle. Yet in Dublin, when the masters issued that humiliating document, asking men—on penalty of dismissal— to swear never to join a trade union, thousands of men who had no connection with the Irish Transport Workers—many among them personally hostile to that organisation—refused to obey. They would not sign away their freedom, their right to choose their own heroes and their own ideas. Most of these men had no strike funds to fall back on. They had wives and children depending on them. Quietly and grimly they took through hunger the path to the Heavenly City. They stand silently about the streets. God alone knows what is passing in the hearts of these men. Nobody in the press in Dublin has said a word about it. Nobody has praised them, no one has put a crown upon their brows.

Yet these men are the true heroes of Ireland today, they are the descendants of Oscar, Cuculain, the heroes of our ancient stories. For all their tattered garments, I recognise in these obscure men a majesty of spirit. It is in the workers in the towns and in the men in the cabins in the country that the hope of Ireland lies. The poor have always helped each other, and it is they who listen eagerly to the preachers of a social order based on brotherhood and co-operation.

I am a literary man and not a manual worker. I am but a voice, while they are the deed and the being, but I would be ashamed ever in my life again to speak of an ideal if I did not stand by these men and say of them what I hold to be true. If you back them up today they will be able to fight their own battles tomorrow, and perhaps to give you an example. I beseech you not to forsake these men.

Other speakers at this meeting were James Connolly, Charlotte Despard, Delia Larkin, Sylvia Pankhurst, and George Bernard Shaw. John Eglinton remarks that 'it must have been an ordeal for Æ, who shrank from public speaking, to rise up before that vast audience, but his speech was received with enthusiasm.'[16]

Russell, in a letter to J. C. Squire, wrote:

I came back to find Dublin one prolonged howl of indignation at my Albert Hall speech. The *Freeman's Journal* leadered my iniquity on Monday, also on Tuesday, also on Wednesday, and only fainted on Thursday through a complete loss of new epithets. The other papers, Unionist and Nationalist, dealt with me good pressed down and frothing over. I am now to have a fight for my continuance in the Co-operative Movement. The Committee of the I.A.O.S. at a special meeting on Monday are to consider my sins. The Hibernians have sent round a circular to stop the [Irish] Homestead. They knew I meant them by my speech about the superhuman. The Church thought I referred to them, and they also had a meeting, hence the I.A.O.S. committee panic to cut me off.[17]

Shortly after the London meeting, Russell wrote a further letter to the *Irish Times*, dated 11 November 1913, which the editor did not publish. However, the letter was published in the *Times* of London on 13 November and immediately reprinted by it as a broadsheet, *The Tragedy of Labour in Dublin*.

Sir, It may seem an audacity on the part of one whose views on the politics of this city are obviously unpopular to attempt once more, through you, to influence public opinion. But the most unpopular council is not necessarily more filled with unwisdom. The masters of Dublin I have addressed in vain. I now ask the citizens of Dublin to consider what effect the policy of the masters is going to have. What has been gained by this resolute refusal of the federated employers to meet the only body with which negotiations can be carried on? Are not the forces on the side of labour becoming more resolute and exasperated week by week?

Nobody in Dublin seems to realise the gigantic power the masters have challenged. As a disdainful attitude is manifested on the one side, the leaders of labour have settled into a grim determination never to submit. The labour leaders, men who have it in their power to do what they threaten, declare that they will rather hold up the industrial system of these islands than see the humiliation of the men completed. Are the citizens content? Do they think it right they should sit silent and have all this brought on them because the masters are too proud to meet the representatives of labour in Dublin? These people seem to read nothing, know nothing, or think nothing of what is happening in respect of labour elsewhere in the world. They do not know that organized labour has become one of the great powers, that its representatives are met by the representatives of capital in industrial countries with the respect that the delegates of great nations meet each other. In Great Britain, the Press, representing all parties, unite in condemning the policy of the employers. What is the position of the men? They have declared always that they wanted arbitration boards such as exist in hundreds in industrial centres where the representatives of organized labour and the federated employers could meet and to which disputes over labour could be referred. Agreements entered into after frank and free discussion as between equals the men will keep. They will not keep agreements into which they consider they are forced. Labour has a sense of honour of its own which is as high as the honour of the masters any day.

I will be met by the famous outburst about contracts and the nether world. That sentence was never uttered in the sense in which it was reputed. Mr. Larkin was speaking not with reference to the contracts between masters and men, but about the masters' complaints that owing to strikes they could not carry out their contracts. It may have been an unfeeling remark, but it was not the defiance of all honour between master and employee that an abbreviated report made it.

Sir, if you will permit me to say something which may irritate the Irish press, but which, I think, is true and necessary to be said. If the Dublin journals had not been so manifestly biased on the side of the employers, reporters would not have come to regard their work, not as the true gathering of strike news, but the making up of a case against the men. Nor would it have been so necessary for me to emphasize one side, as I did in my Open Letter and the much abused speech at the Albert Hall. I am charged with being a revolutionary, I who for seven or eight years past have week by week been expounding an orderly evolution of society. I am charged as being against religion, I the sole poet of my generation who has never written a single poem which did not try to express a spiritual mood. But I am not with those who wish to bring about in Ireland a peace of God without any understanding, and I and all free spirits will fight with all our power against the fanatics who would bludgeon us into their heaven, to bow to their savage conception of a deity. The deity of the infuriated bigot, call him by what holy name they choose, is never anything but the Old Adversary, who can put on the whole outward armoury of God. I have known, worked with, and loved many noble men, true priests of Christ, and they would not, I am sure assert that the spirit that drives a mob to bludgeon and kick parents before the eyes of their children is the spirit which is present at the elevation of the Host. What I say here of the hooligans of religion in Dublin I would say with equal sincerity of the hooligans of religion in Belfast.

But I do not wish now to explain or defend myself, but to point out the danger of allowing the present policy to continue. I tell the citizens of this city that, if the civil authorities, the masters, and their allies in the Press had been trying deliberately and of set purpose to make of Dublin another Barcelona, with the bomb of the Anarchist a frequent blazing terror in the streets, if they wished to empty the churches, and make of Dublin another Paris, they could not devise a policy more certain to bring about the result. The Irish are a gentle people, but history is thronged with evidence that in long exasperated men, suffering from real or fancied injustice, gentleness turns to ferocity. To know that is true we can find ample proof in the story of our own race, whether we begin with mythical Cat Head, in the first far-off uprising of the common people in Ireland, or come nearer our own time to the Dynamitards. Does no one read history nowadays? Is there not a single man in Dublin with knowledge of the human heart? Do not the most kindly and submissive natures change in character through what they believe is injustice or oppression? Natural good is transmuted by some devilish alchemy into hate, and forces are engendered which attract to them all that has been thought by the demoniac outcasts of society, so that the methods of the terrorists seem the only ones which can be adopted.

I ask my fellow-townsmen to think whether it would not have been better for the masters to treat the men as human beings who could be reasoned with than to issue ultimatums like despots to subjects who must be coerced without discussion? I ask whether it is most likely agreements will be kept and good work done if the men are starved into submission or if they are made after the most open interchange of opinions? The state has set up a tribunal which has given its judgement. Ought not public opinion to insist on the recommendation of the Askwith Committee being tried? How can the masters complain of the lawlessness of the workers when they themselves set an example by ignoring the verdict of the only legal tribunal which has tried the case? Dublin seems to be stumbling darkly and blindly to a tragedy, and the silence of those who foresee and do not speak is a crime. It is time for the Chorus to cry out to warn the antagonists in the drama.

Yours, etc.,

Geo. W. Russell ('Æ').

Russell continued as editor of the *Irish Homestead* until 1923 and was editor of the *Irish Statesman* from 1924 until the magazine closed down in 1930, the result of financial difficulties arising from a libel action. Disillusioned with the illiberal direction the new state was taking, Russell went to live in England in 1933 and died in Bournemouth in 1935. He was buried in Mount Jerome Cemetery, Dublin, in the presence of the President of the Executive Council, Éamon de Valera, and W. B. Yeats. Frank O'Connor gave the oration. John Eglinton (William Magee), in *A Memoir of Æ*, records that a woman who had been in service with the Russells and who had once 'got into trouble' and whom they had looked after placed a mass of flowers on the grave. When someone remarked how much the flowers must have cost, she answered: 'I would have died for him.'[18]

In his poem 'Salutations', printed for private circulation in 1917, Russell had written of the execution of the leaders of the Easter Rising. The poem includes the lines:

> The hope lives on age after age
> Earth in its beauty might be won
> For labour as a heritage.
> For this has Ireland lost a son.
> This hope into a flame to fan
> Men have put life by with a smile.
> Here's to you, Connolly, my man,
> Who cast the last torch on the pile.

Writing to his friend Charles Weekes in August 1916, Russell wrote that personally he 'believed there would have been no revolt if the employers and authorities had not been so unmerciful and unjust during the great strike. They left labour inflamed.' He went on:

I wrote then a letter, suppressed here, but which appeared in The Times in which I said 'if the authorities were wanting to make Dublin a place with the bombs blazing in the street they were going the right way about it.' It was labour supplied the personal element in the revolt. It had a real grievance. The cultural element, poets, Gaels, etc. never stir more than one per cent of a country. It is only when an economic injustice stirs the workers that they unite their grievance with all other grievances.

Chapter 30

The Children, the ITGWU, and the Archbishop

Theresa Moriarty has described in her Thomas Davis Lecture (chapter 12) the origin of the idea of sending children from the families of locked-out workers to England for the duration of the dispute so as to alleviate some of the destitution in Dublin. The suggestion was made by Dora Montefiore at a meeting in London in support of the Dublin workers at which Larkin and Frances Greville, Countess of Warwick, spoke. When Larkin had finished speaking, Dora Montefiore passed a slip of paper to him asking if a plan such as she had in mind would work and whether it would have his blessing. He wrote a few words in the affirmative, and Lady Warwick agreed to act as treasurer to a fund to be set up by the Daily Herald League.

Within days, 350 homes were offered to Dublin children and their families. Rebecca West quoted in the *Clarion* (14 November 1913) from some of the letters received: 'A slice off the loaf won't make no difference'; 'We can put another cot in our kiddies' bedroom.'

Dora Montefiore, with Grace Neal and Lucille Rand, came to Dublin, where Delia Larkin was making the arrangements for getting the children to England. What happened when an attempt was made to bring some of the children aboard a ship at the North Wall was reported in the *Daily Telegraph*:

> The attempt to take fifty children to England last night by the Laird Line boat from North Wall was frustrated. A body of about twenty-five Catholic clergy were present to witness the boat's departure, and they surrounded one woman who was going aboard with a child in her arms. As the woman tried to force her way through the crowd a cry of 'Rescue the child!' was raised and a wild scene followed, both the child—about four years of age—and the woman being roughly handled. Ultimately with the aid of the priests, the child was removed to a place of safety by a workman, and subsequently it was explained that the child, whose mother is dead, was being taken to England by its father.

Mary Neill wrote in *Votes for Women* (24 October 1913) of one woman whose child had been brought to England:

> The mother is thirty-three years old and has five children. Her husband went to America four years ago, but for the last year she has heard nothing of him, nor has she received any money from him. She earns 7s. a week at sack repairing. She spends 1s. 6d. on rent, gives 4s. 6d. to a sister to look after and feed the five children while she is at work, and she pays 2d. a week to the Union. During the strike she has only 5s. to do everything. But her courage is high and there is not the slightest sign of giving in.

William Orpen, the painter, was in Liberty Hall when Francis Sheehy-Skeffington arrived with his clothes practically ripped off him. He had come from Kingsbridge (Heuston) Station, where he had been attacked by thugs organised by the AOH, seeking to prevent him from sending children to a home in County Meath.

The Archbishop of Dublin, Dr William Walsh, sent a letter dated 20 October to the newspapers that is so remarkable, even for those times, that it warrants reproduction in full.

> Dear Sir—I have read with nothing short of consternation in some of our evening newspapers that a movement is on foot, and has already made some progress, to induce the wives of the working men who are now unemployed by reason of the present deplorable industrial deadlock in Dublin, to hand over their children to be cared for in England by persons of whom they, of course, can have no knowledge whatever.
>
> The Dublin women now subjected to this cruel temptation to part with their helpless offspring are, in the majority of cases, Catholics. Have they abandoned their Faith? Surely not. Well, if they have not, they should need no words of mine to remind them of the plain duty of every Catholic mother in such a case. I can only put it to them that they can be no longer held worthy of the name of Catholic mothers if they so far forget that duty as to send away their little children to be cared for in a strange land, without security of any kind that those to whom the poor children are to be handed over are Catholics, or indeed are persons of any faith at all.
>
> I am much mistaken if this recent and most mischievous development of our labour trouble in Dublin fails to appeal to all who are involved in the conflict, employers or employed as they may be, or fails to move them to strive with all earnestness to bring the conflict to an end.
>
> William J. Walsh
> Archbishop of Dublin

Thereafter angry crowds were mobilised to prevent any more children leaving Dublin—even for Belfast. Such were the scenes at Kingstown (Dún Laoghaire) and the railway stations that W. B. Yeats was constrained to write the following letter to the *Irish Worker*, which published it under the heading 'Dublin Fanaticism':

> I do not complain of Dublin's capacity for fanaticism whether in priest or layman, for you cannot have strong feeling without that capacity, but neither those who directed the police nor the editors of our newspapers can plead fanaticism. They are supposed to watch over our civil liberties, and I charge the Dublin Nationalist newspapers with deliberately arousing religious passion to break up the organisation of the workingman, with appealing to mob law day after day, with publishing the names of workingmen and their wives for purposes of intimidation.
>
> And I charge the Unionist Press of Dublin and those who directed the police with conniving at this conspiracy. I want to know why the *Daily Express*, which is directly and indirectly inciting Ulster to rebellion in defence of what it calls 'the liberty of the subject', is so indifferent to that

liberty here in Dublin that it has not made one editorial comment, and I ask the *Irish Times* why a few sentences at the end of an article, too late in the week to be of any service, has been the measure of its love for civil liberty?

I want to know why there were only (according to the press reports) two policemen at Kingsbridge on Saturday when Mr. Sheehy Skeffington was assaulted and a man prevented from buying a ticket for his own child? There had been tumults every night at every Dublin railway station, and I can only assume that the police authorities wished those tumults to continue.

I want to know why the mob at North Wall and elsewhere were permitted to drag children from their parents' arms, and by what right one woman was compelled to open her box and show a marriage certificate; I want to know by what right the police have refused to accept charges against rioters; I want to know who has ordered the abrogation of the most elementary rights of the citizens, and why authorities who are bound to protect every man in doing that which he has a legal right to do—even though they have to call upon all the forces of the Crown—have permitted the Ancient Order of Hibernians to besiege Dublin, taking possession of the railway stations like a foreign army.

Prime Ministers have fallen, and Ministers of State have been impeached for less than this. I demand that the coming Policy Inquiry shall be so widened that we may get to the bottom of a conspiracy, whose like has not been seen in any English-speaking town during living memory. Intriguers have met together somewhere behind the scenes that they might turn the religion of Him who thought it hard for a rich man to enter into the Kingdom of Heaven into an oppression of the poor.

The Archbishop's letter had caused consternation. Mobs were mobilised to blockade the North Wall and the pier at Dún Laoghaire. Undeterred for a time, Larkin maintained his support for the scheme, with members of the union—tough dockers and carters—leaving Liberty Hall in procession carrying children on their shoulders. However, he was soon forced to suspend the scheme, subsequently declaring that it had been 'the finest tactical error ever made in the workers' fight.'

The London newspapers incredulously reported what was happening in Dublin. Predictably, the *Daily Herald* (21 October) opened its report by saying that

Dublin is doubly disgraced. A more scandalous exhibition of capitalist oppression of the working class could hardly be given than was comprised in the angry scenes in Dublin and Kingstown yesterday ... Disgraceful scenes took place, and, in their zeal for what no doubt the Dublin priests considered was their religious duty, they went to lengths that can only be described as scandalous. They even used physical violence against Mrs. Rand ... They pursued the mothers and the children, and intimidated them and we hear of excited priests rushing about in taxicabs to strategic points to intercept the babies who were going to be fed with English bread.

The *Daily Mail* referred to a named priest speaking 'in impassioned tones of the dangers of sending young children to Atheistic and Socialistic homes in England.' Another named priest was reported by the same paper as addressing the passengers on the ship to the effect that 'the boys were being taken away by trickery, fraud and corruption, by proselytising, without the permission of their parents.'

There was, it was reported, 'an unseemly struggle.' The police arrested Mrs Rand and took charge of the children; the clergy led the cheering for their victory. Mrs Rand was detained in the local police station and charged with attempting to abduct two children. She was later brought to Liberty Hall by Prof. David Houston.

The *Pall Mall Gazette* commented that 'the clergy have taken up the position that any extremity of suffering should be undergone rather than Catholic children should undergo the risks of temporary detention in Protestant homes.'

At Westland Row (Pearse) Station, as eleven children boarded the train to Dún Laoghaire, priests intervened and removed them from the train. A priest who had taken a prominent part in the scenes told the press that 'Irish people would rather see their children perish by the ditches than that they should be exposed to the risk of being perverted in their religion.'

On 24 October, Dora Montefiore was arrested by an inspector and a detective in her hotel, without a warrant. Later, at the Bridewell, she was charged with feloniously kidnapping a child. As a protest against having been arrested without a warrant, she refused even to give her name. This the police took from the flyleaf of the book she was reading. Later she was bailed by Prof. Houston, Constance Markievicz, and a Mr Sinclair. Typical of the headlines in the Murphy-owned *Irish Independent* during this unsavoury episode were 'Spirited action by the clergy'; 'London lady bailed by Dublin Jews' (referring to Mr Sinclair); 'Children brought back in triumph'.

The role of the *Irish Catholic* (also owned by William Martin Murphy) in the disgraceful reaction to the efforts to bring succour to the starving children cannot be ignored. On 6 September 1913 the editor implored the workers 'while there is yet time, to break loose from the Socialist and subsequently demoniacal influences which are dragging them to ruin.' He concluded that it was 'all awful and deplorable and all provoked and brought about for the sake of some fancied allegiance to the pagan image of a blood-stained hand' (a reference to the ITGWU badge, which in 1913 was the red hand of Ulster).

On 27 September the *Irish Catholic* replied to an open letter from Jim Larkin in the *Irish Worker*, which in turn was a reply to an attack on him by an Augustinian priest, Father John Condon, in a speech before the United Confraternities of Dublin. Father Condon had asked whether Larkin was 'a safe leader to whom our Catholic people may entrust themselves for guidance.' He had answered his own question: 'I say distinctly and emphatically that he is not. And I say that as a priest.'

The heading of the *Irish Catholic* editorial was 'Satanism and socialism', and it declared:

If any corroborative evidence is needed to prove that Socialism is essentially Satanic in its nature, origin and purposes, it is abundantly supplied out of the chief promoter of the unrest and misery now existing in our capital.

It has to be added, in fairness, that this diatribe was answered by an English Dominican priest, Father Vincent McNabb, who supported Larkin's position.

In an article first published in *Publications in the Humanities* (1965) by the Department of the Humanities at Massachusetts Institute of Technology and subsequently reprinted in *Studies* (spring, 1985), Prof. Emmet Larkin revealed that Larkin had been a member of the Catholic Socialist Society, which had been founded by John Wheatley in Glasgow in 1906 and had published a number of pamphlets on socialism and Catholicism. In his paper Prof. Larkin quotes Wheatley (*Forward*, 12 April 1912) to the effect that Larkin was 'the most prominent member of the Catholic Socialist Society in Ireland.' In the same article he quotes from a speech made by Jim Larkin in Manchester and reported in the *Manchester Guardian* (15 September 1913): 'You don't know what we are fighting against, those of you who are not members of the Church I belong to. The men I am fighting for have given good sureties for their belief in their Church, and the man that tells you that it is impossible to be a Socialist and a Catholic is a liar.'

Larkin's comments on the issue of the children were reported in the *Freeman's Journal* (27 October 1913): 'I have tried to kill sectarianism, whether in Catholics or Protestants. I am against bigotry or intolerance on either side. Those who want to divide the workers have resorted to the foulest methods.' He declared: 'I am not frightened by the Archbishop or the priests. No one ever heard me say one word against them, but I say the priest who says I would allow a child to be proselytized is a liar in his heart.'

James Connolly set out his position on the controversy in a long article in *Forward* (1 November 1913):

Our good friend the *Daily Citizen* describes the scenes attendant upon the intended departure of some Dublin children to Great Britain, under the auspices of a committee organised there for the purpose of taking care of children of the locked out workers, as 'the most extraordinary scene in this most extraordinary industrial conflict in this country.'

We do not wonder at our British friends being surprised, nor at them being horrified, nor at them being scandalised and shocked at the treatment to which they have been subjected, and the vile aspersions cast upon their motives. For ourselves we anticipated it all, and have never been enthusiastic towards the scheme.

We realised that their children are about all the workers of Dublin have left to comfort them, that amidst the squalor and wretchedness of their surroundings the love of their little ones shines like a star of redemption, and that to part with their dear ones would be like wrenching their hearts asunder. We realised, further, what it is very difficult to make even the most friendly of the British realise, that Great Britain is still an alien country to Ireland, and that even the splendid comradeship and substantial aid of today can hardly expect to obliterate immediately the evil results upon our intercourse of long generations of oppression during the period when class rule stood in Ireland for Great Britain, and symbolised all Britain's relations with Ireland. And we also knew that some of the darkest memories of Ireland were associated with British attempts to stab the heart of Ireland through systematic abduction of the bodies and corruption of the minds of Irish children.

Therefore we felt instinctively that the well-meant move of Mrs. Montefiore and her colleagues would arouse in Ireland hostilities and suspicions they could not conceive of, and would not believe were we to attempt the task of making the matter clear. Hence, while placing no obstacle in the way of its fulfilment, and feeling deeply a sense of gratitude towards the noble British men and women of our class who have so unreservedly thrown open their homes for the purpose of sheltering our stricken little ones, we have nevertheless felt that the scheme was bound to be taken advantage of to our detriment by all the hostile elements who surround us, but usually fear to reveal their hostility. We know that people 'willing to wound, and yet afraid to strike' swarm everywhere on the flanks of the labour movement in Ireland.

But when we have said this we have said all that our own position demands. Having said it, we must protest in the name of the whole labour movement of this country against the foul and libellous accusations brought against the noble-minded ladies who have been in charge of the scheme. One scoundrel in clerical garb is said to have stated on Wednesday that the children were being 'brought to England by trickery, fraud and corruption for proselytising purposes.' Nothing more venomous and unfounded was ever spewed out of a lying mouth in Ireland since the seoinín clergy at the bidding of an English politician hounded Parnell to his grave. Mrs. Montefiore had given his Grace Archbishop Walsh her assurance that wherever the children went, the local Roman Catholic clergy would be given their names and addresses, and requested to take charge of them, and see that they attended to their duties as Catholic children. His Grace felt that, despite that assurance, and without doubting it in the least, there would still be dangers. But not for one moment did he impugn the motives of the ladies in question

The utterances of his Grace the Archbishop on the question at issue deserve and no doubt will receive, the earnest consideration of every thoughtful man and woman in Ireland. Nobody wants to send the children away—the Irish Transport and General Workers' Union least of all desires such a sacrifice. But neither do we wish the children to starve. We love the children of Ireland, we are sacrificing our own ease and comfort in order that the future of these children may be sweeter and happier than the lot of their fathers and mothers. We know that progress cannot be made without sacrifice, and we do not shrink from the sacrifice involved in fighting for freedom now in order that future generations may build upon the results of our toil. But the master class of Dublin calmly and cold-bloodedly calculate upon using the sufferings of the children to weaken the resistance of the parents. They wish to place us upon the horns of a dilemma. Either the parents should resist, and then the children will starve, or the parents will surrender, and the children will grow up in slavery, and live to despise the parents who bequeathed to them such an evil heritage.

Your Grace, we are resolved to fight Death itself—the death some of us have already suffered, the death your humble servant has in the same cause looked in the face without flinching—it would be preferable to surrendering the Dublin workers again to the hell of slavery out of which they are emerging. Your Grace, we will fight!

But if your Grace is as solicitous about the poor bodies of those children as we know you to be about their souls, or even if you are but one tenth part as solicitous, may we suggest to you or your laymen that your duty is plain. See to it that the force of public opinion, that the power of the press, that all the engines at your command are brought to bear upon the inhuman monsters who control the means of employment in Dublin to make them realise their duties to the rest of the community. We have done our part, we have told the Lord Mayor, we have told Sir George Askwith, we have told the Dublin Industrial Peace Committee, that we are ready to negotiate. All of these admit that our position is reasonable, all of them have been spat upon with scorn by the employers, and all of them shrink in cowardice from taking the next logical step and concentrating public feeling and public financial support in favour of the workers, the only party to the dispute that all along has declared its readiness to bow to public opinion.

These people, we repeat, have shrunk in cowardice from their manifest duty. Will you undertake it? It is your duty equally with theirs. To you we repeat our offer: we are willing to accept the mediation of any party whose functions will be strictly limited to bringing the two parties together in a conference to thrash out their differences. We are prepared to meet the representatives of all the employers, or meet any individual employer, as we have done satisfactorily in many cases already. This is our offer to you. And we repeat to you what we have said to the others:

If the employers reject your offer of mediation and still declare their contempt for any public opinion they cannot rig in advance, then it is your manifest duty to organise public support for the workers to defeat their soulless employers.

We have read your Grace's character in vain if you shrink from that task, or fail in that duty. The plight of the children, and your concern for them should be your warrant for acting, if any warrant other than your high position was needed. Meanwhile, come weal or woe, in good repute or evil, we are prepared to fight, because we feel that this fight is a fight for the future, a brighter future for

> The children who swarm and die,
> In loathsome dens where despair is king;
> Like blackened buds of a frosty spring
> That wither, sunless, remote they lie,
> From the hour that quickens each soul and sense,
> Whilst vice and hunger and pestilence—
> Breast-poisoned nurses—the babes drain dry.

229

Chapter 31

Come off the Fence

James Stephens

In a movement whose objective is to change things as they are into things as they ought to be, it is necessary to be certain of two facts—First: What you are going to do; second: Who you are going to fight; for this is certain, that you can do nothing without fighting something. The entire machinery of life and health has been captured by your enemies and they dole out existence to you with as miserly a hand as they dare. You will never get from these traitors to humanity more than a quarter of what you demand; anything over that you must take for yourselves and you will find that ancient and modern privilege will fight like demons to keep you from the enjoyment of physical, mental or spiritual freedom ...

As to what you are going to do, it can be stated in the smallest space. By bettering your own conditions you are going to better the condition of everyone. Every great human movement, every crusade that had an idea or an ideal for its banner was inaugurated and carried to victory by your class in the teeth of precisely the same opposition as is arrayed against you to-day. And this is equally true, that when your victories had been won the rich people, the glib-tongued professional classes and that other class which croaks for ever on the fence, have sneaked in and stolen the jobs and turned the idealism which was won by your bones and your groans into a new tyranny for yourselves and your children. It is good to remember this and to be prepared for it.

The world-movement in which you are now pioneers, has this happy difference from all others, that the idealism has a prudent alloy of materialism to keep it in ballast. Be certain that this is true; that before you can assist others in the slightest degree you must assist yourselves. Only from your own prosperity can there come any assuagement from the miseries of your class or of humanity.

Be very proud of what you are doing. The whole weary earth is hanging on your fortitude. You are as truly the liberators of the world to-day as were those twelve other workingmen who long ago threw up their jobs to follow the penniless Son of the Carpenter and your battle will not be a bit easier than theirs was. Your leader was in jail through as contemptible a piece of political and social treachery as can be imagined. Every lie that malignity could invent has been used against him for the past seven years. Are you going to desert him? He did not desert you. Was it any fun for Larkin to be rusting in Mountjoy Jail? If he could have been bought his price would have been paid ages ago; but thank heaven, there are still poor men who are not for sale. Can you be bought away from him?

If so, there is money and soft soap for the traitor; but one can live to the height of one's intellect and soul and be a proud man even if one is a hungry man.

Who are you going to fight? Capitalism? It is a beast with ten thousand heads, the legs of a centipede and the arms of an octopus. Its heads are able to speak at once from the boss's office, the Press and the pulpit. Its legs are soldiers and sailors, policemen and renegades of your own class, and its arms are halfpennies and pennies and pounds. Go for it surely, go for it quickly, but tread very warily or those legs and arms and teeth will get you and bite and crush like the devil it is ...

[Extracts from an article in the *Irish Worker*, November 1913.]

The public and the Dublin employers

Pádraic Colum

The Dublin Industrial Peace Committee has dissolved itself. When one party to a dispute is bent on securing, not a settlement, but a surrender, there is no place for honest go-betweens. For over a month the Committee has been striving to bring about direct negotiations between masters and men with a view to ending a dispute that is like a running sore. It found that the workers were willing to act as reasonable beings and good citizens, and that the employers kept to the attitude of the Turkish Government and the Balkan States before the war last October ... Let the public realise that the attitude of the employers is now the sole obstacle to the movement for peace in Dublin. The dissolution of the Industrial Peace Committee and their declaration made this clear.

Be it remembered that the dissolution of the Peace Committee comes at the moment when the established right of picketing is not merely challenged but overborne on the streets of Dublin.

What are we to do with the employers? People have written and spoken about their malignity, but what startles me is their utter lack of intelligence. The projects of a Machiavelli or a Bismarck may be malignant but they are tolerable because they are intelligent.

But what are we to say to the Dublin employers? They solemnly ask organised workmen to sign away a right that they won long ago—the right to join a union that, in their judgment, served their interest best. The employers waved this document in the face of the Dublin public saying, 'see how strong we are; the workers will not stand up to us for a fortnight.' Sir George Askwith assured them that this document was indefensible, but they did not withdraw it; as a matter of fact they stand by it still. Its issue showed that the employers were ignorant of the very condition of modern industrial combinations. It exposed the Dublin employers to contempt. One would think that if the pettiest board of directors had acted in this way, they would be forced to resign. And yet employers of Dublin are still in a position to hamper our business.

231

Let the public be aware of the facts. Ignorant and incompetent generals were taking it upon themselves to prolong or neglect and waste public resources. It is we who have to pay for the carloads of policemen; it is we who have to contribute to the feeding of the children whose natural bread-winners are shut out from employment; it is our liberties that are threatened where the peaceful pickets are overborne. The employers of Dublin have taken it upon themselves to say—'The public: it is us.' They must be given a shock.

[Extract from an article in the *Irish Worker*, 15 November 1913.]

* * *

James Stephens (1880–1950) was brought up in an orphanage and at about the age of sixteen went to work in a solicitor's office in Dublin. He contributed to *Sinn Féin* and the *Irish Worker*. His first book of poetry, *Insurrections* (1909), contains angry pictures of Dublin slum life. Three years later he published *The Charwoman's Daughter* and *The Crock of Gold*. In the following three years there were three further volumes of poetry as well as *Demi-Gods*, the third of his trilogy of novels. He moved to Paris but returned to Dublin to become Registrar of the National Gallery of Ireland, a position he held until 1924.

Stephens published many short stories, notably 'Hunger', about deprivation in Dublin, and further volumes of poetry. In 1916 he wrote an eye-witness account of the Easter Rising, *Insurrection in Ireland*. He moved to London in 1925. More short stories and collections of verse followed.

* * *

Pádraic Colum (1881–1972) was born in Longford, the son of the workhouse manager there. He was a prolific playwright, poet, novelist, and writer of children's books. Three of his plays were produced by the early Abbey Theatre between 1903 and 1910: *Broken Soil*, *The Land*, and *Thomas Muskerry*. His best-known work is *Wild Earth* (1916), which includes such well-loved verse as 'The Old Woman of the Roads' and 'She Moved through the Fair'.

In 1912 he married Mary Gunning, also a writer, who taught at Pearse's school, St Ida's (a sister school of St Enda's), and later moved to America. They both spent some time in Paris, where they were close friends of James Joyce.

Chapter 32

Nineteen-Thirteen

James Connolly

Glorious Dublin

Baton charges, prison cells, untimely death and acute starvation—all were faced without a murmur and in face of them all, the brave Dublin workers never lost faith in their ultimate triumph, never doubted but that their organisation would emerge victorious from the struggle. This is the great fact that many of our critics amongst the British Labour leaders seem to lose sight of. The Dublin fight is more than a trade union fight; it is a great class struggle, and recognised as such by all sides. We in Ireland feel that to doubt our victory would be to lose faith in the destiny of our class.

I heard of one case where a labourer was asked to sign the agreement forswearing the Irish Transport and General Workers' Union, and he told his employer, a small capitalist builder, that he refused to sign. The employer, knowing the man's circumstances, reminded him that he had a wife and six children who would be starving within a week. The reply of this humble labourer rose to the heights of sublimity. 'It is true, sir,' he said, 'they will starve; but I would rather see them go out one by one in their coffins than I should disgrace them by signing that.' And with head erect he walked out to share hunger and privation with his loved ones. Hunger and privation—and honour.

Defeat, bah! How can such a people be defeated? His case is typical of thousands more. Take the case of the United Builders' Labourers' Trade Union, for instance. This was a rival union to the Irish Transport and General Workers' Union. Many sharp passages had occurred between them, and the employers counted confidently upon their co-operation in the struggle; Mr. William Martin Murphy especially praising them and exulting in their supposed acquiescence in his plans. Remember also that they were a dividing society, dividing their funds at the end of each year, and therefore without any strike funds. When the members of their union were asked to sign the agreement, promising never to join or help the Irish Transport and General Workers' Union, not one man consented—but all over Dublin their 2,500 members marched out 'to help the I. T. & G. W. U. boys.' Long ere these lines are written, they have experienced all the horrors of starvation, but with grim resolve they have tightened their belts and presented an unyielding front to the enemy.

It is a pleasure to me to recall that I was a member of their Union before I went to America, and that they twice ran me as their candidate for Dublin City Council before the Irish Transport and General Workers' Union was dreamed of.

What is true of that union is also true of most of the tradesmen. All are showing wonderful loyalty to their class. Coachbuilders, sawyers, engineers, bricklayers, each trade that is served by general labourers, walks out along with the Irish Transport and General Workers' Union boys; refuses to even promise to work with any one who signs the employers' agreement, and, cheering, lines up along with their class.

Or think of the heroic women and girls. Did they care to evade the issue, they might have remained at work, for the first part of the agreement asks them to merely repudiate the Irish Transport and General Workers' Union, and as women, they are members of the Irish Women Workers' Union, not of the Irish Transport and General Workers' Union. But the second part pledges them to refuse to 'help' the Irish Transport and General Workers' Union—and in every shop, factory and sweating hell-hole in Dublin, as the agreement is presented, they march out with pinched faces, threadbare clothes and miserable footwear, with high hopes, undaunted spirit, and glorious resolve shining out of their eyes. Happy the men who will secure such wives; thrice blessed the nation which has such girls as the future mothers of the race! Ah, comrades, it is good to have lived in Dublin in these days!

And then our friends write deprecatingly to the British press of the 'dislocation of trade' involved in sympathetic strikes, of the 'perpetual conflicts' in which they would involve great trade unions. To those arguments, if we can call them such, our answer is sufficient. It is this: If the capitalist class knew that any outrages upon a worker, any attack upon labour, would result in a prompt dislocation of trade, perhaps national in its extent; that the unions were prepared to spend their last copper if necessary rather than permit a brother or sister to be injured, then the knowledge would not only ensure a long cessation from industrial skirmishing such as the unions are harassed by to-day, it would not only ensure peace to the unions, but what is of vastly more importance, it would ensure to the individual worker a peace from slave-driving and harassing at his work such as the largest unions are apparently unable to guarantee under present methods.

Mark, when I say 'prepared to spend their last copper if necessary,' I am not employing merely a rhetorical flourish, I am using the words literally. As we believe that in the socialist society of the future the entire resources of the nation must stand behind every individual, guaranteeing him against want, so to-day our unions must be prepared to fight with all their resources to safeguard the rights of every individual member.

The adoption of such a principle, followed by a few years of fighting on such lines to convince the world of our earnestness, would not only transform the industrial arena, but would revolutionise politics. Each side would necessarily seek to grasp the power of the state to reinforce its position, and politics would thus become what they ought to be, a reflex of the industrial battle, and lose the power to masquerade as a neutral power detached from economic passions or motives.

At present I regret to say labour politicians seem to be losing all reality as effective aids to our struggles on the industrial battlefield, are becoming more and more absorbed in questions of administration, or taxation, and only occasionally, as in the miners' national strike, really rise to a realisation of their true role of parliamentary outposts of the industrial army.

The parliamentary tail in Britain still persist in wagging the British industrial dog. Once the dog really begins to assert his true position, we will be troubled no more by carping critics of labour politics, nor yet with labour politicians' confessions of their own impotence in such great crises as that of the railway strike or the Johannesburg massacres.

Nor yet would we see that awful spectacle we have seen lately of labour politicians writing to the capitalist press to denounce the methods of a union which, with 20,000 men and women locked out in one city, is facing an attempt of 400 employers to starve its members back into slavery.

And thou, Brutus, that you should play the enemy's game at such a crisis! Every drop of ink you spilled in such an act stopped a loaf of bread on its way to some starving family.

[*Forward* (Glasgow), 4 October 1913 (extracts).]

A titanic struggle

What is the truth about the Dublin dispute? What was the origin of the Dublin dispute? These are at present the most discussed questions in the labour world of these islands, and I have been invited by the editor of the *Daily Herald* to try and shed a little light upon them for the benefit of its readers. I will try and be brief and to the point, whilst striving to be also clear.

In the year 1911 the National Seamen's and Firemen's Union, as a last desperate expedient to avoid extinction, resolved upon calling a general strike in all the home ports. At that time the said Union as the lawyers would say, was, more or less, of an Ishmael among trade unions. It was not registered, in most places it was not even affiliated to the local Trades Union Councils, and its national officials had always been hostile to the advanced labour movement. They believed, seemingly, in playing a lone hand. Perhaps the general discredit into which it had been brought by the curiously inconsistent action of its leaders in closely identifying themselves with one of the orthodox political parties, and at the same time calling for the aid in industrial conflicts of the labour men whom they fought and slandered in political labour contests, had something to do with the general weakness and impending bankruptcy of the National Seamen's and Firemen's Union, at the time it issued its call in 1911.

At all events the call was in danger of falling upon vain ears, and was, in fact, but little heeded until the Irish Transport and General Workers' Union began to take a hand in the game. As ships came into the Port of Dublin, after the issue of the call, each ship was held up by the dockers under the orders of James Larkin until its crew joined the union, and signed on under union conditions and rates of pay. Naturally, this did not please the shipowners and merchants of Dublin. But the delegates of the Irish Transport and General Workers' Union up and down the docks preached most energetically the doctrine of the sympathetic strike, and the doctrine was readily assimilated by the dockers and carters. It brought the union into a long and bitter struggle along the quays, a struggle which cost it thousands of pounds, imperilled its very existence, and earned for it the bitterest hatred of every employer and sweater in the city, every one of whom swore they would wait their chance to 'get even with Larkin and his crew.'

The sympathetic strike having worked so well for the seamen and firemen, the Irish Transport and General Workers' Union began to apply it ruthlessly in every labour dispute. A record of the victories it has won for other trade unions would surprise a good many of its critics. A few cases will indicate what, in the hands of Larkin and the Irish Transport and General Workers' Union, it has won for some of the skilled trades.

When the coachmakers went on strike the Irish Transport and General Workers' Union took over all the labourers, paid them strike pay, and kept them out until the coachmakers won. The latter body are now repaying us by doing scab work while we are out.

The mill-sawyers existed for twenty years in Dublin without recognition. The sympathetic strike by our union won them recognition and an increase of pay.

The stationary engine drivers, the cabinetmakers, the sheet metal workers, the carpenters, and, following them all the building trades got an increase through our control of the carting industry. As did also the girls and men employed in Jacob's biscuit factory. In addition to this work for others we won for our own members the following increases within the last two years: cross channel dockers got, since the strike in the City of Dublin Steam Packet Company, an increase of wages of 3s. per week. In the case of the British and Irish Company the increase, levelling it up with the other firms meant a rise of 6s. per week. For men working for the Merchants' Warehousing Company 3s. per week, general carriers 2s. to 3s., coal fillers halfpenny per ton, grain bushellers 1d. per ton, men and boys in the bottle-blowing works from 2s. to 10s. per week of an increase, mineral water operatives 4s. to 6s. per week, and a long list of warehouses in which girls were exploited were compelled to give some slight modification of the inhuman conditions under which their employees were labouring.

As Mr. Havelock Wilson, General Secretary, National Seamen's and Firemen's Union, has mentioned the strike on the City of Dublin Steam Packet Company as an instance of our erratic methods, it may be worth while to note that as a result of that strike some of his sailors got an increase of 5s. 6d. per week.

In addition to the cases enumerated I might also mention that the labourers on the Dublin and South-Eastern Railway got increases of 6s. per week, and those in the Kingstown Gas Works got increases varying from 3s. to 10s. per week per man.

All of these increases were the result of the sympathetic strike policy, first popularised by its success in winning the battle for the Seamen and Firemen—who are now asked to repudiate it.

These things well understood explain the next act in the unfolding of the drama. Desiring to make secure what had been gained, Mr. Larkin formulated a scheme for a Conciliation Board. This was adopted by the Trades Council, at least in essence, and eventually came before the Employers' Executive, or whatever the governing committee of that body is named. After a hot discussion it was put to the vote. Eighteen employers voted to accept a Conciliation Board, three voted against. Of that three, William Martin Murphy was one. On finding himself in the minority he rose and vowed that in spite of them he would 'smash the Conciliation Board.' Within three days he kept his word by discharging two hundred of his tramway traffic employees for being members of the Irish Transport and General Workers' Union, and thus forced on the strike of the tramway men. Immediately he appealed to all the Dublin employers who had been forced into a semblance of decency by Larkin and his colleagues, called to their memory the increases of wages they were compelled to pay, and lured them on to a desperate effort to combine and destroy the one labour force they feared.

The employers, mad with hatred of the power that had wrested from them the improved conditions, a few of which I have named, rallied round Murphy, and from being one in a minority of three he became the leader and organising spirit of a band of four hundred.

I have always told our friends in Great Britain that our fight in Ireland was neither inspired nor swayed by theories nor theorists. It grew and was hammered out of the hard necessities of our situation. Here, in this brief synopsis, you can trace its growth for yourselves. First a fierce desire to save our brothers of the sea, a desire leading to us risking our own existence in their cause. Developing from that an extension of the principle of sympathetic action until we took the fierce beast of capital by the throat all over Dublin, and loosened its hold on the vitals of thousands of our class. Then a rally of the forces of capital to recover their hold, and eventually a titanic struggle, in which the forces of labour in Britain openly, and the forces of capital secretly, became participants.

That is where we stand to-day. The struggle forming our theories and shaping the policy, not only for us, but for our class. To those who criticise us we can only reply: we fight as conditions dictate; we meet new conditions with new policies. Those who choose may keep old policies to meet new conditions. We cannot and will not try.

[*Daily Herald* (London), 6 December 1913.]

A fiery cross or Christmas bells

While we are writing this the one question agitating all Dublin is whether this Christmas will see a relighting of the Fiery Cross or the ringing of Christmas bells of peace and rejoicing. Possibly no more grim commentary upon the so-called civilisation of to-day could be instanced than that fact. Here we have a great city held up by a war between two classes, and in that war the contending classes are represented, on the one hand, by those who control the wealth, the capital, the armed forces and all the means of coercion; whilst, on the other hand, all that is represented is toiling men and women, with no assets except their brains and hands, and no powers except the power and capacity to suffer for a principle they esteem more valuable than life itself.

But to the side of this latter class has been drawn gradually as if by a magnet all the intellect, the soul and the spirit of the nation, all those who have learned to esteem the higher things of life, to value the spirit more than the matter.

Publicists of all kinds, philanthropists, literary men, lovers of their kind, poets, brilliant writers, artists, have all been conquered by the valiant heroism of the Dublin workers, have all been drawn within the ranks of the friends of the fighters of labour—all have succumbed to the magic charm of the unobtrusive men and women whose constancy amidst sufferings has made this fight possible. Whoever signs the document of settlement (if any is ever signed), whosoever is acclaimed as the great one of the treaty of peace (if there ever is a treaty of peace) the real heroes and conquerors are to be found in the slums, and in the prisons where men, women and girls have agonised and are agonising in order that their class may not lose one step it has gained in its upward toil to freedom.

These thoughts come crowding upon us as we write. We think also that, despite all the adhesion of all the brilliant ones and all those in the highest odour of sanctity to the cause of the workers, the settlement is still in the hands of those who control economic power. Poets, artists, authors, humanitarians and archbishops may plead and beg for the ringing of the bells of Christmas for ever. The final word still rests with those who control the money bags; and thus we learn, hard facts teaching us, that in this gross travesty of civilisation under which we live to-day neither soul nor brains is the equal of gold.

> The clinking of the silver dimes life's melody has marred,
> And nature's immemorial chimes are jangled, harsh and jarred.

And so Dublin lies in the grip of the power of the purse; and on this fateful Friday the issue still hangs trembling. A few hours may determine whether the verdict will go forth for the joyous ringing of the Bells of Peace or for the militant call to all lovers of their kind to grasp and pass from hand to hand again the dread but inspiring Fiery Cross.

[*Irish Worker*, 20 December 1913.]

The isolation of Dublin

It is not necessary, I presume, to remind our readers of the beginnings of the Dublin struggle. Let us, just for convenience sake, take up the fight at

Elizabeth and James Larkin at home after Larkin's release from jail in 1913 with their three sons, James, Denis and Fintan. *(Photograph: Le Miroir, Paris)*

Speakers at a meeting organised by Liverpool Trades Council in support of Dublin workers: James Larkin, James Connolly, Big Bill Haywood (IWW) and Mrs Bamber.

Portrait of William Martin Murphy
by Sir William Orpen, RA.

Drawing of Larkin in
Liberty Hall by Sir
William Orpen, RA.

The Daily Herald

HOW TO SETTLE DUBLIN—FOLD ARMS!

Cartoon by Will Dyson in
The Daily Herald (London),
9 December 1913.

Cartoon by the
American artist,
Ryan Walker

Suggestion for today's after dinner debate: "Which is
the biggest crime—"To steal a loaf of bread or to starve
a little child?"

*At his trial Larkin
was indicted on a
charge of "speaking
with the intention of
having the shops
pillaged and robbed"
in that he told the
crowd that "there was
plenty of food in the
shops and if any man
went hungry he was
an idiot."*

*This cartoon by the
American cartoonist,
Ryan Walker, posed
the question "if the
family depicted were
your family, what
would you do about
it?"*

Francis Sheehy Skeffington.

Councillor William P. Partridge.

Æ (George Russell)
from a painting by Jack Yeats.
(National Gallery of Ireland)

Seán O'Casey, Secretary,
Irish Citizen Army, 1913–14.

Constance Markievicz, Treasurer,
Irish Citizen Army, 1913–16.

Countess Constance Markievicz
with her daughter, Maeve Alys,
and stepson, Stanislas.

Lieutenant Constance Markievicz,
Irish Citizen Army.

Captain J. R. White, DSO,
Chairman, Army Council,
Irish Citizen Army, 1914.

Below: Flag of the Irish Citizen Army

Right: Commandant General James
Connolly, Irish Citizen Army, from a
woodcut by Harry Kernoff, RHA.

Irish Citizen Army on parade outside Croydon House, Croydon Park, Dublin, the ITGWU recreation centre.

Delia Larkin, Secretary, Irish Women Workers' Union, 1911–1915.

Delia Larkin signs the anti-conscription pledge in the Mansion House, April 1918.

IRISH TRADES
UNION CONGRESS

Members of the National Executive of Irish TUC, 1914. *From left – standing:* James Connolly, William O'Brien, Michael J. Egan, Thomas Cassidy, W. E. Hill, Richard O'Carroll. *Sitting:* Thomas MacPartlin, David R. Campbell, Patrick T. Daly, James Larkin (President), Michael J. O'Lehane. Thomas Johnson, not in the picture, was also a member of the National Executive.

Thomas Johnson,
Irish TUC President 1916,
Secretary 1921–1928.

Delegates to the 21st annual congress of the Irish Trades Union Congress, City Hall, Dublin, April 1914. The President, James Larkin, is seated eighth from the left on the second row. The three women delegates sitting on either side of the President were from the Irish Women Workers' Union – Bridget Butler and Delia Larkin (Dublin) and Ellen Gordon (Belfast). James Connolly is standing second from right.

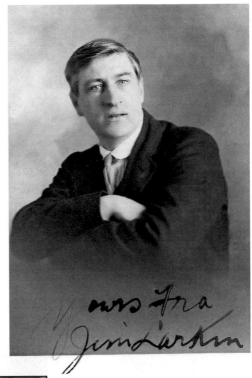

Right: Autographed photograph of James Larkin taken in America.

Below: Jack Carney (photograph taken in Chicago).

LARKIN
IN
AMERICA

Poster for demonstration addressed by
Larkin, Chicago, March 1916.

Larkin with Big Bill Haywood of the International Workers of the World in America.

Convict 50945.
New York police mugshot of Larkin 1919.

James Larkin in Sing Sing Penitentiary,
New York State.

Elizabeth Gurley Flynn.

Joe Hill.

Letter to Elizabeth Gurley Flynn ('The Rebel Girl') from Joe Hill, written a few hours before he was shot by firing squad in Utah State Prison.

Funeral of Joe Hill in Chicago.

Australian police mugshot of Peter Larkin.

Peter Larkin, National Organiser,
Workers' Union of Ireland.

PETER LARKIN

Funeral of Peter Larkin passing the GPO, O'Connell Street, Dublin, November 1931.

ONE BIG UNION

PROPAGANDA LEAGUE

KING,
BEASANT,
LARKIN,
REEVES,
GLYNN,
FAGIN,

MOORE,
BEATTY,
McPHERSON,
GRANT,
TEEN,
HAMILTON.

**1916
to
1931!**

**1916
to
1931!**

Lost their
Liberty that
You and I
Should be
FREE.

Their Fight
was for
Education,
Organisation,
Emancipation.

Demands the Immediate Release

of their Twelve Mates in Jail

Poster of One Big Union Propaganda League (New South Wales) demanding the release of the jailed Twelve including Peter Larkin.

SPECIAL

MAY DAY ISSUE

"An Injury to One an Injury to All"

Special May Day Issue, *Direct Action* (Sydney)
5 May 1917.

ITGWU members at Croke Park, Dublin, May 1923 welcome home from America the General Secretary of the Union, James Larkin, seated fourth from right in the second row with his eldest son, James Junior, on his left and the General President, Thomas Foran, on his right.

LARKIN RETURNS

ITGWU Executive Council 1923.
James Larkin (General Secretary) is at head of table with Thomas Foran (General President) on his left and William O'Brien (General Treasurer) on his right.

the moment it became a subject of national action on the part of the British Labour movement.

A public meeting had been proclaimed in Dublin in a brazen illegal manner. For declaring that this proclamation was illegal, and advising their leaders to disregard it and stand to their rights, a number of leaders of the Irish Transport and General Workers' Union had been arrested and imprisoned. A wholesale batoning of the people had followed, and Dublin was the scene of the most unparalleled police brutality.

An appeal was made to the British Trades Union Congress, then happily sitting, and that body in the name of the British working class nobly rose to the occasion, and pledged the credit of the whole British labour movement to see their Dublin comrades through the fight. As a result, the right of free speech was re-asserted in Dublin, a supply of food was arranged for through the despatch of specially chartered steamers, and a huge amount of money was raised to enable the men and women of Dublin to keep the fight going. Never was seen such enthusiasm in a labour fight. Trade unionists, socialists of all kinds, anarchists, industrialists, syndicalists, all the varying and hitherto discordant elements of the labour movement found a common platform, were joined together in pursuit of a common object. Now, permit me to underscore that point, and emphasise its great importance. For long years we have been preaching to the labour movement the necessity of concerted industrial action, telling it that the time was rotten ripe for industrial unity, and declaring that as the interests of each were the concern of all, our organisations should be rearranged with a view to the conserving of their common interests.

We found that to a large extent these ideas were taking root in the minds of the workers, but that to a still larger extent the tacit acceptance of our ideas failed to evoke concerted action built upon these lines. The forces of our enemies were united and wielded with all the precision and relentlessness with which the general staff of an army would wield the battalions and brigades which formed the component parts of that army, but the battalions and brigades of the army of labour when engaged in battle had no efficient general staff to guide and direct the whole army to the salvation of its individual units; and, worse still, had none of that esprit-de-corps which on the military battle-field would make the desertion of any section to its fate an unthinkable course to the officers of the divisions not engaged. We had seen at London, at Leith and elsewhere that whereas the whole force of the Shipping Federation has been actively engaged in fighting the dockers of these ports, the dockers and seamen of the other ports had maintained the peace, and left their Leith or London brothers to bear alone the full force of the Federation attack, instead of meeting that attack by a movement against the flanks and rear of the Federation in these other ports. We know that although much of this blundering was due to the sectional jealousy of various union leaders, much was also due to the fact that the conception of common action on a national scale by the whole working class had not yet entered the minds of the rank and file as a whole. Something had been wanting—something that would make the minds of the workers more responsive, more ready to accept the broader idea, and act upon its acceptance. That something Dublin supplied.

The dramatic suddenness with which the Dublin fight was thrust upon public attention, the tragic occurrences of the first few days—working class martyrdom, the happy coincidence of a Trade Union Congress, the intervention of British trade unionists to assert the right of public meeting for Irish workers—filling the gap in the ranks caused by the jailing of Irish Trade Union leaders, the brilliant inspiration of a food ship, and last but not least the splendid heroism of the Dublin men and women showing out against the background of the squalor and misery of their houses.

There are times in history when we realise that it is easier to convert a multitude than it ordinarily is to convert an individual; when indeed ideas seem to seize upon the masses as contra-distinguished by ordinary times when individuals slowly seize ideas. The propagandist toils on for decades in seeming failure and ignominy, when suddenly some great event takes place in accord with the principles he has been advocating, and immediately he finds that the seed he has been sowing is springing up in plants that are covering the earth. To the idea of working class unity, to the seed of industrial solidarity, Dublin was the great event that enabled it to seize the minds of the masses, the germinating force that gave power to the seed to fructify and cover these islands.

I say in all solemnity and seriousness that in its attitude towards Dublin the working class movement of Great Britain reached its highest point of moral grandeur—attained for a moment to a realisation of that sublime unity towards which the best in us must continually aspire. Could that feeling but have been crystallised into organic expression, could we but have had real statesmen amongst us who, recognising the wonderful leap forward of our class, would have hastened to burn behind us the boats that might make easy a retreat to the old ground of isolation and division, could we have found labour leaders capable enough to declare that now that the working class had found its collective soul it should hasten to express itself as befitted that soul and not be fettered by the rules, regulations and codes of organisations conceived in the olden outworn spirit of sectional jealousies; could these things have but been vouchsafed to us, what a new world could now be opening delightfully upon the vision of labour? Consider what Dublin meant to you all! It meant that the whole force of organised labour should stand behind each unit of organisation in each and all of its battles, that no company, battalion or brigade should henceforth be allowed to face the enemy alone, and that the capitalist would be taught that when he fought a union anywhere he must be prepared to fight all unions everywhere.

For the first days and weeks of the struggle, the working classes of Great Britain attained to the height of moral grandeur expressed in that idea, all labour stood behind Dublin, and Dublin rejoiced. Dublin suffered and agonised, but rejoiced that even in its suffering it was the medium for the apostolate of a rejuvenating idea. How often have I heard the responsive cheers to the question whether they would be prepared to stand by others as these others had stood by them!

And now? Dublin is isolated. We asked our friends of the transport trade unions to isolate the capitalist class of Dublin, and we asked the other unions to back them up. But no, they said we would rather help you by giving you funds. We argued that a strike is an attempt to stop the capitalist from carrying on his business, that the success or failure of the strike depends entirely upon the success or non-success of the capitalist to do without the strikers. If the capitalist is able to carry on his business without the strikers, then the strike is lost, even if the strikers receive more in strike pay than they formerly did in wages. We said that if scabs are working a ship and union men discharge in another port the boat so loaded, then those union men are strike breakers, since they help the capitalist in question to carry on his business. That if union seamen man a boat discharged by scabs, these union seamen or firemen are by the same reason strike-breakers, as also are the railwaymen or carters who assist in transporting the goods handled by the scabs for the capitalist who is fighting his men or women. In other words, we appealed to the collective soul of the workers against the collective hatred of the capitalist.

We asked for no more than the logical development of that idea of working class unity, that the working class of Britain should help us to prevent the Dublin capitalists carrying on their business without us. We asked for the isolation of the capitalists of Dublin, and for answer the leaders of the British labour movement proceeded calmly to isolate the working class of Dublin. As an answer to those who supported our request for the isolation of Dublin we were told that a much better plan would be to increase the subsidies to enable us to increase strike pay. As soon as this argument had served its purpose, the subsidies fell off, and the 'Dublin Fund' grew smaller and smaller as if by a pre-arranged plan. We had rejected the last terms offered by the employers on the strength of this talk of increased supplies, and as soon as that last attempt at settlement thus fell through, the supplies gradually froze up instead of being increased as we had been promised.

Sufficient to say that the working class unity of the first days of the Dublin fight was sacrificed in the interests of sectional officialism. The officials failed to grasp the opportunity offered to them to make a permanent reality of the union of working class forces brought into being by the spectacle of rebellion, martyrdom and misery exhibited by the workers of Dublin. All England and Scotland rose to it; working class officialdom and working class rank and file alike responded to the call of inspiration; it would have raised us all upward and onward towards our common emancipation. But sectionalism, intrigues and old-time jealousies damned us in the hour of victory, and officialdom was the first to fall to the tempter.

241

And so we Irish workers must go down into Hell, bow our backs to the lash of the slave driver, let our hearts be seared by the iron of his hatred, and instead of the sacramental wafer of brotherhood and common sacrifice, eat the dust of defeat and betrayal.

Dublin is isolated.

[*Forward* (Glasgow), 9 February 1914 (extracts).]

Disturbed Dublin

Disturbed Dublin is the title of a book just published in the interests of the Dublin employers, and with the name of Arnold Wright upon its title page as author. The purpose of this book is to present to the reading public as colourable a presentation as possible of the events from the employers' point of view of the great dispute of 1913–14. We are not saying so because this book is antagonistic to the cause of labour, but we say so because from the very first paragraph of the preface to the last sentence of the volume itself this bias against labour is so pronounced that the idea that it found its inspiration in the councils of the employers springs at once to the mind of the thoughtful reader. For instance, let us quote from the second sentence of the preface, where the author describes the result of the employers' conspiracy as:

> The ignominious defeat of the attempt to establish a peculiarly pernicious form of Syndicalism on Irish soil.

This, one must admit, is a good start for an 'impartial' history, and the same spirit is in evidence all through the book. In this attempt to present a literary justification for the employers the author does not scruple to distort facts, and even to state deliberate untruths.

One feels like congratulating the real literary men of Dublin that the employers could not trust one of them to be sufficiently blind to facts as to present a case that would suit the employers. A stranger, without any knowledge of Dublin people, without any insight into the terrible struggle life involves to a Dublin worker, without any appreciation of the finer elements of character which the Dublin toiler has preserved in spite of the hell of poverty and misery in which he or she was born and reared, without any grasp of the blended squalor and heroism, pride and abasement that environment has woven into the Dublin character, and absolutely blind and deaf to all knowledge of the countless cross-currents, interests and traditions that played their part in moulding and shaping that historic struggle—it is only such a fatuously ignorant stranger that the employers of Dublin could count upon to describe that struggle as they wanted it described.

The achievement of the employers is written of as if the book was dealing with the struggle of a puny David against a mighty Goliath, the employers being David and Jim Larkin the giant Goliath. No epic story of

242

heroism that was ever written could surpass in admiring sentences the description of the employers' battle against the working men and women as this hack writer tells it.

Told by a labour writer, or even told by one of those literary men who, although not of the manual labour ranks stood so grandly by the workers during that titanic struggle, the story would indeed read like an epic, but it would be an epic of which the heroes and heroines were the humble men and women who went out in the street to suffer and starve rather than surrender their right to combine as they chose for the uplifting of their class. Some day that story will be written from that standpoint, meanwhile let us briefly cast up the elements out of which that story will be composed.

It must tell how four hundred Dublin employers covenanted together, and pledged each other by solemn vows, and by still more binding financial pledges, that there would be no more resumption of work in Dublin until the Irish Transport and General Workers' Union was wiped off the map. How they agreed upon a document to be forced upon all workers that they would neither join nor help that union. How they had all the press of every shade of politics and religion upon their side. How they obtained beforehand the promise of swift and relentless use of Government forces, of batons, bullets, and jails to destroy the resistance of the workers. How that promise was faithfully kept by the Government. How they were able to override the law, and to fill the prisons with old and young, men and women, boys and girls, who attempted to exercise the picketing rights guaranteed to them by British law. How they instituted a reign of terror in which the lives of every worker was at the mercy of every callous brute in the uniform of a policeman or the vocation of a scab. How starvation was sent into the homes of thousands of the poor, until their lives were shortened by the sufferings enforced. How one bright young girl was shot, two honest workers batoned to death, and one other destroyed in his bright manhood by the hirelings of the Government. How the domestic privacy of the poor was violated, their poor household treasures ruthlessly smashed and the most sacred feelings of womanhood outraged by hordes of drunken policemen. And how through all this long-drawn-out agony every agency of every organised political, journalistic, social or religious kind in Ireland, not directly controlled by labour, joined in one great unanimous chorus in vilification of the sufferers, and in praise of their oppressors.

When that story is written by a man or woman with an honest heart, and with a sympathetic insight into the travail of the poor, it will be a record of which Ireland may well be proud. It will tell of how the old women and young girls, long crushed and enslaved, dared to risk all, even life itself, in the struggle to make life more tolerable, more free of the grinding tyranny of the soulless Dublin employers. It will tell of how, like an inspiration, there came to those Irish women and girls the thought that no free nation could be reared which tolerated the enslavement of its daughters to the worst forms of wage-slavery, and how in the glow of that inspiration they arose from their seats in the workshop or factory, and went out to suffer and struggle along with their men. It will tell of how the general labourers, the men upon whose crushed lives is built the fair fabric of civilisation, from whose squalid tenements the sweet-smelling flowers of capitalist culture derive their aroma, by whose horny hands and mangled bodies are bought the ease and safety of a class that hates and despises them, by whose ignorance their masters purchase their knowledge—it will tell how these labourers dared to straighten their bent backs, and looking in the faces of their rulers and employers dared to express the will to be free. And it will tell how that spectacle of the slave of the underworld looking his masters in the face without terror, and fearlessly proclaiming the kinship and unity of all with each and each with all, how that spectacle caught the imagination of all unselfish souls so that the artisan took his place also in the place of conflict and danger, and the men and women of genius, the artistic and the literati, hastened to honour and serve those humble workers whom all had hitherto despised and scorned.

And that story will tell how, despite the wealth and the power of the masters, despite jails and batons, despite starvation and death, victory was within sight for the Dublin workers, and only eluded their grasp because of the failure of a part of their allies to remain keyed up to the battle pitch. Because others outside their ranks were not able to realise the grandeur of the opportunity, the sublimity of the issues at stake.

The battle was a drawn battle. The employers, despite their Napoleonic plan of campaign, and their more than Napoleonic ruthlessness and unscrupulous use of foul means were unable to carry on their business without men and women who remained loyal to their union. The workers were unable to force the employers to a formal recognition of the union, and to give preference to organised labour. From the effects of this drawn battle both sides are still bearing heavy scars. How deep those scars are none will ever reveal.

But the working class has lost none of its aggressiveness, none of its confidence, none of its hope in the ultimate triumph. No traitor amongst the ranks of that class has permanently gained, even materially, by his or her treachery. The flag of the Irish Transport and General Workers' Union still flies proudly in the van of the Irish working class, and that working class still marches proudly and defiantly at the head of the gathering hosts who stand for a regenerated nation, resting upon a people industrially free.

Ah, yes, that story of the Dublin dispute of 1913–14 is meet subject for an epic poem with which some Irish genius of the future can win an immortality as great as did the humble fighters who in it fought the battle of labour.

[*Irish Worker*, 18 November 1914 (extracts).]

Chapter 33

After the Battle

William Martin Murphy

On 1 September 1913 the Dublin Chamber of Commerce paid tribute to its president, William Martin Murphy. It passed unanimously a resolution of thanks for 'the energetic manner in which the President had dealt with the present labour unrest in the city.' The president replied:

I wish to express my sincere thanks to the meeting for the resolution. I am particularly proud of it, and I am also proud of the result of my exertions, because of my position as President of the Chamber of Commerce and the interests it represents in the present crisis. That was one of the things that has stimulated me in the action I have taken. I have seen for a long time that the head of this labour agitation in Dublin has been aiming for a position that was occupied some time ago in Paris by a man who was called 'King' Pataud, who was able to hold up the whole business of the city by raising his little finger. That man was driven out of Paris, and the other man will be driven out of Dublin shortly.

The question I have fought in connection with the Tramway Company was not one of wages or the treatment of those employed in the tramway service. The whole issue was the supremacy of Mr. Larkin and whether he was going to rule the trade of Dublin, and whether men could carry on their business and in fact be able to call their bodies and souls their own, unless they went cap in hand to him. The position was becoming intolerable.

It was time to stop this man, and I think I have stopped him. I did not get into the matter in a light-hearted or an haphazard way. I had laid out my plans of campaign, and prepared for any emergency that might arise. Generally, Mr. Larkin was good enough to state in advance what he proposed doing, and thus I was able to take him in anticipation. Larkin is now under the protection of the police. His victims, the employers, have been under the protection of the police for some time, but for the past week Mr. Larkin appeared to have been craving for the police himself and to get inside jail, which would be the safest place for him, when his victims are looking for him and find there is no strike pay for them.

The fight against Larkin was not, after all so difficult: it was easier than it appeared. The prospect of a strike and the anticipation of it had much more terror for the employer, than the actual strike when it took place. An employer who had never been up against a strike was terrorised at the prospect. When the strike actually took place the employer had to get his back to the wall, and the workman had fired his last cartridge. The employer all the time managed to get his three meals a day, but the unfortunate workman and his family had no resources whatever except submission, and that was what occurred in 99 cases out of 100. The difficulty of teaching that lesson to the workman was extraordinary.

One of the helps we have had in this strike, has been that Mr. Larkin has provided an antidote to the poisonous atmosphere which he himself has created. That antidote is the hundreds of men he has thrown out of employment, who can easily be had to take any work and undergo any risks so sad is their plight.

At the annual general meeting of the Dublin Chamber of Commerce on 28 January 1914, William Martin Murphy, its president, had more to say about the lock-out of the previous year (though this was not how he described the dispute). The strike, he asserted,

> had been part of a plot to plunge the city into a state of anarchy and to make all business impossible by means of a system known as 'syndicalism' or 'sympathetic strikes', the avowed object of which was to destroy capitalists and establish what Mr. Larkin called a co-operative commonwealth of which he, no doubt, was to be Cromwell. It was strange enough that even the most ignorant labourer should be caught up by this claptrap, but it is amazing to think how the skilled tradesmen of the city, as represented by the Trades Council, came under the domination of Mr. Larkin, and allowed themselves to be dragged at his heel.

Following the meeting, the Council of the Dublin Chamber of Commerce established a public committee to express their appreciation of 'the great services rendered' by Murphy during 'the recent prolonged labour troubles.' At the annual general meeting the following year (29 January 1915) it was reported that 'the response made in subscriptions showed the citizens' appreciation of the services he had rendered to the city and the widespread feeling of esteem for him.'

The testimonial took the form of a portrait of Murphy by William Orpen. (A replica by the same artist was hung in the office of the Chamber of Commerce.) The portrait was presented to Murphy in February 1915, together with an address 'bearing the signatories of 410 noblemen and gentlemen representative of trade, commerce, and of the professions, not only in Dublin but throughout the country.'

Chapter 34

Ballads of 1913

'It's Murphy's'

I entered a tram and rode all day
On a regal couch and a right of way
Which reached its arms all over the land
In a system too large to understand.
'A splendid property this!' I cried
And a man with a plate on his hat replied—
    'It's Murphy's!'

I went to heaven. The jasper walls
Towered high and wide, and the golden halls
Shone bright beyond. But a strange new mark
Was over the gate, viz. 'Private Park'.
'What is the meaning of this?' I cried
And a saint with a livery on replied:
    'It's Murphy's!'

I went to the only place left. 'I'll take
A chance in the boat on the brimstone lake,
Or perhaps I may be allowed to sit
On the griddled floor of the bottomless pit.'
But the jeering tout with horns on his face
Cried as he forked me out of the place,
    'It's Murphy's!'[1]

Who Fears to Wear the Blood Red Badge?

Who fears to wear the blood red badge
Upon his manly breast?
What scab obeys the vile command
Of Murphy and the rest?
He's all a knave, and half a slave
Who slights his Union thus
But true men, like you men,
Will show the badge with us.

They dared to fling a manly brick
They wrecked a blackleg tram,
They dared give Harvey Duff a kick,
They didn't care a damn.

They lie in gaol, they can't get bail,
Who fought their corner thus,
But you men, with sticks, men,
Must make the Peelers 'cuss'.

We rose in sad and weary days
To fight the workers' cause,
We found in Jim, a heart ablaze,
To break down unjust laws.
But 'tis a sin to follow him
Says Murphy and his crew,
Though true men, like you men,
Will stick to him like glue.

Good luck be with him, he is here
To win for us the fight;
To suffer for us without fear,
To champion the right.
So stick to Jim, let nothing dim
Our ardour in the fray,
And true Jim, our own Jim,
Will win our fight today.[2]

A Song of Swords

G. K. Chesterton

'A drove of cattle came into a village called Swords and was stopped by
the rioters' (daily paper).

In a place called Swords on the Irish road
It is told for a new renown
How we held the horns of the cattle, and how
We will hold the horns of the devil now
Ere the lord of hell, with the horn on his brow,
Is crowned in Dublin town.

Light in the East and light in the West,
And light on the cruel lords,
On the souls that suddenly all men knew,
And the green flag flew and the red flag flew,
And many a wheel of the world stopped, too,
When the cattle were stopped at Swords.

Be they sinners or less than saints
That smite in the street for rage,
We know where the shame shines bright: we know
You that they smite at, you their foe,

Lords of the lawless wage and low,
This is your lawful wage.

You pinched a child to a torture price
That you dared not name in words;
So black a jest was the silver bit
That your own speech shook for the shame of it.
And the coward was plain as a cow they hit
When the cattle have strayed at Swords.

The wheel of the torment of wives went round
To break men's brotherhood,
You gave the good Irish blood to grease
The clubs of your country's enemies,
You saw the brave man beat to the knees:
And you saw that it was good.

The rope of the rich is long and long—
The longest of hangmen's cords;
But the kings and crowds are holding their breath,
In a giant shadow o'er all beneath
Where God stands holding the scales of Death,
Between the cattle and Swords.

Haply the lords that hire and lend,
The lowest of all men's lords,
Who sell their kind like kine at a fair,
Will find no head of their cattle there;
But faces of men where cattle were;
Faces of men—and Swords.

And the name shining and terrible,
The sternest of all man's words,
Still mark that place to seek or shun,
In the streets where the struggling cattle run—
Grass and a silence of judgment done
In the place that is called Swords.[3]

To the 'Villas of Genteel Dastards'

Susan Mitchell

'A city of bellowing slaves! Villas of genteel dastards!'—John Mitchel (*Jail Journal*).

It was a glorious civic boast—civis Romanus sum!
But we—we want no citizens, we have no Orange drum;
We have the Ancient Order and ratepayers of renown,
And publicans and peelers all over Dublin town.

Oh mean and crafty Dublin, the sons you've flung away!
The tale of your iniquity you're filling up today;
You cringe and slink before the lash, I know you for a cur
Who turned on a Lord Edward, who fawned upon a Sirr.

You stood aside while Emmet died, you let John Mitchel go
Across the seas of exile, nor struck one manly blow
To save the ardent hearts who would have set you up on high:
You found the paid informer, you cheered the pensioned spy.

You sit within your villas, genteelly, as of yore,
Unheeding the fierce life that throbs a stone's throw from your door:
Have you no blood to nerve your arm to do the selfless deed?
The portents that surround you have you no eyes to read?

I see a band of shabby men, down in a shabby street,
I see the light in eyes upturned a leader's eyes to meet:
I know that spark of holy fire and bend a reverent knee
Before the light unquenchable of man's divinity.

No prouder sight has Ireland seen since banded peasants stood
Upon her fields for freedom than this famished brotherhood,
Who in their leader's message have caught a distant gleam
Of that far off Holy City, our glory and our dream.

These are the sons whom Dublin should gather to her breast,
These—these her citizens to spread her glory East and West,
Ye cannot quench the spirit, but oh, consider well,
Lest ye should turn the torch of God to light the fires of hell.[4]

The Blackleg

Jim Connell

There's a cuckoo in our household, and he terrifies our young,
For the habits of the traitor have been often told and sung,
Though his feathers flutter softly, there is murder in his heart,
And all down the toiling ages he has played the villain's part.

> *Chorus:*
> Oh, we hate the cruel tiger,
> And hyena and jackal;
> But the false and dirty blackleg
> Is the vilest beast of all.

When we dress our brave battalions, and confront the Lords of Loot,
We behold the Scab desert us ere the guns begin to shoot,
Just to gorge his greedy stomach, and to save his coward skin,
With salvation in the balance he betrays his kith and kin.

You can tell him 'midst a thousand by his cringe and by his crawl,
For of dignity or courage he possesses none at all.
In the aleshop he's a sponger, in the workshop he's a spy;
He's a liar and deceiver with low cunning in his eye.

Let us flout him in the market, let us 'cut' him in the street,
Let us jeer him from all places where the honest workers meet.
When to greet his brazen features every decent door is slammed,
We will leave him burst and broken to go down among the damned.[5]

The Watchword

James Connolly

Oh, hear ye the Watchword of Labour,
The slogan of they who'd be free
That no more to any enslaver
Must labour bend suppliant knee.
That we, on whose shoulders is borne,
The pomp and the pride of the great,
Whose toil they repay with their scorn,
Must challenge and master our fate.
    Then send it aloft on the breeze, boys
    The slogan the grandest we've known
    That Labour must rise from its knees, boys,
    And claim the broad earth as its own.

Oh, we who've oft won by our valour
Empires for our rulers and lords
Yet kneel in abasement and squalor
To the thing that we've made by our swords,
Now valour with worth will be blending
When answering labour's command,
We arise from our knees and, ascending
To manhood, for freedom take stand.

Then out from the fields and the factories,
From workshop, from mill and from mine,
Despising their wrath and their pity
We workers are moving in line
To answer the Watchword and token
That Labour gives forth as its own,
Nor pause till our fetters we've broken
And conquered the spoiler and drone.[6]

Lines to the Brotherhood of Cain

Maeve Cavanagh

Drive them back to their wretched dens
    With brutal baton and sword,
And raise to a patient God your thanks
    That evil and power have scored.

Suffer them not to know of aught
    But squalor and toilsome days;
Live on their little one's sweated toil
    Whilst your own child thrives and plays.

Fetter their minds with ignorance
    With puerile fears and with lies;
Preach glibly 'The poor must always be,'
    Lest they dare to think and rise.

Divide their ranks with bigotry
    Whilst you rob the wealth they made;
Then go to your vaulted church and pray
    Still shameless and unafraid.

Whilst you list to the organ's notes
    A fierce gale shrieks and raves;
Where far from your tranquil church
    Your ships are fighting the waves.

O'erfreighted and ill equipped,
    Death traps for their doomed crew,
With cargo high o'er the load line plied—
    But what is their plight to you?

If she rides the seas 'tis well—
    Should she sink—'tis better still;
The widows' and orphans' curse
    Is powerless to work you ill.

When the writhing and mangled for us
    Are snatched from your burning mine,
Do you think of the desolate homes
    Whilst you languidly dine and wine?

Yet spite of your fiendish wiles—
    And canting blasphemous prayer—
Right shall prevail, on your gilded walls
    The writing is surely there.[7]

252

Chapter 35

The Citizen Army is Born

Seán O'Casey

Discontent had lighted a blazing camp-fire in Dublin. The ruddy light of the flame was reflected by an earnest and ominous glow in the face of every Dublin worker. Men, full of the fire of battle, thronged in dense masses the wide, expansive area facing Liberty Hall. The city was surging with a passion full, daring, and fiercely expectant; a passion strange, enjoyable, which it had never felt before with such intensity and emotion. It was felt, unconsciously, that this struggle would be the Irish Armageddon between Capital and Labour. The workers were exuberantly confident that the unparalleled spread of the sympathetic strike would overthrow the moneyed hosts of Midian. Did you not hear it? It was true, many great scholars had declared in their favour, and even now Captain White, the aristocrat and gentleman, was with their beloved Leader, and had signified his intention to throw in his lot with his socially humbler brothers, abandoning the privileges of position, ignoring the remonstrances of friends, choosing freely and bravely to stand by the people now in their hour of need.

And the eager, toil-worn, care-lined faces of the workers now turned with concentrated uneasy patience towards the window on the left-hand side of Liberty Hall, waiting for it to be raised, that they might listen to their nightly message of hope, progress and encouragement from those Leaders, whom they were convinced would guide them safely through the heavy ordeal that each man must share that there might be preserved to all the elemental right of the workers to choose their Union, and to follow the Leaders in whom alone they placed their whole confidence and trust.

The disappearing Artist sun had boldly brushed the skies with bold hues of orange and crimson, and delicate shades of yellow and green, bordered with dusky shadows of darkening blue, which seemed to symbolise the glow of determination, the delicate hues of hope, and the bordering shades of restless anxiety that coloured the hearts and thoughts of the waiting, watching masses of men that stood silently beneath the oriental-coloured panoply of the sky.

Suddenly the window is raised, and the tense, anxious feelings of the men crowded together burst into an enthusiastic and full-throated cheer that shatters the surrounding air, and sends up into the skies a screaming flock of gulls that had been peacefully drifting along the sombre surface of the River Liffey. Louder still swells the resonant shout as Jim Larkin appears at the window, with an animated flush of human pride on his strong and rugged face, as he brushes back from his broad forehead the waving tufts of dark hair that are here and there silvered by the mellowing influence of Time and the inexorable force of issuing energy from the human structure. Again the cheers ring out, and Larkin quietly waits till the effort to demonstrate their confidence and affection will give place to the lustful desire to hear what he has to say to them, while hidden under the heavy shadows of the towering Custom House a darker column of massive constables instinctively finger their belts, and silently caress the ever-ready club that swings jauntily over each man's broad, expansive hip.

Rumours had been circulated that Jim Larkin had forged a new weapon for the workers, some plan which, when developed, would make their resisting power irresistible, a power that would quickly change their disorganised, clumsy, incohesive units into a huge, immovable, unbreakable Roman phalanx.

Hope's ruddy flame was leaping in their hearts: this day would be an historic one in the unhappy annals of the Irish Labour Movement.

Perhaps this lovely autumn sunset would be followed by the dawn of their social emancipation.

And the lusty cheers died away to a droning echo, which was followed for a few moments by a silence that was so strangely sincere that the mass of people resembled the upright figures of an assembly in the shady and silent regions of the dead.

And then, with a sweeping gesture of his arm, that seemed to pass around that tremendous gathering and make them one with himself in thought and hope and action, Jim Larkin began to speak.

In rugged, passionate, vitalising phrases he told them that 'they were engaged in the fight of their lives; that every conceivable combination had united its forces against the workers; that it would be a long and bitter fight between the Titans of Capital and the Titans of Labour.

'Therefore, the workers must become disciplined, organised, made of the one stuff in thought and action, so that in all that they would essay to do for themselves there would be a spontaneous unity of pressure and a hardened and impenetrable unity of resistance. The men must get to know each other. They must no longer be content to assemble in hopeless, haphazard crowds, in which a man does not know and cannot trust the man that stands next to him, but in all their future assemblies they must be so organised that there will be a special place for every man, and a particular duty for each man to do.

'They knew to their cost that a few determined men, determined because they were imbued with the force of discipline, led by men whom they looked upon as their leaders, could scatter, like spray before the wind, the largest gatherings of men, who, untaught and loosely strung together, would always be dominated by the possibility of fear and panic.

'If they would not agree to bring themselves under the influence of an ordered and systematic discipline, then they could never hope to resist the efforts that were being made to prevent them assembling peaceably to discuss affairs of their Union. By order and discipline only could they hope to secure for themselves the recognition of the sacred heritage bestowed by Nature upon every man born into the world—the right to live. All this must be changed, and he, with the help of Captain White, who would soon address them was determined to begin the work now that would bring about this much-desired improvement in the strength and mutual combination of the various sections of the workers.

'Labour in its own defence must begin to train itself to act with disciplined courage and with organised and concentrated force. How could they accomplish this? By taking a leaf out of Carson. If Carson had permission to train his braves of the North to fight against the aspirations of the Irish people, then it was legitimate and fair for Labour to organise in the same militant way to preserve their rights and to ensure that if they were attacked they would be able to give a very satisfactory account of themselves.

'They were going to give the members of their Union a military training. Captain White would speak to them now and tell them the plans he had to create from among the members of the Labour Unions a great Citizen Army. Captain White would take charge of the movement, and he trusted that the various Trades Unions would see to it that all their members joined this new army of the people, so that Labour might no longer be defenceless, but might be able to utilise that great physical power which it possessed to prevent their elemental rights from being taken from them, and to evolve such a system of unified action, self-control and ordered discipline that Labour in Ireland might march at the forefront of all movements for the betterment of the whole people of Ireland.'

Like the loud rolling of a multitude of drums the cheers broke out again. This was what was long wanted—a Citizen Army! What could not Labour accomplish with an army trained and disciplined by officers who held the affection and confidence of the workers! Now they would get some of their own back; and vivid visions of 'Red-coats and Black-coats flying before them' floated before the imaginative eyes of the Dublin workers filled with and almost intoxicated by the wine of enthusiasm.

And once again the cheers rang out as the tall, athletic figure of Captain White appeared, and his boyish face was aglow with gratification as he listened to the cheers that seemed to proclaim to him a ready realisation of the schemes he contemplated towards the disciplined consolidation of the lower orders in the battalionised ranks of an Irish Citizen Army.

Captain White told them that the work would commence immediately. He told them to attend the very next day at Croydon Park, Fairview, where they would be marshalled, divided into battalions, sub-divided into companies, and put through the elementary stages of military training. 'This was a day of Hope for the workers,' continued Captain White, 'the definite result of their plans depended now on the efforts and sincerity of the workers themselves. The Irish Citizen Army would fight for Labour and for Ireland.' He asked all those who intended to second their efforts by joining the army and training themselves for the fight for social liberty, to hold up their hands.

Almost every hand was silhouetted out against the darkening sky, and a last long deafening cheer proclaimed the birth of the Irish Citizen Army.

[From *The Story of the Irish Citizen Army* by P. Ó Cathasaigh [Seán O'Casey], Dublin: Maunsel 1919, chapter 1. The 'P.' in the author's name in the first edition was a printing error.]

Seán O'Casey (1880–1964) was born in Dublin into a Protestant working-class family. His father died when he was six, and Seán started work at fourteen in manual jobs, including the Great Northern Railway. From an early age he was involved in parish work at St Barnabus and in the Gaelic League, the IRB, the GAA, the Orange Order, and the ITGWU. He was actively associated with Larkin, particularly during the 1913 lock-out, and contributed to the *Irish Worker* from 1912 to 1914. He was secretary of the Irish Citizen Army 1913–14 and secretary of the Larkin Release Committee when Larkin was jailed in America.

O'Casey's three great plays were first performed in the Abbey Theatre in the twenties: *The Shadow of a Gunman* (1923), *Juno and the Paycock* (1924), and *The Plough and the Stars* (1926). *The Silver Tassie* (1928) was rejected by Yeats and the Abbey. O'Casey settled in England. Four of his later plays have a worker-hero: *The Star Turns Red* (1940), *Red Roses for Me* (1942), *The Purple Dust* (1945), and *Oak Leaves and Lavender* (1945). He wrote a further three plays: *Cock-a-Doodle Dandy* (1949), *The Bishop's Bonfire* (1955), and *The Drums of Father Ned* (1959).

O'Casey wrote six volumes of autobiography: *I Knock at the Door* (1939), *Pictures in the Hallway* (1942), *Drums under the Windows* (1945), *Innisfallen Fare Thee Well* (1949), *Rose and Crown* (1952)—which he dedicated 'To the workers of all lands, all colours, all creeds'—and *Sunset and Evening Star* (1954).

Chapter 36

The Irish Citizen Army, 1913–1916

Donal Nevin

The Irish Citizen Army was unique in the Labour Movement: the American historian of labour and nationalism in Ireland, J. D. Clarkson, has described it as the first 'Red Army' in modern Europe. Its exact inception is somewhat obscure but its origins in the great labour upheaval in Dublin in 1913 are clear enough. The strike of the tramwaymen followed by the lock-out of a large part of the city's industrial and transport workers was characterised by savage repression and intimidation by the Dublin Metropolitan Police. Strikers were indiscriminately batoned and set upon, picketing made impossible, tenement homes broken up.

On the very first day of the strike, Jim Larkin, denouncing the police brutality that had already manifested itself advised the workers to take Carson's advice to the men of Ulster. Addressing the huge crowd outside Liberty Hall, 'the old spot by the river,' he thundered 'if Sir Edward can call on the people of Ulster to arm, I will call upon you to arm. If they have a right to arm, the working men have an equal right to arm so as to protect themselves. If at every street corner there is a hired assassin ready to kill you, then you should arm.'

The immediate impetus to the formation of the Citizen Army was provided by Captain J. R. White, DSO, son of the defender of Ladysmith. At a meeting of the Industrial Peace Committee which had been formed by Professor Tom Kettle and which included leading writers, professors and other prominent citizens, Captain White proposed 'the formation of a citizen army, as a means by which to bring discipline into the distracted ranks of labour.' The proposal was ruled out of order but at a subsequent meeting held in the rooms of the Rev. R. M. Gwynn, at 40 Trinity College on 12 November 1913, arrangements were made for 'a drilling scheme' for the locked-out workers and a fund opened to buy boots and staves with Professor David Houston of the Royal College of Science as treasurer.

The proposal was discussed with James Connolly, then in charge at Liberty Hall, Larkin being in jail. He was enthusiastic about the suggestion and on the following night, 13 November, speaking at Beresford Place at a victory rally celebrating the release that day of Jim Larkin, he announced that he was going to talk sedition. 'The next time we are out for a march,' he said, 'I want to be accompanied by four battalions of trained men. Why should we not drill and train our men in Dublin as they are doing in Ulster?' He added that he had competent officers ready to instruct and lead them and they could get arms when they wanted them.

Seán O'Casey in his first book, *The Story of the Irish Citizen Army*, has described the reaction of the crowd when Jim Larkin put to them the idea of forming a Citizen Army. 'Like the loud rolling of a multitude of drums the cheers broke out again. This was what was long wanted—a Citizen Army ... Now they would get some of their own back; and vivid visions of "Redcoats and black-coats flying before them" floated before the imaginative eyes of the Dublin workers filled with and almost intoxicated by the wine of enthusiasm.' When Captain White asked for hands to be raised by those who intended to join the Citizen Army to fight for Labour and for Ireland, 'almost every hand was silhouetted out against the darkening sky and a last long deafening cheer proclaimed the birth of the Irish Citizen Army.'

It is clear that Captain White's idea at the start was merely to drill the workers and make them a disciplined labour force. Indeed, the leader of the employers during the lock-out, Mr. William Martin Murphy, claimed in a statement to the Royal Commission of Inquiry into the Easter Rebellion that Captain White had discussed the idea with him and had pointed out that when the strikers were drilled they would be disciplined and 'it would raise their moral tone.' Larkin and Connolly, however, had other ideas for the new force.

White, a keen and experienced soldier, was not a little naïve and romantic in his notions for the army he had helped to create. In his autobiography, *Misfit*, he points out that he 'certainly had no clear goal of violent revolution, national or social. At first I just enjoyed the fun and excitement of the whole thing. There was so much apparent enthusiasm about it ... The Citizen Army, after teaching the police manners, would be the machine of industrial organization in the new era.'

With tireless energy, he drilled and trained the men at Croydon Park in Fairview which Larkin had purchased as a recreation ground for the members of the Irish Transport and General Workers' Union, and at the Fianna Hall in Camden Street which was lent by Countess Markievicz. He was to complain bitterly of the unpunctuality and irregularity of attendance at drill parades. When, on one occasion, he remonstrated with Connolly about his army being taken off to a political meeting without his being notified, he was told by Connolly 'you're nothing but a great boy.' Nora Connolly recalls White in a great rage, his hands clenched and fairly gnashing his teeth at some misinterpretation of a command he had given and her father remonstrating with him, 'Easy now, Captain, remember, they're volunteers.'

To the men the lock-out and the dire privations it meant to their families was the main preoccupation, not drilling with the Citizen Army. The existence of the army had, it seems, a marked effect on the behaviour of the police. It ensured order at meetings and demonstrations; its members marched with hurleys to protect the band formed during the lock-out by Robert de Coeur; it prevented evictions. To many, the army was in O'Casey's words 'a subject for amusing jokes and quiet laughter,' an army without rifles or uniforms, but Connolly was to recall that its presence had kept the peace at all labour meetings from its foundation and had protected the workers from the 'uniformed bullies'. Apart from what their bitter experience of industrial conflict, squalor and hunger had taught them, the members of the Citizen Army for the most part probably lacked any coherent socialist philosophy. Their aim was not yet revolution. Prophetically, Captain White wrote to the Citizen Army in the *Irish Worker* before the end of 1913: 'Whether the first fruits of your labour is the freeing of yourselves or the freeing of your country, time will show. But ultimately Ireland cannot be free without you nor you without Ireland. Strengthen your hand then for the double task.'

As the great industrial lock-out dragged on into 1914, the army fell on evil days, its membership reduced by hunger and victimization. Many who had attached themselves to the Citizen Army joined the Irish Volunteers, perhaps as Seán O'Casey put it 'preferring Caitlín Ní Houlihan in a respectable dress than a Caitlín in the garb of a working woman.' The dispute ended indeterminately. The ITGWU, though crippled and exhausted by the struggle, had not been broken. The onslaught of the Dublin employers had, however, sown dragons' teeth that were to spring up as armed men in a reorganized Citizen Army. Despair was soon to give place to a new hope.

By March 1914 the numbers in the Citizen Army had been reduced to no more than a single company and Seán O'Casey suggested to Captain White that the army should be reorganized, a constitution drafted and a council elected. A preliminary meeting was held attended by James Connolly, Countess Markievicz, William Partridge and P. T. Daly. Captain White presided and Seán O'Casey acted as secretary. Arrangements were made for a public meeting to be held in Liberty Hall on 22 March. Jim Larkin who presided, announced that the army would have a standard uniform. The constitution (the Army's first) as drafted by O'Casey, was adopted. It declared that 'the first and last principle of the Irish Citizen Army is the avowal that the ownership of Ireland, moral and material, is vested of right in the people of Ireland,' that the army stood for 'the absolute unity of Irish nationhood' and supported the 'rights and liberties of the democracies of all nations,' that one of its objects was 'to sink all differences of birth, property and creed under the common name of the Irish People' and that it was open to all who accepted 'the principle of equal rights and opportunities for the Irish People.' At Larkin's suggestion it was provided that every applicant must, if eligible, be a member of his trade union.

An Army Council was elected with the following officers: Chairman, Captain White; Vice-Chairmen, Jim Larkin, P. T. Daly, W. Partridge, Thomas Foran, Francis Sheehy-Skeffington; Honorary Secretary, Seán O'Casey and Honorary Treasurers, Richard Brannigan and Countess Markievicz. James Connolly, though he had attended the preliminary meeting was not a member of the first Army Council.

Dark-green uniforms and broad slouched hats of the same colour were soon procured and paid for by weekly payments by the men themselves.

In April the distinctive 'Starry Plough' banner was carried for the first time by the Irish Citizen Army at the head of a demonstration and in the same month the Dublin Trades Council officially approved the Army.

The early days of the reorganized Citizen Army were marked by bitter feelings between it and the Irish Volunteers. The deeply held conviction of Seán O'Casey that the workers should 'keep clear of politicians' who would use the workers for their own purpose and that 'not in the shouts of deluded wage-slave Volunteers but in the hunger cry of the nation's poor is heard the voice of Ireland' was undoubtedly a factor in this situation. The Committee of the Volunteers refused to allow the use of their drill halls to the Citizen Army and on one occasion, John MacNeill explained in a letter that the Volunteers could have no association with an organization that had recently been in conflict with the police! A suggestion, prompted by Jim Larkin, that there should be a public debate between the Citizen Army and the Volunteer executive in which the latter would justify their appeal for the support of the Irish working class was brusquely rejected. On the Citizen Army side, Captain White and Countess Markievicz opposed any antagonism towards the Volunteers. In May, Captain White resigned as chairman of the Army Council and Jim Larkin was elected in his place.

Soon the Citizen Army and the Volunteers were to march together. The occasion was the pilgrimage to Wolfe Tone's grave at Bodenstown on 26 June 1914 when Jim Larkin led two companies of the Army and was warmly welcomed by Tom Clarke, the chairman of the Wolfe Tone Memorial Committee. In the following month, at the funeral of the victims of the Bachelor's Walk shooting, the guards of honour were composed of alternate units of the Citizen Army and the Volunteers.

The inclusion of nominees of the Irish Parliamentary Party on the Provisional Executive of the Volunteers widened the gulf between them and the Citizen Army. Jim Larkin denounced this move in the *Irish Worker*. When, however, Seán O'Casey sought to have Countess Markievicz sever her connexion with either the Volunteers or the Irish Citizen Army he was opposed by a majority of the Army Council including Jim Larkin. In consequence, Seán O'Casey resigned as secretary of the Council.

In July 1914 the Citizen Army had one Lee-Enfield rifle and a number of revolvers. The war was to transform the situation. Already on the eve of the outbreak Jim Larkin in the *Irish Worker* had called on 'every man who believed in Ireland a nation to act now. England's need, our opportunity. The men are ready. The guns must be got, and at once.' In the 'Citizen Army Notes' of the same issue the same point was made. 'Now is the time to realize the aspirations of Wolfe Tone ... While we see in the Volunteer movement great possibilities, the Irish Citizen Army is the only armed force in Ireland today standing for the rights of the worker and the complete independence of our country ... Get arms anyhow or anywhere, but get them.'

In Belfast, James Connolly pondering the implications of the war, determined that the opportunity should not pass without a blow being struck for Irish freedom. In his mind may have flashed the thought that the Irish Citizen Army could be the instrument for precipitating a revolt. The outbreak of war cannot have surprised Connolly but the attitude to it of his socialist colleagues in the belligerent countries did. The failure of the socialists to oppose the war appalled him. In the *Irish Worker* of 8 August, writing of 'Our Duty in this Crisis' he addressed himself to the working-class democracy of Ireland. 'Should the working class of Europe, rather than slaughter each other for the benefit of kings and financiers, proceed tomorrow to erect barricades all over Europe ... that war might be abolished, we should be perfectly justified in following such a glorious example and contributing our aid to the final dethronement of the vulture classes that rule and rob the world.' Calling for the stopping of the export of food he warned: 'This may mean more than a transport strike, it may mean armed battling in the streets' and ended his article: 'Starting thus, Ireland may yet set the torch to a European conflagration that will not burn out until the last throne and the last capitalist bond and debenture will be shrivelled on the funeral pyre of the last war lord.'

Little more than twelve months before the Rising Connolly was to declare in the *International Socialist Review* (Chicago): 'The signal of war ought also to have been the signal for rebellion. When the bugles sounded the first note for actual war, their notes should have been taken for the tocsin for social revolution.' Such was the attitude to the war of Connolly, the socialist revolutionary. In the months to come his objectives were to be far wider than those of his allies among the nationalists. Early in September he was to say at a public meeting in Dublin while on a visit from Belfast: 'Revolutions do not start with rifles; start first and get your rifles after. Make up your mind to strike before your opportunity goes.'

Already Connolly had been thinking of a united front of Citizen Army and Volunteers. In the *Irish Worker* of 15 August, noting that imperious necessities 'demand the formation of a committee of all the earnest elements, outside as well as inside the Volunteers, to consider means to take and hold Ireland for the people of Ireland,' he announced that 'we of the Transport Union, we of the Citizen Army are ready for such co-operation.'

An opportunity for such joint action presented itself when plans were made for eighty Volunteers and forty Citizen Army men to seize the Mansion House to prevent Prime Minister Asquith addressing a recruiting meeting there. The attempt had to be abandoned but on the night of the meeting, one hundred Citizen Army men with rifles marched from Liberty Hall to a vast opposition demonstration in Stephen's Green which was addressed by Larkin, Connolly and Countess Markievicz. When on 24 October, the first convention of the Irish Volunteers was held after the split with Redmond, the Citizen Army helped guard the Abbey Theatre while the convention was in progress. On the same day, Pearse and Connolly spoke from the same platform for the first time at a Citizen Army meeting.

Towards the end of October 1914, Larkin left for America and in his farewell message to his comrades of the Irish Citizen Army he bid them remember their constitution and their oath 'Ireland, first, last and all the time' and appointed Jim Connolly to take command in his absence. Connolly while retaining close links with the militants in the Irish Volunteers was determined to maintain the Citizen Army as an independent force as, among other reasons, he was not convinced that the IRB would seize the opportunity of starting a Rising before the war ended.

Now Commandant of the Citizen Army, Connolly appointed Michael Mallin as Chief of Staff. Mallin, a silk weaver by trade and at one time secretary of the Silk Weavers' Union, had served in the British Army and latterly ran a small newsagent's shop in Meath Street. In 1914 he took charge of the Irish Transport Union at Emmet Hall, Inchicore, one of the storm-centres of the 1913 lock-out and formed a branch of the Citizen Army there. By divers means weapons of various kinds were procured and the Army paraded openly with their arms. Later they began to make their own bombs. Military manoeuvres were held in various parts of the city including sham attacks on Dublin Castle. Midnight marches were frequent.

The Citizen Army under Connolly stood for revolution and made no pretence about it. In the last issue of the *Irish Worker* before its suppression in December 1914 Connolly threw down the challenge: 'A resurrection! Aye, out of the grave of the first Irishman murdered for protesting against Ireland's participation in this thrice-accursed war there will rise anew the Spirit of Irish Revolution. Yes, my lords and gentlemen, our cards are on the table ...! If you strike at, imprison or kill us, out of our prisons or graves, we will evoke a spirit that will thwart you and, mayhap, raise a force that will destroy you. We defy you. Do your worst!' Prophetic words, indeed.

Throughout 1915 preparations for revolution were maturing. At the end of May Connolly began publication of the *Workers' Republic* printed in Liberty Hall under an armed guard of the Citizen Army, though not without much misgivings on the part of some of the members of the Transport Union. In the first number he announced his intention of dealing with the lessons of military science as exemplified in campaigns of 'similar bodies of armed citizens' in other countries in the past. The first dealt with the Moscow revolution of 1905. In articles and lectures, Connolly instructed the Citizen Army in the tactics of street fighting and armed revolt. Its military proficiency improved. At Tullow in June 1915 it took first prize for drill and handling of arms in competition with units of the Volunteers from all over Ireland. Under Mallin's leadership they had brought their military training to a high pitch of efficiency. Classes in first-aid were held in Liberty Hall by Dr Kathleen Lynn. Girls under Miss Helena Molony were taught drill and rifle practice while a Scout Corps was formed among the boys under Walter Carpenter. The basement of Liberty Hall became a veritable munitions works where cartridges and bullets were packed and hundreds of bombs manufactured.

In the issue of the *Workers' Republic* of 30 October 1915, Connolly set out the position of the Irish Citizen Army, 'the first publicly organized armed citizen force south of the Boyne,' whose constitution pledged its members to work for an Irish Republic and for the emancipation of labour. He saw it as the army of a class whose aims went much further than the achievement of national freedom.

'An armed organization of the Irish working class is a phenomenon in Ireland. Hitherto the workers of Ireland have fought as part of the armies led by their masters, never as members of an army officered, trained and inspired by men of their own class. Now, with arms in their hands, they propose to steer their own course, to carve their own future. Neither Home Rule, nor the lack of Home Rule, will make them lay down their arms. However it may be for others, for us of the Citizen Army there is but one ideal—an Ireland ruled and owned by Irish men and women, sovereign and independent from the centre to the sea ... We cannot be swerved from our course by honeyed words ... nor betrayed by high-sounding phrases. The Irish Citizen Army will only co-operate in a forward movement. The moment that forward movement ceases it reserves for itself the right to step out of alignment, and advance by itself if need be, in an effort to plant the banner of freedom one reach further towards its goal.'

As the year wore on Connolly increasingly feared that the IRB would back down on its decision made early in the war to start a Rising and considered the possibility of the Citizen Army taking action on its own. In the *Workers' Republic* (6 November 1915) in a scathing article he asserted that Ireland was not really a revolutionary country, its revolutionists 'telling that England's difficulty is Ireland's opportunity, and then when her greatest difficulty comes, postponing action on the opportunity ... We latter-day Irish are great at cheering heroic sentiments about revolution. But we are not revolutionists. Not by a thousand miles.' He concluded by quoting Walt Whitman's 'Once to every man and nation comes the moment to decide ...'

In the last article ('What is our Programme?') that he wrote before his meeting with members of the Military Council of the IRB between January 19/22, 1916, when he came to an agreement with them for the date for the rising he declared that 'the time for Ireland's battle is now ... It is our duty ... to strengthen the hand of those of the leaders who are for action ... we are neither rash nor cowardly. We know our opportunity when we see it and we know when it has gone.' Desmond Ryan has related that Pearse told him in a conversation at St Enda's that Connolly planned to lead out the Citizen Army as a means of forcing the Volunteers into action; that Pearse had learned of this and that he and Seán MacDermott had gone to Connolly and urged him to hold his hand in order not to ruin plans already made. Pearse added that finally, after what Pearse described as a terrible mental struggle, Connolly agreed, saying 'God grant, Pearse, you are right.' A week later Connolly wrote in the *Workers' Republic* (29 January) 'the issue is clear, and we have done our part to clear it ... In solemn acceptance of our duty ... we have planted the seed in the hope that ere many of us are much older, it will ripen into action. For the moment and hour of that ripening, that fruitful blessed day of days we are ready. Will it find you ready too?'

The Citizen Army's preparations for the 'blessed day of days' were pushed forward. Route marches became more frequent. The quest for arms intensified. Liberty Hall was under armed guard day and night.

On the suggestion, it is said, of Councillor William Partridge, the Council of the Irish Citizen Army resolved to hoist the green flag of Ireland over Liberty Hall. 'Where better could that flag fly' wrote Connolly, 'than over the unconquered citadel of the Irish working class, the fortress of the militant working class of Ireland. We are out for Ireland for the Irish. But who are the Irish? Not the rack-renting, slum-owning landlords; not the sweating, profit-grinding capitalists … Not these are the Irish upon whom the future depends. Not these, but the Irish working class, the only secure foundation upon which a free nation can be reared. The cause of labour is the cause of Ireland, the cause of Ireland is the cause of labour. They cannot be dissevered.'

On Palm Sunday, as the culmination of a dramatic and moving ceremony in Beresford Place, the green flag with a golden harp emblazoned on it, was hoisted before a great throng by Miss Mollie O'Reilly of the Citizen Army. Commandant James Connolly gave the order 'Battalion, present arms,' and buglers sounded the general salute. This symbolic ceremony was to be the prologue to a week of high drama, most of it centring on Liberty Hall.

That evening Connolly addressed the Citizen Army. 'The odds are a thousand to one against us,' he concluded, 'but in the event of victory, hold on to your rifles, as those with whom we are fighting may stop before our goal is reached. We are out for economic as well as political liberty. Hold on to your rifles.' Connolly remained a socialist revolutionary.

A week later the Proclamation of the Republic was being printed in Liberty Hall under a guard of the Citizen Army. It declared 'the right of the people of Ireland to the ownership of Ireland' as the constitution of the Citizen Army drawn up three years before had set out as its first principle that 'the ownership was vested of right in the people of Ireland.' In it too the Republic guaranteed 'equal rights and equal opportunities to all its citizens' just as the Citizen Army constitution proclaimed the principle of equal rights and opportunities for the Irish people.

The seven signatories of the Proclamation meeting in Liberty Hall at 9 a.m. on Easter Monday elected Patrick Pearse, President of the Provisional Government and Commandant General of the Army of the Irish Republic; James Connolly was appointed Vice-President and Commandant-General of the Dublin Division. Shortly afterwards Connolly addressed the Citizen Army for the last time and told them that there no longer existed a Citizen Army and a Volunteer force. There was now only the Irish Republican Army.

By about 11.30 a.m. when the 'fall in' was sounded by bugler William Oman of the Citizen Army about 210 Citizen Army men, women and boys had mustered. At 11.35 a.m. the first section marched off under Captain Richard McCormack to seize Harcourt Street railway station. There followed a section under Captain Seán Connolly to occupy the City Hall and other buildings commanding Dublin Castle. A section under Commandant Michael Mallin with Lieutenant Constance Markievicz as his second in command set out for St. Stephen's Green. Finally, at 11.55 a.m. James Connolly with Joseph Plunkett on his left and Pearse on his right led a mixed body of Citizen Army and Volunteers into Lower Abbey Street and O'Connell Street for the attack on the General Post Office.

The 'blessed day of days' had arrived and the Citizen Army had gone into action, leaving a deserted Liberty Hall. It was perhaps symbolic that the first shots of the Easter Rising should have been fired by the Citizen Army in the attack on the Guard Room at the Upper Castle Yard and that the first casualty of the Republican Army should also have been from the Citizen Army (Seán Connolly shot dead on the roof of the City Hall by a sniper). It was symbolic too that while the tricolour flew from the General Post Office Connolly arranged for the flag of the Citizen Army, the Starry Plough, to be hoisted over the Imperial Hotel opposite—the same building from which Jim Larkin had briefly addressed the crowd on Bloody Sunday 1913. In a message sent with the flag, Connolly said that Martin Murphy (who owned the Imperial Hotel) had then triumphed over Labour but that now Labour triumphed over Martin Murphy and his class.

Of the 211 Citizen Army men, women and boys who took part in the Easter Rising, eleven were killed in action: five in Stephen's Green, five in the City Hall area and one at the GPO. Its Commandant James Connolly and Vice-Commandant Michael Mallin were executed.

A couple of months after the Rising, George Russell (AE) was to write to a friend: 'the stirring element in this was Labour. Connolly was the strong man and intellect in the Rising.'[1] It was Connolly who, twenty years earlier, had been the first in his time to raise openly the demand for an Irish Republic when in 1896 he founded the Irish Socialist Republican Party with its explicit demand for absolute independence. 'We are Republicans because we are Socialists,' he subsequently declared. Desmond Ryan has drawn attention to the unity of all Connolly's thought and work and to the fact that he had nearly as clear a view and as firm a philosophy in 1896 as in 1916. His participation in the rising with his comrades of the Irish Citizen Army was not a diversion from his life work. He had no illusions least of all about freedom. 'Our task will only commence when the rifle has done its work,' he once said. In recalling the Easter Rising which Connolly did so much to bring about, one must echo the words of Desmond Ryan: 'There is no need for any maudlin apologies for the most vital and consistent thing about him: his Socialism.'

[Reprinted from Owen Dudley Edwards and Fergus Pyle (editors), *The Easter Rising*, London 1968, 119–31.]

Chapter 37

Each for All and All for Each

Jim Larkin

At the twenty-first annual conference of the Irish Trades Union Congress, held in City Hall, Dublin, on 1 June 1914, William O'Brien, a delegate from Dublin Trades and Labour Council, who had been president of Congress in 1913, moved that Jim Larkin be elected president by acclamation. Larkin, a delegate from the ITGWU, had been a member of the Parliamentary Committee of Congress in 1908 and from 1911. This was the first occasion on which the president's address to Congress was unwritten. The incoming chairman of the national executive of Congress, Thomas Johnson, declared afterwards that the address would mark the Congress as historic.

Comrades—We are living in momentous times, but we who have been elected to take up and carry still further the banner which was hoisted by the pioneers twenty-one years ago in this city cannot afford to make mistakes. The knowledge gained in the bitter days of the past should strengthen us in our deliberations and work in the future.

We are now on the threshold of a newer movement, with a newer hope and new inspiration. The best thanks we can offer those who went before and who raised the Irish working class from their knees is to press forward with determination and enthusiasm towards the ultimate goal of their efforts, a 'co-operative commonwealth for Ireland.' In the meantime the immediate work to hand is the establishment of a new party—a Labour Party—an industrial army; a political party whose politics would be the assurance of bread and butter for all.

We have been told in every mood and tense, throughout the long weary past, that no common denominator could govern the actions of the workers' activities—North and South. The question of Home Rule—the question of what some people call religion—has been used to divide us in the past. Now that the Government of Ireland Bill, which is alleged to be a Home Rule Bill, is on the Statute Book, and will be law in the immediate future, that question was settled once and for all. The question of religion is a matter for each individual's conscience, and in a great many cases was the outcome of birth or residence in a certain geographical area. Claiming for ourselves liberty of conscience, liberty to worship, we shall see to it that every other individual enjoys the same right. Intolerance has been the curse of our country. It is for us to preach the gospel of toleration and comradeship for all women and men.

The day has arrived for us of the Irish working class to reconsider our position. Whatever other classes in Ireland might do, we must march forward to the complete conquest of Ireland, not as representing sections, sects or parties, but as representatives of the organised working class as a whole. No book, no avenue must be closed. By God's help and the intelligent use of our own strong right arms we can accomplish great things.

The Irish working class are now rising from their knees and attaining full stature. The new Irish labour party has come of age, entered into its inheritance, and will stand erect upon its feet from this day forward.

Looking back over the immediate past—more particularly the long months of 1913 and the early months of 1914—we saw there the attempt of an organised, unscrupulous capitalist class composed of men of different political parties and holding different sectarian views who had combined together for the purpose of destroying organised labour in Ireland. The lock-out in 1913 was a deliberate attempt to starve us into submission, and met with well-deserved failure. The workers emerged from the struggle purified and strengthened, with fierce determination and a fixed purpose. The employers' attitude was a direct attack upon the essential principles of trades unionism. The outcome of the attack had been the initiating of a new principle of solidarity inside the unions, and for the first time in the history of the world of labour the beautiful and more human principle had received universal recognition, 'An injury to one is the concern of all.' That motto would be emblazoned on the banner of labour the world over in the future. We have established a great human principle. Once again the Dublin workers stood as pioneers in the upward and onward march of Labour.

The men and women engaged in the struggle had shown magnificent courage, loyalty, and endurance. The history of their bitter sufferings and fortitude had rung like a clarion call throughout all the countries of the world.

In this morning's papers I read with pain and disquietude the report of the utterances of an eminent churchman—a most learned man—a man who claims to be a great educationalist and Christian—who has been speaking foolish words on the industrial question. He would find it necessary to go back to school and learn the ABC of economics. This learned gentleman said unthinkably (we will charitably suppose) that capital must be supplied by the employers—meaning by that the present controllers of capital. That statement had only to be made to prove its absurdity. All capital is supplied by the working class: but to our undoing and to our shame it was controlled by the capitalist class. A statement such as this churchman made should open the eyes of the working class to the want of knowledge of men who claim to be guides and leaders. And as much as I respect the Church to which I belong and the views of those who are interpreters of the dogmas of the Church, and as much as I respect the opinions of members of any and every church, I make this claim—that as long as the working class allow any churchman to abuse his trust and interfere in our affairs in the industrial world so long would they have to submit to hunger, privation, and wage-slavery. In matters spiritual they

267

would obey them, but on the economic and industrial field they would be guided by knowledge gained by long and hard servitude.

I submit that the working class have as much right as any section or class in the community to enjoy all the advantages of science, art and literature. No field of knowledge, no outlook in life, and no book should be closed against the workers. We should demand our share in the effulgence of life and all that was created for the enjoyment of mankind. And here do I appeal to those who cannot see eye to eye with us—who feel they cannot come all the way—to come with us as far as their knowledge will permit. Come at least to the bottom of the boreen, and then if we must part, the pioneers will continue on and up the mountain to meet the dawning of the new to-morrow.

The working class must be free, not only economically but intellectually. Speaking to a priest some time ago he said: 'I agree with some of your views and believe that improvement and alteration is necessary in the world; but,' said he, 'we are determined to build a wall round Ireland and keep out the advanced ideas of Western Europe.' I replied, 'As much as I respect your views, Father, there is no power on earth can build a wall to keep out thought.' The men in this movement are determined to enjoy the fullness of life and of the knowledge and power that the Creator ordained them for.

I desire to bring you back for the moment, and would speak with you on one or two points of the struggle in Dublin last year. We saw too plainly then that sectionalism carried with it defeat amongst the working class. We had thirty-seven unions engaged in the struggle, each acting upon its own line of defence and attack and according to its own methods. Those who were engaged had shown magnificent courage—women and men, aye, and little children—had proven their heroism. Hunger, the gaol, and death itself did not deter them. Let us not forget our comrades, Brady, Nolan and Byrne, who were murdered in the streets of this city by the hired hooligans of the capitalist class—the police. We found that no political party, no church, made a protest against the abuse of the laws by the capitalist class. During that period it was shown clearly then that there was neither Unionist nor Nationalist amongst the employing class; and but two camps—employers and workers. We found no Redmondites, Carsonites, or O'Brienites then. The enemy were all employers, and every weapon they could wield—political, social and administrative—they used unsparingly. Let us not talk of wooden guns or tin guns. What the working class wanted was the gun of intelligence. Let 'solidarity' be the watchword, and a few years will broaden out the liberties curtailed by the most unscrupulous and most vindictive capitalist class that any country was ever cursed with. Police, politicians, the Press, and the judges on the bench were simply the tools of the employing class. No city in the world has a more useless or vicious capitalist class than that of Dublin.

Think of the treatment meted out to the soldiers in the industrial army by judges appointed for their political views. One of these judges gave two years' hard labour to our comrade, Tom Daly, for a common assault on a scab; and the same judge in the same court gave a degenerate who ruined a child of seven years old a sentence of three months. That was the class war they had to submit to. The foul, putrid Press who told of the alleged outrageous attack by Daly published not a word about the foul creature who ruined a beautiful flower of womanhood in this Christian city.

Condemnation and calumny had been poured out upon the heads of the leaders of the working class. I, too, received more than my share. The agitator had been denounced by Press and pulpit, but thank God, the agitator was the salt of the earth. The employers claim a victory, but the employers did not beat back organised labour in this city. I admit we had to retreat to our base, but that was owing to the treachery of leaders in affiliated unions and betrayal in our own ranks. Two of the most influential unions who had undertaken to see the struggle through deliberately sold the pass, made arrangements behind their comrades' backs with the employers, and ordered their members to take other men's jobs. Two unions were guilty of this foul treachery, one of which was represented at the Congress, the other was ashamed to face the music. I will mention no names, in the interest of unity, but we must see to it that such happenings shall never take place in the future. One union is the only way out—one union for all industry. One might say when they hear this suggestion that it is the term of a madman—that it is Larkin again. It is, however, the only sound, logical method and the only way that makes for success.

The employers knew no sectionalism. The employers gave us the title of 'the working class'. Let us be proud of the term. Let us have, then, the one union, and not, as now, 1,100 separate unions each acting upon its own. When one union was locked out or on strike other unions or sections were either apathetic or scabbed on those in dispute. A stop must be put to this organised blacklegging. We saw, too, the workers in Belfast, who in 1907 put up one of the greatest fights in history, owing to the fact that sectarian bigotry had been roused to such a pitch by the organised capitalistic class in that great city, that they who appealed for help to Dublin and other cities in 1907, with a few honourable exceptions, had refused to send ammunition to Dublin during the late struggle.

These cursed lines of sectarian and political demarcation must be wiped away. They must hunt the fomenters of such bigotry and intolerance out of the Trade Union Movement. No employer ever asked a man whether he was a Nationalist or a Catholic, Unionist or Protestant. If a worker entered Queen's Island shipbuilding yard and stated that he would not work with an Orange lathe, a Protestant pneumatic riveter, or a Catholic anvil he would be fired out at once. We must drop these party distinctions. One union is the way out. That union should embrace all departments of industry—engineers, shipbuilders, distributive trades and transport—each of these sections looking particularly after its own work, but all of them bound up together and working for the betterment of all men and women. Those who would not assist in this one-union movement

269

were on the side of the capitalist; they must either be with us or against us. We have no time to argue further with these men and women who stand for sectionalism; we must simply march over them to the conquest and control of industry and our own destiny.

Another side of our lives which has been too long neglected—a line of advance which had not been taken seriously into consideration—the safest line of advance I speak of now—the Co-operative Movement. In this city, at the present moment, the annual congress of the British Co-operative Movement is being held. It is attended by women and men from all parts of the earth. It would be news to many to know that we here in Ireland had been pioneers in co-operation long before the Rochdale pioneers. There had been a communistic colony down at Usher's Quay, but it was crushed out by jealous and restrictive laws. Like every good thing Ireland ever started, England made it its business to put a stop to it.

The working class of Ireland would be compelled to understand the worth of co-operation. Through its agency we could supply all that life needs by ourselves and for ourselves. It needed no further argument to favour it. Life itself was co-operation in its truest sense. Man himself was a social animal and lived by co-operation. We had a great opportunity this week to see in the Co-operative Exhibition in the Rotunda what could be done by co-operative methods. The hard-headed Northerner had appreciated the benefits of co-operation. The Northern missed some of the advantages of the Southern atmosphere in which man lives for a day like a flower of the field. That was a beautiful and inspiring thing; yet the flowers closed up at night to preserve the dew again for the appearance of the morrow's sun. They could start right away to develop Co-operation in the shop and in the home, and eventually they would have no need for an employer as he is to-day; but they themselves would become their own employers; produce, distribute, and consume their own products; and then in that day they would be able to give the employers well-deserved punishment. They would give him a job and he would have to work for his living.

Thanks to the last two Congresses and the resolutions therein carried, to-day we see the birth of an Irish Labour Party in which there would be no room for the old lines of cleavage; no sectional politics, no disagreements, no misunderstandings; cemented by their common needs, a working-class party, that would concern themselves with seeing to it that sufficient food, clothing, and shelter were enjoyed by women, men, and children. We saw, too, during the last few months that the law-breakers in Ulster were allowed to break every law in the land, and, on the other hand, when Labour held a constitutional meeting, the leaders were arrested and cast into prison. That should be a lesson to the workers. The question of Redmondites, O'Brienites, or Carsonites should be a thing of the foolish past. We must unite as Labourites in the three-leaved shamrock of Fellowship; have Faith in our Cause, Hope of its realisation, and Charity to all men.

I have deliberately refrained from writing anything in the shape of an address to this Congress, believing the spoken word coming from the heart is of more value than the written word; and all that I have said I have put my soul into. I recall that only a short time ago I was expelled by those who were opposed to the newer movement; expelled by methods which were a disgrace to the Trade Union Movement. As you all know, I have been in prison on a charge such as no man of my class would be guilty of. I was released, thanks to the efforts of my friends in the Trade Union Movement. I had the honour to sit in this Council Chamber as a member of the City Corporation. My opponents took good care to have me expelled. All of these things strengthened the organisation which I have the honour to be a member of. Some day I hope that I will have the pleasure of returning as an administrator to this Corporation.[1] However, eight good comrades of mine sit here as members, led by our good friend, Councillor O'Carroll of the Bricklayers' Society. Dublin Labour members now have a strong voice in the administration of local affairs. In Ulster we have our comrade, James Connolly, fighting against forces that few realise the strength of. We undertake the transport work of Sligo port, and are active in other towns and cities. Throughout this country we have made a name we need never be ashamed of.

I hope we will see the day when we will take full advantage of our opportunities, cry 'finis' to our differences, and obliterate all jealousies from our ranks. Be truly Irish of the Irish. Give ear to all men who do worthy work. Ireland must no longer be Niobe but Mercury amongst the Nations. Let us be comrades in the true sense of the word, and join with our brothers the world over to advance the cause of the class to which we belong. On that day we will put upon our escutcheon a mark worthy of the trust reposed upon us twenty-one years ago. We are entering upon a new era to do work worthy of the cause to which we are attached. Cathlín Ní Houlihan calls upon us to abolish old jealousies, old intolerances that she may sit enthroned in the midst of the Western Sea. I claim we have an opportunity given us of achieving much in the future in our beloved country, to work and live for, and if needs be die, to win back, in the words of Erin's greatest living poet, for Cathlín Ní Houlihan her four beautiful fields.

Chapter 38

Solidarity for Ever

Manus O'Riordan in his Thomas Davis Lecture (chapter 9) spoke of James Larkin, in the aftermath of his leading Dublin's workers in the epic struggle of 1913, having reached the edge of nervous and physical exhaustion and of how much he required a change of environment. By August 1914 he had decided to go to America on a lecture tour to raise funds for the much-depleted coffers of the ITGWU.

In a farewell message to the members of the union, their general secretary wrote in the *Irish Worker* (24 October 1914):

> I have found it necessary for the benefit of the Union and in the interests of its advancement to go on a lecture tour in the United States of America. It having come to my knowledge that the aims and methods and activities of the Union have aroused an amount of interest amongst the workers of that great Continent, and that advantage has been taken by our enemies to malign the leaders of the Union and the Labour movement in this country generally; to misinterpret our message, and to deliberately misconstrue our ideals, aims, and methods. To you who are with us, and of us, it is hardly necessary to explain that we have always taken a broader outlook on life than the ordinary trade unionist, and keener insight into the causes that affect the welfare of the working classes of this country.
>
> We at all times have been careful to live up to our motto: 'An injury to one is an injury to all.' We have refused under the most severe pressure to any way compromise with the oppressors and exploiters of the working class, and have never watered down our principles. We hold still the same belief in the loyalty, sacrifice and honesty of the Irish working class as on the first day we laid the foundation stone of an Irish working-class movement. We have been and remain truly national in our outlook and work because of our belief in a real international labour movement. Our convictions have been strengthened in that matter by the failure of the labour movement in Great Britain, Germany, France and Belgium to stem the wave of jingoism and the worship of the God of Militarism by our comrades in those several countries; they talked internationalism but refused to live it.
>
> Ours is not an ordinary trade union—our Union is a world movement. We have the honour of inspiring a new spirit into trade unionism. The old apology of the fossilised trades union 'combined to defend, and not to attack,' is gone for ever. We have been defiant. We have defended our class by attacking. We have been constructive by being destructive. We have given a new spirit, a new hope to those without a spirit, and without a hope. We have been pioneers of the newer time—'each for all, and all for each.' That has been the belief animating and inspiring all our efforts. Let us not then come short of our aims and ideals in the future. I leave you in this hope that my absence will cause you to feel called upon to do even more in the future than in the past; that you will rally to the side of the men who are in charge. I desire that no prejudice will exist in the mind of any

member about any little difference with individuals in the past. I go away having full confidence in every man and boy in the Union. To the Old Guard I desire to say, I depend on you not only to carry on but to encourage and help the Young Guard.

Remember, no matter what happens let Ireland's welfare and the betterment of her working class be your aim and object.

'Swiftly spring to the front,
Pioneers, O Pioneers!'

In the Trades Hall in Capel Street, Dublin Trades Council met to bid the chief farewell for what was expected to be a short absence of some months. But it was to be eight-and-a-half years before Larkin was again to set foot on Irish soil. Now almost forty-one years old, he had spent less than seven years in Ireland.

The President of the Trades Council, William O'Brien, spoke of the admiration of the Dublin workers, as they felt that the historian of the future would have to record the activities of Jim Larkin as one of the greatest factors in the uplifting of the Irish working class and in making that class a decisive factor in the future history of Ireland.

The address from the council referred to Larkin's sterling work in the interest of the labour movement since his advent to Dublin, work that was 'magnificent, prodigious and noble.'

When you came on your mission of organisation to Ireland you found the unskilled workers disintegrated, powerless, and practically at the mercy of their taskmasters. The work which you undertook to discharge would have dismayed an ordinary individual, but all obstacles disappeared before your indomitable energy and perseverance until eventually you had the happiness of seeing activity taking the place of lethargy, and manliness replacing despair.

During the period of the historical labour war of the years 1913 and 1914, and in which you were the central figure, the severe strain imposed upon you must have had the inevitable effect of impairing your splendid constitution which Providence had endowed you with, and which in the case of ordinary mortals would have given way, and hence the necessity for rest and recuperation.

The address was signed on behalf of Dublin Trades Council by William O'Brien (president), Thomas Foran (vice-president), John Farren (treasurer), and John Simmons (secretary).

Responding to the address, Larkin spoke of his early resolve, nurtured by his mother's teachings, to do something for Ireland and her people. When he spoke of love of country, he said, he was speaking of a thing that could not exist apart from the people. 'It is not the rocks or soil, or rivers or coasts, or green grass or blue clouds that evoke the love of the patriot; it is all these things combined with the men and women, the boys and girls that draw forth true patriotism. True love of country cannot exist side by side with oppression of the people.'

While away, he assured them, he 'would still be working for the ideal they all held in common, the owning and control of Ireland by the people of Ireland.'

Arriving in New York in a blizzard in early November 1914, Larkin was not to return home until 30 April 1923. During those eight-and-a-half years he was to traverse the United States from east to west, north to south, lecturing, agitating, organising, rousing immigrant workers, denouncing oppression and the denial of freedom, fighting for the right to strike, opposing the barons of industry, calling on the masses to rise from their knees and stand erect as free and equal human beings, seeking to make America truly the land of the free. He was to be arrested many times, with frequent spells in jail, ultimately spending over two years in penitentiaries in New York State. Throughout these years he lived in poverty and endured great privations.

The *New York Times* and James Larkin

To a degree, Larkin's intense involvement in the struggles of American workers and in their industrial and political organisations can be tracked in the columns of the *New York Times*. It is indicative of the international standing of Larkin before the First World War that a report from Dublin at the end of December 1913 that he intended making 'a professional tour of the United States' prompted an editorial in the paper, headed 'Larkin is coming' (26 December 1913).

The editorial described Larkin as 'an orator of great natural endowment' and continued sarcastically: 'To carry on his fiery cross mission among laboring men, who, as everybody knows, are shockingly abused in this country, and under paid, is the idea of Mr. Larkin.' It warned Larkin that 'he must not look for much support from the benighted trades unionists, who are far behind the times and not at all in sympathy with the improved Larkin methods.' His strongest supporters, it said, would be the members of the IWW, but 'they are suffering an eclipse at present, as things have not quite gone their way.' However, the editorial concluded, 'James is unique in his line, the most conspicuous and noisiest of disturbers of the public peace. He is no imitator. He is an original ... Let him come with courage.' And courage Larkin certainly needed.

On 31 December 1913 the *New York Times* carried a letter about Larkin's proposed visit from America's most famous writer, Upton Sinclair. While sympathising with Larkin in the work he had been doing with the Dublin workers, Sinclair felt obliged to draw the public's attention to an aspect of Larkin's propaganda with which he was clearly at odds. He referred to Larkin's refusal to speak on the same platform in England with 'a well-known English gentleman who has given his life to the cause of Socialism,' on the grounds that this gentleman had been divorced. Sinclair ended his long letter with the admonition that 'those members of the American Socialist and labor movements who have happened to break the Church commandments concerning marriage would be advised to avoid the vicinity of Mr. Larkin's cross.' In fact (according to what Jack Carney told Dr Emmet Larkin) the reason Larkin had refused to speak was not that the man was divorced but rather that he had treated his wife in a most shameful fashion, which was unworthy of a socialist.

On 22 May 1916—within a month of the Easter Rising—the *New York Times* reported an incident at a mass meeting held in the Grand Opera House in Chicago to protest at the execution of the leaders of the Rising, which indicated Larkin's way with unwelcome interrupters. A speaker from the Polish Federation had said that the English certainly murdered the Irish in true Russian style, when 'a dapper young man' in the audience [one Matthew Thomas Newman] described the remark as 'bally bunk' and 'ridiculous drivel'. The paper's report went on:

> Larkin, who was sitting far back on the stage, arose, and, in a frenzy of anger, ran to the footlights. He jumped, clearing the orchestra pit and a high brass railing with apparent ease. A woman in the back of the theatre shrieked. When she started down the aisle she was recognised as Mrs. Larkin. 'Be careful what you do to him!' she shouted to her infuriated husband. 'Jim, Jim! Think!'
>
> Larkin seized Newman by the throat and choked him until he gasped for breath. Then he jerked him out of his seat and shook him until the offending one was speechless. After Larkin had torn Newman's collar away, he dragged him to the entrance of the theatre and tossed him out into the lobby. Then the meeting resumed.

In the course of his speech at the meeting, Larkin, dramatically holding aloft one of three rifles stacked on the stage, told the audience: 'Perhaps you don't know who brought this kind of rifle into Ireland. Of course you don't, because the press has never told you. Well, it was Mary Spring-Rice, sister of the British Ambassador, [Sir Cecil] Spring-Rice. It was she who smuggled them in to us.' Larkin was referring to the Howth gun-running in July 1914, when Erskine Childers and Mary Spring-Rice brought in nine hundred rifles for the Irish Volunteers on board the *Asgard*.

On 24 June 1917 the *New York Times* reported the arrest of James Larkin, 'an organiser of labor,' following an attack on the Selective Draft Bill at a socialist meeting in Queens, New York. All those who registered under the laws were 'mules', Larkin had said.

On 3 February 1919, Larkin, described as 'the Sinn Féin leader', was the principal speaker at a Liebknecht-Luxemburg memorial mass meeting in Boston, at which most of those present wore red carnations. According to the *New York Times*, Larkin advised his hearers to go into labour unions and 'try to revolutionize them.' Larkin charged that organised agents of a bourgeois government were responsible for the deaths of Karl Liebknecht and Rosa Luxemburg.

Larkin's speech on this occasion elicited another editorial in the *New York Times* the following day. Larkin, it declared, was 'himself as much of a Bolshevik as he can find time to be in moments when he doesn't have to be a Sinn Féiner and an exponent of what in this country is called the IWW.' 'Mr. Larkin,' the editorial writer added, 'has been credited with ability of a kind and with moving eloquence. This is what makes him dangerous ...'

On 21 June 1919 the *New York Times* reported Larkin speaking at a meeting in Madison Square Garden, New York, under the auspices of the Russian Federation of the Socialist Party and attended by about six thousand people, 'about half of them women.' There Larkin said that he thanked God that he was not an American citizen but 'a citizen of the Irish Republic.' He expressed a wish that the government would deport him to Ireland. His wish was not to be granted, and on 30 October the paper reported protests in Dublin against the action of the government in withholding passports from Larkin for his return from America.

A week later Larkin was reported speaking with the veteran socialist agitator Ella Reeve Bloor at a meeting in Independence Hall in New York celebrating the second anniversary of the Russian Revolution. Larkin criticised the Mayor, Hylan, 'Irish in name only,' saying that while he was receiving de Valera 'the police were smashing the heads of Russian revolutionists.'

The next day the *New York Times* reported that seventy-three 'radical headquarters' in all five New York boroughs were raided by more than seven hundred policemen and federal and state agents for evidence of revolutionary propaganda. One of the first prisoners brought in by the New York State Constabulary was Jim Larkin, the 'Irish labor agitator', regarded as 'one of the most dangerous of the agitators in this country.' When questioned by counsel for the Lusk Committee, Larkin claimed 'the protection of his Government, the Irish Republic. He was detained nevertheless.'

Larkin, 'Irish agitator and strike leader', was held on $15,000 bail on a charge of criminal anarchy, one of 'the two most prominent prisoners caught in the raids by the Lusk Committee.' He and Benjamin Gitlow were charged with being instrumental in the publication in the *Revolutionary Age* of the manifestos of the Communist Party and the Left Wing Socialist Party, Gitlow as the business manager of the paper and Larkin as one of the editors.

While on bail, Larkin proceeded to address a mass meeting under the auspices of the Communist Labor Party of America in the Manhattan Lyceum, where, according to the *New York Times* front-page headline, Larkin 'incited cheers for revolution.' Big Jim had lost none of the old invective. The terms he applied to Senator Lusk and his committee included 'microbes of society', 'men with the mind of an amoeba', and 'a body with the vile odour of the skunk in and about them.' Rejecting allegations that 'combustibles' had been seized by the police in the raids, Larkin declared: 'We don't use such weapons. We use mental bombs to blow a new idea, a new ideal, into life.'

On 29 March 1920 Larkin was reported as addressing a meeting in the Bryant Hall under the auspices of the Labor Union Committee for Irish

Freedom, which called on British workers to compel recognition of demands for the freedom of Ireland by declaring a general strike. Larkin asserted that 'neither Ireland nor any other country would be free in the real sense of the word until capitalism was a thing of the past.'

The following day Larkin, now described as 'an international labor agitator', told Justice Weeks in the Criminal Branch of the New York Supreme Court that he was a citizen of the Irish Republic, that the State of New York had no right to try him, and that he wanted to be deported. 'There is a conspiracy', he said, 'between England and the United States Government to prevent my return to Ireland.'

Larkin's trial opened on 5 April 1920. On 23 April the *New York Times* headlines read:

LARKIN IN CONTEMPT AS LARKIN'S LAWYER
AFFRONTS COURT, BUT IF SENT TO JAIL WOULD LEAVE
NO DEFENDANT TO BE TRIED

This legal imbroglio arose from the fact that Larkin, acting as his own counsel, was ordered to be committed for contempt following his assertion that both the court and the Assistant District Attorney, Rorke, were interfering with the defendant's (Larkin's) questions to prevent a proper examination of a witness (Larkin). The situation, the paper noted, was more embarrassing for the court than for the defendant: 'The Court could send Larkin, the lawyer, to the Tombs until he had purged himself for contempt, but it would be impossible to continue the trial in the absence of the defendant, Larkin.' Larkin had said that he could not prove what he was trying to prove 'if the court and the District Attorney desire to obscure with meaningless interruptions the intercourse of thought between the defendant (Larkin) and the witness (Larkin).'

On 28 April 1920 Larkin was found guilty of criminal anarchy, the jury returning its verdict after not more than an hour's consideration. On 4 May, Larkin 'the agitator' was sentenced by Justice Weeks to from five to ten years in Sing Sing.

Friends of Larkin's in court were warned by Justice Weeks to refrain from demonstrating. All obeyed, except one. Gertrude Nafe, of 264 Waverly Place, stood up when sentence was announced and again when Larkin was led out. She told Justice Weeks that she had been associated with Larkin as a member of the Communist Labor Party.

In the following weeks the *New York Times* reported protests at Larkin's sentence and demands for his release. On 17 July, however, it reported a resolution passed by the District Council of Moira, County Down, which declared that Larkin's conviction was 'just and righteous and the sentence no more than his conduct earned him.' A copy of the resolution was sent to the United States Government.

On 29 December 1920 the *New York Times* reported that in the New York State elections, three votes were cast for Charlie Chaplin for Governor and

277

one for Jim Larkin for Justice of the Supreme Court and one for Lieutenant-Governor.

The paper carried an editorial on 28 March 1922 headed 'Ireland doesn't need him', which welcomed the decision of Governor Miller not to grant executive clemency to Larkin. The editorial concluded: 'That he will not be able to go to Ireland at present cannot be regretted. Too many men like him are there already.'

On 4 December 1922 the *New York Times* reported that Larkin's brother Peter, lately released from jail in Australia, was in Chicago organising public sentiment to bring about his brother's release. The Chicago Federation of Labor voted a resolution demanding Larkin's release. On 10 January 1923 the paper reported that

> before a large audience in the Executive Chamber, Governor Al Smith listened for more than an hour to pleas by Mrs. Muriel MacSwiney, widow of the late Lord Mayor of Cork [Terence MacSwiney], and others for the release of 'Big Jim' Larkin, Irish agitator, having served nearly three years of a five-year sentence. In a voice hardly audible, Mrs. MacSwiney told the Governor that Larkin had done more than any one else she knew in behalf of the working people of the world.
>
> Others who pleaded for a pardon for Larkin at the hearing were: Jeremiah A. O'Leary, Chairman of the Larkin Amnesty Committee; Rev. John H. Dooley in behalf of the American Association for the Recognition of the Irish Republic; Mrs. Malcolm Duncan of the Daughters of the American Revolution; Mrs. Margaret Warner of the Irish Progressive League; Miss Florence McKeon, representing the Speakers' Bureau for American Independence.

On 18 January 1923, the *New York Times* announced that Larkin had been pardoned and had left Sing Sing. 'The initiative in the action to obtain freedom for the Irish agitator was taken by the American Civil Liberties Union, of which Roger N. Baldwin is director.'

Larkin left Sing Sing Prison at 5 o'clock on 17 January and went immediately to New York. It was the first time in five years that a prisoner in Sing Sing had received an unconditional pardon. When the warden conveyed to Larkin the news of his pardon, he told him, 'I never deserved to be sent here in the first place.'

Larkin had entered Sing Sing on 3 May 1920. He was allowed out for three months when his case was on appeal. He would have been eligible for release, with a year and a half off for good behaviour, on 7 January 1924.

In New York, the *New York Times* reported (19 January), Larkin immediately contacted Roger Baldwin, protesting that he would not have accepted the Governor's unconditional release had he not understood that freedom would be granted to four other people convicted with him of criminal anarchy. The four Larkin referred to were Ignatz Mizher, Paul Manko, Minnie Kalnin, and Anna Leisman.

The same day the paper's editorial took issue with the grounds given by Governor Smith for the unconditional pardon for Larkin. It followed this with another editorial the following day (20 January):

James Larkin bears himself and talks just about as might be expected. Imprisonment has not changed in the slightest his opinions or his aspirations ... Of gratitude for the Governor's clemency no word of his gives any hint. Instead he uses his eloquence in denouncing as 'all wrong' the law for the violation of which he was convicted ... His assertion that the Communists left behind, still under lock and key, have a right to liberty as good as his does not seem incredible—indeed the statement is characterized by high plausibility and becomes more and more easily credible the more that Larkin's record and present behaviour are considered.

A week later, in Providence, Rhode Island, Larkin was refused permission by the police to make a public address on the subject of 'America and Human Liberty'. On the same day, 29 January, the *New York Times* was again editorialising on Larkin, under the heading 'Anyhow, he will make trouble':

Larkin is constitutionally opposed to anything that is, and it would be very like him to hold Ireland's present condition insufficiently complicated. If he can do anything to complicate it still further, he can be trusted to do so. Only one thing is next to certain—the Free State will have no charms for such an inveterate rebel as he. It hasn't too many charms for anybody just now.

On 18 April the Assistant Secretary of Labor, Robe C. White, announced that James Larkin was listed by the Federal Government as an undesirable and must leave the country. On 20 April, under the headline 'Larkin arrested as alien anarchist', the *New York Times* reported: 'Larkin was arrested shortly after 3 o'clock at 323 Thirty-third Street by Special Agents Davis and Gurevich of the Department of Justice and Lieutenant Gegan and Detective Kelly of the Bomb Squad on a warrant issued by Secretary of Labor James J. Davis, charging Larkin with being an alien anarchist.'

At Ellis Island one of the attendants laughingly enquired for his luggage. 'Everything I own is on my back,' replied Larkin. 'I'm like the man in Whitman's poem: "Free and light-hearted I take to the open road."' On 21 April Larkin was deported in the White Star Line's *Majestic*—steerage, of course!

On 30 April the *New York Times* carried its last editorial on Larkin. It quoted Larkin's statement to English reporters at Southampton that he did not know whether he would go to Ireland.

'I am a child of circumstances,' said Mr. Larkin. All disturbers of the social order, all agitators for radical changes ... are in the same class—all children of circumstances, but the circumstances generally disown them. Jim Larkin is always a heavy tragedian, a sombre, beetle-browed protagonist of the issues he expounds ... Free spouting in Ireland on any topic, especially in Dublin, is not a safe occupation now. The great question there is not any right of labor, but who shall rule, the Free Staters or the republicans. The Free Staters would not welcome Larkin's type, and if he joined the republicans he could not afford to be caught by the Government. Ireland is no country for him at present.

There are two further references to Larkin in the *New York Times*. Appropriately, perhaps, on 1 May 1923 it reported from Dublin:

Larkin arrived here tonight [30 April] and received a hearty welcome from many thousands of workers, men, women and children. He was cheered and embraced by this vast following as few leaders have been for many a day. The procession moved through the streets to Liberty Hall, two bands playing and red and green flags waving. He addressed the crowd from a window and denied the charge that he came to sow disunion. Larkin went on to talk of the rights of the people and the poor and endeavoured to inspire all with a determination to secure them. He made a reference to the Irish fightings and killings and said the people must see these ended.

Finally, on 14 May the New York paper reported a huge open-air demonstration in O'Connell Street, held in memory of James Connolly, at which Larkin, who spoke bare-headed in a torrential rainfall, dealt with the demand for peace and demanded the release from prison of Connolly's daughter Nora.

This section of the chapter on Larkin in America might be ended with an editorial from a distinguished New York journal, the *Nation*, which in its issue of 2 May 1923 had this to say of James Larkin:

So 'Big Jim' Larkin has been deported to Ireland as an 'undesirable,' only a few months after Governor Smith's courageous pardon. Deportation is always a petty process; it somehow seems doubly petty in the case of such an epic figure as gaunt, gray-haired, long-limbed James Larkin. It was Larkin who built out of the Dublin dock workers Ireland's first great labor union, which was later the heart of the Easter Revolution; his energy built Liberty Hall, which became a symbol of more than labor's struggle for freedom. We seldom agree with Larkin. But there is a genuine bigness of soul behind his bigness of body. He is one of those rare beings—a born leader of men with a sense of the pain of life.

Jim Larkin in America

Jack Carney

In November 1914, the Big Fellow went to the United States, the first lap in a world tour, but the moment that he landed on American soil, the British Government at the request of Lord Kitchener, issued an Order in Council forbidding him to enter any part of the British Empire. The Order in Council only served to spur him to greater efforts. He filled American halls to overflowing but, as in Dublin so in the United States, Jim was frank and outspoken. He never could believe that Irish-American politicians who exploited the workers of America could ever free Ireland. Jim hated war because he knew the source of wars—imperialism. The Irish-American politicians opposed the war for their own selfish, political motives. To most of them their idea of a free Ireland was an enlarged conception of Tammany Hall. 'Boss' Murphy of Tammany Hall once told me: 'Jim Larkin is a great Irishman, but I hate his kind of Ireland.' 'Boss' Murphy thought Tammany politics was the only politics worthwhile and Jim hated Tammany.

America was not yet in the war, but the American imperialists were preparing to enter. This was in 1916. In every large city there were huge demonstrations calling upon the United States Government to build the biggest army and the biggest navy in the world. There is money in war— for some people wise enough to keep out of the front-line. There was a big procession in San Francisco. Thousands lined the streets and on a tall building overlooking the procession, a young man and his wife leaned over the parapet watching the procession below when a bomb exploded down below, killing several people. The next day the young man was arrested and charged with throwing the bomb and killing several persons. He was the son of an Irish-speaking mother. His name was Tom Mooney. A year later he was sentenced to death.

We were sitting together in Jim's Chicago flat when the word came through that Tom Mooney had been sentenced to death. The American edition of the *Irish Worker* was about to go to press. Jim rushed to the telephone and ordered the printers to hold up the paper. Then he asked me to get to the typewriter and there and then he dictated one of the most powerful editorials it has been my privilege to read and in my life I have both read and written quite a few. We worked through the night and the next day every news stand in Chicago carried copies of the *Irish Worker*.

Jim did not rest there. He telephoned to all the delegates he knew in the Chicago Federation of Labour. He held a meeting of them in his flat and in the afternoon he went to the weekly meeting of the CFL and through the support of John Fitzpatrick, its president, a blacksmith from Athlone, a Tom Mooney Release Committee was organised. I was elected secretary. Within a week the members of the Committee had addressed more than a hundred union meetings. In addition, Jim telegraphed to every city where the Irish were strong and inside a week the United States was covered with Tom Mooney Release Committees.

Jim had to act quick because he knew there was a danger that the official labour movement would hang back and Tom Mooney would be executed. There was a reason for this fear. In 1911 the trade unions in Los Angeles were engaged in a general strike to make Los Angeles a closed town, meaning no worker could obtain a job without a union card. The *Los Angeles Times*, just like the *Irish Independent* in 1913, was leading the fight to keep Los Angeles an 'open shop' town, meaning union cards were not recognised. The *Times* was a scab newspaper and none of its employees belonged to a union. The *Times* building was dynamited and twenty-one scabs were killed. Joseph J. McNamara, secretary of the Structural Iron-Workers, and his brother, James B. McNamara, member of the International Typographical Union, were arrested. The American Federation of Labour took charge of their defence. Millions of dollars were raised and spent in their defence. Each brother fearing for the safety of the other, was separately approached and in return for prison sentences they pleaded guilty. James B. McNamara was sentenced to spend the rest of his natural life in prison where he died, and his brother, Joseph, was sentenced to fifteen years. American labour was shocked at the turn of events, so that when Tom Mooney was sentenced to death, official American labour refused to make a move. Without fear of contradiction I make bold to say that more than any other man Jim Larkin was responsible for the release of Tom Mooney. Jim's action in the case of Tom Mooney did not improve his relations with official labour in America, but the son of an Irish mother was in grave peril of losing his life and what else mattered, said Jim.[1]

Jim could not remain long in Chicago. He toured the United States addressing mass meetings and giving striking workers the benefit of his advice. Gunmen followed him from town to town but Jim knew no fear. In Butte, Montana, the Irish lads organised a guard for him. Each night they would maintain guard outside the place where he was sleeping. One night they were surprised to find him coming in at 3 a.m. He had been for a walk around the town. The miners of Butte worshipped him. They had never known such courage and fearlessness. Butte is no seaside resort. In those days the Anaconda Mining Co., the only firm in Butte, employed an army of gunmen more than a thousand strong. They thought nothing of taking a leader of the workers out and hanging him to a railroad trestle so that in the morning the workers would see the hanging body of their leader as they went to work in the mines.[2]

It is not possible to tell of all that Jim Larkin did in the United States. But it would be unfair to the memory of the Big Fellow to leave out his attitude to the Russian Revolution. The Big Fellow was never a coward. In November 1917, the workers and peasants of Russia overthrew the most corrupt regime in Europe, and not without cause. When the word was flashed to the United States that the Russian workers and peasants had left the trenches and established their own form of government, the timid held back and waited to see how official opinion in the United States would respond. Jim did not hesitate. He knew there would perhaps be mistakes and excesses, for revolutions are not the pleasantest of social events, but he also knew that men and women in Russia were crawling out of dungeons, out of the salt mines of Siberia, into the light and were walking into a future of their own making. Jim walked with them. The Irish-American politicians never forgave him. So an Irish-American district attorney had him arrested and an Irish-American prosecuted the case and an Irish-American judge sentenced him to five to ten years in jail. Jim could have kept out of jail if he had repudiated what he believed and knew to be right. Eminent lawyers advised him to plead guilty and get off either with a reprimand or a short sentence. He refused and defended himself. His voice rang clear in court and although he knew that within a few hours he would be on his way to jail, he kept faith with himself and the workers of the world.

Not satisfied with jailing Jim, the authorities tried to destroy him. He was sent to the worst prison in the United States, the dreaded dungeon prison of Dannemora. He was put to work in the basement operating a jute mill. Few emerged from this job without falling a victim to tuberculosis. Due to the pressure of public opinion he was transferred to Sing Sing. The Big Fellow always had a way with him. Notorious American gangsters who practically ran Sing Sing came to him and told their stories. They came to him for advice and were putty in his hands. He laughed at their stories of racketeering and it is not healthy in the United States, inside or outside of jail, to laugh at an American gangster. He told them that only a foul system would permit them to breed. They were not used to such plain speaking, but there was nothing they would not do for him. However, he could not make friends with them, although he mingled with them in the prison exercise ring.

Later on he was transferred to Comstock. This was an open prison for trusted prisoners. I sent the governor of Comstock prison books which dealt with the life and work of the Big Fellow. He wrote to me: 'I have read the books with interest. He is the most amazing man who has come to my attention in the last thirty years. His influence with the rest of the prisoners has to be seen to be believed.' Jim did not enjoy the comforts of Comstock because there were too many convicted politicians among the prisoners so he was transferred back to Sing Sing until, finally, he was released.[3]

Joe Hill: Wobbly bard

Joyce L. Kornbluh

On 19 November 1915, Joe Hill, a thirty-three year old Wobbly writer, was killed by a five-man firing squad in the prison yard of the Utah State Penitentiary.

Hill had been a member of the Industrial Workers of the World for probably only three years before he was arrested for murder in Salt Lake City. He more than any other one writer, had made the IWW a singing movement. He was the author of dozens of Wobbly songs which were printed on song cards and published in the *Industrial Worker*, *Solidarity*, and in the *Little Red Songbook*. They had tough, humorous, sceptical words which raked American morality over the coals.

Joe Hill's songs swept the country; they were sung in jails, jungles, picket lines, demonstrations. IWW sailors carried them to other countries.

Little is known about Joe Hill before he joined the IWW about 1910, since he drifted from job to job like most single migrants. In fact, Joe Hill was a Swede, born Joel Emmanuel Haaglund, who came to the United States about 1901 at the age of nineteen. By 1910, he was an IWW member, active around the port of San Pedro, California, and in the next three years took part in the San Pedro dock workers' strike, the San Diego free speech campaign, and an abortive revolution in Tia Juana [Tijuana], which aimed to make Lower California into a commune.

Hill was charged with the murder of John Morrison, owner of a grocery store, and his son Alving on 10 January 1914. Though suffering from a bullet wound in his left lung, and from a shot fired by the police which had gone through his right hand, Hill was put into a solitary cell at the county jail and imprisoned for four months awaiting trial. He insisted that he had been shot in a quarrel over a woman and not by a shot fired by Alving Morrison.

Confusion and contradiction marked the testimony of witnesses during the trial which started on 10 June 1914. None of the witnesses identified Hill as one of the two armed men who had entered the grocery store. Hill repeatedly refused to testify and declined to give the names of the persons involved in the quarrel which he maintained to his death was the reason for his wound. He would say nothing about his roommate, suspected as the second gunman, who disappeared the night of the murder and was never found.

Ten days after the trial began, despite irregularities and unanswered questions, Hill was declared guilty and sentenced to be executed. Hill and the IWW maintained that he had not had a fair trial.

Despite thousands of letters, resolutions and petitions from all parts of the world and intense efforts by his colleagues in the IWW, Joe Hill was executed on 19 November 1915 by firing squad.

On his last day, Hill wired Bill Haywood [the IWW leader]: 'Goodbye, Bill. I die like a true blue rebel. Don't waste any time in mourning. Organise.'

A second telegram to Haywood read: 'It is only a hundred miles from here to Wyoming. Could you arrange to have my body hauled to the state line to be buried? I don't want to be found dead in Utah.'

Haywood replied: 'Goodbye, Joe. You will live long in the hearts of the working class. Your songs will be sung wherever workers toil, urging them to organize.'

Joe Hill was given a martyr's funeral. Following funeral services in Salt Lake City, his body was shipped to Chicago. There an estimated 30,000 sympathisers marched through the streets to the cemetery. His ashes were later put into small envelopes and scattered to the winds 'in every state of the union and every country in the world' on May Day 1916.[4]

[From Joyce Kornbluh (editor), *Rebel Voices: An IWW Anthology*, 1988, chapter 5.]

Joe Hill's funeral

Ralph Chaplin

On Thanksgiving Day the throngs began to gather in the great West Side Auditorium in Chicago hours before the funeral exercises were to take place. By 10.30 the streets were blocked for blocks in all directions; street cars could not run and all traffic was suspended. The casket was placed on the flower-laden, black and red draped stage, above which was hanging a hand woven IWW label (made by fellow-worker Cline in prison). The floral pieces were inscribed in a medley of languages. Some of these wreaths and flower pieces were elaborate and costly and others were simple and plain, but all were full of the heart-deep spirit of protest and regret.

The funeral exercises were opened with the singing of Joe Hill's wonderful song, 'Workers of the World, Awaken'—members of the IWW leading and the audience swelling out the chorus. This was followed by Jenny Wosczynska's singing of the 'Rebel Girl', after which came two beautiful tenor solos, one in Swedish by John Chellman and one in Italian by Ivan Rodems.

William D. Haywood introduced Judge O. N. Hilton of Denver with a short but powerful appeal, the keynote of which was, 'Don't mourn—organise.' In spite of this brave admonition, however, fellow worker Haywood's clarion voice was strangely husky as he stood beside the silent, flower-covered casket. There followed Judge Hilton's masterful presentation of the legal facts of the case. And when the oration was concluded the thousands in the hall silently marched out to the strains of Chopin's Funeral March.

Slowly and impressively the vast throng moved through the west side streets. The flower-bearers with their bright coloured floral pieces and wreaths tied with crimson ribbons, formed a walking garden almost a block in length. Thousands in the procession wore IWW pennants on their sleeves or red ribbons. Songs were sung all along the way, chiefly Joe Hill's, although some of the foreign-speaking workers sang revolutionary songs in their native tongues. As soon as a song would die down in one place, the same song or another would be taken up by other voices along the line.

The exercises in the cemetery were held in the open air as the chapel was ridiculously inadequate for the accommodation of the vast audience. And on the olive green slope of an evergreen-crested hill they took place. Above—high above the casket were the evergreens and above these, a couple of tall, bare elm trees raised up into the sky their delicately edged trunks and branches. Clutched in one lofty tremulous branch, as in a hand, was one of the last summer's empty birdnests. The sky was somewhat heavy and of a pearly grey tone with tiny dove-coloured clouds flitting across it hurriedly—somewhere. The air was warm and somewhat humid so that the trees were hung with a soft mist that caused the landscape to fade away into a distance that seemed fairly enchanted.

Here Joe Hill's songs were sung and Fellow Workers Haywood and Jim Larkin made short but stirring addresses in English, followed by Fellow Workers in Swedish, Russian, Hungarian, Polish, Spanish, Italian, German, Yiddish and Lithuanian. A few more songs were sung and then the body was removed to the little oak beamed high-roofed chapel, and placed on a bronze stand overhung with live palms and ferns. Here those assembled were given the last opportunity to view the remains of the murdered song-writer with the pale smiling face and the bruised hands folded above the four unseen purple bullet holes in his breast.

The great crowd gathered close around outside joined in one swelling, mighty chorus of song. Each one of Joe Hill's songs was sung over and over again and when the great crimson silk banner of the Rockford local appeared the song of that name was struck up and sung as it was never sung before. Three ringing cheers were then given for the Social Revolution and the IWW and then more songs.

Next day, through an aperture in the far end of the furnace, the committeemen, one at a time and each with feelings all his own, viewed the flame-lashed casket containing the fine body and placid features of Joe Hill, dreamer, poet, artist, agitator, with four purple bullet holes in his young chest as punishment for the crime of being 'true blue' to his class—and to himself.[5]

[From Ralph Chaplin's lengthy article in *International Socialist Review*, December 1915.]

Murder most foul

Jim Larkin

'Fire! Let her go!' With these words on his lips passed to the great beyond a few hours ago Joseph Hillstrom, murdered by the hired assassins of the capitalist class, who, for a few dirty pieces of silver, shot to death a man for the alleged killing of the man Morrison and his son, in what has been well named the City of Undiscovered Crime, Salt Lake City.

While we here respectfully tender our sincere condolences to the bereaved woman Morrison, it must be said, Comrades, that lie as they may, apologize and explain as they may, Joe Hill was shot to death because he was a member of the fighting section of the American working-class, the Industrial Workers of the World.

It is necessary that this should be said by one like myself who is not a member of that organisation. May be I, like many others of its critics, lack the intelligence and requisite courage to fit me for membership in the organization which in its brief life has displayed more real revolutionary spirit, greater self-sacrifice, than any other movement in the world of labor has produced—admitting that at times it has made mistakes due to over zeal on the part of its members and propagandists, and has been somewhat intolerant of less revolutionary sections.

Nevertheless, the I.W.W. has ever hewed true to the line of working-class emancipation. Never at any time or place or under the most adverse conditions can it be charged with having obscured the issue or with ever having preached permanent peace with, or given recognition to, the capitalist system. No! but true to its mission as the pioneer movement of the newer time, it advocated perpetual war on, and the total abolition of the system of wage slavery that blights humanity.

That is a record to be proud of in these days of compromise, when we are cursed with a breed of sycophants masquerading as labor leaders, whose sole purpose in life seems to be apologizing for and defending the capitalist system of exploitation and forever putting forward palliatives and outworn nostrums such as arbitration boards, time agreements and protocols.

Even the Gods cannot fight against stupidity, but when allied with that we have venal graft, lust for power and place, and a deep-seated contempt for the workers who elect them to office, animating the soul-cases of these alleged leaders, it gives us great hope and courage and strength of purpose to know of a movement that can produce a great soul like Joe Hill, whose heart was attuned to the spirit of the coming time and who voiced in rebellious phrases his belief in the working class.

Judge of the type of man he was, who on the verge of eternity, writing to Comrade Elizabeth Gurley Flynn, who with many other good Comrades was making a heroic uphill fight to save that valuable life for the cause, penned the following:

> We cannot afford to drain the resources of the whole organisation and weaken its fighting strength just on account of one individual—common sense will tell you that Gurley—there will be plenty of new rebels coming to fill up the gap.

Never thinking of self, but always of the cause, such was the type of man a vindictive jury, filled with blood lust and desire for revenge, found guilty of an atrocious cowardly murder on circumstantial evidence only. They lied in their verdict, and they knew they lied, but a victim had to be found and so the itinerant IWW propagandist and poet, Joseph Hillstrom, one of the Ishmaelites of the industrial world, was to hand and they 'shot him to death' because he was a rebel, one of the disinherited, because he was the voice of the inarticulate down-trodden; they crucified him on their cross of gold, spilled his blood on the altar of their God—Profit.

Because he cried out in the market place, on the highways and in the dark places where the children of men gathered together, the truth would make men free, for such a crime they crucified the Man of Galilee, for such a crime they crucified John Ball, Parsons, and a million unnamed, aye and for such a crime they will crucify millions unborn, if we cry not halt.

Therefore, Comrades, over the great heart of Joe Hill, now stilled in death, let us take up his burden, rededicate ourselves to the cause that knows no failure, and for which Joseph Hillstrom cheerfully gave his all, his valuable life. Though dead in flesh he liveth amongst us, and cries out:

> Arouse! Arouse! Ye sons of toil from every rank of Labor,
> Not to strife of leaping lead, of bayonet or of sabre.
> Ye are not murderers such as they who break ye day and hour!
> Arouse! Unite! Win back your world with a whirlwind stroke of power!

Let his blood cement the many divided sections of our movement, and our slogan for the future be: 'Joe Hill's body lies mouldering in the grave, but the cause goes marching on.'

[From *International Socialist Review*, December 1915.]

Joe Hill

Ralph Chaplin

High head and back unbending—fearless and true,
Into the night unending; why was it you?

Heart that was quick with song, torn with their lead;
Life that was young and strong, shattered and dead.

Singer of manly songs, laughter and tears;
Singer of Labor's wrongs, joys, hopes and fears.

Though you were one of us, what could we do?
Joe, there was none of us needed like you.

We gave, however small, what Life could give;
We would have given all that you might live.

Your death you held as naught, slander and shame;
We from the very thought shrank as from flame.

Each of us held his breath, tense with despair,
You, who were close to Death, seemed not to care.

White-handed loathsome power, knowing no pause,
Sinking in labor's flower, murderous claws;

Boastful, with leering eyes, blood-dripping jaws …
Accursed be the cowardice hidden in laws!
Utah has drained your blood; white hands are wet;
We of the 'surging flood' never forget!

Our songster! have your laws now had their fill?
Know, ye, his songs and cause ye cannot kill.

High head and back unbending—'rebel true blue,'
Into the night unending; why was it you?

On Larkin in America

A number of American labour leaders, writers and others have left records of Larkin's activities at various stages of his agitational and propagandist activities there between 1914 and 1923.

One of the first visits he made in New York after his arrival there was to 511 East 134th Street in the Bronx, where Thomas Flynn, his wife, Annie, and two daughters, Catherine and Elizabeth, lived up three flights of stairs. One day there was a knock on the door. Elizabeth answered the knock; there stood 'a gaunt man, with a rough-hewn face and a shock of greying hair.' He spoke with an Irish accent. He asked for Mrs Flynn. When Elizabeth's mother went to the door, the man said simply: 'I'm Jim Larkin. James Connolly sent me.' The Flynns had been comrades of Connolly when he was in America between 1903 and 1910.

This was the first meeting between Larkin and the already famous Elizabeth Gurley Flynn. A later symbolic connection between the two may be noted here. About a year after this visit Jim Larkin was to be, with Bill Haywood, the main speaker at the funeral in Chicago of the martyred Joe Hill. Elizabeth was the 'Rebel Girl' for whom Joe Hill had written his famous song. She met him for the first time in his cell in May 1915. It was to her that he wrote his last letter, at 10 p.m. on 18 November 1915, a few hours before he was executed.

> You have been more to me than a Fellow Worker. You have been an inspiration and when I composed 'The Rebel Girl' you were right there and helped me all the time. As you furnished the idea I will, now that I am gone, give you all the credit for that song.

As she left the jail, Joe Hill said to her: 'I'm not afraid of death, but I'd like to be in the fight a little longer.'

Elizabeth Gurley Flynn was not at Joe Hill's funeral: she was awaiting trial in Patterson, New Jersey, on charges arising from the famous strike of silk workers in 1913.

Elizabeth's mother, Annie Gurley, was born in Loughrea, County Galway, and her paternal grandfather was also Irish-born. Elizabeth, though only twenty-two, had been a leader of the Patterson strike. She held special meetings for the women and spoke in the eastern cities in support of the strikers.

In her autobiography, *I Speak My Own Piece* (1955), Elizabeth Gurley Flynn described Larkin as 'a magnificent orator and an agitator without equal.' She wrote of him speaking at anti-war meetings 'where he thundered against British imperialism's attempt to drag the United States into it.'

Her mother gave Larkin the green banner of the Irish Socialist Federation, which had been founded by James Connolly and Patrick L. Quinlan some years before. Quinlan was now a prominent labour agitator and strike organiser. He had served a sentence of two to seven years for his part in the Patterson silk workers' strike. In Elizabeth Gurley Flynn's case the jury had disagreed. Larkin was to speak under the green banner of the ISF innumerable times, especially on the New York waterfront.

'Larkin was very poor,' wrote Elizabeth Gurley Flynn, 'and while in New York, he lived in a small alley in Greenwich Village, called Milligan Place. His ways of life were frugal and austere.'

Another comrade of Joe Hill's, Ralph Chaplin, also wrote about Larkin in his autobiography, *Wobbly: The Rough-and-Tumble Story of an American Radical* (1948). Chaplin had met James Connolly in Chicago as Connolly had completed *Socialism Made Easy*; Connolly was a member of the IWW in 1905 and one of its New York organisers in 1907.

Chaplin, a poet and artist, was drawing the cover design for Connolly's pamphlet for the Charles H. Kerr Company, the well-known radical publishers. 'Any suggestions?' Chaplin asked Connolly. 'None at all boy, just so it's plenty Irish,' he replied. The cover was full of runic decorations, shamrocks, and an Irish harp. Connolly was so delighted that he asked Chaplin to chair one of his open-air propaganda meetings. So it was that at 63rd and Halsted Streets in Chicago, Ralph Chaplin delivered his first soap-box oration. He was not yet twenty-one.

In his autobiography, Ralph Chaplin recalled Bill Haywood, the IWW leader—who had spoken with Larkin in England in the Fiery Cross campaign in 1913—and Jim Larkin having interminable arguments about the philosophy and strategy of class struggle 'around an old round-bellied stove' at the rear of the Radical Book Shop in North Clark Street, Chicago. Sometimes they were joined by the poet Carl Sandburg. Chaplin quoted the famous Prof. Robert Morss Lovett of the University of Chicago as admitting that Larkin could always attract a larger crowd to the IWW educational meetings in the Wobbly hall than any professor in town. On one occasion they put on a big entertainment on a Saturday night, Larkin telling funny stories before and after his short speech: 'he got much applause.'

It was in 1915, when he was twenty-eight, that Ralph Chaplin wrote America's most famous labour anthem, 'Solidarity Forever'.

Another American socialist leader of the time, Bertram D. Wolfe, painted a vivid picture of Jim Larkin in his book *Strange Communists I Have Known* (1966):

> Big Jim Larkin appeared in our midst surrounded by legend. The year was 1917. He was a big-boned, large-framed man, broad shoulders held not too high nor too proudly, giving him an air of stooping over ordinary men when he was speaking to them. Bright blue eyes flashed from dark heavy brows; a long fleshy nose, hollowed-out cheeks, prominent cheek bones, a long thick neck, the cords of which stood out when he was angry, a powerful stubborn chin, a head longer and a forehead higher than in most men, suggesting plenty of room for the brain pan. Big Jim was well over six feet tall. Long arms and legs, great hands like shovels, big rounded shoes shaped in front like the rear of a canal boat, completed the picture.
>
> When Larkin spoke, his blue eyes flashed and sparkled. He roared and thundered, sputtered and—unless a stage separated him from the public—

sprayed his audience with spittle. Sometimes an unruly forelock came down on his forehead as he moved his head in vigorous emphasis. Impulsive, fiery, passionate, swift at repartee, highly personal, provocative, and hot-tempered in attack, strong and picturesque of speech, Larkin's language was rich in the terms of Irish poetic imagery sprinkled with neologisms of his own devising. Particularly in front of an Irish or an Irish-American audience, or an audience of bewildered foreign-born socialists unprepared for poetry and religion in Marxist oratory, he was the most powerful speaker in the left-wing socialist movement. An Irish nationalist to the core of his being, he was at the same time a revolutionary socialist and internationalist. Combative by nature, he was reflective, too, and a romantic who always saw himself as the spokesman and leader of some gallant fight. No one ever heard foul language from his lips. He could be as hot-tempered as any man, indeed hotter, but the temper expressed itself in withering repartee, angry condemnation, and scorn, sputtering, unforgettable epithets, never in obscenity.

He had no taste for theory at all, but made up for that by a strong sense of justice, and a belief in his personal mission to lead men in combat, in all manner of struggles for a better life, a little more dignity, a little more freedom. He made no appeal to reason, advanced no theories, only recited wrongs and outrages in angry tones, labour's wrongs and Ireland's together.

He never seemed to prepare a speech, being always ready with invective and his ad libs. Acoustics, whether of hall or roaring streets, were of no moment. His voice was strong and strident, and at climactic points turned to withering scorn or exultant roar.

Charlie Chaplin and Frank Harris have both written about their visiting Larkin in Sing Sing. In *My Autobiography* (1964), Charles Chaplin wrote:

The last day in New York, I visited Sing-Sing with Frank Harris. Jim Larkin, the Irish rebel and labour union organiser, was serving five years in Sing-Sing, and Frank wanted to see him. Larkin was a brilliant orator who had been sentenced by a prejudiced judge and jury on false charges of attempting to overthrow the Government, so Frank claimed, and this was proved later when Governor Al Smith quashed the sentence, though Larkin had already served years of it.

Frank inquired about Jim Larkin and the warder agreed that we could see him; although it was against the rules, he would make an exception. Larkin was in the shoe factory, and here he greeted us, a tall handsome man, about six foot four, with piercing blue eyes but a gentle smile.

Although happy to see Frank, he was nervous and disturbed and was anxious to get back to his bench. Even the warder's assurance would not allay his uneasiness. 'It's bad morally for the other prisoners if I'm privileged to see visitors during working hours,' said Larkin. Frank asked him how he was treated and if there was anything he could do for him. He said he was treated reasonably well, but he was worried about his wife and family in Ireland, whom he had not heard from since his confinement. Frank promised to help him. After we left, Frank said it depressed him to see a courageous, flamboyant character like Jim Larkin reduced to prison discipline.

Chaplin's companion on the visit to Sing Sing was the writer and journalist Frank Harris (born in Galway in 1855), who had published the first biography of Oscar Wilde in 1920. He included a chapter on Larkin in the fourth series of his 'Contemporary Portraits', published in 1924. In it he wrote of the visit to Sing Sing. The head teacher at the prison, Mr Henzel, had read some of Harris's books and enjoyed them, and he told Harris that if he could do anything for him he would be glad to. 'There is one thing you can do for me,' Harris answered. 'Find out where Jim Larkin is, and let me have a word with him.' Henzel said he would, adding: 'You know, I have to examine all prisoners to find out how they are educated. So I asked Larkin where he had been educated and how many years he had gone to school. He replied casually: "Oh my school days were very short, you can take it that I am unlettered." That "unlettered" told me a great deal, and I soon found out that, wherever he had got his education, he had got a good deal of it.'

'He is one of God's spies,' I cried warmly. 'A wonderful man. He has got the manners of a great gentleman; you have no idea how perfectly he bore himself at the trial, though there were insulting interruptions from the judge at every moment—uncalled for and malevolent when they were not stupid. Not only has he manners and reading, but wisdom and kindness to boot—an extraordinary man, a great man. He and Debs both in prison. Could any criticism of American government be more damning!'

'They were afraid at first,' said Henzel, 'that he might use radical propaganda on the prisoners. If they only knew, this is a worse place for radical propaganda than even Wall Street. The prisoners all think Larkin a damned fool for having come here just because he would stand up for others. 'What have the workmen ever done for him,' they say, 'the poor boob!' They all think him rather a fool. And you call him one of the noblest.'

'Yes' I said. 'We are told pretty early in life to let well alone. It is a good proverb, but no one tells us that it is still more dangerous not to leave ill alone. That's Jim Larkin's fault. He couldn't sit still and see the wrong triumph.'

We went into the boot place. Mr Joyce (the superintendent of the industries) was explaining in advance to Charlie Chaplin all about the making of boots; I with eyes for only one man, for one figure. Suddenly on the other side of the room I caught sight of him. I went across, and our hands met.

'Jim,' I cried, 'I have done my best again and again, but our Government is brutally indifferent!'

'You never sent me your books,' he said.

'I sent them, Jim,' I cried, 'but you shall have them again.'

'I know,' said Jim, 'I know!'

'How are you in health?' I asked.

'Fine,' he said, carelessly raising himself to his full six feet two and throwing out his great chest.

'But you broke your leg?' I questioned again.

'It's first-rate now, they patched it up; I'm all right; but (this in a whisper) is there any chance they might deport us? I want to get back to my people.'

'I'll see what can be done,' I said, 'you may be sure. We'll all do what we can.'

'I know, I know.'

'I want you to meet Charlie Chaplin,' I said, so I brought Charlie across the room and they shook hands. Jim at once excused himself.

'I had better go off,' he said. He didn't want to take up the time of the great visitor; he is the most courteous of gentlemen, with the best of manners—heart manners.

Robert Monteith, who accompanied Roger Casement on his journey to Banna Strand, County Kerry, in April 1916 and who later went to America, also visited Larkin in Sing Sing. A quarter of a century later he was to write about the visit in the socialist monthly *Review* (Dublin), April 1947:

In the United States, Jim continued his work. There were few vacant seats at meetings where he was billed to speak. One naturally looked for fireworks and was seldom disappointed. His outspoken words and direct approach to the problem at issue assured him the support of wingers left and right.

Larkin's speech at his trial in New York where he was committed to Sing Sing, was a classic. His opening words held the attention of everyone. As far as memory serves they were: 'I am a man unused to four walls, the forum or debating chamber. My way has been the way of the worker, the factory, the workshop and the broad high road.' Then the story of the struggle. But what was the use? He was speaking to an audience which did not understand a working man's language. He went to gaol.

I visited him in Sing Sing. He was the same old Jim, a little thinner perhaps, the silver in his hair a little more apparent. But the same old gallant spirit. The flood of memories and the few flying minutes. From Ringsend to the Park, from Liberty Hall to the Howth Road, the rising sun in the east and the warder's tap on Jim's shoulder. 'Time's up, Jim!' then the grey cell and the bars. They still think they can lock up ideas.

The Larkin Defense Committee

After Larkin had been sentenced, a Larkin Defense Committee was set up in Chicago by his old friend John Fitzpatrick of the Chicago Federation of Labor. The committee included Emmett O'Reilly, Eadhmonn MacAlpine, T. J. O'Flaherty, and Jack Carney. Mina Carney, an artist and the wife of Jack Carney, later became secretary of the committee.

Emmett O'Reilly, a lieutenant of Larkin's in New York, was prominent in the James Connolly Socialist Club there. Eadhmonn Mac Alpine, from Belfast, was associate editor of the *Revolutionary Age*, published in Boston in 1918, and in 1919 was associate editor of the *New York Communist* (the editor of which was John Reed) and later the *Voice of Labor*. He had joined with Larkin in founding the Communist Labor Party in September 1919. Tom O'Flaherty, a brother of the writer Liam O'Flaherty, was active with Larkin in the socialist movement in New York.

The James Connolly Socialist Club, which had been set up by Larkin in March 1918, was the centre of left-wing activities among the Irish in New

York. John Reed addressed the club on his return from Russia, where he had witnessed the October Revolution.

It was in large part this address by Reed that was responsible for Larkin's passionate espousal of the Bolshevik cause. Reed was a radical journalist, an opponent of capitalism, a poet, visionary, romantic, who was to inspire a whole generation of American intellectuals. He welcomed the revolution in Russia as the end of a corrupt social order and went on to write his extraordinary account of the October Revolution, *Ten Days that Shook the World*. He died of typhus in Moscow in 1920, at the age of thirty-three, and was buried in the Kremlin. (Warren Beatty's film *Reds* was inspired by the life of John Reed. A fine biography, *Romantic Revolutionary* by Robert A. Rosenstone, was published in 1975.)

The Larkin Defense Committee campaigned actively for Larkin's release. Mina Carney approached Governor Miller of New York in the autumn of 1922, asking for a free pardon for Larkin. He suggested that she secure the signatures of ten important and representative people in the community. With the help of Larkin's lawyer, Jeremiah O'Leary, and Dr Gertrude Kelly she secured the signatures of Father Duffy, the chaplin of the famous 'Fighting 69th' regiment of the US Army, and Monsignor James Power, who was prominent in Irish-American affairs. Mina Carney told Emmet Larkin that she interviewed the Archbishop of New York, Cardinal Hayes, who did not sign the petition but promised to write to the Governor on Larkin's behalf.

There is little evidence that the politically active Irish-American community made any effort to secure Larkin's release or even to support groups seeking a pardon. This is not surprising, given that the alleged offence for which Larkin had been sentenced was not likely to encourage these politically conservative politicians to put their political heads on the block for the sake of a 'red' who despised them anyway.

Most notably, there is no record that the President of the Irish Republic, Éamon de Valera, when he was in America gave any support to the release campaign. Indeed a letter from Jack Carney to the president of the ITGWU, Thomas Foran, recently discovered in the archives of the ITGWU by Theresa Moriarty (a letter that apparently had been excluded from the O'Brien Papers deposited in the National Library) makes an astonishing allegation against de Valera in the matter. The letter, dated 16 September 1920, was written from Duluth, Minnesota, by Jack Carney, then the editor of *Truth*, a paper published in Duluth, to Thomas Foran:

> I am in receipt of your letter of August 31st and owing to the fact that I have been out West conducting meetings of protest on behalf of the Lord Mayor of Cork [Terence MacSwiney] and Jim [Larkin], I have not been able to reply to yours.
>
> I was able to raise over 300 dollars in my tour out west, for the benefit of Jim, but regret to say that my work was hampered by the loose talk of President De Valera. It is to be deeply regretted that men of our own race should be so foolish as to attack other members of the race. In Butte De

Valera made the statement that Larkin was an Englishman and that during the Dublin strike that he attempted to have Irish children sent to England for the purpose of UNDERMINING THEIR RELIGIOUS FAITH. No words of mine are needed to prove to you what effect such statements have on our work.

De Valera arrived in America and stayed at the Waldorf Astoria, in a suite of rooms used by royalty and presidents. The rent of these rooms is $20,000 for three months. Jim was at that time staying in a furnished room at $60 for three months. De Valera was being wined and dined and on the other hand Jim was unable to even have medical prescriptions filled, due to his lack of finance. Jim received 5 to 10 years. I received seven years and a $1,000 fine. Due to my friendship with Jim, we were associated together on the American 'Irish Worker,' I have been the target of aspiring district attorneys and I am at present out on $50,000 bonds. Yet De Valera has the colossal nerve to suggest, prior to Jim's incarceration, that Jim and I were making an 'easy' living.

British propagandists have endeavoured to have me attack De Valera, but I refused to be a tool of British propaganda. I have been silent. I am prepared to remain silent as far as I am personally concerned, but not as far as Jim is concerned. Jim Larkin is too high-minded a person for men like De V to traduce. I want you to take this matter up. These insidious attacks of De Valera must cease or else I shall feel duty bound to resent them publicly.

Jim is now in the best of spirits although his treatment is not to be desired. We are endeavouring to look after that. I am leaving TRUTH, expecting to go out West as editorial writer on a large Western daily.

There is also a question mark over the position taken by the Provisional Government of the Irish Free State in 1922 towards Larkin's release, as is clear from government papers deposited in the State Paper Office (now part of the National Archives) in 1976 (file S2009).

On 15 February 1922 the American Liberty Club sent a telegram to Michael Collins, as Chairman of the Provisional Government, pointing out that all Larkin's avenues of appeal were virtually exhausted and that 'a message supported by the dignity and energy of the great Irish nation' to the US government would underline the feelings of countless Americans 'that Larkin is the victim of an unholy alliance of the enemies of Irish freedom and workers' rights.' Collins referred the letter on 21 February to Thomas Johnson, secretary of the Irish Labour Party and Trades Union Congress, for his opinion. Johnson replied on 8 March, stating on behalf of the National Executive of the ILP and TUC that Larkin's imprisonment was unjust and tyrannical. The organisation had from the first protested against the US action in harassing Larkin during the war and in the charge of seditious utterance, for which he was imprisoned. He added that the ITGWU had repeatedly brought pressure on Dáil Éireann. (The previous day, the paper reveals, Dáil Éireann's meeting of ministers had instructed its American envoy, Prof. Timothy Smiddy, to investigate and report on the case of Larkin.) Johnson also pointed out that Dáil Éireann's representatives had enabled the president of the ITGWU, Thomas Foran, to see Larkin in jail.

There is no evidence that Collins took any action on the matter on behalf of the Provisional Government. At the end of April or the beginning of May, Collins received a document sent by Larkin's prosecutor, Alexander I. Rorke, to Governor Miller of New York. He showed this to George Gavan Duffy, Minister for Foreign Affairs in Dáil Éireann, who returned it on 4 May 1922. On 10 May 1922 Joseph McGrath, Minister for Labour in the Provisional Government (who had been manager of the Insurance Section of the ITGWU in 1920), told his colleagues that he had received copies of a circular being distributed to branches of the ITGWU 'alleging that the representatives of the Provisional Government in the United States had used their influence to prevent Mr. Larkin's release.' As Collins had left the meeting before the matter was dealt with, it was deferred.

The file contains nothing further on the question of Larkin's release.

Conclusion

In an interview with the *New York Call*, a socialist daily, on 7 November 1914, shortly after his arrival in America, Larkin indicated that his main activity would be in the anti-war area: 'We realize in Ireland that this war is only the outcome of capitalistic aggression, and the desire to capture home and foreign markets. Behind the gods of militarism is a foul, grasping and vicious and inhuman power, the god of Mammon.'

Two days later, at a mass meeting in Madison Square Garden celebrating the victory of Meyer London as a socialist congressman from New York city, Larkin, addressing 'women and men of the city of New York,' as he significantly put it, said:

> I want to congratulate the Comrades on the work they have done. Remember, Comrades, this is only an entering wedge. The citadel of capitalism still remains. The task before you is great. You must realize the great responsibility that faces you. It takes great men and women to stand up and say 'We're Socialists.' You are fighting to abolish this system of exploitation. You have the power within yourselves to make Socialists of the people who have the right to vote.

A couple of months later Larkin was to declare: 'I am for the working classes of every country.'

These three themes—anti-war, anti-capitalism, and the solidarity of the workers of the world—were to govern his mission over the next few years. He was to cleave to these with tenacity and with courage in the face of hostility, misunderstandings, and the desertion of colleagues. Emmet Larkin has well expressed the cost to Larkin by his cleaving to the course he had adopted:

> Larkin was one among the many who fought the good fight and suffered in the name of the cause in these years. For the four years that the war continued he agitated and worked against it. The price he paid was poverty, loneliness, and persecution. But it was a small equivalent when the faith

was put in the balance. Larkin embraced the idea of the Bolshevik Revolution with a fervour that would have made St. Paul tremble with ecstasy. For this the price he paid was almost three years in prison on top of the poverty and loneliness. Again he paid the price without regret or complaint.[6]

Larkin's critics, then and later, were quick to point to the many contradictions that frequently lay at the bottom of his fiery words and rumbustious actions. Then might he have said, in the words of one of his favourite poets, Walt Whitman, in *Song of Myself* (1881):

> The past and present wilt—I have filled them, emptied them,
> And proceed to fill my next fold of the future.
> Do I contradict myself?
> Very well then I contradict myself,
> (I am large, I contain multitudes) …

To Larkin

Lola Ridge[7]

Is it you I see go by the window, Jim Larkin—you not looking at me or
    anyone,
And your shadow swaying from East to West?

Strange that you should be walking free—you shut down without light,
And your legs tied up with a knot of iron.

One hundred million men and women go inevitably about their affairs,
In the somnolent way
Of men before a great drunkenness …
They do not see you go by their windows, Jim Larkin,
With your eyes bloody as the sunset
And your shadow gaunt upon the sky
You, and the like of you, that life
Is crushing for their frantic wines.

[From *Sun Up and Other Poems* by Lola Ridge (New York, 1920).]

Chapter 39

The Larkin Affidavit

After the First World War, the United States government lodged claims against the German government involving some $40 million for damages for alleged German sabotage during the war. The case came before the Mixed Claims Commission in 1936.

At the request of John J. McCloy, representing the United States, James Larkin made an affidavit on 21 January 1934. The affidavit, which has never been published, is given in full in the pages following.

Prof. Emmet Larkin had sight of the affidavit when preparing his biography of Larkin, published in 1965. The manuscript was in the Record of Boundary and Claims Commissions and Arbitrations in the National Archives, Washington. He considered that the affidavit, an account of Larkin's associations with German agents in the United States and Mexico between 1914 and the end of 1917, was corroborated by what independent evidence was available and that it was generally accurate, considering the interval of sixteen years. The copy of the affidavit reproduced here was secured by SIPTU in 1997 through the good offices of the US ambassador to Ireland, Jean Kennedy Smith.

The lawyer John J. McCloy, who visited Dublin to secure Larkin's affidavit, was to become president of the World Bank in 1947 and two years later US Military Governor and High Commissioner in Germany, which position he held until 1952.

Affidavit of Mr. James Larkin

I, JAMES LARKIN, general secretary of the Workers' Union of Ireland, whose offices are at 31 Marlborough Street, Dublin, a registered trade union in the Irish Free State, also formerly general secretary of the Irish Transport and General Workers' Union, Liberty Hall, Dublin, age 21 years and upwards, make oath and say.

I left Liverpool, England, on or about October 29th, 1914 in the s.s. St. Louis for the United States my purpose being to interest the workers of the United States in the condition of the Irish labour movement and with a view of getting material and political assistance for the revolutionary movement in Ireland, which had gone on record opposing the government of the British Empire in the then world war, our object being to achieve economic and political freedom for Ireland.

I landed in the city of New York on the fifth or sixth day of November, 1914, presented my credentials to the official head of the Irish revolutionary organisation and of the Socialist Party of America. My first meeting in the United States was in the old Madison Square Gardens to celebrate the return of Meyer London as a member of the Congress of the United States.

Shortly after landing in the United States I set up an organisation known as the 'Four Winds' Fellowship, which was only open to trade unionists and socialists, born in the British Empire and opposed to the government of the British Empire and pledged to resist any participation or give any assistance to the British Empire in its struggle.

I also made contact with the American Labour movement, undertaking organising work for the Western Federation of Miners, International Longshoremen's Association, Coastwise Seamen's Union and the Amalgamated Steel Workers Union, also other unions throughout the forty eight States.

I was also instructed by the official Irish organisation to assist in propaganda work in association with the German American Alliance. My first public meeting, under the auspices of this particular organisation was in the Academy of Music, Philadelphia. After the meeting, at a banquet, I was introduced to certain consuls of Germany and Austria and a number of high German officials.

I then returned to New York City, where I was invited to meet a Captain Boy-Ed and other German officers, both naval and military. At this moment I cannot recollect whether Major or Captain Von Papen was present when I met Captain Boy-Ed but a high official of the Nord-Deutscher Lloyd Steamship Company acted as host on this occasion. The meeting was held in Alliers' restaurant, corner of 3rd Avenue and 18th Street.

Owing to the number of people present Captain Boy-Ed asked me to see him in a house situated at 67 West 88th Street (at this period I believe this was the address). It must be understood at the outset that I am speaking wholly from recollections, without having any recourse to my documents or records, some of which are at present somewhere in the United States if they still exist.

At this meeting there was also present a heavy-built German person, whom I afterwards learned was an officer of the Hamburg Amerika Line. Although a person was introduced as an interpreter, Captain Boy-Ed and his colleague spoke good colloquial English.

Captain Boy-Ed explained to me that a political connection had been arranged, of which, of course, I was aware, between the revolutionary Irish movement and the German government; that a high officer of the German Government was proceeding to the United States, who would have charge of direct negotiations. They were to co-operate under three heads: open propaganda in the interests of Germany and Austria and any other of their allies; political influence to be used jointly at Washington and a special secret department charged with hindering or interfering with the transportation of supplies. Captain Boy-Ed pointed out at this time he was not authorized, as yet, to speak fully about plans and he had been informed by my friends, the official Irish leaders, who he mentioned by name, that I was not under their control; that I had refused to take direction from them since my arrival; that I was an extremist and an inter-nationalist and they would not hold themselves responsible for any action I might undertake.

Captain Boy-Ed laughed and said he understood and knew my position. He said, in substance, we know these men and though my Government has given an undertaking that in event of success they will recognise any de facto Government set up in Ireland, they look upon these leaders in America purely as politicians.

'What we want', Captain Boy-Ed continued, 'are men of extreme views. We are prepared to give you and the movement you represent, official recognition. We want men of serious and extreme view to undertake what we realise will be a dangerous but essential and vital work.' He further said, 'I understand that your work lies mostly in the region of mass propaganda; that is not sufficient. We have gained control of a number of industrial plants. We hope, with the arrival of certain individuals, and further credit, to extend our activities in this sphere, but we have been unable to extend this to certain powerful industrial groups. In connection with the further development of our plans we will ask you to meet us again on a later date.'

Captain Boy-Ed then undertook that two hundred dollars ($200.00) per week would be paid to me, through any person or avenue I would designate. I refused to accept any monies or to have any official connection.

Around Christmas week, by arrangement of Captain Boy-Ed, we met again in Moquin's restaurant, somewhere about 28th Street and 6th Avenue. I believe Von Papen was also present. Paul Koenig, the North-German Lloyd or Hamburg Amerika Steamship Companies' labour agent, was also present. Koenig was charged with organising the men for the crews of the former German vessels. Certain of these men were selected for sabotage work. Koenig was their chief and their paymaster. After dinner we adjourned to another German restaurant, I believe at 29th and 6th Avenue, where we sat until a late hour in the morning. Captain Boy-Ed and myself drove to my lodgings and during the course of the night Captain Boy-Ed told me what the German organisation had been doing and what they hoped to do, in connection with sabotage, such as stopping munition supplies. He asked me to undertake to organise a group of men, non-Germans, to work along the waterfront, as the Germans were under too strict a surveillance.

I had explained to him what my work was and this I did with the official knowledge of my own people. It was working through the trade unions and unorganised workers for the purpose of stopping production and transportation of war supplies.

The 'Four Winds' Fellowship was to be used as a means to getting entrance into the trade unions with a view to control, particularly among longshoremen and seamen. Subsequently it was the intention to get into the basic industries such as steel and copper. I outlined all this for Captain Boy-Ed, told him how far we had progressed and told him that we had already created a number of substantial stoppages at New York, Philadelphia, Newport (Mons) and New Orleans.

Captain Boy-Ed told me that a number of discharged seamen who were reservists of the German Navy, had been distributed around the different ports and that they would receive instructions to co-operate with my work. He stated that they had men working in the I.W.W. (Industrial Workers of the World).

He stated that they had found that these men had no influence in the I.W.W. What the Germans were chiefly concerned about, he said, was direct sabotage work. They wanted men who were prepared to take a risk. To them they would guarantee the best legal protection and they could provide avenues whereby they could escape outside American and Canadian territory. He said that each man would work according to number; that sabotage material would be provided for anyone engaged and full compensation paid to their relatives in case of a 'catastrophe'.

I told him that I would have nothing to do with such an organisation or such methods, that I was working in co-operation with my own people upon lines agreed upon and in accordance with my own views of life; that I had no regard for the German Government as such, nor was I desirous of its success in the World War except that it might result in forcing England to accept Irish independence. My object was to see a deadlock arrived at, hoping that the workers would revolt in the several countries. I was quite aware of the promises held out as to recognition, but I did not wish Ireland to be in any way subject to the German Empire, any more than to the British Empire; that I thought it more important to get recognition and protection from and within the United States from whom we had nothing to fear.

I informed my Irish-American friends that I had been approached behind their backs. I then had occasion to carry out my own itinerary and for a number of months passed up and down through the different States. During my tour in the South I crossed into Mexico, but this had nothing to do with the Irish or German matters.

Upon my return to New York in April, 1915, I received information as to the failure of Sir Roger Casement to carry out successfully within Germany the plan agreed upon. Antagonisms had grown up between the German Government and Sir Roger Casement and the organisation of the Irish Brigade had come to a standstill.

It was suggested that I cross the ocean, the Germans undertaking to get me through via Spain. For various reasons these attempts failed. It was at my suggestion that one of our men from Dublin was instructed to proceed to Berlin and to undertake the enlistment of Irish prisoners of war. This man was a former non-commissioned officer of the British Army. He was successful in getting there and is known through his associations with Sir Roger Casement as Captain Robert Monteith. He is now a resident in the United States.

I was invited by the Germans to proceed to Washington. First, I went to the Capitol buildings with James K. Maguire. Dr. Dernburg and two other German representatives were present. From there we went to the office of Mr. James K. Maguire. This was somewhere about the early Fall of 1915. I was asked and pressed to undertake the work of supervising port groups who were charged with destructive sabotage. I was informed that I would be officially protected and amply compensated. I again definitely refused.

They asked me regarding my success along my own lines. I told them that we had officially organised the workers in the ammunition plants in Bridgeport and had two successful disputes in which we had achieved the eight hour day, an increase in wages, but more important accomplished a substantial retardation in production of war supplies. We also held up the building of an annex or extension to the Remington Plant (I am not certain it was the Remington Plant but believe that it was).

I stated to the Germans at this meeting that we had some difficulties in getting the Germans and Austrians to stand by or strike than we had with others. In Bridgeport the Austrians took advantage of the 8-hour day to work two shifts. Dr. Dernburg, I believed it was, promised that a special order would be issued to all known German and Austrian citizens to the effect that they should withdraw from ammunition, iron and steel plants. If they refused to withdraw when instructed by agents or refused to co-operate with accredited agents, they would forfeit all their citizen rights and at the close of the war if found on German or Austrian control they would be tried by military court martial, as well as lose all citizenship rights. Such an order was actually passed, but my experience was that it proved futile.

Throughout these discussions the greatest emphasis was placed on the necessity of stopping by any means the shipment of munitions from Jersey and Kearny's Point. The Germans were interested in the work I was doing, but considered it of less importance than direct methods.

It was about this time, the latter end of February, 1916, I came into close contact with Von Igel. I first met him in an office in Nassau Street, four doors from Moquin's restaurant on Park Row. From there we proceeded to an office which was in William Street. I proceeded with him from that office to another office located somewhere below the sub-Treasury building in the Wall Street area. At this place there were a number of Germans present. It was a small office with a very large safe in the corner. Some of the Germans present could not speak English. Von Igel expressed himself as the official spokesman for the German Government. He stated that he was very disappointed at the lack of co-operation of the Irish-American group, who were very fond of talking big on platforms but would give him no active assistance in his special work; that this platform talk and the Austro-German Red Cross work was very useful but he had direct orders from Berlin that munitions, especially heavy gun ammunition and T.N.T. had to be stopped; that a deadlock had been reached on the Western Front and if the supply of munitions could be held up, the advantage would be on the side of Germany and her allies and Germany would be able to break through. If they could succeed in getting through to Paris they would suggest an armistice, call upon President Wilson to intervene and Germany would definitely agree to recognise a revolutionary government in Ireland. This latter statement was for my benefit. He asked me to make arrangements to proceed to Washington and he appealed to me to co-operate with him apart from my interest in the Irish organisation and help him to interfere directly with the shipment of munitions. At this particular meeting Von Igel assured me, as had been explained to me previously, that there was no personal danger in carrying out the work. He arranged that we should cross to Hoboken so that his staff could show me by actual demonstrations the means that were being used.

The place we went to was situated behind a rathskellar close to the waterfront in Hoboken. It was raining heavily and I am not quite clear to the exact location of the spot. I was shown how they reduced white phosphorus to liquid. It was done in a tank under water. The operator had to reduce the solid into liquid form under water. It was then put into small bottles, such as contain scent. These bottles could be carried in your waistcoat pocket. The liquid would become inflammable only in a measure of time, for instance, if the stuff was deposited and you wanted to get away in half an hour or one hour you had to judge carefully the strength to be used. They had a German name for this, 'feierwasser' [feuerwasser], or liquid fire. They demonstrated how the stuff could be laid down. They brought out some old rags and laid them alongside some shavings, poured out a quantity of this liquid, opened a window, explaining that it required air to ignite, and just within the time arranged, almost to the minute, the fire burst out and travelled along the line of liquid as it would do in the case of a train of gunpowder. Von Igel was present at this demonstration. They also explained that they had new and improved explosives, especially for attachment to ships in a tideway. They were made conically like eggs, with an attachment that would go into the intake valve or the exhaust of a ship. They could also be attached to the bolts of the propeller boss or under the counter of the ship. They could be attached by a method of suction such as the principle of the barnacle or by expanding grips that entered into the intake valve and they could be timed up to 36 hours. They operated by the action of certain chemicals which burnt away metallic separation points. They had other devices for internal combustion such as concentrated dynamite in the shape and colour of coal. They explained the technical terms of the elements contained in these devices which brought about the explosions or fires. There was a chemist present who explained the formulae. No notes, however, were allowed to be taken. (I saw this same chemist in Mexico City in 1917. He was a red-bearded man of Jewish extraction).

The effect of the demonstration further strengthened my conviction of having nothing to do with this method of sabotage. The liquid fire, it was stated, was mostly to be used for factory operations.

Shortly after I had an appointment with a number of Germans in the Deutscher Verein in the neighbourhood of 88th Street and 3rd Avenue. One of the district representatives either from New Haven or New London there made a report as to conditions along the North-East coast. The bulk of this conversation was in German. The matter discussed was the success or lack of success in the work of interfering with the shipment of munitions. There was money distributed at this meeting, by a man who posed as an assistant of Von Igel. In all the discussions that took place both in Hoboken and Manhattan it was always considered to be of the utmost strategic importance to concentrate upon New Jersey. At one of these meetings a quotation was read from as it stated 'a high political personage' that they had to concentrate all their activities on New Jersey which was known as the chief base for the shipment of munition supplies, particularly in all the conversations I had with the Germans in and about New York special stress was always placed upon the question of destroying the supply of munitions at the New Jersey terminal and Bayonne, N.J. There were a permanent espionage staff located in Lakewood, N.J., which was frequently referred to in their conversations. The agents met there presumably for holidays.

At about this time specific plans had been discussed for destroying the munitions at the Jersey City terminus by means of a loaded barge exploding alongside the pier or jetty. The barge, it was stated, already arranged for was a Lackawanna railroad barge. It being explained that the detonation from these explosions would result in the explosion stored in or about the vicinity.

It was about this period while proceeding to a conference at which Von Igel was to be present, as I entered the office building I saw a group of Federal men and members of the Bomb Squad in the vicinity of the building and withdrew. That evening the papers carried the news that Von Igel had been arrested. I consulted with my friends and left New York hurriedly for the West.

I became engaged in the mining areas in the Western States. I worked among the miners from Tucson right up to the Canadian border, but more especially in Phoenix, Globe and Butte camps. The intermittent stoppages in these camps is a matter of record. In Butte I stayed in the Macdonald apartments in the Lloyd Block. From there I proceeded to the Coast where I arrived early in June, 1916. In or about this time I spoke in the Dreamland Rink, San Francisco, and at an Irish picnic in a park in Oakland. I also met the German Consul, Von Bopp, at his request. At this meeting there was a general discussion about the stoppage of munitions and he expressed himself as being in sympathy with my work. He referred to his successful work in Seattle and along the Pacific Coast. I returned to Chicago where I always had my headquarters.

After being here a short time I received a message from John Devoy to return to New York at once. This I did. I spent the time addressing meetings. On the night of what is now known as the 'Black Tom' explosion I was in lower Broadway at about 2 a.m. I was returning from Jamaica. I had gotten off at Fulton Street. I was somewhere about Trinity Church when a tremendous detonation was felt and glass fell down from the windows of the office buildings. There were very few people about and I proceeded to my apartments in Milligan Place, 10th Avenue. I read of the explosion in the early issues of the morning papers, realised my own danger in connection with it and made a record of the places I had been to, and of the persons I had been with. That record is either in the hands of the police authorities or among my papers in New York City. I was not arrested however and there was no need for me to explain my presence at any place or time. I notified my friends that in case I was picked up and gave them a copy of my statement as to my whereabouts previous to the explosion. I had only been in New York, for a matter of fact, for a few days. From New York I returned to Chicago.

I proceeded from Chicago to Washington where I met three or four Germans in a restaurant on Pennsylvania Avenue. James K. Maguire was again present. We had a long discussion and they asked me if it was possible for me to get into Mexico. I explained that I had already been there on two occasions. They asked me if I had a passport and told me they could fix me up with a passport or provide me with ship's discharges, either English or American. I inquired as to what they wanted me to go into Mexico for and they said that certain high officers had arrived in Mexico and did not dare to come into the United States. I went to Mexico City in accordance with their request and arrived there about September, 1916. I crossed between Laredo and Eagle Pass, through a ranch owned by an Italian-American. We went down to the river in a motor car and crossed it in a flat bottom boat. I was met on the other side by a Mexican and a German who travelled under the name of Walsh. On my arrival in Mexico City I was met at the station by two Germans and the secretary of the Mexican Railwaymen's Union, a Mexican, and taken to the hotel Juarez, which I believe was on the Avendee [Avenida] Juarez. At any rate the General Post Office is at the corner of this avenue. A man named Otto Paglische, whom I afterwards got to know very well owned this hotel.

There were some eighteen to twenty Germans and Austrians, two Polish and a Dane in the hotel. Mexicans very rarely visited the hotel. After I had been a couple of days there was a celebration of some German military success.

The Germans got so enthused about this victory that the police had to be brought down to get them to tone down their enthusiasm. Otto made arrangements for me to meet the German Minister. I arrived at the Ministry and was met by an official in uniform, who gave me a letter of apology, signed by Von Eckhardt himself, stating that he could not see me on account of certain political complications but that one of his officers would arrange to see me at another place and explain what they wish to see me about. I was taken to the hotel Iturbide, where after two days a German officer with a name something like Gratz called and explained that there had recently been a very serious political complication as a result of British objection to German activities in Mexico. They felt it would be much better that since they were so carefully supervised that I should return to the States to San Francisco and there meet certain German officials who would discuss matters with me. I was told to see Von Bopp.

I went back to San Francisco and stopped at the Fresno Hotel, where a German met me and arranged for me to cross to Berkeley to meet, as he said, an important German official. As I did not want to make my visit public in San Francisco, owing to my associations with Thomas Mooney, who was then in serious jeopardy, I kept under cover. They sent a car for me. Von Bopp met me somewhere near the University of California. He expressed his sympathy with Tom Mooney and made a lot of condemnatory statements regarding those who had, as he said, railroaded Mooney. I asked him if Mooney had anything to do with him. He stated that he had had something to do with strikes and Mooney had assisted them to that extent. I asked him what he wanted with me. He said he was in bad odour and that he had been in trouble over sabotage and espionage; that some people he had engaged for intelligence he had discovered were in the pay of the Department of Justice and the British Consulate; that he wished me to reorganise a group to help him. He said that Crowley, O'Connell and others were just hot-air merchants; that certain important local German-American politicians were betraying Germany. He said they were supplying coal to the English cruisers and though they were supposed to give Bopp news as to their destination and rendezvous, they had deliberately misled him and he had gotten into serious trouble with the home government as a result. He offered to provide me with a fast motor yacht and the means to destroy vessels designated by him to me through the accredited official. These messages were to be arranged secretly by means of the use of a small Bible, in which punctures would be made under letters by pin or needle. By holding the page of the Bible to the light the letter shown was to be taken as part of the word and capital letters were to have two punctures. Any message delivered by the agent was to be ignored as merely camouflage, only the puncture letter in the small bible should be considered. Bopp stated that though he was closely supervised he had three places to meet his friends, although he could not and dare not make too many appointments. He pointed out that some of his colleagues had been arrested and interned. These men, he said, he had tried to have released through his Irish-American associations, in San Francisco, but they had either gotten cold feet or were doublecrossing him. He said that it was becoming necessary for him to make arrangements for someone to act in his place.

At this meeting he definitely requested me to confine my activities to the west coast and asked me if I would undertake with the means placed at my disposal to deal with various oilfields, particularly Bakersfield, as well as other well known areas. The local shipyard in San Francisco was also mentioned, as well as the Seattle waterfront. Von Bopp told me he had men working from British Vancouver right down to Guatemala. He stated that all the West Coast was under his supervision; that there were unlimited funds at his disposal and that I would be well taken care of. I told him what I had told them in New York that I would not be a party to any proceedings where human life was involved. He asked me whether I would not engage in sabotage of munition plants, that there was no danger to human life since the means they had were so safe. He also wanted me to become concerned with the stoppage of mules and horses, especially mules, where the concentration shipping point was St Louis. He said they had plenty of Germans living in and around St Louis but they would not take any risks. It was necessary he said to inject disease cultures into the animals, which would bring on fever in a space of time and make utterly incapable of working. It was a slow developing culture which was to affect the animals during the voyage. I told him I would have nothing to do with any such methods; that I was a propagandist and believed in mass action and mass intelligence. He said that he had been informed that I would undertake anything and that he needed someone whom he could rely upon as he had terrible difficulties with his own men who were always drinking and debauching themselves. He said he had agents in the Department of Justice who had made good reports on me and that they could not get anything on me although they felt I was engaged in sabotage. He offered to pay me my hotel expenses and asked me to go and have a holiday in a camp at Lake Tahoe. He again asked me and during the next few days he importuned me for further meetings. He pretended to be a great friend of Ireland. On the next occasion I met him in a house in Oakland. He tried with argument after argument to prevail upon me to accept his offer to immediately commence destructive sabotage work as he said it was hard to get men to take the necessary risks. He showed me a list of some of his agents to establish his bona fides. These men were alleged to be Irish. While on the coast in company with Von Bopp I met Janhke, Von Brinken, as well as a number of other Germans, whose names I cannot for the moment recollect.

I returned to the Middle West and published in Chicago at 1046 North Franklin Street a paper known as the 'IRISH WORKER', copies of which are in the Congressional Library. I continued to carry on my anti-war work and immediately America declared war on Germany, the paper was seized. After the declaration of war I carried on my anti-war work and consistently opposed conscription. I was arrested on a number of occasions, third-degreed and held for trial under the Espionage Act in Jamaica, L.I. before Judge Ryan but was acquitted.

From my actual knowledge of and intimate relations with the revolutionary Irish organisation in America, the leaders of the Irish movement in America had no act, hand or part, if they had the brains to suggest destructive sabotage. I always found them to be without exception, 105% Americans and that opinion was held and expressed by all the Germans, and German officials I met in the United States and Mexico. On the declaration of war by the United States the leaders of the Irish movement instructed all their members and followers to accept the draft and give to the war their utmost support.

The Germans complained bitterly that they had been let down by the Irish and they looked upon the leaders of the Irish group, as they expressed it in their own words, as four-flushers and political grafters.

307

In all the four years up to the close of the war I know of no one who was engaged in destructive sabotage in the United States who was not either a German-born or Austrian-born citizen, with the exception of a few Poles, Italians, Lithuanians and one or two Danes, also some German-Americans.

From December, 1914, repeated proposals to enlist my services and the group I was associated with, were made to me by officials of the German Government, particularly, Captain Boy-Ed, Minister Dr. Dernburg, a high official of the Hamburg-Amerika Line whose name I do not recall, Von Igel and Von Bopp in the United States, and Von Eckhardt, Major Schwartz and Major Schwiertz in Mexico. I cannot recall that Captain Von Papen ever directly requested me to undertake destructive sabotage, although he was present and fully aware of the proposals made to me by Captain Boy-Ed. Dr. Dumba also had a conscious knowledge of these matters. There was also another gentleman, who was an art critic and fine art publisher, with a gallery in 57th St. I was told he was a representative of the German Government though he claimed to be an American citizen with no connection with Germany. This man's name is something like Unstengal and was well-known in New York. He was a tall gentlemanly type, well-spoken and an intellectual.

In the summer of 1917 an emissary came to me direct from San Francisco and urged me to proceed to Mexico City because of complications arising out of the military situation. This man came from Von Bopp or his organisation. I left New York about the latter end of August and was met in San Antonio by two German officials who told me it was very difficult to cross the border since their machinery and line of communication had been destroyed. Their fake passport bureau had been discovered and a number of their agents were under surveillance. They said that though they could give me no assistance, that they had been told to urge me to get through. They gave me seven letters to deliver, one which I distinctly recall was written in Hebrew, others were in code. I first refused to take them and they wired to my friends in New York. I then received a letter from James K. Maguire, requesting me to carry out any task the Germans asked of me, at the risk of my life I then agreed to take and deliver the letters. I made my way to the Coast. Left the letters with a friend near the Border. In San Diego I was arrested under the name of McInerney, but was released in a couple of days. I crossed the border at Tia Juana [Tijuana], proceeding to Ensenada and delivered the letters to an official residing there, which I had picked up after being released.

From here with the assistance of the Governor of Lower California I proceeded to La Paz where I was provided with a motor boat to Guaymass [Guaymas] on the mainland. I was put up at a hotel formerly a monastery, owned by a Dublin man who was a British secret service man.

The German secret service department communicated with me after two days. They told me that a revolution had broken out in Tepiz [Tepic], that all the railway lines were down and the bridges gone. It was suggested that I travel down the coast in a motor boat. I did this and arrived in Matzalan [Mazatlán] and found the Germans in serious trouble. From there I proceeded to Manzalillo [Manzanillo], where I was met and arrangements made to take me through the country. I arrived in Mexico City on September 17th, I believe, after many difficulties. I was taken to the Cosmos Hotel and after a couple hours my former friend, Otto Paglische came for me and took me to the Hotel Juarez. After two or three days I had an interview with Carranza and was then taken to the German Ministry, which is located in an area of Mexico City where the names of the streets are all in English.

At the first interview there, there were present two German officers who were joined by Major Schwartz. He expressed his apologies that the Minister could not be present but said that Von Eckhardt would be in attendance the following day. He asked me where I was put up, whether I was comfortable and suggested that I should stay at the Hotel Iturbide. He was most solicitous. That night, they took me down to the Spanish Club and introduced me to a number of Mexicans. There was very heavy drinking and gambling going on. Of course, in which neither of which I participated. They offered me money which I refused. They then produced a large roll of English sovereigns and tried to force me to accept them though I had not seen an English sovereign for months. The following day they took me for a ride in the country and upon my return we went to the Ministry. After a short space of time, Minister Von Eckhardt, Major Schwartz and two other gentlemen came into the room and began to discuss the general situation. They were very open, explained their situation was very bad, that unless the advance of the Allies was halted, they would have to negotiate for peace. They brought lunch in and an acrimonious discussion took place among themselves. They were very bitter against the Austrians, although an Austrian was present, but were particularly vehement against Americans and the United States. They explained that Carranza had sold them out and gone pro-English. On this occasion I learned for the first time that Carranza was a lodge brother of Von Eckhardt. They stated they were going to instruct all their people in the overthrow of Carranza; that both newspapers had gone pro-Ally and practically speaking they had friends nowhere.

During the course of the discussion another German entered the room and all arose and saluted him. He was a tall individual whose name I can not recollect, spoke very good English and all deferred to him. They said that all of their agents on the North East coast of England had been seized and some executed. They said they were disgusted with their Irish friends, with whom they had associated themselves in the United States because they had turned out to be the most loyal of Americans; that the whole arrangement between the Germans and the Irish had fallen through since America entered the war. Their own machinery and their own men had fallen down and become useless. They made bitter accusations against German-American politicians and German-Americans generally. They

309

asked me for details about the anti-draft and inquired about the trouble among the copper miners and asked other questions since their effective avenues of communication had been destroyed.

They then took out maps and placed them on the table and stated that if I and those associated with me would undertake a certain line which they proposed, they would give me and my group official recognition in Ireland. They stated that they had been deceived so often that they had begun to lose faith in everybody and wanted to make contact with someone on whose loyalty they could rely. On the maps there was marked every oilfield, railway junction and to my knowledge the majority of the ammunition and steel plants in the United States, and port terminals. They openly referred to the names of men that had carried on sabotage in the United States, praising some and blaming others. Von Rintelen, whom they all despised, was mentioned. Von Brinken was referred to and especial credit was given to Von Bopp as a loyal servant though lacking in capacity. They were loud in their denunciation of and blamed the exposure of their early plans on Boy-Ed. They complained bitterly about agents who had been reporting explosions and sabotage work that had never taken place, although the agents had gotten paid for it. They stated however that they had had some important successes considering their difficulties. Their chief success they stated was what they termed the New Jersey terminal explosion. They stated that of the five men who were involved in that explosion, two were then located in Mexico City, one of them would have to be removed as he was giving them a great deal of trouble because they could not keep him away from drink. They stated that even at this late hour if something of such importance could be made to occur again they might be able to accomplish something. They stated that it was not true that there had been any loss of life at New Jersey terminal; that all their agents had gotten clear away and that the mention of men being killed in New Jersey in the explosion had been made only to instil hate against the Germans in the minds of the people of the United States. In the course of the discussion they mentioned several other places where ammunition was made or stored which had been destroyed. They also referred to ships which had been sunk. The discussion also covered a number of men who were interned on Angel's Island or Alcatraz. They were anxious that certain of these men should escape as they were afraid they might be executed. They referred to a 'landsman' of mine who had undertaken to get certain of them away. They stated that they had endeavoured to destroy the oil wells in Tapico, but that Doneny had an army of Mexicans protecting the entire country and they could not accomplish anything in this area.

They then asked me to return to the States and carry out certain destructive sabotage measures which they proposed. They said they could still get money into the States if I could get men to carry out the work they wanted done. They told me that on my return to the States they would communicate with me at an appointed place in San Francisco as to what they wanted done. They said unlimited funds would be available. I told them quite definitely I would have no such arrangement with them. When they became convinced of this, their whole demeanour changed. When I returned to the hotel Juarez, the proprietor of the hotel, who seemed to have been notified beforehand refused me access to my apartment and to association with the German refugees, although previous to my visit to the Ministry all had been very friendly. Paglische in fact had asked me to take up an agency for him on my return to the States for the disposal of his antiques and art objects, of which he had a large collection. A few days later my wallet was gone, containing my money, and I was practically without resources. I was presented with a substantial bill for my stay at the Iturbide and the Juarez. All of my expenses which had been incurred since I set out for Mexico, with the exception of the hospitality which I received in Matzalan and in Manzallo and Guaymass and the conveyance across country I received no reimbursement for, although it was at their expressed request that I had come to Mexico and a verbal undertaking I should be paid. I had sufficient money to pay my hotel expenses at the Iturbide, which can be verified as I paid them in the name of Lawson. When I reported the loss of my wallet in the Juarez they brought in the police but said no trace could be discovered. The day following my bag was missing. This I blamed on the Germans though they charged the Mexicans with the theft of both the wallet and the bag. Practically no Mexicans visited the Juarez. They were nearly all Germans, Austrians and a couple of Poles. At the weekend I was asked for my room. I told them my position and with my last few pesos I wired to New York for money. The money was cabled to me through Joe Donnelly and came through Iselin's and was cashed in the post office. I do not recall whether the money came in the name of Lawson or Larkin.

At this time I was sleeping out having no place to go while I waited for money. On the bench where I used to sleep in the Plaza Madero, a Mexican was stabbed to death during the night I was away from this bench. I found out after I left Mexico City I was under constant surveillance. I was told by one of the refugees in the Juarez, who had been a German marine, that anyone who had ever done anything for the Germans that brought them within the criminal law, if he did not undertake the next job offered, he was threatened he would be refused rations and allowance, as well as handed up to the authorities. On my way to the border I was attacked by three Mexican bullies on the train. The Border officer at Laredo will remember the incident. It is my definite opinion were instigated by the German authorities in Mexico City. After my return to San Francisco I was arrested and questioned by the Department of Justice but released. I was approached by one O'Connell to get in touch with the Germans again but I refused to have anything to do with them.

During the course of my association with the Germans I, of course, came into contact with many of their active agents. Of these I definitely recall in addition to those I have made mention of in this affidavit, Carl

Rodiger. Tauscher. Becker. Gratz (seaman). Rasmussen. Witzke, and many others whose names I cannot recall at the moment. I feel that if I had a list of agents before me I could identify many others.

Witzke I recall as a young man whom I think I met in Los Angeles in October, 1917.

These and other matters of which I have knowledge I am prepared to submit, under oath, for examination and cross-examination before any tribunal.

I make this affidavit in the interests of truth, having no other ulterior motive in view whatsoever and having received no consideration or promise of consideration whatever therefor.

Upon my hurried deportation I could make no arrangements regarding my property, documents, correspondence, etc. It is possible they can be traced through my friends and recovered if not in the possession of the authorities. Some are in the care of James Brennan, Chicago, Albert Hickland, 33rd Street, New York and persons in New England and San Francisco.

This affidavit has been hurriedly prepared without having any time for preparation or for reference to any records because of the urgent need of forwarding to the United States.

James J. Larkin
Sworn to before me, this Second Day of January, Nineteen hundred
and Thirty-Four at 12.:30 A.M. hour.
[Signature]
HENRY H. BALCH
CONSUL GENERAL OF THE UNITED STATES OF AMERICA, DUBLIN, IRELAND.

Chapter 40

Triumph and Disaster

On 27 April 1923 Éamon de Valera, president of the 'Republican Government', and Frank Aiken, on behalf of the Irish Republican Army, ordered 'the suspension of all offensive operations' in the Civil War then raging, from noon on Monday 30 April.

Five hours after the cease-fire, at five o'clock on the Monday evening, James Larkin landed at Carlisle Pier, Dún Laoghaire, from Holyhead. He had been away from Ireland for nearly eight-and-a-half years. The following day the *Irish Times* reported Larkin standing on the deck of the ship in a broad-brimmed black hat, his hands thrust deep in the pockets of his black overcoat. 'A grim-faced, dour looking man of middle age, he seemed wholly unconscious of the excitement which his coming appeared to invoke.'[1]

Some of Larkin's followers who had travelled to the port to greet their chief were prevented from getting onto the pier by armed sentries. The welcoming party, with the leaders of the ITGWU conspicuously absent, travelled by train into Westland Row (Pearse) Station, where some thousands of wildly enthusiastic men and women, 'Larkin's rabble', greeted him. There were five bands, and a wagonette to bring Larkin and his family to Liberty Hall, the 'old spot by the river'. The horses drew the wagonette down Brunswick Street (Pearse Street), past the Antient Concert Rooms, where Larkin had spoken at many meetings, around by Tara Street, across the river to Beresford Place, the bands playing and the crowds cheering and singing the fighting songs of 1913.[2]

From the window of Liberty Hall, Big Jim once more spoke to his excited followers. 'Comrades,' his voice rang out across Beresford Place and over the bridge to the Coal Quay,

> this is a meeting of the old guard and the new guard. You all know the old rule of the Transport and General Workers' Union: 'Each for all and all for each.' Unity is strength but there has been a lack of faith and a limitation of vision. Those who founded this Hall had dreamed great dreams and are going to realise them. Since I have come back I have noticed that the rich are now richer and the poor are poorer. There are many ways to win freedom and liberty and we have not tried them all yet. The three important things for us are Unity, Solidarity and Charity.

In a general message to the members of the union he wrote in its paper, the *Voice of Labour*, within days of his return:

> Now in the crisis confronting the nation, we again speak with no uncertain voice. 'Peace, reconstruction, charity to all,' is the demand we make and to

you this charge is given, unto each and every man, member of Rank and File or Officer entrusted with duties, perfect your organisation. Solidarity the keynote. Get ready, be prepared to enforce peace, to carry out construction measures, and live true to the motto of this Pioneer Union. 'Each for All and All for Each,' steady and be ready!

Peace was again the theme of Larkin's address to a huge Labour Day celebration arranged by the union in Croke Park the following Sunday. After a sports meeting and a concert given by three bands sponsored by the union, Larkin spoke.

It is easy to preach hate and destruction, and you would always get men who would sell themselves for a price to preach hate. For the sake of the new race, the children, we have got to have peace and concord, charity and forgiveness of wrong to all men. Two armies are contending for power in the nation but I am speaking to the greatest army of all of them, and it is the working classes who are going to bring peace … Let us march forward with peace on our banners and victory in our hearts.

That evening, at the Theatre Royal, after a Connolly Commemoration Concert, Larkin again addressed the question of peace.

It is about time that the common people of Ireland who have been so long silent and inarticulate should speak out. The questions of the day should be argued with reason and logic, for the sword, the bayonet and the rifle never proved to be anything but brutality. Force means that might was right. Everybody is sitting down like cowards afraid to speak. People think it is courageous to take a gun or a mine and use it, but it requires more courage to speak the truth. We have had assassination by word and by deed, and the worst form of it is moral assassination. We must get rid of this curse which is bringing our country into the contempt of the world.

When a man in the audience shouted, 'We are for peace with honour,' Larkin curtly answered him: 'There can never be dishonour in peace.'

Larkin's words about peace must have seemed bitter indeed when within a few weeks a veritable civil war was to break out within the ITGWU itself, which was to have disastrous consequences for Big Jim and for the labour movement.

Following the occupation of the ITGWU offices in Parnell Square and Liberty Hall by supporters of Larkin on 11 June 1923 and their refusal to allow the union's officials to enter the premises, the Executive Committee, meeting in the offices of the union's solicitors, suspended Larkin as general secretary and applied for an injunction to prevent him or his agents from interfering with their carrying out their duties as officers of the union. This in effect ended Larkin's official involvement with the union he had founded almost fourteen years before.

Legal proceedings by Larkin against the officials of the ITGWU and the union's counter-proceedings continued during the autumn of 1923. The hearing of a consolidated action arising from four separate actions taken by Larkin and by the union was held before the Master of the Rolls in Dublin Castle in February 1924.

The four actions were: (1) the general president of the union, Thomas Foran, and the members of the Executive Committee sought a declaration that they were the legal trustees, officers and executive of the ITGWU and were entitled to possession of the premises at 35 Parnell Square and Liberty Hall; (2) the same officers sought an injunction to restrain James Larkin from entering the union's premises and obstructing the plaintiffs in the discharge of their duties; (3) Larkin alleged that the new rules of the union were invalid and that the defendants had unlawfully applied funds of the union and that there had been irregularities in regard to the funds; (4) Larkin sought declarations that the rules of 20 December 1918 were invalid, as also the rules of 2 June 1923, and that Thomas Foran and William O'Brien had been illegally applying union funds. In their defence, Foran and O'Brien denied that the funds of the union had been unlawfully or improperly applied. They said that the action was vexatious and that it should be dismissed, with costs.

The proceedings opened on 12 February 1924, with three KCs (Sergeant Hanna, S. L. Brown, and Timothy Sullivan) and a junior (M. Maguire) representing the ITGWU. At the outset Larkin indicated that he had dismissed his counsel and would conduct his own case.

Early exchanges between Larkin and O'Brien were a mild foretaste of the bitter exchanges to come. When O'Brien, in reply to his counsel, gave the dates of Larkin leaving the country and returning, Larkin interjected: 'How does he know when I went away or came back?' with O'Brien declaring, 'I know a good deal about you.'

Larkin's presentation of his case was, to put it mildly, disorganised. Calling a named witness, Larkin was asked by the judge whether he had served a subpoena and got the reply that he had 'sent out' for him. As for the next witness, Larkin said that he would telephone and ask him to come. 'While we are waiting for him, what do you propose we do?' asked the judge. 'I will call some members who were present at branch meetings,' came the reply from Larkin. 'Call whoever you like,' he was told.

After examining a witness, Larkin was told by the judge that he was only wasting his time calling evidence to prove 'absolutely irrelevant facts'. Soon afterwards, following the prolonged questioning of a witness, the judge told him that if he did not confine himself to relevant matters he would have to stop the examination: 'You have not asked a single relevant question now since you commenced.'

Told by the judge that it seemed to him that Larkin had 'a mind so constituted that you cannot distinguish what is relevant and what is irrelevant, what is important and what is unimportant,' and that he would not allow public time to be wasted, Larkin replied that he was not attempting to waste anyone's public time and that anyway 'the judge was paid for his time the same as the rest of public servants.' 'I am paid to serve the public,' admonished the judge. Then, with 'I am sure you will do that, my lord,' Larkin ended the exchange.

When one of Larkin's witnesses (who, it was alleged, had prevented officials of the union from entering the offices in Parnell Square) entered the witness-box he was told by Larkin: 'We will dispose with your services this afternoon. I am afraid you called into too many places on your way down here.' Turning to the judge, he said, 'These men, my lord, have got the usual weakness and take what is called a pint or two.'

At the conclusion of Larkin's evidence in the first part of the proceedings he was asked whether this closed his evidence, to which he replied, perhaps sarcastically, 'My lord, it does, and I must say you have been very good to me,' to which the Master of the Rolls responded that he was 'glad to get that reference from you, Mr Larkin.'

Unfortunately, any light that was shed in the cross-examination of witnesses on the allegations that were the subject of the legal actions was not to Larkin's advantage. Not least was this so when William O'Brien took the stand. The verbal confrontations between the two, by now arch-enemies, gave rise to piquant exchanges. From these, it must be said, O'Brien was usually the victor, certainly in the legal aspect.

Asked by Larkin to show his membership card (which showed, incidentally, that O'Brien had joined the union on 6 January 1917, eight years after its foundation), O'Brien handed the card to Larkin, who then asked for the roll-book. 'I usually carry the card in my pocket, but not the roll-book,' was O'Brien's caustic reply. O'Brien availed of every opportunity to bait Larkin. When asked by Larkin whether he (Larkin) had directed the Executive from the time he went away until he came home, O'Brien replied: 'There was no Executive in your time. You took good care of that.'

The intense bitterness between the two men was palpable in every exchange between them. O'Brien, asked by Larkin whether everything he had sworn in an affidavit was as true as what he had sworn previously, replied that everything he ever swore was true.

> Mr. Larkin: We will test that later on.
> Mr. O'Brien: Test it now. Now is the time. Come on now, James; I will face you as I always did.
> Mr. Larkin: Now, Field Marshal, don't get so warlike.
> Judge: Don't indulge in personalities.
> Mr. Larkin: But he has invited me.

Apart from the main issues that fell to be determined by the Master of the Rolls, a number of matters not wholly germane to the proceedings arose that the judge allowed to be discussed. Some of these only incidentally, if at all, related to the legal questions at stake but were nevertheless of significance to both sides in that they had a relevance to the power struggle in the union and the credibility of the two antagonists in the eyes of the members of the trade union movement.

One of these issues concerned a food ship that Larkin had wanted to sail to Ireland following his release from Sing Sing jail in New York at the beginning of 1923. The origin of the idea is related in the 'Carney Memoir', a nineteen-page typewritten memoir by Jack Carney written at the request of Emmet Larkin, the future biographer of Larkin, in May 1953. Jack Carney was with Larkin in New York and was involved in the planning of the arrangements for the food ship.

The idea of a food ship was first mooted by Larkin in June 1922, when he was on temporary release from jail. The newspapers at the time had carried grim reports of the distress in Belfast arising from the sectarian conflicts raging there. In his book *Labor and Nationalism in Ireland*, published in New York in 1925, the American historian J. Dunsmore Clarkson wrote that in 1920 Belfast was launched 'on a period of murder and arson unparalleled in intensity and brutality anywhere else in Ireland—a period that was to last for more than two years.' Larkin was profoundly affected by the press reports, which suggested that the city had been reduced to almost famine conditions because of the strife.

At the adjourned delegate conference of the ITGWU on 14 May 1923 Larkin was to tell the delegates how, when he had first got out of jail in America, he had read about the state of affairs in Belfast, which, he said, had 'always been dear to him.' He took up the question of the relief ship. Subsequently he had been imprisoned again, but on his later release he had again taken up this matter. According to Jack Carney, Larkin held a meeting in Chicago and raised some $1,500. Carney was chairman of the meeting, and Hanna Sheehy-Skeffington also spoke. Larkin and Carney inspected some ships on Long Island, which they could have bought for $15,000. It was then that Larkin sent the first cable to the president of the union, his closest associate in Ireland, on 23 March 1923.

Require five thousand pounds to complete purchase steamer means one hundred thousand dollars worth food, etc., other values, ship's ownership yours, accept responsibility for refusal.

Foran cabled Larkin at 53 Jane Street, New York, three days later:

Unsigned cable received asking that five thousand pounds be forwarded. If you are sender, Union Executive no official knowledge of your proposal, and cannot vote Union funds without full information. Executive surprised no reply received to its cable of 6th February asking when you proposed returning, and now requests definite information. Foran.

This was a perfectly reasonable response, given the circumstances, but Larkin, no doubt under much strain following his release from jail and his preparations for returning to Ireland, replied in a manner that, to say the least, was unfortunate. It was, however, typical of Larkin's way of doing things, and he was probably wholly unconscious of the reaction it would provoke. He always had a cavalier attitude to money—funds were to be

317

expended if for a worthy cause—and he was impatient of any attempt to control his actions.

Larkin's reply was addressed to 'Foran, acting secretary' and was signed 'Jim Larkin, secretary.'

Cable signed name, appointed you; information for Executive, ship purchase can be completed, Union first mortgage, ownership transferred Union. When purchased placed on berth here loaded with food, clothing, etc. for victims of fratricidal strife, volunteer crew work ship across, loaded free, have monopoly contract certain Eastern Government, after relief work done. Suggest money withheld you, O'Neill and another nineteen thirteen without my knowledge might furnish amount requested. Who are your Executive? Cable their names, districts. What mean you last portion of message? What do your Executive request—definite information about ship or my return? Each member Executive sign cable message for record.

Now it is quite likely that Larkin and his colleagues in New York had either made arrangements or could make them for the supply of food and clothing for the relief ship, for its loading, and for a volunteer crew to sail the vessel to Ireland. It is also probable that an agreement had been reached with representatives of the Russian authorities for the ship to be chartered after its voyage to Ireland: it may be noted that on his earlier release from jail Larkin had received a message from no less than Zinoviev, president of the Communist International in Moscow, sending 'warmest greeting to the undaunted fighter released from the "democratic" prisons.' This being so, it would be understandable that Larkin should have regarded the failure of the union to provide the relatively small amount required to purchase the vessel—which would in any case become the property of the union—as unreasonable.

No doubt Larkin, with his always strong emphasis on the importance of symbolic gestures, saw himself on the bridge of the food ship sailing up the Liffey or the Lagan after a voyage across the Atlantic, when he would reclaim his leadership of the Irish working class. No doubt too he remembered the psychological boost that the arrival of the relief ship *Hare* gave to the hungry families of the locked-out workers in Dublin in 1913.

However, the reference to the money 'withheld' by Foran, O'Neill and another in 1913 had another connotation altogether. This matter too was to be raised in the court actions in 1924 and was to create a deep division with Foran and in effect ensure his adherence to the O'Brien camp in the struggle against Larkin.

Foran called a special Executive meeting to consider Larkin's cable and on 9 April cabled Larkin to inform him that the Executive could not sanction his application for £5,000.

This was not the end of the matter. At the delegate conference held on 24–25 April, on the eve of Larkin's arrival in Dublin, the request from Larkin for £5,000 was brought up. After a short discussion, the seventy-five delegates from forty branches unanimously approved the action of the Executive.

The refusal of his request for money to acquire the food ship rankled deeply with Larkin. No doubt he felt humiliated in the eyes of his American colleagues at the refusal of the union of which he was the general secretary to accede to his request; and Larkin's pride was a formidable trait in his character. It is probable too that his close colleagues in America added fuel to the fire of his anger by seeing in the Executive's action confirmation that at home a conspiracy had developed to exclude him from any control over the union. That he was completely out of touch with the real situation in Dublin and in the union would not have occurred to him.

How dominant in his mind the issue of the food ship was is evident from the fact that when he met the Executive Committee at a special meeting on 4 May, called for the purpose of giving the general secretary an opportunity of meeting the members after nearly nine years' absence, Larkin immediately raised the matter of the food ship, expressing his disappointment that the money had not been sent to him. The members of the Executive should have known him sufficiently well to trust him, he told them.

Larkin then told the surprised members of the Executive that he proposed going to Russia immediately, 'where he had important work to do,' and he would not allow the Executive Committee or any other body 'to prevent him doing the work which he felt it was his duty to do.' He would therefore, he told the astonished members, hand in his resignation as general secretary the following day and would cease to hold any official position in the union and would be simply an ordinary member. Later in the meeting Larkin was prevailed upon to withdraw his resignation, and at his request it was agreed that no public mention should be made of his differences with the Executive Committee.

When the adjourned delegate conference was held ten days later, on 14 May, Larkin again referred to the issue of the food ship, though in a low key and not contentiously. He told the delegates about his original idea to send a food ship to Belfast to relieve the distress there, that he had an offer of a suitable ship, and that if the money had been sent to purchase it, the money would have been quickly repaid. However, he added, the Executive Committee considered that they had not got sufficient particulars before them to warrant them sending the money, and 'he made no complaint on that score.'

The matter was first raised at the court hearing in 1924 by William O'Brien. Larkin in his evidence on 19 February again confirmed that the money sought from the union was for the purpose of completing the purchase of a steamer, of which $25,000 was being provided by a society in New York. His intention, he said, was to fill the ship with food and clothes and take it into Belfast 'as a gesture towards peace.'

Far more serious as a bone of personal contention, and the primary cause of the rift with his oldest comrade, Thomas Foran, was the imputation involved in the controversy about the £7,500 that Larkin referred to in his cable to Foran as having been withheld by Foran, O'Neill and another in 1913 without his knowledge. The matter had been raised at the delegate conference on 24–25 April, when Foran, referring to Larkin's cable seeking £5,000 and his mention of money withheld in 1913, had explained how this arose and had pointed out that the money had gone to the purchase of Liberty Hall and that 'Larkin had agreed to this.' It was raised again at the adjourned delegate conference on 14 May, when Larkin was present.

Larkin was the spirit of conciliation in his comments. He told the delegates that he had never had anything to do with cash or handling the funds of the union. In 1913 he had toured England and Scotland to raise funds, and the money had been sent directly to Dublin, and he did not handle it. At the time he sent the cable in question he had remembered that a balance of money was due, and the collection of some of it at least was due to his efforts. When he saw there was no other means available for raising the necessary funds for the relief ship, it occurred to him that it would be well if this money could be got for the purpose.

That was all that was said about the £7,500 at that conference. Three weeks later, however, at the general meeting of the No. 1 Branch held at the La Scala Theatre, Prince's Street, on 3 June, Larkin, in a fierce onslaught on his opponents in the union and with an invective that must have surpassed his previous denunciations, hurled all kinds of allegations around. In the middle of a tirade about trouble in the union between 'certain people for place and power' he suddenly asked who had withheld money in strike pay in 1913.

Foran immediately replied that it was public knowledge now that he and John O'Neill had laid this money aside and that when the strike was over, portion of the money referred to, £3,000, went towards the purchase of Liberty Hall. With great passion, he told the delegates that neither he nor John O'Neill had ever enriched themselves with one penny of that money, and he challenged the general secretary to say that one penny of it ever went into their pockets.

Larkin did not then comment on the statements made but went on to say that the delegate conferences held in April and May were 'absolutely illegal' and that they had been 'packed for a certain purpose.' He did not blame these two men (Foran and O'Neill) 'but there was another—the man who was behind this, but he was not there that day.' He went on to say: 'I make this charge definitely, that money was deliberately paid for corruption in this union to organise a machine so that one man could be thrown out.' From his earlier statements it would seem probable that Larkin was referring to money paid, as he claimed illegally, to the delegates to the delegate conferences that met that year to formulate new rules. However, having made the statement about corruption, Larkin then asked who gave these two men (Foran and O'Neill) authority to withhold £7,500 in strike pay.

Larkin was to refer again to the £7,500 in his speech to the meeting. If the auditor certified that the papers showed that the money was expended, he was satisfied, he said. Foran interjected: 'It might be in some of their minds, and many would be glad to circulate it, that Tommy Foran and John O'Neill were accused by Jim Larkin of robbing the Union of £7,500.' 'I have not made any such charge,' Larkin replied.

During the court examination of the general president on 18 February 1924, Foran gave a detailed explanation of the position regarding the £7,500. He told the court that in 1913 he had the duty of bringing funds required for dispute pay from the Central Lock-out Committee in the Trades Hall in Capel Street to Liberty Hall. Each week the amounts received were paid in to the general funds of the union. These amounts and other subscriptions received generally exceeded the sum required for dispute pay; as a result, the total union funds in December 1913 amounted to approximately £7,500. Some time before Christmas 1913 Larkin had asked him how the union stood financially and he had answered: 'Well, John O'Neill [secretary of the Dublin No. 1 Branch] and I have discussed the situation and we have agreed not to tell you what the state of the fund is.' Larkin had replied: 'I don't want to know the actual position; I only want to know is the union safe.' Foran then said: 'Well, as to that, I am not breaking any confidence with John by telling you that the union is quite safe.' He had feared that if Larkin knew the sum that was in the union funds, he would squander it away. Furthermore, the union was in danger of eviction from Liberty Hall, and they were anxious to safeguard the union's future by purchasing the premises. (Ironically, the purchase of Liberty Hall was made urgent by the fact that the Ancient Order of Hibernians, a notoriously anti-Larkin organisation, was seeking to acquire the premises.)

An unpleasant aspect of Larkin's attitude to his opponents emerged when he was questioning John O'Neill, the secretary of the No. 1 Branch. O'Neill agreed that he had been employed in Kennedy's bakery before he went to the union. Asked why he had left Kennedy's, he replied that he had to leave it. 'Was there a charge against you?' asked Larkin, to which O'Neill replied that there was, 'of being deficient of money on two books.'

The Master of the Rolls when giving his judgment was severely critical of Larkin regarding this exchange. Recalling that Larkin had called O'Neill a thief, the judge emphasised that there was no evidence whatever that he was guilty of any dishonesty when he was in the employment of Kennedy's. He explained the position of the driver of a bread van who is sometimes asked to give credit to a poor woman whose husband is out of work and for which he may not be paid. That is an unsatisfactory thing to the employer, and he does not want such a man. 'So far as the evidence in this case goes,' he said,

we have got nothing more than that Mr O'Neill was dismissed from his employment because he was in default in paying up the price of the bread delivered to him for distribution. This does not at all involve him in anything like a criminal offence, and I regret very much that very strong accusations are made in this Court by Mr Larkin and levelled against him.

The main thrust of Larkin's case related to the rules of the union. He claimed that the rules of 1918, which replaced those of 1915, had not been properly passed, and similarly the rules of 1923.

The court had no problem in finding that the rules of 1918 had been properly passed and were valid. On 11 November 1918 draft rules were circulated to the branches. Some of the branches held meetings and voted on the draft rules. There were thirty-nine branches at the time, and of these, twenty-four voted for the new rules and only one branch, Sligo, voted against. Twelve branches did not vote, and two made returns that were unsigned and therefore invalid. On the basis of the votes recorded in the returns, 6,876 members voted for and 501 against.

It might be noted that evidence was given in court that the number of members counted as voting in favour of the rules at the branch meetings (6,876) included the total membership of branches recording a unanimous decision. The number of benefit members in the union at the time was given as 'about twenty thousand' by William O'Brien. Evidence was given by James Hughes (correspondence secretary of the union from 1918 to July 1921) that the membership of the Dublin No. 1 Branch was roughly ten thousand and of Dublin No. 3 Branch three to four thousand. A substantial majority of the members of the ITGWU in 1918 therefore were in Dublin. It seemed to have been established in the court that no meeting of the No. 1 Branch had been held to consider the rules, and the secretary of the No. 3 Branch gave evidence that neither he nor the committee had called a meeting to vote on the rules. There was also evidence that some members of No. 1 Branch, including Micheál Ó Maoláin, had protested to the Registrar of Friendly Societies about the registration of the rules, and that no action had been taken.

It is understandable, therefore, that Larkin should have been convinced that the rules of 1918 had not been validly adopted and that they did not have the approval of a majority of the membership. The moral basis for his position is unassailable. But the fact was that the case was being argued in a court of law, and the question to be resolved was whether the rules had been approved in accordance with the previously existing rules of 1915. The fact that a clear majority of the members of the union, who were in the two largest branches, had not voted on the rule amendments was irrelevant in law. As the Master of the Rolls retorted to Larkin, 'If they [Dublin No. 1 Branch] didn't vote it was their own fault.' Yet this branch constituted, on the evidence of Hughes, at least half the union membership (Larkin claimed 70 per cent).

The position regarding the 1923 rules was legally even more clear-cut, and again the court unhesitatingly held against Larkin's arguments, which were not only tenuous in the extreme but in a way absurd. Once the 1918 rules had been shown to be valid—and the Master of the Rolls indicated this at an early stage of the proceedings—there was not a titter of legal substance in the case argued by Larkin about the 1923 rules. The Master of the Rolls had no hesitation in finding that these rules had been properly adopted.

Larkin charged the Executive Committee, and particularly the general president, Thomas Foran, and general treasurer, William O'Brien, with making false and fraudulent declarations for the purpose of having the rules registered by the Registrar of Friendly Societies. It was on this matter that the Master of the Rolls used the strongest language in criticism of Larkin.

> It was very difficult indeed for Mr Foran and Mr O'Brien to remain calm in the box with charges of that kind hurled at their heads, and it only surprised me that they were so composed as they were. They were anxious to have their characters vindicated. I asked them to restrain themselves for the time. The time has now come when their character is to be vindicated, and I must say there was not a shadow of foundation for this gross charge that was made against them of falsely making a declaration for the purpose of having these rules registered, and I may go further and say this, that it brings the utmost discredit on the name of Mr Larkin that without any cause whatever he makes a charge of this kind against these two respectable gentlemen.

The judge was particularly scathing about the union's financial return for 1913, submitted by Larkin himself to the Registrar of Friendly Societies. The return was certainly signed by Larkin but almost certainly prepared by someone else. The return stated that there was a sum of £1,746 6s 9d in the Hibernian Bank; yet it had been proved in the court that there was no such sum in the bank in the union's account. The Master of the Rolls immediately absolved Larkin from any accusation of deliberately making a mis-statement.

> A mis-statement was made, but I am rather inclined to attribute it to an entire want of business capacity, to an entire absence of a sense of duty, to an entire absence of responsibility of the duties of his office. I cannot go further, but there, he signs a document absolutely false and apparently he does not seem to recognise the fact that once that document is shown he is a discredited witness in the case.

The court directed that Larkin should pay all the costs—likely to be very considerable, since the hearing had taken seven full days—except for a small portion in respect of one of the claims, which had been upheld.

For Larkin personally, the case had ended in disaster. It never seemed likely that the claims he had made had the faintest prospect of success from a legal point of view, even if he had retained his counsel. The legal disaster was aggravated by Larkin introducing irrelevant matters, related more to hostility to personalities than to the case but affording opportunities to his opponents to rake up various allegations made against him, including his conduct of the affairs of the union. Further, his wild, unsubstantiated allegations and in some instances unsavoury innuendoes against individuals elicited sympathy for those whom he sought to humble. The exchanges with the judge and with witnesses such as O'Brien and Foran usually resulted in the discomfiture of Larkin and, on occasion, his humiliation. Not a scintilla of a political or moral victory could be gleaned from this legal debacle.

There had long been a traditional objection by trade unionists to recourse to the courts for redressing grievances against colleagues or resolving internal differences within unions. The fact that Larkin had taken the case to the courts would have alienated many of his admirers in the trade unions. He would have been further isolated from colleagues because of his unfounded allegations against individuals who had opposed him and because of some of the revelations that emerged at the trial.

The proceedings in the court were reported at considerable length in the papers and would have been avidly read by active trade union members. To secure the widest dissemination of the evidence in the case, the National Executive Council (as the Executive Committee had become under the new rules) of the ITGWU published a 170-page book entitled *The Attempt to Smash the Irish Transport and General Workers' Union.* The book includes a full report of the court proceedings, with a lengthy introduction that, from internal evidence, was written by William O'Brien at his notoriously most bitter and caustic best (or worst).

The book also includes some sixteen appendixes, containing extracts from minute-books, reports of meetings and conferences, correspondence with Larkin, Connolly, Foran, and others, all carefully selected to present Larkin and his actions in the worst possible light.

On the face of it, the book is an indictment of Larkin, his autocratic attitudes, domineering approach to his colleagues and dictatorial methods in his running of the union, his personal vendettas and flagrant attacks on those who disagreed with him or questioned his judgment, and his bitter invective against enemies, real or imagined.

In the introduction it is claimed that the purpose of the book was to expose Larkin's attempt to 'smash' the union and to help to eject 'Larkinite poison' from the labour movement. In the carefully selected documents (many of them published for the first time) there is indeed a litany of Larkin's shortcomings and failings and an undoubtedly exaggerated portrayal of the more negative qualities that marked Larkin's personality. Larkin was larger than life in his defects as in his merits.

It would not be apparent from reading this ITGWU publication of 1924 that by then Larkin had blazed a trail of revolt for over a quarter of a century in Liverpool, Belfast, Dublin and the United States that had made him a world figure in the labour movement, an orator unsurpassed among his contemporaries, a hero who in a real sense had given a voice to a generation of downtrodden, oppressed people, preaching the gospel of discontent in two continents, achieving miracles among uneducated men and women, whom he contrived to raise from their knees through his leadership and inspiration.

Much of the content of what must be seen as the first round of O'Brien v. Larkin represents a rather squalid attempt to pull down a hero by exposing his failures and his follies and unmasking his pretensions while ignoring completely the enormous contribution he had made to the working-class struggle in Britain and Ireland and across the American continent. Here was a portrait of Larkin—warts only.

The question must be raised why Larkin had come to initiate the legal action against the union and its Executive Committee that was to have such disastrous consequences for Larkin and for the trade union movement and that was in effect to alienate him from almost the entire trade union leadership for a generation.

Larkin was a vain man, who did not tolerate criticism, whose path none, whether foe or friend, dare cross with impunity, a man whose ways were imperious. These characteristics explain in part only Larkin's behaviour on his return to Dublin, determined to take over the reins of office in the union he had founded and had dominated before he left Ireland, just as if he had never released them from his hands. As well, it is abundantly evident that he had no realisation of the many changes, and the magnitude and significance of the changes, that had taken place in his absence arising from the Easter Rising and the War of Independence, followed by the Civil War, and the partition of the country. In the intervening decade the relatively small union, largely Dublin-based, had become a nationwide organisation whose membership had increased tenfold.

On the basis of his leadership of the 1913 uprising, his experiences in America, including his involvement in the setting up of the Communist Party there, his trial and imprisonment, and his pending visit to Russia—to which he attached so much importance—Larkin's local difficulties with Alderman William O'Brien must have seemed a trifling affair. Here was he, a major figure in the international labour movement, beset by little men engaged in petty hostility to him. No doubt his conviction of the certainty of victory for the working class in the world struggle for power—already the revolution had triumphed in the east, with the red flag flying over Moscow's Kremlin, where lately the Russian Tsar had reigned—might well have dominated his vision of the future and put into perspective the petty antagonisms aroused against him by his enemies in Ireland.

It is probable that Larkin was encouraged and incited to seek the elimination of the new leadership, especially William O'Brien, by some of his close supporters, the old-guard Larkinites. Chief among these would have been his brother Peter, returned from Australia, where he had spent years in prison, and his sister Delia (now Delia Colgan), who had already been in bitter disagreement with the union leaders. Others might have included Seán O'Casey, and certainly Micheál Ó Maoláin, who had been employed as a clerk in Liberty Hall in 1915 in the Farm Labourers' Section and later in the Health Insurance Department until 1919. Ó Maoláin was one of Larkin's witnesses in the court case who had testified that he had not seen any notice about a meeting to amend the union's rules in 1918, that there had never been a meeting of the No. 1 Branch (the largest in the union) to pass the amendments, and that he had never received a ballot paper.

Other Larkin supporters, such as P. T. Daly, were personally hostile to O'Brien and may have been mainly concerned with paying off old scores. O'Brien's cold personality, combined with his administrative efficiency and concern for detail and his insistence on officials attending to their duties, provided fruitful soil for dislike of and hostility to him. Seán O'Casey was to write in *Innisfallen Fare Thee Well* (1949): 'He seemed a self-centred man, finding in himself all that was needed to live a cool and concentrated life ... The clever, sharp, shrewd mind at white heat behind the cold, pale mask, was forever boring a silent way through all opposition.'

O'Brien, though nominally the general treasurer of the union, was in effect the chief officer. The prolific capacity for gossip of many of the personalities in the labour movement in Dublin created a widespread belief that O'Brien was at the centre of every conspiracy and that he personified the hostility to Larkin for personal reasons of jealousy and ambition. That O'Brien was ambitious and aspired to ruling the union with an iron hand and, if he could, the wider trade union and labour movement, is not in doubt. Though he seemed not to worry about his personal popularity, or absence of it, he must have felt some jealousy of the position Larkin held in the eyes of the Dublin workers, especially the dockers, carters, labourers, and gas workers, who were the core of the union's membership in the capital city. In any direct confrontation between the two men—both autocratic, vain, opinionated—Larkin would certainly emerge victor in the battle for the hearts of the workers.

Emmet Larkin in his magisterial biography of Larkin had no doubt 'that the responsibility for forcing a split in the Irish Labour Movement was Larkin's, but whether the split was justified is a more difficult question.' He points to the miscalculations made by Larkin in his tussle for power with O'Brien. First of all, Larkin grossly overestimated O'Brien's influence and power in the union. Secondly, he unwisely sought to purge Thomas Foran as well as O'Brien, even though Foran had been the first president of the union and Larkin's closest colleague up to his departure for America, and still was by no means hostile to Larkin. Thirdly, Larkin overestimated his own influence in the union: he would have had little influence on members outside Dublin, who now constituted a majority. Fourthly, Larkin failed to realise that the main officials of the union, such as Richard Corish in Wexford, James Everett in Wicklow, and James Hickey in Cork, as well as many of the Dublin officials, supported the Executive Committee against him, and not because they were 'simply the tools of O'Brien.' Finally, Prof. Larkin points out, Larkin took little notice of the general feeling in the labour movement: two of the most influential men on the political side of the movement, Thomas Johnson and Thomas MacPartlin, sided with Foran and O'Brien and not out of hostility to Larkin—though this may not be wholly true of MacPartlin.[3]

It is true, as Prof. Larkin states, that there were larger questions reflected in the struggle for power, the two men mirroring in their personalities—one radical by temperament, the other conservative—two conceptions of trade unions: revolutionary and reformist. Time and circumstances, he argues, were on O'Brien's side and against Larkin.

One can agree that O'Brien took the view that trade unions should be seen as instruments of social change within the existing fabric of society. It is doubtful if Larkin—apart from the rhetoric—saw them exclusively as instruments to hasten the social revolution; this, however would certainly have been James Connolly's position. It is notable that in America, Larkin, unlike Connolly, was not directly associated with the truly revolutionary Industrial Workers of the World. Rather, in pursuit of the social revolution Larkin associated with the political left, joining the Socialist Party in 1917. Later, after the October Revolution in Russia, he helped to found a Communist Party. Back in Ireland, he was far from identifying with the objectives of the revolutionary wing of the socialist movement, such as it was.

Revolutionary rhetoric came readily to Larkin—indeed it has been said that he seemed to suffer a brainstorm when on a platform. No great insight was required to realise that in 1924 conditions in Ireland were not ripe for social revolution, however the term is construed. (It may be noted that later on Larkin was to lecture the world communist movement's leaders in Moscow about how unreal were their expectations of revolution in Europe.)

No, the disaster that befell Larkin does not need to be explained in terms of conflicting views on the role of trade unions or the part they could play in effecting revolutionary change: rather must it be found in more mundane, non-ideological factors. The reasons are to be found in Larkin's own failings and mistakes: his autocratic temperament—much exploited by O'Brien; his misjudgment of people and events; a deeply rooted antipathy to O'Brien; a belief, probably inculcated by his family and some of his closest colleagues, that he was the victim of a conspiracy by the group who by now controlled the union—his union; and inherent defects of personality that made it impossible for him to share control and accept decisions where these ran counter to his instinctive feelings.

Emmet Larkin's conclusion was that Larkin's position in 1923, 'whether considered from a tactical, practical, or ideological point of view, was untenable,' stands.[4] Of these, the ideological was the least significant.

The Attempt to Smash the Irish Transport and General Workers' Union, and especially the introduction, was a particularly nasty piece of work, calculated to damage Larkin's personal reputation and standing. Besides portraying his character and personality in wholly negative terms, it made no attempt to understand Larkin's position in the light of his well-known erratic and volatile temperament. The selective use of extracts from letters of James Connolly (letters that O'Brien suppressed for over half a century) gave an exaggerated picture of the differences between Larkin and Connolly; likewise the selective extracts from union minutes and reports— all seek to diminish Larkin and call in question his integrity. Nowhere in the introduction is a scintilla of credit given to Larkin for his role in building the union in the dark and difficult days leading to what was an uprising of Dublin's underclass in 1913.

Innuendoes and insinuations abound in the introduction and in many of the sixteen appendixes, not least those relating to members of Larkin's family.

Allegations about Larkin's 'extravagance' in spending, and about his priorities, are well exemplified by the references to what the introduction refers to as the adventure of Croydon Park, Fairview. The house and three acres had been leased for £250 a year by the union and was officially opened on Sunday 3 August 1913 with a 'Grand Temperance Fete and Children's Carnival'. Dancing, singing, music and games for the children marked the day. For Larkin, Croydon Park was to be a symbol of the better quality of life for workers and their families that was the objective of the union's activities on behalf of the working class. At Christmas 1913 three large marquees were pitched on the grounds, where five thousand children were fed and entertained. Sports were encouraged and a boxing team organised.

Here was the first attempt by a trade union in Ireland to bring colour, entertainment and recreation into the drab lives of workers' families. The *Manchester Guardian* certainly saw the leasing of Croydon Park in a positive light and praised the enlightened approach of Larkin, both with regard to the promotion of temperance—drink being a serious social problem in the slums—and a lively social life. In an editorial on 17 November 1913—written in reply to a letter from William Martin Murphy—the paper pointed out that

> with the exception perhaps of the Maison du Peuple in Brussels, no Labour headquarters in Europe has contributed so valuably to the brightening of the lives of the hard-driven workers around it as [Liberty Hall]. It is a hive of social life, keeps a band, and gives concerts and dances which are the delight of the poverty-stricken men and women who flock to it—people whose lives are probably more toil-worn and oppressed than those of any in our own industrial centres ... Croydon Park is to be converted next summer into a camping and recreation ground for the members of the Transport Union, their wives and families.

Much information is given in *The Attempt to Smash the Irish Transport and General Workers' Union* about costs and expenses incurred at Croydon Park, including details about the purchase of 'the cow and calf'. Presumably it was as an example of Larkin's profligacy that a letter to a seed merchant in Liverpool (2 April 1914) is given in an appendix:

> We are running a Co-operative Hostel here in Dublin. We have some 3 acres of gardens. I want to interest our people in the culture of vegetables and flowers, and window-box display.
> The gardens have been neglected for some years. We have vines and hot houses. I myself have not had the experience I would like in these matters.

We have two gardeners employed. I want to get good results, so as to encourage our people. Would it be too much trouble to ask you to interest yourself in the matter by sending me the best seeds, plants, etc., up to the value of £20 0s. 0d., delivered in Dublin, and also any information you could send me?

It was in Croydon Park that the first two companies of locked-out men recruited for a 'Citizen Army' paraded on 23 November 1913 under Captain Jack White. It was to Croydon Park that the men whose heads had been smashed in the police baton charges on Bloody Sunday 1913 were brought.

In the introduction to the book it is stated that 'Larkin with his wife, his family and his sister lived in Croydon Park rent free and that a cow was purchased out of Union funds so that he and his family might have a plentiful supply of milk. Miss Larkin was in full control of the mansion [sic] and gardens.' This brief quotation gives an indication of the level of argument that pervades the introduction. It is not pointed out that the Larkin family went to live there after they had been evicted from their home in Auburn Street as a result of participating in the 'pay no rent campaign', or that the family—including four children, the eldest nine years of age—lived in fact in the stables.

Desmond Greaves, the biographer of James Connolly and historian of the early years of the ITGWU, has given by far the most likely explanation for Larkin's frequently erratic conduct and irrational behaviour, which led to his making wild statements at times. In *The Irish Transport and General Workers' Union: The Formative Years, 1909–1923* (1982), Greaves refers a number of times to Larkin's personal temperament and the consequences of his 'vigorous, rumbustious' character.

A study of his behaviour through the years suggests there was a sensitive, vulnerable streak in his nature. He could be hurt. He kept going by dramatising himself. He caused much mystification on those occasions when he abruptly changed roles, often on the spur of the moment. He was volatile, enthusiastic, gregarious and full of exuberant idealism. But his upbringing in the slums of Liverpool had not been such as would stiffen to complete self-confidence his undoubtedly creative spirit.[5]

Greaves, pointing out that it was Hippocrates who first distinguished the type of person he called 'choleric', notes that in his description we can recognise Larkin.

He could display immense energy, almost superhuman dynamism. Yet he could be plunged into profound gloom and depression ... To be deprived of spontaneous action was a torture to him. It threw him into a self-pitying mood, and this could be broken by sudden explosions of resentment.[6]

Greaves describes Larkin in 1911 as being 'in the high spring of his career, bustling, businesslike and confident.'

He had a vision of a great bloodless revolution in which the half-starved ill-clothed denizens of the slums would win a new life that would include leisure and culture. He thought that all that was necessary was the will, and he made himself the embodiment of that will.[7]

As Greaves rightly asserts, the 'old' Transport Union reached the zenith of its influence in the summer of 1913. The total membership was probably in the region of thirty thousand. Greaves notes that

Larkin had recovered his spirits and was indeed showing an optimism bordering on euphoria. It was as if he had continually to reassure himself. He swung between doubt and uncertainty, each larger than the reality demanded.[8]

From the recollections of those who worked closely with Larkin, it is clear that he did indeed go through periods of acute depression, which as often as not were followed by moments of euphoric exhilaration. Periods of depression are well documented. The seeming failure of the lock-out struggle precipitated one such attack of depression and was so acknowledged by William O'Brien. Emmet Larkin suggests that his self-confidence was severely shaken and that he required reassurance that he was still needed.

Larkin himself testified that he was suffering from overstrain and nervous reaction. In a speech in June 1914 he said: 'No-one under God's sun knows what I have been through.' Explaining that he was speaking under the influence of 'strong emotion and physical disabilities,' he told his colleagues that he had been fighting depression and physical difficulties. When he spoke in Trafalgar Square, London, on 5 July he said he did so 'against doctor's orders.' P. T. Daly contrasted his physical condition then with that of the vigorous young man he was six years before, when he first came to Dublin. James Connolly too conceded that Larkin was overstrung, seeing opposition where there was none, and that he needed a rest.

On this matter of Larkin's temperament, the last word might rest with Greaves, who, pondering what he termed 'the mystery of Larkin's character', concluded:

Was it perhaps the very opposite of what it seemed to be—like the bluster of the small child who says: 'I am big and I am strong and I can knock the house down'?—was it a condition of his activity that he should over-compensate deep uncertainties and inhibitions? If this is so, his life had a tragic aspect. We should perhaps see him as a sensitive spirit deeply hurt by the failure of his plans, a man whose exaggerated self-assurance was required to negate and transform the doubt and immaturity within. His speeches bristled with inaccuracies. He could thrust reality unceremoniously aside. He had a vision of a world remoulded. From his own contradictory character came his capacity, absent in many men of greater intellectual attainment, to personify to the underdog the underdog transfigured, freed from the restraints imposed on his personality by his economic position. It was the softer side of Larkin that attracted the lifelong admiration of a perceptive artist like O'Casey, whose eyes began to sparkle as soon as his name was mentioned.[9]

When considering Larkin's behaviour after his return from America, it must be realised that, apart from his gruelling experiences of poverty and hardship endured through his years of campaigning and agitation throughout the United States, he had also spent years in jail there, for a time in the notorious Clinton jail in Dannemora, where conditions were extremely harsh. The prisoners there were for the most part long-term prisoners, some of them dangerous. The left-wing journalist Agnes Smedley visited Larkin there and wrote that he was ageing fast; he was then only forty-six.

In Sing Sing he had been visited by Frank Harris and Charlie Chaplin, the latter quoting Harris about how it depressed him to see 'a courageous character like Jim Larkin reduced to prison discipline.' Larkin's psychological state and his proneness to periods of depression cannot have been helped by his imprisonment.

Larkin's legal action against the officials of the ITGWU had concluded in February 1924, when judgment was given against him. In the following year he was again involved in legal proceedings, this time a libel action. It was taken by Thomas Johnson, the leader of the Labour Party in the Dáil and secretary of the Irish Labour Party and Trades Union Congress (to give it its formal title at that time), in respect of an alleged libel in the *Irish Worker*.

Johnson, self-effacing and modest in his manner and completely non-confrontational in his relations with those whom he opposed, was a most unlikely person to begin proceedings against an opponent, whatever the provocation. It is most likely that he was pressed by his colleagues to take action more for the purpose of damning Larkin than vindicating himself against the outrageous allegations made against him in Larkin's paper. In the event, the action was to be decisive in isolating Larkin in the labour movement and in preventing him from taking his seat in Dáil Éireann, to which he was to be elected.

The statements made in the *Irish Worker* about Johnson were grossly libellous—as well as patently ridiculous—even when allowance is made for the exaggerated and slanderous language that was the stock in trade of post-Civil War rhetoric in the politics of the time. Although in this instance it was directed at Thomas Johnson, it was simply an exaggerated example of the campaign of vilification indulged in by the *Irish Worker* against a number of the leaders of the labour movement. In the case of Johnson in particular it had no justification, even in the heated political atmosphere that might have afforded some excuse for impassioned rhetoric.

Abuse was typical of the tirades that enlivened the columns of the *Irish Worker*, even if they failed to enlighten its readers. The Labour Party was referred to as 'the God-Save-the-King Irish Labour Party' and as an imperialist appendage to the pro-British Free State government. It jibed that 'Johnson says to the worker, love thy boss, he is a good fellow.'

Ironically, it was Johnson's Liverpool birth that was singled out in the paper as justification for the regular tirades against him. Larkin himself had been born in Liverpool, though he claimed he had been born in Newry and may have convinced himself that he had been born there. After his return from America in 1923, Larkin's enemies contrasted Larkin's birth in Liverpool with the then assumption that Connolly had been born in Monaghan. Though the fact that Connolly had been born in Edinburgh must have been known to close associates, such as William O'Brien, the fact was never revealed publicly until Desmond Greaves published the evidence in the *Irish Democrat* and in his biography of Connolly (1965).

It was an article in the issue of the *Irish Worker* for 24 May 1924 that was the subject of the libel action. The article referred to a speech in the Dáil on unemployment and was headed 'Johnson incites to chaos'. The leader of the Labour Party, also then the leader of the opposition, had said that 'this evil of unemployment was as serious as that other problem that confronted the Government two years ago [the Civil War], and would have to be dealt with in the same manner: they would have to raise a civil and industrial army.' This was perhaps an infelicitous manner of expressing what he had in mind, but the writer in the *Irish Worker* chose to construe it as meaning

> that the workers thrown out of work as a direct result of the murderous and suicidal policy of the government, of which Mr. Johnson is one of the advisers, must be shot down as 'Irregulars' [Republican forces in the Civil War] were, in the event of their agitating for work. It is time labour dealt with this English traitor … Months ago we told our readers that Johnson was going over to capitalism and by that we meant his services were in the market. He has now gone further than any capitalist dare have gone, for his incitement to murder the workers is the most bloody-minded and callous statement in our time …

Pointing out that Johnson was a member of the Irish Union of Distributive Workers and Clerks, the article asked rhetorically what the rank and file of the union intended to do about it, adding that 'if they do not get rid of this scoundrel at once they will get the bullet and the bayonet in reward for their "loyalty" to what he stands for.' Johnson's suggestion for a civil and industrial army was interpreted as a call for 'an army of scabs to break any strike or lock-out precipitated by the bosses of Irish capitalism.' The article concluded:

> If this does not open the eyes of the workers to the chronic ruffianism of Johnson, there is nothing for them but a dose of the lead which Johnson promises to those who dare to look for work.

Before the action came to trial, Johnson was to be the subject of further vituperative abuse by Larkin. In the *Irish Worker* of 7 June 1924 Larkin welcomed the legal action by the 'English anti-Irishman' and promised him 'an experience such as he had never before "enjoyed" when we get him before a jury.' The following week Larkin claimed that 'had it not been for the pestiferous Englishman and his satellites we would never have had the great betrayal, and the massacre of our people by the Cosgravian job-vultures ... Johnson, hostile Englishman, imperialist, aider and abettor of capitalists, has his back to the wall, and we have driven him there. Soon we shall see the end.'

Johnson's claim for damages of £1,000 each against Larkin and the Gaelic Press, the printers of the *Irish Worker*, was heard in the High Court in November 1924. Larkin accepted responsibility for the offending article while admitting that it had been written by his son, James Larkin Junior. If he himself had written the article, he told the court, it would have been written with more bitterness and invective.

The court awarded Johnson £500 damages against Larkin and £500 against the printers. (This would now be equivalent to about £17,500.) Larkin refused to pay the damages and was once again declared bankrupt.

So it was that the failure of Larkin's action against the ITGWU, compounded by the Johnson libel action, marked the end of any hope Larkin may have had of again leading the Irish labour movement. Not only had he alienated practically all the leaders of the movement, he had also distanced himself from the mass of trade union members. For the next twenty years or so he was confined to giving leadership to the newly formed Workers' Union of Ireland, in a measured and far from strident way, with only occasional forays into the wider issues confronting the labour movement. He was to withdraw completely from involvement in the international movement. His future lay almost wholly with keeping his largely Dublin-based union afloat as a viable organisation, served by a few ill-paid officials and maintained by the devoted loyalty of the old-guard Larkinites and a handful of young disciples.

Larkinism had ceased to be an effective force in national life and scarcely any more so in the political and industrial labour movement. It survived only in the hearts of Dublin's working women and men.

Chapter 41

Workers of the World

Early in 1976, hitherto confidential government papers from the setting up of the Provisional Government of the Irish Free State in 1922 were deposited in the State Paper Office (now National Archives), Dublin. Among them was a file (S2009) containing material relating to James Larkin. The last document in the file is dated 18 July 1924 and is from the Director of Intelligence.

> I have the honour to report that the above-named [James Larkin] has been elected as Irish Representative on the Communist Commitern [sic] Third Internationale [sic]. This is the first time that Ireland has been represented on the Council. Larkin is at present in close touch with Arthur McManus, an organiser of the British Communist Party and Representative of Great Britain on the Commitern of the 3rd Internationale. Larkin would appear to be senior to McManus and can vote on occasions when the latter cannot ...

The background to Larkin's first visit to Russia in 1924 and his election to the Executive Council of the Communist International or Comintern must be outlined.

In 1914, V. I. Lenin, writing of Larkin, described the Dublin events of 1913 as 'a turning point in the history of the labour movement and Socialism in Ireland.'

> In the wake of the Irish bourgeois scoundrels who are celebrating their 'national' victory there followed the Irish proletariat that is awakening to class consciousness. It has found a talented leader in the person of Comrade Larkin, the Secretary of the Irish Transport Union. Possessing remarkable oratorical talent, a man of seething Irish energy, Larkin has performed miracles among the unskilled workers ...
>
> A new spirit has been awakened among the Irish labour unions. The unskilled workers have introduced hitherto unparalleled animation in the trade unions. Even the women have begun to organise—a thing hitherto unknown to Catholic Ireland. Dublin showed promise of becoming one of the foremost towns in the whole of Great Britain as far as the organisation of the workers is concerned. This country, bearing a double and triple national yoke, was beginning to be transformed into a land of the organised army of the proletariat.

Larkin's anti-war agitation in America, from his arrival there in November 1914 right up to the end of the war, had put him firmly in the front rank of socialist leaders who were to support the October Revolution. After the return of the famous journalist John Reed, who had witnessed the October events in St Petersburg and who was to become with Larkin a founder of the Communist Labor Party in America, Larkin openly proclaimed himself a Bolshevik.

When on temporary release from jail in New York in May 1922, Larkin had received a congratulatory telegram from Zinoviev, president of the Communist International, who was second only to Lenin in the Bolshevik hierarchy: 'The Communist International sends its warmest greeting to the undaunted fighter released from the "democratic" prisons.' The same year Larkin was elected to the Moscow Soviet.

As a leading international labour figure who had ardently supported the revolution, Larkin's support was more than welcome for the beleaguered Bolsheviks, and on his release from jail early in 1923 his first idea seems to have been to visit Moscow. In the National Archives file referred to there is a despatch dated 20 April 1923 from Gloster Armstrong of the British Consulate-General in New York to Lord Curzon, the Foreign Secretary—and which was sent to the Provisional Government of the Irish Free State on 10 May—indicating that Larkin had requested a passport 'with provision first to visit Germany, Austria and Russia on business matters before returning to his own country.' However, he was granted a passport valid for the United Kingdom only.

Four days after Larkin's arrival in Ireland—he had first spent some days in London with Communist Party leaders—he told the Executive Committee of the ITGWU, of which he was still general secretary, that he was 'going to Russia immediately, where he had important business to do.' He even announced that he would tender his resignation as general secretary on the following day. However, he was persuaded to change his mind on this. It was in fact to be over a year before he travelled to Russia, and by then he had been expelled from the ITGWU.

In Ireland, those in the labour movement in the twenties who supported the international communist movement—a minute number indeed—were in some disarray. In October 1921 the leaders of the Socialist Party of Ireland, William O'Brien and Cathal O'Shannon, were expelled following a take-over by a group led by Roderic Connolly, the 21-year-old son of James Connolly. By this time the SPI had become moribund anyway, even though in 1919 it had proclaimed that its programme was as uncompromisingly Marxian as ever.

In November the name of the SPI was changed to Communist Party of Ireland, with Roderic Connolly as president, Walter Carpenter, the son of an old colleague of James Connolly, as secretary, and Nora Connolly as treasurer. The CPI included in its ranks—briefly—the writer Liam O'Flaherty, who was to lead the occupation of the Rotunda, Dublin, by unemployed workers, hoisting the red flag there, and Seán MacLoughlin, its organiser, the fifteen-year-old boy commandant of Easter Week who had been promoted to that rank by the military command at its last meeting in Moore Street following the evacuation of the GPO. Some support for the party's position was forthcoming from Peadar O'Donnell, a member of the IRA Executive, and Liam Mellows. Ernest Blythe, a minister in the Provisional Government, claimed in the paper *The Free State* (22 April 1922) that the only men among the Republicans who had a definite line of policy were the Bolsheviks. Roderic Connolly was to describe the CPI as more noisy than numerous and admitted that after nearly two years it had a total of between thirty and fifty active members, having made hardly ten converts to the party.

The CPI was accepted as the Irish section of the Communist International, and Connolly attended its Second Congress, when he met Lenin, who showed him his copy of his father's book *Labour in Irish History*. He also attended the Third and Fourth Congresses, in 1921 and 1922.

Harmony did not prevail among the comrades. At the first congress of the CPI, on 20 January 1923, Connolly, its president and editor of the *Workers' Republic*, was not elected to the party executive. However, he was installed as political secretary in November 1923; but shortly afterwards the Communist International ordered the party's dissolution.

Soon after Larkin's return to Ireland he was to attack the CPI members as 'little wasps'. He had his own ideas about who should represent Ireland at the Comintern. Expelled from the ITGWU on 14 March 1924, he departed for Moscow on 27 May to attend the Fifth Congress of the Communist International, held in the Kremlin. He spoke at only two of the more than thirty sessions, and what he had to say was unlikely to have enthused the leadership. His contributions were certainly not what might have been expected of him. Larkin always was his own man.

On the basis of the Abridged Report of the Fifth Congress, quoted by Emmet Larkin in *James Larkin: Irish Labour Leader*, Larkin spoke twice. On 24 June he supported the British Communist Party's contention that it should seek a united front with the Labour Party. To do otherwise, he said, 'we should become sectarian and that was opposed to the whole spirit of Leninism.' (Lenin had died the previous year.) The following week (1 July) he made his second intervention in the discussions.

> I mount this tribune with some deference and only at the request of Comrade Zinoviev [president of the Communist International] who said the Congress was interested in Ireland. I have failed to notice it. The Congress seems interested only with those parties which have the largest membership. The Irish proletariat, however, rose in 1916, not 1917 ... I appeal to you comrades, to turn your eyes to the Irish proletariat. We are not confined to Ireland. We have millions in England, Scotland, the United States, Australia and South Africa. It is the duty of the Communist International to get this great mass, mostly proletarians, interested in the great Communist movement.

This was a theme that Larkin had frequently referred to in America.

At the closing session, Larkin was elected one of the twenty-five members of the Executive Council, which was responsible for the affairs of the International between congresses. He did not, however, attend any meetings of the Executive Council except its last, in 1928, when he was in

Moscow for the Sixth Congress. Incidentally, Larkin was listed as Brown in the English abridgment of the Congress report: this was his wife's maiden name.

In Moscow, Larkin also attended the Third Congress of the Red International of Labour Unions or Profintern, to which the new union founded by his brother Peter in Dublin during his absence in Moscow was later to affiliate, at least nominally. At this congress, Larkin, no doubt to his hosts' surprise, concentrated on the importance of the co-operative movement to the trade unions in their revolutionary struggle, giving as a reason the mistake that trade unions make of throwing 'the masses into the fight without giving a thought to their stomachs.' He also, not surprisingly, given his background, stressed the importance of transport workers as a truly international revolutionary force.

However, in two further contributions Larkin was to refer scathingly to propositions put forward by the leadership of the Profintern, notably its head, Losovsky. He expressed surprise that the Second (Amsterdam) International should have been accused of 'unreality' while 'we have been nursing all the illusions that have been spread' in the course of the session. He referred specifically to the view of some comrades that 'England was on the verge of revolution, that the revolution was already knocking at the door.' This view he openly ridiculed, while accepting that there were some people ready to struggle for revolutionary goals, but these were convinced that the British Empire must be destroyed, 'for otherwise, working-class humanity will have no hope of emancipation.'

It was in a discussion on the 'strategy of strikes', however, that Larkin came most into conflict with the leaders and into a direct clash with Losovsky. Objecting strongly to any firm analogy being drawn between military strategy and the strategy of strikes, he asked:

Is this a new application of Leninism? Does one have to study Klausewitz [sic] in order to galvanise the working classes into action? If so, why not follow the Hindenburg school? I have taken part in a great many strikes and I dare assert that I know their mechanics.

Rubbing salt into the wound, he added:

When some one tells me that a strike is a movement that can be run on paper, or directed from an information bureau, I assert that those who say that don't know what they are talking about. One must see men as they are, one must understand human emotions, the psychology of the workers.

Losovsky would not have approved of what he had heard from Larkin. He was to return the compliment a few years later when he sneeringly asked Larkin 'if Ireland had the very best revolutionaries and the very worst reactionaries in Europe?' as Larkin seemed to imply.

It was during this visit that Larkin was presented with a scarlet banner richly brocaded and embroidered with gold thread. On Larkin's return to

337

Dublin on 25 August 1924 the banner featured in a welcome-home procession. Next day the *Freeman's Journal* reported that on one side of the banner was inscribed in Russian, *Greetings to the Revolutionary Transport Workers of Dublin from the Moscow Transport Workers* and on the other the slogan *Unite in the Soviet Federated Republics*. This banner had long been assumed lost or destroyed, but it was found, in perfect condition, in 1997 and was included in the Larkin Exhibition in the National Library that year.

A wild and strident speech in the Mansion House, Dublin, on his return about his activities in Russia was extensively reported in the *Freeman's Journal*. It could not be taken seriously and certainly not literally. It did great damage to his reputation, helped further to isolate him in the labour movement, and gave fuel to his enemies preparing the pyre for his leadership ambitions.

It soon became clear that any hope the Comintern might have had of Larkin being the focus for a mass communist movement in Ireland was forlorn indeed. The very idea was absurd, given not only the temperament and personality of Larkin but also the objective conditions prevailing in the country. In any case, Larkin's interest lay more in the trade union movement than in politics or ideology. The trade union movement was then in serious decline, and even more so the political labour movement. An industrial base was completely lacking in the Free State, which was overwhelmingly agricultural. Social and political conditions in Britain and in Europe generally were not conducive to mass agitation or social revolution, even though the Continent and America were about to enter the throes of the great depression.

Not least there was the situation in Ireland where an intensely conservative and authoritarian church exercised enormous influence and power in all spheres of activity, a church to which the state made no secret of its abject submission in all temporal spheres.

Seán O'Casey explained his opting out of labour activities in the nineteen-twenties in a letter he wrote to Prof. Ronald Ayling (26 January 1960), which echoes Larkin's position.

> Ireland had altered for Larkin and for me … I saw unconsciously that a change was here; that Ireland would have new masters, and that a battle would begin all over again against different enemies; and that many of these enemies were in the Labour Movement; and that Jim was spancelled; he no longer had the power of past days, that a Home Government backed by the Church, plus the O'Briens and Forans, etc., would hold him in check; tho' I didn't think the Church would get such a grip on Ireland's throat.

An emissary from the Comintern, Bob Stewart, one of the founders of the Communist Party of Great Britain, came to Dublin in January 1925 in the hope that a communist party might be established in co-operation with Larkin. He was to remain some five months, during part of which time he stayed with Larkin. His mission was an utter failure. In his autobiography, *Breaking the Fetters* (1967), Stewart concluded, naïvely, that all that was needed for the successful launching of a mass Marxist party was Larkin's acceptance of a manifesto that had been drawn up but which Larkin neither accepted nor rejected but simply ignored. 'My own opinion is that Larkin would never accept the democracy of a disciplined Marxist party. He always had to be in the centre of the stage all the time, and so to join a party where the emphasis is put on collective work was not for him.'

Larkin had set up the Irish Worker League in September 1923. As its title indicates, it was intended to be a social organisation built around the *Irish Worker*, which Larkin had relaunched the previous June. No doubt he had in mind the pre-war Daily Herald League in Britain, which had been so supportive of the Dublin workers in 1913 and of Larkin's Fiery Cross campaign. In effect the IWL was to be an adjunct of the paper and far from being an active political organisation. Though it could on occasion rouse some enthusiasm among Larkin's supporters, such as the demonstration following the death of Lenin, when six thousand marched in Dublin, its activities, such as they were, were intermittent, ineffectual, and of minor importance.

As an organisation it scarcely existed. About five hundred people attended the founding rally in September 1923, and its first congress took place in April 1924, when it adopted a constitution that declared for a workers' republic. Larkin was its honorary president. Among the executive members were the world heavyweight boxing champion, Jack Dempsey, who knew Larkin in America, and Muriel MacSwiney, the widow of Terence MacSwiney, who had campaigned in America for Larkin's release from jail. It seems to have had only two branches, one in Dublin and the other in London. It was said that the London branch was more active than the one in Dublin! Its secretary was Seán Murray, an IRA commandant in County Antrim during the War of Independence, and among the active members was Captain Jack White, one-time chairman of the Irish Citizen Army. Apparently Larkin seldom attended meetings of the league, even on the few occasions on which they were convened.

The failure of the Irish Worker League as a political organisation, though evident to the Communist International, did not prevent it retaining its official support. However, the league had an important success in the general election of September 1927. It ran three candidates in Dublin: Larkin in North Dublin; his son James Larkin Junior in Dublin County; and John Lawlor, the general president of the WUI, in South Dublin. The three candidates between them won 12,500 votes, compared with 9,000 votes for the Labour Party candidates, who included the leader of the Labour Party, Tom Johnson, who lost his seat.

Larkin had urged first-preference votes for Fianna Fáil in other constituencies and none for Labour. The Labour Party responded, according to Mike Milotte in *Communism in Modern Ireland* (1984), with a campaign of personal abuse depicting Larkin as 'an English communist Orangeman who took his orders from Moscow.'

Larkin was elected to the Dáil on the first count in the eight-seat constituency. However, he was unable to take his seat, because, as an undischarged bankrupt, he was disqualified. Ironically, his bankruptcy was due to the costs incurred in the legal actions taken against him. Johnson's loss of his seat was in no small part due to the intervention of Young Jim Larkin (who polled a respectable 2,126 votes to Johnson's 3,626) in his constituency.

In February 1928 Larkin made his second and last visit to the Soviet Union to attend—for the first time—the Executive Committee of the Comintern, to which he had been elected in 1924. At one of the sessions, during a debate at which both Stalin and Trotsky spoke, Bukharin, who had replaced Zinoviev as president of the International, asked Larkin if he would like to speak. According to Jack Carney, who had been the IWL's representative on the Executive Committee in the years 1925–26, Larkin declined the invitation, explaining that 'the issue was one between the men and women of Russia and that it would be an impertinence on his part to take sides' [in the Stalin-Trotsky debate].

Larkin was unable to remain in Moscow for the Sixth Congress of the International, as he had to return to Dublin to fight the by-election caused by his disqualification. He expected that Fianna Fáil would not contest the election but would throw its weight behind his candidature; he was incensed when that party nominated Kathleen Clarke, who earlier had been an antagonist of Larkin, as its candidate. Larkin came third in the by-election.

Thus ended for a decade Larkin's electoral hopes and effectively ended the hapless existence of the Irish Worker League, which maintained but a nominal existence till 1932. It resulted too in a new departure by the Communist International towards Ireland. Early in 1930 Tom Bell, accompanied by Bob Stewart, arrived in Ireland to attempt to salvage something from the debacle caused by the stubbornness of the Communist International in backing Larkin to lead a communist movement here. Tom Bell had been a close associate of James Connolly in the Scottish Socialist Labour Party early in the century.

The opening up of the hitherto secret files of the Comintern in Moscow in recent years has thrown light on the relations between Larkin and the International. These files have been researched by Dr Barry McLoughlin of the Documentation Centre of Austrian Resistance in Vienna and Dr Emmet O'Connor of the University of Ulster. In *Saothar*, the journal of the Irish Labour History Society (1996), they published some preliminary conclusions from their research.

It now appears that in his relationship with the Comintern and the Profintern, Larkin was really interested in promoting the interests of the Irish Worker League and the Workers' Union of Ireland. The main issues that he or his representative in Moscow, Jack Carney, were concerned with were pretty parochial and neither national nor international. They both quarrelled with the Comintern bureaucracy about four issues: financial assistance to ease the dire financial plight of the WUI; intervention by the Communist Party of Great Britain in affairs in Ireland; the employment policy in Ireland of a commercial company sponsored by the Soviet Union (Russian Oil Products); and the role of British unions in the Free State and particularly the organisation of railway workers. Apparently much of the extensive material now available deals with these issues. What seems to emerge from the article by McLoughlin and O'Connor is that it was Larkin who was seeking to use his Comintern connections to advance the interests of his union, rather than the Comintern using Larkin to advance the cause of communism in Ireland.

In a later issue of *Saothar* (1997), McLoughlin underlines the fact that in the late twenties relations between Larkin and both the Comintern and the Profintern were 'extremely strained'. He explains Larkin's estrangement from the Moscow 'centre' as follows:

> Basically Larkin, like older Communist leaders with a strong trade union or syndicalist background, entered Comintern and Profintern politics when discussion in such bodies … was open and vociferous. He hardly fitted into a working relationship which had not been shaped by developments in the capitalist West but by the exigencies of Russian politics, namely Stalin's consolidation as dictator in the years 1927–29.

James Larkin seems not to have had any association with the Revolutionary Workers' Groups or the (second) Communist Party of Ireland, even though his son, Jim Larkin Junior, stood as a communist candidate in the Dublin Corporation elections in 1930 and was chairman of the founding conference of the Communist Party of Ireland in 1933. Nor had he any connection with the international communist movement after 1930.

Chapter 42

Larkin and the Workers' Union of Ireland

The Irish Transport and General Workers' Union was brought to birth by James Larkin quietly enough in 'a room in a tenement in Townsend Street, with a candle in a bottle for a torch and a billycan of tea with a few buns for a banquet,' as Seán O'Casey put it. By contrast, the Workers' Union of Ireland was born in the stress of industrial struggle on the quays of Dublin.

Larkin had left for Moscow on 27 May 1924. Over the previous weeks there had been dramatic developments in the trade union movement. For one thing, there had been the expulsion of Larkin from the ITGWU, of which he had been general secretary from its foundation in 1909, though for over nine of the years since then he had been in America. A disastrous split in the trade union movement was at hand.

A dispute had broken out in the Alliance and Dublin Consumers' Gas Company in the middle of May 1924. It arose out of the refusal of a clerk who had been promoted to give up his membership of the ITGWU. Strike action had been sanctioned by the secretary of the No. 1 Branch, John O'Neill; but William O'Brien, now general secretary, refused strike pay, on the grounds that the section had placed control of the dispute in 'the hands of a non-member' of the union (O'Brien seemingly could not bring himself even to refer to him by name), James Larkin. The offence of the gas workers was that, by ballot of 407 to 44, they had invited Larkin to attend a meeting in the Mansion House. The Gas Company subsequently made an agreement satisfactory to the workers, to which the union was not a party.

Before the settlement, forty-five of Larkin's supporters, led by Barney Conway, had occupied Liberty Hall, which was promptly surrounded by the military, who arrived with an armoured car and a lorry on which a machine-gun was mounted. The men were arrested. Larkin, for the last time, spoke from the window of Liberty Hall, as he had done so often in the past, and the next morning called a strike that paralysed the port, calling it off only when the arrested men had been released on bail. They were charged with unlawful occupation, but the charges were not sustained. However, on their refusal to post £5 each for their good behaviour, they were sentenced to a month in jail. Reuters news agency reported that 'the police had taken elaborate precautions to prevent a disturbance in the vicinity of the court, where a crowd of several hundred people had collected.'[1]

Three days after Larkin left Dublin for Russia, his brother Peter issued a notice in the name of the Port, Gas and General Workers' Provisional Committee, addressed to members of the ITGWU, stating that it would receive all union contributions until further notice. The split was now open. The *Irish Worker* (14 June 1924) carried the report of a speech by Peter Larkin giving the reasons why the rank and file had decided to take things into their own hands and set up the Provisional Committee. The following day, Sunday 15 June, at a meeting in Beresford Place, Peter Larkin launched the Workers' Union of Ireland.

It should be pointed out that before his departure, Larkin had given explicit directions that there was not to be a break with the ITGWU. Emmet Larkin quotes the 'Memoir' prepared for him by Jack Carney in 1953 to the effect that Larkin had told Peter Larkin that under no circumstances was he 'to allow the members of the Union to break away from the ITGWU.' Young Jim Larkin confirmed this to Dr Larkin.[2]

Larkin did not want a break, possibly deluding himself that the membership would sweep him back into control of the union and oust O'Brien. Even after his expulsion, he described himself as general secretary, and continued to address branch meetings.

With regard to the name of the new union, it is of interest that it was similar to that of the union founded by Tom Mann in 1898, the Workers' Union of Great Britain and Ireland. Jim Larkin had assisted Mann in setting up the Liverpool Branch of that union.

The rules of the Workers' Union of Ireland were registered with the Registrar of Friendly Societies on 15 July 1924 by Peter Larkin on behalf of a provisional executive committee, application for registration having been made on 1 July. The date of commencement of the union was given as 1 June 1924. The first rule was that the union 'existed to organise the workers of Ireland for the attainment of full economic freedom'; otherwise the rules were the usual ones for a trade union.

The trades and occupations organised by the WUI, as listed in the first return to the Registrar, were 'dockers, coal, carters, builders, bakeries, public services, distributive and productive, and miscellaneous.' The members whose signatures were appended to the rules registered by the Registrar were Andrew Baker, George Caliph, Francis Rankin, John Doyle, Vincent Atkinson, Bernard Costello, Michael Costello, and Michael S. Sheppard.

The weekly contribution was six pence for men and four pence for women. Dispute pay was fixed at 15 shillings for men and 10 shillings for women for the first ten weeks of dispute and 10 shillings for men and 7 shillings for women for a further ten weeks.

Rooms were secured by the Provisional Committee at the corner of Luke Street on the south quays. The committee consisted of Michael Whitty, James Mitchell, Denis Redmond, Peter Larkin, and John Kenny. There were five provisional trustees: John Dempsey, Henry Fitzsimon, Bernard Conway, Patrick Forde, and John Ruth.

Soon the head office moved to 31 Marlborough Street, which was named Unity Hall. Jim Larkin was made general secretary, taking up the position on 25 August 1924 on his return from Moscow. The Workers'

Union of Ireland was henceforth to be known proudly by its members as Larkin's Union. John Lawlor was general president and Peter Larkin national organiser. Ciarán King acted as general treasurer.

In its first return to the Registrar for the six months ending December 1924, the union's assets included some office furniture and a Crossley car. Its income for the half-year was £9,478, of which more than half (£5,220) was spent on dispute pay and £3,160 on general working expenses. It ended the year with £472 in its general funds.

The total number of members on its books was given as 15,754. It seems that about two-thirds of the Dublin membership of the ITGWU had joined the WUI on its foundation, though some of these would have returned later. There were twenty-seven branches, all but five in Dublin city and county; the others were in Abbeyfeale, Bray, Dundalk, Nenagh, and Roscrea. For the entire period that Jim Larkin was general secretary, the WUI membership was confined largely to the Dublin area.

Following the setting up of the WUI there developed sporadic conflicts between the two unions, and great hostility was often shown by members to their fellows in the opposing union. Dublin was to be the scene of inter-union disputes that shocked the city. Disputes in the docks, the coal trade, the building industry and the cinemas arose from the ITGWU seeking to oust WUI members from their jobs and the WUI striking against the employment of ITGWU members. Passions ran high, and physical conflict was not rare. Strong loyalties developed in the course of these disputes, which were to leave bitter legacies, persisting for two decades.

The early years of the WUI's existence were spent in disputes with varied employers, with the union resisting wage cuts and resolving workers' grievances arising from the new-found strength of the employers, which was due to the deteriorating economic position, the inter-union rivalries, and the deep divisions in the trade union movement. They were not glorious days for the movement. Emmet Larkin summarised the position: 'The two rival unions continued to engage in a type of guerrilla warfare with jurisdictional sniping and resulting work stoppages the order of the day.'[3]

The climax to these inter-union disputes came in July 1925, just a year after the foundation of the WUI. There was a lock-out by the Coal Merchants' Association, which announced that the lock-out would continue 'until a satisfactory guarantee is obtained that the men employed in the coal yards will work amicably together.'

In August the Dublin Employers' Federation pledged financial aid to the coal merchants. The managing director of the British and Irish Steam Packet Company alleged that 'Mr. Larkin demands the right to become the sole dictator of the wage-earners of Dublin,' words echoing those of William Martin Murphy in 1913. The *Irish Times* thundered editorially that 'Larkin's triumph would be the triumph of anarchy in the Free State' and reminded its readers that 'Mr. Larkin does not conceal his associations with a malignant and "alien power".'[4] By early September the coal merchants had in effect defeated the attempts of the WUI to resist their lock-out, after a physical confrontation between WUI members with men unloading coal at the Alexandra Basin.

During the dispute with the coal merchants the union was to show some business acumen and tactical ingenuity. At the time of the strike there was £130 in the funds. Larkin formed the Unity Coal Company to import coal from Britain and sell it to the poor and needy more cheaply than the merchants and out of the surplus would pay strike pay. But he didn't pay the bills. The merchants in Liverpool threatened that no more coal would be sent unless they got £12,000. The story goes that Larkin crossed to Liverpool to meet the merchants, who offered him a cigar. He took two and pointed out to them that unless they continued to export coal to his co-op in Dublin the strike would collapse and then they would never get any money. He got the coal.

There is no little difficulty in recounting the history of the WUI over its first fifteen years or so, for the simple reason that no records of any kind have survived—neither reports, minutes, nor correspondence—apart from the annual returns made to the Registrar of Friendly Societies. And, notoriously, scarcely a single letter to Larkin from his many correspondents throughout the world has been found. Larkin's way with correspondence, apparently, was to read incoming mail, discard what didn't interest him, and thrust the rest into his commodious pockets, which from time to time he would empty out. Unlike his rival, William O'Brien, he kept no records, letters, or diaries. Seán O'Casey wrote to Jack Carney (2 August 1948): 'I often told Jim Larkin in Dublin that he should keep records; but Jim was too occupied with fighting for his men—not like O'Brien who had time to index everything.'

The fierce opposition of O'Brien to Larkin had the effect of completely isolating the WUI. As Charles McCarthy in his magisterial *Trade Unions in Ireland, 1894–1960* put it, 'Larkin earned the undying hatred of William O'Brien' and thus precipitated the 'tearing row' between the two unions.[5]

The WUI was refused affiliation to the Irish Trades Union Congress and Dublin Trade Union Council, at the behest of O'Brien. In 1934, when the WUI applied for affiliation to the council, the reaction from O'Brien, on behalf of the ITGWU, was vehement: 'So far as we are concerned we will not associate with James Larkin either inside or outside the Council, and if he is admitted this Union will have no option but to withdraw from affiliation.'

But the WUI was accepted into affiliation, and the ITGWU withdrew. As a result Larkin became eligible to attend the annual conference of the ITUC as a delegate representing the trades council, which he did for several years, until O'Brien got the constitution of the Congress amended in 1942. Henceforth a trades council could send as delegates to the Congress only members of unions affiliated to the Congress. It was at this conference in 1942 that Larkin called O'Brien 'an unmitigated liar'. The rift between the two was further from resolution than ever. At the same conference Larkin was to refer to himself: 'I am Ishmael,' adding that he was 'possibly making my swansong today in this particular assembly.'

It was not so, though Larkin's subsequent attendance at the ITUC was brought about in circumstances that Larkin would not have wished. In 1945 the ITUC split, with the ITGWU and other Irish unions disaffiliating and forming the Congress of Irish Unions. Immediately after the disaffiliation the WUI was accepted into membership of the ITUC. Larkin was a delegate to the annual conference of 1945, when Young Jim Larkin was elected to the National Executive. The WUI was now at last fully accepted into the official labour fold.

Since the WUI was not affiliated to the Congress in the thirties, it was not involved in the discussions and conferences held during that period on trade union organisation; but an interesting insight into the union's attitude to reorganisation is to be found in the submission it made to the Commission on Vocational Organisation, which was set up by the Government in 1939. The submission, made in 1940, was certainly prepared by Young Jim Larkin, though it can be assumed to have had the approval of his father, who in fact was nominally a member of the Commission, though he is believed to have seldom if ever attended its meetings and seems to have treated it with contempt. The policy the WUI put forward in its submission was scarcely different from James Connolly's syndicalism: 'We recognise no limit ... to our activities locally or nationally, and our offices are a clearing house, hourly and daily, for all the hardships, troubles and worries, that never cease besetting the common people. We are an industrial organisation, a cultural organisation, a welfare organisation, and a social organisation ...'[6]

Stating that their objective was the creation of 'one big union', a single general union 'composed of industrial sections,' the submission went on:

> Our ultimate object is the realisation of our belief that wealth producers of the nation, the wage earners in industry, commerce, and agriculture, and the working farmer, should own, control and govern the nation, its wealth and resources, and its economy in the interests of the common working people. We strive to organise and educate the workers to the realisation of that objective.

All this could have come straight out of the writings of James Connolly. The union saw in the working class, as he did, the seeds of social revolution.

Up to the death of James Larkin the WUI was organised on very simple lines indeed. It was governed by an annual meeting, at which all members could attend. Its membership remained small. By the outbreak of war it had perhaps eight to nine thousand members, compared with possibly thirty-five thousand in the ITGWU. Its finances were always precarious, the few officials ill-paid but dedicated to a degree that is not believable today. The union was of course dominated by Jim Larkin, but it was not an imposed dominance but one freely accepted by members, who regarded themselves proudly as Larkinites.

Things were to change radically when Young Jim was elected general secretary in succession to his father in 1947. Seán O'Casey had said that 'whenever the workers march forth to demonstrate the great hope that is within them, there will be the big figure steady at their head. It is for us to finish the job that Jim began so mightily and well.' The WUI proceeded to consolidate itself, to develop and grow. This was to be the work of Young Jim.

The change in leadership ushered in a new era of teamwork, in contrast to the dominance of one man in the leadership of the union. When elected general secretary, Young Jim said that one of the conditions for his undertaking the responsibility was 'that we are going to have teamwork, rather than the work of individuals.'

The union was in a parlous state. In 1959 Young Jim was to say: 'Those of us who know the full story were doubtful that the union would last another twelve months. We had less than £5,000 and of that we owed at least half.'

He set about the reorganisation of the union. It may have been strong in spirit, inspiring in its traditions, stout in its class-consciousness, but it was numerically small, its membership still confined largely to Dublin, and had virtually no material assets. Soon it had doubled its effective membership; methods of work and organisation changed; a proper administrative system was introduced. The structure was altered. The annual meeting of members became an annual delegate conference. Organisation was extended into new areas, such as Aer Lingus and hitherto unorganised employments, such as Guinness and the Hospitals Trust.

Methods of negotiation were adapted to meet the new circumstances brought about by the establishment of the Labour Court in the year before Big Jim's death. In fact the first case on behalf of workers heard by the Labour Court, the ESB case, was presented by Young Jim in 1946. His father was proud of this, even though the new conditions were wholly alien to his manner of negotiation.

John Smithers, who had succeeded John Kenny in 1946 as general president—he was the first full-time president—told the 1947 conference of the Union that 'no longer would the merely sentimental appeal or the blunt threats suffice. Now our negotiators not alone have to express the traditional militancy of our class but must employ both the science and art of logic and the cunning of the lawyer.'

The four senior officials who represented a collective leadership were Young Jim Larkin, John Smithers, Christy Ferguson, and Denis Larkin, the second of Big Jim's four sons. Smithers and Ferguson were in sharp contrast: one a traditionalist, the other an iconoclast; Smithers cool, Ferguson fiery. Ferguson told the story of two internees held in Newbridge Camp during the Civil War. One was a 'decent guy', the other a 'smart guy'. The decent guy dug a tunnel, the smart guy escaped. Ferguson happened to be the smart guy who escaped through the tunnel; the decent guy, Smithers, who had dug the tunnel, did not.

Ferguson was small and wiry, full of explosive energy, with a sharp mind; he did not suffer fools gladly. Above all he was a great organiser and a masterly negotiator. He was credited with ghosting in one of the Dublin daily papers what was probably the most influential weekly political column of the time. He died in 1957, nine years after joining the staff of the WUI.[7] It was his unexpected death that was the reason for Jim Larkin not contesting the 1957 general election: he had been a Labour TD for fourteen years. Smithers was a very different type of person, with a wonderful sense of humour but who kept the tightest of control over the purse strings.

At the commemoration in 1974 of the fiftieth anniversary of the foundation of the WUI, Donal Nevin, then the assistant general secretary of the ICTU, spoke of Young Jim and what he had achieved in the twenty-two years he had been general secretary of the WUI: 'Towering over all the others was Young Jim, who was so like his father in his dedication to his life's work in the labour movement, in his loyalty to the working class, his absolute integrity, but so much in contrast to him in temperament, in his personality, and in his way of doing things.'

Throughout the post-war years the voice of Young Jim was heard not in the ringing eloquence that was his father's but clearly, cogently, a voice that was at all times rational, intelligent, coherent, logical. In the pages of the Dáil debates, in the reports of the WUI, the ITUC and the ICTU his views and ideas are recorded. Rereading them, one is struck by how astonishingly relevant much of what he had to say in those years remained, long after the speeches were made.

At the bier of his father, Young Jim had pledged himself to help build a labour movement that would be united in purpose, united in struggle, and united in its objectives. The theme of trade union unity and workers' fellowship and solidarity was to run right through his endeavours. The other main theme was, as he put it, 'the broad human purpose which had been the driving force of the labour movement.'

Young Jim's thought did not rest with the philosophical and the general. Always he was realistic and practical in his approach to problems. Even a cursory survey of some of the main topics to which he addressed himself in his contributions to the annual conferences of Congress in the late forties and fifties gives an indication of this.

— In 1946 he took up the cause of agricultural labourers, then one of the most exploited groups in Irish society. The WUI had organised farm workers in County Dublin, and Seán Dunne became secretary of the Agricultural Workers' Section of the union. In 1946 also, when the Federation of Rural Workers was set up by the ITUC, the WUI transferred some thousands of its members to the new union, and Young Jim became the federation's first president.
— In 1947, the year his father died, he was pointing out that full employment would not be achieved unless a plan for economic development was put into effect and called for a national economic council.

348

—In 1948, as war clouds seemed to be gathering over Europe, he was demanding that Ireland's voice be heard loudly and clearly for peace and that Irish neutrality be reaffirmed.

—In 1949 he was speaking of the necessity for industrial democracy, with workers exercising some control over their work environment and sharing in management.

—In 1950 Larkin's emphasis was on the need for the trade union movement to act on behalf of the low-paid workers and unorganised labour.

—In 1951 he was making a passionate appeal for the trade union movement to take up the cause of the poor and the needy, and especially the aged, in a war against poverty.

With John Conroy, the general president of the ITGWU, Larkin was the prime architect of the reunification of the trade union movement, in a provisional united organisation in 1956 and finally with the establishment of the Irish Congress of Trade Unions in 1959. It is poignant to reflect that they died within a week of each other, just ten years later, in February 1969.

Young Jim had no illusions about utopian formulas or make-believe programmes. 'We have our own social and economic outlook,' he wrote, 'but in our day to day activities we have to make the best of the world as we find it. Our movement is not a static movement; it is made up of men and women who live and have their being in a changing world. The world changes men and women and they in turn change the world. Our movement has got to live and go forward with the world around us.'

Charles McCarthy, who himself was a trade union leader for many years (he was general secretary of the Vocational Teachers' Association and president of the ICTU in 1964), wrote of Young Jim as 'the towering figure in the Irish trade union movement from the war's end onwards.'[8]

Of Young Jim Larkin, Prof. Patrick Lynch writes:

Patrick McGilligan (Professor of Constitutional Law at University College, Dublin), intellectually the most outstanding representative of the first Inter-Party Government, once told him that there were two members of the Dáil at that time always worth listening to, Seán Lemass and Young Jim Larkin. Of the two, he said that Larkin was probably the abler. Larkin's speeches were always well-prepared, his capacity for analysis was very marked and he usually came up with original ideas. His grasp of policy issues were always firm when as Minister for Finance he introduced them. Above all, the content of Larkin's speeches was never predictable.

Young Jim's brother Denis succeeded him as general secretary in 1969. He had been an official of the union for most of his adult life. He died in 1987. He was the shrewdest of negotiators, having a distinctive style, which was quite deceptive and confusing to employers. More often than not his tactics worked to the benefit of the members. Like his brother he had an astute political sense, which got him elected—sometimes against the odds—in both Dáil and municipal elections. He was Lord Mayor of Dublin in 1955.

In its first fifty years, the Workers' Union had only three general secretaries: Big Jim, Young Jim, and Denis Larkin. It had four general presidents, all with the same first name: John Lawlor, John Kenny, John Smithers, and John Foster.

Subsequently the WUI had another general secretary—its last—Patrick Cardiff, who succeeded Denis Larkin. He merged the Federation of Rural Workers and the Irish Women Workers' Union with the WUI to form the Federated Workers' Union of Ireland. Its last general secretary was William A. Attley. In 1990 the FWUI and the ITGWU merged to form a new union, SIPTU.

The first national organiser of the WUI was James Larkin's brother Peter. He was appointed in 1928 and died in November 1931, at the age of forty-eight. He lay in state in Unity Hall in Marlborough Street, the head office of the union, and his coffin, covered with the Red Flag, was borne from there to Glasnevin on a black-draped dray.

The first president of the WUI, John Lawlor, was a cab driver who had been world champion handball player in the late eighteen-eighties and early nineties. He died in June 1930 and was succeeded by John Kenny, a docker, who had been a boxing champion and was a staff major in the WUI Brass and Reed Band.

A notable figure in the union, and earlier in the ITGWU, was Barney Conway. He first went on strike in 1894, when he was twelve years of age. In 1913 he was twice arrested for beating blacklegs. On the first occasion he was sentenced to one month and on the second occasion to six weeks. He was once described by Jim Larkin as the most honest man he had ever met, while to Seán O'Casey, a life-long friend, he was the 'incorruptible Barney'. He died in 1965, the last outstanding member of Larkin's Old Guard.

Another stalwart of the early days of the WUI was Frank Cluskey Senior, the secretary of the Operative Butchers. He told a story of how in 1913 he was living with an aunt who was deeply religious. Over his bed he had put a picture of Jim Larkin but next day found that it was missing. When he spoke to his aunt about it she said that there could be neither luck nor grace where such a picture was. Cluskey was the last person to leave Big Jim home to Wellington Road before he was taken to the Meath Hospital, where he died.

One of Larkin's closest associates in England, Ireland and America was Jack Carney, who worked with the WUI for about nine years in the twenties and thirties. His career as agitator, anti-war militant, revolutionary, trade union official and journalist warrants much more space than can be given to it here.

Jack Carney, like Larkin Liverpool-born, had worked with Larkin in Liberty Hall and helped with the *Irish Worker*. He was also active in Belfast in the ITGWU with James Connolly. (Part of his story over these years will be found in chapter 49.) In 1916 he was helping Larkin to get out an

American edition of the *Irish Worker* in Chicago. Both Larkin and Carney campaigned in 1916 for Eugene V. Debs, the greatest of American labour leaders, then seeking election to Congress, and in fact both spoke with Debs in his birthplace, Terre Haute, Indiana. (Debs had polled 900,000 votes, 6 per cent of the poll, in the 1912 presidential election.)

In December 1919 Carney, then editing a labour paper, *Truth*, in Duluth, Minnesota, was arrested and charged with 'wilfully attempting to obstruct the recruiting and enlistment service of the U.S. by publishing a certain weekly paper known as *Truth* containing an article entitled "Hands off Russia".' The campaign for Carney's release was led by Eugene Debs, who wrote of Carney:

> There is not a truer spirit, a more uncompromising soul in the labor movement than Jack Carney. I know him and love him. He never falters, never wavers, never turns his face from the enemy. He is true to the core of his great heart to the working class. He has never weakened, never whimpered, and never for one moment dipped his colors to the enemy. He has stood like the warrior he is, through the thickest of the battle, and there he stands today.

When Larkin was deported from America in April 1923, Carney signed on as 'French chef' on the *Majestic*, on which Larkin was sailing. He later recalled that they did not mind his not being French, but when they found out that he was not even a chef they put him to work stoking the boilers.

Back in Dublin, Carney remained a colleague of Larkin, working with him in the WUI and helping to edit a new series of the *Irish Worker* in 1925–26 and 1930–32. He accompanied Larkin on his visit to Russia to attend a meeting of the Comintern in 1924 and the following year returned there as Larkin's representative. During the thirties he was an official of the WUI, serving members in a number of employments. He was a member of one of the Trade Boards (now Joint Labour Committees).

During the Spanish Civil War the Executive Committee of the WUI, of which Carney was an official, passed a resolution forbidding officials of the union from appearing on any but a trade union platform. (Carney had spoken at meetings in support of the Spanish Republicans.) This decision of the union must be seen in the context of the atmosphere of the time and the hysterical support by the Catholic Church and elements in the political parties for Franco's rebellion against the legitimate government in Spain, the isolation of the WUI in the trade union movement, and the fierce antagonism to it of some of the most powerful figures in the movement. Carney resigned his position in the union and went to London, where he became a freelance journalist and a member of the House of Commons Press Gallery as a representative of an Australian group of newspapers. He died in 1956 at the age of sixty-eight.[9]

Emmet Larkin dedicated his biography of Larkin to Jack Carney. Of him he wrote: 'Jack Carney more than anyone else, gave me an understanding of what Jim Larkin was all about. No one, perhaps, knew

Larkin better than he did, and though a warm and passionate admirer, he was never blind to the faults and defects in that great man. Jack Carney, then, saw Larkin whole and best.'

Jack Carney's wife, Mina, an American sculptor, was secretary of the Larkin Defense Committee in America in the early twenties. She studied art in Vienna with Oskar Kokoschka and later became a close friend of the famous artist in London. Mina Carney died in London in 1974, when she was in her early eighties. Her husband had died in 1964.

A bust of Jim Larkin by Mina Carney is in the Hugh Lane Municipal Gallery of Modern Art in Dublin, presented to the gallery in the late twenties.

Jack Carney wrote to his old comrade John Fitzpatrick of the Chicago Federation of Labour in 1934:

> Jim [Larkin] is not so active at present. I think he made a mistake in 1923, but he has kept the past. Without him wages and hours would have been terrible. It is no soft job working with him, but one likes it because the man is hopelessly and may I say wonderfully honest. He does understand his people and though at times he would drive you to drink with his generous hand and heart you are glad he is what he is because of what he is. He is not without his faults but I prefer his faults to the virtues of some of the leaders here.

Carney—like Larkin—loved Dublin. In the same letter (24 January 1934), written from 52 Merrion Square, where he was then living with his wife, Mina, he wrote:

> Spring in Dublin. Nowhere do men feel the wonder and exhilaration of spring as here in this great city, and in no city is the glory of Spring so amazing and stimulating as here in Dublin. I love this city. I could do better in London or Paris, but Dublin on bare living is so much better. The very memories of Dublin are sufficient to carry one on through to the heights. Here in this square walked Oscar Wilde, Emmet, Tone and others. The world still speaks of them. Here was born great hopes and here trod aristocrats whom the world has forgotten. Across over the square, beyond yonder tower was born Castlereagh, of whom Byron wrote, 'So he has cut his throat at last! He? Who? The man who cut his country's long ago.'

This letter of Jack Carney is included in *Jim Larkin: In the Footsteps of Big Jim*. (For more about Jack Carney see chapters 38 and 49.)

Chapter 43

Death of a Titan

Big Jim crosses the city

Liam Mac Gabhann

There were crowds at Jim Larkin's funeral—just as there were crowds in Jim Larkin's life. A half century of history marched through Dublin yesterday morning. The years were crowded between Haddington Road and Glasnevin.

You couldn't think of Larkin being in that flower-covered coffin with its Starry Plough flag, just dead.

They all came out, men in dungarees with overcoats buttoned up to the throat, marching erectly as he told them to march. It could have been a Citizen-Army-cum-Irish-Volunteer parade, only for the slowness. The very air of the city seemed to be muffled. You had the feeling that the people were magnetised into the funeral 'as by common instinct.'

And the men in the dungarees and the women grown old who have borne children since they struck instinctively at the 400 bosses at Larkin's will, seemed to be there because they just had to be there.

Just because Big Jim was crossing the city.

Then you wanted to see a big black slouch hat on the coffin and a big black pipe beside it, because all the time you visualised Larkin swinging his huge shoulders, going to a meeting in the North City.

That flag on the Ballast Office symbolised death yet did not stress it.

What does it bring back? Words tramp through the slush of the streets, undertone the music of the dead:

> And Connolly watches ships go out through flags at Kingstown pier;
> A starving Dublin sends its toll of guard and fusilier;
> The Citizen Army is out to-day and if you wonder why,
> Go, ask the lords of the finance boards why the men go out to die.

The south-easterly gale blows up the turbulent river, crashing on the O'Connell Bridge arches like Larkin's fist at the council table.

Boots, heavy and grimy and dirty; boots polished and shiny, tramp, tramp, tramp, joining the long, long crowd, step and slither through the snowy slush.

As the procession passes, blinds come down over the windows, people come out of the shops, swell the funeral.

Groups that line the sidewalks, waiting, saying nothing, move out, walk after the old grey men of the Citizen Army, after the tired women of the hopeful eyes of the Citizen Army.

Children gather around the huge lorry of flowers, red and yellow and blue and lily white.

353

At Beresford Place the bands cry back through the years. Up from the docks small, stocky men walk. They stand beside the coffin as it halts near Liberty Hall.

The deep-sea men seem grimly proud to stand as guard-of-honour.

(Larkin ... tied to a ship's stanchion ... planning revolution ... that's what you're thinking).

The parade moves on, by the Workers' Union old headquarters. Women on tenement steps—(there are brand new bricks on the buildings now)—hold up children to see the parade.

Moladh go deo le Dia! A Kerry policeman is straightening out the crowd and that's not rain on his cheeks. Praise be! At Larkin's funeral I have seen a policeman on duty ... crying!

Corporation men were cleaning slush an hour ago. There are men in the funeral with shovels—and they handle them like military weapons. That band rings through the high houses and the words plod by the horses' feet—

The Citizen Army is out to-day and if you wonder why,
Go ask the lords of the finance boards if the cash returns are high;
It isn't the bosses that bear the brunt and 'tisn't you or I,
'Tis the women and kids whose tears are hid as the Army marches by.

But that is old ... out by O'Connell Street you can't help thinking of Bloody Sunday. Crowds waiting, a D.M.P. man to every two workers and somewhere, silent and disguised, there is hope—*Big Jim is crossing the City!*

So fifty years of history have marched on and so have the D.M.P.

Gardaí in blue are lining the way for Jim Larkin's funeral.

There are wreaths on the coffin from people in Britain too, people who wear dungarees—and frock-coats—girls in offices, men in mines.

The principal men of the State he helped to build, when the foundation stones were being laid, are behind the great coffin that still looks small because one thinks of the fierce statuary of Big Jim.

The Last Post sounds and rifles crash a volley. The people tramp back through the slush and snow, a bit dazed.

They seem dimly aware that above the muffled throbbing of the drums, above the lament of the bugle, and the dull thudding of the marching thousands it was really a voice that called them. Larkin's voice shouting to the people about the history of things they had lost and gained.

Like a thousand times before when the battles were won, he had shouted with a proud command in his words: 'Go back to the job.' Back to the job ... Big Jim has crossed the city.[1]

The lion will roar no more

Seán O'Casey

It is hard to believe that this 'lion' of the Irish Labour movement will roar no more. When it seemed that every man's hand was against him the time he led the workers through the tremendous days of 1913 he wrested tribute of Ireland's greatest and most prominent men. Yeats, George Russell, Orpen and George Bernard Shaw proclaimed him to be the greatest Irishman since Parnell. And so he was; for all thoughts and all activities surged in the soul of this Labour leader. He was far and away above the orthodox Labour leader, for he combined within himself the imagination of the artist, with the fire and determination of a leader of a down-trodden class.

He was the first man in Ireland—and perhaps in England, too—who brought poetry into the workers' fight for a better life. Lectures and concerts, and other activities, he brought into Liberty Hall, and the social centre he organised in Croydon Park coloured the life of the Dublin workers, and was a joyous experience they had never known before, and won for Jim the admiration of many who had but scanty interest in the labour movement.

Before all others, Jim Larkin brought into the Dublin labour strife an interest in the hearts of humanity never associated before with the life of those who had to work hard and long for a living; and today this interest has grown to tremendous proportions, and the workers are swarming to enjoy and to understand the finer things of life.

So Jim Larkin, as well as being a great leader of men and an imaginative artist himself, was a foreseer of things to come. He was the man who first introduced to me the great name of Eugene O'Neill just after that playwright had had his *Hairy Ape* produced in New York. He fought for the loaf of bread as no man before him had ever fought; but, with the loaf of bread, he also brought the flask of wine and the book of verse.

He had the eloquence of an Elizabethan, fascinating to all who heard him, and irresistible to the workers. He was familiar with the poetry of Shakespeare, Whitman, Shelley and Omar Khayyam, and often quoted them in his speeches. In all his imaginative speeches there ran the fiery threat of devastating criticism not only of the employers, but of the workers themselves.

Jim Larkin never hesitated to expose and condemn the faults of his followers. No man ever did more since the days of Father Mathew to persuade the workers to live a more sober and sensible life than this Jim.

Many were jealous of his great fight and of his influence on the working class, and many still are, but the life of this man, so great, so unselfish, so apostolic, will live for ever in the hearts and minds of those who knew him and in the minds of those who will hear of the mission to men, and of all he did to bring security and decency and honour to a class that never knew of these things until Jim Larkin came.

There was a man sent from God whose name was Jim, and that man was Larkin. Jim Larkin is not dead, but is with us, and will be with us always.[2]

Another Irish Chieftain has gone from us. One of the greatest of them all: a Chief of the people—Jim Larkin is his name. The banner and beacon-fire of the Irish Labour Movement. The banner is now furled. The beacon-fire is out—a little heap of ashes only.

But what ashes! Out of it will spring another flame, firing itself from that which Larkin kindled, flaming in Ireland, and flaming everywhere. It is not only that Jim Larkin will never be forgotten (to forget him would be to forget ourselves), it is that he can never be dead.

In the great things he did for the Irish workers is everlasting life. Not life that will remain as it is now; but life growing into a fuller consciousness of its own worth, of its own power, its own right to the ownership of all things.

I heard men, turning aside in moments of quiet from Irish-Ireland work murmur: 'A man has come among the Irish workers.'

Then I heard this man speak to dockers, coalheavers and drivers in Beresford Place. There he was, larger than the life we knew, standing above the Dublin workers, telling them of the story the workers must write themselves. In this man's burning words were the want, the desire, the resolution of the world's workers. Here before me was the symbol of the revolting proletariat. The personal manifestation of 'Each for all, and all for each.' The symbol of a march forward; not in twos and threes; not this union today, that one tomorrow; but a march forward en masse for what the workers never had, but for what they will have and hold for ever.[3]

Feartlaoi

Micheál Ó Maoláin

A Shéamuis, shiubhlas le t'ais ar shráideanna Loch Garman i 1911 nuair a tháinig oibridhthe an bhaile sin amach le fáilte a chur rómhat fhéin agus roimh Phádraig Ó Dálaigh a chaith ráithe i bpríosún ar a son; bhí mé 'do chuideachtain go Sligeach i 1912 nuair a bhunuigheamar beirt Chraobh de'n Transport Union ar an mbaile sin; chaitheas téarma i bpríosún i Mountjoy chomh maith leat féin i 1913 agus b'iomdha cruinniughadh eile dár fhreastal sinn beirt chomh maith. B'iomdha seanchas agus b'iomdha sáruidheacht a bhíodh againn le chéile faoi neithibh a bhain le lucht oibre agus le hÉirinn.

Labhair mé leat san osbidéal cúpla lá sul dar d'éag thú, a Shéamuis. Tá tú imighthe uainn anois agus is uaigneach an chathair í Bláth Cliath i d'eagmais. Tá roinnt mhór dar sheas leat sa nglua   iseacht   fadó imighthe freisin ach feiceamuíd a chéile arís agus déanfamuíd seanchas 'sa' machaire glórmhar ar an taoibh thall de na Réalta. Go dtí sin, a Shéamais, 'mo ghuidhe-se féin agus guidhe Mhic Mhuire leat,' agus go mba soillseach t'ionad i measc na n-aingeal agus na naomh. Leagaim an fhleaschuimhne seo ar t'uaigh.[4]

Jim, I walked with you through the streets of Wexford in 1911 when the workers of the town came out to welcome you and Patrick Daly, who had been in prison on their behalf; I was with you in Sligo in 1912 when we set up a branch of the Transport Union in the town; I was with you in prison in Mountjoy in 1913, and many other meetings too we had together. Many were the yarns we had, and many the arguments about matters affecting the working class and Ireland.

I spoke to you in the hospital a few days before you died, Jim. You have left us, and lonely is Dublin city now that you have gone. A great many of those who stood with you in the movement long ago have now departed, but we'll see one another again and we'll talk together in that bright glade beyond the stars. Till then, Jim, 'My prayer and the prayer of Mary's Son be with you,' and may your place be radiant among the angels and the saints. I lay this garland of memories on your grave.

Oration

William Norton TD

It is nearly fifty years since Larkin first blazed the trail of organising the unskilled workers. It was a gigantic task, calling for dauntless courage, for vision, for faith in men who had lost all sense of faith in themselves, but, above all, for faith in his own ability to insulate himself against the never-ending disappointments, the daily rebuffs, the faithlessness of the weak and timid, and the harsh iron-like tyranny of an employer class of that period which fought as tigers rather than shed their economic stranglehold over the bodies and lives of men and women. It was a task before which even the strongest and bravest might well shudder. But with dynamic energy Jim Larkin threw himself into the fight—for him a never-ending fight—and wherever he went—Liverpool, Belfast, Cork, Dublin, the United States—the same passionate zeal consumed him in a crusade to raise the standard of life for the toiling, exploited masses. Jim's defiant spirit, his fiery eloquence, his rugged, picturesque personality, enabled him to meet adversity with imperturbable courage and perseverance and to impart these qualities to a growing band of men and women by whom he was regarded as an economic Saviour.

Dublin was his main battlefield and here a task almost terrifying in its magnitude confronted him and that small, but gallant band who, in 1908, sought to establish the Transport Union as an instrument of protection against the unbridled exploitation of the workers. From humble beginnings the Union grew in strength, the pioneering spirit of Jim Larkin and his human, emotional appeals winning converts daily. An uneasy feeling gripped the Dublin employers. The Union's growth and Larkin's prestige were a challenge to their privileges, to their exploitation of workers, to their sense of ownership of men and women and they determined that the Union must be destroyed and the power of Larkin broken for ever.

1913 was the year selected by the employers for the onslaught and, having first declared war, they waged it with an unrelenting ferocity that called forth the bitter condemnation of some of the finest minds in Ireland and throughout the world.

Like most pioneers, Jim Larkin was not immune from controversy; indeed in many respects he was a veritable furnace of controversy. Remembering the herculean tasks that confronted him, comparing the conditions of Dublin workers to-day with those of 1913, we can say with every pride that the workers are richer by his services, for he gave them

357

new concepts of independence, a new sense of human dignity and the courage and the weapons to achieve both. Truly, it can be said that if service to one's fellows be the title deeds to a place of honour and affection in the minds and hearts of men and women, Jim Larkin, judged even by the most critical standards, will assuredly enjoy that place of honour.

Jim Larkin, we, your old comrades, bid you goodbye. Death has snapped our earthly friendship with you, but it cannot dim or sever the love and esteem in which we shall ever hold your memory. We thank you for your magnificent work, for the courage and inspiration you gave us in such overflowing measure. We shall look with unceasing pride on your achievements which brought happiness to many homes and brought to the workers a new spirit of independence and manliness.[5]

Epitaph

James T. Farrell

Larkin is no more. He was a brave soldier of the working class. He was a great agitator. He gave his spirit and the best years of his life in their service. Karl Marx spoke of the great heart of the proletariat in his pamphlet on the Civil War in France. Jim Larkin came from this great heart. One bows one's head in memory of this brave Irish labour leader.[6]

Tribute

John Swift

Then came Larkin and his co-workers. Soon thousands of the despised rabble became ennobled with the dignity of trade union organisation. Larkin taught them the duty of struggle, the imperative of rebelliousness. He breathed fire into the dead eyes and the cringing breasts of slaves. They heard him, and their supplications to their masters became defiance, their despair became a challenge. He taught them self-reliance. They followed Larkin because he had convinced them in his person and in his teaching that there was no more noble duty or destiny for men and women than that of raising themselves from bondage.

Some of us are old enough to remember how Dublin throbbed to Larkin's fiery slogans. A Titan of a man, he needed no banners on which to scroll his burning poetry. He made banners of the air: his voice wrought magic patterns compelling attention and exultation. In the city's gutter, in the fetid slum, in the stinking holds of ships, on the quayside, where men fawned and flunkeyed for wretched bread, in the poorhouse, even, and the prison, there was exultation when Larkin spoke. Men and women, made dumb and abject by injustice and destitution, listened. What new hurricane from the heavens was this that said: 'The great appear great because we are on our knees. Let us rise.'

This man of power was loved by little children and was himself throughout his life, in many ways a child. He was a great artist, working towards the ideal that consumed him. His music was livid thunder, hurtled at injustice and hypocrisy. At times his harmonies were strange, as of forces eruptive and elemental. But who could doubt the main chords of the symphony he sought to fashion, with its tones and overtones that told of chains breaking and dungeons tottering, and the wild elation of serfs made free! Let us stand to honour Larkin—Larkin who taught the despised rabble to stand erect, unafraid and hopeful.[7]

Homage to Jim Larkin

Frank O'Connor

Roll away the stone, Lord, roll away the stone
As you did when last I died in the attic room;
Then there was no fire as well, and I died of cold
While Jim Larkin walked the streets before he grew old.

Larkin was a young man then, all skin and bone;
Larkin had a madman's eyes, I saw them through the stone;
Larkin had a madman's voice, I don't know what he said,
I just heard screeches ringing in my head.

Something screeched within my head as in an empty room;
I felt the lightning of the pain run through every bone;
I couldn't even scream, Lord, I just sobbed with pain;
I didn't want to live, Lord, and turned to sleep again.

But with the screeches in my head I couldn't settle right,
At last I scrambled to my knees and turned to the light;
Then I heard the words he spoke, and down crashed the stone
There was I with blind man's eyes, gaping at the sun.

Things are much the same again, damn the thing to eat;
Not a bloody fag since noon and such a price for meat;
Not a bit of fire at home all the livelong day—
Roll the stone away, Lord, roll the stone away![8]

Jim Larkin

Patrick Kavanagh

Not with public words now can his greatness
Be told to the children, for he was more
Than a labour-agitating orator—
The flashing flaming sword merely bore witness
To the coming of the dawn: 'Awake and look!
The flowers are growing for you, and wonderful trees
And beyond are not the serf's grey Docks, but seas—

Excitement out of the Creator's poetry book.
When the Full Moon's in the River and the ghost of bread
Must not haunt all your weary wanderings home,
The ships that were dark galleys can become
Pine forests under winter's starry plough
And the brown gantries will be the lifted head
Of man the dreamer whom the gods endow.

And thus I heard Jim Larkin above
The crowd who wanted to turn aside
From Reality coming to free them. Terrified
They hid in the clouds of dope and would not move.
They eat the opium of the murderer's story
In the Sunday newspapers; they stood to stare
Not at the blackbird but at a millionaire
Whose horses ran for Serfdom's great glory.
And Tyranny trampled them in Dublin's gutter
Until Jim Larkin came along and cried
The call of Freedom and the call of Pride
And Slavery crept to its hands and knees
And Nineteen Thirteen cheered from out the utter
Degradation of their miseries.[9]

Jim Larkin

Brendan Behan

Brendan Behan (1923–1964) wrote only a dozen poems in Irish. 'Jim Larkin', the second of these poems to be published, appeared in *Comhar* in March 1947, a month after Big Jim's death. This version was reprinted in Donal Nevin (editor), *Trade Union Century* (1994). A slightly different version was published by Denis Cotter in *Brendan Behan: Poems and Stories* (Dublin: Liffey Press 1978) and a revised version in *Brendan Behan: Poems and a Play in Irish* (Oldcastle: Gallery Press 1981). The last-mentioned version is the one used here.

There are four known translations of 'Jim Larkin'. One of these is given below. A translation by Theo Dorgan will be found in chapter 13 and another, by Ulick O'Connor, in chapter 59. The fourth translation is by Colbert Kearney in his book *The Writings of Brendan Behan*, published in 1977.

Ba mise é! Ba gach mac máthar againn é!
Sinn féin. Láidir. Mar ab áil linn a bheith,
Mar ab eol dúinn a bheith.
Eisean ag bagairt troda is ag bronnadh fuascailte—
Is sinne ag leanúint a chónra trí chlab na cathrach
I mbéiceacha móra feirge.

Ag leanúint a chónra trí chlab na cathrach aréir
An sinne a bhí sa chónra?
Níorbh ea: bhíomar sa tsráid ag máirseáil
Beo, buíoch don mharbh.

The following is an English version by Manus O'Riordan:

He was us! He was me!
Each and every mother's son!
We ourselves. Self-reliant. Strong.
As we would wish ourselves to be
Knowing such strength could make us free.

Himself fist-clenched confronting oppression
To release from servitude's knee-bending servility
Ourselves to mourn in his funeral procession
Those great angry roars through this open mouth city.

Last night as we followed his coffin
Through Dublin's garrulous din
Were we ourselves in that same coffin?
Not so: on the streets were now marching our ranks
Alive Alive Oh! To the Dead we give thanks.

Jim Larkin, RIP

Anonymous

Come listen a while you Irish men, and hear my mournful news,
Although it is quite sorrowful, I'll know you'll me excuse,
Come join my lamentation for one who was our friend,
He led the tortured workers and made the bosses bend.

A great man like Jim Larkin, we never can replace,
He fought our fight in dark '13 when the Peelers he did face,
We lost our fight, but still we won, for Jim was not outdone,
And as the troubled years rolled on, his fight and ours he won.

When Ireland honours heroes bold, who fought to make her free,
The name of brave Jim Larkin will be there for all to see,
He fought to save the working man from bondage and from woe,
And his name will long be honoured no matter where you go.

He was treated to the batons by the Forces of the Crown;
But bullies' guns or batons they could never keep him down,
The worker is a free man now by his persevering fight,
And his prospects for the future have never been so bright.

So, God rest your soul, Jim Larkin, may Heaven be your home,
May St Patrick take you to the Land from where you'll never roam,
And when a day in Ireland dawns that North and South are free,
We will think of one great fighting man and just say: R.I.P.[10]

Inscription for a Headstone

Austin Clarke

What Larkin bawled to hungry crowds,
Is murmured now in dining-hall
And study. Faith bestirs itself,
Lest infidels in their impatience
Leave it behind. Who could have guessed
Batons were blessings in disguise,
When every ambulance was filled
With half-killed men and Sunday trampled
Upon arrest? Such fear can harden
Or soften heart, knowing too clearly
His name endures on our holiest page,
Scrawled in a rage by Dublin's poor.[11]

Appeal for unity

On the day of his father's funeral, Jim Larkin's eldest son, Young Jim, made a dramatic plea for unity in the sundered labour movement in a letter to the *Irish Times*. The movement had been divided following splits in the trade union and political wings of the movement. In 1945 a number of Irish unions, led by the largest union in the country, the ITGWU, had broken from the Irish Trades Union Congress, which had been the trade union centre for Ireland since 1894, to form the Congress of Irish Unions. This soon led to the formation of a breakaway group from the Labour Party, forming the National Labour Party.

Unfortunately the trade union unity that Young Jim Larkin had so passionately appealed for did not come about until 1959, when the ITUC and CIU united to form the Irish Congress of Trade Unions.

The architects of that united organisation were John Conroy, the general president of the ITGWU, and Young Jim Larkin, then the general secretary of the Workers' Union of Ireland. Big Jim had been general secretary of the ITGWU from 1909 to 1924 and general secretary of the WUI from 1924 to 1947.

> Sir, It is necessary for me to seek the courtesy of your columns because, in the first place, this letter is not and cannot, by its very purpose, be addressed directly to any person or organisation, and in the second place, it is of concern to so many who can only become aware of it through the medium of the Press.
>
> This day a man was laid to rest with the great dead of our race. Of his claim to that resting-place many tongues have spoken during these past

few days, and a deep and wide-flung emotional wave has swept over great numbers of people. That common emotion, that appreciation of loss, has been keenest among working men and women and the organisations, political and industrial, in which they associate. Whatever be the measure of his claim to their thoughts and feelings, Jim Larkin has been mourned and his passing deeply regretted by persons and organisations in every section and division of the Irish Labour movement. Stirred by a common emotion, these diverse groups and persons have found that they hold in common certain simple, yet great, beliefs, which have been brought sharply to the surface by the death of this man. They have found that they possessed a common bond, because being of the Labour movement, they found their common heritage added to by the unique service of the dead man, and the essential unity of Labour has been indicated by the value placed by them on his life work in the broad stream of Irish Labour.

If it be true that Irish workers have suffered a great loss, and if in that loss something common to all in the working-class movement has been manifest, surely now at this moment that which is most essential to Irish Labour can be given to Irish working men and women—a Labour movement, united in purpose, in struggle, and in its objectives. Unity is not such a great benefit that it may be purchased at any price, but today unity of Labour, industrial and political, is so urgently required that the price, even it be costly, can, and should, be paid by those who are in a position to make sacrifices.

The great mass of working men and women who constitute the Irish Labour movement most ardently desire that their strength and purpose should be added to a thousandfold by all that flows from unity, and those in whose hands lies the giving or the withholding of that unity should not deny the living vibrant mass of Labour, made up of the bodies, minds and spirits of living men, that which they need so urgently.

Irish people are emotional, and, perhaps, our common emotion this day may give us that unity we need, where reason and argument has failed in the past.

I have no doubt of the truth of my statement when I declare that unity is the single quality sought for by the working men and women who constitute, and who are, the Irish Labour movement. Why, therefore, when so little stands between them and the unity they desire, should they be denied it.

With this great man's death, the last of the great figures of Irish Labour has passed, and we who remain are little people. If among those of us who occupy leading positions in the Labour movement there be individuals who, for one reason or another, represent obstacles or barriers to unity, let us grow in stature by stepping aside so that unity may be realised; if there are difficulties of policy standing in the way, let us, as we did this day, find the simplest common denominator in policy, and agree upon that as an immediate objective; if there are difficulties of organisation to be overcome, let us overcome them in the understanding that our organisations were built to serve Labour, not to shackle it.

Who shall make the first step? Naturally, those whose devotion to Labour is greatest. If the greater measure of devotion is not expressed by those of us who by chance are playing leading roles, then let the real and living body of Labour—the rank and file—show us and compel us to do our duty; but let it be quick and decisive, whoever takes the first step.

I have, as I stated above, written this letter because I feel it should be written now on this day of mourning and deep and common emotion. I have consulted no person. I speak for no organisation, neither the union of which I am a member nor the political party I support. Neither do I write it because of the name I bear, which is mine by accident of birth, but, being the only possession this dead man had to leave me, an obligation devolves on me of putting in words that which tens of thousands of working men and women felt this day—their common emotion spreading from their common needs and striving in this life and united in that which is known as 'Irish Labour.'

Chapter 44

Inscriptions on a Monument

The great appear great because we are on our knees. Let us rise!
Ní uasal aon uasal ach sinne bheith íseal. Éirímis!
Les grands ne sont grands que parce que nous sommes à genoux. Levons-nous!

These inscriptions, in English, Irish, and French, are engraved on the base of the Jim Larkin monument in O'Connell Street, Dublin. The figure of Larkin is by Oisín Kelly (1915–1981).

The slogan *The great appear great to us, only because we are on our knees. Let us Rise* appeared on the masthead of the *Workers' Republic*, the organ of the Irish Socialist Republican Party, published in Dublin between 1896 and 1903. The ISRP was founded by James Connolly when he came to Ireland in 1896, at the age of twenty-eight. An Irish version of the slogan was also given on the masthead as *Is dóigh linn gur mór iad na daoine móra mar atámaoid féin ar ár nglúnaibh. Eirghimís.*

The slogan is usually attributed to Camille Desmoulins (1760–1794), the French revolutionary and one-time friend of Robespierre, who was beheaded on 2 April 1794. It was used by the *Journal des Révolutions de Paris*, which was published from 1789 and edited by Louis-Marie Prudhomme. While Desmoulins was associated with the *Journal*, and it ceased publication after his death, the slogan has been attributed to the editor, Prudhomme.

The form given by Harbottle's *Dictionary of Quotations* is 'Les grands ne paraissent grands que parce que nous sommes à genoux. Levons-nous.'[1] In Guerlac's *Citations Françaises* (1952) it is given as a motto that appeared at the head of Prudhomme's newspaper *Les Révolutions de Paris*. Guerlac states that some attribute the slogan to Vergniaud, others to Loustalot, the chief editor of Prudhomme's paper, and that it seems to have been inspired by a similar phrase used in 1652 by Dubosc-Montandré in his pamphlet *Le Point de l'Ovale*.[2] The text on the Larkin monument is that given in Guerlac.

The Irish text on the monument is by Seán Mac Réamoinn.

On the west side of the base of the Larkin monument there is a quotation from the poem 'Jim Larkin' by Patrick Kavanagh, first published in the *Bell* (editor, Peadar O'Donnell) in March 1947:

And Tyranny trampled them in Dublin's gutter
Until Jim Larkin came along and cried
The call of Freedom and the call of Pride
And Slavery crept to its hands and knees
And Nineteen Thirteen cheered from out the utter
Degradation of their miseries.

On the east side of the monument there is a quotation from *Drums under the Windows* by Seán O'Casey:

... He talked to the workers, spoke as only Jim Larkin could speak, not for an assignation with peace, dark obedience, or placid resignation; but trumpet-tongued of resistance to wrong, discontent with leering poverty, and defiance of any power strutting out to stand in the way of their march onward.

Unveiling the statue of Larkin on 15 June 1979, the President of Ireland, Dr Patrick Hillery, said:

It is not often in the history of a capital city that the occasion arises for the unveiling of a monument in its principal thoroughfare. This is such an occasion.

Larkin is one of the great men of our race, whose courage and dedication to the task which he set himself will always be remembered. At home and abroad he blazed a trail, rousing by his burning zeal and concern with their lot the poor and the oppressed, inspiring in them hope and confidence in their own ability to mould their future.

In his assaults on oppression and exploitation, Jim Larkin often used barbed words. Indeed he might also have directed harsh words at our commemorating him in granite and bronze. One feels that he would have wished to be remembered rather in the hearts and minds of men and women. And assuredly, his memory will forever live in the respect and affection of our people.

In the ages to come it will stand, a work of art raised to the memory of a great man who spent his energies and talents in the cause of his fellow-man, an inspiration to all who gaze upon it to strive on behalf of their brothers everywhere.

The statue is referred to in Thomas Kinsella's poem 'To the Coffee Shop':

Under Larkin with his iron arms on high,
conducting everybody
in all directions, up off our knees.[3]

Larkin's year of birth as originally engraved on the monument was 1876. It was not until 1980 that the historian C. Desmond Greaves established that Larkin was born in 1874. The correct date has since been substituted.

The statue of Jim Larkin is only the second to be erected in O'Connell Street this century. The other was the Parnell Monument, erected in 1912. Famously, George Bernard Shaw had said of Larkin that he was the greatest Irishman since Parnell.

PART 3

BIG JIM

Promethean Jim Larkin with the voice born of the
bugle and the drum.

Seán O'Casey

And Tyranny trampled them in Dublin's gutter
Until Jim Larkin came along and cried
The call of Freedom and the call of Pride
And Slavery crept to its hands and knees
And Nineteen Thirteen cheered from out the utter
Degradation of their miseries.

Patrick Kavanagh

Mourn not the dead that in the cool earth lie—
    Dust unto dust—
The calm, sweet earth that mothers all who die
    As all men must ...
But rather mourn the apathetic throng—
    The cowed and the meek—
Who see the world's great anguish and its wrong
    And dare not speak!

                                    Ralph Chaplin

Chapter 45

Larkin: A Titanic Figure

Rev. Prof. F. X. Martin

If I were asked to state in one sentence what was Jim Larkin's achievement, I would say that he was a man who gave Dublin, and consequently Ireland, a social conscience, something which it did not have. Secondly, if I were asked could I say in another sentence what he had given Ireland, I would say that he gave the Dublin working man, and therefore, ultimately, the Irish working man, dignity.

Once in a friend's house I saw an inscription on the wall: 'Get down on your knees and thank God you are standing on your feet.' Jim Larkin was the man who got the Dublin workers up off their knees, because they were down permanently on their knees, not praying but simply because they had been beaten there by events and by the unjust social system which prevailed in Dublin.

If we are to appreciate Jim Larkin's achievement we must realise that he was a titanic figure, a great example of what an individual can do in history. No matter how much you talk about movements, social causes, social developments, ultimately it is individuals who determine which turn events will take. Jim Larkin was one of these. But we must realise that he was in a context in which it was possible for him to do so.

Ireland at the time Larkin came here had a great series of orators: John Redmond and his brother Willie, Joe Devlin from Belfast, Tom Kettle, Pearse, and Jim Larkin. And oratory was to be the instrument, Larkin the trumpet voice. Larkin did not arrive on the scene, he burst on it. This burly brass-throated orator with the magnificent frame which helped him, a magnificent face too, ideally made for sculpture, became a boisterous, fearless prophet of the gospel of social justice. He urged the Dublin workers to demand fair wages and lashed the employers into a fury of retaliation. In Belfast in 1907 he had worked a miracle. He brought Catholics and Protestants to unite under the one banner. Dublin he brought to explosion point in 1913, and rightly so.

Larkin was the first to give the urban poor of Ireland a face. He was the first person to make them a powerful force. Above all, he gave the Dublin working man dignity. He had this indomitable courage, magnetic personality, powerful voice, a wonderful turn of phrase. He didn't just give the Dublin workers better wages, he gave them hope, he gave them conviction, he gave them the sense that they were worth something. In him they incarnated their strength.

Larkin had a great sense of the dramatic, as when he publicly burned the police notice forbidding the meeting, or when he appeared on the balcony of the Imperial Hotel, owned by William Martin Murphy, his opponent, or again when he got food ships steaming up the Liffey to the docks, with bands playing, crowds cheering, and speeches. The same when he chose Horse Show Week, Dublin's premier social event, as the occasion to show the contrast between the underpaid worker and the boss.

Larkin's own spirit of defiance gave heart to the people. He was full of energy, full of fire. He had fire in his belly—a Cromwellian phrase. He was a big man, with big faults. He was impetuous; but who wanted a cautious man in Dublin in 1913? What had the cautious men got? What had they done for the workers? He was intemperate in his words—of course he was. What was the point of being temperate? He described William Martin Murphy in some wonderful phrases: an 'industrial octopus', the 'tramway tyrant', 'bloodsucking vampire'. He didn't put all these in one article: he spread the manure fairly evenly. He said Murphy was a 'whited sepulchre', a 'soulless, money-grubbing tyrant'. If you want to rouse people there is no point in speaking in moderate or over-moderate tones.

Larkin was the man who took the poor of Dublin, put food in their bellies, clothes on their backs, fire in their grates. He also put fire into their hearts, and that was what they needed even more than food—fire in their hearts, dignity, a sense of being human beings.

The statements of Larkin are worth recording, because they expressed his mind. One of them was 'You will crucify Christ no longer in this town.' No Christian could have put it better, because to deal iniquitously or unjustly with your fellow-man is, if you are to believe the gospels, to crucify Christ himself. And Larkin sensed that. This is where his humanity came in. Another statement of Larkin's which I think embodies his whole philosophy of action was: 'I have come to preach the divine mission of discontent.' Jim Larkin made it his mission in life to stir up people to be discontented about the iniquitous conditions about them.

There should be erected a monument to Jim Larkin, which he deserves. It should be of bronze, because bronze is the most imperishable, and Jim Larkin was imperishable and, I think, will always be in the history of Ireland.

[From an address to a meeting in Coláiste Mhuire, Parnell Square, Dublin, in 1974 to commemorate the fiftieth anniversary of the founding of the Workers' Union of Ireland.]

Chapter 46

Larkin and the Historians

Prof. Fergus A. D'Arcy

In presenting this essentially tentative paper on Larkin and the historians it is necessary to clearly state at the outset the limits of this review. By 'historians' here is meant simply general historians, not specialists, and one has in mind general survey works on Irish history, not special works on labour history, not labour historians, and not biographers.

The exclusions are deliberate. One simply wanted to gain some sense of how Larkin fits in to the general picture as seen by the broad surveyors: if they were concerned to present the broad story of Ireland, especially of modern Ireland, what estimate would they make of Larkin's role, particularly in relation to the period 1907–14? Firstly, did he in their view figure large, or small, or at all—did he matter or did he not? Secondly and obviously, if he figures large or small, then why? Thirdly, to what extent over the period of general historical writing, from say 1922 to 1997, has the treatment of Larkin in survey histories changed over time: is it from nothing to little, to large? Fourthly and finally, does the product of the answers to these questions in itself tell us more about the historians themselves, or the changing preoccupations of Ireland's culture and society, than it does about Larkin?

This may be an eccentric proceeding and an eccentric paper if in talking and thinking about the writing of Larkin into or out of Irish history it omits the distinguished list of historical and biographical commentators from James Dunsmore Clarkson, through R. M. Fox, John W. Boyle, Emmet Larkin, Donal Nevin, Joe Deasy, Dermot Keogh, Desmond Greaves and Samuel Levenson, Andrew Boyd to Henry Patterson, Austen Morgan, and Emmet O'Connor. So be it: their contributions are matter for a separate commentary.

If then we are to consider Jim Larkin and the general historians, which general histories? For a people who see themselves, or are seen by others, as preoccupied with their past, it should come as a surprise that for a good fifty years after 1922, or after 1916, or 1913, there isn't all that much 'general history'. Paradoxically, as Ireland has become more 'modernised', 'pluralist', 'secularised', 'internationalist' or 'Europeanised' and tries to leave behind the pities and the pieties of its past, especially since 1970, there has been a large growth of historical writing, local and national, and in the production of general histories.

Surveying the scene in 1971, at the end of the fifty-year fallow period and at the beginning of the period of relative plenty, the late Theo Moody in a piece entitled 'Thirty-five years of Irish historiography' was to note a paradox: 'Within its limits Irish historical research since 1936 has produced an impressive body of new knowledge and new thinking,' but, significantly, he was forced to add, 'little progress has been made till recently in the writing of general history.'[1]

Indeed, as far as he was concerned, Irish historians before 1936, such as Dunlop, Wilson, Curtis, McNeill, Phillips, and D'Alton, had at least attempted 'boldly to construct general history' but since then 'the general history of Ireland has received little attention.' Indeed he added, somewhat depressingly, that until recently 'nearly all the general histories available were largely unsatisfactory—narrow in scope and sympathy, amateur in treatment, ill-informed, sadly out of date and often unreadable.'[2]

In surveying the general histories of Ireland that appeared during the period 1922–1960, say, with a particular look-out for Larkin, one is obliged to agree with Moody. The general historian has little time or space for Larkin or for 1913. What little treatment there was wasn't particularly hostile, and the approach tended to be simply factual, short but not unsympathetic. Monsignor E. A. D'Alton of University College, Galway, out of the more than four hundred pages of volume 8 of his *History of Ireland* devoted half a page to Larkin and 1913—a factual, unvarnished account, slightly sympathetic but essentially seeing the man and the events as an isolated episode intruding into the general narrative of events.[3]

As time went on, worse was to follow: neither Dunlop nor Wilson nor McNeill had anything to say, and the major general historian, Edmund Curtis, first published in 1936 and circulating thirty years and more later as a Methuen University Paperback, never once mentioned the labour movement and had a single passing reference to Larkin; he wrote, after referring to the emergence of the Ulster Volunteers: 'a General Strike organised in 1912 by James Larkin had been defeated by the employers, a disastrous victory it was to prove.' We are never told why; there is no other word on Larkin; and we are left with the great strike and lock-out happening a year before it did.[4]

With only one earlier exception, which will be referred to later, we had to wait until 1946 for redress. It was then that T. A. Jackson's *Ireland Her Own* appeared, by courtesy of the Cobbett Press. Jackson was already in his late sixties when this appeared, a lifetime as a left-wing activist behind him. A founder-member of the British Communist Party, he had no connection with Ireland other than a horror of the history of its exploitation and an admiration of the inspirational genius of Connolly. He wrote as an Englishman writing for Englishmen and in the context of the struggle of British and Irish people to free themselves and each other from the imperialism of the British ruling class.

Against that background, his account of Big Jim, with special reference to the period 1907–1914, was described as 'The Larkin Labour War'; his two pages on the subject, out of 443 pages, were brief, but he did at least try to offer an interpretation of the significance of Larkin and the lock-out. For Jackson it left behind 'a great growth in militant class consciousness among the Dublin workers,' 'a great enhancement of the reputations of Larkin and Connolly,' and 'the establishment of close relations between the young neo-Fenian intellectuals and the labour movement.' But, surprisingly, there is no biographical detail of Larkin, no assessment of the man and his impact, no judgment or interpretation of him, save for the cryptic comment that Larkin left Ireland for America in 1914 'to evade arrest and deportation to England.'[5]

Moody's negative comment of 1971 on the comparative paucity of general Irish history surveys had already been firmly remarked upon by Michael Tierney in 1952 when he observed: 'Books on Irish history, good, bad or indifferent, are sufficiently rare to be worth welcome irrespective of their quality.' The occasion was a review of two remarkable works that had appeared from Methuen in London in 1951 and 1952.[6] The more famous and more influential was P. S. O'Hegarty, *A History of Ireland under the Union, 1801–1922*; the less well known, probably less influential but more remarkable, was Erich Strauss, *Irish Nationalism and British Democracy*.

As to O'Hegarty, in his major volume of 811 pages there is only a solitary reference to Larkin, and it reads (p. 699): 'Irish labour was now directed by James Connolly, James Larkin having gone to America.' The only other reference, not to Larkin but to labour, is a short paragraph in reference to the Citizen Army (p. 672):

> This which grew out of a widespread Dublin strike in 1913 was organised in October 1913 by Captain J. R. White. It was not a national organisation but a class-conscious playacting reaction to the baton charges by the police during the strike for the 'defence of the workers'. Certain writers on this period have exaggerated its importance but it was only a playacting bellicosity until the Irish Volunteers put some reality into it, and save as an adjunct to that body, it has no place in the story.[7]

Such a cavalier dismissal of Larkin and Labour by a widely circulating author is significant, but not surprising. Already in his preface O'Hegarty made his position clear: 'I have been concerned almost wholly with political history because that is the important part of history, and social and economic factors are subordinate to it. I am unable to accept either the economic or the class-conscious interpretation of history.'[8]

An ex-IRB man himself, O'Hegarty wrote in the era of the Cold War, and it was as if in direct challenge and rebuttal of Strauss's work, which preceded it by a year. Strauss was a Marxist but not necessarily a communist, like Jackson. He wrote a very detailed and sympathetic account of, and was the first general historian to see, Belfast in 1907 as 'a landmark in British as well as Irish labour history.'[9] He was also the first and one of the few to note how rapidly, and despite setbacks, Larkin and his general labour union associates rose to prominence in and dominance of the trade union hierarchy and the Irish Trades Union Congress. And there is the graphic pen-picture of Larkin as 'a fearless and highly effective strike leader and negotiator with an intense egotism which made him impatient of criticism.'[10]

373

Finally, Strauss makes an original contribution by stressing how Larkin and Connolly, in capturing the Irish labour movement, made it truly independent of the British movement, with one fateful result: that it broke the all-Irish alliance of labour; the conquest of Irish trade unionism by the unskilled and rebellious transport workers made the break inevitable, with the result that 'the failure of the alliance forced the weakened southern working class movement into alliance with the nationalists.'[11]

We may not accept his facile suggestion that the labour movement was, north and south, a united one until the fractures occurred from the pressure of the new militant general trade unionism under Larkin, Connolly, and company. We may prefer to insist that the labour movement in Ireland was already divided in fact if not in name. However, Strauss at least opened up an avenue of thinking on the subject that was new and thoughtful.

There are wider virtues and defects in Strauss's work, but with it at last the place of labour in Irish history appears seriously on the stage of general history. Indeed, given the well-known political conservatism of Michael Tierney, it is a tribute to Strauss that, despite his mechanical application of Marxist theory to Irish history, it was 'a tour de force' and 'as always with Marxist history his work has the basic good qualities of thoroughness and industry,' and 'it often enables us to see familiar events in a new light. Nothing is more valuable for the student of Irish history than to be assisted to step outside the romantic, half-mythological version of it with which he has usually grown up.'[12]

And, strangely, though Tierney shared a good deal with O'Hegarty in outlook, he saw O'Hegarty as just as much a victim of ideology in his writing of history. Of course Tierney as a devout Catholic and Strauss as a Marxist had this much in common: each subscribed to a world view and a philosophy that was essentially global and impatient with the importunity of nationalism when nationalism itself was a creed that in certain extreme forms demanded a primary and exclusive loyalty. O'Hegarty was just such a nationalist, believing in no other god than the manifest destiny of the Irish nation.

Writing in 1971, without any reference to Tierney's views, Helen Mulvey was to echo them in her praise and strictures upon Strauss and in her dismissal of O'Hegarty's massive volume, which, 'despite its late date of publication (1952) already seems a period piece.'

After Strauss and O'Hegarty in 1951 and 1952 there was little new or noteworthy in the appearance of general histories, especially with regard to their treatment, or non-treatment, of Larkin and labour. Of the most noteworthy books to appear between 1932 and 1970 one must include J. C. Beckett's *Short History of Ireland* (1952) and *The Making of Modern Ireland, 1603–1923* (1966), Brian Inglis's *The Story of Ireland* (1956), Nicholas Mansergh's *The Irish Question, 1840–1921* (1965), T. W. Moody and F. X. Martin's *The Course of Irish History* (1967), F. X. Martin's *Leaders and Men of the 1916 Rising* (1967) (in which Edward MacLysaght had an interesting chapter on Larkin and Connolly and the labour movement), Laurence

McCaffrey's *The Irish Question, 1800–1922* (1968), and Oliver MacDonagh's *Ireland, the Union and its Aftermath* (1968).

Not one of these has anything very much to say about Larkin or the labour movement, beyond Inglis's passing description of Larkin as 'a redoubtable demagogue'. Perhaps the sole minor exception is Donal McCartney's few sentences in *The Course of Irish History*, where, covering the period 1891–1921 and referring to 1913 and the emergence of the Citizen Army, he instinctively shares Strauss's conclusion that the far-reaching results of Larkin's defeat in 1913 propelled labour towards the extreme nationalists and saw the emergence of a new sympathy between these persuasions.

From 1970, however, there was a great growth in the publishing of general histories, as the following short list for the seventies alone will indicate:

F. S. L. Lyons, *Ireland since the Famine*, London 1971.
P. F. O'Farrell, *Ireland's English Question*, London 1971.
E. R. Norman, *A History of Modern Ireland*, London 1971.
Robert Kee, *The Green Flag*, London 1972.
Ruth Dudley Edwards, *A New History of Ireland*, Dublin 1972.
J. J. Lee, *The Modernisation of Irish Society, 1848–1918*, Dublin 1973.
John A. Murphy, *Ireland in the Twentieth Century*, Dublin 1975.
M. Hechter, *Internal Colonialism*, London 1975.
Oliver MacDonagh, *Ireland, the Union and its Aftermath*, London 1977.
L. J. McCaffrey, *Ireland, from Colony to Nation State*, Englewood Cliffs (NJ) 1979.

To this list may be added since then the following works:

Roy Foster, *Modern Ireland, 1660–1972*, London 1988.
J. J. Lee, *Ireland, 1912–1985*, Cambridge 1989.
Dermot Keogh, *Twentieth-Century Ireland, Nation and State*, Dublin 1994.
W. E. Vaughan (editor), *A New History of Ireland, volume 6: Ireland under the Union, 1870–1921*, Dublin 1996.

What emerges clearly enough after 1970 is that Larkin and the labour movement, at least for the heroic period 1907–1913, now feature more prominently, though not always so. There is, for example, no mention by name of Larkin at all in Dudley Edwards's *New History of Ireland* (1972). In general, the treatment is slightly more extensive and slightly more sympathetic and a good deal more sensitive to context.

Whereas Helen Mulvey, surveying the scene in 1970, had to observe that 'Irish urban labour history … had been a neglected subject' (although she noted the importance of Emmet Larkin's, Desmond Greaves's and John W. Boyle's works), eleven years later Gearóid Ó Tuathaigh was able to observe that 'labour history has been making considerable progress in the past few years' and predicted a healthy growth for it in the nineteen-eighties.[13]

The results were to be seen in the treatment of Larkin in 1913. There was O'Farrell's identification of Larkin's syndicalism as a huge threat to the

Catholic religion, as seen by the contemporary hierarchy, in his singling out of Bishop Dwyer's condemnation in the pages of the *Catholic Bulletin* of Larkin's acceptance of English aid: 'Larkin has got our entire working population in his hands and out of our hand and he is working hard to accentuate the separation of priest from people' (Bishop Donnelly to Bishop O'Dwyer).[14]

O'Farrell was now able to identify one impact of Larkin and labour on general Irish history: 'to direct clerical attention on to the threat of socialism and away from the growth of revolutionary currents in nationalism,' and secondly, because of the fear of socialism, to dispose the bishops and clergy towards nationalism.

There was Robert Kee's relatively extensive attention to Larkin and one that was sympathetic in a new kind of way: he did not see Larkin and 1913 as an episode within and a digression from the main Home Rule Crisis narrative but as someone and something so powerful as to put these into the shade completely, if temporarily. Furthermore, he stressed that the more than twenty thousand unfortunates who were locked out in 1913 were locked out by employers who were ardent Home Rulers.

Laurence McCaffrey separately, as a general historian, felt it necessary to take into account Larkin as syndicalist and to integrate him and the movement as an essential part of the narrative rather than as an interruption of it.

But the most impressive treatment of Larkin in general histories from 1970 was to be found in the work of F. S. L. Lyons and of Edward Norman.

Lyons was the first major general historian to incorporate trade union history and Larkin extensively and fully into his survey, with a degree of detail and sympathy that is surprising. His description of Larkin as having 'a genius for oratory,' 'simple in his tastes,' 'widely read' and 'deeply compassionate' is new in survey history writing. His conclusions on Larkin's and 1913's legacy, apart from immediate defeat, being among other things a shift in the leadership of the labour movement is unique to him. And unique (almost entirely so) is his attention to Larkin in the twenties and in the forties.

Likewise, Edward Norman in *A History of Modern Ireland*, published in the same year (and scathingly received and reviewed by Irish historians), gives a greater attention to Larkin and to the labour movement than any orthodox general historian did or has done since. Norman's is one of the very few general surveys to mention the Knocklong or Bruree take-overs or the Limerick Soviet, and one of the very few to assert Larkin's stimulus to the growing self-consciousness of labour in Ireland. But it is hard to avoid the conclusion that Norman devotes this attention because it suits his underlying bias: that the union with Britain was not the huge problem that nationalists and nationalist historians made it out to be. Larkin and labour deserve attention, not for themselves but because they offered an alternative to the nationalist agenda.

One is tempted to wonder if something of the same could be said of Lyons: that he felt comfortable with Larkin in a way that he could not be with militant republicans like Collins or de Valera. And one cannot help noting that their attention, Strauss apart, is following in the style of Alison Phillips's remarkable work *The Revolution in Ireland, 1906–1923* (London, 1923). Phillips was at a polar opposite from P. S. O'Hegarty, for example in his assessment of the role of the Citizen Army: whereas O'Hegarty, as seen earlier, had dismissed it as mere 'playacting', Phillips saw it as taking 'the leading part in the Easter Week Rebellion' (p. 70). Phillips, of course, was unique in placing the developments in the labour movement under Connolly and Larkin within a European context, and his assessment of the significance of 1913 was based on this sense of context: 'The strike failed but its consequences were momentous. Liberty Hall became the centre of that spirit which was later to be known as Bolshevist.'

Perhaps Phillips, Lyons and Norman almost constitute a kind of liberal unionist tradition that sees Larkin and labour in almost British terms, as distinct from Ulster unionist or Irish nationalist or Irish-American nationalist historiography: to put it crudely, Larkin deserves attention because he queers the pitch.

Be that so or not, it is clear that after 1970 Larkin features in general historical treatments of Ireland in a fuller and more sympathetic and more integrated way, and that is in no small measure due to the work of Irish labour biographers, editors and historians from the mid-sixties to the present and to the work also of their associates in economic and social history.

Gearóid Ó Tuathaigh's prediction in 1981 that labour history was due a healthy growth in the eighties was well borne out: we have only to list a selection that would include the following:

Henry Patterson, *Class Conflict and Sectarianism*, Belfast 1980.
Donal Nevin (editor), *Trade Unions and Change in Irish Society*, Cork 1980.
J. Anthony Gaughan, *Thomas Johnson*, Dublin 1980.
Dermot Keogh, *The Rise of the Irish Working Class*, Belfast 1982.
C. Desmond Greaves, *The Irish Transport and General Workers' Union*, Dublin 1982.
Seán Redmond, *The Irish Municipal Employees' Trade Union*, Dublin 1983.
John Gray, *City in Revolt*, Belfast 1985.
Séamus Cody, John O'Dowd, and Peter Rigney, *The Parliament of Labour*, Dublin 1986.
John W. Boyle, *The Irish Labor Movement in the Nineteenth Century*, Washington 1988.
Emmet O'Connor, *Syndicalism in Ireland, 1917–1923*, Cork 1988.
Fergus A. D'Arcy and Ken Hannigan (editors), *Workers in Union*, Dublin 1988.
Mary Jones, *These Obstreperous Lassies*, Dublin 1988.
Liam Cahill, *Forgotten Revolution*, Dublin 1989.
Emmet O'Connor, *A Labour History of Waterford*, Waterford 1989.

Gary Sweeney, *In Public Service*, Dublin 1990.

T. J. Morrissey, *A Man Called Hughes*, Dublin 1991.

Austen Morgan, *Labour and Partition*, London 1991.

Emmet O'Connor, *A Labour History of Ireland, 1824–1960*, Dublin 1992.

W. K. Anderson, *James Connolly and the Irish Left*, Dublin 1994.

Donal Nevin (editor), *Trade Union Century*, Dublin 1994.

In the general surveys that followed, from 1980 to the present, it is interesting to note the impact of these labour histories on general history. Notable among these were Roy Foster's *Modern Ireland, 1660–1972* (1988), J. J. Lee's *Ireland, 1912–1985* (1989), Dermot Keogh's *Twentieth-Century Ireland, Nation and State* (1994), and W. E. Vaughan's *A New History of Ireland, volume 6: Ireland under the Union, 1870–1921* (1996). Two of these writers, Keogh and Lee, had already published significant work on aspects of labour history in their own right and might therefore have been expected to attentively integrate Larkin and 1913 significantly into their general survey. As it happened, Lee's starting date of 1912 undoubtedly constricted his treatment—but did so to the extent that there is virtually nothing on Larkin. Lyons's chapter in Vaughan continued the sympathetic and serious consideration of Larkin as a force, now acknowledging specialist influences on him, and gave a very full assessment of the legacy of Larkin and 1913.

Keogh, like Lyons, saw Larkin as important enough to refer to his return in 1923 and to his death in 1947. Finally, Foster gives closer attention to the appalling conditions in Dublin than does any other general historian, attributes to Larkin the fact that labour in Ireland, as evidenced by 1913, had moved into a new phase, and is the only one of the general historians to treat of Larkin in Belfast in 1907. His overall treatment of labour in Irish history is unique in its sensitivity to working-class unionist politics and in its referencing or contextualising Larkin and the labour movement between 1906 and 1913 in the context of European labour history, however briefly.

All this is in sharp contrast to the neglect of Larkin and labour that characterised much of the general presentation of Irish history by Irish historians up to twenty years ago and is a very particular testimony to the impact of specialised research and publication of Irish labour history on the discipline at large.

Chapter 47

Historians on Larkin

John W. Boyle

James Larkin is a figure from the heroic age of trade unionism. From 1907 to 1914, he dominated and transformed the Irish labour movement, infusing it with some of his own gospel of divine discontent. A close examination of his work shows that he organised skilfully, gathering members steadily and negotiating with considerable ability. But when he felt that a crisis was reached he would not give way.

Larkin was determined to establish the right of the labourer to join a union, and was prepared, if it was not conceded, to invoke his doctrine of 'tainted goods' and use the weapon of the sympathetic strike. These tactics called forth his superb gifts as an agitator and incidentally created in the minds of his enemies the image of Larkin as a destructive force. It is true that the organisation proper suffered in these struggles and that the work of his successors consisted of consolidation before expansion, but without Larkin's initial efforts there would have been nothing to build on.

His desire for a socialist society was strong, even if he saw it in less precise detail than his fellow-unionist Connolly. Unlike him he left no body of doctrine—he had not Connolly's powers of detachment or analysis—but what he wrote is still worth reading for his telling phrases, its hatred of cruelty and oppression and its passionate desire for justice, as the files of his paper, the *Irish Worker*, bear witness.[1]

Jesse D. Clarkson

Larkin was ever able at a moment's notice to mingle blistering epithets with literary and classical allusions, knit together with a thoroughly Irish native humour. His outstanding characteristics throughout his life were his quick sympathy for all the downtrodden and his flaming resentment for all forms of injustice. The magnetism and courage that poured from him and the independent life and vigour that surged up among the apparently hopeless casual labourers of Dublin, Belfast, Cork and other Irish towns are well-known phenomena.

From its meagre beginnings (its original assets were a table, a couple of chairs, two empty bottles, and a candle—the Larkin family furniture on occasion was sold to eke out strike pay), the ITGWU rose swiftly to dominate the Irish Trades Union Congress and become the backbone of the nascent Irish Labour Party.

Larkin has sometimes been characterised as a revolutionary syndicalist. Certainly he brought to Ireland the 'new unionism' with all its syndicalist implications. Certainly his methods and his intent were revolutionary, both in Ireland and in America. Yet he regarded himself not as a syndicalist, but as a socialist. He was widely read in socialist literature, but he had an instinctive distrust of any nicely worked-out philosophy. His own activities were ever concerned with trade unions, though not in the old bowler-hatted sense. No mere apostle of divine discontent, he had ever in mind practical existing conditions—and the desire to remedy them in the here and now.

Larkin's nationalism was innate and intense.

Big Jim rose above all 'isms'. He was simply an outstanding human being—a man of universal stature, physically and spiritually—who acted in accord with no jelled body of doctrines, who acted intuitively, sometimes blunderingly but always honestly and fearlessly, in tune with the warmth and breadth of his own nature.[2]

George Dangerfield

Larkin had begun to make his living, at the age of eleven, in one of the most viciously slum-ridden and criminal cities in Europe (Liverpool). Bellicose and imaginative, vindictive and compassionate, Larkin was a marvellous extrusion from that dreadful environment, above which he rose by sheer force of character, and which he longed to dispel.

He was a tall, ungainly man, with blue-black hair and burning eyes. He had a quick wit, an immense voice, a marvellous rhetoric, all uttered in a harsh Liverpool accent. 'You cannot argue with the prophet Isaiah,' said one Dublin employer, after an unprofitable exchange of words with Larkin: but if ever a social Isaiah was needed, surely he was needed here.

Nearly 26,000 families out of a city of 300,000 were huddled together in the Dublin slums, the verminous haunts of drunkenness, immorality, disease and crime. It is no wonder that the Dublin death rate was a horrible 24.8 per thousand, chiefly due to infant mortality and tuberculosis, both higher than anything that could be found in Great Britain, itself no sanitary paradise. And at the root of all this lay unemployment, casual employment, sweated labour, social indifference, and the Dublin Corporation, one of the most corrupt city governments in all Europe.

It is not hard to imagine how inconvenient, to say the least, was the proletarian voice of James Larkin, echoing and re-echoing in such an environment. Larkin was a virtuoso in the use of sympathetic strikes, to which Dublin as a trading city was especially vulnerable. It was for his deployment of such strikes and for his belief in one big union that Larkin was labelled a syndicalist—a heady word in those days.

Whether he really was one is another matter. Since it meant 'Trade Unionism' and implied a belief in class warfare as a fact of life, in the primacy of production, and in the crying need for economic activism, then in these terms Larkin was a Syndicalist indeed. One thing, at any rate, is certain: his importance to the history of Irish insurrection is that he brought revolution into Dublin and this revolution had a distinctly nationalist tendency.[3]

Richard Dawson

At this moment Larkin stepped upon the Irish stage, a man knowing little of philosophy and caring less, heedless of the past, reckless of the future, looking only at the present, and seeing it through eyes glowing with revolutionary fire—no logician, inconsequent, perhaps sometimes incoherent in argument, but gifted with burning speech, violent, coarse, but singularly effective with the people to whom he spoke. Like Connolly, James Larkin was a revolutionary by instinct and bitter experience in the depths …

Whether he was attracted by it or whether he created it, wherever Larkin went there was generally trouble.[4]

R. M. Fox

Into this underworld of Dublin came Jim Larkin, restless, eager, militant—a vital force expressing a burning indignation against social injustice and calling for revolt. To the conservative-minded employers be came as a dreaded, lurid 'strike organiser'.

His methods were crude—as crude as the evils he attacked. Whether Larkin roused hatred or enthusiasm none could deny that he was a force, and that with his coming the whole of the submerged element of Irish Labour stirred. He was a crater through which the rumble of social discontents poured out. The feeling of hopeless stagnation gave place to agitation and unrest.

Always Larkin relied upon defiance, upon individuality, upon a sense of justice and indignation which enabled him to triumph over wrong and to enthuse his followers. Looking at Larkin and listening to him they came to believe in their own strength and they developed a feeling of self-reliance which they never possessed before. It was to the human will and the human spirit that Larkin made his direct appeal.

He was a man of passionate sincerity and rugged poetic eloquence. I often listened to him, framed in the big window of Liberty Hall, one foot up on the sill, his arms holding each side, while a blur of white faces in Beresford Place shone through the gloom.[5]

Larkin was a crater through which volcanic rumblings emerged from the great upheaving force responsible for social tremors throughout the world … a man who could have stood as a model for the Rise of the Underman, the Triumph of Labour, Atlas Bearing the World upon his Shoulders, or any other title which an artist cared to give to an ideal representation of the militant working class.[6]

David Howell

Perceptions of its [ITGWU] distinctiveness was moulded inevitably by the personality of James Larkin. Even many sympathetic to the struggles of the Dublin workers expressed their reservations about his lack of tact. His style posed obstacles for both conventional trade unionists and middle-class sympathisers. A *New Statesman* portrait ['Anarchism in Dublin', 6 September 1913] in the dispute's early days epitomised this distancing:

He is one of those born revolutionaries who know not diplomacy, but who believe that the Kingdom of Heaven must be taken by violence today and tomorrow and the day after ... His utopia, we feel, would be a world where a general strike was going on all the time. Big and black and fierce, he is a Syndicalist of the street corners ... He calls to the surface the very depth of unrest. His theory seems to be that a city should never be allowed a moment's rest so long as there remains a single poor man whose wrongs have not been righted. His genius ... is inflammatory. He preaches turmoil.

Reservations about Larkin were not restricted to the unpredictable consequences of his fiery radicalism. Connolly's revolutionary credentials were unassailable, yet he had severe misgivings about Larkin's autocratic tendencies. [Howell quotes a letter written by Connolly to William O'Brien, 13 September 1912:]

> I begin to fear that our friend Jim has arrived at his highest elevation, and that he will pull us all down with him in his fall ... He must rule or he will not work, and in the present stage of the Labour Movement he has us at his mercy. And he knows it, and using his power unscrupulously I regret to say ... I am sick of all this playing to one man ...

The revolt of the Dublin workers was based on harsh material factors, yet discussion of the dispute, its origins and possible solutions centred around Larkin's volcanic personality.

Such a dominant image is significant, it helped to mould the responses of contemporaries, but it was a caricature. Larkin ... spoke for workers in revolt, not just against employers, but also against cautious trade union officials. He envisaged the union, not simply as an industrial instrument, but as the basis for the flowering of a socialist culture.

But by the summer of 1913, industrial conflict in Dublin had become symbolised in the clash of two individuals. William Martin Murphy was the dominant figure in the city's business community ... his austere style was a universe removed from Larkin's rumbustious agitation ... [Murphy's] antipathy towards the Transport Workers was total. In particular, the doctrine of the 'sympathetic strike' challenged Murphy's perception of managerial prerogatives.[7]

T. A. Jackson

Nobody who ever saw or heard Larkin could fail to be impressed and inspired by his magnificent personality. He was magnificently immovable once he started on a line and he had just the personality which made it possible for him to work the miracle of organising the so-called unorganisable.[8]

Robert Kee

The labour troubles in Ireland were the climax to years of activity in the trade union field by a wild and dynamic organizing genius named James

Larkin ... All sensed in him, rightly, an independent, restless force dangerous to all carefully prescribed modes of thinking. His one concern, manically displayed through a powerful ego, was to organize effectively for their own welfare the wretched urban working classes of Ireland ...

Larkin, lion-hearted and personally erratic, was assisted in his work by two remarkable lieutenants of different character from himself [William O'Brien and James Connolly].[9]

Dermot Keogh

Larkin, as general secretary, was not the easiest man to work with. He was a supremely disorganised person who never tried to conceal his contempt and loathing for the busy bureaucrat. His spirit was administratively uncontainable and not even a battalion of bureaucrats could untangle the list of untended correspondence, unpaid bills, etc. left in his wake. His inside pocket was his filing cabinet, and his spontaneity had its drawbacks ...

Larkin did not exactly convert people to his own image and likeness. The reason for his popularity was partially due to his ability to adapt and sail with the prevailing wind. When he came to Dublin to settle in 1908 he was a comparative neophyte in the trade union movement. During most of his earlier life he had put more faith in politics as a fulcrum for social change ... He was really a trade unionist by accident, a politician by vocation and a socialist by conviction. He did not so much draw his inspiration from the writings of Marx as from Marxist thinkers, pamphleteers, street orators and his personal experience of the 'class struggle'.

There was one other influence which shaped the direction of his thought and that was Christianity. Raised in Liverpool's Irish ghetto, ritualistic Catholicism as he saw it practised there repulsed the young Larkin. Yet, he saw behind the facade a philosophy which offered both an explanation and a remedy for social injustice. Marxist categories, Larkin thought, amplified and best expressed the radical essence of the Christian message. His marriage of secular and sacred thought was that of an eclectic rather than a scientific synthesis. Publicly, Larkin declared himself an avowed Marxist but in no sense was he a purist ...[10]

Emmet Larkin

Words are almost impossible to find to describe Larkin's ascendancy over the workers in this period [1911–14] ... The reasons for the hero worship of Larkin by the Dublin working class are a combination of the historical, personal, and psychological. The psychological need of the inarticulate masses to express themselves is not a new idea. The Dublin masses found their instrument in Jim Larkin. Larkin's ability to identify himself with the masses, to be only one of themselves yet something more than each, was the basis of his power ...

By 1913 Larkin had convinced the Dublin working classes that he was their instrument, working only in their interest and for their welfare. His honesty, integrity and sincerity of purpose in these years is unquestioned.

In these years Larkin made his union something more than an instrument of industrial advance. He made it a vehicle for social and cultural advancement as well.[11]

Joseph J. Lee

Labour appeared poised to at last emerge as a major party after the 1943 election ... It promptly rose to the challenge by tearing itself apart in an internecine struggle between the ancient adversaries, William O'Brien and 'Big Jim' Larkin. O'Brien, the powerful General Secretary of the Transport Union, was mainly responsible. Larkin, the stormy petrel of earlier years, was gradually making his peace with the party. O'Brien was determined to stop him ... O'Brien was a classic case of the successful apparatchik so frequently found in Irish organisations, combining fine administrative abilities with a domineering personality and a narrow mind. He was the type of man, only too common in Ireland, who prefers to wreck a movement rather than lose control of it.[12]

[Prof. Lee in *Ireland, 1912–1985: Politics and Society* (1989), devoted precisely eight lines to Larkin and the events of 1913 in a 754-page book.]

Samuel Levenson

Larkin was fiery revolution incarnate; a man able to set crowds aflame while seeming to speak to each listener individually; a man contemptuous of logic or theory, who identified himself with the cause, and trod on other people's toes mercilessly. Connolly soon came to detest his ebullience and unpredictability. He squirmed when he heard him support sound courses of action with appallingly wrong arguments. Though he applauded publicly Larkin's courage and his ability to come down on the side of the angels, he doubted inwardly that Jim received his instructions directly from God.

The employers attributed all this [the wave of industrial unrest in 1911] to the work of Larkin, an easy error to make as they watched him captivate thousands of workers every night at indoor or outdoor meetings. Over six feet tall, he was a powerful, natural orator, with a 'deep, dark, husky voice and an endless flow of words and sweeping gestures.'[13]

F. S. L. Lyons

Larkin was one of the most remarkable labour leaders to have emerged in these islands in the last hundred years ...

That Larkin was almost larger than life goes without saying; that he was physically a big man, handsome, a marvellous orator, magnetic in the highest degree—all this we know. It is easy to see why the people loved him. It is, alas, also easy to see why he was in the end such a colossal failure. Like many great demagogues who thrive on the plaudits of the crowd, Larkin was at best an erratic administrator, quick-tempered, high-handed and temperamentally unsuited to the day-to-day manipulation of men. Perhaps we do not have to go much farther to understand why control of his movement passed eventually to quieter, more cautious leaders. Even in his heyday there were signs and portents of what was to happen in later life.

The more one studies Larkin's career the more one is led to the conviction that at the centre of this proud, sensitive, flamboyant man there was a kind of chaos.

He had one ruling passion—to achieve a better and a fuller life for his fellow-workers. And for him this meant not simply better wages, hours and working conditions, but enlargement of life by admitting into drab homes whatever could be won of education and beauty. It was this about him which attracted Seán O'Casey ...[14]

Larkin read widely and used his reading to fortify a vivid imagination and a natural gift, or rather genius for flamboyant oratory. Larkin's speeches were larger than life because Larkin himself was larger than life. Physically a very powerful man, he had a big presence and an even bigger voice which allowed him to dominate vast meetings even in the open air. He himself asked little enough of existence—he was simple in his taste, simple in his religion (he may have remained a Catholic though he castigated the Church for its attitude to social problems), simple in his vision of a society that would bring beauty as well as security to the working-class home. 'Here', as Seán O'Casey summed him up, 'was a man who would put a flower in a vase on a table as well as a loaf on a plate!' But his emotions, too, seemed more intense than those of ordinary men. He was driven by a deep compassion and tenderness for the poor to preach 'the divine gospel of discontent.' The other side of that gospel was a *saeva indignatio* against employers who exploited their workers, or against trade union officials who failed to protect their members. Larkin, once enraged, respected neither laws nor conventions nor individuals and his creative years were passed in a frenzy of passionate involvement and controversy. He was the archetypal bull in a china shop and it was a moot point whether irate industrialists or staid trade unionists were more alarmed by his eruption onto the Irish scene.[15]

Nicholas Mansergh

Larkin was a man of crude but fiery eloquence and picturesque appearance whose ability to sow the wind was as undoubted as his inability to control the whirlwind ... But, whatever his extravagances—and a price was enacted for them—he knew well, possibly better than any other man of his time, how to sustain the morale and to stir the emotions of the hungry workless of 1913.[16]

Arthur Mitchell

The establishment of industrial unionism in Ireland and the story of James Larkin are inevitably intertwined. That demagogic, inspiring and controversial figure swept into Ireland like a human tornado, organising, in turn, the neglected unskilled workers of Belfast, Cork and Dublin.

Larkin was a commanding figure in the Irish labour movement from the creation of his union in late 1908 until he left for America in 1914.[17]

Deasún Ó Riain

Ní thuigtear fós i gceart, dar ndóigh, an méid maitheasa a rinne Ó Lorcáin ar son fear oibre na tíre lena linn, agus an méid a rinne sé ar a bhealach féin chun réabhlóid na hÉireann do chur ar siúl. Dúirt an tOllamh Liam Ó Briain uair 'of Larkin it is incontestable that he revived an almost extinct flame of nationalism in thousands of Dublin workmen.' Bhí an bharúil chéanna ag an bPiarsach nuair a dúirt sé sa bhliain 1913 go raibh níos mó déanta ag an Lorcánach chun Caisleán Bhaile Átha Cliath a leagadh agus réim iasachta a scrios taobh istigh de sé míosa ná éinne eile le leath-chéad bliain. Ach caithfear admháil freisin go raibh dhá Lorcánach ann .i. an laoch agus an buachaill báire. Bhí nós meidhreach aige-sin i gcónaí fabhailscéal a mheascadh ina chuid cainte agus go minic mheasc sé an fhírinne fós leis an bhfabhailscéal.

Mar a dúirt R. M. Fox: 'He was a great romanticist and a great romancer. This always put his more mundane critics and enemies in a rage. But Larkin could not help seeing himself as the centre of a thrilling saga. Usually he did hold this position so there was a fundamental truth about his attitude, however uncertain the details might be.' Agus go cinnte b'iontach na 'details' úd!

Ach ar an dtaobh eile den scéal, do bhí an saga féin níos iontaí arís. I mBéal Feirste sa bhliain 1907 rinne se míorúilt nach ndearna éinne roimhe sin ná ó shin. Mharbhaigh sá fearmad creidimh sa chathair sin maol marbh agus shiúil Caitiliceach agus Protastánach, Fíníní agus Fir Oráiste guala ar ghualainn fána gcuid bratacha féin agus iad go léir aontaithe i gcúis an Lucht Oibre.

Inneasfar mar chuimhne ar an Lorcánach go deo an gníomh do rinne sé nuair a labhair sé ó chéimeanna Theach an Chustaim i mBéal Feirste ar an 12 lá de mhí Iúil 1907 leis na sluaite comhaontaithe sin. 'Ní raibh a leithéid ann riamh ná o shin,' arsa Alice Milligan uair, 'ní raibh an fearmad chomh marbh céanna ariamh, ní raibh lucht oibre chomh cairdiúil le chéile, ní raibh an spiorad náisiúnta ariamh chomh láidir is do bhí sna laethe sin.'[18]

W. Alison Phillips

James Larkin, a fiery and somewhat irresponsible demagogue ... The [1913] strike failed, but its consequences were momentous. Liberty Hall became definitely the centre of the spirit which was to be known later as Bolshevist.[19]

Desmond Ryan

Larkin had fanned up the smouldering discontent of the masses and breathed a new spirit into Irish trade unionism and labour political bodies in general. Jim Larkin had much kindliness of heart, and Elizabethan directness of diction, a love for the poetry of Walt Whitman and Francis

Thompson, an immense power of gripping popular audiences. He aroused the vague, incoherent and almost helpless masses and wielded them into harmonious union, articulate, organised and militant.

Jim Larkin, not unjustly struck the popular eye as the inspiration, and indeed, as the fomenter of the revolt. From an open window in Liberty Hall the well-known figure of the strike leader dominated the scene—a strong, sturdy, fighting frame, a face of rare determination and purpose, with fierce blue eyes that drop before no man's, a voice that seemed as the long silent voice of the underpeople, ringing out with a rude, eloquent beauty upon a hitherto listless, now startled world.

Night after night, this husky, roaring giant of labour thunders out the strangest talks that have ever stirred a multitude: no balanced periods, no favourite whimsicalities, no cleverly prepared surprises. Nay, none of these, nor the recondite philosophy of a Karl Marx, the subtle triflings of a George Bernard Shaw, the sentimental trenchant appeals of a Keir Hardie; but rather facts known to the audience, the virtues of temperance, bowelless employers, white-livered curs, adjectived scabs, and other obnoxious individuals. Above all, what was to be done that night, tomorrow, next week.

Dublin workers tighten belts to an enthusiastic murmur; 'Good luck to you, Jim Larkin! We will fight on![20]

W. P. Ryan

Jim Larkin is the greatest figure in Irish Labour mythology. I well remember the swift, strange growth of the marvel, the dire magic of the sinister, tremendous 'Larkin' of the legend, several months before I met the human 'Jim' in the actual world.

Larkin came, agitated Belfast, and generally set to work in far obscure quarters of our Irish world, and soon there was a curious sense of something sinister and haunting in the background of life.

By the hostile he was deemed rude, domineering, turbulent, prone to passion and exaggeration; to the detached he seemed vigorous, reckless, racy; to the sympathetic he was often somewhat distressing, and by no means definite and conclusive in his social and industrial philosophy. What were his ideals, and where lay his goal? His harangues and exhortations suggested different conclusions. He advised, exhorted, struggled, and struck from instinct, from an intense pity for the slave class amongst which he had grown; yet from a feeling of pride in its manhood, depressed and distorted though it might be; and from a stern determination to secure fair play. He did not come with any shapely social scheme, he had not learning or leisure in the way of Utopias; but he had a burning desire to right the immediate wrong, and to go on battling against the next.

He called ugly things by their names, his more than childlike simplicity in this regard being mistaken for calculated daring and the desire to give offence. He said rude blunt things when he and his were cheated and hurt;

the life circumstances did not tend to bring a naturally strong and earnest character, the doubtful graces of finesse and circumlocution. Through all this two of his most decided characteristics were liable to be obscured: his genuine kindliness of heart and—although he was not always easy to work with—his faculty of conciliation.

Larkin went straight to the men in the workshops and the unions—though he also talked to them in ringing tones abroad—and dwelt far more on what was pressing and painful at the moment than on what might be permanently true or ideally right. He told them home-truths on the subject of their own faults and weaknesses; he spared them no more than the masters. He did not suggest the student or the thinker, though he had studied and thought to some purpose, loving poetry at least as much as economics. His experiences in the terrible human (or inhuman) school through which he had passed gave him a unique mould and driving force. Below and beyond all there was a magnetic power not easily described. But the undermen felt it from the first, and that made all the difference.

Jim Larkin had come down on a big adventure, and, though it was not realised till a few years later, something far greater than the starting of a trade union, Irish or English, was at issue.

Jim Larkin, moving amongst despised dockers, carters and land-slaves, lit fires that at one and the same time were beacons, bewildering portents and irritants. It took a long time for even idealists to see that the flame he brought was but part of the Gleam and the Ideal that had never died in his race. The Kingdom of Heaven is within us, we know from the Gospel; but who had sought for it hitherto amongst the slums and unskilled slaves of Dublin?[21]

Erich Strauss

In 1907 Larkin started his conquest of Ireland ... His activities began with the great Belfast strike of 1907 which was a landmark in British as well as in Irish labour history ...

James Larkin combined the qualities of a fearless and highly effective strike leader and agitator with an intense egotism which made him impatient of criticism and difficult to deal with. But his lack of business habits, which infuriated British trade unionists like James Sexton, and his lack of balance, which repelled well-meaning supporters like Captain Jack White, the eccentric founder of the Citizen Army, did not prevent him from recalling James Connolly to Ireland, in order to endow the young movement with all the qualities in which Larkin himself was patently lacking.[22]

John Swift

1913 was an eventful year for labour in Dublin. The events that year brought all the enemies of labour and progress out into the open. The writer is old enough to remember how the slogans of the day filled the streets of Dublin with exultant, often angry, people ... In 1913, the Dublin, nay, the Irish workers, were receptive to noble slogans. They loved to hear them. What is more, they read them. That volcanic periodical, the *Irish Worker*, was a banner of slogans—a banner riding the torrent of a class's anger and struggle. It was not in its black ink, but rather in the livid fervour of the movement's message that the downtrodden read: An injury to one is the concern of all. The Great appear great because we are on our knees. Let us rise! Then the doubting and the timorous were rebuked and heartened: who is it that speaks of defeat? I tell you, a cause like ours is greater than defeat can know. It is the power of powers!

We remember how, when these holy stirrings had stung reaction to calumny, a new noun, connoting everything that was evil, was added to the dictionary of the lackey editors and orators whose task it now was to blacken the Irish Trade Union Movement. The term 'Larkinism' was intended to be synonymous with anarchy and irreligion ...

Outside the craft unions were the masses of the untouchable, the so-called 'unskilled' and 'semi-skilled'. These pariahs of the working class, however, were not untouchable to the heavy harness wherewith their ill-nourished bodies were yoked to the harvest wains and the tumbrils of Irish capitalism.

Some of these helots dug the merchants' boats and hauled the heavy cargoes of the millers and the builders on the quays of Dublin. There was little in their wretched lives of that romance suggested by the Volga Boatman's Song or by that effort of one of our own poets, The Canadian Boatman's Song. The Dublin quay labourer slaved as hard as the Russian serf or the convict-lumberman; and if his back was not bowed to a Cossack's knout, his life was no less burdened by ill-paid drudgery.

At last, under irresistible leadership, the despised found their place in the upward march. Whatever the defeat and confusion in 1913, from 1908 on the great masses of the general workers were now in the ranks—nay, in the vanguard of the Irish Trade Union and Labour movement. The leaders of the newly-organised general workers became the leaders of the Movement.[23]

David Thomson

With Ireland heading for civil war—for the Nationalist Volunteers, like the Ulstermen, were drilling and arming—there grew up in Dublin a new syndicalist movement led by James Larkin and James Connolly. It preached the contemporary European creeds of riot, the general strike, guild socialism, syndicalist revolution. Larkin's Irish Transport Workers' Union fought a great transport strike in Dublin in 1913, and it led to a crop of sympathetic strikes and riots. Linked through Connolly with the Irish Volunteers, this desperate syndicalist movement of the workers seemed for a time yet another element in the forthcoming Irish civil war ... But here, as elsewhere in Europe, the bigger crisis of 1914 swamped all lesser quarrels. In the Summer of 1914 it seemed certain that a general strike would soon occur in Britain. If it had, both Irish syndicalist revolt and Irish civil war would doubtless have merged into it. Sarajevo happened just in time to save the parliamentary system in Britain.[24]

Jacqueline van Voris

Jim Larkin was a spellbinding speaker, the most dynamic ever heard in Dublin. He had the gift of stirring his audiences to action and giving them confidence in him and what he was doing. Most important of all, he gave them confidence in themselves. A fighter by instinct and by training, he inspired strong emotions in anyone who had dealings with him. He was often worshipped by the workers, and just as often hated by the employers. Some of the union officials mistrusted his every move, others followed his lead unquestioningly. But no one ever discounted his courage.

Whether he was a socialist, a syndicalist, or simply a powerful, anarchic personality, no one was sure, but everyone looked on him as a force, which they called 'Larkinism.'[25]

Chapter 48

Writers on Larkin

Dominic Behan

Larkin gave a new meaning to Christianity when he decided to fight his cleric critics with their own cannons—a Bible and a plea for a true brotherhood of man. When they accused him of being a red menace, he threw back the suggestion that they were un-Christian, but it was in Larkin's mouth more than a suggestion, it was an indictment of the Christian soldiers who were prepared to stand by and see the children of Christ starve.[1]

Daniel Corkery

I took him to be a man of ideas, some of them wrong but most of them right, or at least right according to my lights. I saw in him a powerful advocate of temperance and an apostle of nationality. I regarded him as one earnest to a fault, for I never heard him speak to the class for which he stood that he did not half offend them by dwelling on the failings which kept them powerless and timid. And in my estimate was much of pity, because I saw that the man stood alone and guideless; by dint of experience, he had slept in every workhouse from Land's End to John-O-Groats; by dint of reading it was his custom to quote poetry as freely as I would myself if I had more courage; by brooding and thinking on problems that for his companions must practically have had no existence—he had raised himself so much above his fellows that he deceived himself if he believed he could find lieutenants in their ranks. Here is a drama for any Ibsen that cares to write it—the failure of a leader of the democracy to find lieutenants.[2]

Gabriel Fallon

Came a trouble maker called James Larkin, a rabble-rouser if ever there was one, a man with a mission and one armed with the vituperative power of a Leon Bloy. Like Bloy he was on the side of the poor, the downtrodden, the oppressed.

He began to organise the workers, to instil into them the knowledge that they were men and not slaves: he was determined that they should walk erect and not on all fours like beasts of burden. He wanted to give them back their place in society and their dignity as creatures formed in the image of God.

Well-to-do Dublin organised itself against him. Pulpits thundered against his socialism. It was considered that the sacred rights of private property were in danger. No one seemingly knew enough of Aquinas to proclaim the fact that the possession of property carried with it duties as well as rights.

But Larkin raged on, declaring that he spoke and acted in the spirit of the Beatitudes. He was immediately dubbed 'Anti-Christ'.

A paper calling itself Catholic asked if the rats that infested the Dublin tenements were to be allowed to dictate to the respectable citizens of Dublin. Trade unionism took on the scarlet of a newly-discovered deadly sin. Then came the great Lock-Out and thanks to Larkin the hungry children of Dublin's workers were fed by the trade unionists of England.

This in itself was bad enough but the move to send the children to England set the devil's seal on this man's work. Now the Faith was in danger.

The pulpits thundered anew. With the honourable exception of a handful of priests—all of them regulars—the voice of every cleric in the diocese was set against the Red Hand of Larkin and his Union. Hymn-singing bands of Confraternity men marched down the quays determined to snatch from eternal perdition those children whom this Anti-Christ was attempting to deport.[3]

James T. Farrell

Larkin was emotional, impetuous, violent, extravagant. In his speeches and in his actions, he was an improviser. He did not stop to reason or to plan. He spoke with a rapid flow, with sweeping gestures. His speeches were filled with hyperbole, with castigation, with acidity, with sentimentality, and with rousing appeals. In one speech he declaimed that it was his divine mission to preach subversion and discontent to the working classes. This more than suggests his style. He was brave to the point of foolhardiness, and he was self-sacrificing. Again and again, he was ready and willing to give up his life and be a martyr of the working class. In his great days as an organiser and an agitator, he lived a life of danger. He gave his services to the struggle for the emancipation of the working class of the world: at the same time, he refused to appear on the same platform with an American Socialist of international repute because this man was divorced!

In a period when the most depressed sections of the Irish working class were militant, he was peculiarly fitted to play the role of agitator. His ability to lash their enemies, and to rouse and stir them, enabled him to appeal to their manhood, to the will to freedom which slept within their hearts. He added his own daring example to the appeal of his words. And when he led these workers in strikes he was adamant, uncompromising, and in the forefront when danger lurked. His bravery and daring were as extravagant as his foibles. But in a period of letdown, of retreat, of the sodden rule of the middle classes and the clergymen in Ireland, he was like a lost child. In the slums of Dublin after 'the Troubles', he could not repeat what he had done in this same area in the early days of this century. This was apparent when I saw him in Dublin in 1938. He was embittered.[4]

Frank Harris

It is difficult to meet Larkin, even casually, without becoming interested in him. He is very tall, well over six feet, loose built, with the figure of a youth. His hair is greying and there are lines about the eyes and mouth that tell of middle-age. The large grey eyes, however, are still laughing and boyish and the mobile lips humorous, persuasive; the features are all well-cut, Greek rather than Celtic; a very quiet, unassuming, rather handsome fellow, with sympathetic, conciliatory manners. He spoke admirable, quiet English, the English of a well-read man with a gift of fluent expression.

His choice of words reminded me of Galsworthy, his facility of Bernard Shaw. And the marvel was that what he said was as good as his easy way of saying it. He understood labour conditions in Ireland and England and these United States better than anyone with whom I have ever talked—a singularly wise, fair, fine mind, the equal of the best politicians I have met in Washington or in France or even in England, where the politician is sometimes almost a statesman. I say, deliberately, there is no company of the most distinguished in the world where Jim Larkin would not hold his own and have his place.[5]

Francis MacManus

Towards the end of his life, Dublin, which he once ruled, seemed like a cage for the tall, handsome figure of Jim Larkin. Somehow we had met, and on trams and in the street he used to talk to me, in a paternal way, in that deep, purring growl of his that could break out into a roar from the platform. With the broad-brimmed black slouch hat and the dark clothes and the fine face, marked by suffering as by impish humour, he looked more like a poet than the noble raging lion who had transformed, as by magic, the dirty, prostituted biddy of a capital city into an honourable queen. Now the city accepted his presence as if he had always been tame and old and caged.

The 1913 Lock-out was the climax of Jim Larkin's career as leader. He had become the Chief. For this monstrous confrontation of force he, it seems, had been created. Through it he entered the folklore of a city.

In a few months in 1913, Dublin became a world city. Larkin grew in stature until he was a colossus. These were his days of glory and they were given to him, freely, by starving men, women and children who, in the end, would have to taste the defeat of stalemate.[6]

Ulick O'Connor

In January 1947, Jim Larkin died. Nearly forty years before he had arrived as a Messiah to the stricken Dublin proletariat. He had pulled them off their knees and promulgated the message that they were no longer slaves but human beings with rights. A passionate orator with great poetic flair, he had a Trotskyesque gift of igniting words into phrases that spread like a flame through the mob mind.[7]

Seán Ó Faoláin

Larkin had come out of the dark netherworld with the eyes and face of a poet. He burned with a fiery simplicity of belief in his fellow-man and his speech to them was like a lava. He had mild but wide, clear eyes, questioning, almost staring; a long nose; sensuous lips; a sombre lock of hair across his forehead; the hollowed cheeks and high cheekbones of an ascetic.[8]

James Plunkett

James Joyce spoke of Dublin as the centre of paralysis. It was a total paralysis, blinding conscience and soul. It remained to Jim Larkin to see the slum dweller as a human being—degraded, yet capable of nobility; perceptive, capable of living with dignity, capable even, of music and literature. That was the message he began to address to the city at large— a message of love, delivered, one must concede, by a man swinging wildly about him with a sword.

In the course of forty years of social agitation Jim Larkin earned a reputation that was universal. Yet he was no doctrinaire revolutionary in the Continental sense and he was not a great theorist. Perhaps the employers of Dublin found the best name for his movement when they labelled it Larkinism. His lifelong concern was not with theory, but with the immediate needs of the underprivileged, the sweated men, the struggling mothers, the little children born to a life of drudgery in a sunless world. In his efforts to help them he was sometimes arrogant, sometimes unfair to colleagues and often rash beyond the justification of his most indulgent admirers.[9]

Chapter 49

Larkin and Connolly

The unsigned letter that follows, addressed 'Dear Jack' and dated 'May the First 1948,' came into the possession of Donal Nevin some time in the nineteen-sixties. The letter was obviously written by Jack Carney. In reply to a query, Jim Larkin Junior, the general secretary of the Workers' Union of Ireland and a long-time friend of Jack Carney, replied to Donal Nevin on 9 October 1968, only a few months before his death. He was not sure to whom the letter might have been written but felt that it was a close friend and could have been a brother of Eadhmonn MacAlpine, a colleague of Jim Larkin when he was in America. There is a reference in the letter to Violet, and Larkin recalled that Eadhmonn had a sister and his recollection was that her name was Violet, though he did not know her well.

At the end of the letter there is a promise of another letter, but unfortunately the editor has not been able to trace it, if indeed it was written.

The Breon referred to in the final paragraph is Breon O'Casey, the son of Seán O'Casey, born on 30 April 1928. It is known from Seán O'Casey's letters to Jack Carney that Breon stayed with the Carneys in London.

A number of controversial statements are made in the letter, some of which run counter to perceived opinion. (Reference should be made to the notes on page 528.)

In reply to your letter I am sending you R. M. Fox's book on James Connolly[1]: I am also taking the opportunity of criticising the book, because I believe Fox is guilty of the same fundamental error that has resulted in much misunderstanding of the position of the late Jim Larkin. I knew Jim Larkin longer than any man or woman in living memory. Our friendship began as far back as 1906 and strangely enough I was the last man to convey a message to him—at midnight preceding the dawn in which he died. It had just struck midnight on the clock of St Paul's and I was finishing my night's work when I had a feeling that I should ring up the hospital in Dublin and inquire about Jim. The night nurse said she would tell him I had asked for him. The next morning I received a telegram saying he was dead.

I have every reason to feel grateful towards Jim Larkin. I was 18 years of age when I first heard him speak in the town of Widnes. At that time I was working 84 hours a week in a chemical works for 17/6 a week. One week I worked by day and the other by night. One Sunday morning, after I had been working for 18 hours I was gassed with chlorine gas. Stumbling from the bleaching powder chambers, where the gas was escaping, I fell into some slake lime. So blinded and gassed, I made my way home to my lodgings. I slept until 1.0 p.m. Then I walked into the street and across the ground that stood between me and the Town Hall Square I heard the voice of a Socialist speaker. It was the voice of Jim Larkin. He was not the first

Socialist speaker I had heard, but he was the most impressive. At the end of the meeting I timidly approached him and told him of my position. I asked his advice. He took me along for a cup of tea in the home of a Socialist. He said: 'You could not be worse off if you were a tramp.' A week later I took his advice; a step I have never regretted.

At the age of 13 I had passed every book in Euclid. At 11 I had won a scholarship of 36 pounds a year for three years. At the end of the three years I had lost my grandfather with whom I lived and instead of proceeding to the Liverpool University, I had to go to work in a chemical works, working 56 hours for eight shillings. I tried to continue my education by attending night school, where I won several prizes, but owing to my long working day I used to fall asleep at night school. Then in order to earn enough to pay for my lodgings I had to work on harder jobs. Life was pretty hopeless. Never at any time did I have more than a shilling in my pocket. The sky was never darker than the day on which I met Jim Larkin.

What impressed me most about Jim Larkin, was his ability to translate the feelings of his audience in sympathetic speech. One felt that through some mysterious means he had investigated your personal position and was taking the opportunity of saying for you that you could not say for yourself. His language was not the language of tears, but the language of proud hope. And often when I was on tramp, with neither hope of a bed nor a breakfast the following morning, his words echoed back to me making me feel that my tramping was an adventure of high order. More than any other man, Jim Larkin taught me that Socialism does not spread by itself, because of its own inner beauty or logic or even consistency. It spreads because of strong impulsions from the social order and from the alignment of economic power. It spreads when there is something in it that is a response to the needs of the hour or, in the language of the intellectual, to the ethos of the times.

For eight years from the press gallery of the House of Commons I have watched Socialists (?) in action. I have studied their curious fears and their much more curious negativisms. They have never faced the real problems of the masses and often they have resented any expression of these problems, such as unofficial strikes, believing that if they ignored them they would eventually cease to exist and so they crept into their shells, crossed their fingers and waited until the winds and storms of the world had blown over. Later these Socialists took office. And again I watched them, growing daily more resentful at what they termed the embarrassing actions and attitudes of the workers and regarded their stay in office, even without fulfilment of their election programme, as the basic achievement of the movement. Jim Larkin not alone faced problems as they arose, but he anticipated them. He had an uncanny insight into the workers' minds. He even knew where they would fail and why they would fail. It is in no sense of hero-worship that I say that he was without equal in the English-speaking world as an organiser of the masses. I have closely studied him and his work on both sides of the Atlantic and now looking back over the years and making comparisons, I see nothing to cause me to change my opinion.

R. M. Fox, in his book, has not delved very deep in his search for the facts. It is highly superficial and he highlights the commonplace and ignores the important. The failure of Fox is that he is merely a reporter of events, not the actual event, but the writings of people who understood less of the events than even Fox. It is true that Connolly did great work in the early years of 1896 and onwards, but it is untrue to say that the work of Jim Larkin was a continuation of the work of Connolly. There is no co-relation or connection between 1896 in Dublin and 1908 in Dublin.

There is proof of this when you read through the names of the men who assisted Jim Larkin to his work which led to the foundation of the Irish Transport & General Workers' Union. Not one member of the Irish Republican Socialist Party was a founder member of the ITGWU. There was a basic reason for the absence of these men from the early campaigns of Jim Larkin. They were in the main skilled workers, such as bakers, tailors, etc. Socialism to them was a Sunday morning diversion at the end of a week's hard work. It was too academic in character to bear any relation to the lives of the Dublin workers. Jim Larkin came to Dublin as a pioneer of the 'new unionism' in which the unskilled worker was to play the leading role. It was this understanding of Jim that made him so different to other labour leaders.

Of course it is foolish to maintain of Jim that he had powers bordering on the miraculous, but the reason for his success in Dublin was due mainly to the fact that he had been trained in an atmosphere of advanced capitalism, where big combines were coming into being. He had trained himself in the years in which finance-capitalism was taking a more direct share of the control of industry through interlocking directorates of British industries. Backed with this experience he came to a Dublin in which small business had so far remained immune from the influence of finance-capital. So it was that he won his early successes not through the strength of the masses, but the weaknesses of their employers. It was William Martin Murphy who was the first to recognise the secret of Jim's success. It was Murphy who welded the employers of Dublin together and met Jim with a solid army of Dublin capitalists, instead of the usual divisions which Jim had so cleverly employed to his advantage.

The failure of the 1913 struggle was the failure of the trade unions of Dublin to appreciate the significance of the action of Martin Murphy. They had resented the upsurge of the unskilled worker who had now come to dominate the labour movement in Ireland. Through the organisation of the workers on the industrial field, Jim had successes in municipal elections and at one stroke killed the jobbery and graft that was going on. Trade union leaders could no longer play with the Irish Nationalist Party in return for political spoils. So in the combination of these two factors—the rise of the unskilled worker on the industrial and political fields—the trade union leaders could hardly conceal their glee when Murphy took up Jim's challenge.

It was during this period—1911—that James Connolly returned to Ireland. The funds of the ITGWU, through the instrumentality of Jim Larkin, made possible Connolly's return, also his family, from the United States. I was in Belfast when the return of James Connolly was announced. The Belfast Socialists, then organised in the ILP, did not welcome the return of Connolly. None more so than William McMullan, the present president of the ITGWU. Their Socialism was an imitation of the municipal socialism of the ILP. No IRISH speakers appeared on their platforms. So that when Connolly came to Belfast, he and I spoke together in the open air outside the offices of the Belfast Evening Telegraph. Rarely did a member of the ILP appear with Connolly.

The sound industrial organisation that Jim Larkin had created gave Connolly a platform he had never enjoyed at any time either in England, Scotland or America, so far as his written propaganda was concerned. Connolly (I have his own word for it) sold more of his pamphlets during the first two years he was in Ireland, after his return from the USA, than in the whole of his career. During my tour of England and Scotland in 1913, I sold 1,500 copies of Labour, Nationality and Religion and at least two hundred copies of Labour in Irish History. It is regrettable that Connolly envied the success of Jim Larkin, but I can assure you, Jack, that Jim Larkin did not show a similar envy.

Griffith saw in the combination of Larkin and Connolly the co-relation of action on the job and written propaganda. It was Griffith who set out to split this combination by indulging in the usual bourgeois trick of praising one and denouncing the other. I met Griffith but once and heard him often but he never impressed me. Griffith, being of alien stock—Welsh—was more Irish than the Irish, who had so little in his country's history that he had to go to List, the Hungarian economist, for the materials for his political programme. Griffith of 'kings, lords and commons' was never a republican. He was the John the Baptist of Eire's new industrial aristocracy.

Connolly came to Belfast. Fox writes: 'It was his task to kindle again that feeling of solidarity, that belief and hope which labour had possessed. He had no strong well-established union machinery but just a small, weak union growing out of disaster.' This was true. When Connolly came to Belfast he found an office in working order with organisers on the jobs and the dockers in the Belfast branch of the ITGWU had job control. No man could work on a deep-sea ship without a ITGWU card. I know because I worked both as a tally clerk and occasionally a hooker-on on grain boats. Through my speaking in the open air I was victimized. So I did work on the docks. I used to work in a linen warehouse—54 hrs for fourteen shillings, but then ended when Carson went on the rampage. I was also tally clerk in an artificial manure works and was tinplate worker's helper on the 'Titanic'. In 1912 Jim Larkin came to Belfast. He addressed a private meeting of the branch at which I attended. The branch had run into debt to the Dublin office to the tune of 800 pounds. The meeting was hostile to Connolly. The members resented Connolly spending too much time addressing suffragette and other, what they termed 'outside' meetings. The meeting, after a speech from Jim Larkin in which he, too, criticised Connolly, agreed to pay a monthly levy of sixpence to clear off the debt. Then Jim sang a song.

It is true, as Fox says, that these dockers were isolated in Belfast. Here again the Belfast trade unions, overwhelmingly composed of skilled workers, resented the rise of the unskilled workers. The Belfast bosses gave them the best jobs, such as foremen, etc. The unskilled, mostly Catholics, did the dirty work. This position was maintained because the skilled workers were Protestants and the unskilled were Catholics. Fox fails to mention this. Yet it was the militancy of the dockers which forced the bosses to increase the wages of the skilled. The skilled workers always referred to the high wages of the dockers when making demands for higher wages.

Jim Larkin addressing a rally in Upper O'Connell Street, Dublin in 1923.
(Photograph: J. Cashman)

James Larkin (front row, first on left) with colleagues in Moscow.

LARKIN
IN RUSSIA

James Larkin in Moscow (fourth from left in centre row).

Barney Conway (at head of table) with James Larkin Junior, third on his left, and colleagues, Moscow, 1928.

WORKERS' UNION
of IRELAND

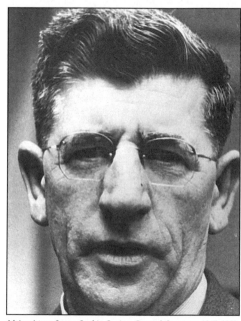

Main picture: James Larkin Junior, General Secretary 1947–1969.
Other pictures *(anti-clockwise from the top):* General Presidents, John
Lawlor 1924–1929, John Kenny 1929–1946, John Smithers
1946–1968, John Foster 1968–1982; and General Secretaries, Denis
Larkin 1969–1978 and Patrick Cardiff 1978–1983.

The Workers' Union of Ireland Brass and Reed Band in the 1920s.
Larkin is standing on left.

The Workers' Union of Ireland Pipe Band in the 1920s.
James Larkin is in centre (front row).

James Larkin

James Larkin

James Larkin
Senior (right)
with James
Larkin Junior.

James Larkin Senior and
James Larkin, TD, in 1945,
outside Dáil Éireann,
Leinster House, Dublin.

James Larkin
in old age.

Drawing of Larkin in 1913
by Sir William Orpen.
*(William Orpen Centenary
Exhibition Catalogue, National
Gallery of Ireland 1978)*

I can't draw him – he's more
like your El greco man
and 6ft 4 high

Head of Larkin
by Mina Carney.
*(Lane Municipal Gallery
of Modern Art, Dublin)*

From a drawing by Seán
O'Sullivan R.H.A. 1942.
(National Gallery of Ireland)

From a pastel drawing
by Seán Keating
R.H.A. 1946. *(Liberty
Hall, Dublin)*

Funeral of James Larkin: Lying-in-state, Thomas Ashe Hall, College Street, Dublin.

His four sons (from left: Denis, Fintan, Bernard and James) follow the cortège.

At the graveside in Glasnevin Cemetery, Dublin. Included in the group are Fr Thomas Counihan SJ and Fr Aloysius OFM Cap.

(Photographs: Irish Times)

Workers' Union of Ireland Banner by Peter Broughal, 1949.

Larkin Monument, O'Connell Street, Dublin.
Statue by Oisín Kelly.

James Larkin c. 1915.

Larkin addressing a meeting in Beresford Place from the centre window of Liberty Hall in 1913.

From a window in the building, leaning well forth, he talked to the workers, spoke as only Jim Larkin could speak, not for an assignation with peace, dark obedience, or placid resignation; but trumpet-tongued of resistance to wrong, discontent with leering poverty, and defiance of any power strutting out to stand in the way of their march onward.

Seán O'Casey

Plaque to the 1913 Dublin
Lockout Martyrs, Alice Brady,
James Byrne, James Nolan
and Eugene Salmon.
(Liberty Hall, Dublin)

Opening of the SIPTU Tribute to James Larkin Exhibition in the National
Library of Ireland, October 1997, to commemorate the fiftieth anniversary
of Larkin's death. *From left:* William A. Attley (SIPTU General Secretary),
the Taoiseach Bertie Ahern, who opened the Exhibition, Jimmy Somers
(SIPTU General President) and Donal Nevin. The Acting Director of the
National Library, Seán Cromien, is on the right of the picture.

Fox dismisses the 1907 strike in Belfast with one page out of 250, yet it was one of the most important periods in the history of the Irish Labour Movement. Jim Larkin arrived in Belfast in 1907 on his birthday, January 11[2] with only 11d. in his pocket. He came to a city in which the only organisation was that of the Ulster branches of British unions of skilled workers, such as the engineers and carpenters and they were mostly in the shipyards. The majority of their members were from the Clyde. In less than six months Jim Larkin had brought Catholics and Protestants together; he had brought skilled workers on the strike platform along with dockers. He forced the return of a policeman to his job. Then on July 12, 1907 he did the impossible: he had Catholics and Protestants walking in the same procession.[3] He turned the spotlight on the sweated industries of Belfast, linen and linen manufactures. Not since the days of the United Irishmen had the overlords of Ulster met with such a challenge. And of such a period and of such events, Fox can only find a single page in which to record its picture; its significance escapes him. The newspapers of these times in Belfast expressed the alarm of the Ulster employers. The shadow of Jim Larkin over Belfast frightened them. The Orange drums were sounded and bitter fights went on between Catholics and Protestants. IF JIM LARKIN HAD DONE NO MORE THAN WHAT HE DID IN BELFAST IN 1907, HIS MEMORY DESERVES TO BE KEPT FRESH AND GREEN IN THE MINDS OF THE IRISH WORKERS.

I am not partisanically critical of Connolly in favour of Larkin. I knew both men intimately. The main defect in Connolly was his shyness. He could not tolerate company. He could not therefore mix with the masses. After lectures or meetings he would rush away because he lacked that human warmth so characteristic of Jim and so essential in the make-up of labour organisers. We all have our touches of vanity. We would be less than human if we had not them. I recall when Connolly was released from Mountjoy in 1913 after going on a hunger-strike. I was in the office of the Transport Union in Belfast when a telegram arrived from him in Dublin. He wanted a band to be on hand at the Great Northern Station in Belfast when he arrived. The band and the crowd was there. That night I was laid out with a brick. There was a pitched battle between the Catholic and Protestant workers. But we had a big meeting at the Custom House steps. I remember setting fire to the Irish Independent which was supporting the '13 lockout. If Connolly had been a wiser man, he would not have had the band. Apart from going on a hunger-strike, he had little to crow about. He had destroyed any chance there was of success in the '13 trouble.

When Jim Larkin went to jail in August, 1913, Connolly was left in charge of the fight. Jim had come to terms with one of the shipping companies, the 'City of Dublin', I believe. Through this company went all the cross-channel trade leaving and entering Dublin. The other shippers were growing alarmed as they saw their trade slipping from them. Connolly withdrew the men from this one shipping company and so united the shippers. It was a fatal move. It was a move that the men never forgot and was climaxed with a demand for the dismissal of Connolly from the Union. Jim intervened and threatened to resign if Connolly was dismissed. The men withdrew their demand.

Connolly was applying his theories, but they did not fit the facts. He knew little of the practical side of union work. This may come as a surprise to you, but it was true. And it was a pity that he should have made the move, more pity he should have held the power to make the move. If the move had not been made, I do not think the '13 lockout would have been won (I shall deal with this later) but the Dublin dockers as one section of the workers would have held their own.

Connolly was a good theoretician (but by no means perfect). Few people have really examined his writings in the light of Marxian understanding. If you get the time, study in detail the pamphlet Labour, Nationality and Religion. Connolly was a peculiar character.

Connolly was a practising Catholic.[4] Few people knew this. He was more of a practising Catholic than Jim Larkin. His Catholicism, unlike that of Jim Larkin's, was an acceptance of the orthodox. He never questioned the religious role of the Church. He believed in Catholicism with all the faith of a simple Irish servant girl. Catholicism to Jim Larkin was an expression of the inherent goodness of mankind. He believed that its spirituality was a state of things to which men and women might come through the creation of sound social conditions. Jim, Bucharin (of the Bolshevik Party) and I sat together in Moscow and for three hours they discussed this side of Jim's life. Jim admitted that there were abuses in the Church and none more freely admitted them but remember, Jack, that Catholicism in Ireland was the religion of the oppressed. Through the destruction of all other agencies in Ireland, the clergy had a free hand. And because the majority of the clergy of Ireland came from peasant stock, they were nearer to the masses than the priests of England. I once aroused the anger of Connolly by questioning his going to Mass when he and I were touring in Scotland. Jim did not attend Mass, not because he did not believe in it, but because those who served it had lined up against the masses. Jim's anti-clericalism was mainly a resentment of the attitude of the clergy towards social problems. Connolly on the other hand did not take his challenge so far, though admittedly he criticised Father Kane, S.J. for his Lenten sermons in Dublin in 1912. This should be the subject of a longer letter.

Now back to the reason for the failure of the 1913 lockout.

Young Jim Larkin was here for the weekend. Breon was 20 yesterday. So all in all we have been busy. The rest of this letter must be held over for some other time.

Best wishes to you both and Violet.

Thine,

Chapter 50

Connolly on Larkin

The *Voice of Labour*, the official paper of the Irish Transport and General Workers' Union, in its issue of 12 April 1924, shortly after the expulsion from the union of its general secretary, James Larkin, carried a remarkable collection of letters, extracts from letters and telegrams, ostensibly dealing with the facts concerning the departure of Larkin to America in October 1914; in effect it was a piece of black propaganda directed towards discrediting Larkin, accusing him of lying, deception, dishonesty, and a range of wrongdoings.

Included in the paper were letters to—of all newspapers—the *Irish Independent* in 1923 from Kathleen Clarke (widow of Tom Clarke, the executed 1916 leader), from Lillie Connolly (widow of James Connolly), and from William O'Brien. There were extracts from several letters written between April and September 1914 concerning projected visits by Larkin to New Zealand, Scotland, South Africa, and America.

Facts about Larkin's departure to America, which was the sub-title of a twelve-page booklet published by the Union in 1927, when William O'Brien was general secretary, under the title *Some Pages from Union History*, constituted a part only of the booklet. There were a number of letters from Connolly to O'Brien written before 1914, or rather extracts from letters. One extract was from a letter of 24 May 1911 that consists of two sentences; the second consists of seven sentences written on 13 September 1912; and there is a somewhat longer extract from a letter written on 29 July 1913—that is, four weeks before the strike of the tramway men in Dublin. The extracts from the three letters are strongly critical of, indeed hostile to, Larkin.

In considering Connolly's criticisms of Larkin, something of their different backgrounds and activities must be noted. Connolly had been born in Edinburgh and served about seven years in the British army—something not uncommon among the children of Irish emigrants. Some part of his service was spent in Ireland.[1] Drawing attention to these two facts might seem irrelevant were it not that both were suppressed by Connolly himself and his close associates, including O'Brien, who must have known about them; they were first revealed as recently as 1961, when C. Desmond Greaves published his biography of Connolly.

After leaving the British army Connolly's first visit to Ireland was in 1896, when he was twenty-eight. He remained here until 1903, though during these years he was away on lecture tours in Scotland and America for much of the time. In 1903 he emigrated to America in disillusionment and with some bitterness; he did not return until 1910. Larkin was one of those who were instrumental in encouraging him to return. In America,

Connolly had written approvingly of Larkin's ideas for building a movement based on the unskilled workers, who were then largely unorganised. His first action on his arrival in Ireland at the end of July 1910 was to visit Larkin in Mountjoy Prison. About a year later, in June 1911, Connolly was appointed by Larkin to be the Ulster organiser of the ITGWU, a post he continued to hold until Larkin's departure to America, a period of little over three years. Thus the period during which the two men were colleagues in the union was a very short one.

By 1914 Connolly—then forty-six—had spent some eleven years altogether in Ireland (excluding his military service) and Larkin—then forty—about seven years.

Larkin had been born in Liverpool and first came to Ireland in 1907, at the age of thirty-three. He had been here therefore only three-and-a-half years when Connolly arrived back from America.

Over the three-year period or so that both were in the union together, Larkin was wholly preoccupied with trade union work, while Connolly was primarily concerned with political work and seeking to spread the socialist gospel.

Apart from the few months that Connolly spent in Dublin during the 1913 dispute, it is unlikely that the two met very frequently, as Connolly was in Belfast. The month before he accepted Larkin's invitation to be an official of the union, Connolly was writing to O'Brien (24 May 1911) in the first of the three letters referred to: 'Do not pay any attention to what Larkin says … The man is utterly unreliable—and dangerous because unreliable.'

In his letter of 13 September 1912 Connolly is much more critical. To quote the extract published in the booklet:

He does not seem to want a democratic Labour movement; he seems to want a Larkinite movement only. The situation will require the most delicate handling … This seems tame and slavish advice, and it is, but it is, I fear, the only way to get him on the move again. He must rule, or will not work, and at the present stage of the Labour movement he has us at his mercy. And he knows it, and is using his power unscrupulously, I regret to say. We can but bow our head and try and avert the storm. I am sick of all this playing to one man, but am prepared to advise it for the sake of the movement.

The extract does not indicate what may have given rise to Connolly's ire. It is likely that the context was political rather than trade union. It was at this time that Larkin was approaching the height of his powers as a leader of the workers in their fight against the employers, and he may well have been irritated by Connolly's preoccupation with theory and political action. It is true, though, that what was developing on the industrial side of the movement was what came to be known as Larkinism.

The extract seems also to indicate not only a clash of personality—the two men were of very different temperaments—but a degree of jealousy on the part of Connolly, who, whatever his great merits, was not a leader of men and loved by the workers as was Larkin. Connolly was often seen as cold and aloof, never staying on after meetings and mixing with the members or engaging in any exchanges with them. How very different it was with Larkin! Both men, moreover, were quite vain.

It is in the third extract, from a letter written on 29 July 1913, that Connolly's exasperation with Larkin becomes evident. The following is the extract, slightly abbreviated:

> To make matters worse, I confess to you in confidence that I don't think I can stand Larkin as a boss much longer. He is simply unbearable. He is forever snarling at me and drawing comparisons between what he accomplished in Belfast in 1907 and what I have done, conveniently ignoring the fact that he was then the secretary of an English organisation, and that as soon as he started an Irish one his union fell to pieces, and he had to leave the members to their fate. He is consumed with jealousy and hatred of anyone who will not cringe to him and beslaver him all over ... He tried to bully me out of the monies due to our branch for administration benefit of the Insurance Act ... He did not succeed ... I told him that if he was Larkin twenty times over he could not bully me ... I would formerly have trusted to his generosity, now I would not trust him at all. Larkin thinks he can use Socialists as he pleases, and then when his end is served to throw them out, if they will not bow down to his majesty. He will never get me to bow to him.

The extraordinary language used in the letter would suggest that purely personal considerations governed Connolly's outburst against Larkin, as if by writing as he did to O'Brien, seemingly his only confidant in Ireland, he could work it out of his system. What has survived of the ITGWU archives for its early years does include quite a number of letters from Connolly to Liberty Hall about financial matters. It may be that the view from head office was that the very small membership in the north did not justify the use of the limited resources of the union on staff costs there.

It was well known in Dublin trade union circles that all was not well in the personal relations between the two men, and the reasons are not very complimentary to either of them. Connolly on more than one occasion acknowledged their differences. Once he said in Larkin's presence: 'Jim knows that I am no follower of Larkin. I stand for Jim because I believe he is the best man our class has turned out in Ireland.' On another occasion he said: 'We speak with different accents but at heart Larkin and I are one.'

In making the use he did of Connolly's personal criticisms of Larkin, O'Brien did a disservice to Connolly. Personal differences between trade union leaders, whether in relation to conflicting styles or behaviour in their relationship with one another, was not uncommon in the years before the First World War in many countries and were accounted as nothing compared with their common purpose and dedication, expressed in different ways by people with conflicting personalities. Connolly was not the petty character that a few sentences written in irritation with Larkin's undoubtedly unreasonable behaviour might imply. If other criticisms of Larkin by Connolly had been available to O'Brien, he would undoubtedly have used them.

The reality is that Connolly was a bigger man than O'Brien portrayed him by using short extracts from three letters written over two years to discredit the man he clearly regarded as an enemy. This is borne out by a speech of Connolly's about Larkin that O'Brien sought to have suppressed. In June 1914 Larkin tendered his resignation as general secretary of the ITGWU, but at a general meeting in Croydon Park he was persuaded to withdraw it. Connolly spoke on that occasion and sent quotations from his speech to the Glasgow socialist paper *Forward*, which it published in the issue for 27 June 1914. The full article is as follows:

As I am writing, the workers of Dublin are rejoicing over the fact that Larkin has withdrawn his resignation which he handed in during the past week. Instantly it became known, a general meeting was called at Croydon Park to consider the situation. The feeling of the meeting, and the general interpretation of the real nature of the crisis is, I think, best summed up in the following quotation from my own speech on that occasion:—

James Connolly asked them to remember that, for seven years, working for the Union, Jim Larkin had every day done ten men's work. He had carried on his own shoulders not only his own responsibilities, but, with his intense desire to see everything well done, had taken on himself, with his overflowing fund of energy, manual work and petty detail work that should have been done by others. That could not last.

He recalled how, during the great lock-out, at the London Conference of December 9th, and again in the Dublin Trades' Hall, the English Labour leaders had been praising him (Connolly) with a view to deposing Larkin and sowing dissension between them. 'At last I could stand it no longer. I told them that, though we spoke with different accents, we spoke with the one voice, and that they could not split the Transport Union.'

He knew the working class of Dublin before Larkin came. He knew them as slaves, most slavish industrially when they were most truculent politically. Contrast that with the heroism they displayed in the recent fight. Jim Larkin had put courage into them, lifted them to their feet, taught them not only their rights, but their duty (which the English Labour leaders were afraid to teach them) to stand by one another.

If there were any friction it meant that the men to whom Larkin had given new power and dignity were taking active interest in every detail of the Union's work instead of leaving Jim to carry it all on his shoulders. The price Jim had paid was that he had broken down physically, run down mentally, and almost worn out. Hence he did not realise himself that what he needed was a rest. Overstrained by anxiety, he, perhaps, saw opposition where there was only an anxious desire to help him.

Let them not only tell him they wanted him back, but that they were more worthy of him than when he came. Let them not—'We'll be beaten if you go,' but let them tell him: 'We were slaves; you made men of us. You trained us to fight but without you we could never carry on so magnificent, so successful a fight.'

They would not accept his resignation, but they were prepared to give him a rest. If he were to go to America and raise funds for the new Irish Labour Party it would recuperate him, and he would be back in seven days, if needed. They had amongst them a man of genius, of splendid vitality, great in his conceptions, magnificent in his courage. Were they to waste this great force in a few months or years? ('No'). Let them give him every possibility of recuperating his strength. They would not part with Jim, but would always co-operate with him in the spirit of loyal comrades.

Another general meeting was held in the Antient Concert rooms, when, with his own consent, and to the intense gratification of the members, the letter of resignation was burnt on the platform.

As Connolly himself put it: 'They had amongst them a man of genius, of splendid vitality, great in his conceptions, magnificent in his courage.' That was Larkin.

Between 1948 and 1951 the ITGWU published three volumes of Connolly's writings, edited by the historian Desmond Ryan. Included in these volumes were twenty articles written by Connolly in *Forward* in the two years 1913 and 1914. The article given above was not among them. Desmond Ryan informed the editor of this book that William O'Brien would not allow it to be included in the selection. (It was Ryan who provided the copy of Connolly's article that is reproduced above.)

Attention might be drawn to Jack Carney's letter (chapter 49) in which he relates that in 1913 union members demanded that Connolly be sacked from the union and that Larkin intervened and threatened to resign if Connolly was dismissed. Carney also refers to an incident in Belfast when the members were hostile to Connolly, and while Larkin too criticised him on this occasion, the matter ended with Larkin singing a song.

Chapter 51

Larkin in Literature and Art

Has any other Irish figure this century inspired so much literary and artistic work as Jim Larkin? A subject for street ballads and verse from the time he came to Belfast in 1907, Larkin had created his own place in the hearts of Irish workers and in the minds of writers, poets, and artists.

The American writer James T. Farrell visited Larkin in Dublin in 1938 and has described the ageing leader kneeling on the floor of the flat where he lived, searching for a book he wanted to give to his guest. 'His books were in dusty cabinets along the floor. Nothing was in order. He flung out piles of books. One's throat became dry and one almost choked because of the dust in the room. And Jim kept looking … This seemed to go on endlessly. Finally, he grunted with pleasure.' Larkin had found the book he was searching for. It was a play by Daniel Corkery, *The Labour Leader*. Jim was the model for the hero of the play.

In the first act of the play, Tim Murphy, the representative of the coal porters on the strike committee, mocking the suggestion that the strike leader, Davna, be given a secretary, asks:

> And if ye give him a secretary his job will be to cut Davna off when he's giving us the history of Ireland in the tenth century, or giving us Shelley: 'Rise like lions after slumber'; 'Shake your manes like thunder'; 'Ye are many, they are few': He was a great lad, that Shelley, and he only a poor sheep of an Englishman and all. And what would we know about him only for Davna? Or about the Red Flag? Or about anything at all.

Daniel Corkery (1878–1964) was the author of several plays, short stories, and a novel, *The Threshold of Quiet* (1917); he is best known as the author of *The Hidden Ireland* (1925). *The Labour Leader* was produced by Lennox Robinson at the Abbey Theatre on 30 September 1919 and published the following year.

Larkin was also to be the inspiration for characters in two of Seán O'Casey's later plays. Already the real-life Larkin had been much written about by O'Casey, notably in the third volume of his autobiography, *Drums under the Windows* (1945):

> Through the streets he strode, shouting into every dark and evil-smelling hallway. The great day of change has come; Circe's swine had a better time than you have; come from your vomit; out into the sun. Larkin is calling you all!

O'Casey dedicated *The Star Turns Red* (1940) to 'the men and women who fought through the great Dublin lock-out in nineteen hundred and thirteen.' The second act of the play takes place in the head office of the General Workers' Union, where a streamer proclaims *An Injury to One is the Concern of All!* (This motto appeared at the top of the editorial in the *Irish Worker*.) In response to the Brown Priest's question why he should stay with the workers in revolt, Red Jim answers: 'To be with us when the star turns red; to help us carry the fiery cross. Join with us. March with us in the midst of the holy fire.'

In the final act of the play, Red Jim declares:

> We fight on; we suffer; we die; but we fight on.
> Till brave-breasted women and men, terrac'd with strength,
> Shall live and die together, co-equal in all things;
> And romping, living children anointed with joy,
> shall be banners and bannerols of this moving world!
> In all that great minds give, we share;
> And unto man be all might, majesty, dominion, and power!

In his autobiographical *Red Roses for Me* (1942), O'Casey again evokes the spirit of Larkin and 1913 when the young strike leader, Ayamonn Breydon, asserts: 'Let us bring freedom here, not with sounding brass an' tinkling cymbal, but with silver trumpets blowing, with a song all men can sing, with a palm branch in our hands, rather than with a whip at our belt, and a headsman's axe on our shoulders.' Later, in the third act, he speaks to the women on the darkened bridge:

> Friend, we would that you should live a greater life; we will that all of us shall live a greater life. Our strike is yours. A step ahead for us today; another one for you tomorrow. We who have known, and know, the emptiness of life shall know its fullness. All men and women quick with life are fain to venture forward. (*To Eeada*) The apple grows for you to eat. (*To Dympna*) The violet grows for you to wear. (*To Finnoola*) Young maiden, another world is in your womb.

At the end of the third act, as the scene darkens and nothing is heard but the sound of tramping feet, through this threatening sound comes the sound of voices singing quietly:

> We swear to release thee from hunger and hardship,
> From things that are ugly and common and mean;
> Thy people together shall build a great city,
> The finest and fairest that ever was seen.

When, towards the end of the fourth act, Inspector Finglas of the Mounted Police responds to a remark that Ayamonn's end was 'a noble an' a mighty death' with the dismissive 'It wasn't a very noble thing to die for a single shilling,' Ayamonn's lover, Sheila, replies, 'Maybe he saw the shilling in th' shape of a new world.'

Earlier in the play, Ayamonn had referred to the shilling:

A shilling's little to me, and less to many; to us it is our schechinals, showing us God's light is near; showing us the way in which our feet must go; a sun ray on our face; the first step taken in the march of a thousand miles.

George Russell, whose searing indictment of the Dublin employers in his famous letter written in 1913 is among the classics of literary protests, based the character Culainn, the socialist, in *The Interpreters* (1922) on Larkin. Culainn is 'a mystic motivated by an absolutely Christian compassion for the slum dwellers of the city,' to quote the American critic William Irwin Thompson, who adds: 'Æ [Russell] knew Larkin well and his portrait of Larkin's religious nature is true to life.'

In *The Interpreters*, Russell describes Culainn as he enters the prison to join the other prisoners:

The figure which emerged from the shadowy into the red air was massive, noble and simple. It might have stood for an adept of labour or avatar of the Earth spirit incarnated in some grand labourer to inspire the workers by a new imagination of society. To the workers this Culainn appeared an almost superhuman type of themselves, a clear utterer of what in them was inarticulate. That deep, slow, thrilling voice myriads had listened to as the voice of their own souls.

Russell's fellow-poet and colleague on the *Irish Homestead*, which he edited, Susan Mitchell, published her poem 'To the "Villas of Genteel Dastards"' in the *Irish Worker* in November 1913.

No prouder sight has Ireland seen since banded peasants stood
Upon her fields for freedom than this famished brotherhood,
Who in their leader's message have caught a distant gleam
Of that far off Holy City, our glory and our dream.

Seven years later, in New York, a Dublin-born American poet, Lola Ridge, the theme of whose poetry was the martyrdom of the downtrodden, wrote her poem 'To Larkin', who was then in Sing Sing jail:

One hundred million men and women go inevitably about their affairs
In the somnolent way
Of men before a great drunkenness ...
They do not see you go by their windows, Jim Larkin,
With your eyes bloody as the sunset
And your shadow gaunt against the sky ...
You, and the like of you, that life
Is crushing for their frantic wines.

Frank O'Connor's poem 'Homage to Jim Larkin' was first published in the *Irish Times* towards the end of 1944, just two years before Larkin's death:

Roll away the stone, Lord, roll away the stone
As you did when last I died in the attic room;
Then there was no fire as well, and I died of cold
While Jim Larkin walked the streets before he grew old.

A month after Larkin's death, Patrick Kavanagh's poem 'Jim Larkin'
was published in the *Bell*:

And Tyranny trampled them in Dublin's gutter
Until Jim Larkin came along and cried
The call of Freedom and the call of Pride
And Slavery crept to its hands and knees
And Nineteen Thirteen cheered from out the utter
Degradation of their miseries.

The same month, Brendan Behan published his poetic tribute in *Comhar*:

Ag leanúint a chónra trí chlab na cathrach aréir
An sinne a bhí sa chónra?
Níorbh ea; bhíomar sa tsráid ag máirseáil,
Beo, buíoch don mharbh.

(Following the coffin through the city's open mouth last night | Was it
we ourselves who were in the coffin? | No; we were in the street marching
| The living grateful to the dead.)

Austin Clarke's 'Inscription for a Headstone' in his *Collected Poems* (1974)
opens with the line 'What Larkin bawled to hungry crowds,' and concludes:

His name endures on our holiest page,
Scrawled in a rage by Dublin's poor.

Many ballads have been written by anonymous scribes of the people
about Larkin and Dublin's women and men who scrawled the heroic tale
that was 1913.

We rose in sad and weary days
To fight the workers' cause
We found in Jim a heart ablaze,
To break down unjust laws.
But 'tis a sin to follow him
Says Murphy and his crew,
Though true men, like you men,
Will stick to him like glue.

The Dublin lock-out of 1913 and the towering figure of Larkin provide
the background to James Plunkett's powerful novel *Strumpet City* (1969)
on which was based a notable television series. Plunkett also wrote the
radio play *Big Jim*, broadcast by Radio Éireann in 1954. His stage play

about 1913, *The Risen People*, had its first production by the Abbey Theatre (playing in the Queen's Theatre) on 23 September 1958. It was produced by Ria Mooney, with settings by Tomás Mac Anna. An Irish translation by Caoimhín Ó Cinnéide, *Múscailt na Lasrach*, was produced by Aisteoirí Bulfin at the Damer Hall, Dublin. The director was Lelia Ní Chinnéide. *The Risen People* was produced at the Lyric Players' Theatre in Belfast in February–March 1976, when the part of Larkin was played by Liam Neeson.

Two other stage productions have commemorated 1913 and Larkin. A masque, *Let Freedom Ring*, by Donagh MacDonagh (1912–1968) was produced at the Gate Theatre, Dublin, in 1963 on the fiftieth anniversary of the lock-out; and in 1974 the fiftieth anniversary of the founding of the Workers' Union of Ireland was celebrated by a production in the Gaiety Theatre, Dublin, of *The Ballad of Jim Larkin* by Eoghan Harris.

Larkin figures in part 5 ('The Great Lock-Out') of *The Non-Stop Connolly Show* by Margaretta D'Arcy and John Arden. The six plays that comprise the show were published in five volumes in 1977 and in a one-volume edition in 1986. The six plays were first given in a 24-hour performance at Liberty Hall, Dublin, in 1975.

Jim Larkin is publicly commemorated in his adopted city by the life-size bronze statue by Oisín Kelly (1915–1981) that stands on a granite base in O'Connell Street, between the GPO on one side of the street and on the other side a department store that in 1913 was the Imperial Hotel, owned by Larkin's great antagonist, William Martin Murphy, at the window of which a disguised Larkin addressed the proclaimed meeting that was to lead to the police baton charges on what came to be known as Bloody Sunday, 31 August 1913.

In the Hugh Lane Municipal Gallery of Modern Art in Parnell Square, Dublin, there is a head of Larkin by the American sculptor Mina Carney (died 1974). She was married to Jack Carney, the close friend and comrade of Larkin over three decades in Ireland and in America. They had been involved together in some of the great working-class struggles of the time and had endured prison spells for their activities there.

A frequent visitor to Liberty Hall in 1913 was the artist William Orpen RA, who made drawings of the food kitchen there and of Larkin. One drawing of Larkin at work in Liberty Hall was reproduced in Orpen's book of reminiscences, *Stories of Old Ireland and Myself*, published in 1924. Another drawing of Larkin by Orpen done around the same time was reproduced in the catalogue for the William Orpen Centenary Exhibition in the National Gallery of Ireland in Dublin in 1978. On the drawing Orpen had written: 'I can't draw him—He's more like your El Greco man and 6 ft 4" high.'

A cartoon drawing of Larkin by the artist Grace Gifford was published in *Irish Opinion*, 12 December 1913. Grace Gifford married Joseph Mary Plunkett on the eve of his execution in Kilmainham Jail on 4 May 1916.

There are other drawings of Larkin, including one by Seán O'Sullivan RHA (1906–1964), which was done in 1942 when Larkin was sixty-eight and which is in the National Gallery of Ireland, and a pastel drawing by

Seán Keating (1889–1977) done in 1946, the year before Larkin's death, which is now in Liberty Hall. Stamps (7p and 11p) designed by Peter Wildbur and incorporating Seán O'Sullivan's portrait of Larkin were issued on 21 January 1974.

There are numerous representations of Larkin on posters and banners, notably the huge banner of the Workers' Union of Ireland done by Peter Broughal in 1949. The maroon border is inscribed in gold, *An injury to one is the concern of all.*

There was a wall painting by Nano Reid (1905–1981), 'Larkin speaking in College Green, Dublin', in Four Provinces House, Harcourt Street, Dublin, the head office of the Irish Bakers,' Confectioners' and Allied Workers' Amalgamated Union, now demolished. A colour slide of the mural is in the Irish Labour History Museum, Dublin.

Chapter 52

Seán O'Casey on Jim Larkin

Jim Larkin was the great hero figure in Seán O'Casey's life. He was to feature in his autobiography, be referred to frequently in his letters to scholars, friends, and newspapers, and be a character in one of his later plays, *The Star Turns Red*.

Apart from two articles on education and on Irish in the *Peasant* and *Irish Nation* (edited by W. P. Ryan) in May and July 1907, O'Casey's first work appeared in the *Irish Worker*, edited by Jim Larkin. He had a letter published in the paper on 8 June 1912—he was then thirty-two years old—and five other pieces were published in that year. In 1913 as many as thirty pieces, including two poems, were published in the *Irish Worker*, and in 1914 eleven pieces, not including 'Irish Citizen Army Notes' (O'Casey being secretary of the Citizen Army) in some ten issues.

The first reference to Larkin in an O'Casey piece in the *Irish Worker* was on 19 April 1913, 'Declenda [*sic*] est Larkinism', a satirical piece about one of Larkin's trade union opponents, William Richardson. O'Casey's first contribution during the 1913 lock-out was 'The gathering' (27 September):

The whole forces of the Transport Union are wheeling into the battlefield. Dressing their ranks, cheering with enthusiasm, deploying to their several places, looking up at the banner that shall never weaken in the grasp of those who carry it, the symbol of their hope—the banner of the Red Hand. Look over in the distance at the army of opposing Generals in their gaudy uniforms, which greed and plunder with deft hands have decorated. Look at Marshal Murphy with his drum-head court-martial at his back, with his manifesto on the drum-head, draped with the Union Jack—swear away the Transport Workers' Union! If not, then starve!

Have a care, Marshal Murphy, Starvation is not a pleasant anticipation, it is always a difficult thing to starve thousands unwilling to suffer where food is plentiful.

Hunger makes men weak; it often makes men desperate, and the ferocity of hungry men and hungry women is a dreadful thing.

Other countries have experienced it. Let Murphy take care that Ireland does not furnish another dreadful example of men mad whom the capitalists would destroy.

'That ancient swelling and desire for liberty' is again stirring in our souls. The workers have lifted up their eyes unto the hills. They have no friends but themselves: but in their own strength they can conquer. Their only hope is their Union.

'Sacrifice the Union,' say the employers, 'and all is gained.'

Sacrifice the Union once—all is lost.

What life would remain in a human body if the heart were plucked out and cast away?

> We know that the Transport Union is the heart of all our strength and all our hope.
>
> We are not deceived. The workers can do as much without their Union as Caesar's body when Caesar's head is off!

On 15 November 1913 O'Casey contributed a piece, 'Ecce nunc', from which the following is an extract:

> What a happy country Ireland would be if Jim Larkin took everybody's advice. The pulpit, the Press and the platform have all echoed, with burning words of counsel, warnings and deprecations to the Labour leader. The clergyman confronts him with the rebuke that his policy and his preaching threatens the tranquillity of the Church; the economist stands at his right hand telling him that his policy will quickly ruin the class he labours to serve; the nationalist stands at his left hand sighing into his ear that no doubt that this policy will shiver into fragments the quivering remains of Ireland's nationality. Terrible man, Larkin! Destroyer of Church and State and Nationality!

Between 1975 and 1992 four volumes of the letters of Seán O'Casey, totalling 3,470 pages, edited by David Krause, professor of English at Brown University, Rhode Island, were published. Some dozens of the 2,445 letters include references to Jim Larkin. The first such letter to an individual was written to William O'Brien, then the treasurer of the ITGWU, in November 1921. It was sent by O'Casey as secretary of the Jim Larkin Correspondence Committee. Larkin was then in jail in America, and the committee was seeking to have Irish workers send Christmas greetings to Big Jim:

> There can hardly be any necessity for us to appeal to you to strenuously assist us in this effort to show Jim we have not forgotten one who did so much for Liberty and Truth. His present condition testifies to his unbreakable fealty to the Cause of the People. His is the prison cell, the convict garb, and the felon's cap. He never sold the workers for a handful of silver, nor even left them for a riband to stick to his coat. There can be said of Jim Larkin that which Boyle O'Reilly, the Irish Rebel, said of a true man—
>
> > 'His reward?—nor Cross, nor ribbon,
> >   But all others high above;
> > They have won their glittering symbols—
> >   He has earned the People's Love.'

It can be assumed that no reply was received.

The next relevant letter (9 October 1922) is one written to Lennox Robinson (1886–1958), playwright and actor, earlier the manager and later a director of the Abbey Theatre, in which O'Casey wrote that he was thinking of writing a play around Jim Larkin—*The Red Star*—in which he would never appear, though responsible for all the action. It was to be almost eighteen years before O'Casey wrote the play, *The Star Turns Red*, published in February 1940, in which Larkin is the basis for the character Red Jim.

In January 1925 O'Casey was writing to Lady Gregory (1852–1932), playwright and founder with W. B. Yeats of the Irish Literary Theatre in 1898 and from 1905 a director of the Abbey Theatre, saying that he would tell Jim Larkin that she had given permission to his union to put on her play *The Rising of the Moon*. Later that year (11 September 1925) O'Casey wrote to Lady Gregory:

> Jim Larkin had a great meeting here on Wednesday night. His men were jubilant, for five boats laden with coal, purchased by the Union, had berthed in the Liffey, and some food ships are expected too.
>
> He spoke again of 'the little Theatre, over the river,' at the meeting, and I know that many coal-heavers, dockers, carters and labourers have been in the Abbey, and good is sure to come from their visits. Many grumbling to me because they couldn't get in, wanted to know 'why the hell we didn't take the Tivoli!' [on Burgh Quay].

Three years later Lady Gregory was to write to O'Casey (31 May 1928) about a meeting to be held in Dublin to press for the building of an art gallery to house the Lane Collection, saying that 'someone (I won't give a name—a woman) had said that the meeting would be broken up by Larkinites.' She went on: 'But I don't think this can be a true prophecy—for J. Larkin was always sympathetic to Hugh Lane … You know what Hugh intended the gallery to be and what it will be—a place full of beauty that is open to all—and that he hoped would be a place of rest and pleasure to the workers above all.' From Lady Gregory's diaries it appears that her informant was Mrs Best (the musician Edith Oldham), wife of the Director of the National Library.

O'Casey replied on 1 June 1928: 'Oh, nonsense, there'll be no interference with the meeting by "The Larkinites". Why not ask "Jim" to be a member of the Citizens' Committee? He knows as much about Literature as most of those on the Council, and more about Art than some of them.'

In December 1936 O'Casey was telling Gabriel Fallon (1898–1983), who had played in the first productions of O'Casey's early plays in the Abbey Theatre in the twenties and was a director of the theatre from 1959 to 1974:

> By the way Francis MacManus (alias Frank) is wrong when he says that the reasoned counsel of Pope Leo XIII was in neglect during the big Lock-out of 1913. This counsel was quoted more frequently than the letter written by AE. Larkin (Jim) often and often sent it flying over the heads and into the ears of the men to whom he spoke. It was quoted in the Irish Worker … He (Frank) is right in saying that it was scorned or ignored (which is worse), but not by the workers.

On 6 February 1938 O'Casey wrote to Horace Reynolds, an American writer, that Larkin had been with him 'the other evening with a friend, and we talked from the early evening to the coming of the morn.' Some years later Larkin, accompanied by another young friend, visited O'Casey. The friend on this occasion was Harry Craig, later assistant editor of the *Bell* and a distinguished BBC script-writer and producer. Writing in the *Irish Times* (30 March 1980) in a tribute to O'Casey on his eightieth birthday, Craig recalled this visit:

> I have only seen Mr. O'Casey once, but perhaps the story of it is worth recounting. It concerns Larkin. As a student, I had crossed over to attend the Fabian Society Summer School at Dartington Hall. Mr. O'Casey lived in the town of Totnes below. One afternoon I was told I was wanted at the door. I went down and there stood Larkin. He had already attracted a crowd, for although he was an old man then he was a great sight. He said he had come over on the spur of the moment to see O'Casey, whom he had not met for many years. But now, at the last mile, he didn't like to go in alone—would I accompany him? O'Casey opened the door and the two men stood for what seemed a long time without saying a word. Then Larkin touched O'Casey's arm. O'Casey smiled, and Larkin slouched past him into the hall.
>
> That August afternoon I will never forget, though I was too young and too nervous to take in all that was said. O'Casey had just written an article about the Irish in the war, which he read to Larkin. It seems to me that, before or since—and radio is now my occupation—I have never heard a man read better. Larkin had him read it twice. There was indeed throughout the afternoon a certain repetition in the conversation, as you would expect from two men of such common experience. When you have climbed, you don't want to talk about the sloblands. Three times, half-hours apart, O'Casey asked 'how is Barney Conway?'

In another letter to Horace Reynolds (6 February 1938), O'Casey refers to an incident in St Vincent's Hospital, Dublin, in August 1915. Following an operation there he was under a Sister Gonzaga but was shifted to a ward under Sister Paul, who didn't like Jim Larkin:

> She asked me if I was to go back to work when I went home. I said work was hard to get, and mentioned one reason why. Then she came out on poor Jim Larkin, and I listened till she had done. Then I said what I felt I had to say, left her, wrapped up brush and comb in a handkerchief, and walked out of the hospital.

In one of many letters to his old friend and comrade (Larkin's too), Jack Carney, on 29 June 1942, O'Casey refers to another visit from Larkin: 'What a remarkable talker Jim is. A bubbling fountain of vitality ... It was delightful to me to see sometimes the flash in Jim's talk that I so often met during the old days in Liberty Hall.' In the same letter O'Casey refers to William O'Brien having set back the labour movement for a generation, adding: 'To set Jim on the one side and Bill O'Brien on the other—good God, what a contrast—the lion and the mangy rat.'

Another visit from Larkin is referred to in a letter to Carney the following year (26 August 1943):

Jim has come and gone again. The same old Jim, the Lion of the Labour Fold. I dare say he's back in Dublin now, sitting opposite Trinity College [in the head office of the Workers' Union of Ireland in College Street] ... Jim tells me he 'designed the flag of the Plough & the Stars' ... I'm inclined to think Jim's fancy first thought of a design like it, suggested by W. P. Ryan's 'Plough & the Cross'[1] of which he sometimes spoke; that AE was asked to draw it & paint it—being a painter of sorts—that [William] Megahy was asked to do it, then.

When Jim Larkin and his son Young Jim were both elected to Dáil Éireann in 1943, O'Casey wrote to Carney (7 February 1944) that 'it must be a bitter thing for William O'Brien to see old Jim and Young Jim members of the Dáil,' and added: 'But he's behind the counter of a Bank and that's something'—a reference to O'Brien being a director of the Central Bank of Ireland, which carried an annual fee of £500, a substantial sum in those years.

Writing to David H. Greene, professor of English, New York University, many years later (8 March 1960), O'Casey again refers to O'Brien. In 1959 the ITGWU had published *Fifty Years of Liberty Hall* (it should more appropriately have been 'Fifty years of the ITGWU': Liberty Hall was not occupied by the union until 1912). He points out that the book 'mentions Jim but once or twice though I was there when Jim plunged into the venture of shifting from the cramped headquarters at 10 Beresford Place to the Mansion on the old spot by the river. These fellows' hatred seems to be pathological or is it just the hatred of the little maneens for the Big Fellow?'[2]

O'Casey refers to Larkin in other letters to Prof. Greene. On 6 December 1957 he wrote that he was sure Emmet Larkin's book on Larkin 'will be a fine one.' (It was not to appear for eight years, after O'Casey's death.) R. M. Fox's book, O'Casey says, 'is a poor one—making Jim look like a lighted match instead of the flaming torch the man was.' On 10 January 1963 he wrote: 'Labour was a large flock of patient baaing sheep till Larkin came and turned the sheep into fiery fighting men.'

Other letters of interest in the Krause collection are ones written to Kay O'Riordan (19 February 1954) and to Michael and Kay O'Riordan (5 April 1955). (Michael O'Riordan was a Communist candidate in Dáil elections in a Dublin constituency in 1951 and 1954. He had fought in the Connolly Column in the Spanish Civil War. Kay O'Riordan was his wife.) In the former O'Casey wrote:

You see, I've worked with Catholics—many of them great Union men, under Larkin—but what a man Larkin was!—I've been on strike with them, went hungry with them, sat in Dispensaries with them, helped them to bury their dead—lived with them and loved them; but did not like their faults, their indifference to their own needs; their ignorance that the world was theirs.

and in the latter:

The labourer's little lad and the labourer's little lass should know the shape of a violin, a piano, and a guitar; should be in a position to handle them and make them speak—one or the other of them; should know something about colour, line and form in a good picture; and should be able to read, recite, and enjoy Shakespeare, and all the richness of literature which is their heritage as well as the heritage of all the others. All these things that Jim Larkin brought into the fight for bread; the great Jim Larkin; Jim Larkin with a loaf under his oxter and a rose in his hand.

O'Casey compares Larkin with Connolly in two of his letters. To Gerald O'Reilly (a War of Independence veteran from Navan, a founder with Mike Quill of the Transport Workers' Union of America in 1934) he wrote on 26 April 1945:

And, by the way, it was Jim Larkin who created the Irish Transport Union, and first made Labour a fighting force in Ireland. Without him there would never have been the great force which the unskilled workers became under his great leadership. Of course, Connolly was a great fellow, too, dogged, true, and incorruptible; but he hadn't the amazing magnetism and loveable personality of Larkin.

In a letter to Shaemus O'Sheel (1886–1954), the Donegal-born poet and writer and long-time resident in New York, O'Casey wrote (26 May 1951): 'Your remarks about not having made a note about Connolly is not surprising: without Larkin, Connolly would have remained a nonentity. His execution was what made him famous. He was incorruptible and able, but very, very limited in mind and imagination.'

When Michael McInerney, later to be the political correspondent of the *Irish Times*, wrote to O'Casey asking him to agree to be a vice-president of the Connolly Club in London, O'Casey wrote (24 January 1939) declining, saying, 'rightly or wrongly, I don't like my name to be too prominent, for I am shy about appearing to pose in any way as a sir oracle,' and suggesting that 'a far more suitable name is the name of Jim Larkin. Jim, as you know, was and is a great Irish Labour leader.'

O'Casey's letters to newspapers were, as is known, many and frequent and nearly always controversial. One of the earliest examples that mention Larkin was one to the *Dublin Saturday Post* (6 October 1917), written following the death from forcible feeding of Thomas Ashe: 'Tom Ashe was always a warm supporter of the Ideals of Labour, voiced then by Labour's great leader, Jim Larkin, and between them there existed a close and unbreakable intimacy. Many times did Jim pronounce the eulogy that Tom Ashe has proved he so well deserved: "Tom Ashe is a man."'

When the Workers' Union of Ireland moved from Unity Hall in Marlborough Street in 1942 to 5A College Street, the head office was named Thomas Ashe Hall.

Referring to a tribute to Larkin in the *Irish Times* (1 December 1941) by Rev. Dudley Fletcher, O'Casey wrote to the *Irish Times* (15 December 1941): 'Jim is a great orator, but he is much more—a great man. God made something when He made Jim Larkin.'

O'Casey's views on Larkin and Connolly were strongly expressed in a number of his letters. One has already been referred to. He wrote to the *Irish Democrat* (London) in February 1946:

> Jim Larkin is the outstanding figure in the Irish Labour Movement; it was he, and he only, who created it. 'The greatest Irishman since Parnell,' said Bernard Shaw, once referring to him; and Bernard Shaw was right ... That Connolly was, relatively, a great man, there is no doubt, but to say that he had the magnetism, the strange organising power, the eloquence of Jim Larkin, or anything like these qualities, is in no way warranted by any fact whatsoever.
>
> The flame that burns in the heart of the Irish Labour Movement, whether we like it or not, was lit by Jim Larkin, and lit by none other.
>
> We should not forget either, that others died in Easter Week, besides Jim Connolly. Peadar Maicín was one; Richard O'Carroll was another; so was Seán Connolly and so was Mallin, not forgetting the splendid Bill Partridge, who died after doing penal servitude. And who wants to forget the indomitable little figure of the valorous Sheehy Skeffington who fell at the hands of a frantic British officer? These I hope, some day, will form a group of statuary in some Irish park.
>
> Connolly was greater than these—bar Sheehy Skeffington, who was as great in his own way; each was great in his own way, but Jim Larkin, from the Labour point of view, was, by far, the greatest of them all; and still is.

Again the following month, April 1946, he wrote:

> There can be no doubt that the flame lit, a great flame too, in 1913 was lit with the torch held by Jim Larkin. It was 'Larkinism' that put the fear into the mean hearts of the employers at that time, and 'Larkinism' alone ... Larkin was far more than just a fiery orator; he had a soul of flame, and lighted every other one that touched his—bar those who were out for their own interests. Not only the workers, but many of the intellectuals, too.

O'Casey credited Larkin with introducing him to the work of the great American playwright Eugene O'Neill. He wrote to the American author Louis Sheaffer (28 January 1957):

> I first heard his [O'Neill's] name from the great Irish Labour leader, Jim Larkin—not unlike O'Neill in stature and one, too, who once went down to the sea in ships. Larkin was a beloved friend of mine, knew I was interested in the theatre, saw The Hairy Ape in New York, told me about it and said, 'You should get this play Seán; O'Neill has a great gift and will be heard of in days to come.' A good prophecy, by God!

Larkin was a great playgoer and regularly attended the Abbey Theatre. Prof. Patrick Lynch in his Thomas Davis lecture (chapter 15) recalled meeting Larkin at the Gaiety Theatre, Dublin, as he smoked his pipe during an interval in Emlyn Williams's play *Night Must Fall*, with Micheál Mac Liammóir in the lead. This was in the early forties. They discussed the play, and then Larkin talked about drama in general and of novels, mainly American.

O'Casey's great encomium to Larkin and most memorable description of the great orator that Larkin was is in the chapter 'Prometheus Hibernicus' in *Drums under the Windows* (1945), the third volume of O'Casey's great autobiography.

Through the streets he strode, shouting into every dark and evil-smelling hallway. The great day of change has come; Circe's swine had a better time than you have; come from your vomit; out into the sun. Larkin is calling you all!

Following afar off for a while, Seán had come at last to hear Larkin speak, to stand under a red flag rather than the green banner.

From a window in the building, leaning well forth, he talked to the workers, spoke as only Jim Larkin could speak, not for an assignation with peace, dark obedience, or placid resignation; but trumpet-tongued of resistance to wrong, discontent with leering poverty, and defiance of any power strutting out to stand in the way of their march onward. His was a handsome tense face, the forehead swept by deep black hair, the upper lip of the generous, mobile mouth hardened into fierceness by a thick moustache, the voice, deep, dark, and husky, carrying to the extreme corners of the square, and reaching, Seán thought, to the outermost ends of the earth. In this voice was the march of Wat Tyler's men, the yells and grunts of those who took the Bastille, the sigh of the famine-stricken, the loud shout from those, all bloodied over, who fell in 1798 on the corn slopes of Royal Meath; here were nursery rhyme and battle song, the silvery pleasing of a lute with the trumpet-call to come out and carry their ragged banners through the gayer streets of the city, so that unskilled labour might become the vanguard, the cavaliers and cannoniers of labour's thought and purpose.

'Who will stand, who will fight, for the right of men to live and die like men?' he called out, the large, strong hand stretched out of the window gesturing over the head of the crowd.

'Gifts of the Almighty,' went on the voice, 'labour—a gift, not a curse— poetry, dancing and principles'; and Seán could see that here was a man who would put a flower in a vase on a table as well as a loaf on a plate. Here, Seán thought, is the beginning of the broad and busy day, the leisurely evening, the calmer night; an evening full of poetry, dancing and the linnet's wings; these on their way to the music of the accordion, those to that of a philharmonic orchestra; and after all, to sleep, perchance to dream; but never to be conscious of a doubt about tomorrow's bread, certain that, while the earth remaineth, summer and winter should not cease, seed time and harvest never fail.

In 1963 the Workers' Union of Ireland wrote to O'Casey asking for a message for the union's commemoration of the fiftieth anniversary of the

1913 lock-out. O'Casey replied to Patrick Dunne, an official of the union (later to be elected Lord Mayor of Dublin) in February 1963:

It is good to hear that the members of your Union and other Trade Unions are to celebrate the great things done for the Irish workers in 1913, the memorable year when the Irish workers got up from their knees, and faced towards the sun.

'Jim Larkin' said Bernard Shaw, 'is the greatest Irishman since Parnell'; and so he was, in spite of the labour pygmies who tried to pull him down, envious of his greatness. He came as a pillar of fire to Dublin, to Cork, to Sligo, and Belfast. Aye, and Wexford too. It was then that those who had nothing begun to frighten those who had all. For the workers of Ireland the bells were ringing the old year out and a new year in, and it took the workers some time to recognise themselves when they stood up straight, and faced the bosses who owned them body and soul.

Before Larkin came it was the bosses determined the hour the workers should begin to work; the time they should end the day; the food they were to eat; the sort of home they'd live in; the kinda clothes they were to wear (I never saw a worker wearing a tall hat!). We workers went through life with our heads down; if one dared lift a head to look a boss in the face, it was time to go, for, if he didn't, a day after he would be handed his docket, and the foreman of the job pointed out the road to him. The bosses are humbler now. Now the workers have a say, a good say about the hours they work, the pay they get, the homes they live in, the clothes they wear, though the cap still suits us far better than the glossy tall hat.

The workers' battle during the great Lock-out in 1913 was the Irish workers' Bunker Hill: the battle sent a thrill through England, Europe, the USA and in all places where workers were gathered together; and it was the great Jim Larkin who lifted us from our knees and set us on our feet, and now we march, Left, left, left! I hope your March of Remembrance may be worthy of our great leader gone.

Overlook the typing errors—I am 83, ill and almost blind, so it is hard to do any work now. Give my love to my old comrade, Barney Conway; he and I went through many hard and trying days.

I am sending a bronze mask of Big Jim by a young sculptor, Sukov. It isn't a first-class work but you might like to have it on a bracket or table in your Union premises. It has Jim's features but there is not much of Jim's amazing fire and energy carved into the face.

Many years ago, I had some photos of Jim, among others, but then had no way of filing things; and all were scattered, lost or destroyed during the Irish wars; now, all I have is one of his pipes—as big as the Big Man himself.

The bronze mask of Big Jim by the Russian sculptor Sukov is now in Liberty Hall, Dublin. It and one of Jim's pipes were on display at the SIPTU 'Tribute to Larkin' exhibition in the National Library in 1997.

In 1963 too Dublin Trades Council invited O'Casey to write a script for a pageant commemorating the 1913 lock-out. He replied on 7 April 1963 to the president of the council, Patrick Donegan. The letter is reproduced here exactly as typed:

Thank you for your letter and for the honour your Council has given me by asking me to write a script for the Pageant commemorating the Golden Jubilee of the heroic and tremendous fight the Irish workers put up against the tyranny and heartlessness of the then bosses, in the great and world-famous LOCK-OUT of 1913; a fight before God and man for vindication of fundamental rights of the working class in Ireland and the rights of workers of all lands; lands where the sun is hottest and lands where the snows never thaw.

I am very sorry that it is impossible for me to do this script. I am 83 now, close to blindness, have a lot of work in hand, and am without the energy to take on such a large and important task.

Were I younger and stronger, nothing would please me better, nothing would honour me more. But as things are, I can but sigh deeply, and say I cannot do it.

It all began when the towering, eagle-like figure we knew as Jim Larkin lighted a candle stuck in a bottle in a tenement room, with a billy-can of tea and a bun, and began that glorious campaign which brought about the wonderful revolution of a new hope, a new life, for dockers, railway worker, lorry drivers, factory worker and all; a change changed the worker from being a slave into the glorious being of a Man as well as a Worker.

Then under Jim Connolly, the Irish Citizen Army came to the front and the rear of the worker, delivering him at long last from the battering assaults of police and thug, and the workers could march the streets of their city in peace, hope, and safety. Oh, I wish I could write the Script but, comrades, I cannot, I cannot.

I don't know whom to suggest for the writing; but should you decide on a film, I suggest that you call on the services of those clever ones who created the film Mise Éire. They are one of the most clever and imaginative groups in Gaelic Ireland—Gael Linn.

I wish your Commemoration every success, a Memorial Service to the men and women of Dublin, Cork, Belfast, Sligo, Limerick and Wexford, who gave a flaming lead to the workers of the world. The fight isnt finished yet, and the workers are out in France. There are a lot here stull who think they can still fling the workers about any God-damn way they like, and tens of thousands ob on the railways here are being told by these purse-proud ones to get reafy to go. So there is going to be a fierce figh on the part of the men—I hope. We workers are steadily learnig that we are content to labor for public service, for all the people, and not to fill the pockets of the profiteers with fresh piles of bank notes.

I am close to blindness now, and type mqinly by quesswork, so there may be mistakes in this letter, mistakes of typing, which I pray you excuse.

I snd you my sincere and best wishes.

Yours very sincerely,

[Signed] Seán O'Casey.

Later the same year O'Casey again wrote to Patrick Donegan, president of Dublin Trades Council (30 August 1963):

Of course, you may use the ballad of THE GRAND OUL' DAME at your Concert, or any other song I may have written.

No, no television appearance for me! I have refused to appear on the BBC television, even to speak about a book of mine about to be published; and about a play of mine to be performed; and I have declined to go on Radio here on several occasions. I have hated publicity in the past, and I hate it now. I have always tried to avoid it. Apart from friends, mostly American, I display myself before no one, except God, and Him only because I can't escape.

By the way does the old Trade Union Headquarters in Capel Street stand? By the way again, Mr. D. McDonagh should do a first-class work in writing the Script for the Ballads. All good wishes for the success of your Concert.

My love to all the Dublin Workers.

    As ever
        Seán O'Casey

The work mentioned in the last paragraph is a masque, *Let Freedom Ring*, by Donagh MacDonagh (1912–1968), which was produced at the Gate Theatre, Dublin, in 1963, to commemorate the fiftieth anniversary of the 1913 lock-out.

Finally, reference should be made to a long letter (26 January 1960) by O'Casey to Ronald Ayling, an O'Casey scholar and critic, professor of English at the University of Alberta. He included it in an article, 'Seán O'Casey and Jim Larkin after 1923', in the *Seán O'Casey Review* of spring 1977.

O'Casey makes it clear that he did not work for labour after Larkin's departure for America. Indeed, as is well known, his relations with the new leadership of Larkin's union were sour indeed and very antagonistic. For example, O'Casey relates how in 1918 during the conscription crisis he gave a song, 'The Call of the Tribe', to Séamus Hughes, an old acquaintance and now an official of the union, who had set Connolly's 'The Watchword of Labour', to music. Hughes was delighted with the verses and agreed to put an air to them. Weeks later O'Casey called to Liberty Hall to Hughes. O'Casey's letter continues:

> Hughes rose from his desk and gripped my arm, handed me the verses back, said he would and could have nothing to do with me as a follower of Larkin's still; four or five others gathered around me (officials), and I was escorted out of the Hall where once I had toiled so often and for nix. However, I was very busy during all the time I could spare as Irish secretary for the Release of Jim Larkin, in cooperation with a similar association in America whose secretary was Robert Emmet O'Reilly. I must have sent out thousands of letters, despatched cards with greetings from thousands of our sympathisers to cheer up Jim …

Returned from America, Jim Larkin found, in the words of O'Casey,

> a very different Labour Movement. He had to create out of apathy, weakness, opposition, hatred of himself and all he had done, envy of his

extraordinary magnetic person, a Union to export his talents to the workers, and a force to keep some life and faith in the future of men.

He did it, O'Casey added, through the new union, the Workers' Union of Ireland. In the union premises, 'a big tenement house' in Marlborough Street, O'Casey saw Larkin a number of times, and once Jim gave him 'a photo of himself in prison garments, showing the bushy hair, once so raven-hued, now as white as snow.'

In September 1950 O'Casey was invited by Belfast Trades Council to attend a peace conference that it was organising in the city. He replied:

> I regret very much that I will not be able to attend the peace conference, but head and heart I am with you for the cause of peace. This is surely a cause for which orange and green can unite. If we don't prevent war, many an orange sash and a green one will be laid aside, for those who wore them will be no more. In the next war, should it come, it will not be a case of one being taken and the other left. Both will be swept away.

He went on to assure the council that he loved Belfast as much as Dublin, Cork, and Galway, and had 'no wish to see it a hill of rubble.'

In February 1963 O'Casey sent a message to a cultural conference organised by the Northern Ireland Committee of the Irish Congress of Trade Unions. In it he wrote:

> Culture begins with the mother teaching a child a nursery rhyme. She and the child must have the environment of a pleasant and colourful home so that culture may be natural all round the family. Then, and only then, can the family know what it is to enjoy music, art and reading. All these delightful things depend on what are called wages. They must be sufficient to provide the things we need.

Sending his blessings to the committee, he told them that he prayed for 'success in every effort and fight Labour makes and everything that Labour does. For the labour of man is the one thing that is eternal. All depends on what the workers do.' He concluded the message: 'God be with you.'

Chapter 53

'Jem' Larkin

Bishop James Kavanagh

I feel like a certain Irish Bishop Donatus, who in the ninth century was invited to a symposium on the Continent. ('Symposium' in the original Greek means a drinking session!) He was the fifth person called upon to speak, and by that time, being a typical Irishman, he was somewhat 'narked'. He stood up and to their dismay he said: 'To hell with the lot of you—you have left me nothing to say.' (I presume he spoke in Latin.)

There have been so many erudite contributions to this fiftieth anniversary of Jim Larkin's death, particularly the SIPTU Commemoration and in an especial way the contribution of Donal Nevin in editing the marvellous volume *Trade Union Century*, which was published in 1994 to commemorate the centenary of the Irish TUC, that it is difficult for me to say anything new about Jim Larkin. So, I thought it better to emphasise what struck myself particularly about him and to bring into sharper focus certain aspects of his character and career which I personally would like to retain in remembrance of him.

As a child I heard so often the name of Larkin (my father always called him Jem Larkin) spoken with admiration, appreciation and love that from early on I wondered about this man who could inspire so much loyalty and affection. Later on I learned that he was branded as a Socialist, a Communist, an anarchist, a Red revolutionary, etc., and some high-ranking clerics spoke and wrote harshly about him. But in our home, which was a devout Catholic one, none of these strictures made any difference. Jim Larkin was idolised as the friend and hero of the working man, and indeed of the non-working man, because of the strikes and lock-outs which were a frequent happening in the struggle for better wages and conditions.

That is the first point I wish to emphasise. Jim Larkin had a magnetic influence on those who followed him—in spite of his faults. James Connolly found him very difficult at times. In 1909, shortly after Larkin started the Irish Transport and General Workers' Union, he wrote to Connolly in America to join him in the union. Connolly wrote to William O'Brien in May 1911: 'The man is utterly unreliable and dangerous. Larkin is only interested in himself. I am fed up with the homage paid to him, but I am happy to praise him for the sake of the movement.' Writing to O'Brien on 13 September 1912 from Belfast, Connolly wrote: 'I am sick of all this playing to one man, but am prepared to advise it for the sake of the movement.'

In 1911 Arthur Griffith attacked Larkin in *Sinn Féin*: 'Due to Larkin, fathers are without work, mothers weeping, children hungry and homes broken.'

Pádraic Pearse, writing in 1913 during the lock-out, wrote: 'I do not know whether the methods of Mr. James Larkin are wise methods or unwise methods (unwise, I think, in some respects), but this I know, that there is a most hideous wrong to be righted and that the man who attempts honestly to right it is a good man and a brave man.'

In 1913 Connolly wrote: 'I don't think I can stand Larkin much longer ... He is forever snarling at me.' However, when in June 1914 Larkin tendered his resignation to the union, because he was tired and worn out, Connolly spoke up: 'Jim knows I am no follower of Larkin ... I am with him as a comrade ... He is the best man our class has turned out in Ireland.' Larkin's resignation was turned down.

Jim Larkin decided to go to the USA on a speaking tour and to have a short break from the work of the union. He left in October 1914 'for a few months.' He was actually away for over eight years and did not come back till April 1923.

He had his faults undoubtedly, but he had great and enormous qualities. Let me speak for a few moments about some of these, which endeared him to the hearts of men and women. He was very brave. The dramatic incident during the 1913 lock-out shows this quality in a remarkable way. He had promised to address a meeting in O'Connell Street (then Sackville Street). It was prohibited by the police. Larkin said he would be there. Crowds assembled on Sackville Street, and a figure appeared in the window of the Imperial Hotel (part of Clery's now)—a hotel owned by Martin Murphy! It was Larkin who had come, dressed as a clergyman. He proceeded to address the crowd before he was arrested. This was bravery of the highest order.

His love of teetotalism. He knew that drink was causing havoc in the homes of the workers. The method of payment for dockers was in the local pub, where the recipient of wages was expected to buy a lot of drink, and the stevedore got a 'cut' from the proprietor. Larkin stopped that abuse.

His wish was to raise workers not only as regards pay but on a general cultural level. The union bought Croydon Park for recreational and cultural activities. This was the vision of a true humanist. The families of the workers enjoyed these pursuits enormously.

His marvellous oratorical skills. He had only formal schooling as a youngster for over three years but he educated himself to heights which were truly remarkable. He was able to quote from Shakespeare and other poets. He threw in allusions to the ancient classics of Greece and Rome, and his audiences were spellbound.

What his hearers made of some of his references, especially to the ancient classics, is debatable. For example, when he addressed the Irish Trades Union Congress in 1914 he said: 'Ireland must no longer be Niobe but Mercury amongst the nations.' Niobe had been changed into a pillar of stone, which shed tears: Mercury, on the other hand, was the messenger of the gods and was extremely active. (Jim forgot that the same Mercury was the patron of thieves!) But these references only cemented the extraordinary hold he had on his hearers; they added a certain spice to the powerful and easily understood message contained in his speeches.

In Professor George O'Brien's biography by Professor James Meenan there is a significant passage re Jim Larkin from O'Brien: 'We occasionally had visitors and I remembered one evening we heard James Larkin who impressed me very favourably. He had a much greater knowledge of literature than I would have expected ... He and Yeats exchanged recollections of the Yellow Book Circle. Larkin also pleased me by his generosity towards his opponents.'

His bravery and oratory were shown when he was in prison in Sing Sing in the USA. On St Patrick's Day he was permitted to speak to the prisoners about St Patrick. He told them how the Saint had driven the snakes out of Ireland. 'And where did they go?' he asked. 'They came to America to become politicians, policemen and prison guards.' It is only a very brave man who would utter these words!

My contribution was meant to highlight certain qualities of Jim Larkin which appealed to me. Details of his life can be found in the excellent biography by Professor Emmet Larkin (who, perhaps, relies too much on the testimony of William O'Brien in some contentious areas—O'Brien, after all, was no friend of Larkin), and I recommend once more the volume *Trade Union Century*, edited by Donal Nevin: this is an absolutely first-class production.

I would like to finish with references to some Churchmen and Jim Larkin. Archbishop Walsh is criticised for the trouble at the Dublin docks when some children were being sent across to England to receive the sustenance they could not get at home. Today one is inclined to think that this was an over-reaction on his part. The same Archbishop Walsh, however, wrote to the last meeting of the contending parties in December 1913 that 'the union's proposals are eminently reasonable'—all to no avail, as the meeting broke down without agreement. The Lock-out (or strike) petered out early in 1914, as the men gradually went back to work.

Archbishop John C. McQuaid, who is not exactly idolised by many journalists nowadays, had a real affection for Jim Larkin. He often spoke to me about him. He always referred to him as 'Mr Larkin'—with great affection—'He is a friend of the poor.' He spent quite a while with him during his last illness in the Meath Hospital.

The famous Capuchin, Father Aloysius, had given Jim the Last Sacraments and was with him often. When Jim died Archbishop McQuaid presided at his funeral Mass in Haddington Road church, and Bishop Wall was the chief celebrant. Emmet Larkin makes no reference to these matters. The funeral, on 2 February 1947, was one of the biggest in Dublin for many years.

It was during the worst winter for over a century. I was in Oxford at the time, and it would have been impossible to travel at that time in England. Not a football was kicked for the whole Hilary term. In Dublin on a bitterly cold day, with frost and snow still on the ground, Jim Larkin was laid to rest in Glasnevin. That was fifty years ago, but his life and labours will always be held in affection and admiration by succeeding generations.

I will conclude with the words of the great Jesuit philosopher Teilhard de Chardin: 'The most satisfactory thing in life is to have been able to give a large part of oneself to others.'

[A talk given to the National Library of Ireland Society, October 1997.]

Chapter 54

Delia Larkin: Relative Obscurity

Theresa Moriarty

The public life of Delia Larkin spans a short decade of Irish trade union history. The relative obscurity of her childhood and youth and the anonymity of her married life throw into sharp relief the intensity of her trade union years. From 1911 until 1921 her life was played out on platforms, pickets, protests and in print, in contrast to the privacy of the years that preceded and followed her years of activism. Both periods are eclipsed by the long shadow of her celebrated elder brother James Larkin, whose trade union and political life encompass the first half of this century. His first biography was already in print in 1909.

Delia Larkin was born on 27 February 1878, at home, as was the custom, in 2 Court, Fermie Street, in the Toxteth Park district of Liverpool. She attended the Chipping Street elementary school and was confirmed in the local Catholic church, Our Lady of Mount Carmel, where she had been baptised. Her given name was Bridget, and her confirmation name was Mary. Her official documents, census form, marriage certificate and death certificate are in the name of Bridget, but she was known throughout her life as Delia.[1]

She was the fifth child, and eldest surviving daughter, of Mary Ann McNulty and James Larkin. An older sister, Agnes, had died in infancy. Their father, James, died in 1887, when she was nine years old. Her oldest brothers, Hugh and James, had to support their widowed mother and the young family. Working lives began early in those days, and it is likely that Delia Larkin began earning at the first opportunity, cutting short chances of schooling that might otherwise have been available to her. A household with two young wage-earners was unlikely to afford a younger sibling taking advantage of any further education.

Though family circumstances militated against her education, Delia Larkin had a lifelong interest in literature and in socialist politics, demonstrated by her knowledge and love of poetry, her commitment to drama, and her small library. Their mother, as Delia Larkin's birth certificate demonstrates, signed her name with the familiar cross, which was the mark of an illiterate woman.

It may have been the experiences of Delia Larkin's elder brothers, especially James, that introduced and nurtured political and literary interests within the family home. His world of the Merseyside docks, union halls and council chambers was exclusively male and would have been almost entirely closed to her. As a young woman she would have been denied direct access to it.

Throughout their lives, James and Delia Larkin shared close interests and retained a strong family bond, which is traced through the events that shape this narrative and identified by the many years that they shared their homes.

Delia Larkin's first official record in Ireland is the census of April 1911, when she is listed as living with her brother James and his family at 27 Auburn Street, near Broadstone, in Dublin. She is remembered as having a nursing career in Liverpool before her trade union appointment, but her occupation on the census form, which was filled out in Irish, is recorded as 'múinteoir'—a teacher. Neither nursing nor teaching required a professional qualification, and she may have worked at either occupation according to inclination or opportunity.

The only glimpse of her life before 1911 is that she had run a hotel in Rostrevor, County Down, about the time that James was an organiser for the National Union of Dock Labourers and strike leader in Belfast in 1907.[2] This suggests that Delia first moved to Ireland with her brother's family close to the Larkin homestead in County Down around this time. Her nephew Denis Larkin, the second child of Elizabeth Brown and James Larkin, was born in Rostrevor in 1908.[3] When James Larkin's family moved to Dublin, Delia may have moved with them.

Delia Larkin joined the roll-call of Irish trade union history in the summer of 1911. It had been decided to start a women's trade union within the ambit of the ITGWU, formed by James Larkin and his comrades from the Dublin docks breakaway from the National Union of Dock Labourers.[4] The Irish Women Workers' Union first advertised for members in the *Irish Worker* on 12 August 1911, followed by a formal launch a month later, on 5 September.

Delia Larkin expressed the programme for the new union succinctly in her weekly column in the *Irish Worker* in October, 1911, which summed up the outstanding grievances of her women members: 'All we ask for is just shorter hours, better pay than the scandalous limit now existing and conditions of labour befitting a human being.' She wrote for the *Irish Worker*, the ITGWU's weekly paper, from the start. One of her earliest contributions was in verse. Her 'Women Workers' Column' began in August 1911; she edited over 120 columns for the next three years, a weekly pattern broken only by her absences from Dublin and the gathering pressure of her daily work during the lock-out in 1913.

Her column dealt with the grievances and both the industrial and domestic conditions of working women and chronicled their struggles and strikes. She was not the column's sole contributor: it was open to women (and men) correspondents and columnists, creating a platform for its readers. Her own contributions often employed a topical anecdote, from which she elaborated on the domestic burdens of tenement life, or temperance, as the theme took her. At festive times the column might include recipes. Here also she elaborated what came closest to expressing her form of socialism in a co-operative system of production. Votes for women were frequently advocated in the column.

For the next four years, between the summers of 1911 and 1915, Delia Larkin lived at a relentless pace of activity. She had come to her task as a sceptical organiser of women, but the enthusiastic launch of the women's union on 5 September 1911 'once and for all dispelled that feeling.' The public world she had entered was almost exclusively male, though by 1911 this predominance was being contested. Women were at their most visible in the suffrage movement, and to an extent within the nationalist movement, where women had gathered around the monthly journal *Bean na hÉireann*.

Socialist women tended to direct their energies into the suffrage movement. They were in effect excluded from the political labour movement that was coming together within the trade union movement. Membership of the Irish Labour Party, formed in 1912, required a prior trade union membership, to which few women were admitted. In the trade union movement women were present, but only emerging into the public gaze. Over the next few years women were to become organised through women's sections, branches, and committees.

Delia Larkin's position on the public stage as the woman leader of women trade unionists was a lonely and isolated place, with only a few hundred members, probably never much more than a thousand or so, with her. She shared with Dublin's young female industrial work force little experience of industrial organisation. She built her union around the members' militancy; what she lacked in negotiating experience or opportunity she made up by enormous energy and commitment.

In Liberty Hall the union rooms were open to members every day, Sunday included, and the secretary advertised her availability to members from 10 a.m. to 10 p.m. The women's union was intimate and informal. Delia Larkin, as secretary, ran the union with complete autonomy and a rule-book. She knew her members and the conditions of their lives: the exploitation of her widowed members; young workers' long hours; the little scope for recreation or entertainment; their unrecognised talents and undervalued skills. Delia Larkin aimed to offer a trade unionism that widened opportunity and broke down barriers by building a united organisation with strong loyalties and where members mixed freely on equal terms. The union programme included discussion groups and weekly socials, annual outings, yearly concerts, and New Year dances.

The women's union embarked on a series of industrial challenges in Dublin work-places. Within its first six months, £172 was paid out in strike pay and idle money and for victimisation. It had recovered £40 in wages and won £70 a week increases in pay for its members. In the early summer of 1912 Delia Larkin won two small but significant strikes, at Keogh's sack-makers and the Pembroke laundry.

Delia Larkin organised large work-places and small, dedicating as much energy to a handful of workers as to employments with a large industrial work force, such as Jacob's biscuit factory, one of the only Dublin factories where the union counted its members in hundreds. Other women workers turned to the union for support, and Delia Larkin championed the cause of domestic workers, waitresses, printers and paper-workers, dressmakers and wig-makers in a variety of Dublin work-places.

The strength of the IWWU was in Dublin. Branches were formed elsewhere: in Belfast (October 1911), Dundalk (January 1912), Wexford (April 1912), and Cork (May 1913). These were all places where the ITGWU was already established. They were started in the aftermath of a local dispute, with the exception of Cork, which was launched when the Irish Trades Union Congress met there.

Delia Larkin seems to have had little or no involvement in the branches, which were left to their own local resources and never survived in any meaningful industrial existence. Only Belfast, where James Connolly recruited linen-workers into an Irish Textile Workers' Union, retained any branch life. This became organised as a branch of the IWWU.

The IWWU affiliated independently from the ITGWU to the ITUC in 1912, with 1,000 members. At the annual congress Delia Larkin's credentials were challenged, because the new union was late registering, delayed by the strike at Keogh's. This led to an attempt by Belfast delegates, who included the only other women in the hall, from the Textile Operatives' Society of Ireland, to object to the organisation of women workers by the ITGWU. Belfast hostility to the new women's union was directed more towards James Connolly than towards Delia Larkin herself, because he had begun a women's organisation for linen-workers, which had led to a drawn-out row on Belfast Trades Council. Mary Galway, secretary of the Textile Operatives, had been a delegate to the ITUC since 1901 and was a former vice-president of the ITUC and still an executive member. Whether as a consequence of this dispute or an unbridgeable divide between their generations of trade unionism, no alliance ever formed between the two women in the few years in which their attendance at the ITUC overlapped.

Delia Larkin represented her union at three annual conferences of the ITUC. In 1912 she attended as the sole IWWU delegate; in 1913 she was accompanied by Ellen Gordon, delegate of the Belfast branch; in 1914 Bridget Butler from Dublin joined Ellen Gordon and Delia Larkin to raise the IWWU delegation to three women.

Her industrial work included representing women workers on Ireland's first trades board, the joint industrial councils formed to regulate pay within the poorly paid manufacturing sectors where women worked. She was unanimously elected as the Dublin representative on the cardboard-box-making trades board at a meeting in the new Labour Exchange on 29 January 1912 and seems to have remained a member over the next two years.

Alongside her industrial activity, Delia Larkin had formed the union choir in February 1912, which first performed publicly at the St Patrick's Night concert. Its success led her to start a drama group four months later. The Irish Workers' Dramatic Class, which she trained herself, started in the first week of June for members of the IWWU and ITGWU; and on St Stephen's Night 1912 the Irish Workers' Dramatic Company made its stage debut in four one-act plays under the direction of A. Patrick Wilson. Delia Larkin featured in three of the plays.

Within the wider political world of women in Dublin, Delia Larkin had represented her members within the suffrage movement. She was among the invited guests to Anna Haslam's celebrations at the election of Sarah Harrison, Dublin's first woman councillor, in February 1912. Delia Larkin represented the IWWU among the platform of women from many organisations at the mass rally in Dublin to demand women's suffrage in the Home Rule Bill, held in the Antient Concert Rooms on 1 June 1912.

This activity did not sustain the membership of the women's union, which fell to about six or seven hundred in 1913. In an effort to raise funds for the union, Delia Larkin arranged a tour for the theatre group in Britain. She appointed Mary Cuddy, a member of the drama company, as a temporary clerk to collect the dues, and left Dublin for a six-week tour.

Two Dublin disputes in the summer of 1913 illustrate the IWWU's committed approach to organising women workers. The union had no members in either Somerset Linen Merchants in Golden Lane or the Savoy Confectionery Company at the start of the disputes. In April, women went on strike at the Savoy. While they were out, a number of them joined the IWWU. The strike was soon settled, but on their return to work four IWWU members were sacked, because of slack trade. Delia Larkin began negotiations, but these broke down when the four victimised workers were replaced.

In May, dressmakers at the Somerset linen factory struck. Although none of them were members, they too joined the IWWU and received four shillings a week strike pay from the union. In June the dispute at the Savoy turned into a strike, which continued into August. The strike was conducted aggressively. Leaflets attacked the adulteration of confectionery, with soot to colour the sweets and rats in the chocolate. In July the *Irish Worker* published photographs of the 'Savoy Scab Octette', eight women who continued to work at the sweet factory. There were arrests and court appearances for intimidation. The conduct of the dispute by the union was to become familiar in the months to come.

On the August holiday Monday in 1913, Croydon Park opened as a suburban social and recreation centre for members of the Liberty Hall unions and their families, with a great festival. But the festive optimism soon evaporated.

Within weeks of the tram strike starting at the end of August 1913 it had spread throughout the city. There were no longer only industrial issues at stake between union and employer: now Dublin was launched on a struggle of life and death as the lock-out paralysed the city and thousands were thrown out of work.

At Jacob's the dispute began on 1 September over the wearing of the IWWU badge. Within a week 310 women were locked out there. Paterson's match factory locked out their women workers.

When James Larkin went to England to seek support from British workers, Delia Larkin took effective charge in Liberty Hall. For the next four months the demands on her organising skills and emotions were relentless. She attended, with Constance Markievicz, the large rallies held almost nightly, usually the only women noted on the platform, although neither are reported among the speakers.

In James Larkin's absence Delia Larkin increasingly became the public face of Liberty Hall. 'Jim's sister' was sought out by visitors to Dublin eager for news of the dispute and of how life fared in the city. She formed and ran the entire undertaking to feed the union members and their dependants throughout the lock-out, with a women's committee of volunteers from among her union members, strikers' relatives, and the circles of political women in Dublin. This huge effort, which provided daily breakfasts for three thousand children, lunches for nursing mothers, and the distribution of clothing, continued until February 1914.

When the Daily Herald League planned to bring Dublin strikers' children to homes in Britain to be looked after during the lock-out, the London organisers turned to Delia Larkin for support with the arrangements. She joined the attempts to escort the children through the angry crowds inspired by the Ancient Order of Hibernians in response to the Catholic Archbishop of Dublin's denunciation of the scheme. She continued to take responsibility in the face of public hostility by visiting the party of eighteen Dublin children who had reached Liverpool, to reassure both the public and their families about their religious instruction, schooling and accommodation during their stay there.

She stood in for her brother, who was in Mountjoy Jail, at a rally in the Albert Hall in London to support the Dublin workers, where she delivered the first speech from the distinguished platform. In the autumn and winter months the resources of Liberty Hall came largely under Delia Larkin's administration. By the end of the year five rooms were taken over by the IWWU for the solidarity action.

Christmas 1913 was another occasion for her considerable mobilising and organising skills, when a huge Christmas party was held at Croydon Park. A great tree was lit in the conservatory of the house, and dinner was provided in shifts for thousands of women, children, and men, 'under the direction of Miss Larkin.'[5] Across the city at Emmet Hall, 'through her kindness and the good friends of the Women Workers' Union,' Christmas dinner was given to the children of Inchicore.

Although the lock-out ended in the early months of 1914, there was little relief from the pressure of Delia Larkin's commitments in the coming year. Four hundred of her own members were not reinstated after the lock-out, and in March she went on tour with the dramatic company she had formed from locked-out workers, taking in Liverpool, Oxford, and London. She hoped to finance co-operatives for Dublin's victimised workers. Each performance comprised two plays, Lady Gregory's *The Workhouse Ward* and either *Birthright* by T. C. Murray (in which she played

Maura Morrisey) or William Boyle's *The Building Fund* (in which she acted as Mrs Grogan). The evenings included Irish songs, dances and selections on the Irish war pipes.

Some of the London venues they played indicate their audiences: the William Morris Hall, Walthamstow, the Co-Op Hall, Penge, and the Social Democratic Club, Willesden. Delia Larkin was away from Dublin for three months. She returned at the end of May to attend the Irish Trades Union Congress annual conference in Dublin with an increased delegation from her union.

In June she contested the Poor Law elections in the North Dock ward of Dublin, the only woman of the thirteen candidates nominated by the Dublin trade unions. While her 561 votes were a couple of hundred away from what was required to get her elected a Poor Law guardian, she polled slightly better than her two fellow-candidates, P. T. Daly (551) and Michael Brohoon (523), a sitting councillor.

By now she was a leading figure in the Dublin working-class movement. But in her absence from Dublin, resentments and difficulties festered in the aftermath of the lock-out. Housekeeping questions began to dominate in Liberty Hall. The drama group tour had not made any money, despite £125 being raised in one night in the King's Hall, London. Running costs had been high. The occupation of the largest room in Liberty Hall by the IWWU, without rent, was resented. Conflict within the demoralised Liberty Hall focused on Delia Larkin. Friction came to a head in June 1914 when the ITGWU No. 1 branch committee demanded back the large room taken over by the IWWU during the lock-out. By August this row had turned into a squabble over the piano that Delia Larkin had installed for the weekly IWWU socials.[6] In September she was ordered to find other premises for the women's union. A month later, in October, James Larkin left for the United States.

When the Chief Secretary for Ireland, Augustine Birrell, met suffrage women to discuss the make-up of the newly appointed Ladies' Advisory Committee to help relief work in Ireland, the women proposed Delia Larkin as a member, in recognition of her public standing; but apparently it was too much to expect the Viceroy's wife, Lady Aberdeen, a familiar target of Delia Larkin's column, to sit with the sister of a man who made such disloyal speeches. Delia Larkin's rejection by the authorities was viewed as a deliberate insult to Dublin's only women's union. Being 'Jim's sister' ensured her an ambiguous celebrity.

Soon after this public rejection Delia Larkin was brought to court by a former member of the IWWU, Mary Cuddy, who alleged that she had not been fully paid for her work as a temporary clerk during Delia Larkin's theatre tour in 1913. The case was dismissed.[7]

By January 1915 the sole activities of the IWWU advertised in special election issues of the *Irish Worker* were Irish dancing twice a week, Sunday socials, and the IWWU co-operative making Irish republican badges and shirts at the shop in Eden Quay. James Connolly had taken charge at

Liberty Hall as acting secretary of the ITGWU since Larkin left for America. Recollections and reminiscences by observers and participants in later quarrels suggest that relations between him and Delia Larkin were poor.

There are conflicting accounts of her role in the Irish Citizen Army. In a series on the life of James Larkin in the *Sunday Chronicle* in 1948, J. Doran O'Reilly describes Delia Larkin as secretary of the Red Cross section of the Citizen Army. Frank Robbins records that she prepared food with her women workers, for a group of men on manoeuvres in September 1914, but this was all he witnessed of her participation.[8]

Her isolation was not as intense as the rows in Liberty Hall suggest. In February 1915 she won 'without difficulty' a newspaper poll as the most popular woman in the movement.

By the summer the bad feeling had worsened. At the end of June the ITGWU decided to give up its lease on Croydon Park, where Delia Larkin had lived with her brother and his family since they had all been evicted from Auburn Street during the lock-out. Towards the end of July she locked up the co-operative shop and left Dublin. Her departure led to a protest by women against Connolly at Liberty Hall.[9]

Delia Larkin's life was, as so many others, interrupted in its pattern by the war. At the end of 1915 James Connolly wrote to Winifred Carney, in language that indicates the breach that had taken place: 'One of Miss Larkin's crowd recently showed a letter from Delia to a third party, which third party reported to us that Delia said in the letter that she had joined the Red Cross, and was nursing Tommies in the military hospitals in London, and was broken down in health as a consequence. It seems incredible. But the woman is positive.'[10]

Nursing Tommies was no indication of wartime sentiment. A single woman arriving back in England without employment or even lodgings—Delia Larkin was now in London and not her home town, Liverpool—may well have opted to take up this work, as many women pressed into the war effort did, as humanitarian, rather than military, service. Her personal views of military recruitment may be more accurately suggested by the photograph of her, back in Dublin in 1918, signing the anti-conscription pledge.[11] She supported the anti-war campaigning of her two brothers, James in the United States and the youngest, Peter, who was imprisoned in Australia from 1916.

When Delia Larkin returned to Dublin in 1918 it was to a very changed political climate. The transformation wrought in Irish politics, and within Liberty Hall and the ITGWU in particular, by the events and aftermath of Easter 1916 had created a different organisation, reordered the priorities, and brought new opportunities to old faces. The Dublin world Delia Larkin had known was gone.

She started work in Liberty Hall in the insurance section that had paid her wages when she was IWWU secretary, under the sponsorship of the Larkin loyalist P. T. Daly, who headed this section since 1914 and at whose invitation some believed she had returned to Ireland. The reorganised

IWWU would not readmit her as a member, saying she should seek membership of the Irish Clerical Workers' Union, which also turned her down. Daly, as secretary of Dublin Trades Council, raised her exclusion by both unions at the council's August meeting.

The IWWU, now an independent trade union under the leadership of Louie Bennett, had fraught relations with the ITGWU, which had begun to recruit women workers. Mary Jones, historian of the IWWU, says the Trades Council minutes discussing this dispute 'bristle with innuendo' but give few clues to the reasons why 'the first General Secretary of the IWWU, and one of the earliest champions of working women in Ireland, found herself so unceremoniously discarded.'[12]

Delia Larkin may have begun to weary of the repeated rejection she felt in Dublin. A letter written in July 1918 to Peter Larkin's wife in Australia reported that she had expressed the intention of going to Australia. According to the Australian police, who had seen this letter, Delia Larkin 'was no improvement on her brothers,' Peter and James. She had written a letter of encouragement to a leading Australian syndicalist, a member of the 'Wobblies' (Industrial Workers of the World), and had taken a prominent part in a Dublin meeting to release the Sydney Twelve.[13] The public meeting, organised by Delia Larkin, called for the release of Peter Larkin and his eleven comrades in Australia and was addressed by Jock Wilson, the Liverpool organiser of the Independent Labour Party, who had himself been deported from Australia. In the chair was P. T. Daly. Motions were moved by M. J. O'Connor and Barney Conway. Once again Delia did not speak herself but, in the words of the newspaper report, acted as secretary to the meeting, reading out letters of support, including one from Éamon de Valera. The meeting was planned for 27 May in the Mansion House; when the meeting there was proclaimed, the venue shifted to 10 Langrishe Place, now becoming the centre of the opposition within the ITGWU.

The following month the ITGWU did not reappoint P. T. Daly to his position in the insurance section. The dispute between William O'Brien, now the ITGWU treasurer, and Daly had come to represent the line on which the political and personal differences within Liberty Hall were divided. On 11 June, Delia Larkin, Michael Mullen and a temporary clerk, Norberry, went on strike against Daly's victimisation. When the ITGWU refused to reinstate them, protest meetings were organised, first at Langrishe Place, then at the Mansion House on 15 June, chaired by Barney Conway. The dispute spread to Dublin Trades Council, where the following day Delia Larkin was prominent among the protesters in the gallery.

From July to September, Delia Larkin edited and wrote for the *Red Hand*, an opposition newspaper to the ITGWU leadership, which advertised its loyalties in each issue with a picture of James Larkin on the front. It was published from Langrishe Place.[14] Shortly after its publication it was halted by James Larkin.

In America, Larkin's application for a passport had been turned down. Dublin Trades Council planned a work stoppage in protest. Within weeks he was on trial and eventually committed to prison. Now Delia Larkin had two brothers in prison, on opposite sides of the world. Both brothers were imprisoned in highly politicised trials and on highly politicised charges: Peter Larkin was tried on treason and conspiracy charges and was serving ten years' penal servitude, while James was charged with criminal anarchy.

In 1920 Peter Larkin and his comrades were released from prison, and Delia Larkin became the moving spirit of the Release James Larkin campaign. The reluctance of the Dublin trade union movement to act on behalf of either of them was probably viewed by her as an act of betrayal. It would almost certainly have exacerbated resentment against the ITGWU leadership, since James Larkin remained its general secretary and Peter Larkin had formerly been an organiser for the union. When Dublin Trades Council launched its Larkin Defence Fund, the ITGWU remained aloof, saying it was responsible for Larkin's welfare.

On 8 February 1921, Delia Larkin married Patrick Colgan, a member of the Citizen Army, at the Pro-Cathedral, Dublin.[15] From then on her public life largely ceased. They lived in a flat at 17 Gardiner Place. In this crowded apartment people came and went constantly, attracting young political writers such as Liam O'Flaherty, Seán O'Casey, and Peadar O'Donnell. Bob Stewart, an emissary from the Communist Party of Great Britain, stayed there, and, on his return to Dublin, so did James Larkin.

The account of Delia Larkin by her grandnephew James Larkin in his family biography recounts that after 1924 she renewed her theatrical activities, running a drama society for the members of the Workers' Union of Ireland. In 1930 and 1931 she wrote occasional pieces for the relaunched *Irish Worker*, including an exchange with another correspondent about domestic workers, when she returned, as 'DLC', to many of the themes she wrote of in her women workers' column twenty years previously.

When Patrick Colgan and Delia Larkin moved to Ballsbridge, James Larkin joined them and lived out his last years in their flat at 41 Wellington Road.

The eclipse of her later years was, by her own account, due to ill-health, which imposed on her 'a very quiet life, quite against my inclination,' as she told R. M. Fox in a letter of acknowledgment to him shortly after her brother's death.[16]

Delia Larkin died at her home in 41 Wellington Road, Dublin, on 26 October 1949 and was buried in Glasnevin Cemetery.

Rouse, Ye Workers

Delia Larkin

Rouse up, ye workers, awake from your dreamings,
Arise in your might, and for liberty strike;
Too long have you dreamt: 'tis pleasant, beguiling,
But life calls for action, which dreamers dislike.

Be up then and doing, time waits not the dreamer,
The morning breaks clear, 'tis a beckoning hand,
To show you the way, for mists to grow clearer
And to strike for your rights, ye valiant band.

What are your rights—mayhap you've forgotten them
So meekly and long to oppression you've bent;
Your rights are to live not as slaves, but as freemen,
Free to think, speak, and act; free to live as God meant.

[*Irish Worker*, 8 July 1911.]

Chapter 55

Peter Larkin

Our Readers will regret to hear that Peter Larkin, Founder and Organiser of the Workers' Union of Ireland, passed away on Friday morning at 9 a.m. in Baggot Street Hospital.

His remains will be taken from the Hospital, on Saturday evening at 5 p.m. to Unity Hall, Marlboro Street.

Public Funeral from Unity Hall on Sunday, at 1 p.m. to Glasnevin Cemetery.

Go ndéanfhaidh Dia Trócaire ar a anam.

Thus the *Irish Worker* (16 May 1931) announced the death of Peter Larkin. The next issue (23 May 1931) contained the following obituary:

Union man, agitator, organiser and fighter for the working class in every part of the globe, on the Five Continents and the Seven Seas. A member and active worker and organiser of National Union of Dock Labourers, National Union of Sailors and Firemen, IWW (America and Australia), ITGWU. Founder and Organiser of the WUI.

Member and agitator in the early days of the Independent Labour Party, Irish Labour Party, Social Democratic Federation, Irish Worker League.

A life of service and struggle, a life bound up with the whole history and struggle of the International Labour Movement. A servant of his class, a leader of his class, a fighter of the working class who died in harness.

Peter Larkin was born in Liverpool on 12 August 1880, the youngest of six children. His brother James was the second-eldest of the family. Peter was extremely delicate during childhood and did not attend school regularly. Once when police arrived at their home to arrest James, who had failed to pay a fine of £5 imposed for obstruction and riotous assembly, Peter went with them to jail in place of his brother, who was the only member of the family working. He was involved with his brother and Fred Bower in burying a message from 'the wage slaves employed on the erection of the cathedral' in the foundations of the Anglican Cathedral in Liverpool in 1904 shortly before the foundation stone was to be laid by King Edward VII.

In the eighteen-nineties, during the so-called religious riots in Liverpool, Peter helped to organise the Catholic Democracy League, composed of workers only. They had a fife and drum band, of which Peter was drum-major. It was during this campaign that he married Annie Traynor of Dublin.

In 1907 he went to Belfast to help James, who related that during the strike the first power-driven vehicle ever used in Ireland was brought in by the Shipping Federation. The strikers could hold up horse vehicle transport, but the 'steam devil' gave them pause. Peter organised the workers to lie down in front of the devil car. As soon as one group was arrested, another group 'composed themselves for a stretch out.'

In 1911 Peter was involved in the great Liverpool dock strike led by Tom Mann. After this, according to his brother, he drifted to the United States and, under his mother's maiden name, McNulty, was active in the IWW during a dispute in the canning industry in Louisiana, among lumber workers, and on the waterfront. He returned to England in 1913 and spoke at meetings in support of the locked-out Dublin workers and was active in agitation work in Belfast and Dublin that year. On the Saturday before Bloody Sunday he barricaded the doors of Liberty Hall to prevent access to the police.

In his autobiography, *New Horizons* (1942), J. T. Murphy, a leader of the Communist Party of Great Britain and of the Comintern in the twenties, wrote of Peter Larkin before the war:

> Was there ever a man with more stentorian tones than Peter? He was not as big a man as Jim, but nevertheless powerful, a rugged, swarthy dock worker and seaman, who had knocked about the ports of the world.

Late in December 1914, while Jim Larkin was speaking at an IWW meeting in New York to organise the men on the waterfront, a voice roared out from the back of the hall, 'Fellow-worker speaker.' It was the voice of Peter.

In 1915 Peter went to Australia. There he became active in the IWW. In 1911, the Chicago headquarters had granted a charter to a group of socialists in Adelaide and 'from this small band grew the strongest and most significant revolutionary movement the Australian working class had yet known.'[1] The Sydney branch, with which Peter Larkin was to become associated, was led by Tom Glynn, a blacksmith by trade, who had emigrated to Australia from Wexford and was known by his associates as 'the intellectual of the bunch.' Thirty-five years old, he had been editor of the paper *Direct Action* and by the time Larkin arrived in Sydney was full-time secretary of the IWW branch there.

The Australian historian Ian Turner in his book *Sydney's Burning* describes Larkin as 'heavily built, with an untidy mop of hair surmounting a moon face dominated by a great bulbous nose.' Larkin worked on the waterfront, 'spending his spare time agitating for Home Rule for Ireland and industrial democracy.'[2]

Arriving in Sydney in the autumn of 1915, Larkin soon had convictions arising out of his agitational activities on Sydney Domain. In September, with eleven others, he was arrested on charges of arson and treason. The Twelve, as they were to become known, were tried before Mr Justice Prior in the Central Criminal Court. In the dock, Larkin was reported to have been belligerent. The only evidence against him was that of two policemen, who claimed to have seen him demonstrating the use of fire-dope on the footpath outside the IWW rooms. Larkin denied any knowledge of arson and had an alibi for the date the police gave for the alleged demonstration: he was at home at the time with his wife, and this was confirmed by her and by a fellow-worker, Pat O'Brien.

Larkin was found guilty of conspiracy to commit arson and seditious conspiracy. Asked by the judge if he had anything to say, he retorted:

> You ask me have I anything to say! Have I anything to say against a Star Chamber? ... Why, I ask you, should I bring to this country but a few months ago the wife of my bosom and the child of her womb and then perpetrate the foul crimes with which you charge me. No such thing as crime can be laid at my door. I am not guilty, even if all the juries in the world say I am. I leave it to my own class who know me.

In passing sentence, the judge described the Twelve as members of 'an association of criminals of the very worst type, and a hotbed of crime.' Larkin was sentenced to ten years' hard labour. Early in 1917 the sentence was confirmed by the Court of Criminal Appeal.

A Release the Twelve campaign was mounted, supported at first by colleagues of the prisoners but later to embrace the entire labour movement in Australia. The pressure of public opinion compelled the government of New South Wales to establish in July 1918 a Royal Commission, headed by Mr Justice Street. It examined the evidence, noting in the Larkin case that his alibi had been supported by his wife, who had stated that they were at home counting tickets for a lecture he was to give the following night. Mr Justice Pring cynically said of the alibi that he had no doubt that Mrs Larkin was correct that on some occasion they were counting tickets, 'but it may not have been the 14th.'

Ian Turner insists that the case against Larkin was very thin and that even if his alibi is not accepted it seems extremely unlikely that he would make a public demonstration of fire-setting when the privacy of the IWW hall was close behind him.[3] With regard to the case against the Twelve, Turner concludes that 'there can be little doubt' that it was a frame and that in the case of Larkin the only evidence against him was 'concocted'.[4] The Royal Commission, however, did not recommend any change in the verdicts or the sentences on the Twelve.

In the summer of 1920 another inquiry by a judge of the Tasmanian Supreme Court was held. This time Mr Justice Ewing had no difficulty in finding very differently from Mr Justice Street. In the case of Peter Larkin he found that there was adequate evidence to support the charge of seditious conspiracy, but that the time he had served was sufficient punishment. The State Premier, John Storey, accepted the report of Mr Justice Ewing.

Larkin, with nine others, was released on 3 August 1920, after serving nearly four years of the sentence. The ten freed men, with their defenders and supporters, celebrated their release in Sydney Town Hall, where women distributed red camellias; it ended with the singing of 'The Red Flag'. Larkin wore what the police report of the celebration described as 'Sinn Féin colours'.

441

Peter Larkin's subsequent activities in Australia were recorded in police reports.[5] The following are extracts from these reports:

Peter Larkin is an Irishman and a brother of James Larkin, an erstwhile Irish agitator who achieved much notoriety in connection with Home Rule and strike rioting in Dublin prior to the outbreak of war.

Larkin came to Australia in 1915 and was undoubtedly sent out by the IWW to push forward that body's work. He became one of its most prominent officials and speakers. He was arrested in 1916 with eleven other IWW members on a charge of treason and conspiracy arising out of various fires which had occurred in Sydney. He was convicted on two charges and was sentenced in all to 10 years penal servitude and was incarcerated in the Parramatta Gaol.

While in jail he was safe enough, but certain doings of persons interested in his release are worth noticing and throw a little light on his antecedents and connection with Irish 'troublers'. On 25 July 1917 a cable from London was published that James Larkin was on his way to Australia via USA. His entry into Australia was prevented as it was thought that from his previous record for disturbances, the visit was for the purpose of creating strife in this country to secure his brother's release.

Mrs. May Wilson (wife of 'Jock' Wilson, a deported IWW member) wrote to Mrs. P. Larkin on 22 July 1918 stating that they, the Wilsons, had been in touch with Miss Delia Larkin who expressed the intention of coming to Australia.

Delia Larkin was no improvement on her brothers, Peter and James. She wrote a letter of encouragement to J. B. King for his part in IWW matters, and took a prominent part in the organisation of a meeting in Dublin on 27 July 1919 on behalf of the 12 IWW men. At this meeting 'Jock' Wilson was to speak.

As a result of ceaseless agitation, and after two Royal Commissions had reviewed the cases, 10 of the 12 IWW conspirators, including Larkin, were released on 3 August 1920.

Larkin's compulsory retirement did not improve him or his views which are essentially anti-British. On 2 July 1918, and while still in gaol he wrote to one Thos. O. Byrne, Fermanagh, Ireland, expressing admiration for Sinn Féin, and certain of its leaders; at the same time uttering the hope that the workers of Ireland would become organised into one big union and so bring about a state of affairs best described as 'Ireland for the Irish workers.'

A banquet was given to the released IWW prisoners at Trades Hall, Sydney, 9 August 1920; Larkin was present but said little. He wore the Sinn Féin colours, however.

After his release he set out for a trip to Broken Hill and en route visited Adelaide and other South Australian industrial centres in company with Tom Glynn. He was in Adelaide on 10 and 31 October 1920; he spoke the usual revolutionary jargon and claimed that the industrial movement was at the bottom of Sinn Féin trouble in Ireland.

Returning to Sydney he identified himself with the Communist Party and by May 1921 was so far advanced in the Australian CP that he was bracketed with Glynn and Garden as the leading Communists at the back of an effort to turn the Trades Hall May Day procession into a Communist demonstration.

In August 1921, he went to Queensland, and at a CP meeting at Brisbane on 18 August 1921 he was a speaker. A fortnight after this he left for an organising tour in Northern Queensland, and while engaged in this work he was afforded assistance by Donald Grant.

On 12 December 1921 he reported to the Brisbane Branch that he had enrolled 150 new members. 52 being Russians. He was called back to Sydney on 19 December 1921 by his wife, owing to a cable said to have been received from Ireland.

On 8 January [1922] he attended a Communist unity conference held in Sydney at the instigation of the Small Bureau, Comintern, Moscow. His excuse for being at this meeting was a delegation for the Cairns branch.

Larkin is a dangerous and fanatical revolutionary with a dash of Sinn Féin thrown in. He keeps up his connection in Ireland where his family seems to have a vested interest [in] strife. A determined organiser, he is the kind of man to make the CP a real menace to the community.[6]

The dossier of Peter Larkin's papers in the Attorney-General's Department of the Commonwealth of Australia contained a press report of an address delivered on 12 May 1922 on Larkin's way back to Ireland. The title of the address was 'Capitalism or the Workers' Republic in Ireland'. It was given under the auspices of 'the Revolutionary movement in South Australia embracing the OBU, the Industrial Union Propaganda League and the Communist Party.'

Larkin's application for a passport was referred by the Home and Territories Department to the Department of External Affairs. It stated that he desired to proceed to England for the purpose of residence, accompanied by his wife, Annie, and daughter, Esther, aged eleven. He gave his occupation as seaman and his place of residence as 27 Richard's Avenue, Sydney. He was stated to be five feet eight inches in height, with broad forehead, long nose, square chin, florid complexion, oval face, grey hair, and blue eyes.

Larkin left for England on the *Hobson's Bay* on 10 May 1922. On 21 May the Investigation Branch of the Attorney-General's Office was informed by the Prime Minister's Department that 'Peter Larkin, after travelling through America, recently arrived in England from Canada' and that his movements in Great Britain would be advised to the Investigation Branch.

In a further report, on 16 February 1923, Larkin was said 'to be touring the United States in an endeavour to arouse the workers there to demand the release of his brother.' On 6 April the Australian High Commissioner in London was informed that 'Peter Larkin, formerly interested in the Communist movement in Australia, has recently arrived in this country from Canada.'

On his return to Ireland he became involved in his brother's campaign to gain control of the ITGWU. After James Larkin's expulsion from that union and during his absence in Russia, in the summer of 1924, Peter Larkin founded the Workers' Union of Ireland. (See chapter 42.)

One of the first places outside Dublin that Peter Larkin sought to organise into the WUI was Limerick. He was wholly unsuccessful. The trade union movement in the city had already come into conflict with the Arch-Confraternity of Limerick, and members were advised by the priests to leave the union. Sermons were preached against 'Larkinism' and against Peter Larkin in particular. His comment was that 'there was a time when timber ships sailed up the Shannon and there were men of iron. Now we have iron ships and timber men.'

Shortly after the WUI was founded, probably as a result of differences between the brothers about the tactics to be followed by the new union, Peter went to London and became involved in agitation on the docks there. Peter Larkin might be described more as an anarcho-syndicalist, in comparison with his brother, who held to a more traditional socialist view. However, by 1927 Peter had returned to Dublin, becoming the national organiser of the Workers' Union of Ireland.

C. Desmond Greaves, in *The Irish Transport and General Workers' Union* (1982), considered Peter Larkin a political leader in his own right, though he lacked his brother's charisma. He had represented the Liverpool dockers at the 1910 syndicalist conference in Manchester, and he was well read in Irish history. (For more about Peter Larkin see chapter 42.)

Chapter 56

As I Remember Big Jim

Dr John de Courcy Ireland

I frequently heard Larkin's name mentioned when I was a child, but the message it brought then was confused. I had an ultra-conservative step-father, who insisted that I should be sent to an English boarding-school to learn discipline and become an expert in Latin and Greek and so qualify for a full-time, pensionable job in the British civil service. I hated it—the school, not so much the Latin and Greek. The moment I was seventeen I left school, took a scholarship in history at Oxford University, and went off for a spell in various insignificant categories at sea.

I decided to take up my scholarship, arrived at Oxford, and joined the University Irish Club forthwith. The members of this club and of the University Labour and Liberal Clubs used to frequent an Oxford café called Sheila's, run by two Irishwomen. It was in the never-ending arguments in Sheila's Café that I first came up against serious arguments in favour of a radical transformation of society by the establishment of socialism. I was particularly impressed by the clarity of thought of a notorious young lecturer (several years older, of course, than most of us) who, when in 1926 Britain had been smitten by the only general strike in its history, had refused the request, amounting almost to a demand, by the university authorities to volunteer to do 'essential' work, like bus and lorry driving, shifting coal etc. to help break the strike. It was this man who detailed to me the extraordinary achievements of Larkin in my own country before the 1914 war, his activities and persecution while in the United States, and his efforts to inspire socialist ideas in the labour movement here since his return.

Not long after, I joined the British Labour Party and very quickly made contact with the left-wing grouping around Aneurin Bevan, who formed the Socialist League.

It was when I had a temporary job in Manchester in 1934 that I read that Jim Larkin Junior, who was later to become the greatest friend I ever had, was going to speak locally about the Anglo-Irish crisis. I was deeply impressed, as all who heard either Jim Larkin speak invariably were, totally different though their styles were. I spoke to Young Jim after the meeting and immediately sensed the vast admiration that he had for his father. I asked him if he would introduce me to Big Jim next time I managed to get to Dublin, and he promised he would.

Next year, recently married, I found myself with three spare weeks on my hands and so went straight to Dublin. Within hours of arriving we were in touch with Young Jim, who met us at Amiens Street (Connolly)

Station and brought us straight to the head office of the Workers' Union of Ireland, and there we met Big Jim.

From that day I have been, and shall always remain, a Larkinite. I was astonished by the patience and courtesy with which this world-famous labour leader treated two obscure young people who had been introduced by his son into his office in the midst of its morning's business. He immediately asked detailed questions about my experiences at sea, the ports and countries I had visited, what in particular my impressions had been of Italy, which I knew well, Germany, where Hitler had only recently become ruler, and South America, of which he had a profound knowledge. He asked my wife about her experiences in the restaurant business in England (she had worked at Sheila's at Oxford, among other places). His ability to note at once (quicker than we did) the most significant details in the rambling narratives with which we answered his questions was, I soon realised, a characteristic of the man.

When we were beginning to think that we had intruded more than enough on the big man's time he said we should accompany him to Wellington Road (where he lived with his sister and brother-in-law, the Colgans) and get some lunch, and, if we would like, we could spend our three free weeks as his guests. It is probably true to say that of all the surprises received in my eighty-six years, that was the greatest, and certain that no holiday before or since was ever so fascinating.

Larkin lived very simply. By far the most striking feature of his way of life was the regularity with which, at 10 p.m. every night when he was not out at a meeting, he gathered an armful of books and took them up to bed, announcing that he would keep reading them till 3 a.m., by which time he would have got through most of them.

As the result of his wide reading, his many travels and his numerous and unusual adventures in the struggle to improve the conditions of ordinary people, the evening meal and the interval between it and 10 p.m. was in Wellington Road an educational treat, which has been one of the very greatest privileges of my life. From those discussions I gained a vision of what the socialist movement must irremovably stand for, which has never left me, as well as an understanding of the situation as it was in 1935 at home and in other parts of the world, which Jim had studied on the spot, through reading, or both, which I could never otherwise have got.

The socialist leader from the time of his pre-1914 activities to whose memory Jim Larkin introduced me was Jean Jaurès, the great French left-winger whose murder in July 1914 made the outbreak of the First World War unavoidable. Jim was sure, and many contemporaries of Jaurès and some historians of the time are inclined to agree, that, Jaurès being as popular with the German working class as with that of his own country, had he made the visit to Germany to speak on the gathering crisis that his death made impossible the combined refusal of the workers in the two main belligerent states to support their governments' military moves would have prevented the outbreak of war.

Two other matters that came up in discussion with Larkin in that memorable summer of 1935 left conceptions in my mind that, like an understanding of the importance of Jaurès, grew into convictions only with the experience of years. I would certainly not have reached those convictions as soon as I did, if at all, if the clarity, sincerity and confidence of Larkin's expression of them had not left a permanent impression upon me. These were the 1916 Rising and the Soviet Union.

I had told Larkin several times that I would like to hear what he had to say about 1916, and he had been non-committal. When we had only a couple of nights more to stay with him I asked him, as he went to bed one night with the load of books, if we could talk on the matter next day. He was already on the stairs, and he told me what he had to say from there, in little more, I am sure, than ten minutes.

The substance of what he said was that the 1916 Rising was not the rising he would have advocated, because the working-class movement was not, as such, involved and the numbers of workers who took part were not great. But it was the rising we had had, which had given us eventually the Ireland of 1935, with which we were now having to deal. He said, which of course was not original, that in essence we had changed one exploiting class for a new, exclusively native one.

When I mentioned the liberal passages in the Easter Proclamation, he compared them with the celebrated declaration of social aims (drawn up by Tom Johnson, but I was not then fully acquainted with the bitterness of the feud that had divided Larkin and Johnson since the twenties—not that that really affected the core of the argument). Larkin said that the liberal ideas in both the Proclamation and the Democratic Programme, whatever the intentions of their writers, had in practice proved to be illusions, which neither the Sinn Féin movement that developed after 1916 nor the same, more consolidated movement in the first Dáil had any wish to make real, though they were useful for recruiting popular support. Only the presence in the Rising and in the first Dáil of an active and well-organised Labour representation could have given reality to what he dismissed as pious hopes.

I vividly recalled these words of Larkin when, on RTE, on the fiftieth anniversary of the opening of the first Dáil, one of its better-known participants, Ernest Blythe, in answer to a question said categorically that the Democratic Programme was never meant to be taken seriously.

On that and other occasions I mentioned Connolly to Larkin, but he never expressed an opinion on him, favourable or unfavourable. My impression, for what it is worth, is that he had a high opinion of Connolly as a trade union organiser but felt that his political activities, after his initial cry when the 1914 War began, that the Irish worker served 'neither King nor Kaiser but Ireland,' were in practice deviations from the spirit of that famous slogan. The orthodox socialist and more particularly the Leninist version of Connolly's activities in 1915 and 1916 was, and for well over half a century remained, that Connolly was 100 per cent correct.

About the Soviet Union, Larkin was more forthcoming. He had of course been lionised there and had become for a time one of the listed leaders of world communism. It is not easy for people in the last decade of the twentieth century to realise what a mighty inspiration the Russian Revolution became for progressive-minded people throughout the world, not least in Ireland, where the labour and trade union movement openly welcomed it and Irish workers had no hesitation in creating local 'soviets' in opposition not only to British imperial rule but to a number of the activities initiated by Sinn Féin and the newly formed IRA.

Larkin retained his admiration for the Russian Revolution to the end of his days. When in the nineteen-forties meetings of the Central Branch of the Labour Party in Dublin drew to a close and the members set about discussing the news from the war zones, so far as Mr de Valera's rigid press censorship let us know it, Larkin listened, contributed to the often passionate discussion about the peril of fascism conquering the world (and the Central Branch, with his support, was for many months involved in a long series of public meetings in and off O'Connell Street in denunciation of the briefly flourishing Irish Hitlerite organisation, Ailtirí na hAiséirí), but often reminded us that it was the extraordinary defence that the Soviet people were putting up against the greatest military machine in history that was making and would make it impossible for fascism to triumph.

But Larkin, though in the popular sense of the word by far the greatest idealist I ever met, and probably as great an idealist as any human who ever lived, was also a realist. So far back as 1935 in Wellington Road, Larkin warned me, in his words, which I heard painfully but could never forget, that the Soviet leaders 'were losing their idealism.' He spoke not only of autocratic behaviour by Russian communist officials, but more practically, typically Larkin, and evidently particularly to impress me, he detailed faults that he had noticed in Soviet ships: rust, skimped paint, unpolished brass—numerous evidences of working people not striving for excellence, and not being taught by their leaders to strive for excellence. I have read a lot about Larkin but I do not remember anyone writing about him emphasising the passion for excellence in that most essential of human activities, work, which was such a characteristic of this man.

During that summer of 1935 Larkin revealed to us many parts of that Dublin with which he was so intimately acquainted, including the area around Fishamble Street, with its echoes of the capital in days of Swift and Sheridan.

In that very Fishamble Street, where we think it was he who first told us of Handel's famous visit, the Workers' Union of Ireland then had a meeting-hall. There he brought us to a long mass meeting of union members. He got a most attentive listening, not only when he assured his members that they never need doubt that he would stand with them against any injustice, and for every improvement that they and he in consultation believed they might get, but he castigated some for doing skimpy work, as he had been castigating some Russian seamen to me, in their absence, a couple of nights before. With his wonderful voice he assured his hearers he would never stand by them if they deliberately worked at standards lower than their best. He reminded them that the labour movement was created to make it possible for workers to live in a comfortable and agreeable world. They would make that world; nobody else would make it for them. They should strive ever to improve their best, and the time would surely come when, by right, the full value of their best work would automatically come back to them. This was one of the most impressive and unexpected of the hundreds of speeches it has been my lot to hear.

In 1935, when the great economic slump was still on, there was much unemployment in Dublin, and Larkin brought us to visit the co-operative tool factory that the union had established for unemployed members. It was a cheerful and certainly very busy place, the details of which I no longer remember, nor do I know how long it lasted. However, the visit gave Larkin the chance to talk to us at some length about the kind of 'co-operative commonwealth' (the common term for the sort of society Larkin's type of socialist visualised for the future) that he wanted to see develop in Ireland. I do not believe that when he fought elections and took part in party politics Larkin felt really at home. He had little faith in parliaments and in most of those who enjoyed parliamentary politics, as I understood him. He had infinite faith in ordinary people doing their own thing together and, by their innate ingenuity, in which he trusted, ultimately by-passing capitalist business and creating their own co-operative enterprises. Looking back, I suppose he was by nature an anarcho-syndicalist. I am sure he had not worked out in any great detail how society would transform itself from dependence on greed-driven private enterprise to universal co-operationism, but certainly in 1935, and so far as I could judge for the rest of his life, he believed that transformation had to come, and he seemed to see state enterprises, though preferable to capitalist-owned ones, as only transitional, on the way to becoming great co-operative societies.

The next time I was in direct contact with Larkin was in the summer of 1938, when the Irish Trades Union Congress had its annual conference at Bangor. I had got a job as organiser for Ireland and north-west England, through H. J. Timperley, the *Manchester Guardian's* China correspondent, of relief for China, which was being invaded and occupied by Hitler's ally, imperial Japan. I had a long family connection with and personal interest in China, and I had undertaken to report on the Congress meeting (where I hoped to make contacts who would help organise meetings against Japanese aggression) for the British Socialist League's weekly paper.

Larkin was very much interested in the Chinese situation and had read the dramatic despatches of the North American journalist Edgar Snow, who was the first person to alert the general public in his own country and Europe to the emergence of the Chinese Red Army under Mao Zedong as the real anti-fascist force in China.

Larkin's chief contribution to the deliberations of the Congress was a typically dramatic Larkinite episode. When it came his turn to speak he whipped the tablecloth off the speakers' table and held it up for all to regard, pointing a finger at a tab that announced that the linen cloth had been manufactured abroad. (It was Croatian.) This gave Larkin a chance to make a short but moving and quite devastating speech on the run-down condition of the Ulster linen industry, the part played by the greed of the mill-owners in weakening their own industry, and the iniquity of the trade union leadership in not ensuring that all linen in use in Bangor throughout the conference was of local origin. This was a typically practical Larkinite way of emphasising the need for solidarity between the workers of the two parts of Ireland, worth a score of abstract speeches on the morality of solidarity or the politics of national unity.

I was living in County Donegal very near the border when the 1939 war began, having received a suggestion from a London publisher I knew that a book on partition and the border might be a success in England. When the war stopped being 'phoney' in the spring of 1940, the publisher decided a book on partitioned Ireland would be no help to Britain's war effort. I had to find another way of earning a living and after a number of adventures got a job teaching in Dublin.

I had been contributing to various Dublin socialist papers: *Labour News*, the *Torch*, the *Irish Workers' Weekly*. As soon as I got to Dublin I sought out Young Jim Larkin and told him that, with the world in crisis and Ireland in the grip of serious shortages and an authoritarian veto on any rise in wage or salary, I felt I should get into labour politics.

There had been a reshuffle on the left in Dublin's politics. Young Jim had dropped his membership of the Communist Party, and he and his father, aware of the rising discontent of many workers, had applied to join the Labour Party, with which Larkin had had a feud—much described and from a multitude of different angles—since soon after he returned from the United States. About the same time the Communist Party had (south of the border) wound itself up, and most of its ex-members joined the Labour Party; so also in Dublin did a number of active trade unionists who had hitherto distrusted the Labour Party but felt, now that the country's condition was so critical, that a poor tool was better than none to help right it with. This group of diverse leftists proceeded to form the Labour Party's Central Branch, not attached to any special area but meeting and operating essentially in the city centre. Young Jim suggested I join this Central Branch, which I did early in 1942 and quickly became very active.

Larkin attended more or less all the Central Branch's very regular and well-run meetings. The branch chairman was Ned Tucker of the Brushmakers' Union, a man of vast wisdom and experience and very real charm. He was a Larkinite socialist, quiet, determined and infinitely patient. Harry Ryan, an engineer, much younger, very fiery but, like Ned, meticulously efficient, was the branch secretary.

The branch's activities were more or less infinite. I have mentioned the long campaign of meetings against the local fascists. We had to give what lead we could against black-marketeers, for fairness in the rationing system, for a campaign against an appalling scourge that hit wartime Dublin, tuberculosis. All these matters came up for discussion at branch meetings, and Larkin's advice was always sought. Whether or not he was dictatorial in his younger days, as a member of the Central Branch he was anything but, rarely speaking until asked to, and then briefly and incisively. His very great knowledge of Dublin municipal affairs—he was long a city councillor—was invaluable.

Larkin was also remarkably quick to spot a fake socialist, and it was a treat to listen to him demolish their pretensions. I remember three: one who turned out to be a plant in the branch from the notorious right-wing weekly of the period, the *Catholic Standard*; another who was a very fashionable psychologist in Blackrock and Rathmines, whose arguments, elegantly though arrogantly expressed, flew to pieces under Larkin's scornful counter-attacks, so marshalled that I began to suspect that Hegel had been among the authors he read at night. Then there was a particularly odious doctor, a self-proclaimed lady-killer and one-time Fianna Fáil TD.

What made the uninspiring Norton, then Labour Party leader, accept this character into the Labour Party I do not know, but one of my vivid memories is of a large public meeting in O'Connell Street, presided over by Norton and addressed by the Labour candidates for the 1943 general election. Larkin was one, as will be related. So was the doctor. Larkin deliberately took his place on the platform beside the doctor and as ostentatiously as possible—he was a very big man, with unforgettably striking features—turned his back on his neighbour, and so kept it throughout the proceedings. With all the other candidates looking dutifully frontwards and only Larkin out of order, and manifestly so, the message to the voters of Dublin was unmistakable.

Young Jim and I were the delegates sent by the Central Branch to join two from each Dublin branch to form the Dublin Executive of the party, which had considerable freedom of action and its own weekly paper, the *Torch*. The only time I saw Larkin really angry at the Central Branch was over some obstinate personal difference of opinion between two members. Larkin pointed out that Labour Party members called each other 'comrade'. Larkin gave the miscreants a lecture on the meaning of the word, ending by reminding us all that if we really believed in the creation of a newer and better society of comrades, we must realise that our movement of today was a microcosm of the new, comradely society we would make, and so we should in our movement act like comrades as well as addressing each other as such. This was an ideal that Jaurès also held.

Needless to say, Larkin and Jaurès, like lesser mortals, sometimes fell short of their ideal, but I can never forget that during 1942–1944 not only the Central Branch but the Dublin Labour branches generally, though containing Connollyites, Trotskyites, Stalinists, and all kinds of social democrats, did co-operate in a comradely way, and consciously so. I think that the constant sense of national and international crisis around us induced a strong sense of the need to pull together. But it is also true that in those short years Larkin, who had once been considered the very symbol of division in the labour movement, was now genuinely revered, not only by the old Larkinites like Tucker and Barney Conway but more especially by the young activists like Harry Ryan who came in large numbers into the wartime Dublin Labour Party.

When Young Jim and I came onto the Dublin Executive I think there were ten Dublin branches, perhaps twelve. Young Jim became chairman of the Executive and I its secretary. The whole team worked extremely hard, and by half way through 1943 there were twenty-six Labour Party branches in Dublin, each meeting at least once a month, and at the regular public meeting of each branch either Young Jim or I attended, to bring to the members for discussion the proposals of the Executive. We advised each branch to produce its own duplicated local monthly paper. Several did this, selling it from house to house along with the *Torch*. I remember particularly how active the branch at Whitehall was.

Very much of this activity was inspired by the presence of Larkin, now widely revered in the Labour Party, and by news of his continuous activities for the people's good on the now Labour-dominated Dublin Corporation. Among proposals fought for was the idea of the corporation making it possible for the city's national schools to have a glass of milk and a slice of bread for each pupil. (The Archbishop of Dublin objected that this was a threat to the solidarity of families through joint meals.) Later the future of Dublin transport came up for discussion. Larkin and his supporters wanted a municipal transport service to replace the bankrupt tramway company, but, despite many meetings and conferences, the CIE concern was set up by the Fianna Fáil Government.

All in all, Larkin's prestige grew and grew throughout the city from 1941 right through 1942 and into 1943, and veterans of 1913 began to recall the all-permeating influence of Larkin back in those days. An important consequence was that a strong movement developed for proposing both Larkins as candidates for the general election due in 1943.

It was at the selection conference for candidates for the 1943 election that I realised the depth of the hatred of Larkin that had grown up in the leadership of the then very dictatorially led Irish Transport and General Workers' Union (the presentation by which of £100,000, a huge sum then, to the Government to help in the 'Emergency' had particularly irked Larkin). Larkin's name was proposed all right as a candidate, but William O'Brien, his bitterest critic, general secretary of the ITGWU, the largest union, made a vicious attack on Larkin, who reminded the conference, but in vain, that it was he who had moved the motion originally founding the Labour Party. O'Brien related with relish how he had driven Larkin from the ITGWU, and amidst uproar a vote was called. Larkin's nomination was defeated, largely by the virtually solid vote of the ITGWU delegates.

As soon as the selection conference was over, the Dublin Executive met, and Young Jim told me as the meeting began that a group of Larkinites had come straight to him and his father proposing that, if they would agree, they would seek that the emergency meeting they were calling of the Executive would have a motion before it for the Executive itself to put up Jim Larkin as its own candidate (which of course was in contradiction to the Labour Party constitution). That the Dublin Executive had no right to put up a candidate of its own was eloquently argued by Cathal O'Shannon, but all of us Larkinites were in no mood to listen, and Big Jim's candidature as Dublin Labour candidate for Dublin North-East was approved overwhelmingly.

All the hard work done by the Central Branch, the Dublin Executive and the twenty-five other branches now paid off. The 1943 general election in Dublin was in general something of a festival; in Jim's constituency it was a regular carnival. The opening meeting at the Five Lamps, at which I was asked to preside, is one of the most unforgettable events in a life fairly studded with events. There was a vast crowd assembled before I opened the proceedings by simply introducing the candidate, who got loud and long applause.

When Larkin at last got silence, he made a truly remarkable oration in the style, I am sure, of his great orations in the period leading up to 1913, his rich, cavernous voice reaching easily to every corner of the multitude, his vocabulary simple but voluminous, his imagination deliberately let loose to kindle his hearers' curiosity, and behind it all, and ready to be brought out as the ultimate weapon, his huge range of totally relevant facts, leading up to the final call for the crowd's support in the struggle he was entering upon to alter the shameful facts he had recounted.

Jim's opening sentences were the most bizarre I ever heard at a political meeting. He started by pointing at a nearby building, where a friend of his called Murphy had lived. He and Murphy, he said, had been firemen in a ship bound to the West Indies—'it was the year of the Martinique earthquake—now you know how old I am.' The other firemen were Germans and not very efficient. As they approached the West Indies they were struck by a hurricane, and the ship was lost with all hands save himself. He walked a long way along a barren shore till he saw a large building. Here the Governor of the island lived, who was Irish and lived when home in a big house, the upper part of which he could see from the platform on which he was speaking.

How much of this had any relation to truth I have never been able to discover, but the vividness of its telling—he was always mind-gripping speaking on the sea and ships—got the whole audience palpably straining to hear the next slice of the drama.

The Larkins ran through that election like a whirlwind and pulled in a third (already sitting) Labour candidate, Martin O'Sullivan, wiping out the shame of Ireland's capital having one Labour deputy only in the national parliament.

The two Larkins raised points in the Dáil that would otherwise not have been raised, and Young Jim began to create for himself the reputation for clear thinking and decisive action that would enable him in the next twenty-five years to create a far better-organised and better-informed trade union movement. But the forces that had received such a set-back with Big Jim's election in 1943 were determined to hit back. And (in my opinion, as one who was myself in too much of a hurry) some of the younger Larkinites gave O'Brien and his henchmen too much valuable ammunition in the campaign they immediately opened to reverse the situation in the Labour Party, which they succeeded in splitting, and also the Irish Trades Union Congress.

Some of us were expelled from the party, primarily for having induced the Dublin Executive (which, along with the Central Branch, was dissolved) to break the rules and field its own candidate. We were denounced as dangerous reds. The former Dublin communists thought it not worth while to challenge their expulsion; I did, and I was at the door of the Labour Party annual conference hall, where I had made my defence (brilliantly elaborated by Young Jim), when Sam Kyle of the Amalgamated Transport and General Workers' Union slipped out to tell me my expulsion had been annulled by the conference, with only a dozen supporting it. But it was four years before I was officially notified that I was not expelled and could sign up again as a party member. By that time Big Jim was dead.

The other outstanding though much lesser Labour leader of Larkin's epoch in Ireland was Tom Johnson, who survived him. The two, as noted, had been involved in a bitter feud. During the years while I was waiting for the Labour Party head office to obey its own annual conference and restore me my party membership, I was editor of a left-wing monthly, *Review*, which ran lectures on various topics of interest to the left, chiefly at Four Provinces House in Harcourt Street, which one of the staunchest and ablest Larkinites, John Swift, general secretary of the Bakers' Union, had inaugurated, with a lecture-hall, a splendid library, and a reading-room, all of which was to be destroyed, to Dublin's eternal shame, by anti-'red' fanatics bred by the Cold War. Johnson was often at the Four Provinces: he came to many of the lectures, Big Jim more rarely. It happened that they once were both there together when I was, and I had the pleasure of getting them to indulge in a short and friendly conversation together.

In 1957 I went for a long walk with Young Jim over Bray Head, discussing with him the possibility of his standing for the leadership of the Labour Party. The climax of the conversation was when we were each on opposite sides of a stile. Jim said categorically: 'There will only ever be one Jim Larkin, my father.' He had gone right over his father's career, had analysed his relations with O'Brien and with Johnson, and with Norton, with some of the Russian and Continental communist leaders, with socialists in North America. He did not pretend his father was always right, but he had a total and unshakable conviction of his father's honesty and sincerity; and he, who was so pragmatic and so down to earth, though in a way as much of a visionary as Big Jim, clearly saw in him something almost superhuman. It was in a way uncanny, but Big Jim was himself uncanny.

Larkin was an idealist; but he was not a utopian. He thought a co-operative commonwealth was a noble aim proper for human beings to aspire to, but he knew it could not be perfect, if infinitely perfectible. Like a famous contemporary of his, Terence MacSwiney, he felt, 'B'fhéidir go sroichfimid barr na sléibhte ar lorg na réaltaí.'

Breda Cardiff

I went to work as a shorthand-typist in the Workers' Union of Ireland in July 1944, at a wage of three pounds per week (in those days 2s 6d secured a four-course lunch in Arnott's!).

The union offices were in Thomas Ashe Hall, which consisted of the top floor, ballroom, and ground floor. The top floor contained two rooms, one large and one small. Big Jim Larkin and Jim Junior, as they were known, occupied the smaller office. In the large room Seán Dunne had a desk, and the delegates, as they were called then—Jack Connolly, Jack Byrne, Paddy Donegan, and Tony Brack—came in and out at various times during the day and sat at the big table making out their reports. Seán Nugent was a branch secretary and Billy Eustace his assistant. The cash office, on the ground floor, was staffed by Paddy Dwyer and Charlie McEvoy, who worked under the direction of Ralph James. John Brady was the union's cashier, and Mick McKeown acted as driver. Joe Smith was the caretaker. Three weeks after I joined the staff, Margaret McLoughlin swelled our ranks.

At that time Big Jim was a councillor in Dublin Corporation and Jim Junior a member of Dáil Éireann. Big Jim was in his seventies, and his greatest achievements were behind him. He was now mainly concerned with housing cases, and Margaret and myself spent many hours interviewing people and typing out their statements. I remember on one occasion there was an outbreak of food poisoning on the Belfast train, and Big Jim took up the compensation claims of those involved.

Dozens of people called into the office to make statements, and from time to time Big Jim would come out of his office and say to those calling in: 'Just give the girls the facts, not your life history!' Any time he felt a housing case required the attention of the husband, he would say to the women: 'Send down your husband to see me. Why isn't he dealing with this?'

He personally saw everyone who called into the office and enquired for him, and he always interviewed them in order of their appearance, rather than their standing in society. To him each person had an equal dignity. He had a great respect for women and felt they should be protected.

Sometimes he would call me into the office and say he wanted to send a letter off to a friend in America. One letter, I remember, ran to over twenty pages of shorthand. As I struggled to type it back he would come out and say, 'Have you finished it yet?' In order to reach the end I skipped whole pages at a time. When I eventually brought it in he said, 'Did I say all this?' He evidently did not miss the pieces I left out. He had a habit of dropping his 'h's, and, being young and ignorant, I often spent ages looking up non-existent words in the dictionary. Two that come to mind are 'hiatus' and 'homologate', which he pronounced 'iatus' and 'omologate.'

He was always very kind to us and never took us to task, and despite his commanding size we were never in awe of him. We were a happy and contented staff.

In the summer of 1945 the union served a claim for a fortnight's holidays for workers. The beef and pork butchers' sections of the union were on strike for three months to secure this concession. The strike pay involved emptied the reserves of the union, and we had to start up again from scratch financially.

Joe Deasy

Jim Larkin was first elected to the Dublin Corporation in 1912. Because of a court conviction he was debarred from taking his seat and was disqualified from membership of the City Council for a term of seven years. Other Labour councillors during those years included Richard O'Carroll, who became leader of the Labour group after Larkin's disqualification and who was fatally shot during the 1916 Rising, and William Partridge, who fought with the Irish Citizen Army in the Rising.

It was eighteen years before Larkin again stood for a Dublin City Council election. In 1924 the council was abolished and replaced with Commissioners. It was reconstituted in 1930, and Larkin contested the resulting election. He was elected on behalf of the Irish Worker League. He was then fifty-six years old. His son Jim Larkin Junior was also elected, but he stood on behalf of the Revolutionary Workers' Group. There were then clearly some differences between father and son. Their council tenure lasted until 1933.

James Larkin Senior again successfully contested the Dublin City Council election in 1936 and was re-elected in 1942 and 1945. He remained a city councillor until his death in 1947.

During Larkin's membership of the City Council in the thirties, official Labour Party representation was almost non-existent. For many years the sole Labour Party councillor was Martin O'Sullivan of the Railway Clerks' Association, who was first elected in 1930. There was a chasm between their philosophical and political beliefs. Martin O'Sullivan was a Labour person of an extremely conservative hue. He was very close to Catholic Church thinking on most issues. A high-ranking railway official, he was capable, articulate, and personable, with a distinct middle-class bearing. In the nineteen-fifties he was elected a Labour TD and an alderman and became the first Labour Lord Mayor of Dublin. Larkin's strong socialist beliefs and militant background placed him at a very different point of the labour spectrum. Although fellow-councillors for years, there was undoubtedly little dialogue between them.

Larkin was, therefore, for many years one of only two Labour representatives on the City Council. He was certainly the lone radical leftist voice. Even in the excellent biography by Prof. Emmet Larkin his outstanding role in that capacity does not receive adequate recognition. No longer the towering figure he once was, his Corporation contribution was, however, powerful.

His membership of the City Council was clearly the central aspect of Larkin's political role during the last ten years of his life. His special interest was the Dublin housing crisis, which, despite some significant progress during the thirties, was still a revolting scandal. In 1939 a special Dublin Housing Inquiry was established by order of the Minister for Local Government and Public Health. The inquiry sat from April 1939 to February 1940. Its report filled a volume of huge proportions. Larkin claimed in his submission that 'this inquiry was set up because of some ten years of agitation by me within the Housing Committee and the Council itself.'

He addressed the inquiry on two occasions, in two different capacities. On the first occasion he spoke as a member of the building trade group attached to Dublin Trades Council. Later he addressed it as a member of the City Council.

Dublin housing statistics revealed at this inquiry were horrendous and were comparable, despite some progress, to pre-1914 conditions. The central slum problem was almost unchanged. The City Manager, Dr P. J. Hernon, stated that 18,049 families were living in dwellings (including tenements, basements and cottages) that were unfit for human habitation. A further 4,223 families were living in overcrowded dwellings that were otherwise habitable. These were the years when the dreaded tuberculosis was rampant, especially in the slums and working-class households. Some authorities regarded Dr Hernon's figures as conservative. There were 33,000 families living in tenements. Such was the context in which Larkin made Dublin housing a central issue of his public life in his later years.

His extensive evidence and cross-examination at the inquiry absorbed substantial space in the resulting report. As a spokesperson for the building group, he directed much attention to a direct labour scheme that was organised as a result of the great building stoppage of 1937. He said it had its birth in the needs of the people arising out of the prolonged building stoppage. After some weeks we convinced the Housing Committee that we should proceed to build houses ourselves.

The scheme, he said, had to be organised from the 'bottom up', as a direct labour organisation that once existed had been abolished. They were obstructed by building contractors, who, he alleged, tried to stop them obtaining materials. A housing scheme, however, was completed.

He had harsh words for some of the workers. When the strike was over the men gave an undertaking to finish the job. Immediately the strike was over, 35 per cent of our men, mostly skilled men of the most active units, went back to their old employers, although they had taken advantage of the direct labour scheme in a time of stress. Whether this criticism was just or not, I cannot say. It is an example, however, of Larkin's readiness to criticise working people when he deemed it justified. Other examples could be cited. It could help to explain why his success as a politician was so erratic. He never shirked the task of criticising his own class.

In his testimony as a councillor he frequently became involved in acrimonious exchanges with the chairman of the Housing Inquiry and some of the Corporation officials. The latter often contested the accuracy of his statements, and, it seems, with some justification. Yet his familiarity with all facets of the building industry was impressive.

He tackled questions of finance, differential rents, direct labour, administration, and housing allocations. On this issue he seemed to make an impact, and he kept harping on the alleged removal of a certain allocation officer to support his suggestions of irregularities. On occasion in Larkin's career, apparently reckless statements eventually proved to have some basis in fact. He did suspect some irregularities in housing allocations, and there were grounds for the suspicion.

In 1941 he and James Larkin Junior joined the Labour Party. In 1942 there was a municipal election, which resulted in thirteen Labour Party candidates being elected, including Larkin himself. This was a historic Labour breakthrough and made possible the election of Larkin to the chairmanship of the Housing Committee. He was to remain chairman until his death in 1947. The result also made possible the election in 1943 of Martin O'Sullivan as Lord Mayor.

On Larkin's death, Helen Chenevix, a pioneer official of the Irish Women Workers' Union and one of the Labour councillors elected in 1942, put on the record her admiration for his role on the Corporation and his chairmanship of the Housing Committee. She outlined four measures that he strongly advocated: the employment of direct labour; housing for newly-weds; removal of the Cattle Market and abbatoir to the East Wall; and the development of St Anne's Estate, Clontarf. He also supported the introduction of differential rents.

The present writer was elected a Labour councillor in 1945 and must share her admiration of Larkin's work. To be present at a Housing Committee with Larkin as chairman was quite an experience.

It was a committee of the entire forty-five Council members. He sat at the head of a very long table, flanked by the City Manager and various officials. True to character, he never allowed his chairmanship to inhibit his participation in debate. Yet he presided with courtesy, impartiality, and style. He had a thorough grasp of the issues on the agenda, while his great voice and imposing physique commanded attention. His countenance was striking, and to my eyes there was a certain nobility in its features.

Perhaps not the Larkin of all seasons, but to someone in his early twenties a very real impression!

From the chair he occasionally erupted. We were once discussing some evictions by a private landlord when one councillor rashly tried to extenuate the latter's action by alleging bad treatment of the premises by the tenant's children. Larkin blasted the speaker with a roar: 'Councillor, all God's children haven't got wings!' Another example of his style surfaced when an evicted farm worker with a large family succeeded in attaining an interview with some members of the committee. He was seeking accommodation. There was a lull in the exchanges while the officials made some enquiries to assist our judgment. It was the time when Larkin's union was organising farm workers. Suddenly, but calmly, he asked the man: 'Are you a member of the union?' 'No, sir,' was the reply. Larkin then said sharply but with civility: 'How do you expect others to help you if you don't help yourself?'

Larkin was especially committed to solving the housing crisis, particularly slum clearance. On behalf of a housing study group within the Labour Party I interviewed him in his spartan union office in Thomas Ashe Hall. He was friendly, informative, and, I also realised, a little expansive. I also learned a little more of his character. In the course of his remarks he mentioned Thomas Johnson, with whom in the past he had a hostile relationship (and not to Larkin's credit). He was now full of praise for Johnson, of whom he said that he 'had worked and studied all his life at housing problems.'

As I was leaving, he was speaking to a young artist to whom he was allowing the use of the hall to exhibit his work. He had always demanded the right of workers to have access to a higher quality of life: books, paintings, music, the theatre. Here he was actively promoting his ideal.

There was often humour in his council speeches. He once invited the City Manager to a guided tour of the slums: 'Dr Hernon, you can have your dinner or your tea with the mice, the rats, and the cockroaches.' Dr Hernon managed an embarrassed smile.

He made many memorable contributions to council debates. Before my time he had made an eloquent plea for the release of Frank Ryan from a Spanish jail.

Despite his great qualities there was a contra side to Jim Larkin. He was often described as dictatorial and reckless with facts. He could be generous in his remarks about people but could often be very abusive and vitriolic. The Labour group of eleven, which was elected in 1945 to the City Council and which included Larkin and myself, again experienced both sides of his character. I personally had one unpleasant experience. He abruptly left a group meeting in protest at some comment I had made. I still do not know how I offended him. Perhaps it was my sheer inexperience. Yet later at a public council meeting he made favourable reference to me in very complimentary, even flattering, terms. Later still I learned how supportive he could be to a Labour Party comrade. Such was the great Larkin enigma.

Our most painful memory was the mayoral election of 1945. The group decided to propose Larkin for Lord Mayor. It was known that he so aspired to crown his days by this distinction. The composition of the

Council required assistance from another party if his nomination was to succeed. The politics of the time ruled out Fianna Fáil; the votes of Fine Gael would be needed to achieve Larkin's election. Then came the setback. Fine Gael would be prepared to support a Labour Party nominee, but not Jim Larkin. We resolved to persist with the nomination. John Breen, our group leader, duly nominated Larkin, and Helen Chenevix seconded. Fianna Fáil nominated Cormac Breathnach TD and Fine Gael Peadar Doyle TD, who, like myself, was from Inchicore.

Then Jim, without any prior warning, dropped his bombshell. He withdrew his nomination and launched into an attack on Fine Gael. Raising his great voice to its stentorian heights, he denounced Richard Mulcahy, the Fine Gael national leader, who had sent word from Leinster House to his Dublin councillors that on no account should they support Jim Larkin. Jim concluded by urging the Labour group to abstain.

He then withdrew from the council chamber and was accompanied by three Labour councillors, who were also nominees of the Workers' Union of Ireland: Barney Conway, John Smithers (president of the WUI), and Thomas Doyle. They then took their seats in the visitors' gallery.

The Labour group had decided that if our nominee was eliminated we would support the Fine Gael nominee in preference to that of Fianna Fáil. This was done with much heart-searching and can only be understood in the context of the politics of the period. The outcome was the election of the Fine Gael candidate, Peadar Doyle TD, as Lord Mayor.

On the announcement of the result, a voice from the gallery shouted, 'Shame on Labour.' Then Larkin was heard to say: 'Not shame on Labour but those we have got in the Labour Party.'

Our group had supported Doyle, without any joy. The motive was to defeat Fianna Fáil, who were then perceived by many as the arch-enemy. Our tactics may have been wrong, but Larkin's reaction was indefensible. It revealed the anarchic side of his character, which impaired his ability to work closely with colleagues when contentious decisions were inescapable. It was the second successive year in which Jim was abusive towards his Labour colleagues. In 1944 he had also been troublesome—though with some justification—during the mayoral election.

The year 1946 was to be Larkin's last full year on the Corporation. It was the year of a national teachers' strike, which lasted from March until October. I listened to Larkin expounding on the issue both at Dublin Trades Council and on the Corporation. He was on both occasions extremely constructive and a model of restraint.

His contribution to the City Council debate was interrupted from the Fianna Fáil benches. Councillor Comyn SC shouted: 'We want no solutions from Moscow, Mr Larkin.' Larkin paused and then retorted: 'Well, they have done some mad things in Moscow, but this affair takes some beating.'

In March 1946 he proposed at the City Council that the honorary freedom of the city of Dublin be conferred on George Bernard Shaw, who was a Dubliner and a socialist. Larkin, like James Connolly, was a self-educated working-class intellectual. This was often very evident, and his proposal speech exemplified it. He began humorously: 'We have some beauties as honourable freemen of the city. This proposal is among the serious.' His speech included a reason for Shaw's refusal of the Nobel Prize in 1925 that does not appear in his biographies. Larkin alleged that Shaw refused to accept the money because of Nobel's invention of dynamite. Shaw hated war, and the reason is credible; either it was Larkin's wishful thinking or he knew something Shaw's biographers did not.

With only three against, the proposal was carried, and Shaw accepted the invitation with a typical Shavian reply: 'I have hitherto evaded credentials from foreign sources. Dublin alone has a right to affirm that in spite of my incessantly controversial past and present I have not disgraced her.' To Larkin he wrote: 'My dear Jim, Nothing could have pleased me more in the Freedom Honour that is being initiated by you nor made it surer of acceptance. You have been a leader and a martyr while I have never had a day's discomfort.'

One of the three dissidents was Alderman Bernard Butler, who was a teacher by profession. He lamented the influence of Shaw at the expense of teachers like St Thomas Aquinas. Larkin replied very kindly to Butler, remarking that he had endured as much grief in his life as Larkin himself.

After the meeting I walked down Dame Street with himself and Barney Conway. Jim was pleased with the outcome. On Butler he remarked: 'A very decent man, but he would burn you at the stake for the good of your soul.'

My last recollection of Jim Larkin is a very personal and special one. I had initiated a special inspection of Crooksling TB Sanatorium, which was the main sanatorium in Dublin and run by the Corporation. I wrote the resulting report, which was signed by the other inspecting members, including Alderman Alfie Byrne TD, nine times Lord Mayor of Dublin. A special meeting of the Health Committee (a committee of the full council) was convened, which was attended by Dr Walsh, the Medical Superintendent at Crooksling. Larkin sat at the end of the long table. I remember vividly his reaction to the report. 'Dr Walsh,' he thundered, 'is this report true? Are conditions this awful?'

The report was not challenged, and improvements were promised, some of which were implemented.

It was then late 1946, and I had the impression at the meeting that Jim was unwell. But the incident showed his determination to the end to respond with great anger to any ill-treatment of working people. I was grateful for his powerful presence. He never hesitated to be supportive of a comrade when such was sorely needed.

As the poet Austin Clarke wrote,

His name endures on our holiest page,
Scrawled in a rage by Dublin's poor.

As I conclude, I realise that I am his last remaining fellow Labour councillor. Personally, I am grateful and intensely proud that he so closely passed my way.

Chapter 57

On Larkin: A Miscellany

Principles and persons
In his first editorial in the *Irish Worker* (27 May 1911), Larkin set out the paper's platform and principles: freedom to govern this land called Ireland by Irish people in the interests of all the Irish people; a determination to accomplish not only national freedom but a greater thing—individual freedom; and freedom from the degradation of economic or wage slavery. He warned:

> And forget not, workers, that principles are better than persons. It was persons who sold the Nation in the past! Put your trust in no man, you will therefore never be confounded. Stand by your principles. Let them be fixed as the sun.

Two weeks later Larkin was writing:

> I, personally, a man who has more enemies than any other man in this country—a man who totally disagrees with the present system, and lives for the day when there will be no employee nor employer, when we will all be workers, working together like brothers believing in the brotherhood of man, and fulfilling the fatherhood of God.

In the same issue Larkin quoted the verse used by David Campbell from Belfast to conclude his presidential address to that year's conference of the Irish Trades Union Congress:

> Come ye that listen, rise and gird your swords,
> Win back the fields of Ireland for the poor.
> Give roses to your children's fading cheeks
> And to the hearts of women hope again,
> Bring back content unto the lives of men.

Larkin in Belfast
[In Belfast] a new power appeared in the person of Jim Larkin, the most dynamic personality that ever swept over the Irish labour stage in modern history. In a very short time by his personality and his eloquence he had fired the minds and imagination of his followers. For the first time in modern Belfast history the contending parties were not orange and green, nor Catholics against Protestants, but the combined forces of labour, against the hard-boiled and unyielding Belfast employers. It was an incredible position to witness in our city.

The strike failed or seemed to have failed, but actually it did not ...
Larkin was a highly controversial figure in Irish Labour and indeed in Irish

life generally. Many of his colleagues would protest that, while as an orator who could inspire the masses he had no equal, he was extremely difficult if not altogether impossible to work with as a member of a team.

This, I think, is probably a reasonable enough estimate. I met him many years later but let me say now that if he was impatient of routine and discipline and tended to dominate the leadership, surely these were the defects of his great qualities. To me he had the burning urge to improve the lot of the under-privileged and faced opposition of every type to get them to assert their manhood and their rights.

Let it not be argued that Larkin failed in either Dublin or Belfast. The strikes may have 'petered out' but they were not failures. Incidentally, it was ironical that Jim Larkin's career in Belfast was practically ended by the cry that he was a papist, while later he was denounced in Dublin for the very opposite reason.

From *The Memoirs of Senator Joseph Connolly* (edited by J. Anthony Gaughan, 1996).

Joseph Connolly (1885–1961) was born in Belfast. A leader of the Irish Volunteers in that city in 1914–16, he was imprisoned after the Easter Rising. A member of Seanad Éireann from 1929 to 1936, he was a minister in the first Fianna Fáil government, from 1932 to 1936.

Forth the banners go

The reminiscences of William O'Brien, as told to Dr Edward MacLysaght, in *Forth the Banners Go* (1969) contain the following passage:

> Larkin came to Dublin in July 1907 and addressed a meeting in Beresford Place. I was favourably impressed. It struck me he was the kind of man to rouse up the workers in a way that had not been done before … I attached myself to Larkin.

One hundred per cent organised

Intelligence notes in the Chief Secretary's Office in Dublin Castle refer to Larkin's work in Belfast:

> Larkin set to work with great energy to organise all branches of Dock and Quay Labourers as well as Carters in Belfast, with the result that in three months' time 2,978 Dock Labourers out of 3,100 employed had joined. All the Carters, numbering 1,500 also joined.

Clearing the public house

Tommy Healy was working in Liverpool in 1892 when he first heard Jim Larkin speak at a socialist meeting. Returning to Ireland, he went to work in the Dublin Port and Docks Board. In 1910 he again heard Larkin speak, this time in Beresford Place. Joining the ITGWU, he became a follower of Larkin.

Healy was in Liberty Hall one night when a woman came in with a child in her arms and enquired for Mr Larkin. She was shown up to room 7. She reported that her husband was in a public house drinking and she had nothing for the children.

> Larkin came down the stairs like a lion. I was standing on the steps of Liberty Hall, and he caught me by the arm and brought me along with him. He brought me down the South Quays and we came to Pat Butler's Public House. He went in there. There were about seventy men drinking there. He cleared the public house in less than five minutes.

The men were dockers and they used to be paid in Pat Butler's public house when their day's work was done, and if they did not spend much of their wages there on drink, their likelihood of getting work on the quays was reduced.

Since the incident related by Tommy Healy, no docker has been paid in a public house.

Episcopal ban

The following is an extract from a letter from the Bishop of Achonry, Dr Clancy, referring to a meeting in Sligo that 'the noted leader of the socialistic movement in this country' was to address in March 1912. The letter was addressed to 'the Catholic people of Sligo and the adjacent parishes.'

> I avail myself of this opportunity to state that Larkin's public utterances since he assumed to himself a prominent position in the direction of Irish affairs have been distinctly of a socialistic tendency; that in consequence he is distrusted by the members of the Irish Parliamentary Party, and that his name is associated in many minds with incidents which render it highly undesirable that the good people of Sligo should allow themselves to be allured into a false position by his pretended sympathy with the poor. I therefore expect and hope that no respectable citizen of our town or county and no faithful member of the Church will take part in the meeting at which this man is advertised to speak ...

Larkin was present in the church in Sligo when the bishop's letter was read.

Waiting for Larkin

R. M. Fox, Larkin's first biographer, wrote an article in 1913, when he was at university in England, about Larkin and the fight of the Dublin workers. The methods adopted by Larkin with employers were, he wrote, short and vigorous. He instanced one employer who was informed by postcard that when he wanted the dispute ended he should come round to Liberty Hall and accept terms.

The employer went round all right and was told to get outside and wait: Liberty Hall was for workers. Larkin went out to him when he was ready.

Paying for the strike pay

One of the earliest pamphlets on the Irish labour movement was *The Story of Irish Labour* by J. M. McDonnell, published in London in 1919. In it there is a story that indicates the sacrifices made by Larkin, as by others, at the expense of their families, in order to advance the working-class cause.

> During the Wexford strike [in 1911] every penny that could be raised in Dublin was spent to support the strikers, and when Jim came to look for his wages all that could be found was £1. Walter Carpenter and he split it between them, but even Jim shrunk from offering Mrs. Larkin 10s. for her weekly housekeeping, and begged Carpenter to call round and leave the money with her.

The American historian of the Irish labour movement, J. D. Clarkson, wrote of the Larkin family furniture being sold to raise funds for strike pay.

At a later stage, the general president of the ITGWU, Thomas Foran, arranged for Larkin's wages to be brought to his wife by a colleague, as Jim had the habit of giving much of the money away to poor families on his way home.

Belt of a baton

A children's street song from 1913, sung to the air of the popular 'Alexander's Ragtime Band', runs as follows:

> Come on along, come on along
> And join Jim Larkin's union.
> Come on along, come on along
> And join Jim Larkin's union.
> You'll get a loaf of bread and a pound of tea
> And a belt of a baton from the DMP.
> Other street songs were:

> It's a wrong thing to crush the workers,
> It's a wrong thing to do

and

> Bring your own bread and butter,
> Bring your own tea and sugar,
> And join Jim Larkin's union.

*　*　*

> …'Wait till I tell you,' Mrs. Hennessy said. 'He goes off to Sackville Street a few weeks ago to see will Larkin turn up and comes home to me with his head in a bandage and his arm dislocated. 'What happened to you, Hennessy?' say I, when he came to the door. 'I was caught in a charge in Sackville Street,' says he, 'and got a belt of a baton. And when I fell I think I was walked on be a horse.' Right enough, when he took off his shirt he was black and blue all over. 'That's what you get,' says I, 'for playing the Red Hand hayro. Now your wife and your unfortunate children can go hungry.'

(From James Plunkett, *Strumpet City*, 1969.)

Larkin and 'King' Pataud

In his address to the Dublin Chamber of Commerce on 1 September 1913, the president, William Martin Murphy, told the members:

> I have seen for a long time that the head of this labour agitation in Dublin has been aiming for a position that was occupied some time ago in Paris by a man who was called 'King' Pataud, who was able to hold up the whole business of the city by raising his little finger. That man was driven out of Paris, and the other man will be driven out of Dublin shortly.

Pataud was a leader of the electricians' union who, during a strike that had plunged Paris into darkness, held a press conference in the union's brightly lit offices. On another occasion the electricians at the Paris Opera took strike action minutes before a gala performance for some royal person was to begin. Immediate negotiations—in the dark—secured the electricians the pay increase they had sought.

Larkinism

The following is an extract from the editorial in the *Irish Independent* of 2 September 1913:

> It is necessarily incident to the 'sympathetic strike' ordered by the Transport Union despot that skilled workmen may be peremptorily bidden to leave their work. Was ever grosser tyranny attempted to be set up in the name of freedom of combination? Yet this is what Larkinism means and stands for ...
>
> It is this attempted tyranny that Independent Newspapers and others are now out to overturn and destroy. If the employers of Dublin join forces to complete the work it can be done in a comparatively short time. Sooner or later it must be done. It is infinitely better for Dublin that whatever suffering and loss may be involved should be endured for a few weeks at most than that the city should be left helpless in the toils of Larkinism for an indefinite term of years.
>
> The employers of Dublin must lead the way in emancipating the city from the thraldom of the international Socialist disguised as a Labour leader. In fighting their cause the employers will be battling for the real liberty of labour. This will never be until the pernicious influence of Larkinism has not merely been scotched, but killed.

Secretary to the archbishop

During the lock-out in 1913 the Catholic Archbishop of Dublin, Dr William Walsh, was convalescing from an illness in France. His secretary, Rev. J. J. Curran, kept in touch with him by post. In one of his letters he wrote:

> The disorder here has grown very seriously since Saturday. It is no longer a question of a tram strike. It is simply the scum of our slums versus the police. Unfortunately the mob have the sympathy of the working classes and nobody helps the police. I think it is a scandal that the military have not

yet been utilised. It would free the hands of the police immensely if the soldiers were stationed on the principal thoroughfares.

It is really surprising to see how much support Larkin commands among the artisans. Even the printers who refused to come out on strike at his command are very largely loyal to him. The workmen have gone mad over Larkin and will do almost anything for him, even respectable carpenters and bricklayers.

Anarchism in Dublin — a London view

An article with this title appeared in the *New Statesman* (London) on 6 September 1913, just before the lock-out by the 404 employers:

> Larkin is one of those born revolutionaries who know not diplomacy, but who believe that the Kingdom of Heaven must be taken by violence today and tomorrow and the day after. His utopia, we feel, would be a world where a general strike was going on all the time. Big and black and fierce, he is a Syndicalist of the street corners. He calls to the surface the very depth of unrest. His theory seems to be that a city should never be allowed a moment's peace so long as there remains a single poor man whose wrongs have not been righted. His genius is inflammatory. He preaches turmoil.

A good man and a brave man

Patrick Pearse, writing in *Irish Freedom* in October 1913 about the terrible housing conditions in the Dublin slums, with twenty thousand families living in one-room tenements, commented:

> These are the grievances against which the men in Dublin are beginning to protest. Can you wonder that the protest is crude and bloody? I do not know whether the methods of Mr. James Larkin are wise methods or unwise methods (unwise, I think, in some respects), but this I know, that there is a most hideous wrong to be righted and that the man who attempts honestly to right it is a good man and a brave man.

Barney Conway

Larkin gave everything that was in him to the service of the poor.

Captain Jack White

In those days, at the height of his influence, Larkin was, what God meant him to be, great.

James Connolly

Larkin is a man of genius, of splendid vitality, great in his conceptions, magnificent in his courage.

A nun writes about Larkin

Douglas Bennett, in *A Dublin Anthology* (1994), includes two letters from a Sister of Charity nun in Gardiner Street, written in October 1913. One of the letters includes the following sentence:

Tell Johnny when you write that the Dublin people think Jim Larkin, the leader of all the strikes in Dublin, is either Anti-Christ or in the pay of the Tories to prevent us getting Home Rule.

The second letter concluded:

Jim Larkin has, I think, at last overstepped his mark. The people are wild at the kidnapping of the children. The last description I got of him is that he is the devil in human flesh. The women hate him, the men on the whole so far worship him.

Upsetting the scientists

On 28 October 1913 Larkin, convicted of sedition, was sentenced to seven months' imprisonment. In the *Irish Worker* (1 November 1913) George Russell explained why Larkin deserved his sentence:

He was preventing a sociological experiment of great importance to Ireland from being carried out. We have never accurately determined how little human beings can live on, and how little air space is necessary for families. It is quite possible that after exhaustive experiments had been carried out we might have found out that human beings could be packed comfortably in rooms like bees in a hive, and could generate heat to warm themselves by their very number without the necessity for coal.

Nothing is more annoying to scientific investigators than the unscientific, humanitarian-like James Larkin, who comes along and upsets all calculations and destroys the labours of generations in the evolution of the underman, which was going along so well.

A career of destruction

Arthur Griffith wrote about Larkin in his paper, *Sinn Féin*:

In Dublin the wives of some men that Larkin has led on strike are begging in the streets. The consequences of Larkinism are workless fathers, mourning mothers, hungry children and broken homes. Not the capitalist but the policy of Larkin has raised the price of food until the poorest in Dublin are in a state of semi-famine—the curses of women are being poured on this man's head.

Mr. Larkin's career of destruction is coming to a close, but when it has closed it will have established his name in the memory of Dublin as the man who did the maximum of injury to trade unionism and the industrial revival.

A rebel's wife

On 15 November 1913 the *Daily Sketch* described Elizabeth Larkin as 'well-featured, and with a mass of red-gold hair.' Its correspondent was reporting from Dublin on her husband's release from jail.

While Liberty Hall was celebrating the release by fireworks, processions and speeches, Jim Larkin himself was at home minding the babies. Severe pains in his head had driven him to his modest little house in Auburn-

469

street, and as he was too unwell to risk the strain of speaking, his wife came down to explain his absence, and herself walked in the parade round the city. 'I don't often get the chance to go down,' Mrs. Larkin told me on her doorstep, 'because I don't like to leave the children in bed; so last night I thought I would take the chance when Jim had to be at home.'

She seems to feel the strain of being a rebel's wife, although she is herself keenly enthusiastic for the cause of labour. She has three children, the eldest boy at school, but smilingly declared that they were young to be rebels yet.

Fiery cross

J. T. Murphy, later a leader of the Communist Party in Britain, heard Larkin speak in Sheffield during his Fiery Cross campaign in 1913. He recorded his impressions of Larkin at the demonstration in his autobiography, *New Horizons* (1941).

The struggle of the poorest of Dublin's workers against the combined forces of all the Dublin employers, led by Martin Murphy, stirred all sections of the working class movement as never before since the days of Chartism.

A great demonstration, urging sympathetic action with Dublin was organised in Sheffield at which Jim Larkin and George Lansbury were the speakers. What a contrast! Six-foot Jim Larkin and his powerful, torrentially passionate eloquence swept the audience off its feet. He finished his speech with a rendering of William Morris's The Day is Coming.

I had never heard an orator of his calibre before, nor seen an audience so roused to demonstrative enthusiasm. It was not the kind which greatly appealed to me at that time. I preferred the colder analytical speeches and was sceptical of emotionalism. But it was impossible to be unimpressed by this man. Here was the fighting leader, bearing in his person all the marks of battle, who would storm hell itself.

A painful necessity

On 29 December 1913 Maud Gonne, in a letter to John Quinn in New York, gave her opinion of James Larkin. He was, she confided,

a painful necessity but a necessity and had done great work in many ways. Though she had admired his magnetic influence on crowds she expressed her fear that he was 'too vain and too jealous and too untruthful to make a really great leader.'

Arrests in 1913

Between 19 August and 20 December 1913 the number of arrests in connection with the labour disturbances in Dublin was 656 and the number imprisoned was 416.

No dividend for Heiton's

In September 1914 William Hewat II, the chairman of Heiton's, one of the main importers and suppliers of coal, iron and building supplies in Dublin, reported to his board that, as a result of the dispute the previous year, profits had fallen by two-thirds and that for the first time since the company had been incorporated in 1896 no dividend would be paid on the ordinary shares. (From Tony Farmar, *Heitons: A Managed Transition*, 1996.)

Rupert Brooke and the Dublin lock-out

On 7 January 1914 the English poet Rupert Brooke wrote to his mother from Wellington, New Zealand:

> I got to Wellington two days ago and have been reading up the Times etc. for a month. I'm catching up! I feel wild about Dublin. I always feel in strikes that 'the men are always right' as a man says in Clayhanger [the novel by Arnold Bennett]. Of course the poor are always right against the rich. But often enough the men, in any particular strike, are in the wrong over some point of the moment (it's not to be wondered at). But Dublin seems to be one of the clearest cases on record, where the employers are in the wrong even by Conservative standards—in refusing the Askwith suggestion. When the Times begins saying that the employers are in the wrong, they must be very unpardonably and rottenly so indeed. I do hope people are contributing for the wives and children in Dublin. I saw an appeal from a lot of people including George Trevelyan and [John] Masefield. Erskine Childers is a treasurer for it. Could you send two guineas in my name? I'll settle when I get back. But I'd like it done immediately. I expect you'll have sent some yourself.

(From *The Letters of Rupert Brooke*, chosen and edited by Geoffrey Keynes, 1968.)

Money and food for workers' families

Financial support for the locked-out workers in Dublin in 1913 was to come from many countries, including England, France, and America. Huge sums were contributed by British trade unionists. For a time the Miners' Federation was sending £1,000 a week. The British Trades Union Congress raised over £90,000. The Co-operative Movement in Britain made substantial contributions and despatched food ships to Dublin, the first, *Hare*, arriving on 27 September and a second, *Fraternity*, on 4 October.

In all, around £150,000 in cash was subscribed. It is difficult to express this sum in present-day money, but since 1914 consumer prices, as measured by the official indices, have risen from 100 in 1914 to about 6,700 in 1998, suggesting that the £150,000 in 1913 would be equivalent to approximately £10 million today. Fourteen shiploads of food were sent from the Co-operative Wholesale Society in Manchester (*Co-operative News*, 27 December 1913).

In London, a Dublin Distress Fund was organised by, among others, the Bishop of Oxford, the historian G. M. Trevelyan, E. D. Morel of the Union of Democratic Control, John Masefield (later the Poet Laureate), Lord Henry Bentinck MP, Lady Barlow, Mrs Humphry Ward, and W. B. Yeats. The treasurers of the fund were Erskine Childers (who the following year was to sail his yacht *Asgard*, laden with guns for the Irish Volunteers, into Howth) and Mabel Dickinson (with whom Yeats had begun an affair in 1908). (From the *Times*, 13 November 1913.)

Lord Salisbury wrote to Sir Horace Plunkett, head of the co-operative movement in Ireland, expressing a wish to subscribe to the alleviation of distress in Dublin without seeming to take sides in the dispute. On Christmas Eve 1913 Plunkett replied:

> The condition of the Dublin slums I always knew to be bad but had only realised one half the truth ... My feeling is that the poverty and destitution which has been revealed owing to Larkin's agitation are so awful that temporary amelioration can be provided without any appearance of taking sides in the Dublin labour dispute.

At the 1914 annual congress of the Irish Trades Union Congress the president, James Larkin, singled out for special thanks for the financial help given during the Dublin lock-out of the previous year the Limerick Pork Butchers, who had 'sent more every week in proportion to their strength than any other union.'

Larkin and the suffrage cause

The *Irish Citizen*, which was edited by Francis Sheehy-Skeffington, was the organ of the Irish suffragists. In its issue of 6 September 1913 it wrote about the tramway strike:

> Almost everyone of the Labour leaders involved has in some way or other helped the Suffrage cause, or shown his adhesion to it. Mr. Larkin was the initiator of the vigorous resolution passed by the Irish Trades Union Congress in condemnation of the Government's attack upon freedom of speech and freedom of the press. He has also assisted to carry suffragist resolutions at the Dublin Trades Council and his paper, the *Irish Worker*, has repeatedly attacked the Government for its coercive policy towards the suffragists. The men of Mr. Larkin's union also frequently interfered at the rowdy meetings in Dublin last year, to protect Suffragettes from the hooliganism of the AOH—the body that is now organising strike-breakers.

'Three cheers for Larkin'

By the end of the 1913 dispute the ITGWU had perhaps five thousand members. David Fitzpatrick in his essay 'Militarism in Ireland, 1900–1922' in *A Military History of Ireland*, edited by Thomas Bartlett and Keith Jeffery (1996), suggests that the ITGWU lost as many men to the trenches as it retained in the union.

One company of the 7th Dublins (Royal Irish Fusiliers) composed largely of dockers were called the 'Larkinites'. During the second battle of Ypres in April 1915 one company of the Dublin Fusiliers that had suffered heavy losses during an attack at Saint-Julien went over to the attack to shouts of 'three cheers for Jim Larkin.' (From Tom Johnstone, *Orange, Green and Khaki*, 1992.)

The Cross and Socialism

Benjamin Gitlow was, with Larkin, one of the founders of the American Communist Labor Party and was arrested at the same time as Larkin on 8 November 1919 and charged with criminal anarchy. At his trial Gitlow was defended by the famous lawyer Clarence Darrow (Larkin defended himself), but he too received a sentence of five to ten years in Sing Sing.

Twenty years later Gitlow very publicly recanted his beliefs in the notorious *I Confess*, published in 1939. In a second book, *The Whole of Their Lives* (1948), Gitlow recalled how Larkin at one of his first meetings in New York shocked a socialist audience by unbuttoning his shirt and producing a golden cross. Holding the cross before him, he shouted at the audience:

> There is no antagonism between the Cross and Socialism. A man can pray to Jesus and be a better militant Socialist for it. There is no conflict between the religion of the Catholic Church and Marxism. I stand by the cross and Marxism. I belong to the Catholic Church. In Ireland that is not held against a Socialist. I defy any man to challenge my standing as a socialist and a revolutionist!

In the circumstances, a brave speech by a very courageous man.

Gitlow did not like Larkin. In his book he relates how in one room in a small alley in Greenwich Village,

> the towering man held court. On the small stove, tea was usually brewing, a dark concoction which Larkin drank by the bucketful. His was an informal court. The haughty Larkin did not insist on ceremony, but he did insist on dominating the scene.

To jail with a cigar

Lady Gregory in her journals records Frank Harris telling her about seeing Larkin being brought to trial in New York.

> He was wearing a slouch hat and a long sort of frock coat and was smoking a cigar. And all the way from the Courthouse there were people eight or nine deep along the streets to take a look at him. They thought of him as a god.

Charlie Chaplin and the slippers

When Larkin was in Sing Sing he was visited by Charlie Chaplin, who wrote in *An Autobiography* (1964) that 'prisons have a strange atmosphere, as if the human spirit were suspended.' On leaving the prison he quotes Frank Harris, who had accompanied him on the visit, that 'it depressed him to see a courageous, flamboyant character like Jim Larkin reduced to prison discipline.'

Denis Larkin, Jim Larkin's second son, recalled in an interview with Michael McInerney in the *Irish Times* (30 April 1977) the family getting a package at the time his father was in jail. It was from Charlie Chaplin and contained 'beautiful moccasin-beaded slippers' for his mother.

473

A dogged struggle

In *Review*, April 1947, Captain Robert Monteith, who landed at Banna Strand, County Kerry, with Roger Casement on Good Friday 1916, wrote about Jim Larkin:

> If ever a man suffered the full penalty of leadership, Larkin is that man. This writer watched his dogged struggle from 1910 to 1913 in organising and holding together the Irish Transport and General Workers' Union. Despite the demoralising barrage of mud and filth from the Dublin Press, regardless of the thunders from platform and pulpit, he kept on with the good work. Industrial unionism was on the march. Larkin being no superman made some mistakes, 'even as you and I,' but these mattered little in the great measure of success he achieved in asserting the right not only of Dublin workers but of the workers of all Ireland to live in decency and comfort. His few errors may be likened to the dust kicked up by a troop of cavalry: it does not impede the march but it does give the enemy a denser target to aim at. When Ireland comes into her own he will have a chapter in her history.
>
> The establishment of *The Irish Worker* was an important incident in the march of the Irish workers to industrial unionism. Only those who were on the ground at the moment can fully appreciate the tremendous influence of that labour sheet. It brought about those much to be desired discussion groups of people who either through fear or a feeling of that dear Irish respectability did not attend Larkinite meetings. There was real progress here. Many 'settled' people began to have their doubts about the righteousness of continuing a drab existence 'in that state of life to which God had been pleased to call them.' Through the medium of *The Irish Worker* much seed was sown. Some of it, of course, fell by the wayside, some among thorns, but much fell upon good ground.

Larkin at St Enda's

In an article in the *Irish Times* (9 August 1973) John Swift, the retired general secretary of the Irish Bakers' Union, recalled the fine summer day when he made a pilgrimage to St Enda's School in Rathfarnham.

> Jem Larkin had returned from America and here in the playing-field of the Hermitage the Larkinites of the city had assembled to welcome him home.
>
> The preliminary jubilation seemed more restrained than the event itself suggested. It was the solemn merry-making of the feis, the measured clatter of young feet moving, perhaps impatiently, to the grave music of pipe and fiddle. Then Jem appeared. We thought that in spite of his long harassment in and out of American jails, he was still much the Hercules that, a decade before, bestrode Dublin's streets baiting the DMP, RIC and military. And when he spoke there was still evident the same volcanic source, the same fiery vehemence that, in the struggle of '13, spat challenge and contempt at the Dublin employers and their protectors in the Castle.
>
> Jem's message at St. Enda's was still of challenge and contempt. We had now our own Government, Saorstát Éireann. But Larkin was showing himself no more respectful of the new authority than he had been a decade earlier to the Viceroy whose writs sought to ban the Larkin meetings. Big

Jem's invective had other targets, one of them being the new structure of the organisation he had founded, the ITGWU.

Both Jim Larkin Junior and Denis Larkin were at school at St Enda's when Patrick Pearse was its head.

Reflections on a photograph

The famous Cashman photograph of Jim Larkin addressing a meeting in Upper O'Connell Street at the Parnell Monument soon after his return from America in 1923 is well known, though some assume that it was taken in 1913.

Opening his review of Emmet Larkin's biography of James Larkin in the *New Statesman* (7 May 1965), Dr Conor Cruise O'Brien wrote:

> His great head thrown back, his hair blown by the wind, mouth full open for a roar, arms flung wide and high with the palms turned upward and the fingers spread, he looks a heroic revolutionary symbol, a sculpture from the Arc de Triomphe come to life. Around and below the epic figure is a little knot of ordinary unheroic Dubliners, not terribly beautiful, not changed utterly. But the interesting thing about the group is not the contrast of its ordinariness with James Larkin's superhuman style; it is the apparent relation of the group to the speaker. Of the dozen figures whose faces or attitudes we can make out, only one shows any clear sign of listening to the orator; the others seem elsewhere …
>
> The one man who is watching the speaker with obvious interest and appreciation is a bandsman. He is smiling faintly, and scratching the underside of his chin; his expression is affectionate and, in a way, admiring. But it is not the expression of a revolutionary militant looking at a revolutionary leader. Simply, the bandsman is watching and memorising a performance by a great performer. One guesses he will mimic it and add: 'A star turn, Jim! Oh a st-ar turn!'

Interestingly, in the light of the last sentence of Dr Cruise O'Brien's remarks on the picture, there is another comment on the same picture in the *Seán O'Casey Review* (spring 1977) by Prof. Ronald Ayling:

> The picture is emotionally charged, even explosive in its impact. High above his supporters, a tight group of whom are gathered closely around him, Big Jim has both hands raised in a large outgoing gesture and his mouth is wide open—presumably exhorting them in equally dramatic terms. Agitated by his movements, or caught by the wind, his open jacket swirls above their heads like a cloak. One cannot doubt the fiery rhetoric that must have accompanied the gesture, which is beautiful in an almost balletic sense in its frozen moment of climax. The crowd is interesting too. The few faces that we can see clearly are those close to Larkin: looking out to the crowd, mostly, they have on their features (with two exceptions) what look like set even determined expressions. The exceptions, apart from two anonymous men who are looking at the ground, include a man with a somewhat vacant (even stupid) countenance and a man in uniform who wears an enigmatic smile.

For all the tenseness on most of these faces, however, the crowd cannot be said to reflect Larkin's upward-urging rhetoric.

Larkin and the Legion of Mary

In 1965 Frank Duff brought members of the Legion of Mary around Myra House, 100 Francis Street, in the Liberties of Dublin, where the Legion had been founded in 1921. (The founders were Frank Duff and Matt Lalor.) He told them that in the early thirties, as a result of a dispute with the parish priest of the church of St Nicholas of Myra, also in Francis Street, the Legion was obliged to seek other premises in which to hold their meetings. Somehow or other Jim Larkin was approached, and he readily offered them the use of the nearby office of the Workers' Union of Ireland. One of the members at the time jokingly suggested that members of the Legion should walk in procession with their religious banners and insignia from Myra House to Larkin's union premises.

Larkin had been regarded by many as the anti-Christ in 1913. Now twenty years later he was the arch-red.

Later, Larkin allowed branches of the Legion of Mary to use rooms in Unity Hall, the head office of the WUI, in Marlborough Street (opposite the Pro-Cathedral). He would look in to the room in which they were meeting 'to see if they were quite comfortable.' The house had been a tenement and by all accounts was scruffy and badly kept, with a single unshaded lamp bulb in each room and the stairs in danger of collapsing.

(From a tape-recording of Frank Duff's talk at Myra House made by Enda Dunleavy, who was president of the Concilium of the Legion of Mary when Frank Duff died in 1980, at the age of ninety-one.)

Storming the Dáil ...

Dr Owen Sheehy-Skeffington, lecturer in French in Trinity College, Dublin—a brave liberal in an oppressive era—recalling memories of the College Historical Society in the *Irish Times* (5 March 1970), thought of 'a magnificent meeting' of the 'Hist' in May 1931 on individual freedom, which Larkin chaired. His speech 'made us all feel that if he had asked us there and then to storm the Dáil, we would at once have done so.'

... Lighting a flame

On a famous occasion at a protest meeting in College Green in 1941 against a Trade Union Bill, Larkin, repeating a gesture from 1913, when he had burned the proclamation of Swifte the magistrate banning a meeting in O'Connell Street, took a copy of the Bill out of his pocket and, striking a match on the seat of his trousers, set fire to it.

Some time afterwards Sheehy-Skeffington expressed his admiration to Larkin at the confidence needed to pull off the trick. What, he asked Larkin, if the match went out, or the paper wouldn't light? 'No fear of that,' Larkin replied, 'with ten matches tied together, sandpaper on the seat of the trousers, and paper well soaked in paraffin.' This story is told by Andrée Sheehy-Skeffington in her book on her husband, *Skeff* (1991).

Larkin's last days

The Capuchin priest Father Aloysius, who was the provincial of the Irish province of the order in 1916, when he attended both Patrick Pearse and James Connolly before their execution, was a lifelong friend of Jim Larkin, whom he once described to Father David as a 'big baby', which he intended as a compliment and which Father David took to mean of an ebullient simplicity.

When Larkin was in the Meath Hospital during his last illness, Father Aloysius visited him. One day, according to Father Aloysius's account, he said to him: 'Now, Jim, what about Number One?' He replied: 'Time enough at the end of the week.' That night Father Aloysius woke up with a strangely vivid image of Jim on his mind. He decided to go to see him again the following day. He said: 'Do you know, Jim, I wasn't able to sleep last night because of you. Won't you go to Confession? I'll get you any priest you want.' Jim said: 'I'd rather yourself, father.' There and then Father Aloysius heard his confession. When it was over Jim took hold of both his hands and kissed them. As he did so, tears rolled down the old warrior's cheeks.

According to Father David, Father Aloysius considered that the reconciliation of the great labour leader with the church was a matter of sufficient importance to inform the Archbishop of Dublin, which he did, with Larkin's permission. It was then that Dr McQuaid visited the hospital to see Larkin.

Dr McQuaid had met Larkin previously when, during the national teachers' strike the previous year, he had been on a deputation from Dublin Trades Council that met the archbishop at his house in Drumcondra. Four years before, Larkin had been a member of the Commission on Youth Unemployment, set up by the Minister for Industry and Commerce, Seán Lemass, in 1943, which had been chaired by the archbishop. The commission did not report until 1951, four years after Larkin's death. Among the original members of the commission were two friends of Jim Larkin's, Father Aloysius and Rev. Thomas Counihan, as well as two old trade union antagonists, Helena Molony and Cathal O'Shannon.

In a letter to the *Irish Times* (12 April 1973) Gabriel Fallon wrote that Dr McQuaid had told him that the rosary beads wrapped around the hands of the dead labour leader had been given him by the archbishop the evening before his death. The letter went on:

> On the day of the funeral, in mentioning this fact to me, he [Dr McQuaid] suggested that the gesture was not an unfitting one, particularly in the light of what the clerical attitude had been in the early days of Larkin's attempt to lift Dublin's working men off their knees.

Defiant nature

Nature was in a defiant mood the night before the Big Fellow was buried. Bitter, biting winds, in all their fury, swept through the city of Dublin and its streets were snowbound. Nature seemed to say to the thousands of men and women of Dublin who were mourning their dead Leader: now let us see if you really loved and believed in him; if your tears really betoken your grief at his passing. These men and women of Dublin met the challenge and, in the worst wintry weather that Dublin had experienced in years, in their thousands they walked behind his coffin to Glasnevin. Old men and women said Dublin had never witnessed such a tribute since the days when Parnell came home to take his long last sleep in Glasnevin. The comparison was its own tribute to the Big Fellow. It was not the statesmen, nor the leaders in all walks of life, who shaped the funeral of the Big Fellow into a drama, awe-inspiring in the sense of having naive awe and tears without shame; it was the thousands of ordinary men and women, whose names are never listed in the newspapers as being among those present, who gave to the funeral of the Big Fellow a magnificence and beauty, whose tale will be told around the firesides of Dublin and the rest of Ireland for many years to come. Men and women in those far-off days will feel proud when they tell this tale and say 'I was there!'

(Jack Carney.)

Contrast

Press extract, 15 May 1947:

> Mr James Larkin, the Labour leader, Wellington road, Dublin, who died intestate on January 30th, left personal estate of the gross value of £16 2s. 6d. Letters of administration of the estate were granted to his son, Mr. James Larkin, T.D., Galtrim road, Bray, Co. Wicklow.

William Martin Murphy, who died in 1919, left a personal estate of £264,000, of which £2,000 was left to charity. A sum of £264,000 in 1919 would be the equivalent of over £9 million today.

Philistines and the gallery

In the *Irish Homestead* (9 August 1913), George Russell commented on the controversy about the building of an art gallery for the Lane collection of French Impressionist paintings that the businessmen (headed by William Martin Murphy) responsible for the refusal of Dublin Corporation to build the gallery 'had revealed themselves as the meanest, most uncultured, most materialistic and canting crowd that ever made a citizen ashamed of his fellow-countrymen.'

Larkin's comment was that Murphy should be condemned to keep an art gallery in Hell.

Prof. Roy Foster, in *W. B. Yeats: A Life* (1997), quotes a letter from Stephen Gwynn to John Quinn (5 November 1913) in which he hoped to God that 'Murphy and the Ardilauns [a Guinness family] may be damned to an eternity of Dublin Corporation.' Foster quotes another letter to

Quinn, this time from Lady Gregory (12 August 1913), to the effect that the Lord Mayor was being 'bullied by a vulgar man called Murphy.'

Louie Bennett at Liberty Hall

Louie Bennett came from a prosperous business background. She 'listened half-fascinated, to Jim Larkin thundering his flaming gospel of discontent,' as her biographer, R. M. Fox, put it. She was to write about her visits to Liberty Hall:

> At that time I belonged to the respectable middle-class and I did not dare to admit to my home circle that I had run with the crowd to hear Jim Larkin, and crept like a culprit into Liberty Hall to see Madame Markievicz in a big overall, with sleeves rolled up, presiding over a cauldron of stew, surrounded by a crowd of gaunt women and children carrying bowls and cans.

Louie Bennett admitted that she never felt any personal magnetism about Larkin, as so many others did, and that 'Larkin disgusted me by his wild ravings.'

Kevin Barry on Larkin

In 1919, in his last year at Belvedere College, Kevin Barry, then seventeen, wrote an essay on 'Industrial unrest', in which he gave his views on the 1913 lock-out. Referring to the great industrial upheavals of the time, including major strikes in Belfast, which he regarded as 'the Triumph of Labour, of Trade Unionism and—as Martin Murphy's rag has it—of syndicalism,' he wrote in the essay:

> We here in Dublin had an experience of a strike which has been looked upon by all the world as the 'model strike'. When W. M. Murphy refused to recognise the tramwaymen as a union they went out on strike bringing out every trade union man in Dublin with them. The Socialists all over the world backed them ... The men held out doggedly till they won, or virtually won, since the tramway union was recognised. Thus we received a forcible demonstration of the power of Labour and had an experience also of the power of agitation in the person of that marvellous leader James Larkin and his able lieutenant, Commandant James Connolly.

Kevin Barry's English teacher, who had also taught James Joyce, gave him sixty marks out of a hundred for his essay.

(From Dónal O'Donovan, *Kevin Barry and his Time*, 1989.)

Larkin and John Devoy

In the National Library of Ireland there is a letter written on 9 December 1914 by Prof. Kuno Meyer, the great German Celtic scholar, to Joseph McGarrity (ms. 17465):

We had a great meeting at Brooklyn the other night, when Mr [John] Devoy and Mr Larkin spoke splendidly.

(From Seán Ó Lúing, *Kuno Meyer, 1858–1919: A Biography*, 1991.)

Larkin and the Countess

In the spring of 1922 Constance Markievicz was sent by Éamon de Valera to America to plead the case for the Republic against the Free State. Her attitude to the Treaty was little different from Larkin's. In her speech to the Dáil on 3 January 1922 she had said:

> I rise today to oppose with all the force of my will, with all the force of my own existence, this so-called Treaty. O'Connell said that Ireland's freedom was not worth a drop of blood. Now I say that Ireland's freedom is worth blood, and worth my blood, and I will willingly give it for it.

Larkin's first manifesto on the Treaty had stated:

> We pledge ourselves, now and in the future, to destroy this plan of a nation's destruction. We propose carrying on the fight until we make the land of Erin a land fit for men and women—a Workers' Republic or Death.

In America, Markievicz visited Jim Larkin in Sing Sing. Afterwards she wrote to her step-son Stanislaus, then twenty-six years old and married; he appears to have been imprisoned by the Russian authorities, because in her letter she told him that Jim Larkin had promised 'to try and get certain Bolshie friends of his to try and get you set free.' She added:

> He is in prison here, I think because he is too revolutionary and made wild speeches. But he's awfully decent and promised to do all he could to get you out.

Platitudes and action

Dr Douglas Hyde, the first President of Ireland, wrote about Larkin:

> Larkin mounted the wagonette and spoke from beside me. A tall black-haired, powerfully built man, with a great resounding voice and much fluency and energy, seeming to say a lot with great emphasis but really speaking platitudes, the gist of his speech being that if Irishmen really wanted Irish taught to their children there was no power on earth that could stop them!
>
> Patrick Pearse, who spoke also, pronounced a great eulogy on Larkin, he at least he said was doing something, he was making history. So he was, for he had closed the port of Dublin, and the workers of Dublin have not yet got over the effects of the general strike into which he plunged them—apparently without counting the cost.

(From manuscripts of Hyde's memoirs in the Folklore Department in UCD, quoted by Ruth Dudley Edwards in *Patrick Pearse: The Triumph of Failure*, 1977.)

A primeval force

Constance Markievicz first heard Larkin speak in 1909. Fourteen years later she was to write in the journal *Éire* (16 June 1923):

> Sitting there listening to Larkin I realised that I was in the presence of something that I had never come across before, some great primeval force rather than a man. A tornado, a storm-driven wave, the rush into life of Spring, and the lasting breath of Autumn, all seemed to emanate from the power that spoke. It seemed as if his personality caught up, assimilated, and threw back to that vast crowd that surrounded him every emotion that swayed them, every pain and joy that they had ever felt made articulate and sanctified. Only the great elemental force that is in all crowds had passed into his nature for ever.
>
> Taller than most men, every line of him was in harmony with his personality. Not so much working man as primeval man. Man without the trickeries and finickiness of modern civilisation, a Titan who might have been moulded by Michelangelo or Rodin, such is Jim Larkin, and this force of his magically changed the whole life of the workers in Dublin and the whole outlook of trade unionism in Ireland. He forced his own self-reliance and self-respect on them; forced them to be sober and made them class conscious and conscious of their nationality.

Impressing the professor

During the nineteen-twenties a group of intellectuals in Dublin— including W. B. Yeats, Lennox Robinson, Desmond FitzGerald, Thomas McGreevy, and Brinsley MacNamara—who were known as the Twelve Apostles met regularly in the Moira Hotel in Trinity Street. It was their practice to invite visitors, and in his reminiscences Prof. George O'Brien, the long-time professor of political economy at University College, Dublin, remembered one evening when they had Larkin as a guest. O'Brien admitted that Larkin had a much greater knowledge of literature than he would have expected, and that he and Yeats exchanged recollections of the Yellow Book literary circle of the nineties in London. 'Jim Larkin impressed me very favourably,' O'Brien recorded.

'The greatest bloody man since O'Connell'

Desmond Ryan, in *Remembering Sion* (1934), wrote of Larkin's espousal of temperance and of his throwing 'inebriated backsliders' down the steps of Liberty Hall. One person so treated

> rose from the cobblestones and shouted at Jim Larkin's retreating back: 'There goes the greatest bloody man since O'Connell!'

In the same book, Ryan wrote that it was a pity that Larkin's speeches had never been collected, 'for no such speeches have ever been delivered in any city before or since.'

Visiting Seán O'Casey

Eileen O'Casey in her book *Seán* (1971) recalled two particular visits to her husband. One was in the summer of 1939, when Jim Larkin had travelled down to Devon for the afternoon, arriving at mid-day and returning in the evening to London:

> Jim had always been Seán's hero, often he had told me of him and of how even his prison sentence had left him undaunted; they seldom come like Jim nowadays. Probably seventy [in fact he was then sixty-five], he was a tall man, finely built, with a lovely head of hair and a compelling force. I remember that he and Seán, who was overcome by emotion at seeing him, sat in the kitchen to eat their meal and to talk over the past in a racing torrent of words.

Eileen O'Casey also recalled an earlier visit to Seán in London, when Jack Carney brought with him Barney Conway,

> a docker known well in Dublin, a huge man whose voice was beery and husky, and who certainly loved his pint; he and his frail, small friend made a remarkable pair, and with Seán they talked far into the night of the days with Larkin.

James T. Farrell on Larkin

During the thirties the American James T. Farrell (1904–1979), author of *Studs Lonigan* and other notable novels, was one of the leaders of the Fourth (Trotskyist) International. Following a visit to Ireland before the war, he wrote a letter critical of Larkin to Leon Trotsky (11 December 1938).

> This summer I was in Ireland, and I saw Jim Larkin. All men have weaknesses, but all men are not the victims of their weaknesses. Jim Larkin is a victim of his own weaknesses, and his own temperament. He is untheoretical and unstable intellectually. He is always a direct actionist, and his direct actionism takes whatever turn that his impulses lead him toward. He is very garrulous, human and humane, witty, vindictive, vituperative, and he is Irish. At times, he is almost like an embittered version of the stage Irishman. Larkin was a great and courageous agitator, but not a leader of a defeated army, and he could not work with anyone. Gradually, he lost influence, and now he is old and embittered.

Parnell or Larkin?

> Idolatry encouraged the arrogance. He preferred to break rather than mend. His speaking tours attracted large audiences. He would disappear for days without feeling any obligation to explain his absence. He was never a team player. Splendid in his obduracy. On one occasion he was described as 'erect amid the whole standing cheering crowd. He took no notice of it whatever.' The hauteur was magnificent. But it was the quality which was to drag him down. He could make sudden turns and expect the rest to follow him without question. The charisma worked as long as his self-

482

confidence and certainty lasted. Arrogance and integrity often go hand in hand. Because of the complications of his character his career was bound to end in tragedy.

This passage is not related to James Larkin but to Charles Stewart Parnell. It is based on a review by Roy Hattersley of Robert Kee's *The Laurel and the Ivy*.

Fighting for children's rights

The *Freeman's Journal* (17 October 1913) reported Larkin addressing a meeting and telling the crowd that they were fighting for rights for themselves and their little children. Larkin held up a little child in his arms, declaring: 'We will never lay down the Red Hand we have raised in Ireland until we have secured a better prospect for those who will come after us.'

Tarzan of the slum jungles

In a book review in the *New Statesman and Nation* in 1938 the distinguished writer David Garnett wrote of Jim Larkin:

He was incomparably one of the finest orators I have ever heard. He was absolutely unselfconscious and seemed to care nothing for his audience. I cannot remember any appeal to reason in his speech, which was a recital of wrongs and assaults on persons. There, striding about the platform one beheld the whole of the sweated, starved, exploited working class suddenly incarnate in the shape of a gigantic Tarzan of all the slum jungles of the West.

Elsewhere the same writer wrote:

Larkin was the greatest orator I heard until Winston Churchill began to voice our thoughts in June 1940.

'This bloody incredible man'

For years the actor Peter O'Toole was fascinated by Jim Larkin. In 1979 he had an opportunity to play Larkin in an adaptation for television of James Plunkett's *Strumpet City*, made by RTE.

During the filming he was interviewed by John Feeney (*Sunday Independent*, 17 June 1979), who wrote that he felt certain that 'at last O'Toole had met his master in Larkin—an imperious, charismatic, even vain man, just as O'Toole is himself.' Feeney quoted O'Toole:

Larkin had a madness. He was such an enigmatic man who engaged on the most mad and impossible of revolutions in Ireland. I came to the part because of years of fascination with this bloody incredible man. He was a man who loved the show; arrogant and enigmatic, he loved captivating an audience. He was quite, absolutely unique.

John Kelleher, who was involved in the television production of *Strumpet City*, has told a story about the filming of the riot scene in O'Connell Street early one morning in which an old man was really trampled in the mock riot after O'Toole had so excited the extras that they were mad for a fight: 'We rushed to the man and found him whispering that he knew Larkin in his youth. We offered him help, but he shook his head and was running back to the fray. Larkin had come alive for him again.'

His own man

The same journalist, John Feeney, who had interviewed Peter O'Toole, had his own view of Larkin, which he set out in the *Evening Herald* (12 October 1979).

> Larkin's life was to be the search for justice for all. A steely man, he forged his own views; often intolerant, often irritable, but his own man. He was a Christian Socialist long before Pope John XXIII made such a creature possible. He was damned by bishops as an atheist, damned by atheists in America and Russia as an idealist Christian, always his own man.
>
> Never more so than in 1913 when his voice raised the imagination of a people—and artists since in word and stone have tried to capture the power of this big man, and his might—never quite getting there. Larkin had the vibes that Martin Luther King had and his speeches rolled over the crowds.
>
> A man with a vision, with genius, streaked like a comet across the world, he knew the jails in America, sat in the deposed Tzar's throne in Russia. Ireland and its mean ways was too small for him. As Yeats said of post liberation Ireland 'Great hatred, little room.' Yeats, like Larkin, both men of genius, found the new Free State stifling and dull. The world was their domain.

Method in his madness

The famous British columnist Hannen Swaffer wrote about Larkin in *Forward* (8 February 1957), ten years after Larkin's death:

> A film director who went so far in breaking the rules as to plan a talkie dealing with that greatest of all human dramas—the struggle of the underdog—would find, if he made Jim Larkin his hero, not one tensely thrilling story, but a dozen.
>
> From his early youth, until a few years before his death as a septuagenarian in 1947, he was an agitator ablaze with righteous indignation. At a time when in other parts of the British Isles, trade unionism had become respectable, Jim was the embodiment of the class war, a man who, until his closing years, could see virtue only in the workers. Frequently he was bitter and intolerant. Yet, such was his self-sacrificing honesty of purpose that he was beloved by millions who had been aroused from a lethargic acceptance of their fate by his inspiring and fervid oratory. His enemies called it 'Larkinism', a cult of personality.
>
> The end, in his view, justified the means. So it was that he was constantly at war, not only with all employers but with official Labour leaders, who frequently saw madness in his method—to him method in his madness.

An editor on Larkin

Robert Maire Smyllie was editor of the *Irish Times* for twenty years, up to his death in 1954. After Larkin's death he wrote in the paper (1 February 1947):

My journalistic career has brought me into contact with many great orators. I think that during the last thirty years I have heard most of the world's most famous public speakers, from President Woodrow Wilson to Mr. Winston Churchill. I have listened to them all. But I never heard anybody who moved me quite so much as Jim Larkin.

Of course I was very young at the time. It was in 1912. Naturally I was impressionable. I had just come to Dublin from the country as a student. But I fell for Larkin's spell-binding oratory. And I was not altogether in bad company. He was a wonderful speaker. I heard him speaking outside Liberty Hall, outside the Ballast Office and in various other places: and I came to the youthful conclusion that Jim Larkin was one of the greatest men in the world.

Doubtless, that was youthful enthusiasm. But ever since I have had a hankering respect for a man who seemed to me at the time to be a single-minded idealist. I may be wrong; but, somehow, I do not think so even now. Larkin was a queer, wayward creature, who never sought popularity, although he achieved it in abundant measure.

He had a terrific personality. His detractors say that he was merely a mob orator, which he probably was; but there was more to him than that. He believed in what he was doing, and had the knack of making other people believe in it as well.

Go down, Moses

The journalist James Downey contributed an article, 'James Larkin: the slum prophet,' as the second in a series, 'Leaders and Rulers,' in the *Irish Times* (5 April 1973). He opened the article:

Bigger than life, less than angelic, Jim Larkin inspired adoration but never hagiography. He was a terrible man, terrible both in the Irish and in the literal sense. The literal terror that he struck into the hearts of the bourgeoisie is almost forgotten now, but the loving awe of the Dublin workers whom he thundered at, bullied and dragged off their knees and onto their feet lives vividly in the folk memory.

Neither his remarkable physical aspect, nor his courage, nor yet his immense humanity (and his faults were almost as much loved as his virtues) can quite explain his extraordinary *mana*. It may be that his English birth, his theatrical descent first on Belfast and then on Dublin, helped to form the image—visible on the first appearance, grown larger in the legend, still inescapable—of the messianic prophet, the hero-leader:

Go down, Moses
Way down in Egypt land
And tell old Pharaoh
To let my people go.

The Larkin family

James Larkin, then living at 37 Roche Street, Toxteth Park, Liverpool, married Elizabeth Brown of 58 Ashbourne Road, Toxteth Park, at the Register Office, Liverpool, on 8 September 1903. Elizabeth was the daughter of Robert Brown, described on the marriage certificate as 'Manager Cocoa Rooms,' a dockside café. Larkin's age was given as twenty-seven and his wife's as twenty-four. (In fact he was twenty-nine at the time.) He was described as 'Foreman Dock Porter.' The column for Elizabeth under 'Rank or profession' was left blank.

Elizabeth's father was a Baptist lay preacher, while James Larkin was a Catholic. Intermarriage was uncommon in the sectarian city that Liverpool was at that time. Probably it was because of this that there was little if any contact between Elizabeth and her family after her marriage.

When Larkin left Liverpool, the family lived successively in Rostrevor, County Down, and at various addresses in Dublin, including Auburn Street, North Strand, and Upper Beechwood Avenue in Ranelagh.

Elizabeth twice joined her husband when he was in America, in 1915 for a short period and in 1919 for an even briefer period. Some time after Larkin's return from America in 1923 the couple separated and henceforward lived apart. She died at her eldest son's home in Bray on 2 December 1945, just over a year before her husband died. She was buried in Mount Jerome Cemetery.

Apart from Beechwood Avenue, Elizabeth Larkin lived for many years at St Agnes's Park, Crumlin, with a Citizen Army veteran, Bridie Goff, and later in a flat in Warrington Place on the Grand Canal near Baggot Street Bridge. (Bridie Goff was among the thirty or so Citizen Army members in the College of Surgeons in St Stephen's Green in 1916 with Michael Mallin and Constance Markievicz. A Cumann na mBan colleague, Nora O'Daly, recalled how she kept making the most comical remarks about the snipers who were disturbing her sleep.)

Elizabeth Larkin's granddaughter Hilda Breslin, the daughter of her eldest son, Young Jim, remembers her as a loving, quiet, gentle person who loved children and welcomed visits from her grandchildren to her flat in Warrington Place. Another grandchild, Stella McConnon, the daughter of Mrs Larkin's second son, Denis, remembers that she painted landscapes and portraits, of which unfortunately only two seem to have survived. These show evidence of more than a little talent for painting.

Her grandson Jim Larkin, a brother of Stella, writing about his grandparents' separation, relates in his book *In the Footsteps of Big Jim* that after his grandfather's imprisonment and the hardship he had endured in America 'it became obvious that he and Elizabeth had grown apart and could no longer live together,' but that 'for the rest of his life he held her in great affection as she did him.' Her life, he adds, 'had been one of great difficulty as she had, almost single-handedly, raised four sons who all loved their mother.'

The four sons were James (1904–1969), born in Liverpool, Denis (1908–1987), born in Rostrevor, Fintan (spelt Finton on his birth certificate) (1909–1981), and Bernard (1914–1978), both born in Dublin.

Young Jim succeeded his father as general secretary of the Workers' Union of Ireland, while Denis in turn succeeded his brother. Jim was elected to Dublin City Council in 1930 and was a TD for Dublin South-Central from 1943 to 1957. Denis was a member of Dublin City Council from 1947 to 1964 and TD for Dublin North-East for a number of years. He was Lord Mayor of Dublin in 1955.

James Larkin Senior was president of the Irish Trades Union Congress in 1914; Young Jim was also president in 1949 and again in 1952 and president of the Irish Congress of Trade Unions in 1960, while Denis was president of the ICTU in 1974.

Jim's daughter Hilda served for several years on the Executive Council of the ICTU, while Denis's son Jim was an official of the Workers' Union of Ireland, FWUI and SIPTU for many years.

After what was to be Larkin's last visit to Seán O'Casey, the playwright wrote to Jack Carney, their mutual friend and colleague, on 10 January 1946, a few weeks after Elizabeth Larkin's death:

> We said all we could to persuade Jim to stop the night: but he was obstinately determined to go back. He doesn't realise yet that a man of 70 [in fact seventy-two] can't do what a man of 25 can do easily. I daresay, he'll die with harness on his back. Of course, Jim was always religious—in the good sense of the word. I don't think he acted quite justly to Mrs L. After all it must have been a tough job to have been tied to Jim. He had very little time for any home-life. I think he made a mistake in not living with her when he came back [from America]. But I never said so to him—that sort of thing's too private to be discussed with anyone. Of course, he would dream about her, for his mind is full of her now; and all associations would come into the dreams—there's nothing supernatural in these things.

This poignant letter must be the only occasion on which Seán O'Casey ever expressed the least disapproval of his hero, Jim Larkin.

Chapter 58

Songs of Social Revolution

No revolutionary movement is complete without a poetical expression. If such a movement has caught hold of the imagination of the masses, they will seek a vent in song for the aspirations, the fears and hopes, the loves and hatreds engendered by the struggle. Until the movement is marked by the joyous, defiant singing of revolutionary songs, it lacks one of the distinctive marks of a popular revolutionary movement; it is a dogma of a few, and not the faith of the multitude.

So wrote James Connolly in the introduction to his *Songs of Freedom*, published in New York in 1907.

For over a hundred years 'The International', with its rousing music, has been the anthem of the world's workers struggling against exploitation and fighting for a socially just society under the banner of 'Liberty, equality, fraternity':

C'est la lutte finale,
Groupons-nous et demain
L'Internationale sera le genre humain …

Arise, ye starvelings, from your slumbers!
Arise, ye criminals of want!
For reason in revolt now thunders,
And at last ends the age of cant …
Then, comrades, come rally
And the last fight let us face.
The International
Unites the human race.

This song was written by Eugène Pottier in 1871, following the suppression of the Paris Commune; it was set to music by Pierre Degeyter about 1891.[1] It soon became the most popular of songs at workers' demonstrations in France after 'La Marseillaise'. It has been translated into many languages, including Irish, in a translation by Máirtín Ó Cadhain:

Is í an troid scoir í, a bhráithre,
Éirímis chun gnímh,
An tInternational
Snaidhm comhair an chine dhaonna.

Individual countries also have their own labour anthems. In Italy, for example, it is 'Avanti Popolo', also known as 'Bandiera Rossa':

Avanti popolo, a la riscossa,
Bandiera rossa, bandiera rossa.
Avanti popolo, a la riscossa,
Bandiera rossa trionfarà.
Bandiera rossa trionfarà,
Bandiera rossa trionfarà,
Bandiera rossa trionfarà,
Evviva il socialismo e la libertà!

The peoples on the march, the road they're treading
It leads to freedom and liberty.
Our leaders leading, our banners waving,
Victory proceeding towards liberty.

In Ireland, Connolly was to write what became the anthem of the Irish labour movement, 'The Watchword of Labour':

Then send it aloft on the breeze, boys,
The slogan the grandest we've known,
That labour must rise from its knees, boys,
And claim the broad earth as its own.

The verse first appeared in the *Irish Worker* (6 December 1913) as 'Watchword: A Rallying Song for Labour', with music by Frank Doyle. This was a pseudonym of J. J. Hughes (Séamus Hughes), who became an official of the ITGWU in 1917 and was assistant secretary when he resigned in 1921. He later became the first general secretary of Cumann na nGaedheal, the government party up to 1932.

Connolly wrote at least nineteen songs, including 'A Rebel Song', which first appeared in the *Socialist* (Edinburgh) in May 1903; the original music was by G. W. Crawford, a member of the Edinburgh Branch of the Socialist Labour Party. (Connolly was born in Edinburgh, and it was there that he first became active in the socialist movement.) According to Connolly's biographer C. Desmond Greaves, 'A Rebel Song' became the marching song of the young Scottish socialist rebels whose enthusiasm inspired it.

Then sing a rebel song, as we proudly sweep along,
To end the age-long tyranny that makes for human tears;
Our march is nearer done with each setting of the sun,
And the tyrant's might is passing with the passing of the years.

Another of Connolly's songs was 'Slaves of Toil':

O, slaves of toil, no craven fear
Nor dread of fell disasters
Need daunt ye now, then up, and clear
The earth of lords and masters.

Apart from 'The Watchword of Labour', Connolly's best-known song is 'Be Moderate', one verse of which is:

Some men faint-hearted ever seek
Our programme to retouch
And will insist when e'er they speak
That we demand too much.
'Tis passing strange, yet I declare
Such statements cause me mirth,
For our demands most modest are:
We only want the earth.[2]

Another of Connolly's songs is 'Freedom's Pioneers', which appeared in 1904 after he had settled in America.[3]

Oh, slaves may cringe and cowards whine,
We scorn their foolish fears,
Be this our plan, to lead the van
With Freedom's Pioneers.

In England the best known of workers' rallying songs was, of course, 'The Red Flag':

Then raise the scarlet standard high—
Within its shade we'll live and die!
Though cowards flinch and traitors sneer,
We'll keep the Red Flag flying here!

'The Red Flag' was written by Jim Connell, who was born in Kilskyre, County Meath, in 1852; it was first published in the Christmas 1889 edition of *Justice*, the paper of the Social Democratic Federation. Connell told Tom Mann that in writing it he had been inspired by the Paris Commune, the heroism of the Russian nihilists, the firmness of the Irish Land League, and the devotion to death of the Chicago anarchists. The immediate occasion was the great London dock strike of 1889 for the 'dockers' tanner.'[4]

In Liverpool, his native city, James Larkin would have been familiar with songs and ballads about the workers' struggles, such as 'The Red Flag' and 'The Song of the Lower Classes' by the Chartist Ernest Jones:

Our place we know, we're so very very low,
'Tis down at the landlord's feet:
We're not too low the grain to sow
But too low the bread to eat.

Larkin, with his love of poetry, would have been even more familiar with the poems of William Morris, such as 'The March of the Workers':

What is this, the sound and rumour? What is this that all men hear
Like the wind in hollow valleys when the storm is drawing near,

Like the rolling on of ocean in the eventide of fear?
  'Tis the people marching on.

Hark the rolling of the thunder!
Lo the sun! and lo thereunder
Riseth wrath, and hope, and wonder,
  And the host comes marching on.

—or Percy Bysshe Shelley's 'Mask of Anarchy'[5]:

Rise like lions after slumber
In unvanquishable number,
Shake your chains to earth like dew
Which in sleep has fallen on you.
Ye are many—they are few.

Larkin regularly quoted from Morris and Shelley in his speeches and in the *Irish Worker*. Seán O'Casey wrote in the *Irish Times* on the day after Larkin's death that Larkin was 'the first man in Ireland—and, perhaps, in England, too—who brought poetry into the workers' fight for a better life.' Larkin, he added, had 'the eloquence of an Elizabethan, fascinating to all who heard him, and irresistible to the workers. He was familiar with the poetry of Shakespeare, Walt Whitman, Shelley and Omar Khayyam, and often quoted them in his speeches.'

It was in the United States, however, that the finest flowering of workers' songs of protest took place, especially following the setting up of the Industrial Workers of the World, the 'Wobblies', in 1905. This was particularly true of the second decade of the century, when Larkin was in America. Foremost among the song-writers known as Labour's troubadours of song were Joe Hill and Ralph Chaplin, with both of whom Larkin was associated. Joe Hill was to be executed, and both Chaplin and Larkin were to serve terms of imprisonment.[6]

Among Joe Hill's best-known songs are 'Workers of the World, Awaken', 'Casey Jones—the Union Scab', and 'The Rebel Girl'. These three songs are included in the selection of songs, poems and ballads at the end of this chapter.

Ralph Chaplin's best-known song is 'Solidarity Forever', written in 1915 and sung to the air of 'The Battle Hymn of the Republic'. It soon became the anthem of the IWW; in the thirties it became the organising song of the Congress of Industrial Organisations.

In our hands is placed a power greater than their hoarded gold,
Greater than the might of armies, magnified a thousand-fold.
We can bring to birth a new world from the ashes of the old.
For the Union makes us strong.

Two other songs of Ralph Chaplin's may be mentioned. The first verse and chorus of 'Commonwealth of Toil' are as follows:

In the gloom of mighty cities
'Mid the roar of whirling wheels
We are toiling on like chattel slaves of old,
And our masters hope to keep us
Ever thus beneath their heels
And to coin our very life blood into gold.

But we have a glowing dream
Of how fair the world will seem
When each man can live his life secure and free;
When the earth is owned by Labor
And there's joy and peace for all
In the Commonwealth of Toil that is to be.

The second song was written by Ralph Chaplin in Leavenworth Prison,
'All Hell Can't Stop Us':

Down with greed and exploitation!
Tyranny must fall!
Hail to Toil's emancipation
Labour shall be all.

Scorn to take the crumbs they drop us
All is ours by right!
Onward, men! All Hell can't stop us!
Crush the parasite!

The main creed of the IWW was summed up in its Preamble:

The working class and the employing class have nothing in common. There
can be no peace so long as hunger and want are found among millions of
working people and the few, who make up the employing class, have all the
good things of life. Between these two classes a struggle must go on until
the workers of the world organise as a class ... and abolish the wage system
... We must inscribe in our banner the revolutionary watchword, 'Abolition
of the wage system.' It is the historic mission of the working class to do
away with capitalism ... By organizing industrially we are forming the
structure of the new society in the shell of the old.

A famous American song that has been adopted as the anthem of women
trade unionists is 'Bread and Roses'. The song came out of a famous strike
in 1912,[7] one of the leaders of which was the 22-year-old Elizabeth Gurley
Flynn, whose mother, Annie Gurley, a colleague and friend of Connolly's in
New York, was born in Loughrea, County Galway, and whose paternal
grandfather was also Irish-born. She was the Rebel Girl for whom Joe Hill
wrote his famous song. (More about her will be found in chapter 38.)

On their marches the women strikers at the Lawrence textile mills
carried banners with the slogan *We want bread and roses too*, and it was this
that inspired James Oppenheim to write the song, the music for which was
composed by Caroline Kohlsaat.

Our lives shall not be sweated
From birth until life closes;
Hearts starve as well as bodies:
Give us bread, but give us roses.

Finally, another American song, 'The Banner of Labor', first published in October 1908, author unknown. It was sung to the tune of 'The Star-Spangled Banner'.

Oh, say, can you hear, coming near and more near
The call now resounding: 'Come all ye who labor?'
The Industrial Band, throughout all the land
Bids toilers remember, each toiler's his neighbor.
Come, workers, unite! 'tis Humanity's fight.
We call you come forth in your manhood and might.
And the Banner of Labor will surely soon wave
O'er the land that is free, from the master and slave.

Larkin, like Connolly, was a socialist revolutionary and an internationalist. These songs of protest and social revolution expressed in a general way their world view and reflect the world as they experienced it in the first decades of the century.

The March of the Workers

William Morris

What is this, the sound and rumour? What is this that all men hear,
Like the wind in hollow valleys when the storm is drawing near,
Like the rolling on of ocean in the eventide of fear?
    'Tis the people marching on.

Whither go they, and whence come they? What are these of whom ye tell?
In what country are they dwelling 'twixt the gates of Heaven and Hell?
Are they mine or thine for money? Will they serve a master well?
    Still the rumour's marching on.

Hark the rolling of the thunder!
Lo the sun! and lo thereunder
Riseth wrath, and hope, and wonder,
    And the host comes marching on.

Forth they come from grief and torment; on they wend towards health and
    mirth,
All the wide world is their dwelling, every corner of the earth.
Buy them, sell them, for thy service! Try the bargain what 'tis worth,
    For the days are marching on.

493

These are they who build thy houses, weave thy raiment, win thy wheat,
Smooth the rugged, fill the barren, turn the bitter into sweet,
All for thee this day—and ever. What reward for them is meet
    Till the host comes marching on?

Many a hundred years passed over have they laboured deaf and blind;
Never tidings reached their sorrow, never hope their toil might find.
Now at last they've heard and hear it, and the cry comes down the wind,
    And their feet are marching on.

O ye rich men, hear and tremble! for with words the sound is rife:
'Once for you and earth we laboured; changed henceforward is the strife.
We are men, and we shall battle for the world of men and life;
    And our host is marching on.'

'Is it war, then? Will ye perish as the dry wood in the fire?
Is it peace? Then be ye of us, let your hope be our desire.
Come and live! for life awaketh, and the world shall never tire;
    And hope is marching on.'

'On we march then, we the workers, and the rumour that ye hear
Is the blended sound of battle and deliv'rance drawing near;
For the hope of every creature is the banner that we bear,
    And the world is marching on.'

The Red Flag

Jim Connell

The people's flag is deepest red,
It shrouded oft our martyr'd dead,
And ere their limbs grew stiff and cold,
Their heart's blood dyed its every fold.

Then raise the scarlet standard high—
Within its shade we'll live and die!
Though cowards flinch and traitors sneer,
We'll keep the Red Flag flying here!

Look round!—the Frenchman loves its blaze,
The sturdy German chants its praise;
In Moscow's vaults its hymns are sung,
Chicago swells the surging song.

It waved above our infant might
When all ahead seemed dark as night;
It witnessed many a deed and vow—
We must not change its colour now!

It well recalls the triumphs past,
It gives the hope of peace at last;
The banner bright—the symbol plain
Of human right and human gain.

It suits today the weak and base,
Whose minds are fixed on pelf and place,
To cringe before the rich man's frown
And haul the sacred emblem down.

With head uncovered swear we all
To bear it onward till we fall;
Come dungeon dark or gallows grim,
This song shall be our parting hymn.

Solidarity Forever

Ralph Chaplin

When the union's inspiration through the workers' blood shall run,
There can be no power greater anywhere beneath the sun.
Yet what force on earth is weaker than the feeble strength of one?
But the union makes us strong.

   Solidarity forever!
   Solidarity forever!
   Solidarity forever!
   For the union makes us strong.

All the world that's owned by idle drones is ours and ours alone,
We have laid the wide foundations; built it skyward stone by stone,
It is ours not to slave in but to master and to own,
While the union makes us strong.

They have taken untold millions that they never toiled to earn,
But without our brains and muscle not a single wheel can turn,
We can break their haughty power, gain our freedom when we learn
That the union makes us strong.

In our hands is placed a power greater than their hoarded gold;
Greater than the might of armies, magnified a thousand-fold.
We can bring to birth a new world from the ashes of the old,
For the union makes us strong.

Bread and Roses

James Oppenheim

As we come marching, marching,
In the beauty of the day,
A million darkened kitchens,
A thousand mill lofts gray,
Are touched with all the radiance
That a sudden sun discloses,
For the people hear us singing,
'Bread and roses, Bread and roses.'

As we come marching, marching,
We battle too for men,
For they are women's children,
And we mother them again.
Our lives shall not be sweated
From birth until life closes,
Hearts starve as well as bodies:
Give us bread, but give us roses.

As we come marching, marching,
Unnumbered women dead
Go crying through our singing
Their ancient cry for bread.
Small art and love and beauty
Their drudging spirits knew.
Yes, it is bread we fight for—
But we fight for roses, too!

As we come marching, marching,
We bring the greater days;
The rising of the women means
The rising of the race.
No more the drudge and idler—
Ten that toil where one reposes,
But a sharing of life's glories:
Bread and roses! Bread and roses!

Workers of the World, Awaken

Joe Hill

Workers of the World, awaken
Break your chains, demand your rights
All the wealth you make is taken
By exploiting parasites.
Shall ye kneel in deep submission
From your cradle to your graves?
Is the height of your ambition
To be good and willing slaves?

> Arise, ye pris'ners of starvation
> Fight for your own Emancipation
> Unite, ye slaves of ev'ry nation
> In One Union Grand
> Our little ones for bread are crying
> And millions are from hunger dying
> The end the means are justifying
> 'Tis the final stand.

If the workers take a notion
They can stop all speeding trains
Every ship upon the ocean
They can tie with mighty chains
Every wheel in the creation
Every mine and every mill
Fleets and armies of the nation
Will at their command stand still.

Join the Union, Fellow-Workers,
Men and women side by side,
We will crush the greedy shirkers
Like a sweeping surging tide.
For united we are standing
But divided we will fall;
Let this be our understanding:
All for One and One for All

Workers of the World, awaken,
Rise in all your splendid might,
Take the wealth which you are making,
It belongs to you by right.
No one will for bread be crying,
We'll have Freedom, Love and Health
When the Grand Red Flag is flying
In the Workers' Commonwealth.

Casey Jones—the Union Scab

Joe Hill

The workers on the S.P. line to strike sent out a call;
But Casey Jones, the engineer, he wouldn't strike at all;
His boiler it was leaking and its drivers on the bum,
And his engine and its bearings they were all out of plumb.

Casey Jones kept his junk pile running;
Casey Jones was working double time;
Casey Jones got a wooden medal,
For being good and faithful on the S.P. line.

The workers said to Casey: 'Won't you help us win this strike?'
But Casey said: 'Let me alone, you'd better take a hike.'
Then Casey's wheezy engine ran right off the worn-out track,
And Casey hit the river with an awful crack.

Casey Jones hit the river bottom;
Casey Jones broke his blooming spine;
Casey Jones was an Angeleno,
He took a trip to heaven on the S.P. line.

When Casey Jones got up to Heaven to the Pearly Gate,
He said: 'I'm Casey Jones, the guy that pulled the S.P. freight.'
'You're just the man,' said Peter, 'our musicians went on strike;
You can get a job a-scabbing any time you like.'

Casey Jones got a job in Heaven;
Casey Jones was doing mighty fine;
Casey Jones went scabbing on the angels,
Just like he did to workers on the S.P. line.

The angels got together and they said it wasn't fair
For Casey Jones to go around a-scabbing everywhere.
The Angel Union No. 23 they sure were there,
And they promptly fired Casey down the Golden Stair.

Casey Jones went to Hell a-flying;
'Casey Jones,' the Devil said, 'Oh fine;
Casey Jones, get busy shoveling sulphur—
That's what you get for scabbing on the S.P. line.'

The Rebel Girl

Joe Hill

There are women of many descriptions
In this queer world as every one knows
Some are living in beautiful mansions
And are wearing the finest of clothes.
There are blue-blooded queens and princesses
Who have charms made of diamonds and pearl
But the only and thoroughbred lady
Is the Rebel Girl.

> That's the Rebel Girl,
> That's the Rebel girl,
> To the working class she's a precious pearl
> She brings courage, pride and joy
> To the fighting Rebel Boy
> We've had girls before but we need some more
> In the Industrial Workers of the World
> For it's great to fight for freedom
> With a Rebel Girl.

Yes, her hands may be harden'd from labor
And her dress may not be very fine
But a heart! in her bosom is beating
That is true to her class and her kind
And the grafters in terror are trembling
When her spite and defiance she'll hurl
For the only and thoroughbred lady
Is the Rebel Girl.

The Commonwealth of Toil

Ralph Chaplin

In the gloom of mighty cities
'Mid the roar of whirling wheels
We are toiling on like chattel slaves of old,
And our masters hope to keep us
Ever thus beneath their heels
And to coin our very life blood into gold.

But we have a glowing dream
Of how fair the world will seem
When each man can live his life secure and free;
When the earth is owned by Labor
And there's joy and peace for all
In the Commonwealth of Toil that is to be.

They would keep us cowed and beaten
Cringing meekly at their feet.
They would stand between each worker and his bread.
Shall we yield our lives up to them
For the bitter crust we eat?
Shall we only hope for heaven when we're dead?

They have laid our lives out for us
To the utter end of time.
Shall we stagger on beneath their heavy load?
Shall we let them live forever
In their gilded halls of crime
With our children doomed to toil beneath their goad?

When our cause is all triumphant
And we claim our Mother Earth,
And the nightmare of the present fades away,
We shall live with Love and Laughter,
We, who now are little worth,
And we'll not regret the price we have to pay.

All Hell Can't Stop Us

Ralph Chaplin

Now the final battle rages;
Tyrants quake with fear.
Rulers of the New Dark Ages
Know their end is near.

Scorn to take the crumbs they drop us,
All is ours by right!
Onward, men! All Hell can't stop us!
Crush the parasite!

With a world-wide revolution
Bring them to their feet!
They of crime and persecution—
They must work to eat!

Tear the mask of lies asunder,
Let the truth be known,
With a voice like angry thunder
Rise and claim your own!

Down with greed and exploitation!
Tyranny must fall!
Hail to Toil's emancipation!
Labor shall be all.

Stand Up! Ye Workers

Ethel Comer

Stand up! Stand up! Ye workers;
Stand up in all your might.
Unite beneath our banner,
For liberty and right.
From victory unto victory
This army sure will go,
To win the world for labor
And vanquish every foe.

Stand up! Stand up! Ye workers;
Stand up in every land.
Unite, and fight for freedom
In ONE BIG UNION grand.
Put on the workers' armor
Which is the card of Red,
Then all the greedy tyrants
Will have to earn their bread.

Arouse! Arouse! Ye toilers,
The strife will not be long.
This day the noise of battle,
The next the victor's song.
All ye that slave for wages,
Stand up and break your chain:
Unite in ONE BIG UNION—
You've got a world to gain.

Union Maid

Woody Guthrie

There once was a union maid
Who never was afraid
Of the goons and the ginks and the company finks
And the deputy sheriff who made the raid.
She'd go to the union hall
When a meeting it was called,
And when the company guards came 'round
She always stood her ground.

> Oh you can't scare me, I'm stickin' to the union,
> I'm stickin' to the union, I'm stickin' to the union,
> Oh you can't scare me, I'm stickin' to the union,
> I'm stickin' to the union 'til the day I die.

501

This union maid was wise
To the tricks of the company spies,
She'd never be fooled by the company stools,
She'd always organize the guys.
She'd always get her way
When she struck for higher pay,
She'd show her card to the National Guard,
And this is what she'd say—

A woman's struggle is hard
Even with a union card,
She's got to stand on her own two feet,
And not be a servant of a male elite.
It's time to take a stand,
Keep working hand in hand,
There is a job that's got to be done
And a fight that's got to be won.

Hold the Fort

We meet today in Freedom's cause
And raise our voices high;
We'll join our hands in union strong,
To battle or to die.

Hold the fort, for we are coming—
Union men, be strong.
Side by side we battle onward,
Victory will come.

Look, my Comrades, see the union
Banners waving high.
Reinforcements now appearing,
Victory is nigh.

See our numbers still increasing;
Hear the bugles blow.
By our union we shall triumph
Over every foe.

Fierce and long the battle rages,
But we will not fear,
Help will come whene'er it's needed,
Cheer, my Comrades, cheer.

Chapter 59

Larkin Commemoration, 1997

Since James Larkin's death in 1947, an annual Larkin Commemoration has been held in Dublin, organised by, in turn, the Workers' Union of Ireland, the Federated Workers' Union of Ireland, and, since 1990, SIPTU, the union resulting from the merger of the ITGWU and FWUI. For the fiftieth anniversary of Larkin's death special commemoration events were organised by the Larkin Commemoration Committee of SIPTU.[1]

The fiftieth anniversary Mass, in St Saviour's Church, Dominick Street, Dublin, was celebrated on 26 January 1997 by Monsignor Arthur Bradley, Father Austin Flannery, and Father Henry Peel.

Two of the readings were by James Larkin's grandchildren. Stella Larkin McConnon read from Luke's Gospel (1:46–55), the Magnificat, and Jim Larkin read from Paul's Epistle to James (2:14–18). The Gospel reading was from Matthew (5:1–12), the Sermon on the Mount.

The homily was given by Father Henry Peel:

> It was Seán O'Casey who wrote: 'There was a man sent from God whose name was Jim. That man was Larkin.' I think that the adaptation of the text is appropriate, for there was something about Larkin that evokes the image of an Old Testament prophet. One might, indeed, continue the adaptation: 'What went ye out to see. A reed shaken by the wind? But what went ye out to see? A man clothed in soft garment? Those who are clothed in soft garments live in palaces. But what went ye out to see. A prophet?'
>
> In his fierce denunciation of injustice, Larkin evokes the image of a prophet from the Old Testament. He does the same in his championing of the cause of the poor, the downtrodden, and the oppressed—themes which resonate also in the Beatitudes. An adversary said of Larkin: 'I don't know how you can argue with that fellow Larkin. You can't argue with the Prophet Isaiah.' Larkin proclaimed himself as having come on a divine mission of discontent. And in a memorable phrase he said: 'Christ will not continue to be crucified on the streets of Dublin.'
>
> Prophets, notoriously, are disturbing and difficult people. Small wonder that people stone the prophets! I doubt if any of us can listen to the Beatitudes without a sense of unease. When he was accused of being Antichrist, Larkin said that he spoke and acted in the spirit of the Beatitudes.
>
> Being denounced from the pulpit does not make one a sinner, no more than being praised from the pulpit makes one a saint. Larkin certainly does not conform to the conventional image of a holy man. It could be, of course, that it is our imagery that is faulty. Larkin certainly was a man who hungered and thirsted for what is right.
>
> To hunger and thirst for what is right means to long for it as someone who is starving longs for food. To hunger and thirst for what is right means to long for it as someone who is dying of thirst longs for a drink. Our Lord says that such people are blessed. The blessing is not because of what they

achieve or fail to achieve: it is because of what is in the heart. God and God alone judges the heart.

On the day of judgment the Lord will say to the righteous: 'Come whom my Father has blessed. For I was hungry and you gave me food; thirsty and you gave me drink; a stranger and you made me welcome. I was naked and you clothed me; sick and in prison and you came to visit me.' And the just will say: 'Lord, when did we see you hungry and gave you food; thirsty and gave you drink; a stranger and made you welcome. When did we see you naked and clothed you; sick and in prison and came to visit you?' And the Lord will say: 'As long as you did it to the least of these you did it to me.'

I am sure that Jim Larkin has heard these words spoken to him by the Lord.

The Mass was followed by a wreath-laying ceremony at Larkin's grave in Glasnevin Cemetery, where addresses were given by Jimmy Somers, vice-president of SIPTU, and Jack Harte, chairperson of the Larkin Commemoration Committee.

Lectures

The Larkin Commemoration Lecture, 'James Larkin: Labour Leader,' was delivered on 30 January 1997, the fiftieth anniversary of his death, in Liberty Hall, Dublin, by Dr Emmet Larkin, professor of British and Irish history at the University of Chicago. The lecture was chaired by the general secretary of SIPTU, William A. Attley.

The Larkin Commemoration by the Irish Congress of Trade Unions was held during the biennial delegate conference on 3 July 1997. At the commemoration, which was held in the Assembly Hall of Transport House, High Street, Belfast, talks were given by John Gray, Librarian of the Linen Hall Library, Belfast ('Larkin in Belfast, 1907'), and by Donal Nevin, former general secretary, ICTU ('Big Jim: Orator, Agitator, Revolutionary'). John Freeman, the president of Congress, chaired the talks.

In his introduction, John Freeman remarked that no location in Ireland could be more fitted to honour Big Jim than Belfast.

It was here in Belfast that Larkin experienced the horrors that the absence of organisation among the unskilled workers created; here that he recognised that division and sectarianism were the major difficulties to be overcome in the struggle for workers' liberation; here that Larkin joined the workers of the Falls and the Shankill in a united programme for workers' rights. It was just across the road from Transport House, at the famous Custom House steps, that the fiery voice of Larkin was first heard in Ireland defending workers' right to be union members.

Transport House stands on the spot where Larkin organised the workers and led the strike in 1907. The first general secretary of the Transport and General Workers' Union, Ernie Bevin, who became the British Foreign Secretary in 1945, insisted that if the corner site ever became available it was to be purchased by the union for its Irish head office as a memorial to Larkin. It was after Bevin's death that the site was purchased by the union and Transport House built. It is now a designated building, both because of its nineteen-fifties architecture and its association with Larkin.

504

Salute to Big Jim

As part of the Larkin fiftieth anniversary commemoration, SIPTU presented 'Salute to Big Jim', a celebration in poetry, prose, music, and song, in Liberty Hall, Dublin, on 30 January 1997, the anniversary of Larkin's death, and in Transport House, Belfast, on 3 July 1997. The programme was devised by Donal Nevin.[2]

'Salute to Big Jim' opened symbolically with the Song of the Hebrew Slaves from act 3 of *Nabucco* by Giuseppe Verdi:

Let our plea rise to thee, Jehovah;
Hear at last the voice of thy people
And lead thy people home.

It was followed by a recording by Marc Ogeret of 'L'Internationale' in French.

Readings included articles and addresses by Jim Larkin, read by Emmet Bergin in Dublin and Ian McElhinney in Belfast. These were: 'We are living in stirring times' from the *Irish Worker* (12 August 1911); his speech to the Askwith Commission of Inquiry in Dublin Castle (5 October 1913), 'Christ will not be crucified any longer in Dublin by these men'; his address at the memorial service for Joe Hill in Chicago (25 November 1915), 'Though dead in flesh, he liveth among us'; and an extract from Larkin's address to the jury at his trial in New York (23 April 1920), 'And then I had occasion to go out in the world and found there was no fatherhood of God, and there was no brotherhood of man.'

Other readings were from Seán O'Casey (*Drums under the Windows*: 'Through the streets he strode …'); the *Irish Times*, 31 January and 1 February 1947 ('The lion will roar no more'); James Connolly (*Forward*, 4 October 1913, and *Irish Worker*, 18 November 1914: 'Glorious Dublin'); George Russell (from his speech in the Albert Hall, London, 1 November 1913: 'Humanity, long dumb, has found a voice'); John Swift (from his presidential address to the Irish Trades Union Congress, 29 July 1947: 'Then came Larkin …'); and Liam Mac Gabhann ('Big Jim crosses the city').[3]

The ballads sung included 'In Dublin City in 1913' (Donagh MacDonagh) and 'Who Fears to Wear the Blood-Red Badge', both sung by Jimmy Kelly, and 'Jim Larkin, RIP', sung by Manus O'Riordan, who also set to music and sang Frank O'Connor's poem 'Homage to Jim Larkin'.

The poems read were 'To Jim Larkin' by Lola Ridge, read in Dublin by Mary Maher and in Belfast by Marie Jones; 'Jim Larkin' by Patrick Kavanagh, read in Dublin by Macdara Woods and in Belfast by Marie Jones; and 'Jim Larkin' by Brendan Behan, read by Manus O'Riordan with his English translation.

Other items on the programme in Dublin and Belfast were harp solos played by Brenda Ní Ríordáin and tunes on the uilleann pipes played by Noel Pocock.

There were recordings of 'I Dreamed I Saw Joe Hill Last Night', sung by Paul Robeson, and 'The Red Flag', recorded by Kathleen Behan when she was ninety-two. In the Belfast programme there was also an excerpt from an archive recording of the 1976 production of James Plunkett's *The Risen People* at the Lyric Players' Theatre, directed by Mary O'Malley, in which Larkin was played by Liam Neeson, as well as 'Bread and Roses', sung by Eileen Webster.

The Dublin performance of 'Salute to Big Jim' concluded with the playing of James Connolly's 'The Watchword of Labour' by the SIPTU Band and in Belfast with the singing of 'The Red Flag' to the air of 'The White Cockade' (to which Jim Connell intended the anthem to be sung).

Larkin Exhibition

An exhibition, 'SIPTU Tribute to James Larkin: Orator, Agitator, Revolutionary, Trade Union Leader', was opened by the Taoiseach, Bertie Ahern TD, in the National Library of Ireland, Dublin, on 25 September 1997. The exhibition patron was Mary Robinson, President of Ireland. In opening the exhibition, Bertie Ahern said:

> Every time I pass by that great statue by Oisín Kelly in O'Connell Street I think of the words of Dean Swift: 'Positiveness is a good quality for preachers and orators, because whoever would obtrude his thoughts and reasons upon a multitude, will convince them the more, as he appears convinced himself.'
>
> That is the picture of Big Jim Larkin which leaps out at us from the early black-and-white photographs from the time of the Dublin lock-out in 1913. That's the picture we have of him, two hands aloft, convincing the cheering crowd.
>
> I was very privileged, I believe, in that I was once an active member of Jim Larkin's union, the Workers' Union of Ireland, because Jim Larkin's name will always be remembered for his magnificent leadership of the Dublin workers during the epic struggle of 1913.
>
> From then on, employers had to concede that workers had rights and were entitled to human dignity. The 1913 lock-out was a great uprising by one-third of the people of Dublin, revolting against the quality of their lives and the denial of basic rights.
>
> Larkin had no narrow, parochial or insular approach to fighting injustice. In Belfast, as in Dublin, Cork, Sligo, Wexford, England, and America, he brought his extraordinary talents of oratory to the cause of emancipating the working class.
>
> Larkin's legacy is enduring and continues to give enlightened insights to today's generation of the sacrifices made by those who pioneered most of the liberties we now enjoy as a people and take for granted.
>
> In conclusion, may I quote the words of James Connolly in 1914. He said: 'We have amongst us a man of genius, of splendid vitality, great in his conceptions, magnificent in his courage.' These words of praise refer, of course, to Big Jim Larkin, and I agree fully with the sentiments expressed so pithily by one of our greatest working-class heroes and republicans.

The exhibition was in thirteen main sections: the Larkin family; Belfast, 1907; the ITGWU and the Irish Trades Union Congress; Dublin: Tenement City; 1913; Delia Larkin and the Irish Women Workers' Union; the Irish

Citizen Army; the Road to Sing Sing; Return to Strife-Riven Ireland; Larkin in Russia; the Workers' Union of Ireland; Larkin's Later Years; Larkin Dead, Larkin Lives. These sections in the Exhibition Room included 147 pictures and 56 texts. The design was by Caroline Moloney.

In the library entrance hall were sculptures and plaques, banners and posters, artefacts and memorabilia, books about Larkin, Larkin in drama and poetry, copies of the *Irish Worker*, documents, leaflets, and anniversary programmes. Notable among the artefacts were an inscribed gold watch presented to Larkin by the Belfast Branch of the National Union of Dock Labourers in 1907 (purchased at auction by the Workers' Union of Ireland in 1982), one of Big Jim's pipes, and the originals of letters from Seán O'Casey and George Bernard Shaw. Among the books displayed were two sent by James Larkin from Sing Sing to his son Jim: *Ancient Society* by Lewis Morgan and *The Republic of Plato*, on which he had inscribed the words 'This is a grate book' and 'This is a classic.'[4]

Larkin Plaque

On 2 September 1997 the Lord Mayor of Dublin, Councillor John Stafford, with W. A. Attley, general secretary of SIPTU, unveiled a plaque at 41 Wellington Road, Ballsbridge, where James Larkin lived for thirteen years, from 1934 to 1947.

Red Roses for Me

The final event in SIPTU's fiftieth anniversary celebration was the production in Liberty Hall, Dublin, on 28–31 January 1998 of Seán O'Casey's play *Red Roses for Me*. The play is based on a railway strike in 1911 in which the playwright was involved, making the play partly autobiographical. Published in 1942, it is suffused with the spirit of Larkin and Larkinism. The play was presented by Red Rose Productions and directed by Conor O'Malley. Mrs Breydon was played by Frances Blackburn and Ayamonn Breydon by Kevin Forsythe.[5]

The programme note for the performances of *Red Roses for Me* recounted the connections of the old Liberty Hall with drama. In June 1912 the *Irish Worker* announced the start of a dramatic class, and on St Stephen's Night the Irish Workers' Dramatic Company, founded by Delia Larkin, made its debut in Liberty Hall. The first programme included one-act plays by three Abbey Theatre playwrights: Rutherford Mayne, Séamus Kelly, and A. Patrick Wilson.

On occasions in Liberty Hall such as Citizen Army social gatherings, according to Seán O'Casey, 'the audience would imperiously demand a song from Big Jim, who, after some coaxing would, like the shy boy he sometimes was, sing in hoarse and tremulous voice amid a tense and reverent silence, The Red Flag or The Risin' o' the Moon.'

One of two plays written by James Connolly, *Under Which Flag?*, had its first (and only) production by the Workers' Dramatic Company in Liberty Hall on 26 March 1916. It was reviewed by Francis Sheehy-Skeffington in the *Workers' Republic* on 8 April 1916. The play, he wrote, 'breathes the true spirit of patriotism ... The dialogue was excellent, the parts competently filled while the dancers executed theirs with zest.' He singled out as the best-acted role the part of the blind man, taken by an Abbey actor, Seán Connolly. Within nine weeks of the production in Liberty Hall, Seán Connolly, a captain in the Irish Citizen Army, was dead, the first casualty of the Easter Rising; Francis Sheehy-Skeffington was murdered by a British officer in Portobello Barracks; James Connolly was shot by firing squad in Kilmainham Jail; and Liberty Hall had been all but destroyed by shelling from the gunboat *Helga*.

The script of Connolly's play, long believed to be lost, was discovered in the National Library in 1969, and on 13 May that year it was read in the new Liberty Hall by an Abbey Theatre cast: Máire Ní Dhomhnaill, Bernadette McKenna, Peadar Lamb, Patrick O'Callaghan, John Kavanagh, and Éamonn Kelly. It was directed by Alan Simpson.

Special programmes for 'Salute to Big Jim', the Larkin Exhibition and the production of *Red Roses for Me* were designed by Séamas Sheils and produced by SIPTU. On the back cover of the programme for *Red Roses for Me* was reproduced, for the first time, Gerard Dillon's poster for the first Abbey Theatre production of the play in 1967.

Impressions of an exhibition

Ulick O'Connor

We wait for the Taoiseach, Bertie Ahern, to open this 'SIPTU Tribute to James Larkin' Exhibition after he has opened the new National Museum in Arbour Hill. But the story is around that there's an official trade union picket on that multi-million-pound edifice. Will Bertie pass the picket? is the question among the many trade union officials gathered in the foyer of the National Library. A cheer went up as we saw Ahern's head moving through the crowd at the door. He hadn't gone within a mile of Arbour Hill. 'Stanch' is the word Dubliners use.

As the Taoiseach spoke in the foyer one thought of how Larkin himself would have relished the idea of being commemorated in the National Library, where he had sat in the same Reading Room used by James Stephens, Seán O'Casey, Pádraic Colum, Æ, and Yeats.

After the speech we troop upstairs to the exhibition. It is laid out in chronological order, evoking through texts, photographs and memorabilia images of Larkin's life as selected by Donal Nevin, who has devised the presentation.

In the first display case is a photograph of Delia Larkin, who founded the Irish Women Workers' Union in 1911 and ran the soup kitchens in Liberty Hall during the 1913 lock-out. She had a Larkin organising gift and in this picture bears an uncanny resemblance to Gareth Peirce, the English solicitor who worked so courageously to free the innocent Birmingham Six.

Next there is a copy of a portrait by the artist Sir William Orpen of William Martin Murphy, who led the Dublin business cabal against Larkin in 1913. The comment beneath of the English poet G. K. Chesterton sums up perfectly the personality which Orpen has captured on canvas: 'More like some morbid Prince of the fifteenth century, full of cold anger, but not without perverted piety.'

Next we see Larkin on his first visit to Ireland, in Belfast in 1907 (he was born in Liverpool of County Down parents). Here he is haranguing a crowd. By 1909 he had founded the Irish Transport and General Workers' Union in Dublin. A photograph of the Irish TUC executive committee outside the City Hall in Dublin shows Larkin in the middle and William O'Brien and Thomas MacPartlin, earnest socialists, on either side. As earnest as Larkin, one wonders, or that small man standing at the back of the photograph, slightly apart, who would meet his death, though badly wounded, from a firing squad in Kilmainham a few years later—an event described with Swiftian savagery by the poet Monk Gibbon, who noted that James Connolly's captors had provided the prisoner 'with the amenity of a chair so that he could be shot sitting up.'

There are two display cases devoted to the 1913 lock-out. The famous photograph is here with the fleeing workers looking like a Lowry painting gone demented, an image for posterity, the baton crushing the cloth cap. As the DMP had refused to take on the job, RIC men from the country had been drafted in. They were armed (unlike the DMP) and accustomed to dealing with stroppy peasants, evictions, rascally Fenians. Jim is seen here being carted away by two bobbies after he had slipped in (disguised as an old man) to the Imperial Hotel in O'Connell Street to address the crowd from a window. From their point of view the British were right to arrest Big Jim. He could ignite words so that his phrases spread like a flame through the mass mind. Men such as Larkin can undo an empire.

'Big Jim': the words toll us back like a bell to the suffering of the workers during the lock-out. William Orpen (he who had painted William Martin Murphy's portrait) came down to Liberty Hall to serve Larkin soup to the hungry. While he was at it he did a remarkable sketch of the big man. The Countess (Constance Markievicz) is here too, not yet in her Citizen Army commandant's uniform but doing one of the things her landed gentry upbringing had taught her to do well, organising meals. Her photograph in the case in front of me brings out, as many other snaps fail to, her rare beauty. Constance, they say, had a soft spot for Séamus eile; more luck to him.

Captain Jack White's photograph is in the same display case as Constance. He was an Ulsterman who won a DSO in the Boer War, where his father, Sir George White, had entered history as the defender of Ladysmith. An image comes to the mind's eye of a room in Trinity College where Jack White is making a proposal to raise an army to defend the Dublin workers. He would see that they are trained by the best military standards. These are the rooms of a clergyman, R. M. Gwynn, from a famous Trinity family (someone once suggested that it should be called Gwynnity College). The treasurer of the new army will be the Countess, while the secretary will be Seán O'Casey. Seán will later write the history of this Citizen Army.

Jim's visit to America is well documented in the next two cases. He had only meant to stay a short while to raise money for his union; but he was to become a leading figure in American socialism, along with Eugene Debs, Bill Haywood, Elizabeth Gurley Flynn, Emma Goldman, and other stalwarts of the Industrial Workers of the World.

Such was Larkin's status in the United States that he was chosen to give the oration at the funeral of Joe Hill, who was executed on a trumped-up charge in Utah in 1915. Here is a photograph of Jim in full oratorical flight. Never a man to waste a good phrase caught on the wing, Jim had adapted a well-worn phrase of his about the Dublin slums to an American setting. 'The ruling classes', he told the mourners, 'crucified Joe Hill on their cross of gold, and spilt his blood on the altar of their God, Profit.' Larkin himself might have spoken Joe Hill's last admonition: 'Don't mourn. Organise.'

In the nineteen-seventies, wherever I went in the United States I found Larkin's name still revered by American socialists and activists of the civil rights movement. James T. Farrell, the novelist, author of *Studs Lonigan*, and, like Larkin, a member of the American Communist Party, would occasionally reminisce about the big man's oratory and once remarked to me in relation to the 1913 lock-out that 'Larkin's great heart beat in time to the pulse of the working class.'

These American activities got Jim a stiff sentence in Sing Sing in 1920. A photograph of him in prison shows him looking remarkably like the film star Gary Cooper, and one thinks what a marvellous actor he would have been.

In the next case we see Larkin in 1923, after having been released from jail and deported back in Ireland. De Valera had found the same problem as Jim when he returned two years before. When the cat's away … Jim had now become an international socialist—while some of his former colleagues were more concerned with local infighting than with the liberation of the workers of the world. It didn't help Larkin (though it should have) that the president of the Comintern, Zinoviev, had singled him out for special praise in May 1922. In the British general election of 1924 English Tories would forge Zinoviev's name on a letter allegedly sent to the Labour Party leader, which resulted in Ramsay MacDonald losing the 1925 election. But Larkin's letter from Zinoviev wasn't forged. Neither did Larkin feel the need to disown it.

Ireland for the next twenty years would be a nightmare for him. He would lose his Dáil seat in the general election in 1944. Even in remote Rathgar and playing on an under-thirteen rugby team in Rathmines, I sensed some sort of betrayal at work. Much later and more street-wise I translated a poem from the Irish, written in tribute to Jim Larkin by Brendan Behan. The original Irish version by Brendan, along with two excellent translations by Manus O'Riordan and Theo Dorgan and the one below, are on display in a cabinet in the foyer as I pass on the way out.

Jim Larkin

From the Irish of Brendan Behan by Ulick O'Connor

He was me—he was every mother's son of us,
Ourselves—strong as we would wish to be
    As we knew we could be
And he bellowing battle and promising redemption
Following his coffin through the mouth of the empty city,
    In great roars of fury.

Following his coffin through the mouth of the city last night.
Is it we who are in the coffin?
Certainly not; we are in the street marching
Alive—and thankful to the dead.

Remembering James Larkin, 1997

Francis Devine

Fifty years from that shivering
February morning when respectful
flakes of silence enveloped
a grieving city,
there are those
that would not have us
know your name.

Stock-stiff in O'Connell Street
you serve as meeting point
and roost for winter wagtails,
your rage stifled by stone,
London planes surreptitiously shrouding
your honoured place in a people's heart.

Questioning commemoration quickly
rediscovers that divine discontent,
appreciates its continuing significance
and quakes the modern temple dwellers
for fear they may once more be forced
disgorge their horribly tainted bounty.

In abandoning you
we have abandoned ourselves.
We will erect not more statues
but organise to take Larkinism
from the limitations of history
to the imaginations of tomorrow.

For, in remembering Jim,
we must not forget what it is
he would have it
that we do.

[From *Red Star, Blue Moon: A Collection of Poems* by Francis Devine (1997).]

Sun Through Shadows

Stella Larkin McConnon

The sunbeams danced as I trudged up
Those worn old steps so long ago
My small hand in my mother's clasped
Safely with loving confidence.

Suddenly a man appeared
A giant silhouette he seemed
The light shone round him as he spoke
This was my granddad called 'Big Jim'.

This was my first memory of him
I did not know then what he'd done
To help to lift the city's poor
Up from the mud to see the sun.

Some would say dust had settled there
In Unity Hall on those old steps
To me those sunbeams sparkled on
Then while I watched they came to rest.

It was much later on I'd learn
How hard he'd worked for a just wage
For the people who had to endure
A life of work with little pay.

Some years passed by and then once more
I walked again up other steps
In College Street to see him lie
In a quiet sleep—peaceful. At rest.

There were no sunbeams on that day
The snow lay heavy on the ground
Men joined in as his funeral passed
With brush and shovel, heads were bowed.

There is a time in every life
For joy and sorrow—this I know.
But I could hear my granddad say
Look to the sun, not the shadows.

(Stella McConnon is the granddaughter of James Larkin.)

Citations for an exhibition

Among the citations used in the SIPTU 'Tribute to James Larkin' exhibition
at the National Library in 1997 were the following:

For a' that, and a' that,
It's coming yet for a' that
That man to man the world o'er
Shall brothers be for a' that.
(Robert Burns)

Yet, Freedom! yet thy banner, torn but flying,
Streams like the thunder-storm against the wind.
(Lord Byron)

They have taken untold millions that they never toiled to earn.
But without our brains and muscle not a single wheel can turn.
We can break their haughty power, gain our freedom when we learn
That the Union makes us strong.
(Ralph Chaplin)

His name endures on our holiest page,
Scrawled in a rage by Dublin's poor.
(Austin Clarke)

Then send it aloft on the breeze, boys,
The slogan the grandest we've known,
That Labour must rise from its knees, boys,
And claim the broad earth as its own.
(James Connolly)

By fraternity only will liberty be saved.
(Victor Hugo)

And Tyranny trampled them in Dublin's gutter
Until Jim Larkin came along and cried
The call of Freedom and the call of Pride
And Slavery crept to its hands and knees
And Nineteen Thirteen cheered from out the utter
Degradation of their miseries.
(Patrick Kavanagh)

Mankind will yet be masters of the earth.
(James Fintan Lalor)

It has so happened, in all ages of the world, that some have laboured, and others have without labour enjoyed a large proportion of the fruits. This is wrong and should not continue.
(Abraham Lincoln)

No prouder sight has Ireland seen since banded peasants stood
Upon her fields for freedom than this famished brotherhood,
Who in their leader's message have caught a distant gleam
Of that far off Holy City, our glory and our dream.
(Susan Mitchell)

What is this, the sound and rumour? What is this that all men hear,
Like the wind in hollow valleys when the storm is drawing near,
Like the rolling on of ocean in the eventide of fear?
    'Tis the people marching on.
(William Morris)

You, Promethean Jim Larkin with the voice born of the bugle and the drum.
(Seán O'Casey)

And I say to my people's masters: Beware …
    beware of the risen people
Who shall take what ye would not give.
(Patrick Pearse)

Rise, like lions after slumber
    In unvanquishable number
Shake your chains to earth like dew,
    Which in sleep had fall'n on you.
Ye are many, they are few.
(Percy Bysshe Shelley)

Liberty, let others despair of you—
I never despair of you.
(Walt Whitman)

Notes and References

Chapter 2 (p. 8–16)

1. Mary E. Daly, 'Working-class housing in Scottish and Irish cities on the eve of World War I' in Connolly, Houston and Morris, *Conflict, Identity and Economic Development*, 218.
2. Cited by Daly in *Dublin, the Deposed Capital*, 311; see also Daly, 'Working-class housing in Scottish and Irish cities on the eve of World War I' in Connolly, Houston and Morris, *Conflict, Identity and Economic Development*, 223–7.
3. Emmet Larkin, *James Larkin: Irish Labour Leader*, 40.
4. Reports of the Fiscal Inquiry Committee, appendix A.
5. Swift, *History of the Dublin Master Bakers*, 305, 332, 341; *Statistical Abstract, 1951*, 254; Ó Gráda, *Ireland: A New Economic History*, 238.
6. *International Labour Review*, vol. 58, no. 5 (Nov. 1948), 699–700. K. O'Rourke, 'Did labor flow upward?' in Grantham, McKinnon and Roche, *Labour Market Evolution*.
7. Deeny, *To Cure and to Care*, 127; see also Deeny, *End of an Epidemic*.
8. Deeny, *End of an Epidemic*, 60–72.
9. *Commission on Emigration, Report*, 128.
10. The following few paragraphs are based on my book *The Irish Economy since the 1920s*, chap. 1.
11. Humphries, *New Dubliners*, 204.
12. Humphries, *New Dubliners*, 211. On family limitation in middle-class Dublin early in the century see Cormac Ó Gráda and Niall Duffy, 'Fertility control early in marriage in Ireland a hundred years ago', *Journal of Population Economics*, vol. 8 (1995), 423–31.
13. Birrell, *Things Past Redress*, 210–11; *Annual Register, 1909*, 31, 113; Brenda Collins, 'The Edwardian city' in Beckett et al., *Belfast: The Making of the City*, 175; Tomás de Bhaldraithe (ed.), *Seanchas Thomáis Laighléis* (Dublin, 1977), 61.

Chapter 3 (p. 17–22)

This contribution is drawn largely from my article 'James Larkin and the National Union of Dock Labourers: the apprenticeship of a revolutionary' in *Saothar: Journal of the Irish Labour History Society*, no. 4 (1978), and my book *The Dockers' Union: A Study of the National Union of Dock Labourers, 1889–1922*, chap. 6.

1. For a full account of the foundation and development of the union see Taplin, *The Dockers' Union*.
2. George Milligan, 'Mersey dockers' 30 years' struggle', *TGWU Record*, no. 2 (1923).
3. For a more extended account of Sexton's early life see Taplin, *The Dockers' Union*. For an account of his career see J. Bellamy and J. Saville (eds.), *Dictionary of Labour Biography*, vol. 9 (London, 1993).
4. Sexton, *Sir James Sexton, Agitator*, 79.
5. For a more detailed treatment of the 1905 dispute see Taplin, *The Dockers' Union*, chap. 6.
6. *Liverpool Weekly Courier*, 22 July 1905, 9.
7. Sexton, *Sir James Sexton, Agitator*, 203–4.

Chapter 4 (p. 23–29)

My own *City in Revolt: James Larkin and the Belfast Dock Strike of 1907* remains the only book-length work on the Belfast dispute. Primary sources for that book include the Chief Secretary's Recorded Papers, 1907 (5541) and 1908 (20333), now in the National Archives, Dublin; transcripts of interviews with strike veterans undertaken by Sam Hanna Bell and David Bleakley, available in the Public Record Office of Northern Ireland, Belfast (D3358/1); and William McMullen's unpublished history of the dispute, now in the possession of SIPTU. The Belfast newspapers also provided copious detail. Otherwise the following books contain chapters on the dispute: Clarkson, *Labour and Nationalism in Ireland*; Keogh, *The Rise of the Irish Working Class*; Emmet Larkin, *James Larkin*; and (published after the appearance of my own book), Austen Morgan's *Labour and Partition*. Boyle, *The Irish Labor Movement in the Nineteenth Century*, provides a good account of the preceding labour movement in Belfast.

Chapter 5 (p. 30–37)

1. Coates and Topham, *History of the Transport and General Workers' Union, vol. 1,* 246.
2. For details of Fearon's career see McCamley, *The Third James.*
3. Coates and Topham, *History of the Transport and General Workers' Union, vol. 1,* 272.
4. Cody, O'Dowd, and Rigney, *Parliament of Labour,* 60, citing the official report in the National Archives (CSORP 26,870,1908).
5. O'Brien, *Forth the Banners Go,* 56.
6. Emmet Larkin, *James Larkin,* 49–50.
7. Cited by Clarkson in *Labour and Nationalism in Ireland,* 225
8. Greaves, *Irish Transport and General Workers' Union,* 64.
9. Greaves, *Irish Transport and General Workers' Union,* 68.
10. Belfast produced a paper in 1907; Dublin Trades Council produced one in March 1908; Cork Trades Council published the *Cork Trades and Labour Journal* in the spring of 1908; and Dublin Trades Council echoed this with the *Dublin Trades and Labour Journal* in May 1909, which became the *Irish Labour Journal* before collapsing in September 1909.
11. Greaves, *Irish Transport and General Workers' Union,* 64.
12. Keogh, *The Rise of the Irish Working Class,* 163.
13. John Newsinger, 'A lamp to light your feet: Jim Larkin, the *Irish Worker* and the Dublin working class', *European History Quarterly,* vol. 20 (1990), 63–9.
14. O'Connor, *Labour History of Ireland,* 68–70.

Chapter 6 (p. 38–46)

1. De Vallance to his mother, 13 Sep. 1913, Vane de V. M. Vallance Papers, NLI (ms. 17883).
2. Among the many accounts see Emmet Larkin, *James Larkin*; Greaves, *Irish Transport and General Workers' Union*; Nevin, *1913: Jim Larkin and the Dublin Lock-Out*; Keogh, *The Rise of the Irish Working Class*; Morrissey, *A Man Called Hughes.*
3. The fullest and most recent account of Murphy is Morrissey, *William Martin Murphy*; see also Dermot Keogh, 'William Martin Murphy and the origins of the 1913 lock-out,' *Saothar,* no. 4 (1979), 15–34.
4. Emmet Larkin, *James Larkin.*
5. Eric Taplin, 'James Larkin, Liverpool and the National Union of Dock Labourers: the apprenticeship of a revolutionary', *Saothar,* no. 4 (1979), 1–7.
6. Cody, O'Dowd, and Rigney, *Parliament of Labour,* 82–5.

7. Boyd, *The Rise of the Irish Trade Unions*, 86.
8. Keogh, 'William Martin Murphy and the origins of the 1913 lock-out', *Saothar*, no. 4 (1979), 199–201.
9. De Vallance to his mother, 19 Oct. 1913, Vane de V. M. Vallance Papers, NLI.
10. De Vallance to his mother, 5 Oct. 1913, Vane de V. M. Vallance Papers, NLI.
11. Keogh, 'William Martin Murphy and the origins of the 1913 lock-out', *Saothar*, no. 4 (1979), 218.
12. De Vallance to his mother, 26 Oct. 1913, Vane de V. M. Vallance Papers, NLI.
13. De Vallance to his mother, 14 Nov. 1913, Vane de V. M. Vallance Papers, NLI.

Chapter 7 (p. 47–55)

The main sources for information on Murphy's early years are an article 'The other side of William Martin Murphy: a loyal son of Beara' by Gerard Harrington in the *Cork Holly Bough*, Christmas 1976, and a contribution by William Martin Murphy, 'Reminiscences of fifty years ago', in *The Belvederian*, vol. 11, no. 1 (summer 1909). I am grateful to my colleague in the History Department of University College, Cork, Dr Andy Bielenberg, for referring me to both these sources.

1. 'The Late Wm Murphy', *Irish Independent*, 30 June 1919.
2. 'William Martin Murphy: an appreciation' by 'Abbeyfeale', *Irish Independent*, 30 June 1919.
3. Wright, *Disturbed Dublin*.
4. Harrington, 'The other side of William Martin Murphy', 49.
5. Murphy, 'Reminiscences of fifty years ago', 35.
6. Wright, *Disturbed Dublin*.
7. Callanan, *T. M. Healy*.
8. Murphy, 'Reminiscences of fifty years ago', 35.
9. Keogh, *The Rise of the Irish Working Class*.
10. Keogh, *The Rise of the Irish Working Class*.
11. Wright, *Disturbed Dublin*.
12. 'Tram monopoly', *Irish Worker*, 7 Sep. 1912.
13. See *Irish Catholic*, 6 Sep. 1913.
14. Quoted by Callanan in *T. M. Healy*.
15. Both the above are quoted by Callanan in *T. M. Healy*.

Chapter 8 (p. 56–63)

1. Quoted by E. Halevy in *The Rule of Democracy, 1905–1914* (1932), 92.
2. Cited by J. Cronin in *Industrial Conflict in Modern Britain* (1979), 100.
3. G. Askwith, *Industrial Problems and Disputes* (1920), 150.
4. E. David, *Inside Asquith's Cabinets: From the Diaries of Charles Hobhouse* (1977), 113.
5. L. Masterman, *C. F. G. Masterman: A Biography* (1939), 234.
6. Charles MacCarthy, *Trade Unions in Ireland*, 26.
7. Emmet Larkin, *James Larkin*, xii, 116.
8. Cited by P. Thompson in *The Edwardians* (1975), 252.
9. G. Dangerfield, *The Strange Death of Liberal England, 1910–1914* (1934), viii.
10. N. Stone, *Europe Transformed, 1878–1919* (1983), 74–153.

Chapter 10 (p. 74–83)

1. Emmet Larkin, *James Larkin*.
2. Wolfe, *Strange Communists I Have Known*.
3. Lowery, 'Seán O'Casey and the Irish Worker'.

4. The Irish Worker League is frequently referred to erroneously as the Irish Workers' League.

5. See Greaves, *Irish Transport and General Workers' Union*, and Stewart, *Breaking the Fetters*.

6. See McLoughlin and O'Connor, 'Sources on Ireland and the Communist International'.

Chapter 12 (p. 93–101)

1. US Bureau of Labour, *The Women's Trade Union Movement in Great Britain*, Washington, 1909; Nevin, *Trade Union Century*, 433.

2. *Irish Citizen*, 6 Sep. 1913.

3. ITUC annual report, 1914.

4. Leah Levenson, *With Wooden Sword*, 190.

5. *Irish Worker*, 9 Sep. 1911.

6. William O'Brien, 'The ITGWU and IWWU: a bit of history', O'Brien Papers, NLI (ms. 13970).

7. Eoin O'Leary, 'The Irish National Teachers' Organisation and the marriage bar for women national teachers, 1933–59', *Saothar*, no. 12 (1987), 47; O'Connell, *100 Years of Progress*, 14.

8. *Evening Herald*, 16 Nov. 1914.

9. Fox, *Jim Larkin*, 151.

10. *Votes for Women*, 24 Oct. 1913. All Mary Neal's quotations are from this report.

11. James Connolly, 'Glorious Dublin', reprinted in *Workers' Republic* (1951), 124.

12. Montefiore, *From a Victorian to a Modern*, 156. Other quotations of Dora Montefiore come from the *Daily Herald*, Oct.–Nov. 1913.

13. Louie Bennett to James Larkin, 29 Mar. 1947, WUI Archive, Irish Labour History Museum.

Chapter 15 (p. 116–124)

1. Letter from Jack Carney to a close friend, probably J. MacAlpine, 1 May 1948 (Donal Nevin Papers).

2. Emmet Larkin, *James Larkin*.

3. I am indebted to Prof. Kieran Kennedy for this information.

4. James Meenan (ed.), *History of the Literary and Historical Society, University College, Dublin*, 1956, 181.

5. James Meenan, *George O'Brien, A Biographical Memoir* (Dublin, 1980), 103.

Chapter 17 (p. 133–143)

1. W. P. Ryan, *The Irish Labour Movement*, 172.

2. National Archives, Dublin, CEN 1911 Dublin 46/a form no. 27.

3. Letter from Jim Larkin TD to Joe Deasy, 25 June 1956, *Saothar*, no. 21 (1996).

4. After 1916, and particularly in the course of the strife within the trade union movement in the twenties, it was not uncommon for Larkin's enemies to contrast the Liverpool-born Larkin with the Monaghan-born Connolly. This contrast seemed to carry weight in certain quarters; it was not known then that Connolly was in fact born in Edinburgh. It was again C. Desmond Greaves who discovered Connolly's birth certificate; details were given in his biography, *The Life and Times of James Connolly* (1961). As was the case with Larkin, Connolly was shown to have been two years older than had been thought, having being born in 1868 and not 1870, as had been assumed; ironically, as was also the case

with Larkin, some of Connolly's family refused to accept the evidence. Samuel Levenson records in his biography, *James Connolly: A Biography* (1973), that even then Connolly's son, Roddy, was reluctant to accept the fact of Connolly's Scottish birth, established by Greaves twelve years earlier.

5. The editor is indebted to Pádraig Ó hÉanacháin of the James Larkin Society, Liverpool, for procuring the copies of the birth certificate and the entry in the baptismal records.

6. The Jack Jones referred to was the father of Jack Jones, the British trade union leader who was general secretary of the Transport and General Workers' Union.

7. *The People of the State of New York v. James J. Larkin*, New York Supreme Court, Extraordinary Term, 16 Apr. 1920, Library of the Supreme Court of the State of New York (ms. 3436). A copy of this 772-page document is in the Gilbert Library, Dublin.

8. *Forward* (Glasgow), 9, 16 and 23 Oct. 1909.

Chapter 18 (p. 144–148)

1. Clarkson, *Labour and Nationalism in Ireland*, 215.
2. W. P. Ryan, *The Irish Labour Movement*, 182.
3. Clarkson, *Labour and Nationalism in Ireland*, 291.
4. Sexton, *Sir James Sexton: Agitator*, 204.
5. Gray, *City in Revolt*, 231.
6. Gray, *City in Revolt*, 204, 205–6.
7. Emmet Larkin, *James Larkin*, 39–40.

Chapter 19 (p. 149–151)

1. O'Brien, *Forth the Banners Go*, 37.
2. *Irish Times*, 23 Dec. 1908.
3. Diary of William O'Brien, O'Brien Papers, NLI (ms. 15705).
4. Clarkson, *Labour and Nationalism in Ireland*, 221, note 4.
5. O'Casey, *Drums under the Windows*, 223.
6. The text of this ballad was given to the editor by Tom Geraghty.

Chapter 20 (p. 152–158)

1. *Irish Worker*, 27 May 1911.
2. *Irish Worker*, 17 June 1911.
3. *Irish Worker*, 10 June 1911.
4. *Irish Worker*, 24 May 1913.
5. *Irish Worker*, 12 Aug. 1911.
6. Lowery, 'Seán O'Casey and the *Irish Worker*', 33, 42.
7. Cathal O'Shannon, *Evening Press*, 28 May 1965.
8. Lowery, 'Seán O'Casey and the *Irish Worker*', 47–114.
9. Lowery, 'Seán O'Casey and the *Irish Worker*', 34.
10. *Irish Worker*, 21 Oct. 1911.
11. Lowery, 'Seán O'Casey and the *Irish Worker*', 42–3.
12. Lowery, 'Seán O'Casey and the *Irish Worker*', 46.
13. *European History Quarterly*, vol. 20 (1990), 63–99.
14. Emmet Larkin, *James Larkin*, 76–7.
15. *Irish Worker*, 10 June 1911.
16. *Irish Worker*, 29 July 1911.
17. *Irish Worker*, 7 Oct. 1911.

Chapter 21 (p. 159–162)

1. *Ulster Guardian*, 21 Sep. 1907.
2. Emmet Larkin, *James Larkin*, 42.
3. Emmet Larkin, *James Larkin*, 43.
4. Emmet Larkin, *James Larkin*, 47–8.
5. Joseph O'Brien, *Dear, Dirty Dublin*.
6. *Freeman's Journal*, 14 Oct. 1910.
7. Joseph O'Brien, *Dear, Dirty Dublin*, 216.
8. *Irish Worker*, 20 Sep. 1913.

Chapter 22 (p. 163–168)

1. Extracts from depositions of police witnesses at trials in Dublin City Commission, 1913.
2. Extracts from depositions of police witnesses at trials in Dublin City Commission, 1913. It was at this meeting that Larkin advocated a no-rent campaign, getting the meeting to recite after him the following pledge: 'I will pay no rent until tramway men have got the conditions they demand.' As a result of his own refusal to pay rent, Larkin, his wife and their three sons were evicted from their home in Auburn Street later in the year.
3. *Irish Worker*, 27 Sep. 1913. Some of O'Casey's earliest writings were published in Larkin's paper, to which he contributed up to fifty articles, ballads, and letters, apart from 'Irish Citizen Army Notes', which appeared in twelve issues. The more important of O'Casey's contributions to the *Irish Worker* between the issue for 9 Mar. 1912 and his last contribution, in the issue for 8 July 1914, will be found in Hogan, *Feathers from the Green Crow*.
4. *Irish Worker*, 30 Aug. 1913.
5. Letter from the Chief Secretary to the Prime Minister, Herbert Asquith, 8 Sep. 1913, quoted by Ó Broin in *The Chief Secretary*, 75. Elsewhere in the letter, Birrell referred to the whole atmosphere being charged with gunpowder. In a further letter (26 Sep.) he told Asquith that the police were very overworked and that he had to release a number of them from the duty of guarding tram depots by substituting soldiers. The hours of the other members of the force, he added, would remain, as before, quite intolerable.

Chapter 23 (p. 169–178)

1. The reference is to Michael Davitt, founder of the Land League.
2. Fair rent, fixity of tenure, and free sale.
3. Now Pearse Street.
4. Now Clery's department store.
5. Later to become the first Governor-General of the Irish Free State.
6. The text of Larkin's address is given on p. 195–8.
7. The text of Russell's letter to the *Irish Times* is given on p. 212–14.
8. The text of Russell's Albert Hall address is given on p. 216–18.
9. Extracts from Connolly's article in the *Irish Worker* are given on p. 242–4.

Chapter 24 (p. 179–189)

1. Wright, *Disturbed Dublin*, 136–7. In a footnote on p. 174 of *The Workers' Republic*, 1951 (the selection from the writings of Connolly that he edited for the ITGWU), Desmond Ryan stated that Wright was paid £500 by the Federated Employers of Dublin for writing *Disturbed Dublin*. This was a considerable amount of money at the time.

2. Information given to Emmet Larkin by William O'Brien. See *James Larkin*, 124 (footnote).
3. In some accounts of the events of that Sunday morning it has been stated that Helena Molony was the 'niece'. This was not so: the 'niece' was Sidney Gifford (a sister of Grace Gifford, the artist who married Joseph Plunkett in Kilmainham Jail on the morning of his execution in May 1916), later Sidney Czira, who wrote an account of the incident in the *Irish Digest*, December 1951, under her pen-name John Brennan.
4. Wright, *Disturbed Dublin*, 141–2.
5. In 1942 the Workers' Union of Ireland, whose general secretary was James Larkin, purchased 5A College Street, Dublin, premises that had been the police station, to replace the original head office, Unity Hall, Marlborough Street. The cell in which Larkin had been held after his arrest in 1913 was preserved. The building has since been demolished.
6. Greaves, *The Life and Times of James Connolly*, 250
7. Wright, *Disturbed Dublin*, 144.
8. O'Casey, *Drums under the Windows*, 263. O'Casey's account of the events of 1913 will be found in the chapter 'Prometheus Hibernica', 219–41.

Chapter 25 (p. 190–198)
1. Letter from Chief Secretary, Augustine Birrell, to Prime Minister, Henry Asquith, 8 Sep. 1913, quoted by Ó Broin in *The Chief Secretary*.
2. *Dublin Strikes*, 1913.
3. Eglinton, *Memoir of Æ*, 86. (Thersites was a Greek officer during the Trojan War who, according to Homer, was fond of sneering at his fellow-soldiers.)
4. O'Flaherty, *Life of Tim Healy*.
5. Chesterton, *Irish Impressions*, 75.
6. Callanan, *T. M. Healy*, 711.
7. Callanan, *T. M. Healy*, 488.
8. Callanan, *T. M. Healy*, 490.
9. Callanan, *T. M. Healy*, 489.
10. Callanan, *T. M. Healy*, 489.
11. Callanan, *T. M. Healy*, 489.
12. Callanan, *T. M. Healy*, 490.
13. Ó Broin, *The Chief Secretary*, 75.
14. The *Irish Catholic* was established in May 1888. It was edited by William F. Dennehy (1853–1918), the son of a Dublin merchant who owned an estate in Longford. In the Parnell split he became, in Frank Callanan's words, 'Parnell's most pietistical vituperative assailant,' referring to him on one occasion as 'a notorious, convicted, shameless and unrepentant adulterer.'
15. *Irish Catholic*, 6 Sep. 1913.
16. Callanan, *T. M. Healy*, 488.
17. Callanan, *T. M. Healy*, 489.
18. Lyons, *John Dillon*, 334.
19. Walsh to Lord Aberdeen, 10 Oct. 1913 (Dublin Diocesan Archives, Laity File), quoted by Morrissey in *William Martin Murphy*.

Chapter 26 (p. 199–202)
1. Ó Broin, *The Chief Secretary*, 79.
2. *Manchester Guardian*, 17 Nov. 1913.
3. *Review*, Mar. 1947.

Chapter 29 (p. 211–222)

1. Æ [George Russell], *Collected Poems*.
2. Eglinton, *A Memoir of Æ*, 1.
3. *Oxford Companion to Irish Literature* (ed. Welch), 503.
4. *Irish Homestead*, 10 Feb. 1912.
5. W. P. Ryan, *The Irish Labour Movement*, 227.
6. Letter to F. S. Oliver (quoted by West in *Horace Plunkett*).
7. *Irish Homestead*, 19 Aug. 1913.
8. Letter to Yeats (quoted by Foster in *W. B. Yeats, vol. 1*, 499).
9. Letter to John Quinn, 12 Aug. 1913 (quoted by Foster in *W. B. Yeats, vol. 1*, 495).
10. Quoted by Nevin in *1913*, 49.
11. The dates of composition of the poems by Yeats quoted in this and the following paragraph are as given by A. Norman Jeffares (ed.) in *Yeats's Poems*, Dublin: Gill and Macmillan 1989, 543–5.
12. *Irish Worker*, 1 Nov. 1913.
13. The session of the Peace Meeting referred to by Russell was that of 27 October 1913, at which the Lord Mayor presided. Other prominent citizens on the platform, besides Yeats, were the Protestant Archbishop of Dublin and the Warden of Trinity Hall. According to the *Irish Times* (28 October), Yeats's speech, which had largely been devoted to attacking the press, and William Martin Murphy in particular, was interrupted by the Lord Mayor, who told him he would find opportunity elsewhere to 'express contempt for anyone he liked.' The notes Yeats made for his speech are in the National Library (ms. 30,615); they will also be found in Foster, *Yeats, vol. 1*, 500.
14. Alan Denson (ed.), *Letters from AE*, 91.
15. Dr Monk Gibbon's remark is quoted by Nevin in *1913*, 72.
16. Eglinton, *Memoir of Æ*, 88. Elsewhere (p. 102) Eglinton quotes an unidentified newspaper cutting: 'I have only once seen and heard Æ. That was when he was in London, a while ago, one of several speakers at a public meeting discussing the social and economic condition of Ireland, and when his turn came, he spoke with much evident depth of feeling, so simply, that, for me, he made all the other speakers seem slight and ineffective …'
17. Eglinton, *Memoir of Æ*, 89–90. Squire was then the literary editor of the *New Statesman*.
18. Eglinton, *Memoir of Æ*, 285.

Chapter 34 (p. 247–252)

1. 'It's Murphy's' was first published in the *Irish Worker*, 30 Sep. 1913.
2. 'Who Fears to Wear the Blood Red Badge?' by 'Macha'—adapted from 'The Memory of the Dead' ('Who Fears to Speak of Ninety-Eight?') by John Kells Ingram (1843)—was first published in the *Irish Worker*, 11 October 1913. The ITGWU badge in 1913 was the red hand of Ulster.
3. 'A Song of Swords' by G. K. Chesterton was first published in the *Daily Herald* (London), 11 October 1913. The *Daily Herald* was then edited by George Lansbury, and the assistant editor was W. P. Ryan. The ballad refers to an incident at Swords, Co. Dublin, during a strike of farm workers in August 1913, which was led by Larkin, his brother Peter, and Michael Mullen.
4. 'To the Villas of Genteel Dastards' by Susan Mitchell was first published in the *Irish Worker*, 1 Nov. 1913. Susan Mitchell (1866–1926) worked as sub-editor of the *Irish Homestead* (organ of the Irish Agricultural Organisation Society, edited

by George Russell) and the *Irish Statesman*. Her books of poetry include *The Living Chalice* (1908).

5. 'The Blackleg' was first published in the *Irish Worker*, 22 Nov. 1913. Jim Connell (1852–1929), born in Killskeer, Co. Meath, was the author of 'The Red Flag', which first appeared in the Christmas 1889 issue of *Justice*, organ of the Social Democratic Federation in Britain.

6. 'The Watchword' by James Connolly was first published in the *Irish Worker*, 6 Dec. 1913, as a 'Rallying Song for Labour'. It later became known as 'The Watchword of Labour'.

7. 'Lines to the Brotherhood of Cain' by Maeve Cavanagh was first published in the *Irish Worker*, 31 Jan. 1914.

Chapter 36 (p. 257–265)

1. Denson, *Letters from AE*, 118–19.

Chapter 37 (p. 266–271)

1. Twenty-two years later Larkin did return to City Hall, being a member of Dublin City Council from 1936 until his death in January 1947. He was chairman of the Housing Committee from 1943. His son Denis was elected Lord Mayor of Dublin in 1955.

Chapter 38 (p. 272–297)

1. Tom Mooney, a 34-year-old labour leader, was convicted and sentenced to death for the bomb explosion during a 'Preparedness Day' parade in San Francisco on 16 July 1916, in which nine people were killed. Mooney protested his innocence. The sentence was commuted to life imprisonment, but he served twenty years in jail before being pardoned in 1936. He died in 1962.

2. One IWW leader who was taken out and hanged was Frank Little. Elizabeth Gurley Flynn described Little as 'tall and dark, with black hair and black eyes, a slender, gentle and soft-spoken man.' He was half-Cherokee, one-eyed, one-legged (by the time he came to Butte), and 'all Wobbly.' On 1 August 1917 masked gunmen took the crippled Little from his bed, tied a rope round his neck, and dragged him to the outskirts of Butte, where they strung him up from a railway trestle.

3. This article is an extract from an unpublished pamphlet written by Jack Carney in 1948 for the Larkin Memorial Fund.

4. In the distribution of Joe Hill's ashes, one container was held by a postmaster, who would not deliver 'subversive' mail. Somehow the container ended up in the National Archives in Washington. On 19 November 1988, exactly seventy-three years after Hill's execution, the National Archives forwarded the ashes to the IWW office in Chicago. In 1979 the AFL-CIO made an appeal to the Governor of Utah seeking a pardon that would 'remove the stain of injustice that surrounds the memory of Joe Hill.' There was no response. (In 1977, fifty years after their execution, Sacco and Vanzetti were vindicated by a proclamation from the Governor of Massachusetts, Michael Dukakis.)

5. At his last interview in the death cell, Joe Hill was asked by a reporter about his will. He scribbled on a piece of paper:

My will is easy to decide,
For there is nothing to divide.

My kin don't need to fuss and moan—
'Moss does not cling to a rolling stone.'

My body? Ah, if I could choose,
I would to ashes it reduce,
And let the merry breezes blow
My dust to where some flowers grow.

Perhaps some fading flower then
Would come to life and bloom again.
This is my last and final will.
Good luck to all of you.—Joe Hill.

Joe Hill is immortalised in the song by Alfred Hayes and Earl Robinson written in 1925, made famous in a recording by Paul Robeson. It was sung by Joan Baez at Woodstock in 1970.

I dreamed I saw Joe Hill last night
Alive as you and me,
Says I, 'But, Joe, you're ten years dead!'
'I never died,' says he.
'I never died,' says he.

'In Salt Lake City, Joe,' says I,
Him standing by my bed,
'They framed you on a murder charge.'
Says Joe, 'But I ain't dead.'

'The copper bosses killed you, Joe,
They shot you, Joe,' says I.
'Takes more than guns to kill a man,'
Says Joe. 'I didn't die.'

And standing there as big as life,
And smiling with his eyes,
Joe says, 'What they forgot to kill
Went on to organise.'

'Joe Hill ain't dead,' he says to me,
'Joe Hill ain't never died.'
Where working men are out on strike,
Joe Hill is at their side.

'From San Diego up to Maine,
In every mine and mill,
Where workers strike and organise,'
Says he, 'You'll find Joe Hill.'

I dreamed I saw Joe Hill last night
Alive as you and me.
Say I, 'But, Joe, you're ten years dead.'
'I never died,' says he.

6. Emmet Larkin, *James Larkin*, 188.

7. Lola Ridge was born in Dublin and went to America in 1907. Her first volume of poems, *The Ghetto and Other Poems*, was published in 1918. This was followed by *Sun-Up* (1920), *Red Flag* (1927), *Firehead* (1929)—which was inspired by the execution of Saccho and Vanzetti—and *Dance of Fire* (1933). The constant theme of her poetry was the martyrdom of the downtrodden.

The *Nation* (New York) commented editorially on Larkin's deportation in its issue of 2 May 1923:

> Deportation is always a petty process; it somehow seems double petty in the case of such an epic figure as gaunt, gray-haired, long-limbed James Larkin. We seldom agree with Larkin. But there is a genuine bigness of soul behind his bigness of body. He is one of these rare things—a born leader of men, with a sense of the pain of life.

Quoting from Lola Ridge's poem, the editorial writer noted that 'Lola Ridge understood the man.'

Chapter 40 (p. 313–333)
1. *Irish Times*, 1 May 1923.
2. *Freeman's Journal*, 1 May 1923.
3. Emmet Larkin, *James Larkin*, 271–2.
4. Emmet Larkin, *James Larkin*, 273.
5. Greaves, *Irish Transport and General Workers' Union*, 15.
6. Greaves, *Irish Transport and General Workers' Union*, 56.
7. Greaves, *Irish Transport and General Workers' Union*, 64.
8. Greaves, *Irish Transport and General Workers' Union*, 91.
9. Greaves, *Irish Transport and General Workers' Union*, 13.

Chapter 41 (p. 334–341)
The main sources for this chapter were Gaughan, *Thomas Johnson*; Emmet Larkin, *James Larkin*; Milotte, *Communism in Modern Ireland*; Nevin, 'Radical movements in the twenties and thirties' in Williams (ed.), *Secret Societies in Ireland*; Stewart, *Breaking the Fetters*; McLoughlin and O'Connor, 'Sources on Ireland and the Communist International'; McLoughlin, 'Proletarian academics or party functionaries?'; *Irish Worker* (new series), 1923–1925.

Chapter 42 (p. 342–352)
1. The *Irish Worker* carried a full report of the court proceedings (7 June 1924) and a report on their release (5 July 1924).
2. Emmet Larkin, *James Larkin*, 283.
3. Emmet Larkin, *James Larkin*, 284.
4. *Irish Times*, 14 Aug. 1925.
5. Charles McCarthy, *Trade Unions in Ireland*, 192.
6. Submissions to Commission on Vocational Organisation, 1939–43, vol. 18, doc. 136 (NLI).
7. Ferguson was active in the Labour Party in Dublin. In his autobiography, *West Briton* (1962), Brian Inglis—a recruit to the Labour Party—describes Ferguson as 'a sardonic old-young man with the ability to make us feel that we were ignorant nuisances, but that he bore us no resentment.'
8. On 17 February 1948 the main story on the front page of the *Irish Times* was headed 'Inter-Party Cabinet candidates named'. Included among the prospective Government members named in the article was James Larkin as

Minister for Education. On the following day, when the new Taoiseach, John A. Costello, announced the members of his Government, James Larkin was not included. It is known that the WUI had agreed to leave of absence for Larkin as general secretary. The editor is indebted to Proinsias Mac Aonghusa for permission to publish the following note, prepared at his request (18 April 1997): 'Some time after the 1957 election was called I happened to meet General Seán Mac Eoin, the Minister for Defence, at the corner of O'Connell Street and Lower Abbey Street in Dublin. As a journalist I had met him on a number of previous occasions and we had become friendly. We talked about Jim Larkin's decision to leave Dáil Éireann. He said that Larkin was "a fine fellow with a great brain" but, pointing to a red car parked beside us, said, "That's his colours; he was always like that." General Mac Eoin then told me that when the first Inter-Party Government was in process of being formed in 1948, Jim Larkin was to be Minister for Education. When I said I had never heard of that proposal, General Mac Eoin said: "It had to be stopped. It could not be allowed." He did not say who had successfully opposed Larkin in Government or being nominated as Minister for Education. But I got the impression that opposition had come from outside the leadership of the proposed Coalition (Seán MacBride, William Norton, Richard Mulcahy, James Dillon, Jim Everett and John A. Costello) and that some influential group or person vetoed Larkin.' (The recently released archives of the late Dr John Charles McQuaid, Archbishop of Dublin, may well throw further light on the matter.)

9. Some 150 or so letters from Seán O'Casey to Jack Carney are included in vols. 2 and 3 of Krause's *Letters of Seán O'Casey*.

Chapter 43 (p. 353–364)

1. *Irish Press*, 5 Feb. 1947.
2. *Irish Times*, 31 Jan. 1987.
3. *Irish Times*, 1 Feb. 1947.
4. *Ar Aghaidh*, Mar. 1947.
5. Oration at graveside, 3 Feb. 1947.
6. *New International*, no. 13 (Mar. 1947).
7. Extract from presidential address to 53rd annual conference of Irish Trades Union Congress (Olympia Ballroom, Waterford), 29 July 1947.
8. First published in the *Irish Times*, 9 Dec. 1944. It was recited by Harry Craig, then assistant editor of the *Bell*, at the first Jim Larkin Memorial Meeting and Concert (Olympia Theatre, Dublin), 8 Feb. 1948.
9. First published in the *Bell*, Mar. 1947.
10. Included by Colm Ó Lochlainn in *More Irish Street Ballads* (1965). Ó Lochlainn states that it was sold in the streets of Dublin on the day of Larkin's funeral.
11. First published in *Collected Poems*, Dublin: Dolmen Press 1974.

Chapter 44 (p. 365–366)

1. P. B. Harbottle, *Dictionary of Quotations, French and Italian*, London 1901.
2. Othon Guerlac, *Les Citations Françaises: Recueil de Passages Célèbres, Phrases Familières, Mots Historiques*, Paris: A. Colin 1953.
3. Thomas Kinsella, 'The Pen Shop, Dublin', *Peppercanister*, no. 19 (1997).

Chapter 46 (p. 371–378)

1. Moody, *Irish Historiography*, 137–50, 137.

2. Moody, *Irish Historiography*, 146.

3. E. A. D'Alton, *History of Ireland from the Earliest Times to the Present Day, vol. 8*, London 1925, 175–6, 428, 433.

4. E. A. Curtis, *A History of Ireland*, London 1936 (6th ed., 1950), 405.

5. Jackson, *Ireland Her Own*, xvi, 364–5, 377, 443.

6. Tierney, 'Modern Ireland', 257–67.

7. O'Hegarty, *History of Ireland*, 672.

8. O'Hegarty, *History of Ireland*.

9. Strauss, *Irish Nationalism and British Democracy*, 226.

10. Strauss, *Irish Nationalism and British Democracy*, 227.

11. Strauss, *Irish Nationalism and British Democracy*, 228.

12. Tierney, 'Modern Ireland', 261–2.

13. Gearóid Ó Tuathaigh, 'Ireland, 1800–1921' in J. J. Lee (ed.), *Irish Historiography, 1970–1979*, Cork: Cork University Press 1981, 85–131.

14. P. O'Farrell, *Ireland's English Question: Anglo-Irish Relations, 1534–1970*, London 1971, 269–70.

Chapter 47 (p. 379–390)

1. Boyle, *Leaders and Workers* (1986).

2. Earle, Edward Mead (ed.), *Nationalism and Internationalism*, 1950.

3. Dangerfield, *The Damnable Question* (1976).

4. Dawson, *Red Terror and Green* (1920).

5. Fox, *Jim Larkin: The Rise of the Underman* (1957).

6. Fox, *Smoky Crusade* (1938).

7. Howell, *A Lost Left* (1986).

8. *Daily Worker*, 4 Feb. 1967.

9. Kee, *The Green Flag* (1972).

10. Keogh, *The Rise of the Irish Working Class* (1982).

11. Emmet Larkin, *James Larkin* (1965).

12. Lee, *Ireland, 1912–1985* (1989).

13. Levenson, *James Connolly* (1973).

14. Lyons, *Irish Historical Review*, Mar. 1967.

15. Lyons, *Ireland Since the Famine* (1971).

16. Mansergh, *The Irish Question* (1940).

17. Mitchell, *Labour in Irish Politics* (1974).

18. Ó Riain, *Comhar*, Oct. 1957.

19. Phillips, *The Revolution in Ireland* (1923).

20. Desmond Ryan, *James Connolly* (1924).

21. W. P. Ryan, *The Irish Labour Movement* (1919).

22. Strauss, *Irish Nationalism and British Democracy* (1951).

23. Swift, *History of the Dublin Bakers* (1948).

24. Thomson, *Europe since Napoleon* (revised edition, 1966).

25. Van Voris, *Constance de Markievicz* (1967).

Chapter 48 (p. 391–394)

1. *Bulletin*, Dublin Unemployed Association, 1953.

2. *Leader*, 1 July 1910.

3. *Hibernia*, Aug. 1963.

4. First appeared in *New International*, no. 13 (Mar. 1947), as 'Jim Larkin, Irish revolutionist: fighter for freedom and socialism'. In revised form it was

included by James Farrell in 'Lest we forget: Jim Larkin, Irish labour leader' in *Flynn* (ed.), *On Irish Themes*, from which this extract is taken.

5. Harris, *Contemporary Portraits* (fourth series), London 1924.
6. *Irish Press*, 24–27 Feb. 1965.
7. O'Connor, *Brendan Behan*, London 1970.
8. Ó Faoláin, *Constance Markievicz*.
9. Boyle, *Leaders and Workers*.

Chapter 49 (p. 395–400)

1. Fox, *James Connolly: The Forerunner*, published in 1947.
2. According to John Gray in his authoritative work *City in Revolt* (1985), the date was 20 January 1907. Larkin believed his birthday was 21 January 1876; in fact it was 28 January 1874.
3. The procession Carney refers to was not on the 'Twelfth' but on 26 July, when Belfast Trades Council organised a massive demonstration two or three miles long in which an estimated 200,000 people took part; it passed down Ann Street, Queen's Bridge, Ballymacarrett, Albert Bridge, May Street, Howard Street and Falls Road to the Shankill Road, Crumlin Road, Clifton Street, North Queen Street and York Street, down Royal Avenue, and then to the City Hall.
4. In a letter dated 30 January 1908 to J. Carstairs Matheson, probably his closest colleague and friend in Scotland, Connolly wrote: 'For myself, though I have usually posed as a Catholic I have not gone to my duty for 15 years, and have not the slightest tincture of faith left.' The letter is in the William O'Brien Papers in the National Library of Ireland. The visit to Scotland referred to in Carney's letter may have been in 1913 or early 1914, when Connolly might have been at pains to retain the support of the Catholic emigrants for the 1913 struggle and not be seen to affront their faith by not attending Mass. With regard to Carney's reference to himself, Larkin and Bukharin discussing religion, Emmet Larkin in his biography of Larkin quotes from the 'Carney Memoir', which Carney wrote at his request: 'The Russians looked upon Jim [Larkin] as some kind of enigma. Bukharin had asked him about his Faith, being under the impression that Jim Larkin avowed himself a Catholic for opportunistic reasons. To the surprise of Bukharin, Jim said he had faith that there was a God. Bukharin had asked him if he believed there was a God. Jim insisted that he had Faith there was a God and he would hold to such a Faith until he had been proved to be wrong. There was no shaking him. Although he had the opportunity of going to Mass in Moscow he did not go, which added to the mystery.'

Chapter 50 (p. 401–405)

1. Greaves (*The Life and Times of James Connolly*, 20) speculated that Connolly was in the King's Liverpool Regiment, while Levenson in his biography of Connolly (*James Connolly: A Biography*, 23) quoted research by David Stewart of Edinburgh to the effect that Connolly served in the Royal Scots Regiment, the same regiment in which his eldest brother, John, served. John Connolly died in June 1916 and was buried with military honours. It was John who had introduced James to socialism.

Chapter 52 (p. 412–423)

1. W. P. Ryan, *The Plough and the Cross: A Story of New Ireland*, a novel, published in 1910.

2. This reference is to Cathal O'Shannon, who compiled the book, and William O'Brien, who contributed an article about 1913 he had written in *An Díon* in 1934 in which he succeeds in not mentioning the name of Larkin at all.

Chapter 54 (p. 428–438)

Information about Delia Larkin's years as secretary of the Irish Women Workers' Union, 1911–15, is drawn from the *Irish Worker*, 1911–14. Other sources include ITUC annual reports, 1912–14; *Daily Herald*, 1913–14; and ITGWU, *The Attempt to Smash the Irish Transport and General Workers' Union*; other sources are cited in the notes. The only extensive study of Delia Larkin is 'Delia Larkin and the Founding of the Irish Women Workers' Union' by Alison Buckley (thesis for M Phil in women's studies, TCD, 1996). My thanks to Rosemary Bashford, Lesley Clarke, and Donal Nevin, who provided me with information.

1. C. Desmond Greaves, 'Jim Larkin's earliest years', *Irish Democrat*, Sep. 1980. Greaves, whose research placed the Larkin family in Liverpool, wrote: 'There was another child called Delia Larkin born in Toxteth Park in 1881. If she survived (and she is the only Delia in volumes of the index) Bridget may have known her and fancied her name.' In fact Delia and Della were widely used alternative forms or pet names for Brigid or Bridget.
2. William O'Brien Papers, NLI (ms. 15676 (ii), part 1).
3. James Larkin, *In the Footsteps of Big Jim*, 24.
4. Some reasons for forming the IWWU are discussed by Jones in *These Obstreperous Lassies*, chap. 12.
5. *Daily Herald*, 29 Dec. 1913.
6. Greaves, *Irish Transport and General Workers' Union*, 135–6.
7. *Evening Herald*, 16 Nov. 1914.
8. Robbins, *Under the Starry Plough*, 21.
9. Greaves, *Irish Transport and General Workers' Union*, 148–9.
10. James Connolly to Winifred Carney, 9 Dec. 1915, Cathal O'Shannon Papers, Irish Labour History Museum (COS 90).
11. Patricia Lynch and R. M. Fox Papers, NLI.
12. Jones, *These Obstreperous Lassies*, 30.
13. Peter Larkin (Sydney Travels), Australian Archives (A402; W235). (See chapter 55.)
14. Seven issues survive in the O'Brien Papers in the National Library.
15. My thanks to Lesley Clarke for this item.
16. Delia Larkin to R. M. Fox, 11 Apr. 1947, Patricia Lynch and R. M. Fox Papers, NLI.

Chapter 55 (p. 439–444)

1. Turner, *Sydney's Burning*, 12.
2. Turner, *Sydney's Burning*, 30.
3. Turner, *Sydney's Burning*, 180.
4. Turner, *Sydney's Burning*, 196, 199.
5. The editor is indebted to Theresa Moriarty for providing copies of the police dossiers on Peter Larkin in the Australian Archives, Canberra.
6. John B. King, Tom Glynn and Donald Grant, referred to in the dossier, were among the Twelve. John Garden was secretary of Sydney Labor Council and a leading campaigner for the release of the Twelve.

Chapter 58 (p. 488–502)

1. Denis Brogan, *The Development of Modern France, 1870–1939*, London 1967, 752.
2. Text as given in John McDonnell (ed.), *Songs of Struggle and Protest* (Dublin, 1979). The verse quoted here is not included in *The Legacy and Songs of Freedom* published by the Socialist Party of Ireland in 1919, nor in *The James Connolly Songbook*, published by Cork Workers' Club in 1972, which was based on a selection of songs that were to have been performed at a concert in the Mansion House, Dublin, on 5 June 1919 but which was proclaimed by the police; it was held in the Trades Hall, Capel Street, under the protection of armed members of the Irish Citizen Army.
3. The years 1903 and 1904 were Connolly's most prolific as far as his poems were concerned. His verse owes much to John Leslie's *Proletarian Lays and Lyrics*. Leslie was Connolly's mentor in his early years. Connolly also admired Freiligrath, who was known as 'the poet of the people.' Desmond Greaves has pointed out that Connolly's songs were not at first to Irish airs but to popular tunes.
4. Connell died on 6 February 1929, at the age of seventy-seven. 'The Red Flag' came to be sung to the air of a German Christmas carol, 'Tannenbaum' ('fir tree'), though Connell intended it to be sung to the air of the Jacobite song 'The White Cockade'. George Bernard Shaw famously likened the air of 'Tannenbaum' to 'the funeral march of a fried eel'. Jim Larkin used to sing 'The Red Flag', in a not very melodious voice, at social gatherings in Liberty Hall. Singing it in Moscow on one occasion, he found himself rebuked by his German communist comrades for singing a German hymn!
5. Shelley wrote *Mask of Anarchy* (hailed by his biographer Richard Holmes as 'the greatest poem of political protest ever written in English') on learning in Livorno of the 'Peterloo Massacre', when a peaceful demonstration at St Peter's Fields, Manchester, was attacked by the Yeomanry, who rode into the crowd and hacked away with their swords, killing eleven people, including a mother and her baby, and seriously injuring 141. Overcome by 'the torrent of my indignation,' Shelley wrote the ninety-two verses in five days; but it was not published until 1832, ten years after his death. The poem was recited by the Chartists and in this century was quoted by Gandhi at the beginning of the century when agitating among the Indian population in South Africa, and towards the end of the century by Chinese students demonstrating in Tian'anmen Square in Beijing in 1989.
6. For more about Joe Hill see chap. 38.
7. 'It was the first strike I ever saw which sang,' a journalist wrote. 'I shall not soon forget the curious lift, the strange sudden fire of the mingled nationalities at the strike meetings when they broke into the universal language of song. And not only at the meetings did they sing, but in the soup houses and in the streets. I saw one group of women workers who were peeling potatoes at a relief station suddenly break into the swing of the Internationale. 'The strikers were always marching and singing,' wrote another journalist. 'The tired, gray crowds ebbing and flowing perpetually into the mills had waked and opened their mouths to sing.' Carrying their placards with the slogan *We want bread and roses too*, they sang, as they marched, Jim Connell's 'The Red Flag', the 'Marseillaise', 'Hold the Fort', Joe Hill's 'Casey Jones', and 'On the Good Old Picket Line'. On one occasion, when the IWW leader Bill Haywood (who a year later was to address mass meetings in England with Jim Larkin in support of the locked-out Dublin

workers) spoke to a crowd of 25,000 on Lawrence Common, the strikers sang the 'International' in each of their many languages in turn. The strike at the Lawrence mills of the American Woolen Company involved 23,000 workers of at least twenty-five different nationalities and languages. Teenage girls made up half the strikers from the four mills. A young woman, Anna Lo Pezzi, was killed by police fire as they tried to break up a picket line. The cause of the strike was the decision of the employers to cut weekly wages by two hours' pay when a new state law reduced weekly hours from 56 to 54 for women and children under eighteen. 'Better to starve fighting than to starve working' was their battle-cry. The workers won a great victory after nearly three months; the employers agreed to increase wages by at least 5 per cent (15 per cent for the lower-paid), to pay time-and-a-quarter for overtime, and to rehire strikers without discrimination.

Chapter 59 (p. 503–514)

1. The members of the SIPTU Larkin Commemoration Committee were Jack Harte (chairperson), Tom Dunne (secretary), William Attley, Francis Devine, Tom Geraghty, Des Mahon, Theresa Moriarty, Donal Nevin, Manus O'Riordan, Jim Quinn, and Séamas Sheils.
2. 'Salute to Big Jim' was devised by Donal Nevin and arranged by Tom Dunne, Donal Nevin, and Manus O'Riordan.
3. Readers of these pieces were Brendan Cauldwell in Dublin and Sam Nolan in Belfast (Seán O'Casey), Francis Devine (James Connolly), Paul Bennett in Dublin and Kevin O'Connor in Belfast (George Russell), Francis Devine (John Swift), and Kevin O'Connor (Liam Mac Gabhann).
4. Larkin Exhibition, National Library of Ireland, Sep.–Oct. 1997. *Sponsors:* National Library of Ireland, Irish Congress of Trade Unions, SIPTU, Linen Hall Library (Belfast), and Irish Labour History Museum (Dublin). *Advisory panel:* Dr Fergus D'Arcy (UCD), David Craig (National Archives), John Gray (Linen Hall Library, Belfast), Prof. Emmet Larkin (University of Chicago), Prof. Patrick Lynch, Rev. Prof. F. X. Martin, James Plunkett. *Organising committee:* Donal Nevin (chairperson), Tom Dunne (secretary), Theresa Moriarty (exhibition organiser), Hilda Larkin Breslin, Charles Callan, Joe Deasy, Francis Devine, Tom Geraghty, Jack Harte, Des Mahon, Dr Jack McGinley, Manus O'Riordan, Jim Quinn, Séamas Sheils. *Exhibition design:* Caroline Moloney, Geraldine Martin. *Exhibition displays* constructed by Kingram Studies, Woodprint Finishing Ltd, and Display Contracts. *Scanning and photo enhancement:* Eugene Hogan (NLI) and Deirdre Price and Séamas Sheils (SIPTU). *Design and layout of souvenir programme:* Séamas Sheils. *Texts and captions:* Donal Nevin. *Irish translations:* Seán Mac Réamoinn. *National Library of Ireland advisers:* Catherine Fahy (Education Officer), John Farrell (Preservation Officer).
5. The other members of the cast were Michael Thornton, Eileen Dowling, Alan Leach, Alan Carey, Marie Gallaher, Miriam Gallaher, Sandra O'Hanlon, John Walsh, Noel Lynch, Paul O'Shea, Peter Mahoney, Robert Keogh, Martin Maher, Martin MacDonagh, Anna O'Malley, Eoin O'Malley, Jimmy Kelly, Noel Pocock. *Set visualisation* was by Irish Museum of Modern Art; *lighting* by courtesy of the Abbey Theatre; *sound* by courtesy of Radio Telefís Éireann; *staging and set construction* by Arena Staging; *sound operation* by Tim O'Donovan; *stage management* by Mary Dermody; *movement sequence* arranged by Evelyn O'Malley. The programme was designed by Séamas Sheils.

Bibliography

In general, books and articles have been included that refer, other than in passing, to James Larkin and his activities in Ireland, Britain, and America. A number of books dealing with the historical background and contemporary trade union, social and political developments, as well as with Larkin's associates and colleagues, are also included.

Unless otherwise stated, periodicals and newspapers referred to were published in Ireland.

The year of publication of the books listed is usually that of the first edition. The name of the publisher is given only in the case of books published in Ireland.

Æ [George Russell], *Collected Poems*, London 1913.

Anderson, W. K., *James Connolly and the Irish Left*, London 1994.

Askwith, Lord, *Industrial Problems and Disputes*, London 1920.

Ayling, Ronald (ed.), *Blasts and Benedictions: Articles and Stories by Seán O'Casey*, London 1967.

Ayling, Ronald (ed.), *Seán O'Casey*, London 1969.

Beckett, J. C., et al., *Belfast: The Making of the City*, Belfast 1983.

Bell, Tom, *Pioneering Days*, London 1941.

Bennett, Douglas, *A Dublin Anthology*, Dublin: Gill and Macmillan 1994.

Berresford Ellis, Peter, *A History of the Irish Working Class*, London 1972.

Bew, Paul, 'Politics and the rise of the skilled man' in J. C. Beckett et al., *Belfast: The Making of the City, 1800–1914*, Belfast: Appletree Press 1983.

Birrell, Augustine, *Things Past Redress*, London 1937.

Bloor, Ella Reeve, *We Are Many*, New York 1940.

Bower, Fred, *Rolling Stonemason*, London 1936.

Boyd, Andrew, *The Rise of the Irish Trade Unions, 1729–1970*, Tralee 1972 (new edition, 1985).

Boyle, John, 'Industrial conditions in the twentieth century' in T. W. Moody and J. C. Beckett (eds.), *Ulster since 1800: A Social Survey*, London 1957.

Boyle, John. *The Irish Labour Movement, 1880–1907*, Paris 1961.

Boyle, John (ed.), *Leaders and Workers*, Cork 1986.

Boyle, John, *The Irish Labor Movement in the Nineteenth Century*, Washington 1988.

Bradley, Daniel, *Farm Labourers' Irish Struggle, 1900–1976*, Belfast: Athol Books 1988.

Brissenden, Paul, *The Industrial Workers of the World: A Study of American Syndicalism*, New York 1919 (reissued 1957).

Broom, J., *John Maclean*, Midlothian 1973.

Callanan, Frank, *T. M. Healy*, Cork 1996.

Cannon, James, *The First Ten Years of American Communism: Report of a Participant*, New York 1962 (new edition, 1973).

Carney, Jack, *Report on Ireland: The Communist International between the Fifth and Sixth World Congresses, 1924–28*, London 1928.

Carney, Jack, *Convict No. 50945: Jim Larkin, Irish Labour Leader* (Historical Reprints, no. 12), Cork: Cork Workers' Club 1975.

Carr, E. H., *The Twilight of the Comintern, 1930–1935*, London 1983.

Carroll, Denis, *They Have Fooled You Again: Michael O'Flanagan, 1876–1942: Priest, Republican, Social Critic*, Dublin: Columba Press 1993.

Carroll, Francis, *American Opinion and the Irish Question, 1910–23: A Study in Opinion and Policy*, Dublin: Gill and Macmillan 1978.

Chaplin, Ralph, *Wobbly: The Rough-and-Tumble Story of an American Radical*, Chicago 1948.

Chesterton, G. K., *Irish Impressions*, London 1919.

Clarke, Austin, 'Inscription for a Headstone', *Collected Poems*, Dublin: Dolmen Press 1974.

Clarkson, J. Dunsmore, *Labor and Nationalism in Ireland*, New York 1925 (revised edition, 1970).

Clarkson, Jesse, 'Big Jim Larkin: Footnote to Nationalism' in Edward Mead Earle (ed.), *Nationalism and Internationalism*, New York 1950.

Claudin, F., *The Communist Movement from Comintern to Cominform*, London 1975.

Coates, Ken, and Topham, Tony, *A History of the Transport and General Workers' Union, vol. 1: The Making of the TGWU: The Emergence of the Labour Movement, 1870–1922*, Oxford 1991, part 1, '1870–1911: From Forerunners to Federation'; part 2, '1912–1922: From Federation to Amalgamation'.

Cody, Séamus, O'Dowd, John, and Rigney, Peter, *The Parliament of Labour: 100 Years of the Dublin Council of Trade Unions*, Dublin: Dublin Council of Trade Unions 1986.

Coleman, McAllister, *Eugene V. Debs*, New York 1930.

Collins, J., *Life in Old Dublin*, Dublin: James Duffy 1913.

Colum, Pádraic, *Arthur Griffith*, Dublin: Browne and Nolan 1959.

Connolly, James, *Labour in Ireland [Labour in Irish History* (1910) and *The Reconquest of Ireland* (1915) in one volume], Dublin: Maunsel and Roberts 1922 (reprint, Dublin: Three Candles 1950).

Connolly, James, *Socialism and Nationalism* (selections from his writings edited by Desmond Ryan), Dublin: Three Candles 1948.

Connolly, James, *The Workers' Republic* (selections from his writings edited by Desmond Ryan), Dublin: ITGWU 1951.

Connolly, James, *Selected Political Writings* (edited and introduced by Owen Dudley Edwards and Bernard Ransome), London 1973.

Connolly, S. (ed.), *The Oxford Companion to Irish History*, Oxford 1998.

Connolly, S., Houston, R., and Morris, R. (eds.), *Conflict, Identity and Economic Development: Ireland and Scotland, 1600–1939*, Preston 1995.

Connolly O'Brien, Nora, *Portrait of a Rebel Father*, Dublin: Talbot Press 1935.

Coote, Stephen, *W. B. Yeats: A Life*, London 1997.

Costello, Peter, *James Joyce: The Years of Growth, 1882–1915: A Biography*, London 1992.

Cowell, John, *Dublin's Famous People and Where They Lived*, Dublin: O'Brien Press 1980.

Cradden, Terry, *Trade Unionism, Socialism and Partition: The Labour Movement in Northern Ireland, 1939–1953*, Belfast: December Publications 1993.

Crean, Tom, 'From Petrograd to Bruree' in David Fitzpatrick (ed.), *Revolution in Ireland, 1917–1923*, Dublin: Trinity College Workshop 1990.

Cruise O'Brien, Conor (ed.), *The Shaping of Modern Ireland*, London 1960.

Cullen, L. M., *An Economic History of Ireland since 1660*, London 1962.

Cullen, L. M., *Eason and Son: A History*, Dublin: Eason 1989.

Cunningham, John, *Labour in the West of Ireland: Working Life and Struggle, 1890–1940*, Belfast: Athol Books 1995.

Curriculum Development Unit, *Dublin: Divided City: Portrait of Dublin, 1913*, Dublin: O'Brien Educational 1978 (new edition as *Dublin, 1913: A Divided City*, 1982).

Czira, Sidney, *The Years Flew By*, Dublin: Gifford and Craven 1974.

D'Arcy, Fergus, and Hannigan, Ken (eds.), *Workers in Union: Documents and Commentaries on the History of Irish Labour*, Dublin: National Archives 1988.

D'Arcy, Margaretta, and Arden, John, *The Non-Stop Connolly Show: A Dramatic Cycle of Continuous Struggle in Six Parts*, London 1986.

Daly, Mary E., *Dublin, the Deposed Capital: A Social and Economic History, 1860–1914*, Cork 1984.

Dangerfield, George, *The Strange Death of Liberal England*, London 1936.

Dangerfield, George, *The Damnable Question: A Study in Anglo-Irish Relations*, London 1976.

Dawson, Richard, *Red Terror and Green*, London 1920 (reprinted 1972).

Deasy, Joseph, *The Fiery Cross: The Story of Jim Larkin*, Dublin: New Books 1963.

DeCaux, Len, *The Living Spirit of the Wobblies*, New York 1978.

Deeny, James, *To Cure and to Care*, Dublin: Glendale Press 1989.

Deeny, James, *The End of an Epidemic: Essays in Irish Public Health, 1935–65*, Dublin: A. and A. Farmar 1995.

Denson, Alan (ed.), *Letters from AE*, London 1961.

Devlin, Paddy, *Yes, We Have No Bananas: Outdoor Relief in Belfast, 1920–39*, Belfast: Blackstaff Press 1981.

Dewar, H., *Communist Politics in Britain: The CPGB from its Origins to the Second World War*, London 1976.

Diggins, J. P., *The American Left in the Twentieth Century*, New York 1973.

Draper, Theodore, *The Roots of American Communism*, New York 1957.

Dublin Strikes, 1913: Facts Concerning the Labour Disputes Contained in Speech of Mr. T. M. Healy, K.C., M.P., at Court of Enquiry held in Dublin Castle on Wednesday 1st October 1913, Dublin 1913.

Dubofsky, David, *'Big Bill' Haywood*, Manchester 1987.

Dubofsky, Melvyn, *We Shall Be All: A History of the Industrial Workers of the World*, Chicago 1969.

Dudley Edwards, Owen, *The Mind of an Activist: James Connolly*, Dublin: Gill and Macmillan 1971.

Dudley Edwards, Ruth, *Patrick Pearse: The Triumph of Failure*, London 1977.

Dudley Edwards, Ruth, *James Connolly*, Dublin: Gill and Macmillan 1981.

Egan, Terry, *Dublin, 1913: Commemorative Edition of 'Union News'*, Sep. 1983, Dublin: IDA Section Committee, No. 15 Branch, Federated Workers' Union of Ireland.

Eglinton, John [W. K. Magee], *A Memoir of Æ: George William Russell*, London 1937.

English, Richard, *Radicals and the Republic: Socialist Republicanism in the Irish Free State, 1925–1937*, Oxford 1994.

Enright, Michael, *Men of Iron: Wexford Foundry Disputes, 1890 and 1911*, Wexford: Wexford Council of Trade Unions 1987.

Fallon, Gabriel, *Seán O'Casey: The Man I Knew*, London 1965.

Farrell, James, 'Lest We Forget: Jim Larkin, Irish Labor Leader' in Dennis Flynn (ed.), *On Irish Themes*, Philadelphia 1982.

Ferguson, C., 'Larkin and the WUI', *Silver Jubilee Souvenir, 1924–1949*, Dublin: Workers' Union of Ireland 1949.

Fitzpatrick, David, 'Militarism in Ireland, 1900–1922' in Thomas Bartlett and Keith Jeffery (eds.), *A Military History of Ireland*, Cambridge 1996.

Foster, R. F., *Modern Ireland, 1600–1972*, London 1988.

Foster, R. F., *W. B. Yeats: A Life, 1: The Apprentice Mage, 1865–1914*, Oxford 1997.

Foster, William Z., *American Trade Unionism*, New York 1947.

Fox, R. M., *Rebel Irishwomen*, Dublin: Progress House 1935.

Fox, R. M., *Smoky Crusade*, London 1938.

Fox, R. M., *The History of the Irish Citizen Army*, Dublin: James Duffy 1943.

Fox, R. M., *James Connolly: The Forerunner*, Tralee: Kerryman 1947.

Fox, R. M., *Jim Larkin: The Rise of the Underman*, London 1957.

Fox, R. M., *Louie Bennett: Her Life and Times*, Dublin: Talbot Press 1958.

Freyer, Grattan, *Peadar O'Donnell*, New Jersey 1973.

Garnett, David, *Golden Echo*, London 1953.

Gaughan, J. Anthony, *Thomas Johnson, 1872–1963: First Leader of the Labour Party in Dáil Éireann*, Dublin: Kingdom Books 1980.

Gaughan, J. Anthony, *Alfred O'Rahilly, vol. 3: Controversialist*, Dublin: Kingdom Books 1992.

Gaughan, J. Anthony, *Memoirs of Senator Joseph Connolly, A Founder of Modern Ireland*, Dublin: Irish Academic Press 1996.

Gilmore, George, *1934: Republican Congress*, Dublin: Dóchas Co-op Society 1968.

Gitlow, Benjamin, *I Confess*, New York 1940.

Gitlow, Benjamin, *The Whole of Their Lives*, New York 1948.

Grantham, G., McKinnon, M., and Roche, K. (eds.), *Labour Market Evolution*, London 1994.

Gray, John, *City in Revolt: James Larkin and the Belfast Dock Strike of 1907*, Belfast 1985.

Greaves, C. Desmond, *The Life and Times of James Connolly*, London 1961.

Greaves, C. Desmond, *Liam Mellows and the Irish Revolution*, London 1971.

Greaves, C. Desmond, *Seán O'Casey: Politics and Art*, London 1979.

Greaves, C. Desmond, *The Irish Transport and General Workers' Union: The Formative Years, 1909–1923*, Dublin: Gill and Macmillan 1982.

Gurley Flynn, Elizabeth, *I Speak My Own Piece: Autobiography of the 'Rebel Girl'*, New York 1955.

Harris, Frank, *Contemporary Portraits* (fourth series), London 1924.

Haywood, William D., *Bill Haywood's Book: The Autobiography of William D. Haywood*, London 1929.

Healy, Tim, *Dublin Strikes, 1913* [speech at Court of Inquiry, October 1913], Dublin 1913.

Hicks, Granville, *John Reed*, New York 1936.

Hobsbawn, Eric, *Labouring Men* (second edition), London 1971.

Hogan, James, *Could Ireland Become Communist?: The Facts of the Case*, Dublin: Cahill 1935.

Hogan, Robert (ed.), *Feathers from the Green Crow: Seán O'Casey, 1905–1925*, London 1963.

Holt, Edgar, *Protest in Arms: The Irish Troubles, 1916–1923*, London 1960.

Holton, B., *British Syndicalism, 1900–1914: Myths and Reality*, London 1976, chap. 14, 'Syndicalism and Larkinism'.

Hone, Joseph, *W. B. Yeats, 1865–1939*, London 1943.

Howell, David, *A Lost Left: Three Studies in Socialism and Nationalism*, Manchester 1986.

Humphries, Alexander, *New Dubliners: Urbanization and the Irish Family*, London 1966.

Irish Labour Party and Trades Union Congress, *Ireland at Berne*, Dublin: Talbot Press 1919.

Irish Times Sinn Féin Rebellion Handbook, Dublin: Irish Times 1916.

Irish Trades Union Congress, *Annual Reports*, 1908–1914, 1942, 1946, 1947, Dublin: ITUC.

Irish Transport and General Workers' Union, *The Attempt to Smash the Irish Transport and General Workers' Union*, Dublin: ITGWU 1924.

535

Irish Transport and General Workers' Union, *Some Pages from Union History: The Facts Concerning Larkin's Departure to America*, Dublin: ITGWU 1927.

Irish Transport and General Workers' Union, *Fifty Years of Liberty Hall, 1909–1959*, Dublin: Three Candles 1959.

Jackson, T. A., *Ireland Her Own: An Outline History of the Irish Struggle for National Freedom and Independence*, London 1946.

Johnstone, Tom, *Orange, Green and Khaki: The Story of the Irish Regiments in the Great War, 1914–18*, Dublin: Gill and Macmillan 1992.

Jones, Mary, *These Obstreperous Lassies: A History of the Irish Women Workers' Union*, Dublin: Gill and Macmillan 1988.

Kain, Richard, *Susan L. Mitchel*, New Jersey 1972.

Kee, Robert, *The Green Flag: A History of Irish Nationalism*, London 1972.

Kendall, Walter, *The Revolutionary Movement in Britain, 1900–1921*, London 1969.

Kennedy, Kieran A., Giblin, Thomas, and McHugh, Deirdre, *The Economic Development of Ireland in the Twentieth Century*, London 1988.

Keogh, Dermot, *The Rise of the Irish Working Class: The Dublin Trade Union Movement and Labour Leadership, 1890–1914*, Belfast 1982.

Keogh, Dermot, *The Vatican, the Bishops and Irish Politics*, Cambridge 1986.

Keogh, Dermot, 'Foundation and early years of the Irish TUC, 1894–1912' in Donal Nevin (ed.), *Trade Union Century*, Dublin: Mercier Press (with ICTU and RTE) 1994.

Kiberd, Declan, *Inventing Ireland: The Literature of the Modern Nation*, London 1996.

Kohfeldt, Mary Lou, *Lady Gregory: The Woman Behind the Irish Renaissance*, London 1985.

Konody, P., and Dark, Sidney, *Sir William Orpen: Artist and Man*, London 1932.

Kornbluh, Joyce (editor), *Rebel Voices: An IWW Anthology* (second edition), Chicago 1988.

Kostick, Conor, *Revolution in Ireland: Popular Militancy, 1917 to 1923*, London 1996.

Krause, David, *Seán O'Casey: The Man and His Work*, London 1960.

Krause, David, 'Towards the end' in Seán McCann (ed.), *The World of Seán O'Casey*, London 1966.

Krause, David (ed.), *The Letters of Seán O'Casey, vol. 1: 1910–1941*, London 1975; *vol. 2: 1942–1954*, New York 1980; *vol. 3: 1955–1958*, Washington 1989; *vol. 4: 1959–1964*, Washington 1992.

Krinitz, Stanley, and Haycraft, Howard, *Twentieth-Century Authors*, New York 1942.

Laffan, Michael, 'Labour must wait: Ireland's conservative revolution' in Patrick J. Corish (ed.), *Radicals, Rebels and Establishments* (Historical Studies, 15): Belfast: Appletree Press 1985.

Larkin, Emmet, *James Larkin, 1876–1947: Irish Labour Leader*, London 1965 (new edition 1989).

Larkin, Jim, *In the Footsteps of Big Jim: A Family Biography*, Dublin: Blackwater Press n.d. [1996].

Larkin, Peter, 'Irish Crisis and Jim Larkin' in Jack Carney, *Convict No. 50945* (Historical Reprints, no. 12), Cork: Cork Workers' Club 1975.

Lee, J. J., *Ireland, 1912–1985: Politics and Society*, Cambridge 1989.

Levenson, Leah, *With Wooden Sword: A Portrait of Francis Sheehy-Skeffington, Militant Pacifist*, Dublin: Gill and Macmillan 1983.

Levenson, Samuel, *James Connolly: A Biography*, London 1973.

Lewenhak, Sheila, *Women and Trade Unions: An Outline History of Women in the British Trade Union Movement*, London 1977.

Linklater, Andro, *An Unhusbanded Wife: Charlotte Despard, Suffragette, Socialist and Sinn Féiner*, London 1980.

Luddy, Maria, *Women in Ireland, 1900–1918*, Cork: Cork University Press 1995.

Lynch, Florence Monteith, *The Mystery Man of Banna Strand: The Life and Death of Captain Robert Monteith*, New Jersey 1959.

Lyons, F. S. L., *John Dillon: A Biography*, London 1968.

Lyons, F. S. L., *Ireland since the Famine*, London 1971.

Lysaght, D. R. O'Connor, *The Republic of Ireland*, Cork: Mercier Press 1970.

Lysaght, D. R. O'Connor, 'The existence of Irish syndicalism', *Dublin History Workshop Millennium Edition, 1988* (reviews of Dermot Keogh, *The Rise of the Irish Working Class*, and C. Desmond Greaves, *The Irish Transport and General Workers' Union: the Formative Years*).

Mac an Bheatha, Proinsias, *Tart na Córa: Saol agus Saothar Shéamais Uí Chonghaile*, Dublin: Foilseacháin Náisiúnta 1963.

McCamley, Bill, *The Third James: The Story of the Irish Labour Pioneer James Fearon*, Dublin 1984.

MacCarthy, Charles, *Trade Unions in Ireland, 1884–1960*, Dublin: Institute of Public Administration 1977.

MacCarthy, Charles, *James Larkin as the Embodiment of the Working Classes, 1907–1913* (Discussion Papers in Industrial Relations, vol. 2), Dublin: School of Business and Administrative Studies, Trinity College, 1984.

McDonnell, J. M., *The Story of Irish Labour*, London 1919.

McDonnell, John (ed.), *Songs of Struggle and Protest*, Dublin: Gilbert Dawson 1978.

McDowell, Maeve Kavanagh, *Sheaves of Revolt*, Dublin: City Printing Works 1914.

Mac Giolla Choille, Breandán (ed.), *Chief Secretary's Office, Dublin Castle: Intelligence Notes, 1913–1916*, Dublin: Stationery Office 1966.

McInerney, Michael, *Peadar O'Donnell: Irish Social Rebel*, Dublin: O'Brien Press 1974.

MacManus, M. J., *Éamon de Valera: A Biography*, Dublin: Talbot Press 1944.

Mann, Tom, *Tom Mann's Memoirs*, London 1923 (new edition, 1967).

Manning, Maurice, *Irish Political Parties: An Introduction*, Gill and Macmillan 1972.

Mansergh, Nicholas, *The Irish Question, 1840–1921*, London 1940.

Marreco, Anne, *The Rebel Countess: The Life and Times of Constance Markievicz*, London 1967.

Martin, F. X., 'MacNeill and the foundation of the Irish Volunteers' in F. X. Martin and F. J. Byrne (eds.), *The Scholar Revolutionary: Eoin MacNeill, 1867–1945, and the Making of the New Ireland*, Shannon: Irish University Press 1973.

Marx, Karl, and Engels, Frederick, *Ireland and the Irish Question*, Moscow 1971.

Matthews, James, *Voices: A Life of Frank O'Connor*, Dublin: Gill and Macmillan 1983.

Maye, Brian, *Arthur Griffith*, Dublin: Griffith College 1997.

Meenan, James, *George O'Brien: A Biographical Memoir*, Dublin: Gill and Macmillan 1980.

Merrigan, Matt, *Eagle or Cuckoo?: The Story of the Amalgamated Transport and General Workers' Union in Ireland*, Dublin: Matmer Publications 1989.

Millar, David A., *Church, State and Nation in Ireland, 1898–1921*, Dublin: Gill and Macmillan 1973.

Milotte, Mike, *Communism in Modern Ireland: The Pursuit of the Workers' Republic since 1916*, Dublin: Gill and Macmillan 1984.

Milton, Nan, *John Maclean*, London 1973.

Mitchell, Arthur, *Labour in Irish Politics, 1890–1930: The Irish Labour Movement in the Age of Revolution*, Dublin: Irish University Press 1974.

Mitchell, Arthur, and Ó Snodaigh, Pádraig, *Irish Political Documents, 1916–49*, Dublin: Irish Academic Press 1985.

Montefiore, Dora, *From a Victorian to a Modern*, London 1927.

Monteith, Robert, *Casement's Last Adventure*, Chicago 1932.

Moody, T. W. (ed.), *Irish Historiography, 1936–1970*, Dublin: Irish Committee of Historical Sciences 1971.

Morgan, Austen, *James Connolly: A Political Biography*, Manchester 1988.

Morgan, Austen, *Labour and Partition: The Belfast Working Class, 1905–1923*, London 1991.

Morrissey, Thomas, *A Man Called Hughes: The Life and Times of Séamus Hughes, 1881–1943*, Dublin: Veritas 1991.

Morrissey, Thomas, *William Martin Murphy*, Dundalk 1997.

Mulvihill, Margaret, *Charlotte Despard: A Biography*, London 1989.

Munch, Ronnie, and Rolston, Bill, *Belfast in the Thirties: An Oral History*, Belfast: Blackstaff Press 1887.

Murphy, J. T., *New Horizons*, London 1942.

Murphy, Patrick, *The Federation of Rural Workers, 1946–1979*, Dublin: Federated Workers' Union of Ireland 1988.

Nevin, Donal (ed.), *1913: Jim Larkin and the Dublin Lock-Out*, Dublin: Workers' Union of Ireland 1964.

Nevin, Donal, 'Labour and the political revolution' in Francis MacManus (ed.), *The Years of the Great Test, 1926–39*, Dublin: Mercier Press (with RTE) 1967.

Nevin, Donal, 'The Irish Citizen Army' in Owen Dudley Edwards and Fergus Pyle (eds.), *The Easter Rising*, London 1968.

Nevin, Donal, 'Industry and Labour' in Kevin B. Nowlan and T. Desmond Williams (eds.), *Ireland in the War Years and After, 1939–1951*, Dublin: Gill and Macmillan 1969.

Nevin, Donal, 'Radical movements in the twenties and thirties' in T. Desmond Williams (ed.), *Secret Societies in Ireland*, Dublin: Gill and Macmillan 1973.

Nevin, Donal, 'Marx, Connolly and the Irish Labour Movement' in Kevin B. Nowlan (ed.), *Karl Marx: The Materialist Messiah*, Cork: Mercier Press 1984.

Nevin, Donal (ed.), *Trade Union Century*, Dublin: Mercier Press (with ICTU and RTE) 1994.

Nolan, Seán, *Outline History of the Communist Party of Ireland*, Dublin: New Books n.d. [1973].

Norman, Diana, *Terrible Beauty: A Life of Constance Markievicz, 1868–1927*, London 1987.

Norman, Edward, *A History of Modern Ireland*, London 1971.

O'Brien, Joseph, *'Dear, Dirty Dublin': A City in Distress, 1899–1916*, Los Angeles 1982.

O'Brien, William (as told to Edward MacLysaght), *Forth the Banners Go: Reminiscences of William O'Brien*, Dublin: Three Candles 1969.

Ó Broin, León, *The Chief Secretary: Augustine Birrell in Ireland*, London 1969.

Ó Broin, León, *Revolutionary Underground: The Story of the Irish Republican Brotherhood, 1854–1924*, Dublin: Gill and Macmillan 1976.

Ó Broin, León, *Just Like Yesterday: An Autobiography*, Dublin: Gill and Macmillan n.d. [1986].

O'Casey, Eileen, *Seán*, Dublin: Gill and Macmillan 1971.

O'Casey, Seán, *Drums Under the Windows*, London 1945.

O'Casey, Seán, *Innisfallen, Fare Thee Well*, London 1949.

O'Casey, Seán, *Sunset and Evening Star*, New York 1961.

Ó Cathasaigh, P. [Seán O'Casey], *The Story of the Irish Citizen Army*, Dublin and London 1919.

Ó Ceallaigh, Seán T. (ed. Proinsias Ó Conluain), *Seán T.: Scéal A Bheatha*, Dublin: Foilseacháin Náisiúnta 1963.

Ó Cíosáin, Éamon, *An tÉireannach, 1934–37: Nuachtán Sóisialach Gaeltachta*, Dublin: Clóchomhar 1993.

O'Connell, T. J., *100 Years of Progress: The Story of the Irish National Teachers' Organisation, 1868–1968*, Dublin: INTO 1968.

O'Connor, Emmet, *Syndicalism in Ireland, 1917–1923*, Cork: Cork University Press 1988.

O'Connor, Emmet, *A Labour History of Waterford*, Waterford: Waterford Trades Council 1989.

O'Connor, Emmet, *A Labour History of Ireland, 1824–1960*, Dublin: Gill and Macmillan 1992.

O'Connor, Garry, *Seán O'Casey*, London 1988.

O'Connor, Ulick, *Oliver St John Gogarty: A Poet of His Times*, London 1963.

O'Donovan, Donal, *Kevin Barry and His Time*, Dublin: Glendale Press 1989.

Ó Faoláin, Seán, *Constance Markievicz*, London 1934.

O'Flaherty, Liam, *The Life of Tim Healy*, London 1927.

Ó Gráda, Cormac, *Ireland: A New Economic History, 1870–1939*, Oxford 1994.

Ó Gráda, Cormac, *The Irish Economy Since the 1920s*, Manchester 1997.

O'Hegarty, P. S., *A History of Ireland under the Union, 1801–1922*, London 1952.

Ó Lúing, Seán, *I Die in a Good Cause: A Study of Thomas Ashe*, Tralee: Anvil Books 1970.

O'Malley, Ernie, *On Another Man's Wound*, London 1936 (new edition 1979).

O'Neill, Brian, *Easter Week*, New York 1939.

O'Riordan, Manus, *The American Trial of Big Jim Larkin, 1920*, Belfast: Athol Books 1976.

O'Riordan, Manus, *Larkinism in Perspective: From Communism to Evolutionary Socialism*, Dublin: Labour History Workshop 1983.

Orpen, Sir William, *Stories of Old Ireland and Myself*, London 1924.

O'Shannon, Cathal (ed.), *Fifty Years of Liberty Hall: The Golden Jubilee of the ITGWU, 1909–1959*, Dublin: Three Candles 1969.

Owens, Rosemary Cullen, *Smashing Times: A History of the Irish Women's Suffrage Movement, 1889–1922*, Dublin: Attic Press 1984.

Pankhurst, Sylvia, *The Suffragette Movement*, London 1977.

Patterson, Henry, *Class Conflict and Sectarianism: The Protestant Working Class and the Belfast Labour Movement, 1868–1920*, Belfast: Blackstaff Press 1980.

Patterson, Henry, 'Industrial labour and the labour movement, 1820–1914' in Liam Kennedy and Philip Olleranshaw (eds.), *An Economic History of Ulster, 1820–1940*, Manchester 1985.

Patterson, Henry, *The Politics of Illusion: Republicanism and Socialism in Modern Ireland*, London 1989.

Pelling, Henry, *A History of British Trade Unionism*, London 1963.

Pethick, Lawrence, *My Part in a Changing World*, London 1938.

Phelan, Jim, *Phelan's the Name*, London 1948.

Phillips, W. Alison, *The Revolution in Ireland, 1906–1923*, London 1923.

Pimley, Adrian, 'The working-class movement and the Irish revolution, 1896–1923' in D. G. Boyce (ed.), *The Revolution in Ireland*, London 1988.

Plunkett, James, 'Jim Larkin' in John Boyle (ed.), *Leaders and Workers*, Cork: Mercier Press 1966.

Plunkett, James, 'Seán O'Casey and the trade unions' in Micheál Ó hAodha (ed.), *The O'Casey Enigma*, Cork: Mercier Press 1980.

Plunkett, James, *The Boy on the Back Wall and Other Essays*, Dublin: Poolbeg 1987.

Plunkett, James, 'Jim Larkin and the risen people' in Donal Nevin (ed.), *Trade Union Century*, Dublin: Mercier Press (with ICTU and RTE) 1994.

Postgate, Raymond, *The Life of George Lansbury*, London 1951.

Pyle, Hillary, *Jack B. Yeats: A Biography*, London 1989.

Redmond, Seán, *The Irish Municipal Employees' Trade Union, 1883–1983*, Dublin: IMETU 1983.

Reeve, Carl, and Reeve, Ann Barton, *James Connolly and the United States: The Road to the 1916 Irish Rebellion*, Atlantic Highlands (NJ) 1978.

Renshaw, Patrick, *The Wobblies: The Story of Syndicalism in the United States*, London 1967.

Reports of the Fiscal Inquiry Committee, Dublin 1923, appendix A.

Ridge, Lola, 'To Larkin' in *Sun-up and Other Poems*, New York 1920.

Robbins, Frank, *Under the Starry Plough: Recollections of the Irish Citizen Army*, Dublin: Academy Press 1977.

Robinson, Lennox (ed.), *Lady Gregory's Journals, 1916–1930*, London 1946.

Rosenstone, Robert, *Romantic Revolutionary: A Biography of John Reed*, London 1982.

Ruane, Medb, 'Rosie Hackett' and 'Hanna Sheehy-Skeffington' in *Ten Dublin Women*, Dublin: Women's Commemoration and Celebration Committee 1991.

Rumpf, E., and Hepburn, A., *Nationalism and Socialism in Twentieth-Century Ireland*, Liverpool 1977.

Russell, George, *The Dublin Strike*, London 1913.

Ryan, Desmond, *James Connolly: His Life, Work and Writings*, Dublin: Talbot Press 1924.

Ryan, Desmond, *Remembering Sion: A Chronicle of Storm and Quiet*, London 1934.

Ryan, W. P., *The Labour Revolt and Larkinism*, London 1913.

Ryan, W. P., *The Irish Labour Movement from the 'Twenties to Our Own Day*, Dublin: Talbot Press 1919.

Sexton, James, *Sir James Sexton, Agitator: The Life of the Dockers' MP: An Autobiography*, London 1936.

Sheehy-Skeffington, Andrée, *Skeff: A Life of Owen Sheehy-Skeffington, 1909–1970*, Dublin: Lilliput Press 1991.

Smith, Gibbs, *Joe Hill*, Salt Lake City 1969.

Stewart, Bob, *Breaking the Fetters*, London 1967.

Stone, Irving, *Clarence Darrow for the Defence*, London 1949.

Strauss, Erich, *Irish Nationalism and British Democracy*, London 1951.

Summerfield, Henry, *That Myriad Minded Man: A Biography of George William Russell, 'AE'*, London 1975.

Swift, John, *History of the Dublin Bakers and Others*, Dublin: Irish Bakers', Confectioners' and Allied Workers' Union, n.d. [1948].

Swift, John P., *John Swift: An Irish Dissident*, Dublin: Gill and Macmillan 1991.

Taplin, Eric, *The Dockers' Union: A Story of the National Union of Dock Labourers, 1889–1922*, Leicester 1986.

Thompson, Fred, *The IWW: Its First Fifty Years (1905–1955)*, Chicago 1955.

Thompson, Lucinda, 'Strikes in Galway' in David Fitzpatrick (ed.), *Revolution in Ireland, 1917–1923*, Dublin: Trinity College Workshop 1990.

Thompson, William Irwin, *The Imagination of an Insurrection: Easter 1916: A Study of an Ideological Movement*, New York 1967.

Thomson, David, *Europe since Napoleon*, London 1957 (revised edition, 1966).

Thorne, Will, *My Life's Battles*, London 1927.

Townshend, Charles, *Political Violence in Ireland: Government and Resistance since 1848*, Oxford 1983.

Tressell, Robert, *The Ragged-Trousered Philanthropists*, London 1918 (new edition, 1955).

Turner, Ian, *Sydney's Burning*, London and Melbourne 1967.

van Voris, Jacqueline, *Constance de Markievicz: In the Cause of Ireland*, Amherst (Mass.) 1967.

Vaughan, W. (ed.), *A New History of Ireland, vol. 6: Ireland under the Union, 1870–1921*, Oxford 1996.

Walsh, P. J., *Archbishop William Walsh of Dublin*, Dublin 1928.

Ward, Margaret, *Hannah Sheehy-Skeffington: A Life*, Dublin: Attic Press 1997.

Welch, Robert (ed.), *The Oxford Companion to Irish Literature*, Oxford 1996.

West, Rebecca (selected and edited by Jane Marcus), *The Young Rebecca: Writings of Rebecca West, 1911–17*, London 1982 (includes two articles from the *Clarion*, 31 Oct. and 14 Nov. 1913, that deal with the events in Dublin).

West, Trevor, *Horace Plunkett: Cooperation and Politics*, Gerrards Cross (Bucks.) 1986.

White, J. R., *Misfit: An Autobiography*, London 1930.

Whyte, J. H., *Church and State in Modern Ireland, 1923–1970*, Dublin: Gill and Macmillan 1971.

Williams, Francis, *Magnificent Journey: The Rise of the Trade Unions*, London 1954.

Wolfe, Bertram, *Strange Communists I Have Known*, London 1966.

Wright, Arnold, *Disturbed Dublin: The Story of the Great Strike of 1913–14*, London 1914 (included in the appendixes are the report of the Askwith Enquiry, the Employers' Reply to the Findings, and report of the Dublin Disturbances Commission).

Documents and reports

Report of the Court of Enquiry (chairman, Sir George Askwith), October 1913.

Dublin City Commission, Crown Files 1913.

Dublin Disturbances Commission Report, 1914 (Cd. 7269), Parliamentary Papers XVIII, 1914.

Report of the Departmental Inquiry into the Housing of the Dublin Working Classes (Cd. 7273), Parliamentary Papers XIX, 1914.

Articles

Anon., 'James Connolly and his epoch', chap. 6 (Larkin), *Irish Worker*, 23 Aug. 1924.

Anon., 'Jim Larkin: his spirit goes marching on', *Review*, Mar. 1947.

Anon., 'Larkin's strike', *News Letter* (Belfast), 19 Aug. 1953.

Ayling, Ronald, 'Portrait of the artist as a slum gutter-snipe', *Seán O'Casey Annual*, (Atlantic Highlands, NJ) no. 1 (ed. Robert Lowery) 1982.

Ayling, Ronald, 'Seán O'Casey and Jim Larkin after 1923', *Seán O'Casey Review* (New York), vol. 3, no. 2 (spring 1977).

Bedarida, François (translated by Catherine Burke), 'Syndicalism in Ireland' (Review of Emmet O'Connor, *Syndicalism in Ireland, 1917–1923*), *Saothar*, no. 14 (1989).

Boyle, J. W., 'Irish Labor and the Rising', *Éire-Ireland* (St Paul, Minn.), vol. 2, no. 3 (1967).

Boyle, John W., 'The Irish TUC' (review essay on Charles MacCarthy, *Trade Unions in Ireland, 1894–1960*), *Bulletin of the Society for the Study of Labour History* (Sheffield), autumn 1980.

Brennan, John [Sidney Czira], 'How the Countess trained an army', *Irish Digest*, Dec. 1951.

Brown, Kenneth, 'Labour and the strikes of 1913: their place in British history', *Saothar*, no. 9 (1983).

Carney, Jack, *Irish Democrat* (London), Mar. 1947 (Larkin Memorial Number).

Cluskey, Frank, Snr, 'Recollections', *Workers' Union of Ireland Report*, Aug., Sep. and Oct. 1953.

Cluskey, Frank, James Larkin, *Ireland Today*, 16 Jan. 1976.

Cody, Séamus, 'The remarkable Patrick Daly', *Obair*, no. 2, Jan. 1985.

Cody, Séamus, 'Dublin Trades Council and the 1913 Lock-Out', *Labour History News*, summer 1987.

Cole, Margaret, Review of Emmet Larkin, *James Larkin, Irish Labour Leader*, *Listener* (London), 1 Apr. 1965.

Connolly-Heron, Ina, '1913 Strike', *Liberty*, July 1966.

Connolly-Heron, Ina, 'James Connolly' (series of eight articles), *Liberty*, Mar.–Oct. 1966.

Corkery, Daniel, 'Jim Larkin', *Leader*, 2 July 1910.

Cradden, Terry, Review of John Gray, *City in Revolt: James Larkin and the Belfast Dock Strike of 1907*, *Saothar*, no. 11 (1986).

Craig, H. A. L., 'A Burning Man: Seán O'Casey', *Irish Times*, 30 Mar. 1960.

Cronin, Anthony, 'The failure of Jim Larkin' in *An Irish Eye* [first published in *Irish Times*], Dingle: Brandon 1985.

Cronin, Seán, 'The rise and fall of the Socialist Labour Party of North America', *Saothar*, no. 3 (1977).

Cruise O'Brien, Conor, 'Big Jim' (review of Emmet Larkin, *James Larkin: Irish Labour Leader*), *New Statesman* (London), 7 May 1965.

Cruise O'Brien, Conor, 'Larkin's devotion to workers', *Irish Times*, 22 Mar. 1977.

Cruise O'Brien, Conor, 'The truth about Big Jim' (review of new edition of Emmet Larkin, *James Larkin: Irish Labour Leader*), *Irish Times*, 10 Sep. 1977.

Dallas, George, 'Larkin's life history', *Forward* (Glasgow), 9–30 Oct. 1909.

Dawson, Charles, 'The housing of the people, with special reference to Dublin', *Journal of the Statistical and Social Inquiry Society of Ireland*, vol. 9 (1900–01).

Dawson, Charles, 'Dublin housing question: sanitary and insanitary', *Journal of the Statistical and Social Inquiry Society of Ireland*, vol. 13 (1913).

Deasy, Joe, 'The Fiery Cross and letters from James Larkin Junior', *Saothar*, no. 21 (1996).

Devine, Francis, 'Jim Larkin', *Liberty*, January 1976.

Devine, Francis, Review of Emmet Larkin, *James Larkin, Irish Labour Leader*, *Saothar*, no. 4 (1978).

Devlin, Patrick, 'Michael McKeown: a founding father', *Liberty*, June 1984.

Downey, James, 'James Larkin: the slum prophet', *Irish Times*, 5 Apr. 1973.

Dudley Edwards, Owen, 'The saga of James Larkin: imprisonment in Sing-Sing, and 'peace' challenge to Cosgrave', *Irish Times* (supplement), 21 Apr. 1976.

Fallon, Gabriel, 'Remembering 1913, the year of the great lock-out', *Hibernia*, Aug. 1963.

Feeney, John, 'Big Jim Larkin: the man of vision', *Evening Herald*, 12 Oct. 1979.

Ferguson, Chris, 'Larkin', *Impact*, April 1951.

Ferguson, C., 'Larkin and the union', *Workers' Union of Ireland Report*, nos. 1–4 (July, Aug., Sep. and Oct.–Nov. 1952).

Fox, R. M., 'Jim Larkin' (obituary), *Dublin Magazine*, Apr.–June 1947.

Fox, R. M., 'Jim Larkin', *Bell*, Jan. 1952.

Gallacher, William, 'Larkin made the hard way easier for many', *Review*, Mar. 1947.

Greaves, C. Desmond, 'Jim Larkin's earliest years', *Irish Democrat* (London), Sep. 1980.

Gwynn, Denis, 'Jim Larkin', *Cork Examiner*, 22 Feb. 1957.

Haywood, William, 'Jim Larkin's call for solidarity', *International Socialist Review* (Chicago), Feb. 1914.

Hone, J. M., 'James Larkin and the Nationalist Party', *Contemporary Review* (London), Jan. 1914.

Howell, David, Review of Emmet O'Connor, *A Labour History of Ireland*, *Saothar*, no. 18 (1993).

Hywel, Francis, Review of Emmet O'Connor, *A Labour History of Ireland*, *Saothar*, no. 15 (1990).

Jackson, T. A., 'Larkin', *Daily Worker* (London), 31 Jan. 1947.

Kavanagh, Patrick, 'Jim Larkin', *Bell*, March 1947.

Keogh, Dermot, 'Bloody Sunday, 1913', *Irish Press*, 10 and 11 Sep. 1973.

Keogh, Dermot, 'William Martin Murphy and the origins of the 1913 lock-out', *Capuchin Annual*, 1977.

Keogh, Dermot, 'William Martin Murphy and the origins of the 1913 lock-out', *Saothar*, no. 4 (1978).

King, Carla, 'A separate economic class?: the Irish Women Workers' Union' (review of Mary Jones, *These Obstreperous Lassies: A History of the IWWU*), *Saothar*, no. 14 (1989).

Larkin, Emmet, 'The man who became the Irish labour movement incarnate', *Irish Times*, 30 Jan. 1997.

Larkin, Emmet, 'Socialism and Catholicism in Ireland', *Church History* (Chicago), vol. 33 (1964) (also *Studies*, spring 1985).

Larkin, Jim, 'Joe Hill: murder most foul', *International Socialist Review* (Chicago), Dec. 1915.

Larkin, James, 'The story of a man [James Fearon] by his comrade', *Irish Worker*, 22 Nov. 1924.

Larkin, James, 'The story of a man' [Peter Larkin], *Irish Worker*, 6, 13, 20 and 27 June 1931.

Lowery, Robert, 'Seán O'Casey and the *Irish Worker*' (with an index to the *Irish Worker*, 1911–1914), *Seán O'Casey Annual*, no. 3 (ed. Robert Lowery), London 1984.

Lyons, F. S. L., Review of Emmet Larkin, *James Larkin, Irish Labour Leader*, *Irish Historical Studies*, Mar. 1967.

Lysaght, D. R. O'Connor, 'The rake's progress of a syndicalist: the political career of William O'Brien', *Saothar*, no. 9 (1983).

McCaffrey, Patricia, 'Jacob's women workers during the 1913 lock-out', *Saothar*, no. 16 (1991).

McCamley, B., 'The third James' [Fearon], *Liberty*, Jan. 1982.

MacCarthy, Charles, 'From division to dissension: Irish trade unions in the 1930s', *Economic and Social Review*, vol. 5, nos. 3 and 4 (1974).

MacCarthy, Charles, 'The impact of Larkinism on the Irish working class', *Saothar*, no. 4 (1978).

McCarthy, W. E. J., 'A syndicalist tragedy' (review of Emmet Larkin, *James Larkin: Irish Labour Leader*), *New Society* (London), 10 June 1965.

MacCormack, Dara, 'James Larkin' (Review of Emmet Larkin, *James Larkin: Irish Labour Leader*), *Administration*, winter 1965.

McInerney, Michael, 'Larkin: the name scrawled in rage', *Irish Times*, 20 Jan. 1976.

McKay, Enda, 'Changing with the tide: the Irish Labour Party, 1927–1933', *Saothar*, no. 11 (1986).

McLoughlin, Barry, and O'Connor, Emmet, 'Sources on Ireland and the Communist International, 1920–1943', *Saothar*, no. 21 (1996).

McLoughlin, Barry, 'Proletarian academics or party functionaries?: Irish communists at the International Lenin School, Moscow, 1927–1937', *Saothar*, no. 22 (1997).

MacMahon, Joseph, 'The Catholic clergy and the social question, 1891–1916', *Studies*, winter 1981.

MacManus, Francis, 'James Larkin' (review of Emmet Larkin, *James Larkin: Irish Labour Leader*), *Irish Press*, 25–27 Feb. 1965.

McMullen, William, 'The day Larkin was arrested', *Irish Independent*, 2 and 3 Sep. 1963.

McMullen, William, 'Early days of ITGWU in Belfast', *Liberty*, June and July 1977.

MacWhite, Eoin, 'A guide to Russian writings on Irish history, 1917–1963', *Melbourne Slavonic Studies* (Melbourne), no. 3 (1969).

Markievicz, Constance, 'A few memories', *Éire: the Irish Nation*, 16 June 1923.

Markievicz, S. D., 'Madam Markievicz', *Irish Worker*, 17 Oct. 1931.

Martin, Patrick, 'Jim Larkin and the constable,' *Garda Review*, Nov. 1974.

Mitchell, Arthur, 'Thomas Johnson, 1972–1963: a pioneer labour leader', *Studies*, no. 18 (winter 1969).

Mitchell, Arthur, 'William O'Brien, 1881–1968, and the Irish labour movement', *Studies*, autumn–winter 1971.

Monteith, Robert, 'Jim Larkin: an appreciation', *Review*, Apr. 1947.

Moran, Bill, 'The Dublin lock-out, 1913', *Bulletin of the Society for the Study of Labour History* (Sheffield), autumn 1973.

Moran, Bill, '1913, Jim Larkin and the British labour movement', *Saothar*, no. 4 (1978).

Morgan, Austen, 'James Connolly in Belfast, 1910–1914', *Society for the Study of Labour History Bulletin*, no. 35 (autumn 1977).

Morrissey, Thomas, 'The 1913 lock-out: letters for the archbishop', *Studies*, no. 75 (297) (spring 1986).

Murphy, J., 'Ireland and the international working class', *Labour Monthly*, May 1923.

Murray, P., 'Electoral politics and the Dublin working class before the First World War', *Saothar*, no. 6 (1980).

Murray, Peter, 'A militant among the Magdalens?: Mary Ellen Murphy's incarceration in High Park Convent during the 1913 lock-out', *Saothar*, no. 20 (1995).

Murray, Seán, 'Larkin symbolised Labour's invincibility', *Review*, Mar. 1947.

Nelson, Caroline, 'Jim Larkin', *International Socialist Review* (Chicago), Dec. 1913.

Nevin, Donal, 'Larkin in Belfast … and in America', *Labour*, Jan. 1955 (supplement).

Nevin, Donal, 'Big Jim: a tornado helping the poor' (review of Emmet Larkin, *James Larkin: Irish Labour Leader*), *Sunday Press*, 11 Apr. 1965.

Nevin, Donal, 'James Larkin: a bibliography', *Trade Union Information*, winter 1976/77.

Nevin, Donal, 'Bibliography of writings about James Larkin', *Saothar*, no. 4 (1978).

Nevin, Donal, 'The birth of the Workers' Union of Ireland', *Obair*, May 1984.

Newsinger, John, 'A light to guide your feet: Jim Larkin, the *Irish Worker* and the Dublin working class', *European History Quarterly* (London), Jan. 1990.

Newsinger, John, 'The devil it was who sent Larkin to Ireland: the *Liberator*, Larkinism and the Dublin lock-out of 1913', *Saothar*, no. 18 (1993).

Nichevo [R. M. Smyllie], 'Larkin', *Irish Times*, 1 Feb. 1947.

Nichevo [R. M. Smyllie], 'Larkin', *Times Pictorial*, 8 Feb. 1947.

O'Brien, William, 'Nineteen thirteen: its significance, *An Díon*, Dec. 1934.

O'Connor, Emmet, 'The reformation of the labour movement in Waterford: from New Model Unionism to Larkinism', *Decies*, Sep. 1979.

O'Connor, Emmet, reviews of Dermot Keogh, *The Rise of the Working Class: The Dublin Trade Union Movement and Labour Leadership, 1890–1914*, and C. Desmond Greaves, *The Irish Transport and General Workers' Union: The Formative Years*, *Saothar*, no. 9 (1983).

O'Connor, Frank, 'Homage to Jim Larkin', *Irish Times*, 9 Dec. 1944.

O'Flaherty, Liam, 'Jim Larkin the rebel', *Plain People*, 1 (2), 18 June 1922.

O'Reilly, J. Doran, 'The story of Big Jim Larkin' (eleven-part series), *Sunday Chronicle* (Irish edition), 23 and 30 Nov., 7, 14, 21 and 28 Dec. 1947, 4, 11, 18 and 25 Jan. and 1 and 8 Feb. 1948.

O'Riordan, Manus, 'Larkin in America', *Saothar*, no. 4 (1978).

O'Shannon, Cathal, 'Gathering of the storm clouds', *Irish Times*, 17 Sep. 1963.

Papke, Mary, 'Juno and the Paycock as a Larkinite stage parable', *Seán O'Casey Review* (New York), vol. 3, no. 2 (spring 1977).

Patterson, Henry, 'The new unionism and Belfast', *Bulletin of the Society for the Study of Labour History* (Sheffield), autumn 1977.

Patterson, Henry, 'James Larkin and the Belfast dockers' and carters' strike of 1907', *Saothar*, no. 4 (1978).

Payne, Elizabeth, 'Jim Larkin' (poem), *Workers' Union of Ireland Report*, Jan. 1954.

Phipps, Charlie, 'Memories of Mallin Hall', *Workers' Union of Ireland Report*, May 1954.

Plunkett, James, 'Nineteen Thirteen', *Labour*, January 1955 (supplement).

Plunkett, James, '"Big Jim": the mission of discontent', *Irish Times*, 31 Jan. 1957 (review of R. M. Fox, *Jim Larkin: The Rise of the Underman*).

Plunkett, James, 'Big Jim', *Sunday Express* (Irish edition), 30 Dec. 1956, 6, 13, 20 and 27 Jan. and 3 Feb. 1957.

Plunkett, James, 'Larkin and the great lock-out', *Irish Times*, 26 Aug. 1963.

Plunkett, James, 'Witness' (review of Donal Nevin (ed.), *1913: Jim Larkin and the Dublin Lock-Out*), *Irish Times*, 6 Oct. 1964.

Rigney, Peter, 'Some records of the ITGWU in the National Library of Ireland', *Saothar*, no. 3 (1977).

Ryan, Desmond, 'The great lock-out', *Sunday Press*, 8, 15, 22 and 29 Sep. 1963.

Ryan, Ken, 'Day O'Casey got the sack for backing union', *Irish Independent*, 21 Apr. 1980.

Stevenson, James, 'Clashing personalities: James Connolly and Daniel de Leon, 1896–1909', *Éire-Ireland* (St Paul, Minn.), fall 1990.

Swaffer, Hannen, 'Lone Jim Larkin: the man with a fiery cross for the underman', *Forward* (London), 8 Feb. 1957.

Sweeney, Gary, Review of Emmet Larkin, *James Larkin: Irish Labour Leader*, *Saothar*, no. 4 (1978).

Sweeney, Gary, 'The rise and fall of Larkinism', *Civil Service Review*, July–Aug. and Sep.–Dec. 1981.

Sweeney, Jimmy, 'The Dublin lock-out of 1913: the response of British labour', *Saothar*, no. 4 (1978).

Sweeney, Jimmy, '1913 lock-out', *Liberty*, Dec. 1981.

Swift, John, 'Remembering Jim Larkin', *Irish Socialist*, Sep., Nov. and Dec. 1984 and Jan. 1985.

Taplin, Eric, 'James Larkin, Liverpool and the National Union of Dock Labourers: the apprenticeship of a revolutionary', *Saothar*, no. 4 (1978).

Tierney, Michael, 'Modern Ireland: two interpretations', *Studies*, vol. 41 (1952).

Workers' Union of Ireland Bulletin, Feb.–Mar. 1963, 1913 Supplement.

Index

548

Fianna Fáil, 10, 81, 87, 339, 340, 460
FitzGerald, Desmond, 481
Fitzpatrick, David, 472
Fitzpatrick, John, 281, 293, 352
Fitzsimon, Henry, 343
Fletcher, Rev. Dudley, 150, 155, 418
Flynn, Annie Gurley, 289
Flynn, Elizabeth Gurley, 65, 287–92
Flynn, Thomas, 289
Foran, Thomas, 75–8, 149, 259, 273,
   294–5, 315–26, 466
Forde, Patrick, 343
Forward, 133, 138, 227, 235, 242, 404–5, 484
Foster, John, 350
Fox, R. M., 91, 96, 134, 138, 371, 381, 386,
   395–8, 416, 437, 465, 479
Fraina, Louis C., 68
Frankfurter, Felix, 71
Free State, The, 336
Freeman, John, 504
Freeman's Journal, 34, 58, 182–4, 219, 227,
   338, 483
Freiligratt, Ferdinand, 530 n3 (chap. 58)

Gael Linn, 421
Gaelic American, 65
Gaelic League, 178, 256
Gageby, Robert, 25
Gallacher, William, MP, 200
Gallaher, Thomas, 24–5
Galway, Mary, 431
Gambell, Alexander, 27
Garda Review, 146
Garden, John, 442–4, 529 n6 (chap. 55)
Garmett, David, 201, 483
Garthale, Fr Edward, 135
Gas Workers' and General Labourers'
   Union, 191
General Federation of Trade Unions, 20,
   26–7
George, David Lloyd, 60, 74, 199
German American Alliance, 299
Gibbon, Monk, 216
Gifford, Grace, 410
Gifford, Sydney, 182
Gilligan, Stephen, 180
Gitlow, Benjamin, 68–70, 276, 473
Glynn, Tom, 440, 442, 529 n6 (chap. 55)
Goff, Bridie, 486
Gonne, Maud, 115, 155, 209, 470
Gonzaga, Sr, 415
Gordon, Ellen, 97, 431
Gralton, Jim, 73
Grant, Donald, 443–4, 529 n6 (chap. 55)

Gray, John, 23, 144, 147
Greaves, C. Desmond, 33, 81–2, 116, 134,
   145–7, 185, 329–30, 366, 371, 375,
   401, 444, 489, 530 n3 (chap. 58)
Greene, David H., 416
Gregory, Lady Augusta, 112, 115, 215,
   414, 473
Greville, Frances (Countess of Warwick),
   98, 223
Grey, Sir Edward, 58
Griffith, Arthur, 34, 120, 424, 469
Gurley, Annie, 492
Guthrie, Woody, 107, 501
Gwynn, Fr John, 160
Gywnn, R. M., 257
Gywnn, Stephen, 154, 214–16, 478

Hagarty, Fr, 143
Hanna, Serjeant, KC, 191, 315
Hannay, Canon James Owen (George A.
   Birmingham), 155
Hardie, James Keir, 59, 144, 173, 187, 387
Harriman, Ben, 143
Harrington, Gerard, 51
Harris, Eoghan, 410
Harris, Frank, 72, 76, 291, 331, 393, 473
Harris, Joseph, 28, 32
Harrison, Sarah C., 93, 432
Harte, Jack, 504
Haslam, Anna, 432
Hayes, Cardinal, 294
Haywood, William D., 155, 201, 284–90,
   530 n7 (chap. 58)
Healy, Maurice, 194
Healy, T. M., 43, 175, 191–6
Healy, Tommy, 464
Henderson, Arthur, 44, 144, 193
Henzel, 292
Hernon, Dr P. J., 457, 459
Hewat, William, 470
Hickey, James, 326
Hill, Hugh O'Halloran, 26
Hill, Joe, 65, 283–92, 497–9, 523 n4–5
   (chap. 38), 524
Hillery, Dr Patrick J. (President of
   Ireland), 135, 366
Hilton, Judge O. N., 285
Holmes, Richard, 530
Hoover, J. Edgar, 68
Houston, David, 226, 257
Howell, David, 381
Hughes, James J. (Séamus), 78, 322, 422,
   489
Hugo, Victor, 513

Humphries, Alexander, 14
Hunter, Billy, 147
Hyde, Douglas, 204, 480
Hylon, Mayor, 276
Hyndman, Henry, 140

Igel, Wolf von, 302–3, 308
Independent Labour Party, 17, 30, 36, 39, 117, 128, 137, 397–8, 439
Independent Orange Order, 26, 29
Industrial Workers of the World, 59, 64, 107, 201, 276, 283–6, 290, 301, 436, 440, 491–2
Inglis, Brian, 525 n7 (chap. 42)
International Longshoremen's Association, 299
Ireland, John de Courcy, 89, 445
Irish Agricultural Organisation Society, 211, 219
Irish Catholic, 50, 54, 194, 226, 521 n14 (chap. 25)
Irish Citizen, 93–4, 113, 472
Irish Citizen Army, 44, 255–65, 353, 373, 377, 412, 421
Irish Clerical Workers' Union, 436
Irish Congress of Trade Unions, 91, 349, 423
Irish Co-operative Labour Press, 155
Irish Democrat, 134, 418
Irish Foundry Workers' Union, 34
Irish Freedom, 186, 468
Irish Homestead, 211, 214–19, 221, 408, 478
Irish Independent, 36–41, 48–54, 153, 166, 170, 215, 226, 246, 399, 401, 467
Irish Labour Party, 30, 430
Irish Labour Party and Trades Union Congress, 79, 295
Irish Nation, 412
Irish National League, 140
Irish National Teachers' Organisation, 95
Irish News, 26, 146
Irish Opinion, 410
Irish Parliamentary Party, 260
Irish Party, 39, 54–5, 160, 194–5
Irish Press, 88
Irish Progressive League, 278
Irish Republican Brotherhood, 186, 256, 263
Irish Review, 178
Irish Socialist Federation, 65
Irish Socialist Republican Party, 265, 365, 397
Irish Statesman, 221
Irish Textile Workers' Union, 34, 96, 431

Irish Times, 9, 34, 103, 147, 169, 211, 215, 219, 225, 313, 344, 415, 418, 473, 476–7, 485, 491
Irish Trades Union Congress, 23, 30–35, 40, 87–97, 117, 176, 191, 348, 362, 373, 379, 425, 431
Irish Transport and General Workers' Union, 1, 5, 17, 21, 29–45, 52–3, 74–5, 80, 87, 90–97, 120, 129, 149–51, 164–72, 192, 198, 206, 228, 233–9, 256–62, 295–6, 313–17, 324, 329–35, 342–50, 379, 397, 436
Irish Volunteers, 259–65, 275, 389
Irish Women's Reform League, 94
Irish Women Workers' Union, 33–5, 52–5, 94–7, 100–101, 234, 350, 429–31
Irish Worker, 6–7, 34–40, 53–6, 66, 79–83, 94–6, 120, 152–6, 177, 186, 193, 206, 216, 224–6, 232, 243–4, 256–62, 272, 281, 307, 331–3, 339, 343, 350–51, 412, 428, 432–9, 463, 469, 472–4
Irish Worker League, 80–81, 339–40, 439, 456
Irish Workers' Dramatic Society, 5, 112, 432

Jackson, T. A., 372–3, 382
James, Ralph, 455
Jaurès, Jean, 155, 446–7
Jennings, Tom, 139
John XXIII (pope), 484
Johnson, Jack, 142
Johnson, Thomas, 11, 79, 114, 145, 155, 191, 266, 295, 331–3, 339, 447, 454, 459
Jones, Ernest, 490
Jones, Jack, 137, 139
Jones, Mary, 436
Joyce, James, 232, 394, 479
Justice, 490

Kalnin, Minnie, 278
Kane, Fr Robert, SJ, 400
Kavanagh, Bishop James, 424
Kavanagh, Marcus, 158
Kavanagh, Patrick, 102, 105, 107, 359, 365, 367, 409, 513
Kearney, Colbert, 360
Keating, Seán, 411
Kee, Robert, 376, 382
Kelleher, John, 484
Kelly, Dr Gertrude, 294
Kelly, Oisín, 365, 410
Kelly, Samuel, 24

Lynch, Patrick, 116, 349, 418
Lynn, Dr Kathleen, 262
Lyons, F. S. L., 195, 376, 378, 384

McAdoo (Chief City Magistrate, New York), 69
MacAlpine, Eadhmonn, 67–8, 293, 395
MacAonghusa, Proinsias, 526 n8 (chap. 42)
McAteer, Anna, 135
McCaffrey, Laurence, 376
McCaig, Inspector, 181
MacCarthy, Charles, 30, 58, 345, 349
McCartney, Donal, 375
McCloy, John J., 298
McConnon, Stella, 486
McCormack, John, 66
McCormack, Richard, 264
MacDermott, Seán, 263
MacDiarmid, Hugh (C. M. Grieve), 108
MacDonagh, Donagh, 410, 422
MacDonagh, Thomas, 177
MacDonald, James Ramsay, 144
McDonnell, Sir Anthony, 25, 146
McDonnell, J. M., 465
McEvoy, Charlie, 455
MacGabhann, Liam, 47, 353
McGarrity, Joseph, 479
McGilligan, Patrick, 349
McGrath, Joseph, 296
McGreevy, Thomas, 124, 481
McInerney, Michael, 417, 473
McIntyre, J. P., 133
McKeon, Florence, 278
McKeown, Michael, 207
McKeown, Mick, 455
McLoughlin, Barry, 340–41
McLoughlin, Margaret, 455
McLoughlin, Seán, 335
McManus, Arthur, 334
MacManus, Francis, 393, 414
McMullen, William, 397
McNabb, Fr Vincent, OP, 155, 227
MacNamara, Brinsley, 124, 481
McNamara, James B., 282
McNamara, Joseph J., 282
MacNeill, Eoin (John MacNeill), 260, 372
McNulty, Mary Ann, 428
MacPartlin, Thomas, 45, 172, 326
McQuaid, Dr John Charles (Archbishop of Dublin), 47, 426, 452, 477
MacRéamoinn, Seán, 365
MacSwiney, Muriel, 278, 339
MacSwiney, Terence, 278, 294, 455

Macken, Peadar (Peadar Ó Maicín), 153
Madden, Mr Justice, 199
Maguire, James K., 301, 305, 308
Maguire, M., 315
Mallin, Michael, 155, 162, 262–5, 418, 486
Manchester Guardian, 199–200, 227, 328
Manko, Paul, 278
Mann, Tom, 59, 127, 190, 343, 440, 490
Mansergh, Nicholas, 385
Manson, Bob, 140
Markievicz, Constance (Countess Markievicz), 6, 42, 94, 108, 115, 155, 162, 174, 182–3, 207, 220, 258–61, 265, 433, 479–81, 486
Markievicz, Stanislas, 480
Martin, Rev. F. X., OSA, 369
Martin, Mary Ann, 49
Marx, Karl, 103, 121, 358, 387
Masefield, John, 471
Matheson, J. Carstairs, 528 n4 (chap. 49)
Megahy, William, 416
Mellows, Liam, 335
Meyer, Kuno, 479
Miley, D. O'Connell, 149
Miller, Nathan L., 278
Milligan, Alice, 386
Milotte, Mike, 339
Miners' Federation, 43, 190, 471
Mitchel, John, 154, 218
Mitchell, Arthur, 385
Mitchell, Jack, 108
Mitchell, James, 343
Mitchell, Susan, 154, 249, 408, 514, 522 n4 (chap. 34)
Mizher, Ignatz, 278
Molony, Helena, 100, 182, 477
Montefiore, Dora, 44, 97–100, 155, 175, 223–8
Montieth, Robert, 76, 155, 181, 293, 301, 474
Moody, T. W., 371–3
Mooney, Tom, 281–2, 523 n1 (chap. 38)
Morel, J. D., 471
Morgan, Austin, 371
Moriarty, Theresa, 93, 223, 294
Morris, William, 83, 154, 200, 490–93, 514
Morrison, Alving, 284
Morrison, John, 284
Morrissey, Fr Thomas, SJ, 49
Mortished, R. J. P., 154
Moser, Ms, 94
Mulcahy, Richard, TD, 460
Mullen, Michael (Miceál Ó Maoláin), 75, 133, 155, 436
Mulvey, Helen, 374–5

553